高等学校经济类双语教学推荐教材

ECONOMICS CLASSICS

经济学经典教材·金融系列

Economics Classics

国际投资

（第六版）

Global Investments

(Sixth Edition)

布鲁诺·索尔尼克（Bruno Solnik）
丹尼斯·麦克利维（Dennis McLeavey） 著

中国人民大学出版社
·北京·

出版说明

随着金融全球化进程的不断加快，金融人才的竞争日益激烈，用国际通用的英语来思考、工作、交流的能力也越来越重要。如何顺应这一潮流，培养和造就专业知识和语言水平都具有竞争力的金融人才，一直是各大高等院校和一些主要教材出版单位思考的重要问题，开展双语教学是教育界的共识。双语教学在我国主要指采用汉语和国际通用的英语教学，目的是培养全面的适合国际交流的高素质人才。由于我国长期以来缺乏英语交流的环境，开展双语教学面临着特殊的困难，我们认为双语教学从一开始就应该使用原版的优秀教材，保证语言的原汁原味。

顺应这一潮流，中国人民大学出版社携手国际著名的出版公司，推出了适合经济金融专业的双语系列教材。本套教材具有如下几个特色：

第一，精选教材。本套教材遴选了一批国外优秀的教材，涉及金融学、投资学、公司理财、金融市场与机构、国际货币与金融、国际投资、跨国公司财务管理、金融工程、银行管理、保险学等多门课程，涵盖了金融专业开设的主要必修科目。

第二，保持原教材的特色。本套双语教材广泛听取了一线任课教师的意见和建议，考虑到课时要求，部分图书采用了删减影印的形式，主要是删减了一些相互重复的以及不适应我国国情的内容，但在体系结构和内容特色方面都保持了原教材的风貌。

第三，内容紧扣学科前沿。本套教材基本上都选择国外最流行教材的最新版本，有利于老师和学生掌握国外教学研究的最新发展趋势。

第四，提供强大的教学支持。依托国外大出版公司的力量，本套教材为教师提供了配套的网上教辅资料，如教师手册、PPT 课堂演示文稿、试题库等，从而使教学更为便利。

本套教材主要适用于高等院校经济金融专业的本科教学，同时也适用于金融行业从业人员以及对金融专业感兴趣的人士。

本套教材是对双语教学的积极探索，错误遗漏之处在所难免，恳请广大读者指正。

中国人民大学出版社

目　录

Contents

Chapter 4 International Asset Pricing 117

Chapter 5 Equity: Markets and Instruments 157

Chapter 6 Equity: Concepts and Techniques 203

Chapter 7 Global Bond Investing 259

Chapter 8 Alternative Investments 317

Chapter 9 The Case for International Diversification 385

Chapter 10 Derivatives: Risk Management with Speculation, Hedging, and Risk Transfer 433

Chapter 11 Currency Risk Management 485

Chapter 12 Global Performance Evaluation 523

Chapter 13 Structuring the Global Investment Process 581

Glossary 629

Preface

Global Investing: The Current Perspective

More than thirty years ago, Bruno Solnik published an article entitled "Why not diversify internationally rather than domestically?" in the *Financial Analysts Journal* (July/August 1974). At the time, the combination of poor information, low expertise, stringent regulations, and high costs inhibited global investing. Thirty years later, the investment scene has changed dramatically.

The benefits of international diversification in terms of risk and return have increasingly been recognized, as detailed in this book. This has led to a push toward guidelines and legislation more favorable to foreign investment. A second factor in the rapid pace of global investing is the deregulation and internationalization of financial markets throughout the world. This global integration of financial markets has led to reduced costs, easier access to information, and the development of worldwide expertise by major financial institutions. Computerized quotation and trading systems that allow global round-the-clock trading have been developed. Restrictions to capital flows were removed within the countries of the European Union (EU); European-based investment management firms can freely market their products to residents of any EU member state. Hence, American or Japanese asset managers established in London can easily provide their services to any European client. This globalization of investment management has led to increased competition among money managers of all nationalities. It has also led to a wave of alliances, mergers, and acquisitions among financial institutions seeking to extend their global management expertise and the geographic coverage of their client base. The rapid pace of global investing is further accelerated by the general acceptance of a common set of standards and ethical principles by investment professionals. Debt issues are rated by the same rating agencies worldwide. Listed corporations are progressively adopting common or related international accounting standards. The Chartered Financial Analyst® (CFA®) designation of CFA Institute has progressively been adopted as a standard by the worldwide investment profession. A majority of the CFA candidates are non-U.S. citizens. The Global Investment Performance Standards (GIPS®), developed and administered by CFA Institute, are adopted by asset managers worldwide and are recognized as the leading global industry standard for ethical presentation of investment performance results.

Target Audience

This book is designed for MBA students, advanced undergraduates, investment professionals, and financial managers. It is appropriate for undergraduate and graduate business school electives in international finance as well as for master's courses in fields such as engineering or economics. The book is self-contained and does not take a specific national viewpoint; hence, it has been successfully used in courses and professional seminars throughout the world.

Why is the book good for these students? In a global environment, students need to grapple with such concerns as how to value global companies as well as when and how (1) monetary and fiscal policies affect exchange rates; (2) foreign exchange risk affects companies and investment portfolios; (3) global correlations collapse; (4) foreign exchange risk should be hedged; and (5) multiperiod performance attribution distinguishes skill from luck. Today all investing is global and this edition of *Global Investments* gives the student the tools needed to operate in an environment of global finance, investments, and competition. Indeed this book can be summarized by updating the globalization argument to "Why not learn internationally rather than domestically?"

Structure of This Book

The global investor is faced with a complex task. The financial markets throughout the world are quite different from one another, and information on them is sometimes difficult to obtain. Trading in different time zones and languages further complicates the task. But the most important aspect of global investment is the use of multiple currencies. An American investing in France must do so in euro; therefore, the performance (and risk) of the investment will depend in part on changes in the euro to U.S. dollar exchange rate. Because of the importance of exchange rates in global investment, this book begins with a description of foreign exchange transactions.

In this text, we develop the analysis needed for the global investment and portfolio management process. The first three chapters lay the foundation of exchange rates, which link the economies of different countries and regions. In Chapter 1, we introduce the basic facts of foreign exchange quotation, their interpretation, and arbitrage implications. In Chapter 2, we develop the theory of international parity conditions. The theory helps in defining real foreign currency risk, an important factor to be managed in global investing and portfolio management. Chapter 3 then discusses the empirical validation of the theories introduced in Chapter 2 and explores the techniques and empirical results in the difficult task of exchange rate forecasting.

The next five chapters explore the various assets available for global investing. Chapter 4 is the lead chapter in a series of chapters on international assets. In it we develop international asset pricing in general with attention to foreign currency risk. Chapter 5 places a particular focus on the transaction costs involved in various equity markets and instruments allowing entry into global investments. Following this general introduction to international asset pricing, Chapters 6, 7, and 8 focus on the available international assets and investments themselves: equities, bonds, and alternative investments, respectively.

The final five chapters develop the techniques and perspective of global portfolio management. After building the case for and against international diversification in Chapter 9, we move into the foreign currency risk and return analysis needed for international portfolio management. We develop the risk control techniques available with derivatives in Chapter 10 and then apply these techniques in currency risk management in Chapter 11. In Chapter 12, we examine the performance measures to judge the risk and return contributions of global diversification. Finally, we summarize the global investment and portfolio management process in Chapter 13. Throughout the text, we attempt to isolate those elements of the process that have unique international aspects.

Pedagogical Approach

To operate in a complex, multicurrency, multimarket, multicultural environment, you need a strong conceptual framework as well as a working knowledge of institutional aspects. Presenting concepts without resorting to lengthy theoretical expositions full of equations is a challenge. We have attempted to present all the major concepts and theories by illustrating their applications with numerous examples. Our guiding principle has been that rigor and intuition are equally necessary for a good understanding of the subject.

The "model-in-action" approach is used to integrate the chapter content. In the model-in-action approach, each chapter is motivated with questions of how to solve a valuation or portfolio management problem. These questions reflect the chapter's learning outcome statements found on the first page of each chapter. Examples are provided throughout the chapter to demonstrate answers to the questions and also to preview end-of-chapter problems. Thus the end-of-chapter problems should be familiar reinforcements for those students who have followed the learning outcome statements and worked through the examples of the chapter.

A basic investment course is a useful prerequisite to this text. Some knowledge of international economics may also help in the early chapters. Familiarity with discounting techniques and basic statistics (e.g., standard deviation, correlation, and regression) will make some of the chapters easier to read. However, this book is intended to be accessible to students and portfolio managers without recent training in portfolio theory.

New to the Sixth Edition

The new title *Global Investments* (formerly *International Investments*) reflects general acceptance that asset management is now global rather than categorized as domestic or international. The book's refocused emphasis builds on a foundation of accessible coverage of the world's capital markets and continues to employ contemporary examples to illustrate the application of concepts and theories. Incorporating feedback from the use of fifth edition chapters in the CFA Program curriculum, the sixth edition is the ideal text to help you succeed in financial management and global asset management.

As with the previous editions, this new edition provides students and practitioners with comprehensive yet accessible coverage of global investments. The authors have revised the book in a way that serves the needs of practitioners such as CFA candidates, while continuing to provide the coverage and accuracy our higher education adopters have come to expect. The sixth edition is a major revision in terms of both content and presentation. Specific revisions include the following:

- The sixth edition is considerably shorter than the previous edition. However, we have maintained the same level of conceptual rigor and real world orientation. This has been achieved by simplifying several chapters. For example, in Chapter 3, "Foreign Exchange Determination and Forecasting," the treatment of exchange rate quotations as well as global investment theories has been simplified. In general, we have put less emphasis on formulas while preserving the same level of rigor found in previous editions.
- Chapter 8, "Alternative Investments," has been extensively rewritten and expanded.
- Multiperiod performance measurement has been added in Chapter 12, "Global Performance Evaluation."
- Chapter 13, "Structuring the Global Investment Process," has been streamlined but also made more operational.
- All solutions to end-of-chapter problems have been moved to the Instructor's Resource Center at **http://www.prenhall.com/irc.** However, all important aspects are illustrated in the main text by examples with solutions.

Web Site

The Web site **http://www.prenhall.com/solnik_mcleavey** contains a database that can be used by the instructor to assign various projects related to some of the chapters. This database includes monthly stock indexes, bond indexes, interest rates, exchange rates, and inflation rates for major countries and a sample of emerging countries. This allows students to conduct tests of various theories presented in the text.

Instructor Resources

Instructor resources can be downloaded from the Instructor's Resource Center at **http://www.prenhall.com/irc**. The resources for this text include:

- *PowerPoint® Lecture Slides,* developed by Bonnie Buchanan of University of South Carolina. The PowerPoint slides include lecture notes and all art and tables from the text.
- *Online Solutions Manual,* written by the authors and containing solutions for all end-of-chapter problems.
- *Online Test Bank,* written by the authors, containing additional problems (with solutions) as well as a list of cases that can be used for various chapters of the book.

1

Currency Exchange Rates

LEARNING OUTCOMES

After completing this chapter, you will be able to do the following:

- Define direct and indirect methods of currency exchange rate quotations
- Define and calculate the spread on an exchange rate quotation
- Explain how spreads on exchange rate quotations can differ as a result of market conditions, bank/dealer positions, and trading volume
- Convert direct (indirect) exchange rate quotations into indirect (direct) exchange rate quotations
- Calculate cross rates, given two spot exchange rate quotations involving three currencies
- Calculate the profit on a triangular arbitrage opportunity, given the bid–ask quotations for the currencies of three countries
- Distinguish between the spot and forward markets for currency exchange rates
- Define and calculate the spread on a forward currency exchange rate quotation
- Explain how spreads on forward currency exchange rate quotations can differ as a result of market conditions, bank/dealer positions, trading volume, and maturity/length of contract
- Define forward discount and forward premium
- Calculate a forward discount or premium on an exchange rate and express either as an annualized rate
- Explain covered interest rate parity
- Define and illustrate covered interest arbitrage

The international investor is faced with a complex task. The financial markets throughout the world are quite different from one another, and information on them is sometimes difficult to obtain. Trading in different time zones and languages further complicates the task. But the most important aspect of international investment is the use of multiple currencies. An American investing in France must do so in euros; therefore, the performance (and risk) of the investment will depend in part on changes in the euro/U.S. dollar exchange rate. Because of the importance of exchange rates in international investment, we begin this book with a chapter describing foreign exchange transactions.

In this text, we develop the analysis needed for the international investment and portfolio management process. The first three chapters lay the foundation of exchange rates, which link the economies of different countries and regions. The next five chapters explore the various assets available for international investing. The final five chapters develop the techniques and perspective of global investment and portfolio management.

In Chapter 2, we develop the theory of international parity conditions. This theory helps in defining real foreign currency risk, an important factor to be managed in global investing and portfolio management. We also introduce the various theories of exchange rate determination. In Chapter 3, we then explore techniques and empirical results in the difficult task of exchange rate forecasting.

Chapter 4 introduces a series of chapters on international assets. In that chapter, we develop international asset pricing in general, with attention to foreign currency risk. Then, Chapter 5 places a particular focus on the transaction costs involved in various equity markets and instruments allowing entry into international equity investments. Following this general introduction to international asset pricing, Chapters 6, 7, and 8 focus on the available international assets themselves: equities, bonds, and alternative investments, respectively.

After building cases for and against international diversification in Chapter 9, we move into the foreign currency risk-and-return analysis needed for international portfolio management. We develop the risk-control techniques available with derivatives in Chapter 10 and then apply these techniques to currency risk management in Chapter 11. Then, in Chapter 12, we examine the performance measures to judge the risk-return contributions of international diversification. Finally, we summarize the global investment and portfolio management process in Chapter 13. Throughout the text, we attempt to isolate those elements of the process that have unique international aspects.

Chapter 1 deals with foreign exchange quotes and the relationships between different types of quotes, as well as the nature of bid–ask spreads in the foreign exchange market. The exchange rate quotes for current and future delivery must be aligned with the risk-free interest rates in the two countries for which the quotes are given. Chapter 1 presents the basic facts of foreign exchange involving quotation interpretation and arbitrage. Foreign exchange theories are saved for subsequent chapters.

Currency Exchange Rate Quotations

A currency exchange rate is the rate used to exchange two currencies. An exchange rate states the price of one currency in terms of units of another currency.

Before reviewing the international currency market, we will develop some basic notation. Over time, exchange rates change, so we will assume values for the current exchange rate, knowing that the actual values can be quite different by the time the reader views our printed page.

Suppose now that we are told that the current exchange rate between the dollar ($) and the euro (€) is 0.8. That information is unhelpful because we have not been told whether this is a price quote for the dollar or for the euro.

By convention, we will present all quotes in this book as a:b = S where

a is the quoted currency

b is the currency in which the price is expressed

S is the price of the quoted currency a in units of currency b

For example, $:€ = 0.8 indicates that one dollar is priced at 0.8 euros. Sometimes newspapers will report this as 0.8 euros per dollar.

Conversely, we can also express the exchange rate between the dollar and the euro as €:$ = 1.25, where the euro is the quoted currency in units of dollars. The euro is priced at 1.25 dollars. Hence, we have

€:$ = 1.25 and

$:€ = 0.80

Similarly, the dollar may be quoted as 120 Japanese yen (¥) per dollar, so that 100 yen are worth 0.8333 dollars. Quotations for the yen are usually indicated for 100 yen rather than for one yen because of the small value of the yen. Using the notation a:b, the quotations are

$:¥ = 120 and

¥:$ = 0.8333

Abbreviations are used to refer to the various currencies. These abbreviations could be commonly used symbols or "official" three-letter codes. Financial newspapers such as the *Financial Times* generally use symbols, while traders use three-letter codes. Symbols include $ (U.S. dollar), ¥ (Japanese yen), € (euro), £ (British pound), A$ (Australian dollar), and Sfr (Swiss franc). Three-letter codes for the same currencies are USD, JPY, EUR, GBP, AUD, and CHF. We will alternatively use in this book the various currency abbreviations that are commonly encountered. For example, the Japanese yen can be referred to as ¥, JPY, or yen.

In our discussion so far, we have used the natural terminology *dollars per euro* when referring to €:$ = 1.25 because the quoted currency is the euro. However, newspaper and trader terminology varies, and it is useful to be aware of different exchange rate treatments. It must be stressed that different news and trading services use different notations to refer to the same exchange rate. Actually, the notation $/€ = 1.25, meaning 1.25 dollars per euro, is intuitive and we used this notation in previous editions, but we changed notation in the present edition to be consistent with what has become the most widely used convention. *Readers familiar with previous editions should be aware of the change in notation.* To repeat, we will use €:$ to mean the price of one euro in dollars (number of dollars per euro). With this notation, the *quoted currency* is the first one (here, €) and its price is measured in units of the second currency (here, $).

Direct and Indirect Quotations

As an exchange rate can be quoted with a as the domestic currency or with a as the foreign currency, it is useful to introduce the nationality of the investor.

If a in $a{:}b$ is the foreign currency and b the domestic currency, then the quote is termed a *direct quote*—naturally enough, the price of the foreign currency in which we are interested. An American investor seeing a quote €:$ = 1.25 expects to pay $1.25 for one euro. He is viewing a direct quote, the price of the foreign currency. For the European investor, $:€ = 0.8 is the direct quote that the price of one dollar is 0.8 euros.

If a in $a{:}b$ is the domestic currency and b the foreign currency, then the quote is termed an *indirect quote*, the amount of foreign currency that one unit of the domestic currency will purchase. To an American investor, $:€ = 0.8 indicates that one dollar (the domestic currency) will purchase 0.8 euros. To a European investor, €:$ = 1.25 indicates that one euro (the domestic currency) will buy $1.25.

A direct quote tells us how much it will cost to purchase amounts of foreign currency, and an indirect quote tells us how much foreign currency we can get for an amount of domestic currency. If a European must pay 100 dollars for an American product, he will use a direct quote $:€ = 0.8 to know that it will cost him 80 euros. If a European is making a donation to a U.S. charity and wants to donate 100 euros, he will use an indirect quote €:$ = 1.25 to know that he is contributing 125 dollars.

Direct quotes and indirect quotes are reciprocals of each other. The price per unit of the foreign currency is the reciprocal of the number of units of foreign currency received for a unit of the domestic currency. Just as €:$ = 1.25 tells an American investor that one euro costs 1.25 dollars, so the reciprocal 1/€:$ = 1/1.25 = $:€ = 0.8 tells her that one dollar will purchase 0.8 euros. Of course, the direct euro quote for an American is the indirect dollar quote for a European, and vice versa.

Direct quotes and indirect quotes have directional differences when it comes to price appreciation. Because the direct quote tells us the price of the foreign currency, an appreciation of the foreign currency causes an increase in the direct quote, but an appreciation of the foreign currency causes a decrease in the indirect quote. An appreciation of a currency is considered a strengthening and a depreciation of a currency is considered a weakening. The following table lays out these two alternatives for a foreign and domestic currency.

Domestic Currency	Foreign Currency	Direct Exchange Rate (Foreign currency quoted)	Indirect Exchange Rate (Domestic currency quoted)
Appreciates	Depreciates	Decreases	Increases
Depreciates	Appreciates	Increases	Decreases

Example 1.1 may help ensure familiarity with the terminology.

EXAMPLE 1.1 DIRECT AND INDIRECT EXCHANGE RATES

On April 1, the British pound is quoted as £:$ = 1.80. What are the direct and indirect quotes from the viewpoint of an American and a British investor? A month later, the exchange rate has moved to £:$ = 1.90. Which currencies appreciated or depreciated?

SOLUTION

The pound is quoted in terms of dollars. This quote is a direct quote from the American viewpoint and an indirect quote from the British viewpoint. Conversely, $:£ = 0.55556 is an indirect quote from the American viewpoint and a direct quote from the British viewpoint.

In £:$, the pound is the quoted currency. Over a month, its price increased from $1.80 to $1.90, so the pound appreciated and the dollar depreciated.

Cross-Rate Calculations

A *cross rate* is the exchange rate between two currencies inferred from each country's exchange rate with a third currency, the reference currency. From the quotation of two currencies against a reference currency, we can derive a cross exchange rate. Of use for us in manipulating exchange rates will be the recognition that the : sign in $a{:}b$ can be interpreted as a "divide" sign, and we interpret $a{:}b$ as b/a.

Consider how two currencies, a and c, against a third, b, can give us $a{:}c$. In this form, $a{:}b$ times $b{:}c$ equals $a{:}c$. Of course, $b{:}a$ times $c{:}b$ then gives us $c{:}a$. Consider also how two currencies against a third $a{:}b$ and $a{:}c$ can give us $c{:}b$. In this form, $a{:}b$ divided by $a{:}c$ equals $c{:}b$. Our conclusion then is that

$$(a{:}b) \times (b{:}c) = a{:}c \text{ and}$$

$$(a{:}b) \div (a{:}c) = c{:}b$$

From the quotation of two currencies against the U.S. dollar, for example, we can derive the cross exchange rate between the two currencies: €:$ and $:¥ can give us €:¥. Assume that the euro is quoted as 1.25 dollars and the dollar is quoted as 120 Japanese yen (¥) per dollar. From these quotes, we can calculate the €:¥ rate.

$$€:\$ = 1.25 \text{ and } \$:¥ = 120$$

implies that (€:$) × ($:¥) = €:¥, or

$$€:¥ = 1.25 \times 120 = 150$$

In this example, one euro is worth 150 yen, or 100 yen are worth 0.6667 euros.

Now consider the *a*:*b* and *a*:*c* case in the following quotes for the Korean won and the Brazilian real against the dollar, with $:won = 1012.5 and $:R$ = 2.297. We calculate the won per real rate equal to the won per dollar rate (2012.50) divided by the real per dollar rate:

$$\text{R\$:won} = (\$\text{:won}) \div (\$\text{:R\$}) = 1012.5/2.297 = 440.79$$

Forex Market and Quotation Conventions

The international currency market can be seen as having two components:

- A worldwide *foreign exchange (Forex) market* where participants are major banks and specialized currency dealers (market makers). This is a "wholesale" interbank market for large transactions.
- A "retail" market where investors and corporations deal with local banks.

The Forex market is the driving force on the currency market. Banks quote foreign exchange rates to their clients based on the Forex quotations. The Forex market is a worldwide market in which dealers, mostly large commercial and investment banks, trade large orders (typically several million dollars). This is an *over-the-counter (OTC)* market in which trading is done by telephone and on electronic platforms. Trading takes place 24 hours a day, 5 days a week. A typical daily transaction volume is well above $1 trillion, making it the largest and most liquid market in the world.

In the Forex market, quotations are generally given with five significant digits and three-letter codes. For example, the USD:JPY quote could appear as 120.10 and the EUR:USD as 1.2515.[1]

The worldwide Forex market observes some specific trading conventions. *First*, there is no need to maintain a market in both euros against dollars and dollars against euros. For any pair of currencies, it is sufficient to trade in a single

[1] The most active currencies are sometimes quoted with six significant digits.

exchange rate. History mostly dictates the exchange rate direction that is selected. There is a decreasing order of seniority with the British pound as the senior currency. The Forex convention is to trade British pounds in units of other currencies, so the quote showing on Forex trading screens is the foreign exchange value of one GBP, that is, GBP:EUR, GBP:USD, or GBP:JPY. For exchange rates involving the British pound, the quoted currency is always the pound. For example, the exchange rate between the pound and the dollar is quoted as the dollar price of one pound. When the euro was introduced in 1999, it was given "seniority" just behind its British neighbor. Thus, the quote showing on Forex trading screens is the foreign exchange value of one euro, EUR:USD or EUR:JPY. For exchange rates involving the euro, the quoted currency is always the euro except for the exchange rate with the pound, where the quoted currency is the pound. Finally, the dollar is quoted in units of all other currencies, for example, USD:JPY.[2]

Second, not all exchange rates are traded. In a world with a large number of currencies, there are a very large number of cross exchange rates. For example, with 20 currencies, there are 380 bilateral exchange rates. The exchange rates between two minor currencies are not traded on the Forex market, so a Forex trader could not find on her trading screen the exchange rate between the South Korean won (won or KRW) and the Brazilian real (R$ or BRL). There would be too few transactions between the won and the real to maintain an active and liquid market. Actually, all currencies are simply traded against the U.S. dollar. To buy Korean won with Brazilian reals, an investor must do two Forex transactions: first buy dollars with reals, and then sell those dollars for won. To create liquidity on this interbank market, all transactions involving the Brazilian real are therefore conducted against the U.S. dollar. We can derive the cross rate won:R$ from the two exchange rates $:won and $:R$. Hence, all currencies are quoted against the U.S. dollar, which remains the dominant Forex currency of quotation, although there are such regional exceptions as the yen in Asia and the euro and pound in Europe.[3]

Third, Forex quotes always include a *bid price* and an *ask price* (or *offer* price), and there is no commission or fee added on a trade. The bid price is the price at which the foreign exchange dealer is willing to buy the quoted currency in exchange for the second currency. The ask price is the price at which the dealer is willing to sell the base currency in exchange for the second currency. The difference between the bid and the ask prices is referred to as the *spread.* As an example, assume that a dealer provides the following quote for the $:¥ (value of the dollar in yen):

$:¥ = 120.17–120.19

[2] There is one exception, however. The Australian dollar (AUD) and New Zealand dollar (NZD) are traded in units of U.S. dollars (e.g., AUD:USD or NZD:USD). This is probably a remnant of the British Empire and there is pressure to change this convention for the AUD and NZD.

[3] For example, there are active markets between the euro and the Swiss franc and between the euro and the pound.

The dealer is willing to buy dollars at a price of 120.17 yen per dollar (bid) and willing to sell dollars at a price of 120.19 yen per dollar (ask). We now provide more details on bid–ask quotes.

Bid–Ask (Offer) Quotes and Spreads

As mentioned above, the foreign exchange dealer quotes not one but two prices. The *bid* price is the exchange rate at which the dealer is willing to buy a currency; the *ask* (or *offer*) price is the exchange rate at which the dealer is willing to sell a currency. The *midpoint* price is the average of the bid and ask price: $(ask + bid)/2$. The *bid–ask spread* is the difference between the bid and ask prices. For example, a bank could quote the euro in dollars as

€:$ = 1.2011–1.2014

The dealer is willing to buy euros at a price of 1.2011 dollars per euro (bid) and willing to sell euros at a price of 1.2014 dollars per euro (ask). Forex traders would say that the spread is equal to 3 *pips*. A *pip*, which stands for *price interest point*, represents the smallest fluctuation in the price of a currency. Hence, a pip refers to one unit of the final digit of the quoted exchange rate. This is similar to the concept of "tick" for stocks. The spread is sometimes expressed as a percentage of the ask price (or midpoint price). In the example, the percentage spread is about 2.5 *basis points*:

$$\text{Percentage spread} = \frac{1.2014-1.2011}{1.2011} = 0.00025 = 0.025\% = 2.5 \text{ basis points}$$

Spreads differ as a result of market conditions and trading volume. The size of the bid–ask spread increases with exchange rate uncertainty (*volatility*) and lack of liquidity because of bank/dealer *risk aversion*. When a dealer posts a quote, she does not know whether the customer will buy or sell the quoted currency. Hence, the dealer could end up with an unexpected currency position, depending on the customer's decision. It could take some time for the dealer to offset that position with another customer or on the Forex market. When markets are volatile, there could be a large adverse price movement during that time period. Dealers increase their quoted spreads in volatile times. For thinly traded currencies, it will take longer to offset a currency position at reasonable prices. The length of that time period increases the risk of an adverse price movement. Dealers quote larger spreads for illiquid currencies relative to major currencies with active trading.

The bank/dealer position should not have a significant influence on the size of the bid–ask spread quoted by that dealer. Rather, the midpoint of the spread moves in response to dealer positions. For example, a dealer with excess supply of a specific foreign currency would move the midpoint of that quoted currency down rather than adjust the size of his spread. A dealer quoting a large spread relative to other dealers will basically not trade, so that would not help to reduce the position. Neither will the dealer want to quote a smaller spread because that would mean raising his bid price when he does not want to buy. Basically, the dealer will lower both his bid and ask prices in order to induce customers to buy this specific currency rather than sell it. For example, a dealer with excess euros will try to sell them and therefore lower his ask price of \$1.2014 to, say, \$1.2012 and will probably also lower his bid to avoid having to buy more euros, from \$1.2011 to, say, \$1.2009.

The Forex market quotes exchange rates only in one direction (e.g., €:\$, not \$:€). But it is easy to infer the bid–ask prices for the same pair of currencies quoted in the other direction. Two principles apply:

- The *\$:€ ask* exchange rate is the reciprocal of the *€:\$ bid* exchange rate.
- The *\$:€ bid* exchange rate is the reciprocal of the *€:\$ ask* exchange rate.

In the example above, the dealer is willing to buy euros for dollars at a bid price of 1.2011 dollars per euro. This would be equivalent of the dealer selling dollars for euros at a rate of 1/1.2011 = 0.83257 euros per dollar. Hence, the €:\$ quote of

€:\$ = 1.2011–1.2014

is equivalent to a \$:€ quote of

\$:€ = 0.83236–0.83257

A customer wishing to convert \$100,000 into euros could simply buy the euros from the dealer at the ask price of €:\$ = 1.2014 and hence obtain 100,000/1.2014 = €83,236. This is identical to selling \$100,000 at the bid \$:€ = 0.83236.

A local bank will happily quote bid–ask exchange rates in any direction requested by a customer. Of course, spreads quoted to "retail" customers tend to be wider than those found on the "wholesale" Forex market.

Example 1.2 may help to show how a transaction is initiated.

EXAMPLE 1.2 EXCHANGE RATE QUOTES AND FRENCH BONDS

A U.S. portfolio manager wants to buy \$10 million worth of French bonds. The manager wants to know how many euros can be obtained to invest using the \$10 million. The manager calls several banks to get their €/\$ quotation, without indicating whether a sale or a purchase of euros is desired. Bank A gives the following quotation:

€:\$ = 1.24969–1.25000

Bank A is willing to buy a euro for 1.24969 dollars or to sell a euro for 1.25000 dollars. These quotes are consistent with the following quotes for the \$:€:

\$:€ = 0.80000–0.80020

Note how the ask price for \$:€ of 0.80020 is the reciprocal of the bid €:\$, giving the ask price equal to 1/1.24969 = 0.80020.

To make the quote faster, only the last digits, called the *points*, are sometimes quoted. The preceding quote would often be given as follows:

\$:€ = 0.80000–20

or even

$:€ = 000–020

Assume that the portfolio manager gets the following quotes from three different banks:

	Bank A	Bank B	Bank C
$:€ =	0.80000–20	0.79985–05	0.79995–15

Note that the ask for all three quotes adds 0.00020 to the bid. How many euros will the portfolio manager get to invest?

SOLUTION

The manager will immediately choose Bank A and indicate that he will buy 8 million euros for $10 million. Both parties indicate where each sum should be transferred. The portfolio manager indicates that the euros should be transferred to an account with the Société Générale, the manager's business bank in Paris, whereas Bank A indicates that it will receive the dollars at its account with Citibank in New York. Electronic messages and faxes are exchanged to confirm the oral agreement. The settlement of the transaction takes place simultaneously in Paris and in New York two days later.

Cross-Rate Calculations with Bid–Ask Spreads

Recall that a cross rate is the exchange rate between two currencies inferred from each currency's exchange rate with a third currency, the reference currency.

Earlier we examined a case of $(a{:}b) \div (a{:}c) = c{:}b$, where we assumed that the exchange rate of the Brazilian real per dollar was $:R$ = 2.2970 and that the won per dollar rate was $:won = 1012.50. We calculated the won per real cross rate by dividing the won per dollar rate (1012.50) by the real per dollar rate (2.2970):

R$:won = ($:won) ÷ ($:R$) = 1012.50 / 2.2970 = 440.79

Let's now consider the case where currencies are quoted with a bid–ask spread, as follows:

$:R$ = 2.2960–2.2980

$:won = 1012.0–1013.0

To compute bid–ask cross rates, we follow the same procedure but need to think of the direction of the money flow. For simplicity, assume that we are an investor interrogating a currency dealer. Hence, we take the view of a client, not of the dealer. First, think of the bid price as being the price when we (an investor) hold the quoted currency and want to sell it to the dealer, who is quoting us a price at which he is willing to purchase the quoted currency. Similarly, think of the ask price as the price when we want to buy the quoted currency from the dealer, who is quoting a price at which he will sell the quoted currency. In short, *bid* means we "have" the quoted currency (and wish to sell it) and *ask* means we "want" it as an investor.

For $(\text{R\$:won})_{bid}$ the dealer is willing to buy reals in exchange for won, and the investor desires to sell his reals to buy won. But, if we thought of the underlying two-step process, the investor would *use his reals to purchase dollars* (want dollars) at the $(\$:\text{R\$})_{ask}$ price and *use dollars* (have dollars) *to purchase won* at the $(\$:\text{won})_{bid}$ price. This means the investor faces the ask price for ($:R$) and the bid price for ($:won).

$$(\text{R\$:won})_{bid} = (\$:\text{won})_{bid} \div (\$:\text{R\$})_{ask}$$

For $(\text{R\$:won})_{ask}$ the dealer is willing to sell reals in exchange for won, and the investor desires to buy reals using won. But in a two-step process, the investor would *use his won to purchase dollars* (want dollars) and then *use his dollars* (have dollars) *to purchase reals*. This means the investor faces the ask price for ($:won) and the bid price for ($:R$).

$$(\text{R\$:won})_{ask} = (\$:\text{won})_{ask} \div (\$:\text{R\$})_{bid}$$

We first calculate the bid–ask cross rates when the Brazilian real is quoted in terms of won:

$$(\text{R\$:won})_{bid} = (\$:\text{won})_{bid} \div (\$:\text{R\$})_{ask} = 1012.0/2.2980 = 440.38 \text{ won per real}$$

$$(\text{R\$:won})_{ask} = (\$:\text{won})_{ask} \div (\$:\text{R\$})_{bid} = 1013.0/2.2960 = 441.20 \text{ won per real}$$

As an exercise, we now calculate the bid–ask cross rates when the won is quoted in terms of Brazilian reals:

$$(\text{won:R\$})_{bid} = (\$:\text{R\$})_{bid} \div (\$:\text{won})_{ask} = 2.2960/1013.0 = 0.0022665 \text{ real per won}$$

$$(\text{won:R\$})_{ask} = (\$:\text{R\$})_{ask} \div (\$:\text{won})_{bid} = 2.2980/1012.0 = 0.0022708 \text{ real per won}$$

Of course, it is much easier to calculate these second two quotes from the first two by using our relation that $(\text{won:R\$})_{bid} = 1 \div (\text{R\$:won})_{ask} = 1/441.20 = 0.0022677$ and $(\text{won:R\$})_{ask} = 1 \div (\text{R\$;won})_{bid} = 1 \div 440.38 = 0.002271$.

We have to be careful when different quotation conventions are used. For example, the euro is usually the quoted currency against the dollar in the Forex market. The equations given above should be adapted to reflect the quotation convention. Example 1.3 provides an illustration.

As mentioned above, it would be inefficient to maintain a market between two "minor" currencies (such as the won and the real). Because there would be too few direct transactions between them, the spread would need to be very large to induce a *market maker* to provide continuous quotes. Centralizing all transactions involving those two minor currencies against one single major currency (the dollar) is much more efficient from a cost viewpoint. However, there is a direct market between a few major currencies, meaning that the dollar is not necessarily used as the reference currency. For example, the spread quoted on a direct transaction from euros to Swiss francs could be less than the cross-rate spread.

EXAMPLE 1.3 CROSS RATES WITH THE WON, EURO, AND DOLLAR

You wish to calculate the cross rate between the euro and the South Korean won (€:won). A major dealer on the Forex market provides the following quotes:

$$\$\text{:won} = 1012.0-1013.0$$

$$€\text{:}\$ = 1.24969-1.25000$$

Calculate the bid and ask cross exchange rate €:won.

SOLUTION

Because the euro is quoted in terms of dollars, the won per euro exchange rate is given by

$$€\text{:won} = (€\text{:}\$) \times (\$\text{:won})$$

Hence, the bid and ask cross rates are

$$(€\text{:won})_{\text{bid}} = (€\text{:}\$)_{\text{bid}} \times (\$\text{:won})_{\text{bid}} = 1.24969 \times 1012.0$$
$$= 1264.69 \text{ won per euro}$$
$$(€\text{:won})_{\text{ask}} = (€\text{:}\$)_{\text{ask}} \times (\$\text{:won})_{\text{ask}} = 1.25000 \times 1013.0$$
$$= 1266.25 \text{ won per euro}$$

To verify that the calculations have been made correctly, there are two checks.

The *first check* to make sure that you measure the cross rate in the right direction is to look at the symbols. Notice that the $ symbol disappears in the equations above if you recall that $a{:}b$ times $b{:}c$ equals $a{:}c$.

A *second check* on the result is to make sure that you *maximize* the bid–ask spread. To get the bid cross rate, which is the smaller rate, you should use the combination of bid and ask exchange rates that yields the lowest cross rate.

No-Arbitrage Conditions with Exchange Rates

The foreign exchange market is highly liquid and efficient. If some riskless arbitrage became available, it would be quickly eliminated. Hence, quotes are immediately aligned. For example, several banks provide a market for the dollar in terms of euros, but it would be strange to see an *arbitrage* opportunity available between them. An arbitrage could be created if it were profitable to buy from one bank and sell to another. Such a profitable arbitrage would happen only if the ask price quoted by one bank were below the bid price quoted by another bank. If you saw the following quotes, what would look strangely attractive?

	Bank A	**Bank B**	**Bank C**
$:€ =	0.80000–20	0.79985–95	0.79995–15

You could buy dollars from Bank B for 0.79995 euros per dollar and simultaneously sell them to bank A for 0.80000 euros per dollar. The gain per dollar is very small, but it is riskless and does not require any invested capital. Currency traders are careful that such arbitrage situations do not arise, and quotes are adjusted on a continuous basis. In highly volatile periods, the adjustment can take place every few seconds as the spread on exchange rates is very small compared to a typical exchange rate move.

Arbitrage aligns exchange rate quotes throughout the world. The quote for the €:$ rate must be the same, at a given instant, in Frankfurt, London, Paris, and New York. If quotes were to deviate by more than the spread, a simple phone call would allow a trader to make enormous profits. There are enough professionals in the world watching continuous quote fluctuations to rule out such riskless profit opportunities.

Triangular arbitrage ensures consistency between exchange rates and cross rates, but spreads have to be taken into account, as suggested in Example 1.4.

EXAMPLE 1.4 TRIANGULAR ARBITRAGE ON CROSS RATES

On the Forex market, an American bank gives the following quotes:

$$€:\$ = 1.2000–1.2050$$

$$£:€ = 1.7950–1.8000$$

A British bank gives the following quote:

$$£:€ = 1.5050–1.5070$$

Is there an arbitrage opportunity?

SOLUTION

We can find the £:€ quotes implicit in the American bank's quotes:

$$(£:€)_{bid} = (£:\$)_{bid} \div (€:\$)_{ask} = 1.7950/1.2050 = 1.4896 \text{ euros per pound}$$

$$(£:€)_{ask} = (£:\$)_{ask} \div (€:\$)_{bid} = 1.8000/1.2000 = 1.5000 \text{ euros per pound}$$

The resulting cross-rate quote by the American bank is:

$$£:€ = 1.4896–1.5000$$

There is an arbitrage opportunity because the ask cross-rate of the American bank's quote is below the bid £:€ quoted by the British bank. An arbitrage sequence would be to

- Use 1.8 dollars to buy one pound from the American bank at $(£:\$)_{ask}$.
- Simultaneously sell the American bank 1.5 euros for dollars at $(€:\$)_{bid} = 1.2000$. This would yield 1.8 dollars. These first two transactions are equivalent to buying one pound with 1.5 euros at the American bank's cross rate of $(£:€)_{ask} = 1.5$ euros per pound.
- Sell one pound to the British bank at its $(£:€)_{bid}$ of 1.5050 euros per pound.

The net profit is 0.05 euro used in the arbitrage. This is a riskless profit that requires no initial investment. Such an arbitrage opportunity cannot remain on an efficient currency market.

Forward Quotes

Spot exchange rates are quoted for immediate currency transactions, although in practice the settlement takes place 48 hours later. Spot transactions are used extensively to settle commercial purchases of goods as well as for investments.

Foreign exchange dealers also quote *forward exchange rates*. These are rates contracted today but with delivery and settlement in the future, usually 30 or 90 days hence. As with spot rates, forward rates are quoted by a bank with a bid and an ask price. For example, a bank may quote the one-month €:$ exchange rate as 1.24688–1.24719. This means that the bank is willing to commit itself today to buy euros for 1.24688 dollars or to sell them for 1.24695 dollars in one month. In a *forward contract* (or futures contract), a commitment is irrevocably made on the transaction date, but the exchange of currency takes place later on a date set in the contract. The origins of the forward currency market may be traced back to the Middle Ages, when merchants from all over Europe met at major trade fairs and made forward contracts for the next fair.

Forward exchange rates are commonly used by asset managers to manage their foreign currency positions. By investing in foreign assets, an investor takes a currency position that can suffer (or benefit) from exchange rate movements. For example, a German investor might wish to invest in attractive American stocks but fear a depreciation of the U.S. dollar. In order to hedge the dollar risk, the German investor will sell dollars forward against euros. Currency risk management is a topic addressed in Chapter 11. But it is important first to get an understanding of the pricing of the forward exchange rate and its relation to the spot exchange rate.

Forward exchange rates are often quoted as a premium, or discount, to the spot exchange rate. With the convention of giving the value of the quoted currency (the first currency) in terms of units of the second currency, there is a premium on the quoted currency when the forward exchange rate is higher than the spot rate and a discount otherwise. Clearly, a negative premium is a discount. If the one-month forward exchange rate is €:$ = 1.24688 (1.24688 dollars per euro) and the spot rate is €:$ = 1.25000, the euro quotes with a discount of 0.00312 dollar per euro. In the language of currency traders, the euro is "weak" relative to the dollar, as its forward value is lower than its spot value. Conversely, the dollar is traded at a premium, as the forward value of one dollar ($:€ = 1/1.24688 = 0.80200) is higher than its spot value ($:€ = 0.80000).

Consequently, when a trader announces that a currency quotes at a premium, the premium should be added to the spot exchange rate to obtain the value of the forward exchange rate. If a currency quotes at a discount, the discount should be subtracted from the spot exchange rate to obtain the value of the forward rate.

The forward discount, or premium, is often calculated as an annualized percentage deviation from the spot rate. Given an exchange rate of $a{:}b$, the annualized forward premium (discount) on the quoted currency a is equal to

$$\left(\frac{\text{Forward rate} - \text{Spot rate}}{\text{Spot rate}}\right)\left(\frac{12}{\text{No. months forward}}\right)100\% \qquad (1.1)$$

If (Spot rate − Forward rate) replaces (Forward rate − Spot rate) in Formula 1.1, we have the forward discount (premium) on the measurement currency in which the price is expressed.

The percentage premium (discount) is annualized by multiplying by 12 and dividing by the length of the forward contract in months. For example, the annualized forward premium on the dollar as quoted above is

$$\left(\frac{0.802-0.800}{0.800}\right)\left(\frac{12}{1}\right)100\% = 3.0\%$$

Interbank quotations are often reported in the form of an annualized premium (discount) for reasons that will become obvious in the next section. However, forward rates quoted to customers are usually outright (e.g., €:$ = 1.24688–1.24719).

Spot and forward dollar exchange rates can be found in newspapers around the world, such as the London-based *Financial Times*. For example, the spot $:SFr exchange rate could be $:SFr = 1.2932–1.2939. The midpoint is equal to 1.2936. At the same time, $:SFr for delivery three months later could be quoted at a midpoint of 1.2823. The dollar (the quoted currency) quotes at a discount and the Swiss franc at a premium. The annualized percentage premium of the Swiss franc would then be equal to 3.5 percent. Because the Swiss franc is the measurement currency in the quote, this premium is obtained by taking the difference between the spot and the forward rate and dividing it by the spot rate:

$$\text{Annualized three-month forward premium} = \left(\frac{0.0113}{1.2936}\right)\left(\frac{12}{3}\right)100\% = 3.5\%$$

Interest Rate Parity: The Forward Discount and the Interest Rate Differential

As mentioned earlier, arbitrage plays an important role in the worldwide currency market. Spot exchange rates, forward exchange rates, and interest rates

CONCEPTS IN ACTION *STRONG CURRENCIES*

The sign of the premium as reported in newspapers such as the *Financial Times* (FT) must be considered carefully. This is because the convention for quotation of the dollar exchange rate differs across currencies and because the layperson associates a premium with strength. For all currencies except the euro and British pound, the dollar is the quoted currency, and this leads the FT to reverse the formula and report a calculation based on *spot minus forward* so that a positive premium can indicate that the measurement currency on the line is "strong" relative to the dollar. For example, with $:Sfr, a dollar worth fewer future Swiss francs means a premium on the Sfr currency line. For the euro and the pound, the euro and the pound are the quoted currencies, so a euro worth fewer future dollars (a positive spot minus forward premium as reported) indicates that the currency on the line is "weak" relative to the dollar, while a discount (a negative premium) indicates that the currency is strong.

Foreign Exchange Quotations
Dollar Spot Forward Against the Dollar

Aug. 30		Closing Midpoint	Bid/Offer[1]	Three Months Rate	%PA[2]
Euro	(€)	0.9841	839–842	0.9802	1.6
UK	(£)	1.5492	490–494	1.541	2.1
Switzerland	(SFr)	1.4926	922–929	1.4887	1.1
Canada	(C$)	1.5612	610–614	1.566	−1.2
Japan	(¥)	118.185	160–210	117.655	1.8

[1]Bid/offer spreads show only the last three decimal places. UK £ and euro are quoted in U.S. currency.

[2]Means % per annum.

Source: Data from the *Financial Times* and WM/REUTERS.

are technically linked for all currencies that are part of the free international market.

Interest rate parity (IRP) is a relationship linking spot exchange rates, forward exchange rates, and interest rates. For two currencies, the IRP relationship is that the forward discount/premium equals the discounted interest rate differential between the two currencies. Stated more simply, the product of the forward rate multiplied by one plus the risk-free rate for the quoted currency equals the product of the spot exchange rate multiplied by one plus the risk-free rate for the measurement currency in which the price is expressed. The relation is driven by arbitrage as illustrated here. Assume that the following data exist for the dollar (quoted currency) and the euro:

Spot exchange rate	$:€ = 0.8000
One-year forward exchange rate	$:€ = 0.8080

One-year interest rates (purposely unrealistic at present to show numerical effects) are

$$r_{€} = 14\% \text{ and } r_{\$} = 10\%$$

To take advantage of the interest rate differential, a speculator could borrow dollars at 10 percent, convert them immediately into euros at the rate of 0.8 euros per dollar, and invest the euros at 14 percent. This action is summarized in Exhibit 1.1. The speculator makes a profit of 4 percent on the borrowing/lending position but runs the risk of a large depreciation of the euro.

In Exhibit 1.1, borrowing dollars means bringing money from the future to the present. Lending euros means the reverse. At the end of the period, at time 1, the speculator must convert euros into dollars at an unknown rate to honor the claim in dollars borrowed.

This position may be transformed into a covered (riskless) interest rate arbitrage by simultaneously buying a forward exchange rate contract to convert the euros into dollars in one year at a known forward exchange rate of $:€ = 0.808. In the process shown in Exhibit 1.2, the investor still benefits on the interest rate

EXHIBIT 1.1

Currency Speculation

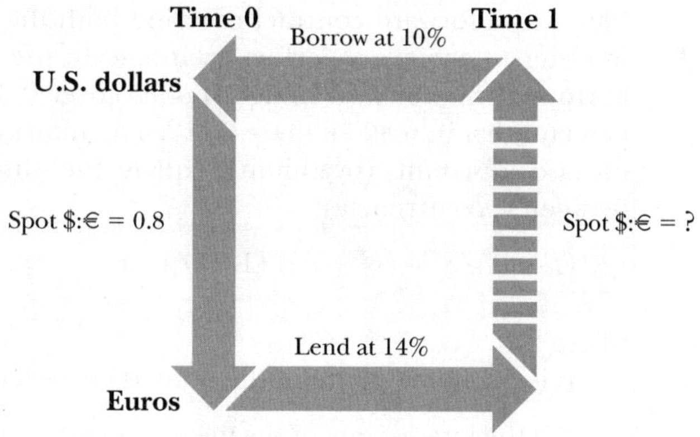

EXHIBIT 1.2

Covered Interest Rate Arbitrage

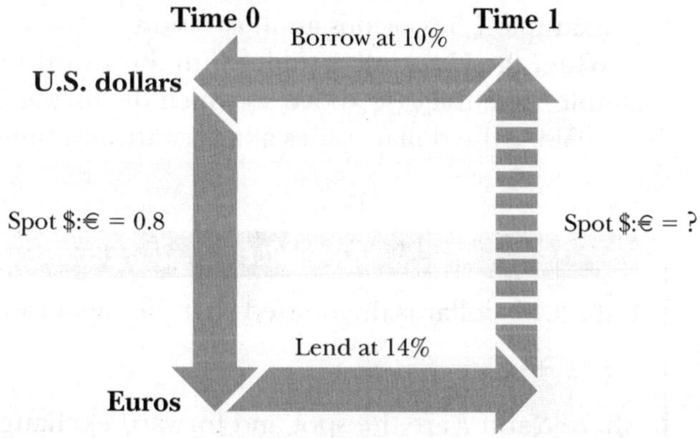

differential (a gain of 4 percent) but loses on the conversion of euros to dollars. In one year, the rate of change in the exchange rate will be equal to

$$\frac{0.800-0.808}{0.800} = -0.01 \text{ for a loss of } 1\%$$

Per dollar borrowed, the net gain on the position is 3 percent. This gain is certain at time 0 because all interest rates and exchange rates are fixed at that time.

No capital is invested in the position, which is a pure *swap* with simultaneous borrowing and lending. If such rates were quoted in reality, banks would arbitrage to exploit this riskless profit opportunity. Enormous swaps could occur, because no capital needs to be invested. To prevent this obvious arbitrage (riskless profit), the forward discount (premium) must exactly equal the interest rate differential. The various rates must adjust so that interest rate parity holds. Note that if the forward discount (premium) were larger than the interest rate differential, the arbitrage would simply go the other way. Arbitrageurs would borrow euros and swap them for dollars.

The exact mathematical relationship is slightly more complicated, because one must buy a forward contract covering both the principal and the accrued interest in order to achieve a perfect arbitrage. In the previous example, for every dollar borrowed, the forward hedge should cover 0.8 euros plus the interest rate of 14 percent, that is, 0.80 (1.14) = 0.912. The interest rate parity relationship is that the forward discount (premium) equals the discounted interest rate differential between two currencies:

$$(F - S)/S = (r_b - r_a)/(1 + r_a) \tag{1.2}$$

where

r_a is the interest rate of the quoted currency

r_b is the interest rate of the measurement currency in which the price is expressed.

S and F are the spot and forward exchange rates; for example, $s = a{:}b$

Equivalently, we have the relation

$$F(1 + r_a) = S(1 + r_b) \quad \text{or} \quad F = S(1 + r_b)/(1 + r_a) \tag{1.3}$$

Example 1.5 provides an illustration.

When the U.S. dollar trades with a forward premium relative to the euro—for example, as in the case above, in which the forward rate is €1.0668 and the spot rate is €1.0500—the dollar trades at a forward premium relative to the euro; conversely,

EXAMPLE 1.5 INTEREST RATE PARITY

If the U.S. dollar is the quoted currency against the euro, arbitrage ensures that

$$F(1 + r_\$) = S(1 + r_€)$$

where S and F are the spot and forward exchange rates (euro price of one U.S. dollar) and $r_€$ and $r_\$$ are the interest rates in euros and U.S. dollars. This relation implies that the forward premium (discount) will be

$$\frac{F - S}{S} = \frac{r_€ - r_\$}{1 + r_\$}$$

If the spot exchange rate is \$:€ = 1.05 and the dollar and euro interest rates are 1.76 percent and 3.39 percent, what is the forward exchange rate, and what is the forward premium (discount)?

SOLUTION

Using equation 1.3, we have

$$F = S(1 + r_€)/(1 - r_\$) = 1.05(1.0339/1.0176) = 1.0668, \text{ or } \$:€ = 1.0668$$

and

$$\frac{F-S}{S} = \frac{r_€ - r_\$}{1 + r_\$}$$

$$= \frac{0.0339 - 0.0176}{1.0176}$$

$$= 1.6\%$$

the euro trades at a forward discount relative to the U.S. dollar. Notice that a forward premium is associated with a lower interest rate.

A similar arbitrage relation holds for maturities of less than a year, provided that the right interest rates are used. Whatever the maturity, the convention for interest rates and yields is to quote annualized rates. To perform the forward exchange rate calculations, annualized interest rates must first be converted into rates over the investment period. For a contract with n months' maturity, the quoted interest rate must be divided by 12 and multiplied by n. This is because short-term interest rates are quoted using a linear convention for annualization. Example 1.6 illustrates the calculations for maturities of less than one year.

EXAMPLE 1.6 INTEREST RATE PARITY WITH MATURITIES OF LESS THAN ONE YEAR

Consider the following data:

Spot exchange rate $:€ = 1.058

Annual risk-free interest rates (three-month maturity)

3.39% for the euro

1.76% for the U.S. dollar

What is the three-month forward exchange rate $:€?

SOLUTION

Three-month interest rates over the period are

$r_€$ 3.39% (3/12) = 0.8475%

$r_\$$ 1.76% (3/12) = 0.44%

The three-month forward exchange rate is equal to

$$\text{Forward exchange rate} = \text{Spot exchange rate} \times \frac{1 + r_€}{1 + r_\$}$$

$$= 1.058(1.008475/1.0044) = 1.0623$$

Thus, the three-month forward rate is €1.0623 per dollar, or $:t= 1.0623.

One can also calculate forward exchange rates for maturities longer than a year, although that is more rarely done.[4] One should be aware that annual interest rates, or yields, for longer maturities are typically quoted using a compounding, or actuarial, convention, not a linear convention as for money rates.

Forward Exchange Rate Calculations with Bid–Ask Spreads

When an investor calls a bank to get a forward exchange rate quote, the bank will quote a bid and ask price. As with spot exchange rates, bid–ask spreads differ as a result of market conditions, bank/dealer positions, and trading volume. Unique to forward transactions is the feature that liquidity decreases with the increasing maturity of the forward contract. Consequently, bid–ask spreads increase with the increasing maturity of the contract.

Actually, a bank will usually construct a forward contract by doing the three transactions outlined above: a spot foreign exchange transaction, coupled with borrowing and lending in the two currencies. Hence, the spread on a forward rate is derived from the spreads on the spot rate and on the two interest rates. As for exchange rates, banks quote interest rates with a bid–ask spread. The bid interest rate is the rate at which the bank is willing to borrow money from the client, and the ask interest rate is the rate at which the bank is willing to lend money to a client. Of course, the bid interest rate is lower than the ask interest rate. In what follows, we calculate the ask forward $:€ and then the bid forward $:*t*.

For example, a transaction in which an investor is buying forward dollars (having to pay the ask forward $:€) with euros is equivalent to $:*t*.

- Borrowing euros (and hence having to pay the ask interest rate, ask $r_{€}$)
- Using these euros to buy dollars spot (and hence having to pay the ask spot exchange rate, ask spot $:€)
- Lending those dollars (and hence receiving the bid interest rate, bid $r_{\$}$)

To obtain the bid forward exchange rate, we perform the reverse calculations:

- Borrowing dollars (and hence having to pay the ask interest rate, ask $r_{\$}$)
- Selling these dollars to buy euros spot (and hence receiving the bid spot exchange rate, bid spot $:€)
- Lending those euros (and hence receiving the bid interest rate, bid $r_{€}$)

The result will constitute the bid price of the forward exchange rate, bid forward $:€.

Example 1.7 illustrates the calculations.

---

[4] As mentioned above, forward contracts are typically offered for maturities ranging from a day to three months, but it is easy to roll over 90-day contracts.

EXAMPLE 1.7 FORWARD QUOTATIONS WITH BID–ASK SPREADS

Consider the following data:

Spot exchange rate $:Sfr = 1.2932–1.2939

Annual risk-free interest rates (one-year maturity) are

Swiss francs	1.42%–1.44%
U.S. dollar	4.50%–4.52%

What should be the bid–ask quote for the one-year forward exchange rate $:SFr?

SOLUTION

Let's first make sure we calculate the forward rate in the proper direction. The one-year forward rate $:Sfr is given by equation (1.3), where the dollar is the quoted currency measured in Swiss francs:

$$\text{Forward exchange rate} = \text{Spot exchange rate} \times \frac{1 + r_{SFr}}{1 + r_{\$}}$$

A bank will quote bid-ask forward rates, where the bid is lower than the ask. The ask forward rate (ask forward $:SFr) is the SFr price at which an investor can buy dollars forward, and the bid forward rate is the price that an investor can obtain for dollars. Buying dollars forward (paying the ask forward) is equivalent to

- Borrowing Swiss francs (and hence having to pay the ask interest rate, ask r_{SFr})
- Using these Swiss francs to buy dollars spot (and hence having to pay the ask exchange rate, ask spot $:SFr)
- Lending those dollars (and hence receiving the bid interest rate, bid $r_{\$}$)

The resulting ask forward exchange rate ($:SFr) is

$$\text{Ask forward}(\$:\text{SFr}) = 1.2939 \frac{1 + 1.44\%}{1 + 4.50\%} = 1.2560$$

The bid forward exchange rate ($:SFr) is

$$\text{Bid forward }(\$:\text{SFr}) = 1.2932 \frac{1 + 1.42\%}{1 + 4.52\%} = 1.2548$$

Thus, the one-year forward rate should be $:SFr = 1.2548–1.2560.

Finally, we note that interest rate parity is sometimes called *covered* interest rate parity (covered by a forward contract) to distinguish it from *uncovered interest rate parity*. *Uncovered interest rate parity* is based on economic theory rather than on arbitrage and involves expected exchange rates rather than forward rates. Uncovered interest rate parity is an economic theory that links interest rate differentials and the difference between the spot and expected exchange rate. We leave it and other parity theories for Chapter 2. On the other hand, interest rate parity, discussed in this chapter, is a pure arbitrage condition imposed by efficient markets.

Summary

- A direct exchange rate is the domestic price of foreign currency. An indirect exchange rate is the amount of foreign currency equivalent that one unit of the domestic currency purchases.
- The spread on a foreign currency transaction is the difference between the rate at which the bank is willing to commit itself today to buy (bid) foreign currency and to sell (ask). When given as a percentage, this spread is given as $100 \times (ask - bid) / ask$.
- Spreads differ as a result of market conditions and trading volume but not dealer positions. The size of the bid–ask spread increases with exchange rate uncertainty (volatility) because of bank/dealer risk aversion. Spreads are larger for currencies that have a low trading volume (thinly traded currencies).
- To work with currency cross rates and bid–ask spreads, we can use two principles: The ask exchange rate for the quoted currency is the reciprocal of the bid exchange rate for the measurement currency in which the price is expressed.
- To calculate the profit on a triangular arbitrage opportunity, the basic step is to determine whether the quoted cross rate is different from the implied cross rate.
- Spot exchange rates are quoted for immediate currency transactions, but forward change rates are rates contracted today for delivery and settlement in the future.
- As with spot rates, forward contract bid–ask spreads differ as a result of market conditions and trading volume but not bank/dealer positions. Bid–ask spreads increase with increasing maturity of the contract.
- The forward discount (negative) or premium (positive) is defined as the forward rate minus the spot rate expressed as a percentage of the spot rate.
- The forward discount or premium is often calculated as an annualized percentage deviation from the spot rate as given by the discount or premium multiplied by 12 over the number of months forward.
- The interest rate parity relationship is that the forward discount (premium) equals the interest rate differential between the two currencies: what is gained on the interest rate of a currency is lost on its discount.

- Covered interest arbitrage is the process of simultaneously borrowing the domestic currency, transferring it into foreign currency at the spot exchange rate, lending it, and buying a forward exchange rate contract to repatriate the foreign currency into domestic currency at a known forward exchange rate. The net result of such an arbitrage should be nil.

Problems

1. If the exchange rate value of the British pound goes from U.S. $1.80 to U.S. $1.60, then
   a. The pound has appreciated, and the British will find U.S. goods cheaper.
   b. The pound has appreciated, and the British will find U.S. goods more expensive.
   c. The pound has depreciated, and the British will find U.S. goods more expensive.
   d. The pound has depreciated, and the British will find U.S. goods cheaper.

2. If the exchange rate between the Australian dollar and the U.S. dollar, $:A$, changes from A$1.60 to A$1.50, then
   a. The Australian dollar has appreciated, and the Australians will find U.S. goods cheaper.
   b. The Australian dollar has appreciated, and the Australians will find U.S. goods more expensive.
   c. The Australian dollar has depreciated, and the Australians will find U.S. goods more expensive.
   d. The Australian dollar has depreciated, and the Australians will find U.S. goods cheaper.

3. Over a period of time in the past, the exchange rate between the Swiss franc and the U.S. dollar, $:SFr, changed from about 1.20 to about 1.60. Would you agree that over this period, Swiss goods became cheaper for Americans?

4. Over a period of time in the past, you noticed that the exchange rate between the Thai baht and the dollar changed considerably. In particular, the $:baht exchange rate increased from 25 to 30.
   a. Did the Thai baht appreciate or depreciate with respect to the dollar? By what percentage?
   b. By what percentage did the value of the dollar change with respect to the Thai baht?

5. A foreign exchange trader with a U.S. bank took a short position of £5 million when the £:$ exchange rate was 1.45. Subsequently, the exchange rate changed to 1.51. Is this movement in the exchange rate good from the point of view of the position taken by the trader? By how much did the bank's liability change because of the change in exchange rate?

6. A financial newspaper provided the following midpoint spot exchange rates. Compute all the cross exchange rates based on these quotes.

€:$ = 0.9119

$:SFr = 1.5971

$:¥ = 128.17

7. You visited the foreign exchange trading room of a major bank when a trader asked for quotes of the euro from various correspondents and heard the following:

Bank A	1.1210–15
Bank B	12–17

What do these quotes mean?

8. Do you think the dollar exchange rate of the British pound or the Polish zloty has a higher percentage bid–ask spread? Why?

9. Here are some historical quotes of the USD:JPY (yen per dollar) exchange rate given simultaneously on the phone by three banks:

Bank A	121.15–121.25
Bank B	121.30–121.35
Bank C	121.15–121.35

Are these quotes reasonable? Is there an arbitrage opportunity?

10. At a certain point in time, the euro is quoted as EUR:USD = 1.1610–1.1615, and the Swiss franc is quoted as USD:CHF = 1.4100–1.4120. What is the implicit EUR:CHF quotation?

11. At a certain point in time, a bank quoted the following exchange rates against the dollar for the Swiss franc and the Australian dollar.

$:SFr = 1.5960–70

$:A$ = 1.8225–35

Simultaneously, an Australian firm asked the bank for a A$:SFr quote. What cross rate would the bank have quoted?

12. At a certain point in time, a bank quoted the following exchange rates against the dollar for the Swiss franc and the Australian dollar.

$:SFr = 1.5960–70

$:A$ = 1.8225–35

Simultaneously, a Swiss firm asked the bank for an SFr:A$ quote. What cross rate would the bank have quoted?

13. Based on historical Japanese yen and Canadian dollar quotes by a bank, the implicit yen per Canadian dollar cross rate quotation was C$:¥ = 82.5150–82.5750. What would be the implicit Canadian dollar per yen cross rate quotation, ¥:C$?

14. Suppose that a quote for the dollar spot exchange rate of Danish kroner (symbol DKr or code DKK) is DKr8.25 per dollar, and a quote for the dollar spot exchange rate of Swiss Franc is SFr1.65 per dollar.

a. What should be the quote for the SFr:DKr cross rate so that there are no arbitrage opportunities (ignore transaction costs)?

b. Suppose a bank is offering a quote for the SFr:DKr cross rate as DKr5.20 per SFr. In this quote, which currency is overvalued with respect to the other?

15. Suppose that at a point in time, Barclays bank was quoting a dollars per pound exchange rate of £:\$ = 1.4570. Industrial bank was quoting a Japanese yen per dollar exchange rate of \$:¥ = 128.17, and Midland bank was quoting a Japanese yen per pound cross rate of £:¥ 183.
    a. Ignoring bid–ask spreads, was there an arbitrage opportunity here?
    b. If there was an arbitrage opportunity, what steps would you have taken to make an arbitrage profit, and how much would you have profited with \$1 million available for this purpose?

16. Jim Waugh specializes in cross-rate arbitrage. At a point in time, he noticed the following quotes:

    U.S. dollar in Swiss francs = SFr1.5971 per \$

    U.S. dollar in Australian dollars = A\$1.8215 per \$

    Swiss franc in Australian dollar = A\$1.1450 per SFr

    Ignoring transaction costs, did Jim Waugh have an arbitrage opportunity based on these quotes? If there was an arbitrage opportunity, what steps would he have taken to make an arbitrage profit, and how much would he have profited with \$1 million available for this purpose?

17. You notice the following hypothetical exchange rates in the newspaper.

    £:\$ spot = 1.46

    £:\$ three-month forward = 1.42

    \$:SFr spot = 1.60

    \$:SFr three-month forward = 1.65

    In the language of currency traders, would the £ be considered strong or weak relative to the dollar? What about the Swiss franc?

18. Suppose that the spot pound in dollars exchange rate is £:\$ = 1.4570–1.4576 and the six-month forward pound exchange rate is \$/£ = 1.4408–1.4434.
    a. Is the pound trading at a discount or at a premium relative to the dollar in the forward market?
    b. Compute the annualized forward discount or premium on the pound relative to the dollar.

19. Suppose that the spot Swiss francs per dollar exchange rate is \$:SFr = 1.5960–70 and the three-month forward exchange rate is \$:SFr = 1.5932–62.
    a. Is the Swiss franc trading at a discount or at a premium relative to the dollar in the forward market?
    b. Compute the annualized forward discount or premium on the Swiss franc relative to the dollar.

20. On the Forex market, you observe the following hypothetical quotes.

    Spot \$:¥ = 110.00−110.10

    One-year interest rate \$ = $4\%-4\frac{1}{4}\%$

    One-year interest rate ¥ = $1\%-1\frac{1}{4}\%$

What should be the quote for the one-year forward exchange rate \$:¥?

2

Foreign Exchange Parity Relations

LEARNING OUTCOMES

After completing this chapter, you will be able to do the following:

- Explain how exchange rates are determined in a flexible (or floating) exchange rate system
- Explain the role of each component of the balance of payments accounts
- Explain how current account deficits or surpluses and financial account deficits or surpluses affect an economy
- Describe the factors that cause a nation's currency to appreciate or depreciate
- Explain how monetary and fiscal policies affect the exchange rate and balance of payments components
- Describe a fixed exchange rate and a pegged exchange rate system
- Define and discuss absolute purchasing power parity and relative purchasing power parity
- Calculate the end-of-period exchange rate implied by purchasing power parity, given the beginning-of-period exchange rate and the inflation rates
- Define and discuss the international Fisher relation
- Calculate the real interest rate, given interest rates and inflation rates and the assumption that the international Fisher relation holds
- Calculate the international Fisher relation, and its linear approximation, between interest rates and expected inflation rates
- Define and discuss the theory of uncovered interest rate parity and explain the theory's relationship to other exchange rate parity theories
- Calculate the expected change in the exchange rate, given interest rates and the assumption that uncovered interest rate parity holds
- Discuss the foreign exchange expectation relation between the forward exchange rate and the expected exchange rate

- Calculate the expected change in the exchange rate, given the forward exchange rate discount or premium, and discuss the implications of a foreign currency risk premium
- Calculate the forward exchange rate given the spot exchange rate and risk-free interest rates, using interest rate parity or its linear approximation
- Discuss the implications of the parity relationships combined
- Explain the role of absolute purchasing power parity and relative purchasing power parity in exchange rate determination
- Discuss the elements of balance of payments and their role in exchange rate determination
- Discuss the asset markets approach to pricing exchange rate expectations
- Calculate the short-term and long-run exchange rate effects of a sudden and unexpected increase in the money supply

Fluctuations in exchange rates are generated by a large variety of economic and political events. Exchange rate uncertainty adds an important dimension to the economics of capital markets. This chapter starts with a review of foreign exchange fundamentals. In the flexible (or floating) exchange rate system of all major currencies, the foreign exchange rate is freely determined by supply and demand. Many international transactions affect foreign exchange demand and supply, and these are detailed in the country's balance of payments. After a brief review of the interaction between the two major components of the balance of payments (current account and financial account), we list the major factors that cause a currency to appreciate or depreciate.

Nevertheless, a detailed analysis of exchange rates and their importance in asset management requires a strong conceptual framework. Many domestic and foreign monetary variables interact with exchange rates. Before presenting the basic models of exchange rate determination, it is useful to recall well-known international parity conditions linking domestic and foreign monetary variables: inflation rates, interest rates, and foreign exchange rates. The relations among these are the basis for a simple model of the international monetary environment and are discussed in the second part of this chapter. Given the complexity of a multicurrency environment, it is most useful to start by building a simplified model linking the various domestic and foreign monetary variables. The third part of this chapter then discusses exchange rate determination theories and their practical implications.

Foreign Exchange Fundamentals

Supply and Demand for Foreign Exchange

Just as the value of money is determined by supply and demand in the domestic economy, its value in relation to foreign currencies is also determined by supply and demand. Major currencies, such as the dollar, euro, yen, British pound, or

Swiss franc, belong to a *flexible* or *floating* exchange rate system. These currencies are freely exchanged on the foreign exchange market, and their exchange rate depends on supply and demand.

Let's assume that the equilibrium exchange rate between the euro and the U.S. dollar is €:$ = 1.25. The $1.25 price of one euro results from the supply and demand for euros. American investors wishing to buy European goods or assets need to sell dollars to buy euros. Conversely, Europeans wishing to buy American goods or assets need to sell euros to buy dollars. If the exchange rate were artificially higher, say €:$ = 1.50, European goods would look more expensive to Americans. More dollars would be needed to spend the same amount of euros to buy European goods, and Americans would decrease their purchase of European goods and their quantity demanded of euros. American goods would look cheaper to Europeans, who would increase their purchase of American goods and the quantity of euros supplied.

In this two-country example, Exhibit 2.1 illustrates the demand and supply curves for euros. In the marketplace, the current exchange rate of $1.25 per euro is the price that equilibrates demand and supply. If the exchange rate were set higher, say $1.50 per euro, there would be an excess supply of euros, a market disequilibrium.

The illustration presented in Exhibit 2.1 is simple, as we referred only to transactions motivated by trading demand between two countries. In general, there are many types of transactions that affect the demand and supply of one national currency. From an accounting viewpoint, each country keeps track of the payments on all international transactions in its balance of payments.

EXHIBIT 2.1

Foreign Exchange Market Equilibrium

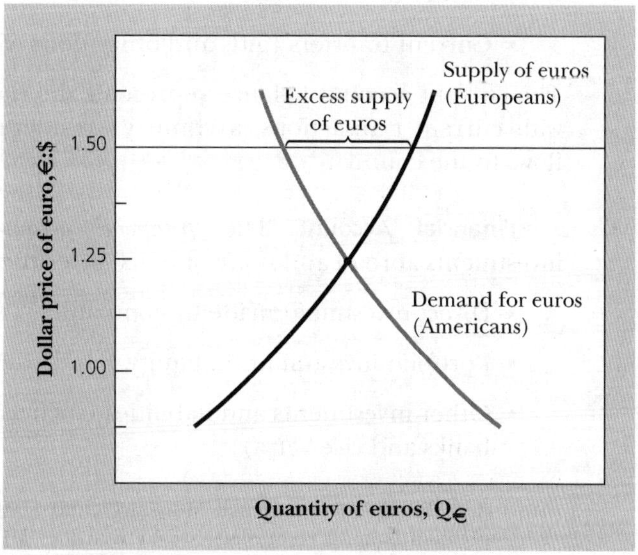

Balance of Payments

The *balance of payments* tracks all financial flows crossing a country's borders during a given period (a quarter or a year). It is an accounting of all cash flows between residents of a country (called the home country in the discussion that follows), and non residents. For example, an export creates a financial inflow for the home country, whereas an import creates an outflow (a negative inflow). A resident's purchase of a foreign security creates a negative financial inflow, whereas a loan made by a foreign bank to a resident bank creates a positive financial inflow. The convention is to treat all inflows (e.g., exports or sale of domestic assets) as a credit to the balance of payments.

For example, assume that a resident imports 100 currency units worth of goods from a foreign country and uses trade credit from the foreign exporter. There will be two accounting entries:

100 debit for the goods (imports)

100 credit for the loan obtained

International transactions such as these are further grouped into two main categories: the current account and the financial account.[1]

Current Account The *current account* covers all current transactions that take place in the normal business of residents of a country. It is dominated by the *trade balance,* the balance of all exports and imports. It also includes various other current transactions. To summarize, the current account is made up of

- Exports and imports (the trade balance)
- Services (such as services in transportation, communication, insurance, and finance)
- Income (interest, dividends, and a variety of investment income from cross-border investments)
- Current transfers (gifts and other flows without quid pro quo compensation)

The current account balance represents the net value of all these flows associated with current transactions, a country's resident's flows abroad and nonresidents' flows to the country.

Financial Account The *financial account* covers a country's residents' investments abroad and nonresidents' investments in the country. It includes

- Direct investment made by companies
- Portfolio investments in equity, bonds, and other securities of any maturity
- Other investments and liabilities (such as deposits or borrowing with foreign banks and vice versa)

[1] We follow the 1993 International Monetary Fund (IMF) presentation and terminology, which is currently used by most countries. A revision in the IMF presentation is expected in 2008. A more detailed description of the balance of payments is given later in this chapter.

The financial account balance represents the net value of all these flows associated with investments and liabilities, a country's residents' flows abroad and nonresidents' flows to the country.

The sum of these two accounts, called the *overall balance*, should be zero.[2] If it is not zero, the monetary authority must use reserve assets to fill the gap. If the overall balance is negative, the central bank can use up part of its reserves to restore a zero balance. The *official reserves* account tracks all reserve transactions by the monetary authorities. By accounting definition, the sum of all the balance of payments accounts must be zero.

Current Account Deficits and Financial Account Surpluses

The trade balance, the primary component of the current account, receives major attention in the media of all countries. Monthly trade figures are widely discussed when they are released. The usual undertone is that a current account deficit is "bad." This simple value judgment is based on some economic arguments that are often incorrect. We now discuss the reasons that a current account deficit is not a bad thing in its own right.

A Current Account Deficit Is Offset by a Financial Account Surplus The current account is only one component of a country's balance of payments. A current account deficit should not be confused with an overall balance deficit. A current account deficit has to be offset by a financial account surplus. Of course, official reserves can be used to offset a current account deficit in a given quarter or year, but this can be only a temporary measure, as the country's reserves will quickly be depleted. To be sustained, a current account deficit must be financed by a financial account surplus. This has been the case for the United States since the mid-1990s. Exhibit 2.2 reports the 2004 balance of payments for the United States.

The large current account deficit of the United States is mostly caused by its trade deficit. But foreigners are large investors in the U.S. economy. They are attracted by a stable country with good investment opportunities and a major currency.

In Exhibit 2.2, we can see that domestic investments in the United States exceed domestic savings, and collaterally, imports exceed exports. The excess demand for investments is met by financial inflows from foreign countries. The exchange rate clears the market with respect to these other countries, for example China. China has a current account surplus (exports exceed imports) and is a net foreign investor (domestic savings exceed domestic investments).

---

[2] Two other small accounts also exist in the balance of payments terminology. They are the *capital account*, which tracks capital transfers (i.e., capital gifts to other countries, such as debt forgiveness), and *net errors and omissions* (to adjust for statistical discrepancies). These accounts are small in magnitude and are usually added to the financial account balance for analysis purposes. We follow this convention. A more detailed presentation of the balance of payments is proposed in the third part of this chapter.

EXHIBIT 2.2

U.S. Balance of Payments for 2004

Current Account (CA, in billions of dollars)			Capital Account (KA, in billions of dollars)		
Goods		−$665	Net capital transfers		−$2
Services	+$48		**Financial Account (FA)**		
Net income		+ $30	Net foreign direct investment	−$145	
Current transfers		−$81	Net portfolio investment		+$660
Total		−$668	Net banking and other flows	+ $67	
			Net statistical discrepancies	+ $85	
			Official Reserves		
			Net change in official reserve assets	+ $3	
			Total		+$668

U.S. Savings and Investment 2004 (in billions of dollars)		
Gross domestic saving		+$1,572
Gross domestic investment	−$2,301	
Net other flows		+ $61
Total		−$668

Source: Modified from the *Economic Report of the President*, 2004

Is a Current Account Deficit a Bad Economic Signal? A country faces a trade deficit when its imports exceed its exports. As long as foreign investors are willing to finance this difference by net capital flows into the country, the situation poses no economic problem. The depreciation pressures from the current account deficit are balanced by the appreciation pressures from the financial account surplus.

A current account deficit is sometimes caused by economic growth. When a country grows faster than its trading partners, it tends to need more imports to sustain its output growth. Because other countries do not have the same growth rate, demand for exports does not grow as fast as that for imports. Higher economic growth also yields attractive returns on invested capital and attracts foreign investment. This capital inflow provides natural financing for the current account deficit.

Large current account imbalances can have social implications, however. Countries with trade deficits will face political pressures against free trade, and those with surpluses will be singled out as targets for tariffs.

Is a Large Current Account Deficit Sustainable? First, we need to judge the size of a deficit relative to some benchmark. This deficit can be compared with total imports or *gross domestic product (GDP).* Deficits ranging from 2 percent to 8 percent of GDP can be observed in different countries, but the sustainability question arises at the high end, particularly when foreign investment comes more from foreign government debt investments rather than from foreign private investors. Recall also that the income payments are part of the current account, so too large a foreign debt burden can exacerbate current account deficits. A large current account deficit can be sustained if nonresidents are willing to finance it continuously. As long as a country offers attractive investment opportunities and a stable "investment climate," it can keep attracting additional financial flows. The situation is no different for a corporation that relies on debt and equity financing to generate more activity. External financing is a normal recourse for a growing corporation. But as with corporations, external financing of a country also increases the risk of a crisis. As soon as foreign investors reduce their financial flows, or seek to repatriate their invested capital, the financing of the current account deficit will disappear and adjustments will need to take place, usually in the form of a depreciation of the currency to restore trade balances. We now detail factors that induce a financial account surplus.

Factors Affecting the Financial Account

Changes in Real Interest Rates Financial flows are attracted by high expected return. For debt securities, investors search for high real interest rates. The *real interest rate* is the difference between the interest rate and expected inflation. If exchange rates do indeed adjust to inflation differentials, the country offering the highest real interest rate will provide the highest expected return after an exchange rate adjustment and will attract international loanable funds.

An increase in a country's real interest rate will lead to an appreciation of its currency, and a decrease in its real interest rate will lead to a depreciation of its currency. Of course, if the real interest rate movement is matched by a similar real interest rate movement in another country, the two currencies' exchange rates should stay unchanged. It is the relative movement in the real interest rate that is of importance for the exchange rate change. The influence of interest rates is detailed later in the chapter.

Differences in Economic Performance Financial flows are attracted by high expected return. For equity securities, investors search for high performance of individual firms and of the economy as a whole. So, good news on the prospect for growth of a nation should attract more international equity capital, and the nation's currency should appreciate.

Although growth should boost the financial account of a nation, there is also an opposite effect on the current account. As mentioned, a fast-growing economy has a fast-growing demand for imports. Demand for exports, however, does not grow at the same rate (because other countries are not growing as quickly). This situation will put a downward pressure on the current account, which could lead to a depreciation of the nation's currency.

The direction of the cumulative effect is unclear. In the early 1990s, Asian emerging countries grew at a very fast rate with stable currencies. Their imports grew rapidly to sustain the growth in production and to satisfy the consumption needs of their wealthier residents. But this deficit was offset by foreign financial flows, so the net result was a stable exchange rate.

It is important to stress that capital flows are motivated by *expected* returns. Thus, it is expected future long-run economic growth that affects investment flows. As indicated by its name, the *current* account reflects the influence of current economic growth on imports and exports. Current economic growth affects the current account; future economic growth affects the financial account (see Example 2.1).

EXAMPLE 2.1 POOR RELATIVE ECONOMIC PERFORMANCE AND DEPRECIATION

Suppose there are disappointing domestic economic data reports about a country that has a significant current account deficit and a relatively high level of foreign indebtedness. What are the likely effects on the domestic currency? To illustrate your answer, take the example of Thailand during the Asian crisis of 1997. In 1996, Thailand exhibited strong economic growth. Rapid growth created a large 1996 current account deficit equal to $15 billion, some 10 percent of its GDP. This was offset by large foreign capital inflows with a 1996 financial account surplus equal to $16 billion. The exchange rate was 25 Thai bahts per dollar. In 1997, some disappointing reports were published on the economic prospects in Thailand. What are the likely effects on the Thai baht?

SOLUTION

The disappointing domestic economic data may lower expectations of future growth and hence put downward pressure on the financial account. At the same time, a significant current account deficit might not be reduced without some depreciation. The level of foreign indebtedness and the sensitivity of imports to economic conditions can reduce the sensitivity of the current account deficit to disappointing domestic economic data. The likely effects, then, are a depreciation of the domestic currency.

This deterioration of the economic prospects of Thailand in 1997 led to a rapid withdrawal of foreign capital and a negative financial flow balance. The overall balance became a huge deficit in 1997, as both the current account and financial account came in deficit. The baht was forced to be devalued to a level above 40 bahts per dollar. The financial crisis also affected the local real estate and stock markets, and a severe recession took place. Imports were cut back because of the economic recession and because of their increased price due to the baht depreciation. Exports increased as they became very competitive internationally with the large depreciation of the currency. By 1998, the current account had moved back to a $14 billion surplus, which helped absorb a continuing deficit in the financial account.

Changes in Investment Climate Financial flows are attracted not only by high expected return but also by low risk. Investors favor countries with a good investment climate and dislike uncertainty. Among desired attributes are

- A stable political system
- A rigorous but fair legal system that protects the rights of all investors
- A tax system that is fair to foreign investors
- Free movements of capital
- Monetary authorities that favor price stability

An improvement in a country's investment climate will lead to increased financial inflows and a currency appreciation. Negative news will worsen investment risk perception and tend to lead to capital outflows and a depreciation of the currency.

Government Policies: Monetary and Fiscal

Many of the previously mentioned factors are affected by government policies, such as monetary and fiscal policies. In this section, we sketch the reaction of the exchange rate and components of the balance of payments to an unanticipated change in monetary or fiscal policy. This is a complex issue, and we have to assume that everything else remains the same, including policies of other governments.

Monetary Policy and the Foreign Exchange Rate Suppose that a country decides to shift to a more expansionary monetary policy. This is a shift that was not anticipated. Most economists would agree that this monetary shock would have, at least, two effects on the domestic economy:

- The real interest rate will temporarily drop.
- There will be an upward pressure on the domestic price level, and inflation will accelerate.

As discussed, both factors would lead to a depreciation of the domestic currency relative to other currencies. Otherwise, both the current account (because of inflation) and the financial account (because of the low real interest rate) would be in deficit.

Whether an expansionary monetary policy creates economic growth in the short and long run is a matter of debate among economists. Many would argue that an unanticipated monetary expansion would induce a short-run boost in economic growth, but no long-run stimulation. Because this boost is not likely to be long-lived, it will hardly motivate additional foreign financial flows, but it will put additional pressures on the current account (imports will grow faster than exports).

For all these reasons, an expansionary monetary policy will lead to a depreciation of the home currency, while a restrictive monetary policy will lead to an appreciation of the home currency.[3]

[3] A detailed analysis of the dynamics of the exchange rate response to a monetary shock is given in the last part of this chapter on the asset market approach.

Fiscal Policy and the Foreign Exchange Rate Suppose that a country decides to use a mix of budget and fiscal policy to finance government expenditures. *Everything else equal,* a more restrictive fiscal policy means that a government increases the share of taxes and reduces the share of borrowing to finance government spending. A more expansionary fiscal policy means that a government reduces taxes while increasing the budget deficit.

A more restrictive fiscal policy implies less government borrowing, which should induce a reduction in the domestic real interest rate. In turn, this drop in the domestic real interest rate should lead to a depreciation of the home currency (investment outflows). However, a more restrictive fiscal policy should also slow down economic activity and inflation. These two factors should lead to an appreciation of the home currency (current account improvement).

These influences are conflicting, and it is hard to draw general conclusions on the link between fiscal policy and exchange rates. Many economists believe that the interest rate factor will dominate and that the net result of a more restrictive policy will be a depreciation of the home currency.

A more expansionary fiscal policy has the reverse effect. It will induce a higher domestic real interest rate, which should lead to an appreciation of the currency. However, this expansionary fiscal policy should also induce a rise in output and inflationary pressures, which tend to put depreciation pressure on the home currency. The net result is usually expected to be an appreciation of the home currency. The reaction will be somewhat stronger if the shift in fiscal policy is expected to be permanent rather than temporary.

Exchange Rate Regimes

The previous discussion was conducted assuming that exchange rates were flexible. Historically, exchange rates have operated under three different types of regimes:

- Flexible (or floating) exchange rates
- Fixed exchange rates
- Pegged exchange rates

Flexible (or Floating) Exchange Rates A *flexible exchange rate regime* is one in which the exchange rate between two currencies fluctuates freely in the foreign exchange market. Today, all major currencies are freely traded, and their pairwise exchange rates fluctuate in the foreign exchange market in a flexible manner. A central bank can intervene on the foreign exchange market, but it is only one of the many players that contribute to total currency supply and demand, albeit an important one. A government can announce what it believes to be the "normal" exchange rate of its currency, and this announcement will be taken into account by the marketplace.[4] But governments have neither the power nor the will to set

[4] There is some similarity with a CEO announcing that a corporation's share price is undervalued. The company could decide to use cash reserves to buy back shares.

official exchange rates (usually called *parities*). In a "pure" floating exchange rate system, governments intervene in the foreign exchange market only to smooth temporary imbalances. If a government has some exchange rate target, it will try to achieve the target by adopting the proper macroeconomic policies.

The *advantage* of a flexible exchange rate system is that the exchange rate is a market-determined price that reflects economic fundamentals at each point in time. Governments do not intervene to defend some exchange rate level, so there is no incentive to speculate "against" them. Because exchange rates are flexible, governments are free to adopt independent domestic monetary and fiscal policies.

The *disadvantage* is that flexible exchange rates can be quite volatile. This volatility is unpleasant for agents engaged in trade and investment, but currency risk-hedging strategies are available.

Fixed Exchange Rates A *fixed exchange rate regime* is one in which the exchange rate between two currencies remains fixed at a preset level, known as *official parity*. In a truly fixed system, the exchange rate is expected to remain at its fixed parity forever. It is not sufficient for a country to announce that it will keep a fixed exchange rate with other currencies. To be credible, it must put in place some disciplined system to maintain the official parity at all times.

Historically, the first international exchange rate regime was one of fixed exchange rates, in which all currencies had a value fixed in terms of gold content (*gold standard*). In such a gold standard, the domestic money supply is fully backed by an equivalent of gold reserves. This system worked well in the 1800s and up to the conclusion of World War I, but it progressively disappeared thereafter. Today, some countries still attempt to maintain a fixed exchange rate against the dollar or the euro. This is usually done by adopting a *currency board*. In a currency board, a country (say, Argentina) commits to keep a fixed exchange rate with a major currency (say, one peso per U.S. dollar), and the supply of home currency is fully backed by an equivalent amount of that major currency.

Suppose there is a deficit in the balance of payments of the home country. It must be financed out of reserves: The amount of dollars held as reserves will be reduced, and so will the domestic money supply (100 percent dollar backing). As the country's money supply is reduced, prices of goods must drop and interest rates must rise. In turn, these adjustments make domestic goods more competitive internationally, and the balance of payments equilibrium is restored.

The *advantage* of a fixed exchange rate is that it eliminates exchange rate risk, at least in the short run. It also brings discipline to government policies; this is particularly useful for emerging countries, which are prone to running inflationary policies.

The *disadvantage* of a fixed exchange rate is that it deprives the country of any monetary independence: Its monetary policy is dictated by the "defense" of its parity. It also constrains the country's fiscal policy. A major problem with a fixed exchange rate is its long-term credibility. As soon as a country runs into economic problems, there will be strong speculatory and political pressures to remove the fixed rate system and a push toward a sizable devaluation, with major economic disruption (as happened in Argentina).

Pegged Exchange Rates A *pegged exchange rate regime* is one characterized as a compromise between a flexible and a fixed exchange rate. A country decides to peg its currency to another major currency (the dollar or euro) or to a basket of currencies. A target exchange rate is set (the peg), but this is not a fixed exchange rate to be defended at all costs. First, the exchange rate is allowed to fluctuate within a (small) band around this target. Second, periodic changes in the target exchange rate can take place to reflect trends in economic fundamentals (mostly higher inflation in the home country).[5]

Smaller countries, especially emerging countries, frequently use a pegged exchange rate. To defend a target exchange rate against speculation pressures, a country can resort to a variety of measures. Central bank intervention, possibly coordinated with other countries, is one method. The demand and supply for its currency can also be constrained by imposing various restrictions on trade flows (tariffs and quotas) and on capital flows (capital and currency repatriation restrictions, taxes). In the end, aid from international agencies could be requested. But artificially defending a pegged exchange rate could be a costly process for a central bank if devaluation ultimately happened. Speculators would benefit, and this chain of events would also deter foreign investments in the future.

The *advantage* of a pegged exchange rate is that it reduces exchange rate volatility, at least in the short run. This is beneficial to international trade. Setting a fixed exchange rate target also encourages monetary discipline for the home country.

The *disadvantage* of a pegged exchange rate system is that it can induce destabilizing speculation. The more rigid the application of a pegged exchange rate system, the more likely it is that speculators will try to take advantage of the lack of adjustment in the exchange rate.

International Parity Relations

We now introduce a simple theoretical framework that is useful to understand the interplay between exchange rates, interest rates, and inflation rates. Traditionally, different nations use different currencies, allowing each nation some independence in setting its national interest rate and monetary policy. Thus, inflation rates and interest rates can differ markedly among countries, implying that the currencies' exchange rates will not stay constant over time.

International parity relations detail how exchange rates, interest rates, and inflation rates would be linked in a simple and perfect world. The set of parity relations of international finance is as follows:

1. the *interest rate parity relation*, linking spot exchange rates, forward exchange rates, and interest rates

[5] For example, Brazil had a "crawling peg" with the U.S. dollar for many years, whereby the target exchange rate (peg) was automatically adjusted for the inflation differential between Brazil and the United States.

2. the *purchasing power parity relation*, linking spot exchange rates and inflation
3. the *international Fisher relation*, linking interest rates and expected inflation
4. the *uncovered interest rate parity relation*, linking spot exchange rates, expected exchange rates, and interest rates
5. the *foreign exchange expectation relation*, linking forward exchange rates and expected spot exchange rates

These theoretical relationships lead to predictions for exchange rate appreciation or depreciation in a simple world. This basic framework can then be enriched to accommodate more complex situations.

Some Definitions

First, we need to recall some notation introduced in Chapter 1 and introduce notation for the inflation rate.

- *The spot exchange rate S:* The rate of exchange of two currencies tells us the amount of one currency that one unit of another currency can buy. *Spot* means that we refer to the exchange rate for immediate delivery. For example, the €:$ spot exchange rate might be $S = \$1.25$, indicating that one euro is worth 1.25 dollars (one U.S. dollar is worth 0.8 euros).

- *The forward exchange rate F:* The rate of exchange of two currencies set on one date for delivery at a future specified date, the *forward* rate is quoted today for future delivery. For example, the €:$ forward exchange rate for delivery in one year might be $F = \$1.2061$, (\$1.2061 per euro).

- *The interest rate r:* The rate of interest for a given time period is a function of the length of the time period and the denomination of the currency. Interest rates are usually quoted in the marketplace as an annualized rate. With the euro as the domestic currency and the U.S. dollar as the foreign currency, for example, the one-year rate in the domestic country (DC) might be $r_{DC} = 14\%$, and the one-year rate in the foreign country (FC) might be $r_{FC} = 10\%$. In this case, the *interest rate differential* is equal to −4 percent ($r_{FC} - r_{DC} = 10 - 14$).

- *The inflation rate I:* This is equal to the rate of consumer price increase over the period specified. The *inflation differential* is equal to the difference of inflation rates between two countries. For example, if the inflation in the FC is $I_{FC} = 8.91$ percent and the inflation in the DC is $I_{DC} = 12.87$ percent, the inflation differential over the period is approximately −4 percent ($I_{FC} - I_{DC} = 8.91 - 12.87 = -3.96\%$).

- *The forward discount or premium f:* This is equal to the forward minus spot rate as a percentage of the spot rate; $f = (F - S)/S = (1.20 - 1.25)/1.25 = -4\%$.

Interest Rate Parity

As discussed in Chapter 1, spot exchange rates, forward exchange rates, and interest rates are linked by the interest rate parity relation

$$F/S = (1 + r_{FC})/(1 + r_{DC}) \text{ or } (F - S)/S = (r_{FC} - r_{DC})/(1 + r_{DC}) \quad (2.1)$$

where S and F are quoted as DC:FC (the amount of foreign currency that one unit of domestic currency can buy) and r_{DC} and r_{FC} are the domestic and foreign risk-free interest rates, respectively.

Defining $f = (F - S)/S = (r_{FC} - r_{DC})/(1 + r_{DC})$, we have a linear approximation for interest rate parity:[6]

$$f \cong r_{FC} - r_{DC} \quad (2.1')$$

This relation states that the percentage difference between the forward and the spot exchange rates is equal to the interest rate differential. This parity relation results from riskless arbitrage and must be true at any point of time (within transaction cost band).

In practice, interest rate parity says that what we gain on the interest rate differential we lose on the discount in the forward contract. Calculations are illustrated in Example 2.2.

Purchasing Power Parity: The Exchange Rate and the Inflation Differential

Purchasing power parity (PPP) is a well-known relation in international finance.[7] It states that the spot exchange rate adjusts perfectly to inflation differentials between two countries. There are two versions of PPP: absolute PPP and relative PPP.

EXAMPLE 2.2 THE INTEREST RATE PARITY RELATION

Suppose that the Eurozone is the domestic country and the United States is the foreign country. The spot exchange rate quote is S = \$1.25. Suppose further that the U.S. risk-free interest rate is 10 percent and the Eurozone risk-free interest rate is 14 percent. Calculate the forward rate and the forward discount.

SOLUTION

With the domestic currency quoted (euro), we have S = DC:FC = 1.25.

Using Equation 2.1, we have $F/S = (1 + r_{FC})/(1 + r_{DC})$, and $F/1.25 = (1.10)/(1.14)$ gives $F = 1.2061$, \$1.2061 per euro. For a linear approximation with Equation 2.1′, we have $f \cong r_{FC} - r_{DC} = 10\% - 14\% = -4\%$. The forward discount is −4%. Then we have the approximate forward rate given by $F = (1 + f) \times S = (1 - 0.04) \times 1.25 = 1.20$, \$1.20 per euro.

---

[6] All parity equations numbered with a prime are expressed in percentages rather than level. This presentation helps to gain an intuitive understanding of the various parity relations.

[7] This theory was originally presented by Cassel (1916). A review of purchasing power parity may be found in Rogoff (1996).

Absolute PPP The version of PPP, inspired by a basic idea know as the law of one price, states that the real price of a good must be the same in all countries. If goods prices rise in one country relative to another, the country's exchange rate must depreciate to maintain a similar real price for the goods in the two countries. This argument is obvious for traded goods with no trade restrictions. Consider the following scenario: Suppose the price of wheat in the Eurozone is 2.68 euros per bushel, and the U.S. price is 2.55 dollars per bushel; the exchange rate is 1.05 euros per dollar. In the next year, suppose the euro price of wheat rises by 3.03 percent, whereas the U.S. dollar price of wheat rises by only 1.4 percent. If the euro depreciation does not offset this hypothetical 1.63 percent inflation differential, Eurozone wheat will be less competitive in the international market and trade flows from the United States to Europe will increase to take advantage of this price differential. If trade could take place instantaneously, at no cost and with no impediments, we would expect the law of one price to hold exactly for all traded goods.

If we take a weighted average of the prices of all goods in the economy, absolute PPP claims that the exchange rate should be equal to the ratio of the average price levels in the two economies. So absolute PPP is some "average" version of the law of one price. If the weights differ among countries, absolute PPP could be violated even if the law of one price held for each individual good. In practice, determining an average national price level is a daunting task that is never undertaken. Rather than calculating average price levels, expressed in euros in Europe and dollars in the United States, countries calculate movements in price indexes. A price index can be based on a representative sample of produced goods (GDP deflator) or a representative basket of consumed goods such as the *consumer price index (CPI)*. A price index is a pure number, without meaning in itself. Its purpose is to calculate price increases, or inflation rates, from one period to the next.

Relative PPP Most economists are concerned with relative PPP when they talk about purchasing power parity. Because of domestic inflation, a currency loses some of its purchasing power. For example, a 6 percent annual inflation rate in a country implies that one unit of the country's currency loses 6 percent of its purchasing power over a year. Relative PPP focuses on the general, across-the-board inflation rates in two countries and claims that the exchange rate movements should exactly offset any inflation differential between the two countries.

The purchasing power parity relation might be written as

$$S_1/S_0 = (1 + I_{FC})/(1 + I_{DC}) \tag{2.2}$$

where

S_0 is the spot exchange rate at the start of the period (the foreign price of one unit of the domestic currency)

S_1 is the spot exchange rate at the end of the period

I_{FC} is the inflation rate, over the period, in the foreign country

I_{DC} is the inflation rate, over the period, in the domestic country

Suppose the exchange rate is DC:FC = 2.235 and inflation rates are $I_{FC} = 1.3$ percent and $I_{DC} = 2.1$ percent. Then the end-of-period spot exchange rate "should" be equal to S_1, such that

$$S_1 = S_0(1 + I_{FC})/(1 + I_{DC})$$

$$S_1 = 2.235(1 + 0.013)/(1 + 0.021) = 2.2175$$

Thus, we have DC:FC = 2.2175. Here, the higher domestic country inflation rate means that the domestic currency depreciates as seen by a decline in the exchange rate from 2.235 to 2.2175.

The PPP relation is often presented as the linear approximation stating that the exchange rate variation is equal to the inflation rate differential. Let's define s to represent the exchange rate movement:

$$s = (S_1 - S_0)/S_0 = S_1/S_0 - 1$$

$$s = S_1/S_0 - 1 \cong I_{FC} - I_{DC} \qquad (2.2')$$

For the preceding example, we would have $I_{FC} - I_{DC} = 1.3 - 2.1 = -0.8$, and we would expect the exchange rate to decline by 0.8 percent to give $S_1 = (1 - 0.008) \times 2.235 \cong 2.2171$, DC:FC = 2.2171 compared with 2.2175 from the exact formula. This is close to the exact figure, even though Equation 2.2′ gives us only a first-order approximation of the exact relation in Equation 2.1.

This PPP relation is of major importance in international portfolio management. If it holds, PPP implies that the real return on an asset is identical for investors from any country. For example, consider a foreign asset with an annual rate of return equal to 20 percent in a country with an inflation rate of 2.5 percent. If the domestic country has an inflation rate of 1.3 percent and PPP holds, the foreign currency should depreciate over the year by about 2.5 − 1.3 = 1.2 percent. With the linear approximation, the asset return for the domestic investor will be the foreign asset return (in foreign currency) minus the depreciation of the foreign currency relative to the domestic currency, or roughly 20 − 1.2 = 8.8 percent. PPP implies that the real return (or inflation-adjusted return) on the foreign asset is the same for investors in both countries. The real return on an asset is equal to the asset return minus the inflation rate of the investor. For the foreign investor the real return is 20 − 2.5 = 17.5 percent For the domestic investor the real return is also 18.8 − 1.3 = 17.5 percent. Hence, the real return on a specific asset should be equal for investors from all countries. Of course, PPP is only an economic theory and the relation does not necessarily hold, especially in the short run.

In practice, purchasing power parity says that we should expect the foreign currency movement (appreciation or depreciation) to be equal to the inflation differential between the two countries. Calculations are illustrated in Example 2.3.

International Fisher Relation: The Interest Rate and Expected Inflation Rate Differentials

Inspired by the *domestic* relation postulated by Irving Fisher (1930), the *international Fisher relation* states that the interest rate differential between two countries should

EXAMPLE 2.3 THE PURCHASING POWER PARITY RELATION

Suppose that the Eurozone is the domestic country and the United States is the foreign country. The spot exchange rate quote is $S=€:\$=\$1.25$. Suppose further that the expected annual U.S. inflation rate is 8.91 percent and the expected Eurozone annual inflation rate is 12.87 percent. Calculate the expected spot rate and the approximate expected spot rate one year away.

SOLUTION

Using Equation 2.2, we have $S_1/S_0 = (1 + I_{FC})/(1 + I_{DC})$, and $S_1/1.25 = (1.0891)/(1.1287)$ gives $S_1 = 1.2061$, or $€:\$ = 1.2061$. For a linear approximation with Equation 2.2′, we have $s \cong I_{FC} - I_{DC} = 8.91$ percent $- 12.87$ percent $= -3.96$ percent. This indicates that the exchange rate should decline by approximately 3.96 percent to $(1 - 0.0396) \times 1.25 = 1.20$, or $€:\$ = 1.20$.

be equal to the expected inflation rate differential over the term of the interest rate. In the domestic relation, the nominal interest rate r is the sum (or rather, the compounding) of the real interest rate ρ and expected inflation over the term of the interest rate $E(I)$:

$$(1 + r) = (1 + \rho)(1 + E(I)) \tag{2.3}$$

The nominal interest rate is observed in the marketplace and is usually referred to as *the interest rate,* while the real interest rate is calculated from the observed interest rate and the forecasted inflation. For example, consider a nominal interest rate of 10 percent and an expected inflation rate of 8.91 percent. The real interest rate is equal to 1 percent because

$$1 + 0.10 = (1 + 0.01)(1 + 0.0891)$$

This relation is often presented with the linear approximation stating that the interest rate is equal to a real interest rate *plus* expected inflation:

$$r \cong \rho + E(I) \tag{2.3'}$$

The economic theory proposed by Fisher is that real interest rates are stable over time. Hence, fluctuations in interest rates are caused by revisions in inflationary expectations, not by movements in real interest rates.[8] The *international* counterpart of this domestic relation is that the interest rate differential between two countries is linked to the difference in expected inflation:

$$(1 + r_{FC})/(1 + r_{DC}) = ((1 + \rho_{FC})/(1 + \rho_{DC})) \times (1 + E(I_{FC}))/(1 + E(I_{DC}))$$

[8] Many economists would disagree with this simple approach. They claim that real interest rates vary with liquidity conditions and with the business cycle. Real interest rates would be higher in periods of strong economic growth than in recession periods: High economic growth sustains high real interest rates. See Dornbusch, Fischer, and Startz (2001).

The international Fisher relation claims that real interest rates are equal across the world; hence, differences in nominal interest rates are caused only by differences in national inflationary expectations. The international Fisher relation can be written as

$$(1 + r_{FC})/(1 + r_{DC}) = (1 + E(I_{FC})/(1 + E(I_{DC})) \tag{2.4}$$

or, with the linear approximation, as

$$r_{FC} - r_{DC} \cong E(I_{FC}) - E(I_{DC}) \tag{2.4'}$$

Suppose that the foreign country has a 4.74 percent interest rate and 2.3 percent expected inflation while the domestic country has 2.39 percent interest rate and zero expected inflation. The real interest rate will then be equal to 2.39 percent in both countries because

$$\begin{aligned} 1 + \rho &= (1 + r)/(1 + E(I)) = (1 + 0.0474)/(1 + 0.023) \\ &= (1 + 0.0239)/(1 + 0) = 1 + 0.0239 \end{aligned}$$

With equal real rates, the ratio of the nominal rates equals the ratio of expected inflation rates:

$$(1 + r_{FC})/(1 + r_{DC}) = 1.0474/1.0239 = 1.023$$

and

$$(1 + E(I_{FC})/(1 + E(I_{DC})) = 1.023/1 = 1.023$$

In practice, the international Fisher relation indicates that what we lose by having a higher domestic inflation rate, we can *expect* to gain on the nominal interest rate differential, leaving us with the same real rate of return regardless of whether we invest domestically or in the foreign country. Calculations of the real rate are illustrated in Example 2.4.

Again, many economists would not agree that real interest rates should be equalized worldwide, simply because national business cycles are not fully synchronized. Countries with different levels of economic growth could sustain different real interest rates.

Uncovered Interest Rate Parity

Purchasing power parity combined with the international Fisher relation implies that the expected currency depreciation should offset the interest differential between the two countries over the term of the interest rate. To see this, take the expected values of the future exchange rate and the inflation in the PPP equation (Equation 2.2). PPP applied to expected values implies

$$E(S_1)/S_0 = (1 + E(I_{FC}))/(1 + E(I_{DC}))$$

Combining with Equation 2.4, we get the theory of uncovered interest rate parity:

$$E(S_1)/S_0 = (1 + r_{FC})/(1 + r_{DC}) \tag{2.5}$$

EXAMPLE 2.4 THE INTERNATIONAL FISHER RELATION

Suppose that the Eurozone is the domestic country and the United States is the foreign country. The spot exchange rate quote is $S = €:\$ = 1.25$. Suppose further that the expected annual U.S. inflation rate is 8.91 percent and the expected Eurozone annual inflation rate is 12.87 percent. Interest rates are 10 percent in the U.S. and 14 percent in the Eurozone. Demonstrate how interest rates are related to expected inflation rates exactly and by approximation, and calculate the real interest rate for each country.

SOLUTION

Using Equation 2.4, $(1+r_{FC})/(1+r_{DC}) = (1+E(I_{FC}))/(1+E(I_{DC}))$, we have

$$(1+0.10)/(1+0.14) = 0.96491 \text{ and } (1+0.0891)/(1+0.1287) = 0.96492$$

With Equation 2.4′, $r_{FC} - r_{DC} = E(I_{FC}) - E(I_{DC})$, we have

$$10 - 14 = -4\% \text{ and } 8.91 - 12.87 = -3.96\%$$

To calculate the real rate of interest, we use Equation 2.3 and solve for ρ: $(1+r) = (1+\rho)\ (1+E(I))$. Arbitrarily using the Eurozone, we have $\rho = (1+r)/(1+E(I)) - 1 = 1$ percent. The real rates are the same in both countries by the international Fisher assumption.

or, with the linear approximation,

$$E(s) \cong r_{FC} - r_{DC} \tag{2.5'}$$

Example 2.5 demonstrates interest rate parity with Equations 2.5 and 2.5′. *Uncovered interest rate parity* refers to exchange rate exposure not covered by a forward contract. In practice, uncovered interest rate parity says that we expect the foreign currency movement (appreciation or depreciation) to be equal to the interest differential between the two countries. This parity relation is illustrated in Example 2.5. Although the relation looks similar to interest rate parity, the difference is dramatic. Interest rate parity must hold by arbitrage. Uncovered interest rate parity is an economic theory about expectations, and the theory's empirical validity can be tested.

From the linear approximation in Equation 2.5′, the expected movement in the exchange rate should offset the interest rate differential. The international Fisher relation assumes that differences in real interest rates among countries would motivate capital flows between countries to take advantage of these real interest rate differentials. These capital flows would lead to an equalization of real interest rates across the world.

Consider for a moment a simple world in which goods and financial markets are perfect. Throughout the world, costless arbitrage can take place instantaneously for physical goods and financial assets. Further assume that all nationals consume the same goods and that there is *no uncertainty*. Hence, we know *exactly* what the inflation and the exchange rates will be in the future. In this simple world, arbitrage

EXAMPLE 2.5 THE UNCOVERED INTEREST RATE PARITY RELATION

Suppose that the Eurozone is the domestic country and the United States is the foreign country. The spot exchange rate quote is $S = €:\$ = 1.25$, the one-year rate in the Eurozone $r_{DC} = 14$ percent, and the one-year rate in the United States is $r_{FC} = 10$ percent. Calculate the exact expected spot rate and the approximate expected spot rate one year forward.

SOLUTION

$E(S_1) = 1.25 \times 1.1/1.14 = 1.2061$, using Equation 2.5. By linear approximation, $s = r_{FC} - r_{DC} = 10\% - 14\% = -4$ percent. This means that the spot rate is expected to decline by 4 percent to $(1 - 0.04) \times 1.25 = €:\$ = 1.20$.

guarantees that the previous parity relations hold exactly. If the exchange rate does not adjust to the inflation differential as claimed by PPP, one would simply buy goods in the country with the lower real price and ship them for sale in the country with the higher real price to make a certain profit. In a perfect world with costless and instantaneous shipping, such attractive situations cannot exist for long; arbitrage will make the exchange rate movement adjust exactly to inflation in both countries. In the same spirit, if the interest rate differential does not reflect the anticipated and certain exchange rate movement exactly, an arbitrageur would simply borrow in one currency, transfer the amount to the other currency, and lend it at that currency interest rate. By doing so, the arbitrageur would make a certain profit with no capital investment. This riskless profit opportunity would attract huge arbitrage capital, and market rates would adjust to "prevent" such an arbitrage.

In reality, the future exchange rate is uncertain, and arbitrage in the goods market cannot be instantaneous and costless. So, the parity relations developed here are only *theories* claiming that real prices and interest rates should be equalized across the world. The empirical evidence on the validity of these relations is presented in Chapter 3.

Foreign Exchange Expectations: The Forward Premium (Discount) and the Expected Exchange Rate Movement

The *foreign exchange expectation* relation states that the forward exchange rate, quoted at time 0 for delivery at time 1, is equal to the expected value of the spot exchange rate at time 1. This can be written as

$$F = E(S_1) \tag{2.6}$$

This relation would certainly hold if the future values of exchange rates were known with certainty. If one were sure at time 0 that the exchange rate would be worth S_1 at time 1, the current forward rate for delivery at time 1 would have to be S_1; otherwise, a riskless arbitrage opportunity would exist.

Assume, for example, that we know for certain that the spot exchange rate will be $€:\$ = 1.2061$ in a year but, surprisingly, the one-year forward rate is $€:\$ = 1.25$.

This arbitrage opportunity would be exploited (sell forward at €:$ = 1.25 and buy spot at the certain expiration rate of €:$ = 1.2061) until the forward exchange rate was established at €:$ = 1.2061.

Of course, this parity relation depends strongly on the certainty assumption. Some economists claim, however, that the forward exchange rate should be an unbiased predictor of the future spot exchange rate in the presence of uncertainty, thereby leading to Equation 2.6. Others claim the existence of a risk premium appended to this relation (see Chapter 4).

The foreign exchange expectation relation is often stated relative to the current spot exchange rate. If we subtract S_0 on both sides of Equation 2.6 (remember that the current spot exchange rate is known with certainty) and divide by S_0, we get

$$(F - S_0)/S_0 = E((S_1 - S_0)/S_0) = E(s) \tag{2.7}$$

As mentioned in Chapter 1, the left-hand side is usually referred to as the forward discount, or premium, and is denoted f. It is the percentage deviation of the forward rate from the current spot rate. This relation states that the forward discount (or premium) is equal to the expected exchange rate movement and can be written as

$$f = E(s) \tag{2.7'}$$

In practice, the foreign exchange expectation relation says that we expect the spot exchange rate to be equal to the current forward rate. This parity relation is illustrated in Example 2.6. If verified, it means that there is on average no reward for bearing foreign exchange uncertainty. If a risk premium were to be added to the relation, the symmetry of the exchange rate means the risk premium will be paid by some investors (e.g., those selling forward euros for dollars) and received by other investors (e.g., those buying forward euros for dollars). A zero-risk premium means that a forward hedge (the use of forward currency contracts to hedge the exchange risk of a portfolio of foreign assets) will be "costless" in terms of expected returns (except for commissions on the forward contracts).

EXAMPLE 2.6 THE FOREIGN EXCHANGE EXPECTATION RELATION

Suppose that the Eurozone is the domestic country and the United States is the foreign country. The spot exchange rate quote is S = €:$ = 1.25. Suppose further that the U.S. risk-free interest rate is 10 percent and the Eurozone risk-free interest rate is 14 percent. Calculate the exact expected spot rate and the approximate expected spot rate one year away.

SOLUTION

Using Equation 2.1, we have $F/S = (1 + r_{FC})/(1 + r_{DC})$, and $F/1.25 = (1.10)/(1.14)$ gives $F = 1.2061$. Using Equation 2.6, we have $E(S_i) = F = 1.2061$, €:$ = 1.2061, the expected spot rate. Using the linear approximation in Equation 2.1′, $f \cong r_{FC} - r_{DC} =$ −4 percent. Hence, using Equation 2.7′, the exchange rate is expected to depreciate by 4 percent to $(1 - 0.4) \times 1.25$ = €:$ = 1.20.

Combining the Relations

The relations link the forward discount to the interest rate differential, the exchange rate movement to the inflation differential, the expected inflation differential to the interest rate differential, and the interest rate differential to the expected currency depreciation, and back to the forward discount.

- *Interest rate differential:* The forward discount (premium) equals the interest rate differential.
- *Interest rate differential:* The interest rate differential is expected to be offset by the currency depreciation.
- *Inflation differential:* The exchange rate movement should exactly offset any inflation differential.
- *Expected inflation rate differential:* The expected inflation rate differential should be matched by the interest rate differential, assuming (Fisher) real interest rates are equal.
- *Expected exchange rate movement:* The forward discount (or premium) is equal to the expected exchange rate movement.

These relations can also be organized in the following manner to show the linkages discussed.

Factor	Related to	By
Forward discount	Interest rates	Interest rate parity
Exchange rate movement	Inflation rates	Purchasing power parity
Interest rates	Expected inflation rates	Fisher relation
Expected exchange rate movement	Interest rates	Uncovered interest rate parity (PPP plus Fisher)
Forward discount	Expected exchange rate movement	Foreign exchange expectation

Recall that the *interest rate parity* relation states that the interest rate differential must equal the forward discount (or premium). This is a financial arbitrage condition that does not involve any economic theory. It must hold. Purchasing power parity also relies on some international arbitrage, but in the physical goods markets. Given the heterogeneity in goods and transaction costs, we cannot expect it to hold precisely. All other relations involve expectations on exchange rates and prices; they are based on simple economic theories about agent behavior. The various parity relations are illustrated in Exhibit 2.3 using the linear approximation.

International Parity Relations and Global Asset Management

The multicurrency dimension adds great complexity to global asset management. Interest rates differ among currencies. A foreign investment carries currency risk in

EXHIBIT 2.3

International Parity Relations
Linear Approximation

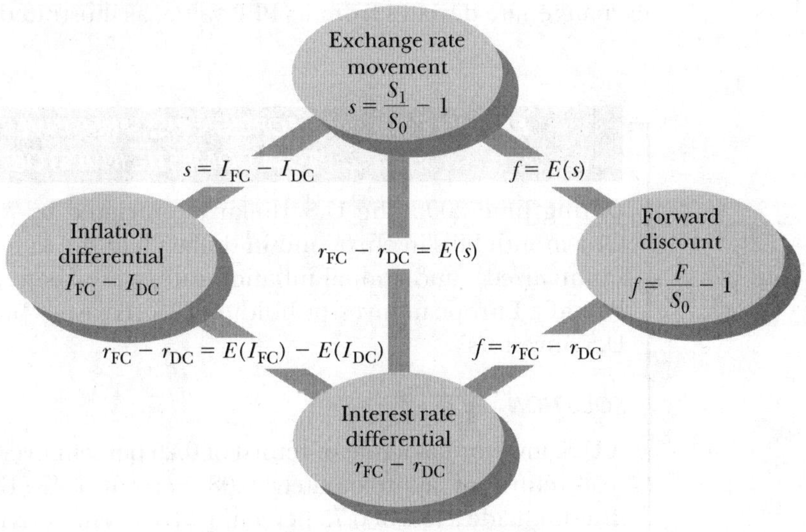

addition to market risks. Because of exchange rate fluctuations, an investment could have a positive return when measured in one currency, but a negative one when measured in another currency. International parity relations provide the simplest framework to gain a better understanding of global investing in the presence of various exchange rates. From this basic framework, various complexities can be incorporated as done later.

International parity relations provide a useful base for the relationship among exchange rates, inflation, and interest rates. Using this simple framework as a starting point, an international investor can draw several practical implications:

- Interest rate differentials reflect expectations about currency movements. The expected return on default-free bills should be equal among countries whether measured in a common currency or in real terms.
- Investing in a country with a high interest rate is not necessarily an attractive option. The high interest rate is expected to be offset by currency depreciation. Nevertheless, the interest rate is a sure thing and the depreciation is only expected.
- Investors from different countries expect the same real return on a given asset, once currency is taken into account.
- Exchange risk reduces to inflation uncertainty if all these relationships hold perfectly, and, in this instance, an investor concerned with real returns would not be affected by exchange rate uncertainty.
- Currency hedging allows investors to eliminate currency risk without sacrificing expected return, because the forward exchange rate is equal to the expected spot exchange rate.

In this simplified world, currency risk is basically of little real importance; however, deviations from parity relations can introduce complexities. Of primary importance is the observation that currency fluctuations can have real effects if the exchange rate deviates from its PPP value, as illustrated in Example 2.7.

EXAMPLE 2.7 ARE FOREIGN RISK-FREE INVESTMENTS RISK-FREE TO A DOMESTIC INVESTOR?

During June 2002, the U.S. dollar depreciated by 7 percent against the euro. One-month bills in euros and in dollars had the same interest rate of 3 percent (annualized), and annual inflation rates were about 2 percent in both regions. Would a European investor holding U.S. Treasury bills have the same return as U.S. investors?

SOLUTION

A U.S. investor has a rate of return of 0.25 percent over the month (3%/12) and a real return of approximately 0.08 percent (1%/12). However, a European investor made a loss of 6.75 percent (7% currency loss minus 0.25% dollar interest rate) when measured in euro. The real return for European investors is −6.92 percent (−6.75% return in euro minus 0.17% monthly European inflation rate). The exchange rate movement has a dramatic real impact.

It could also be that real interest rates differ between two countries that are at different stages of the business cycle. Similarly, investors are not risk neutral and could append a risk premium to the foreign exchange expectations relation (see Chapter 4). We now go one step further and give a brief review of the simple economic models of the exchange rate that could induce deviations from the international parity relations.[9] The empirical validity of these relations is discussed in Chapter 3.

Exchange Rate Determination

In this chapter so far, the traditional view indicates that exchange rates should adjust the purchasing power of two currencies. After we discuss purchasing power parity in a long-term context, we will introduce other economic variables affecting the exchange rate.

---

[9] These models are detailed in standard international economics textbooks. See, for example, Dornbusch, Fischer, and Startz (2001).

Purchasing Power Parity Revisited

The short-run behavior of exchange rates does not conveniently conform to PPP. The empirical evidence to be introduced in Chapter 3 demonstrates that yearly exchange rates can deviate significantly from the inflation differentials between countries. The *real exchange rate* is the observed exchange rate adjusted for inflation. Hence, movements in the real exchange rate are equal to movements in the exchange rate minus the actual inflation differential between the two countries. These movements in the real exchange rate are not explained by PPP. However, the theory, supported by extensive empirical evidence, claims that such real exchange rate movements (deviations from PPP) will be corrected in the long run. So, one approach to understanding the path of the exchange rate is to compute its long-run "fundamental" (or "equilibrium") value based on PPP, and to assume that any observed deviation of the current exchange rate from this fundamental value will be progressively corrected. To provide a forecast of the future short-run movement in exchange rates, we must first estimate the *fundamental PPP value* of a currency.

Fundamental Value Based on Absolute PPP

Ideally, we would like to compare directly the price of goods in two countries to see whether an exchange rate conforms to absolute PPP or whether it is overvalued or undervalued in real terms. This can only be done for some individual goods that are clearly comparable, and the estimation for different goods can lead to opposing conclusions.

For more than twenty years, *The Economist* has run a Big Mac Index, giving the price of the MacDonald's Big Mac hamburger in 120 countries. There is a wide dispersion in the dollar prices of the Big Mac throughout the world ranging from \$1.45 in China to \$5.20 in Switzerland. The article reprinted in the Concept in Action box, "Big Mac Index: Sizzling" shows the price of a Big Mac in local currency and in dollars. The implied PPP given in the third column is the exchange rate that makes the dollar price of a burger the same in each country. Let's take the example of China; the implied PPP exchange rate is simply the ratio of the Big Mac price in yuan divided by the Big Mac price in the United States, or $11/3.41 = 3.23$ yuan per dollar. The actual exchange rate in July 2007 is 7.60 yuan per dollar, which means that the yuan is undervalued by $(3.23 - 7.60)/7.60 = -58$ percent. Differences in taxes, rents, and labor costs partly contribute to these differences, but several studies have shown that Big Mac PPP is a useful predictor of future exchange rate movements because deviations tend to be corrected over the long run. This adjustment takes place either by a change in the exchange rate or by a change in the local-currency price of a Big Mac. For example, Cumby (1996) states that after correcting for currency-specific constants, "a 10 percent undervaluation according to the hamburger standard in one year is associated with a 3.5 percent appreciation over the following year" (p. 13).

In practice, no one would estimate the fundamental value of a currency by applying absolute PPP to a single good, especially a nontraded one, and the preceding discussion is only anecdotal. Some attempts have been made to compare the prices of

CONCEPTS IN ACTION *BIG MAC INDEX: SIZZLING*

American politicians bash China for its policy of keeping the yuan weak. France blames a strong euro for its sluggish economy. The Swiss are worried about a falling franc. New Zealanders fret that their currency has risen too far.

All these anxieties rest on a belief that exchange rates are out of whack. Is this justified? *The Economist's* "Big Mac Index," a light-hearted guide to how far currencies are from fair value, provides some answers. It is based on the theory of purchasing-power parity (PPP), which says that exchange rates should equalize the price of a basket of goods in any two countries. Our basket contains just a single representative purchase, but one that is available in 120 countries: a Big Mac hamburger. The implied PPP, our hamburger standard, is the exchange rate that makes the dollar price of a burger the same in each country.

Most currencies are trading a long way from that yardstick. China's currency is the cheapest. A Big Mac in China costs 11 yuan, equivalent to just $1.45 at today's exchange rate, which means China's currency is undervalued by 58%. But before China's critics start warming up for a fight, they should bear in mind that PPP points to where currencies ought to go in the long run. The price of a burger depends heavily on local inputs such as rent and wages, which are not easily arbitraged across borders and tend to be lower in poorer countries. For this reason PPP is a better guide to currency misalignments between countries at a similar stage of development.

The most overvalued currencies are found on the rich fringes of the European Union: in Iceland, Norway and Switzerland. Indeed, nearly all rich-world currencies are expensive compared with the dollar. The exception is the yen, undervalued by 33%. This anomaly seems to justify fears that speculative carry trades, where funds from low-interest countries such as Japan are used to buy high-yield currencies, have pushed the yen too low. But broader measures of PPP suggest the yen is close to fair value. A New Yorker visiting Tokyo would find that although Big Macs were cheap, other goods and services seemed pricey. A trip to Europe would certainly pinch the pocket of an American tourist: the euro is 22% above its fair value.

The Swiss franc, like the yen a source of low-yielding funds for foreign-exchange punters, is 53% overvalued. The franc's recent fall is a rare example of carry traders moving a currency towards its burger standard. That is because it is borrowed and sold to buy high-yielding investments in rich countries such as New Zealand and Britain, whose currencies look dear against their burger benchmarks. Brazil and Turkey, two emerging economies favoured by speculators, have also been pushed around. Burgernomics hints that their currencies are a little overcooked.

Cash and carry: The hamburger standard

	Big Mac prices				
	in local currency	in dollars	Implied PPP† of the	Actual dollar exchange rate July 2nd	Under(−)/over(+) valuation against the dollar, %
United States‡	$3.41	3.41			
Argentina	Peso 8.25	2.67	2.42	3.09	−22
Australia	A$3.45	2.95	1.01	1.17	−14
Brazil	Real 16.90	3.61	2.02	1.91	+6
Britain	£1.99	4.01	1.71§	2.01§	+18
Canada	C$3.88	3.68	1.14	1.05	+8
Chile	Peso 1,565	2.97	459	527	−13
China	Yuan 11.0	1.45	3.23	7.60	−58
Czech Republic	Koruna 52.9	2.51	15.5	21.1	−27
Denmark	Dkr 27.75	5.08	8.14	5.46	+49
Egypt	Pound 9.54	1.68	2.80	5.69	−51
Euro area**	€3.06	4.17	1.12††	1.36††	+22
Hong Kong, China	HK$12.0	1.54	3.52	7.82	−55
Hungary	Forint 600	3.33	176	180	−2
Indonesia	Rupiah 15,900	1.76	4,663	9,015	−48
Japan	¥280	2.29	82.1	122	−33
Malaysia	Ringgit 5.50	1.60	1.61	3.43	−53
Mexico	Peso 29.0	2.69	8.50	10.8	−21
New Zealand	NZ$4.60	3.59	1.35	1.28	+5
Peru	New Sol 9.50	3.00	2.79	3.17	−12
Phillippines	Peso 85.0	1.85	24.9	45.9	−46
Poland	Zloty 6.90	2.51	2.02	2.75	−26
Russia	Rouble 52.0	2.03	15.2	25.6	−41
Singapore	S$3.95	2.59	1.16	1.52	−24
South Africa	Rand 15.5	2.22	4.55	6.97	−35
South Korea	Won 2,900	3.14	850	923	−8
Sweden	SKr33.0	4.86	9.68	6.79	+42
Switzerland	SFr6.30	5.20	1.85	1.21	+53
Taiwan, China	NT$75.0	2.29	22.0	32.8	−33
Thailand	Baht 62.0	1.80	18.2	34.5	−47
Turkey	Lire 4.75	3.66	1.39	1.30	+7
Venezuela	Bolivar 7,400	3.45	2,170	2,147	+1

†Purchasing-power parity; local price divided by price in United States ‡Average of New York, Chicago, Atlanta and San Francisco §Dollars per pound **Weighted average of prices in euro area ††Dollars per euro

baskets of goods, but goods consumed in different countries are seldom identical, so a direct comparison of their prices is not realistic. How, for example, can one directly compare the value of a nineteenth-century Parisian house and that of a suburban Dallas home?

Fundamental Value Based on Relative PPP

Instead, *relative PPP* is most commonly used to explain and forecast currency movements. Remember that relative PPP considers across-the-board movements in prices over time rather than absolute price levels. Several steps are required to implement this approach:

- Select an inflation index for each country.
- Select an historical period for which to compute long-run PPP.
- Determine the fundamental PPP value of the exchange rate and hence the current amount of over- or undervaluation of the currency.

The definition of a proper inflation index is open to question. The estimation of the inflation rate depends on the basket of goods chosen for the index. Different baskets of goods will exhibit different price increases as the relative prices of the goods change over time. An inflation rate measured from an index of consumed goods (CPI) will be different from an inflation rate measured from an index of produced goods (*wholesale price index* or *WPI*) because of differences in imported and exported goods.

Differences in price movements between tradable and nontradable goods can also make a difference as illustrated in the case of Japan. Japan has experienced remarkable growth in productivity in many manufacturing industries whose products trade internationally. However, productivity gains for nontradables, such as services and locally consumed agricultural products, have lagged considerably. Locally produced nontradables are a significant share of the Japanese consumption basket (CPI). Because of cultural and regulatory restrictions on imports of competing goods and services (including agricultural products), prices of Japanese nontradables can remain high in the long run. The relative price of nontradables versus tradables has also risen in other countries, but to a much smaller extent.

The historical period selected to compute the fundamental PPP exchange rate value is important. For example, assume that you are at the start of 2007 and you wish to determine the fundamental PPP value of the yen/dollar exchange rate. You can select December 31, 1972, as the base year. Then, the current fundamental PPP value will be equal to the December 1972 exchange rate, adjusted by the inflation differential over the period 1973–2006. As of the end of 2006, the fundamental PPP value would have been equal to the December 1972 spot exchange rate, S_{1972} = ¥302 per dollar, multiplied by the ratio of Japanese price indexes at the end of 2006 and at the end of 1972 ($CPI¥_{2006}/CPI¥_{1972}$), and

EXHIBIT 2.4

Fundamental Value for the Japanese Yen

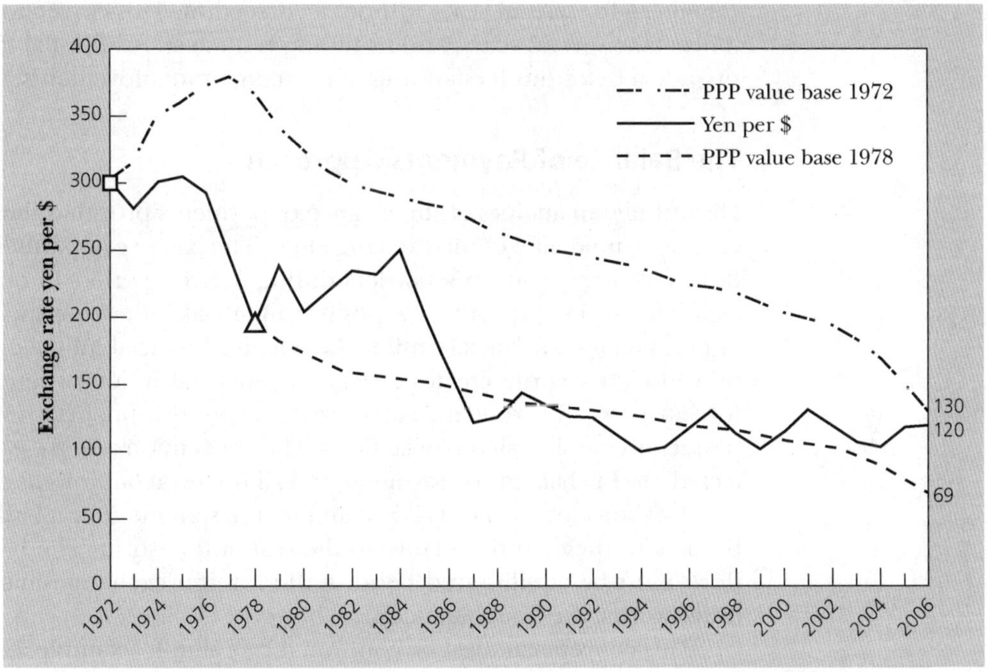

divided by the ratio of U.S. price indexes at the end of 2006 and at the end of 1972 ($CPI\$_{2006}/CPI\$_{1972}$).

This yields a fundamental value of $:¥ = 130 for year-end 2006, compared with an actual spot rate of ¥120 per dollar. This is shown in Exhibit 2.4, in which the solid line is the actual spot exchange rate at year-end, and the top dotted line is the PPP value using 1972 as base year. When the dotted line (PPP value) is above the solid line (actual value), the yen is overvalued (or the dollar is undervalued). Conversely, the yen is undervalued when the dotted line is below the solid line. The yen seemed slightly overvalued at the end of 2006. Based on PPP, you can only conclude that the yen should depreciate relative to the dollar.

If a different base year had been selected, however—for example, 1978—the conclusion would have been markedly different. The bottom dotted line in Exhibit 2.4 plots the PPP value using 1978 as base year: 1978 is a year in which the yen was strong relative to 1972. Hence, calculations using 1978 as a base year lead to a fundamental PPP value equal to only $:¥ = 69 at the end of 2006, a value well below the actual spot rate of ¥120 per dollar at the end of 2006. The conclusion would have been that the yen was strongly undervalued in 2006. Clearly, the choice of base year can make a significant difference.

To summarize, estimating a currency's fundamental PPP value should help explain future short-term movements in the exchange rate. Such estimation is not an easy task, however, and exchange rates can become grossly misaligned and remain so for several years without a correction. This correction will take place, but it may take several years, and its timing is unclear. Additional models are needed to provide a better understanding of exchange rate movements.

The Balance of Payments Approach

Historically, an analysis of the balance of payments provided the first approach to the economic modeling of the exchange rate. The balance of payments tracks all financial flows crossing a country's borders during a given period (a quarter or a year). For example, an export creates a positive financial inflow for the country, whereas an import creates a financial outflow (a negative financial inflow). A resident's purchase of a foreign security creates a negative financial inflow, whereas a loan made by a foreign bank to a resident bank creates a positive financial inflow. The balance of payments compiles all financial flows. The convention is to treat all financial inflows as a credit to the balance of payments and all financial outflows as debits.

A balance of payments is not an income statement or a balance sheet but a cash balance of the country relative to the rest of the world. The balance of all financial flows must be equilibrated because the foreign exchange market always clears. In other words, the final balance *must* be zero.

This concept can best be confirmed by a simple example. Consider a small country whose only international transactions consist of exports and imports of goods. Its central bank has a large reserve of foreign currencies accumulated over the years. Assume that in the year 2000, this country runs a trade deficit of $1 million (imports greater than exports). Then the central bank will need to use $1 million of reserves to offset this deficit. The net balance will then be zero. Of course, the importers could instead borrow $1 million abroad to finance the payment of the trade balance; this will create a financial inflow that will be recorded in the balance of payments as a positive inflow offsetting the trade deficit. Again, the balance of payments will be equilibrated.

A parallel can be drawn with an individual's cash balance. If expenses exceed receipts at the end of the month, an individual must use his reserves to cover the deficit, borrow money from the outside world, or sell some assets to the outside world. The net balance must be zero. Hence, what is interesting is to analyze and interpret the various components of the balance of payments because we know that the final balance must be zero.

The tradition is to separate the balance according to the type of transaction involved. There are many types of international transactions, including the following:

- International trade, leading to payment for goods imported and exported
- Payment for services such as tourism and consulting contracts
- Income received (and paid) on loans and existing investments
- Direct investments made by domestic corporations abroad and by foreign corporations at home

- Portfolio investments, such as purchase of foreign securities by domestic investors and purchase of domestic securities by foreign investors
- All types of short-term and long-term capital flows
- Sale of foreign currency reserves by the central bank

Several chapters could be devoted to the accounting details of the balance of payments and to the controversy surrounding the various accounting conventions. The establishment of a balance of payments requires the collection of statistics from many sources, such as customs data, central bank statistics, and bank reports of transactions. Some countries, such as the United States, construct their balance of payments from a sampling of transactions. Most other countries attempt to trace every single international transaction. It is common to see the balance of payments figures revised periodically after a few months or years to reflect corrected data or changes in accounting conventions.

To simplify the presentation of a balance of payments, it is useful to consider four component groups of lines:

- Current account
- Capital account
- Financial account
- Official reserve account

The *current account* includes the balance of goods and services and income received or paid on existing investments. Exports, or income received from abroad, will appear as credits to the balance. It must be stressed that the current account does not include the amounts paid for investments abroad but only the income received on current holding of foreign assets, usually in the form of dividends or interest payments. Actual investments are reflected in the financial account section. The current account also includes current *transfers*, which are transactions without compensation, such as gifts to relatives living abroad, grants to foreign students, or government aid to developing countries.

An important component of the current account, often mentioned by the news media, is the *trade balance*, which is simply the balance of merchandise exports minus merchandise imports. Many economists believe that the merchandise trade balance is given too much importance and that services should be added to the trade balance. Altogether, the current account gives a more global view of all current (i.e., noninvestment) transactions. Introducing straightforward notation, the current account (CA) is the sum of the following:

Trade balance	TB
Balance of services	BS
Net income received	NI
Current transfers	CT
Current account	CA

The *capital account* (*KA*) section reflects unrequited (or unilateral) transfers corresponding to capital flows entailing no compensation (in the form of goods, services, or assets). These capital transfers are different from current transfers and cover, for example, investment capital given (without future repayment) in favor of poor countries, debt forgiveness, and expropriation losses. It is generally a very small account, whose title is a bit misleading.

The *financial account* (*FA*) includes all short-term and long-term capital transactions.[10] The definition in this textbook excludes transactions made by the central bank, which will be assigned to the official reserve account. The financial account includes direct investment, portfolio investment, other investment flows (especially short-term capital). Direct investment is the net amount of cross-border purchases of companies and real estate made by residents and foreigners. *Direct* means that the purchase did not go through the capital market and involves some form of control in the foreign company, as opposed to portfolio investment. The purchase (sale) of a foreign company by a resident is treated as a debit (credit) because it corresponds to a financial outflow (inflow). The purchase (sale) of a domestic company by a foreign resident is treated as a credit (debit) because it corresponds to a financial inflow (outflow). Portfolio investments correspond to the balance of investments made on financial markets by domestic and foreign investors.[11] The account called *other investment flows* captures many types of private and official capital flows, including short-term deposits made by foreigners at domestic banks and vice versa. Introducing straightforward notation, the financial account (*FA*) is the sum of these three items:

Direct investment	*DI*
Portfolio investment	*PI*
Other investment flows	*OI*
Financial account	***FA***

Net errors and omissions is very embarrassing for balance of payments accountants. At the end of the day, when all statistics are collected from many different sources, the balance of payments must balance, just as any cash balance. Net errors and omissions may include a few unaffected transactions but consists mostly of whatever is needed to equilibrate the final balance to zero. Apparently disliking this terminology, the United States in 1976 changed it to *statistical discrepancy*. This line is often assigned to the financial account because transactions in the current account are more reliably tracked than are capital transactions. Aggregating all these items in the *capital and financial account* (*KFA*), we get

[10] Although the term *current account* is standard in the balance of payments literature, many terms have been used to refer to the sum of all capital flows, defined here as *financial account*. Hence, the reader should be careful in applying the concept of financial account to published balance of payments data. Here we use the IMF terminology adopted in 1993 and applied since 1995 by most countries (see IMF, 1995).

[11] The balance of payments tracks investment flows. It does not take into account changes in value of foreign investments or liabilities caused by changes in market prices of securities.

Capital account	*KA*
Financial account	*FA*
Net errors and omissions	*NE*
Capital and Financial account	***KFA***

The sum of the current account, the capital account, and in IMF terminology the financial account is generally called the *overall balance* (*OB*):

$$OB = CA + KFA$$

The *official reserve account* reflects net changes in the government's international reserves.[12] These reserves can take the form of foreign currency holdings and loans to foreign governments. Conversely, liabilities that constitute foreign governments' reserves come in the deduction of the domestic reserves. When the U.S. Federal Reserve Bank sells foreign currencies to equilibrate a deficit in the current and financial accounts, it will receive dollars in exchange. This inflow of dollars is treated as a credit to the balance of payments. Thus, a *reduction* in the official reserves has a *positive* sign in the balance of payments accounting. This is often a source of confusion because most of us tend to regard a drop in reserves as "bad" or "negative." However, the convention is quite logical. If a country sells goods or services, it receives a financial inflow in exchange. If its government sells foreign currencies, the country also receives a financial inflow. Similarly, if a government is forced to borrow abroad to finance a deficit, the loan will induce a financial inflow and hence create a credit to the balance of payments. This credit is treated as an increase in official liabilities and therefore as a reduction in official reserves.

By definition of a balance of payments, the sum of the current account (*CA*), the capital and financial account (*KFA*), and the change in official reserves (*OR*) must be equal to zero:

$$CA + KFA + OR = 0$$

In other words, the change in official reserves simply mirrors the overall balance:

$$OR = -OB$$

The traditional approach to foreign exchange rate determination is to focus on the influence of balance of payments flows. Let's consider a country in which capital flows are restricted, as is often the case with developing nations. A trade deficit would lead to a reduction in the country's reserves and ultimately to a depreciation of the home currency. In turn, this depreciation would improve the terms of trade. National exports would become cheaper abroad and more competitive: Exports should increase. Imported goods would become more expensive: Imports should drop. This should lead to an improvement in the trade balance, and the currency should stabilize.

For example, the drop in oil prices in 1985 and 1986 led to a Mexican trade balance deficit; the value of the oil that Mexico exported suddenly dropped, without a corresponding reduction in imports. This deficit forced the Mexican government to

[12] The official reserve account is sometimes included as a subcategory of the financial account

borrow abroad to offset the imbalance; it also led to a depreciation of the peso. This devaluation helped restore the terms of trade.

This analysis requires us to estimate the trade flow elasticities in response to a movement in the exchange rate: How will imports and exports react to an exchange rate adjustment? The answers have to be built on often complex models of the economy. For example, oil imports by an emerging country are necessary for the domestic production process, as well as other domestic needs. A devaluation of the home currency is unlikely to strongly affect the demand for oil. Conversely, the demand for some imported goods, such as liquor or luxury items, is going to decrease if such goods become more expensive in home-currency terms.

J-curve Effect: Depreciation Means Trade Balance Gets Worse Before It Gets Better Furthermore, the model must be dynamic, because devaluation-triggered improvement in the trade balance will only be progressive. The immediate technical effect is not a quantity adjustment (more exports and less imports) but a price adjustment. Because imports are more expensive in terms of the home currency, as soon as the devaluation takes place, the trade deficit will immediately increase, given the new exchange rate. This is known as the *J-curve effect*: The trade balance will first deteriorate following devaluation before improving. Of course, this scenario is not always rosy: The rise in import prices can feed higher inflation at home, leading to further depreciation of the currency. The monetary authorities will have to adjust their monetary/fiscal policy to control this "imported" inflation.

The analysis becomes even more complex when we consider capital flows in a necessary look at the various components of the balance of payments. We must draw the line between flows that are autonomous—caused by current economic or political conditions—and those that are created to compensate for a potential imbalance.

The United States has run systematic, large trade deficits without a structural depreciation of its currency because of a financial account surplus. Foreign investors were happy to hold an increasing amount of dollar assets. The 1980s marked an important period for the United States as the dollar developed into the major international reserve currency: The U.S. dollar value swung widely, and the U.S. overall balance (*OB*) moved into a large deficit during the second half of the 1980s. Studying data from the late 1970s to the early 1990s leads to a better understanding of the current situation. The story is told in Exhibit 2.5, which gives the three major components of the U.S. balance of payments, as well as the real effective exchange rate index, as calculated by the IMF. The real effective exchange rate index is the weighted average of the currencies of selected U.S. trading partners, adjusted for relative inflation differentials. It is more representative of the value of the U.S. dollar than any single exchange rate. A real appreciation of the dollar would lead to an increase in the effective exchange rate index. To analyze Exhibit 2.5, remember that a positive official reserve account means a drop in reserves. In 1977 and 1978, the combined deficits of the current and capital accounts led to a drop in official reserves as well as a depreciation of the dollar. The improvement in the balance of payments (stable reserves, no trade deficit) from 1979 to 1982 led to an appreciation of the dollar. From 1983 to 1985, the United States started to run a huge trade and current account deficit. However, this current deficit was offset by fast-growing foreign investments, and the

EXHIBIT 2.5

Balance of Payments and the Dollar Exchange Rate

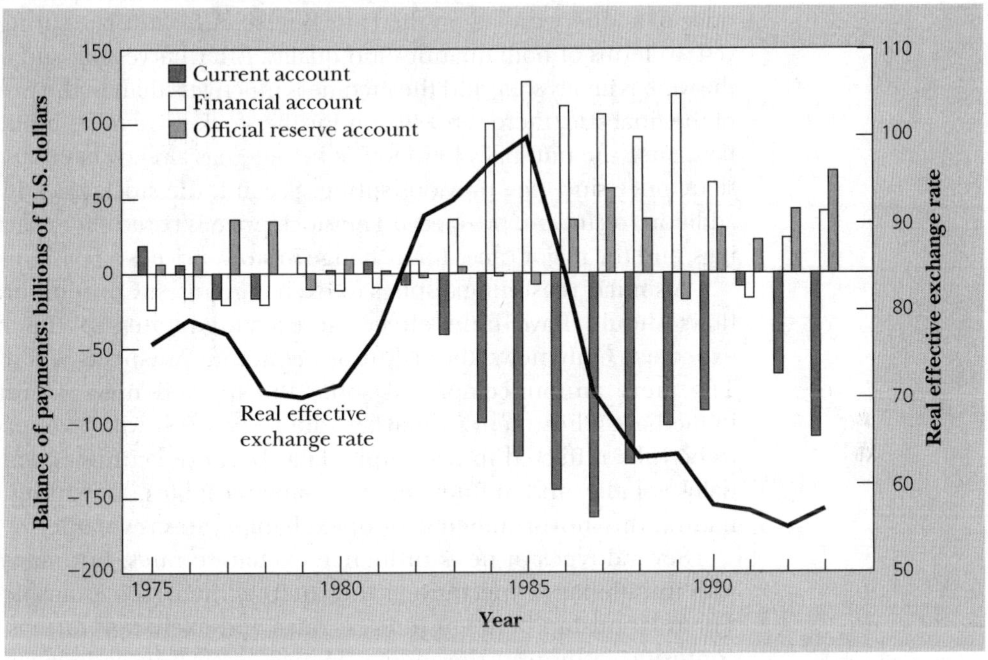

reserves did not deteriorate: The dollar kept rising. By 1986, the capital flows became insufficient to cover the current account deficit, the official reserve position deteriorated, and the dollar started to slide.[13] In 1990, the financial account began to deteriorate; it recovered in the mid-1990s. The big surge in capital investment in the 1980s came partly from Japanese investors who engaged in real estate and business acquisitions in the United States. The Japanese were running huge surpluses in their trade and current account balances, which allowed them to invest extensively in the United States and other countries (a Japanese deficit of the financial account). This situation of a huge U.S. trade deficit offset by foreign capital flows still prevails now.

The Asset Market Approach

The General Idea Many economists reject the view that the short-term behavior of exchange rates is determined in flow markets. Exchange rates are financial prices traded in an efficient asset market. Indeed, an exchange rate is the relative price of two currencies and, therefore, is determined by the willingness to

[13] Remember that the IMF changed its accounting convention for official reserves in 1997 and back-calculated all its balance of payments statistics. *Liabilities constituting foreign authorities reserves* were moved from official reserves to the financial flows account. This move has been questioned because its main implication is to drastically reduce the apparent overall balance deficit of the United States. Here, we use data under the old convention because it is better suited for our analysis.

hold each currency. The exchange rate is determined by expectations about the future, not by current trade flows.

A parallel with other assest prices may illustrate the approach. Consider the stock price of a winery traded on the Paris Bourse. A frost in late spring results in a poor harvest, in terms of both quantity and quality. After harvesting and a year of wine making, the wine is finally sold, and the income is much less than in the previous year. On the day of the final sale, there is no reason for the stock price to be influenced by this low cash flow. First, the unusually low level of income has already been discounted in the winery stock price since the previous spring. Second, the stock price is affected by future, in addition to current, prospects. The stock price is based on expectations of future earnings, and the major cause for a change in stock price is a revision of these expectations.

A similar reasoning applies to exchange rates: Contemporaneous international flows should have little effect on exchange rates to the extent that they are expected. Only news about future economic prospects will affect exchange rates. The mere announcement of some unexpected news is sufficient to trigger an immediate adjustment in market value, even if it will take several months or years to be fully reflected in economic data. Because economic expectations are potentially volatile and influenced by many variables, including those of a political nature, the short-run behavior of exchange rates is volatile.

Several types of news influence exchange rates, but many of them have to do with inflationary expectations and interest rates (see Example 2.8, opposite page). The relationship between interest rates and exchange rates is often presented in a confusing fashion in the media. Hence, we will introduce some simple models to help explain this relationship. In particular, we need to distinguish between short-run and long-run effects.

More on Interest Rates As mentioned, the interest rate can be separated into an *expected inflation* component and a *real interest rate* component, as in Equation 2.3′:

$$r \cong \rho + E(I)$$

The relation introduced by Irving Fisher is a *long-run* equilibrium relation. It states that an increase in expected inflation causes a proportional increase in money rates. Over the long run, the real interest rate is assumed constant.

But monetary policy affects the real interest rate in the *short run*. To illustrate this point, it is useful to introduce a simple domestic monetary model. Equilibrium in the money market requires that money supply M^S equals money demand M^D. The money supply is provided by the central bank. Money demand by all agents can be written as the product of the price level P and real money demand. Real money demand M^D/P can be a function of many variables, but it is generally supposed to be an inverse function of the interest rate.[14] So we can write

$$M^D/P = L(r)$$

This inverse relation between money demand and interest rate is intuitive. Higher interest rates mean that it becomes more costly to hold money balances than to

---

[14] Demand for real cash balances is also a function of economic activity. To simplify the analysis, we do not explicitly introduce the real sector here, but real output (real GDP) is implicit in L.

EXAMPLE 2.8 INFLATION-PRESSURE EBB AND DEPRECIATION

Suppose a central bank chairman announces that inflation pressures have ebbed. Explain why such an announcement could lead to a depreciation of the domestic currency.

SOLUTION

The return on investing in a currency is the sum of the (sure) interest rate plus the (uncertain) currency movement. So investors tend to be attracted to high interest rates (sure component of return), especially given the empirical evidence that subsequent depreciation is not necessarily associated with high interest rates. More importantly, inflation moves very slowly; on the other hand, central banks make serious adjustments to (real) interest rates to quell emerging inflation pressures. When a central bank raises short-term interest rates, it is not to adapt to current inflation (that would be a movement in nominal interest rate with no movement in real interest rate) but to slow down growth that could lead to an inflationary environment. Hence, most interest rate moves by a central bank are real, not nominal, moves in interest rates. A small increase in current inflation, then, could lead to a steep increase in the interest rate (mostly real). That would be attractive for domestic currency investments in real terms, at least in the short run. Conversely, the announcement that inflation pressures have eased means that the bank will not increase the real interest rate and might even lower it. The domestic currency investment becomes less attractive, hence the depreciation.

invest in interest-bearing assets. This opportunity cost reduces the demand for money. Equilibrium implies that money supply equals real money demand times the price level:[15]

$$M^S = P \times L(r) \tag{2.8}$$

The interest rate will adjust so that the quantity of money demanded by agents will equal the money supply. For example, assume that the central bank decides to provide more liquidity (unexpected increase in money supply). Agents will have additional cash balances to invest. The supply of loanable funds will increase and the interest rate will drop.

It must be stressed that the money equilibrium equation, Equation 2.8, is commonly used in two very different contexts:

- In the *long run*, monetarists use Equation 2.8 as an equilibrium relation between the money supply and the price level. Everything else equal, an increase in the money supply will cause a proportional increase in the price level. For example, if the money supply doubles, without any change in real

[15] M^S/P is called the real money supply.

output, the price level must also double. In the long run, goods prices adjust to a change in money supply, and real interest rates revert back to their normal equilibrium level.

- In the *short run*, goods prices are inelastic. They react only slowly to monetary shocks and changes in interest rates. An unexpected increase in money supply will not immediately translate into a proportional price increase for physical goods. Goods prices are generally slow to adjust ("sticky prices") and the price level will only increase progressively. This is quite different for financial prices, such as interest rates, which react immediately to new information that affect expectations. So, Equation 2.8 is used, assuming that the price level P remains unchanged in the short run. An increase in money supply translates immediately into a drop in the interest rate. This is a drop in the *real* interest rate because expected inflation has clearly not decreased (but rather increased).

This difference between short-run and long-run effects is equally important for the exchange rate.

Exchange Rate Dynamics: Asset Market Approach The asset market approach is generally used to estimate the impact of some disturbance on the current value of a currency. Typically, a monetary shock (disturbance) such as a central bank intervention on the interest rate will take time to propagate through the economy, but its expected impact will be immediately reflected in current exchange rates. The asset market approach first determines the new equilibrium value of the exchange rate once the influence of the monetary shock has been fully reflected in the economy (long run). Then, knowing that this equilibrium exchange rate is expected to prevail in the long run, one can infer the current exchange rate using uncovered interest parity.

The typical asset market approach to the exchange rate assumes that the parity relations described previously will apply in the long run. The equilibrium value of the exchange rate is driven by PPP, but goods prices are sticky and PPP will not hold in the short run. Because exchange rates are financial prices, however, they will immediately reflect expected changes in this long-run equilibrium value. So, we must clearly differentiate between the long-run and short-run effects. Thus, the asset market approach studies the dynamics of the exchange rate and proceeds in two steps:

1. Determine the *long-run* expected value of the exchange rate, $E(S)$, based on PPP. This is its fundamental PPP value expected to prevail in the long run.

2. Infer the *short-run* value of the exchange rate S_0 assuming that the uncovered interest rate parity relation holds. Using Equation 2.5, we get Equation 2.9.

$$S_0 = E(S) \times (1 + r_{DC})/(1 + r_{FC}) \tag{2.9}$$

If the expected long-run exchange rate $E(S)$ were known with certainty, Equation 2.9 could be viewed as an arbitrage condition. S_0 would have to be equal to the expected exchange rate adjusted by the interest rate differential; otherwise, arbitrage would occur.[16]

Exchange Rate Dynamics: A Simple Model A simple model reflects the economic reasoning behind the asset market approach. Assume that the foreign currency is the U.S. dollar and the domestic currency is the euro. $M_\$$ and $M_€$ are the money supplies, and $P_\$$ and $P_€$ are the price levels in both countries. S is the €:\$ spot exchange rate. For the sake of simplicity, assume that there is no inflation in either country and that the money supplies have been constant over time and are expected to remain so in the future. Further, assume that the yield curves are flat in both countries, with $r_\$ = r_€$.

An unexpected increase in money supply takes place in the United States, at time t_0, from $M_\$$ to $M_\$^*$. This is a one-time but permanent money expansion. In other words, the U.S. money supply is now expected to remain at $M_\$^*$ for the foreseeable future. Nothing has changed in Europe: the money supply, interest rate, and price level remain constant at $M_€$, $r_€$, and $P_€$. How should the exchange rate react to this money supply shock?

The time path of the various variables is described in Exhibit 2.6.

- The money supply jumps *permanently* from $M_\$$ to $M_\$^*$ at time t_0 (Exhibit 2.6a).
- The *long-run* equilibrium price level in the United States must increase proportionally to the increase in money supply. In the long run, it will reach a level $P_\$^* = P_\$ \times M_\$^*/M_\$$, as implied by Equation 2.8. Once the price level reaches $P_\$^*$, it will remain at that level because there is no expected monetary expansion beyond the one-time shock. The real money supply will get back to its equilibrium level: $M_\$^*/P_\$^* = M_\$/P_\$$. But goods prices are sticky in the short run, so it will take time for the price to reach the level $P_\$^*$. The increase in price level will be progressive (Exhibit 2.6b).
- Once the monetary shock is fully absorbed, the U.S. interest rate will revert, in the *long run*, to its normal level of $r_\$$. But in the *short run* the price level does not move, so the real money supply increases to $M_\$^*/P_\$$. This increase in money supply will lead to a drop in the U.S. interest rate (say, to a level $r'_\$$), which will progressively get back to its long-run equilibrium value in line with the increase in price level (Exhibit 2.6c).
- The exchange rate started at its PPP value of $S = P_\$/P_€$. In the long run it is expected to rise to its new equilibrium PPP value of $E(S) = S^* = P_\$^*/P$. The long-run exchange rate of the euro (number of dollars per euro) will appreciate in proportion to the increase in U.S. money supply, which is also the percentage increase in U.S. price level. Knowing what the exchange rate will be in the long run, we can infer its short-run value using uncovered interest parity. The short-run value (S_0) should be equal to the expected long-run value adjusted by the interest rate differential. Because the U.S. interest rate has dropped,

[16] Note that Equation 2.9 does not specify the time period necessary for the long-run adjustment. So, the interest rates r_{DC} and r_{FC} are compounded over the whole time period; they are not annualized. For example, assume that it takes two years for the exchange rate to reach its new fundamental value; then the interest rates should be equal to the annualized rates compounded over two years.

EXHIBIT 2.6

Exchange Rate Dynamics

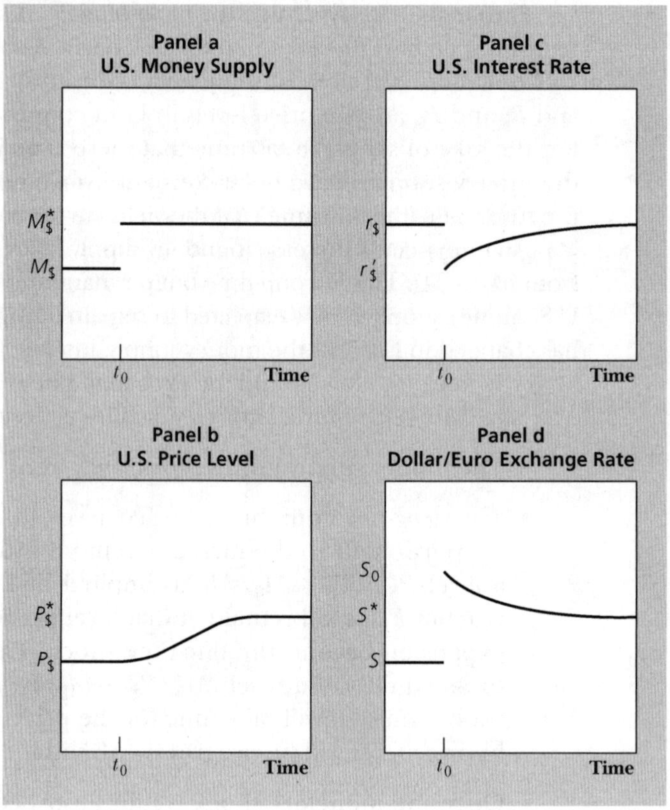

the exchange rate will be higher than its new long-run expected value. The exchange rate will progressively move to its long-run PPP value (Exhibit 2.6d).

The immediate result of this U.S. monetary shock is a depreciation of the U.S. dollar (appreciation of the euro) beyond its new fundamental PPP value. This phenomenon, caused by the U.S. interest drop, is known as *overshooting*: The short-run reaction to a shock is larger than its long-run reaction. Here we see two phenomena at play:

- The dollar depreciates from S to S^* because of the long-run increase in the U.S. price level (*expected inflation*).
- The dollar depreciates even more in the short run (from S to S_0) because of the drop in the U.S. interest rate (drop in the *real interest rate*). As shown in Equation 2.9, the exchange rate S_0 is equal to the long-run expected exchange rate S^* compounded by the domestic interest rate (euro) and discounted at the foreign interest rate (dollar). A drop in the dollar interest rate implies that S_0 is higher than S^*.

A numerical illustration is provided in Example 2.9.

EXAMPLE 2.9 EXCHANGE RATE DYNAMICS

The United States and Europe have no inflation, a constant money supply, and (annualized) interest rates equal to 3 percent for all maturities. The exchange rate is equal to one dollar per euro; this is its PPP value, and the price indexes can be assumed to be equal to one in both countries.

Suddenly and unexpectedly, the United States increases its money supply by 2 percent. This is a one-time but permanent shock. Immediately on the announcement, the U.S. interest rate drops from 3 percent to 2 percent for all maturities. It is expected that it will take two years for the shock in money supply to translate fully into a price increase. There is no effect on the real sector, nor any effect on Europe. Assume that the Eurozone is the domestic country. What will be the exchange rate dynamics?

SOLUTION

First, determine the long-run exchange rate. After two years, the U.S. price level will rise by 2 percent to 1.02. The exchange rate expected to prevail at that time, *E(S)*, is the new fundamental PPP value of the exchange rate:

$$S^* = 1 \times \frac{1.02}{1.000} = 1.02 \text{ dollars per euro}$$

After two years, the U.S. interest rate will be back to 3 percent. In the short run (immediately after the announcement), the exchange rate will move to

$$S_0 = E(S) \times (1 + r_{DC})/(1 + r_{FC}) = 1.02 \times \frac{(1 + 3\%)^2}{(1 + 2\%)^2}$$

$$= 1.04 \text{ dollars per euro}$$

Following the money supply shock, the short-run effect on the dollar is a depreciation of 4 percent. This is caused by two phenomena:

- The fundamental PPP value depreciates by 2 percent because of the 2 percent long-run increase in the U.S. price level.
- The drop in the U.S. interest rate leads to an additional 2 percent dollar depreciation (a total of 4 percent).

This second phenomenon is caused by the drop in U.S. interest rates. If the exchange rate S_0 had settled at its long-run value of \$1.07 per €, an arbitrage could be constructed. Rather than investing dollars at a 2 percent interest rate, it is much more attractive to exchange dollars for euros spot at 1/1.02 euros, invest those euros at 3 percent, and repatriate the euros into dollars two years from now at the exchange rate of $S^* =$ \$1.02 per €. This would enable a speculator to "pocket" the interest rate differential and put pressure on the spot exchange rate until it reaches $S_0 =$ \$1.04 per €. Of course, such reasoning relies on the assumption that the future exchange rate S^* is known with certainty.

To summarize:

- An increase in expected inflation in the foreign country leads to a depreciation of the foreign currency.
- A drop in the real interest rate in the foreign country leads to a depreciation of the foreign currency.

This simple model illustrates how an exchange rate reacts immediately, and in a volatile fashion, to monetary news. More complex monetary expansion scenarios could be modeled. For example, we could consider an unexpected, but permanent, increase in the *rate of growth* in money supply rather than a quantity shock in its level. Then the long-run interest rate would rise because of the permanent increase in expected inflation, but there would also be short-run effects.

Difficulties The challenge of the asset market approach is to specify the news that should affect the exchange rate and quantify its a priori influence in the short run and the long run. One of the important components of such an approach is modeling the behavior of monetary authorities, because investors will try to guess their reactions. Another important component is risk perception. Investors discount expected events, and a change in risk perception affects the pricing of the exchange rate, as in any forward-looking pricing model. The influence of uncertainty is particularly important for the currencies of weaker economies.

Central banks usually convey their attitude by interest rate announcements. We have to evaluate the content and credibility of interest rate announcements carefully. If the rise in interest rates simply reflects an increase in home inflation, not a rise in the real interest rate, it should not have a positive effect on the currency. Even worse, it could carry some negative information. For example, during currency crises, a rise in interest rates is often interpreted as evidence that the currency is under speculative attack, that the central bank has had serious problems defending the exchange rate, and that its foreign exchange reserves are being exhausted. This situation prompts other speculators to join the attack and basically sends a negative signal for the home currency.

Summary

- In a flexible exchange rate regime, exchange rates are determined by supply and demand.
- In the balance of payments accounts, the current account includes the balance of goods and services, the income received or paid on existing investments, and current transfers. The financial account includes short-term and long-term capital transactions.
- Current account deficits can be balanced by financial account surpluses, and these deficits have a negative effect on the economy only if the country cannot attract financial inflows.

- Factors causing a country's currency to appreciate include lower inflation rates and higher real interest rates, but the effect of differences in economic performance is indeterminate.
- Expansionary monetary policy will generally lead to a depreciation of the home currency.
- Expansionary fiscal policy will generally lead to an appreciation of the home currency.
- A fixed exchange rate system is one in which the exchange rate between two currencies remains fixed at a preset level known as official parity.
- A pegged exchange rate system is one in which a target exchange rate (the peg) is set against a major currency, the exchange rate is allowed to fluctuate in a narrow band around the peg, and the peg is adjusted periodically to take account of economic fundamentals.
- Interest rate parity is the relation that the forward discount (premium) equals the interest rate differential between two currencies.
- Absolute purchasing power parity (PPP) claims that the exchange rate should be equal to the ratio of the average price levels in the two economies.
- Relative purchasing power parity claims that the percentage movement of the exchange rate should be equal to the inflation differential between the two economies.
- Purchasing power parity implies that the ratio of the end-of-period exchange rate to the beginning-of-period exchange rate (in indirect quotes) equals the ratio of one plus the foreign inflation rate to one plus the domestic inflation rate.
- The real interest rate can be approximated for all countries by subtracting the expected inflation rate from the nominal interest rate.
- The international Fisher relation claims that real interest rates are equal across the world, and hence differences in nominal interest rates are caused by differences in national inflationary expectations. Interest rate differences approximately equal expected inflation rate differences if the international Fisher relation holds.
- One plus the real interest rate for any country equals one plus the nominal rate divided by one plus the expected inflation rate for that country.
- Uncovered interest rate parity claims that the expected change in the exchange rate approximately equals the foreign minus the domestic interest rate.
- Uncovered interest rate parity is a theory combining purchasing power parity and the international Fisher relation.
- The forward exchange rate equals the expected exchange rate under the condition of no foreign currency risk premium.
- The forward exchange rate discount or premium equals the expected change in the exchange rate under the condition of no foreign currency risk premium.

- Combining all the parity relations indicates that the expected return on default-free bills should be the same in all countries, and exchange risk reduces to inflation uncertainty because there is no real foreign currency risk.
- Deviations from purchasing power parity should be corrected in the long run.
- The elements in the balance of payments are the current account, the capital account, the financial account, and the official reserves account; without central bank intervention, a current account deficit must be balanced by a financial account surplus. Exchange rate adjustments can be needed to restore balance of payments equilibrium.
- The asset market approach to pricing exchange rate expectations claims that the exchange rate is the relative price of two currencies, determined by investors' expectations about these currencies.
- The long-run exchange rate effect of a sudden and unexpected increase in the money supply is a depreciation of the currency so that purchasing power parity is maintained as the percentage increase in the price level matches the percentage increase in the money supply. Given sticky-goods prices, the short-run exchange rate effect is an immediate drop in the real interest rate and more depreciation of the currency than the depreciation implied by purchasing power parity.

Problems

1. Consider two countries, A and B, whose currencies are α and β, respectively. The interest rate in A is greater than the interest rate in B. Which of the following is true according to the expected exchange rate movement relationship and interest rate parity, respectively?
   a. α is expected to appreciate relative to β, and α trades with a forward discount.
   b. α is expected to appreciate relative to β, and α trades with a forward premium.
   c. α is expected to depreciate relative to β, and α trades with a forward discount.
   d. α is expected to depreciate relative to β, and α trades with a forward premium.
2. Suppose that the spot €:$ is equal to 1.1795. The annual one-year interest rates on the Eurocurrency market are 4 percent in euros and 5 percent in U.S. dollars. The annualized one-month interest rates are 3 percent in euros and 4 percent in U.S. dollars.
   a. What is the one-year forward exchange rate?
   b. What is the one-month forward exchange rate?
3. You are given the following hypothetical quotes.
   Spot exchange rates:

   €:$ 1.1865–1.1870

   $:¥ 108.10–108.20

Three-month interest rates (percent per year):

in \$ 5–5¼

in € 3¼–3½

in ¥ 1¼–1½

What should the quotes be for the following?

a. €:¥ spot exchange rate.
b. €:\$ three-month forward ask exchange rate. *Hint*: Buying euros forward is equivalent to borrowing dollars to buy euros spot and investing the euros.
c. \$:€ three-month forward bid exchange rate.
d. \$:¥ three-month forward bid and ask exchange rate.

4. Jason Smith is a foreign exchange trader. At a point in time, he noticed the following quotes.

Spot exchange rate	\$:SFr = 1.6627
Six-month forward exchange rate	\$:SFr = 1.6558
Six-month \$ interest rate	3.5% per year
Six-month SFr interest rate	3.0% per year

a. Ignoring transaction costs, was the interest rate parity holding?
b. Was there an arbitrage possibility? If yes, what steps would have been needed to make an arbitrage profit? Assuming that Jason Smith was authorized to work with \$1 million for this purpose, how much would the arbitrage profit have been in dollars?

5. At a point in time, foreign exchange arbitrageur noticed that the Japanese yen to U.S. dollar spot exchange rate was \$:¥ = 108 and the three-month forward exchange rate was \$:¥ = 107.30. The three-month \$ interest rate was 5.20 percent per annum and the three-month ¥ interest rate was 1.20 percent per annum.
   a. Was interest rate parity holding?
   b. Was there an arbitrage possibility? If yes, what steps would have been needed to make an arbitrage profit? Assuming that the arbitrageur was authorized to work with \$1 million for this purpose, how much would the arbitrage profit have been in dollars?

6. Suppose the following chart illustrates the domestic prices of three items (shoes, watches, and electric motors) of similar quality in the United States and Mexico.

Items	**United States (dollars)**	**Mexico (pesos)**
Shoes	20	80
Watches	40	180
Electric motors	80	600

If one dollar exchanges for five Mexican pesos and transportation costs are zero, Mexico will import

a. shoes and watches, and the United States will import electric motors.
b. shoes, and the United States will import watches and electric motors.
c. all three goods from the United States.
d. electric motors, and the United States will import shoes and watches.

7. A group of countries decides to introduce a common currency. What do you think would happen to the inflation rates of these countries after the introduction of the common currency?

8. Suppose that the current Swiss franc to U.S. dollar spot exchange rate is \$:SFr = 1.60. The expected inflation over the coming year is 2 percent in Switzerland and 5 percent in the United States. According to purchasing power parity, what is the expected value of the Swiss franc to U.S. dollar spot exchange rate a year from now?

9. Let us consider a utopian world in which there are only three goods: sake, beer, and TV sets.
   - Japanese consume only a locally produced food, called sake, and an industrially produced and traded good, called TV sets.
   - Americans consume only a locally produced food, called beer, and an industrially produced and traded good, called TV sets.

   TV sets are produced in both countries and actively traded; their local prices follow the law of one price. Foods are produced only locally and are not traded. The consumption basket of a Japanese individual consists of two-thirds sake and one-third TV sets. The consumption basket of an American consists of one-half beer and one-half TV sets. Prices of beer and TV sets in the United States are constant over time in U.S. dollars. Japanese are very competitive and export a lot of TV sets. Japanese farmers want to share in the increased national wealth, and the price of sake is rising at a rate of 10 percent per year in yen. Assume that the yen/dollar exchange rate stays constant.
   a. What is the consumer price index inflation in Japan?
   b. Does relative PPP hold between Japan and the United States?

10. a. Explain the following three concepts of purchasing power parity:
      i. The law of one price
      ii. Absolute PPP
      iii. Relative PPP
    b. Evaluate the usefulness of relative PPP in predicting movements in foreign exchange rates on a
      i. short-term basis (e.g., three months).
      ii. long-term basis (e.g., six years).

11. A French company is importing some equipment from Switzerland and will need to pay 10 million Swiss francs three months from now. Suppose that the current spot exchange rate is €:SFr = 1.5543. The treasurer of the company expects the franc to appreciate in the next few weeks and is concerned about it. The three-month forward rate is €:SFr = 1.5320.
    a. Given the treasurer's expectation, what action can he take using the forward contract?
    b. Three months later, the spot exchange rate turns out to be €:SFr = 1.5101. Did the company benefit because of the treasurer's action?

12. Suppose the international parity conditions hold. Does that mean that the nominal interest rates would be equal among countries? Why or why not?

13. Suppose that you are given the following information about Australia, Switzerland, and the United States. The Australian dollar is expected to depreciate relative to the United States dollar. The nominal interest rate in the United States is greater than that in

Switzerland. Can you say whether the Australian dollar is expected to depreciate or appreciate relative to the Swiss Franc?

14. Suppose that there were some statistics about the Swedish krona and the dollar:

	SKr		$
Inflation (annual rate)	6%		?%
One-year interest rate	8%		7%
Spot exchange rate ($:SKr)		?	
Expected exchange rate in one year ($:SKr)		6	
One-year forward exchange rate ($:SKr)		?	

Based on the linear approximations of the international parity conditions, replace the question marks with appropriate answers.

15. Suppose that the one-year interest rate is 12 percent in the United Kingdom. The expected annual rate of inflation for the coming year is 10 percent for the United Kingdom and 4 percent for Switzerland. The current spot exchange rate is £:SFr = 3. Using the precise form of the international parity relations, compute the one-year interest rate in Switzerland, the expected Swiss franc to pound exchange rate in one year, and the one-year forward exchange rate.

16. Following are some statistics for Malaysia, the Philippines, and the United States.

Inflation Rates: Annual Rates in Percent per Year

	1991	1992	1993	1994	1995	1996
Malaysia	4.40	4.69	3.57	3.71	5.28	3.56
Philippines	18.70	8.93	7.58	9.06	8.11	8.41
United States	4.23	3.03	3.00	2.61	2.81	2.34

Exchange Rate per U.S. Dollar: Annual Average

	1991	1992	1993	1994	1995	1996
Malaysia	2.75	2.55	2.57	2.62	2.50	2.52
Philippines	27.48	25.51	27.12	26.42	25.71	26.22

In 1997, Malaysia and the Philippines suffered a severe currency crisis. Use the numbers in the preceding tables to provide a partial explanation.

17. Paf is a small country whose currency is the pif. Twenty years ago, the exchange rate with the U.S. dollar was 2 pifs per dollar, and the inflation indexes were equal to 100 in both the United States and Paf. Now, the exchange rate is 0.9 pifs per dollar, and the inflation indexes are equal to 400 in the United States and 200 in Paf.

a. What should the current exchange rate be if PPP prevailed?

b. Is the pif over- or undervalued according to PPP?

18. Paf is a small country. Its currency is the pif, and the exchange rate with the United States dollar is 0.9 pifs per dollar. Following are some of the transactions affecting Paf's balance of payments during the quarter:

- Paf exports 10 million pifs of local products.
- Paf investors buy foreign companies for a total cost of $3 million.
- Paf investors receive $0.1 million of dividends on their foreign shares.
- Many tourists visit Paf and spend $0.5 million.
- Paf pays 1 million pifs as interest on Paf bonds currently held by foreigners.

- Paf imports $7 million of foreign goods.
- Paf receives $0.3 million as foreign aid.

Illustrate how the preceding transactions would affect Paf's balance of payments for the quarter, including the current account, the financial account, and the official reserves account.

19. The domestic economy seems to be overheating, with rapid economic growth and low unemployment. News has just been released that the monthly activity level is even higher than expected (as measured by new orders to factories and unemployment figures). This news leads to renewed fears of inflationary pressures and likely action by the monetary authorities to raise interest rates to slow the economy down.
    a. Based on the traditional flow market approach, discuss whether this news is good or bad for the exchange rate.
    b. Based on the asset market approach, discuss whether this news is good or bad for the exchange rate.

20. Even though the investment community generally believes that Country M's recent budget deficit reduction is "credible, sustainable, and large," analysts disagree about how it will affect Country M's foreign exchange rate. Juan DaSilva, CFA, states, "The reduced budget deficit will lower interest rates, which will immediately weaken Country M's foreign exchange rate."
    a. Discuss the direct (short-term) effects of a reduction in Country M's budget deficit on
        i. demand for loanable funds.
        ii. nominal interest rates.
        iii. exchange rates.
    b. Helga Wu, CFA, states, "Country M's foreign exchange rate will strengthen over time as a result of changes in expectations in the private sector in country M." Support Wu's position that Country M's foreign exchange rate will strengthen because of the changes a budget deficit reduction will cause in
        i. expected inflation rates.
        ii. expected rates of return on domestic securities.

Bibliography

Cassel, G. "The Present Situation on the Foreign Exchanges," *Economic Journal*, 1916, pp. 62–65.

Cumby, R. E. "Forecasting Exchange Rates and Relative Prices with the Hamburger Standard: Is What You Want What You Get with McParity?" NBER Working Paper No. 5675, 1996.

Dornbusch, R., Fischer, S., and Startz, R. *Macroeconomics*, 9th ed., New York: McGraw-Hill, 2004.

Fisher, I. *The Theory of Interest*, New York: Macmillan, 1930.

IMF, *Balance of Payments Textbook*, International Monetary Fund, Washington, D.C., 1995.

Krugman, P., and Obstfeld, M. *International Economics: Theory and Policy*, 7th ed., New York: Addison-Wesley, 2005.

Rogoff, K. "The Purchasing Power Parity Puzzle," *Journal of Economic Literature*, 34, June 1996, pp. 647–668.

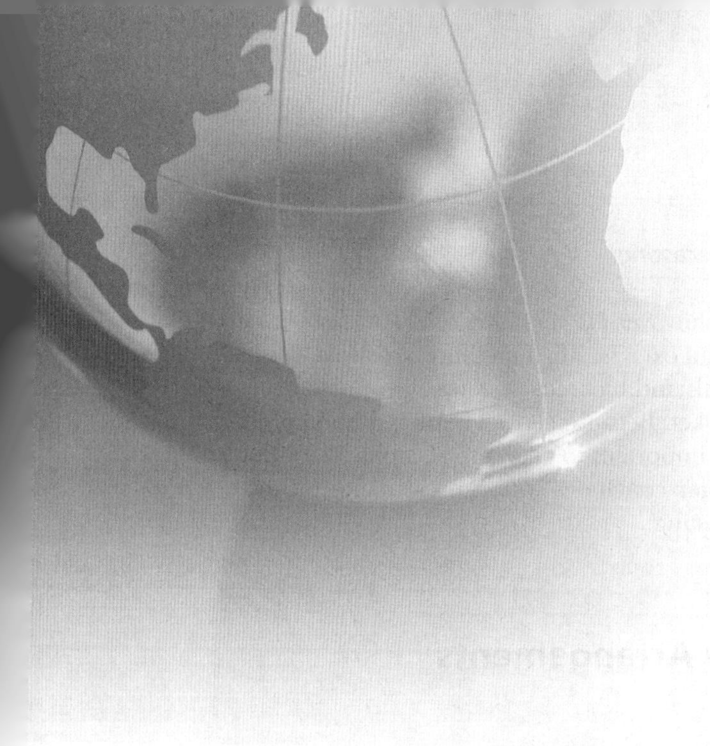

3

Foreign Exchange Determination and Forecasting

LEARNING OUTCOMES

After completing this chapter, you will be able to do the following:

- Discuss the evolution of international monetary arrangements
- Discuss the empirical evidence on the various parity conditions
- Contrast the findings for purchasing power parity in the short run and in the long run
- Draw the implications for international management in terms of risk and return
- Discuss the various methods used in exchange rate forecasting
- State why possible central bank intervention should be considered when forecasting exchange rates
- Discuss the use of forecasts for different types of investors
- Define how you would measure the performance of foreign exchange forecasters

In previous chapters, we presented a theoretical framework that helps to analyze the international monetary environment and the contribution of currencies to international investment returns. *Parity relations* combine inflation rates, interest rates, and foreign exchange rates in a simple manner to guide investing in a global environment. In real life, exchange rates deviate from their parity values. This creates exchange rate uncertainty to be managed, as well as profit opportunities, if exchange rate forecasting can be implemented.

The behavior of exchange rates is constrained by some international institutional arrangements, so we first briefly review these monetary arrangements. The next section discusses the empirical evidence on the parity relations introduced in Chapter 2. Although there appears to be a lot of exchange rate volatility in the short run, currencies tend to revert to their fundamental value over the very long run. This result suggests that currency forecasting could be a fruitful exercise. Two methods are actively used to forecast exchange rates: economic analysis and technical analysis. Central banks are active players on the foreign exchange market. Because central bank motivations differ from the usual risk–return motivating, it is important to take into account their interventions in any forecasting model. This chapter concludes with a presentation of the use and performance of exchange rate forecasting.

International Monetary Arrangements

An Historical Perspective

An exchange rate (i.e., a *spot exchange rate*) must be set in order for trade in goods and assets to occur between countries that use different currencies. The traditional method has been to use a common standard for assessing the value of each currency. Over the centuries, various commodities have served as the international standard, including small seashells, salt, and such metals as bronze, silver, and gold (the best known and most recent). Silver played an important role until the middle of the nineteenth century, when gold was found in Transvaal and in California. Thereafter, an international monetary system started to prevail.

Gold Standard In the nineteenth century, most countries had decided that their currency would be exchangeable into gold bullion at a fixed parity. This system, known as the *gold standard,* prevailed quite informally and was not sanctioned by an official international treaty. During the era of the gold standard, gold was the international means of payment, and each currency was assessed according to its gold value. At the time, one could exchange French francs for British pounds in exact proportion to their gold value. For example, if one ounce of gold bullion was worth ten francs in France and two pounds in the United Kingdom, the exchange rate was five French francs per British pound, or 0.2 British pounds per French franc. The domestic monetary authorities set the domestic purchasing power of a currency by establishing its gold content, and they thereby controlled the exchange rate.

To maintain equilibrium in the system, gold bullion was used to settle international transactions. Gold made up all the international reserves of a country. National bank notes and coins were backed by the gold reserves of the country. The balance of all monetary flows in and out of a country is referred to as the *balance of payments.* These flows were linked to either trade (payments of imports and exports) or financial flows (borrowing and lending abroad). Under the gold standard, a deficit in the balance of payments resulted in an outflow of gold and a reduction in the domestic reserves; this was equivalent to a reduction in the domestic money supply, because the gold stock of a country was its real money supply. As a country's money supply was reduced, prices of goods had to drop and interest rates had to rise. In turn, this adjustment made domestic goods more competitive internationally. Similarly, higher interest rates attracted foreign capital. Both phenomena served to replenish the country's national gold reserves. Hence, the adjustment in the balance of payments was automatic. *Purchasing power parity* (PPP) held by construction. Inflation was basically absent, and the last three decades of the nineteenth century witnessed negative inflation in all major countries.

One problem with this gold standard system was that the world money supply could grow only at the rate of new gold mining. The economic growth rate in the early 1900s became much larger than the physical growth in gold reserves. Another major problem was that national economic policies were totally subordinated to the fixed exchange rate objective. A country could not have a flexible monetary policy. While exchange rates remained stable, any sudden disequilibrium in the balance of payments led to severe shocks in domestic economies. With the industrial revolution at the start of the twentieth century, the gold standard system's rigidity became a problem.

CONCEPTS IN ACTION *ECONOMICS FOCUS PLUS ÇA CHANGE*

The Lessons of Sound Money from One Thousand Years' Experience

This month [January 2002] has seen progress in one bold monetary experiment, the issuance of euro notes and coins, and the failure of another, Argentina's currency board. In the history of money, this is all par for the course. Currencies, and systems for managing them, have come and gone with striking frequency ever since Croesus, king of Lydia, first minted coins in the sixth century B.C.

Might the euro also fail? A new book, *The Big Problem of Small Change,** underscores how little has been learnt from more than a millennium of monetary experiment. This fascinating new history of money shows that the key ingredients of a sound currency were identified in Europe hundreds of years ago. The mystery is why, even today, so many governments fail to put this knowledge to work.

The authors, Thomas Sargent of the Hoover Institution and François Velde of the Federal Reserve Bank of Chicago, argue that today's monetary orthodoxy has its origins in an ancient puzzle. For several centuries after 1200, when Charlemagne's famous silver penny was supplemented throughout Europe with coins of other denominations, there were inexplicable shortages of small change, which curiously coincided with a fall in their value, apparently defying the laws of supply and demand. Why?

Most of the value of a coin derived from the amount of precious metal in it. The amount by which the value of a coin could vary had an upper and lower limit. One reflected the cost of turning, say, an ounce of silver into a coin (this included minting costs plus a government coinage tax known as seigniorage). The other was what could be bought if the coin were melted down and the metal it contained used as payment. The supply of each denomination depended on how much silver people took to the mint.

A shortage might occur because of an unexpected rise in national income or its distribution, causing ordinary people to increase their purchases of bread, beer and so on. Small coins, not big ones, were needed for these transactions, which would often be for far less than the denomination of a high-value coin. At the same time, the value of small coins relative to big coins would often fall.

The authors explain this using modern monetary theory—which, alas, is somewhat counterintuitive. Broadly, instead of using simple supply and demand, it explains changes in the demand for one asset (a small silver coin, say) relative to another (a large coin) in terms of changes in the rate of return that the holder of the assets can expect from each. Depreciating smaller-denomination coins—which lowered the expected return from holding them—was the market's way to encourage holders of money to ease the shortage by getting rid of their small coins, the authors reckon. But this often made things worse, because the depreciation took the value of small coins below the point at which it paid to melt them down.

For centuries governments responded to a shortage of small coins by debasing them, i.e., reducing the amount of silver required to make a penny. This provided an incentive for people to turn silver into pennies, but it generated inflation.

Eventually an ingenious way was found out of the mess. Instead of each denomination containing precious metal, only one higher-denomination coin would do so. All other denominations would be tokens, made of a metal too cheap to be worth melting down, that could be exchanged for higher-denomination ones (or for a set amount of the precious metal) at a rate fixed and guaranteed by the government.

Following the invention of the Boulton steam press in 1787—which raised the cost of forgery—a British token currency flourished, initially issued by private firms before being nationalized in 1816. By the late 19th century, most other leading countries had token currencies, mostly pegged to the value of gold. Hence the rise of the gold standard.

A question is left unanswered. If the problem of small change led economists to understand how to run a system of token money, did some of the greatest economists of the early 20th century learn the wrong lesson from the system's success? John Maynard Keynes and Irving Fisher, among others, opposed the gold standard as a waste of valuable resources. They argued for a currency based entirely on tokens, with no link to an underlying physical commodity. Governments, greedy to spend their gold reserves, warmed to this idea, particularly during the 1930s depression. When America belatedly and finally abandoned the gold standard in 1971, it was history.

Abandoning the link to gold meant that it was entirely up to governments to ensure that their token-based currencies kept their value. In the event, for most of the 20th century they failed. They presided over levels of inflation that were seldom seen when money was backed by precious metal, debasement notwithstanding. Does history teach that a token-based currency works only if it is anchored to some unambiguous real store of value that a government cannot inflate away? Ironically, this was the logic behind Argentina's currency board, anchored to the American dollar rather than to gold. In the end, Mr. Sargent says, that failed in part because even anchored systems cannot co-exist with unsustainable government debts, as in Argentina; the temptation to reduce debts by tampering with the value of money is too great. Even economic insights developed over hundreds of years cannot work their magic without the requisite political will.

---

* *The Big Problem of Small Change,* by Thomas Sargent and François Velde. Princeton University Press, 2002.

Pegged Exchange Rates The twentieth century saw many attempts to establish international currency regimes under the global coordination of the *International Monetary Fund (IMF).* In 1944, the *Bretton Woods* agreement created the IMF and a system of *pegged* exchange rates. The objective was to create a stable system in which countries would have more autonomy in setting their domestic economic policies. This Bretton Woods system, also called the *gold exchange standard,* was distinguished by two characteristics: an enlargement of international reserves and the design of stable but adjustable exchange rates or pegged exchange rates.

- In order to soften the impact of balance of payments deficits or surpluses on domestic economies, hard currencies were introduced to increase international reserves. These currencies—the U.S. dollar, later followed by the British pound and the Deutsche mark—were freely convertible into gold.
- This Bretton Woods system also allowed exchange rates to fluctuate within a band around fixed parities. It further allowed infrequent devaluation or revaluation of the fixed parities, requiring the IMF's agreement.

Hence, exchange rates were semifixed, or *pegged,* around official parities set in global cooperation. To understand how the system worked, consider the example of a country facing a sudden balance of payments deficit. First, it could use its international reserves of gold and convertible currencies to cover this balance of payments deficit. It could also let its exchange rate drop within the assigned band (typically 1%) around the fixed parity. Both options gave a nation more time to implement policies to restore equilibrium in the balance of payments. For example, a country could tighten its monetary policy and raise interest rates. It could also introduce various forms of capital controls to limit currency speculation. If the deficit turned out to be structural and permanent, the country had to ask the IMF's permission to devalue its currency (i.e., adjust the parity). This devaluation made its goods more competitive in the international markets, improving the trade balance and removing the motivation for speculative capital flows.

This international system did not work for long. National economic policies and inflation rates quickly became so diverse that it was difficult to maintain these pegged exchange rates. The internationalization of financial markets led to an increase in the amount of capital trying to take advantage of currency swings. A fixed exchange rate, defended by central banks, offered great profit opportunities for speculation. Gold stopped playing a role and the U.S. dollar became de facto *the* international currency. After several failed attempts at an improved system of global coordination, a system of floating exchange rates became the rule, with each currency's value determined in the marketplace.

The Current Situation: Floating Exchange Rates and Pegged Exchange Rates The international monetary system progressively evolved toward a system of *floating* exchange rates. Under the current system, the price of each currency is freely determined by market forces. Exchange rates are not fixed by governments, but fluctuate according to supply and demand. Of course, governments attempt to "manage" their exchange rates through central bank intervention in the foreign exchange market and various policy and regulatory measures. However, the exchange rate is determined at each instant in the marketplace without reference to an "official" parity. All major currencies, including the U.S. dollar, the British pound, the yen, and the euro, are floating.

In this world of flexible exchange rates, some governments have linked their currency to others. Sometimes the link is rigid. For example, a *currency board* was adopted by Argentina in 1991. In a currency board, the exchange rate is fixed (one Argentinean peso per U.S. dollar) and the supply of domestic currency is fully backed by an equivalent amount of U.S. dollars. This system is comparable to the gold standard, with the dollar replacing gold. De facto, Argentina abandoned an independent monetary policy. Indeed, the peso remained equal to one dollar for several years following the introduction of the currency board, and Argentinean inflation dropped down from more than 100 percent per year to a figure comparable to that of the United States. However, even a slight annual inflation differential can lead to deterioration in competitive position if it is accumulated over several years with a fixed exchange rate. To be operational, a currency board requires a full and credible commitment of present and future governments; otherwise, speculative pressure will build on the domestic currency. This happened in Argentina, which ran large budget deficits in the late 1990s and was forced to abandon the currency board with a severe devaluation in 2002. Argentina's dollar currency board also suffered strong pressures in the early 2000s when Brazil, a major trading partner, devalued its currency against the dollar. Currency boards have also been implemented in Lithuania (backed by U.S. dollars), Bulgaria, and Estonia (backed by euros).

On the other hand, Hong Kong presents an interesting case in that it did not formally put a currency board in place but rather announced a total commitment to maintain a parity of the Hong Kong dollar with the U.S. dollar within the band of 7.75 to 7.85 H.K. dollars per U.S. dollar. The Hong Kong Monetary Authority stands ready to use its reserves to defend the fixed rate, despite pressures brought by the appreciation of the Chinese yuan.

Many other currencies are linked, tightly or loosely, to the U.S. dollar. Many emerging countries attempt to maintain a link between their currencies and the U.S. dollar or the euro, but maintaining a fixed exchange rate, when not justified by economic fundamentals, inevitably leads to currency speculation. Other pegged currencies are linked to a basket of currencies. By far the most important linkage affecting major investment currencies is the original system put into place by the European Union, which led to the euro.

The Euro *The European Union (EU)* is the name given to the former European Economic Community. Fifteen countries belonged to the EU in 1999, but twelve of those abandoned their national currency on January 1, 1999, to replace it with the euro, denoted as € or more formally EUR. Denmark, Sweden, and the United Kingdom decided to retain their national currencies. Other countries have joined the EU since 1999 and are considering joining the euro at a later stage. As of 2007, there were 27 member countries of the EU, but only 13 used the euro. The list is given below.

Euro Countries

Austria	Greece	Netherlands
Belgium	Ireland	Portugal
Finland	Italy	Slovenia
France	Luxembourg	Spain
Germany		

Other Possible Euro Countries Already Members of EU

Cyprus and Malta (planned for 2008)	Latvia
Slovakia (planned for 2009)	Poland
Bulgaria	Romania
Czech Republic	
Estonia	Denmark
Lithuania	Sweden
Hungary	United Kingdom

As of January 1, 1999, the euro was introduced for all official and interbank transactions, as well as for securities quotations and transactions. The exchange rate between each of the 12 national currencies (e.g., the French franc or the Deutsche mark) and the euro was set on January 1, 1999, and remained fixed until the disappearance of the national currencies in 2002. These fixed exchange rates were called *legacy rates.* On January 1, 2002, euro bank notes were introduced and all former legacy currencies ceased to exist. The euro is now the sole currency of the Eurozone countries.

Established in Frankfurt, the European Central Bank (ECB) is an independent central bank. Board members are appointed by the various EU governments with an eight-year term of office. The ECB sets the monetary policy for the Eurozone. The ECB's primary objective is to maintain price stability in the Eurozone. Without prejudice to the objective of price stability, the ECB will support the general economic policies of the EU. The euro has a floating exchange rate against other currencies, such as the U.S. dollar, the Japanese yen, and the British pound (at least in these early years).

Although these countries have adopted a common currency, their national budgets and fiscal and socioeconomic policies differ, so tensions within the European monetary system could easily develop before full harmonization of policies is reached.

CONCEPTS IN ACTION *THE CASE FOR COOPERATING*

Euro Threatened with 2007 Meltdown, as French Economy Slumps

The resurgent strength of the euro in the international currency market could, ironically, be the agent of its demise in 2007. Problems caused by the lack of fiscal maneuverability that the "one-currency-fits-all" approach imposes saw Italy considering a return to the lira just last year. But in October, when French car manufacturing output dropped to 14 percent for the year, with the country's monthly trade deficit running at a staggering $2.7 billion, and economic growth shuddering to a standstill, it left one of the EU's biggest guns warning of possible withdrawal—a move which would signal the end for European monetary union.

French Trade Minister Christine Lagarde has recently criticized the German-based European Central Bank (ECB), which, by raising interest rates six times in a year to 3.5 percent, has been instrumental in pushing up the value of the euro. During 2006, the euro rose 11 percent against the U.S. dollar and most Asian currencies, and a staggering 20 percent against the yen. Complaining about only selling one Airbus, and no satellites or ships at all, during the year, Lagarde pointedly told the ECB it needed to stop worrying about inflation and start "thinking about growth." French Premier Dominique de Villepin even called for limits on the power of the ECB, espousing the need to reassert national control over the economy. "We must clarify matters in exchange rate policy, which means taking back our sovereignty," he said. A clause in the EU's Maastricht Treaty (111-4) could allow them to do exactly that. The "get-out" clause allows EU states to set their own interest rates, effectively stripping the ECB of independent control.

Paradoxically, it was the strait-jacket fiscal approach of the ECB-controlled single currency, and concern over its impact on national sovereignty, that persuaded Britain and Sweden not to join the euroland group of EU member nations. It is hard to deny, however, that such fears have been realized. Italy has lost 40 percent in competitiveness against Germany since the exchange rates were fixed ten years ago. France has lost over 20 percent, and Germany has emerged as the big winner with burgeoning exports to China, Eastern Europe and the Middle East.

The Bruges Group, a neoliberal think-tank, has warned against European federation and monetary union, especially for Britain. The group has long refuted the EU's consistent claims that the euro has the ability to "deliver stability." The euro was launched at the exchange rate of $1.17. It quickly dropped to 80 cents. As I write it is now worth over $1.30. Stability in relation to its main competitor, the U.S. dollar, has in fact proven as elusive as the economic stability that was predicted for euro-zone member nations. The British pound has, on the other hand, remained remarkably stable against the U.S. dollar.

The euro was created in 1999 as "heir apparent" to the U.S. dollar's world reserve currency status. While in its first decade it has remained a shaky currency, its recent rise—courtesy of the ECB's regular interest rate hikes—has encouraged many of the world's central banks to diversify away from the U.S. dollar. Consequently, many countries now hold vast reserves of euros. If the euro were to collapse it could well precipitate a global financial crisis in an already precariously balanced system of international currencies.

Source: Peter C. Glover from *World Politics Review.*

The Empirical Evidence

The international parity relations presented in Chapter 2 provide a useful framework for analyzing the international interplay of monetary variables. The parity theory relies on restrictive assumptions about uncertainty, as well as about the perfection of trade and money markets. In the real world, future inflation and exchange rates are uncertain and physical arbitrage cannot take place instantly. In developing a forecasting methodology, the next step is to evaluate the extent to which each parity condition holds true and to examine the causes of any deviations. A better understanding of parity condition deviations can help in forecasting exchange rates and in estimating currency risks.

Interest Rate Parity

As demonstrated in Chapter 1, the interest rate parity (IRP) relation is derived from riskless financial arbitrage among the various money markets. If these markets are free and deregulated, interest rate parity must hold, within a transaction cost band: The interest rate differential must be equal to the forward discount/premium. Because the bid–ask spreads are minuscule on the *Eurocurrency market,* interest parity is always verified within a few basis points. By arbitrage, IRP *must hold* for all major investment currencies. However, some countries, especially developing ones, still impose various forms of capital controls and taxes that impede arbitrage. Furthermore, some smaller currencies can be borrowed and lent only domestically; the domestic money markets are often subject to political risk and various types of costly regulations and controls.[1] The continuing deregulation and international integration of financial markets throughout the world are certain to reduce these deviations in the future, even for emerging markets.

International Fisher Relation

Although it has exchange rate implications, the international Fisher relation does not directly involve the exchange rate. The question raised is whether real interest rates are equal among countries. This question is illustrated in Exhibit 3.1, which plots the real interest rate for three-month bills for the three major international currencies over the period 1973–2006. Because it requires a measure of expected inflation, the calculation of the real interest rate is somewhat difficult. In Exhibit 3.1, expected inflation is simply replaced by the realized inflation over the life of the three-month bill; real rates observed each quarter have been averaged over the year. Real rates differed markedly during the first oil shock of 1973–1974. Real rates were very high in the 1980s and became lower on the U.S. dollar than on other currencies in the early 1990s. Japan witnessed a period of economic slowdown in the 1990s, with dropping real interest rates, while the United States witnessed a period of sustained economic growth, which could accommodate much higher real rates. Real rates went down in early 2005 but moved up in 2006. Averaged over the 1973–2006 period, the real interest rates in the United States and Germany are

EXHIBIT 3.1

Real Interest Rates: United States, Japan, and Germany, 1973–2006

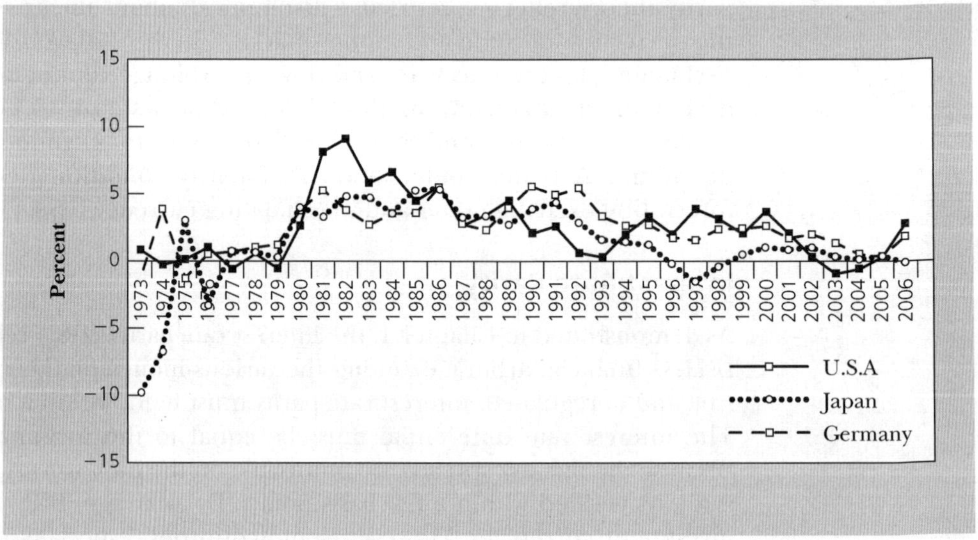

[1] Frankel and MacArthur (1988) have confirmed that deviations from interest rate parity can be quite large for what they call "closed less-developed countries."

almost identical (a few basis points difference), as is the case with other European countries. However, Japan had lower real rates.

A casual observation of Exhibit 3.1, confirmed by more sophisticated econometric tests, suggests that real interest rates tend to move up and down together worldwide as a function of the world business cycle. Because national business cycles are not fully synchronized, however, significant differences in real rates can exist in any time period.

An investment strategy that takes advantage of such deviations from parity would be to invest in high-interest-rate currencies. In terms of risk and return, the results of this strategy would depend on the evolution of the exchange rate. We now turn to the empirical evidence on parity relations involving the exchange rate.

Purchasing Power Parity

Purchasing power parity is one of the economic subjects that has attracted the largest number of empirical articles. The empirical findings on the validity of PPP in the short run can be characterized as disappointing in the sense that they are unsupportive.[2] Regressions of monthly or quarterly exchange rate movements on inflation differentials yield low explanatory power (R^2) for the recent period of floating exchange rates. Typically, inflation differentials explain less than 5 percent of monthly exchange rate movements in major currencies. This means that 95 percent of currency movements were not caused by current inflation. Some researchers have even suggested that short-term movements in the real exchange rate tend to follow a random pattern. Deviations from PPP may not be corrected unless by chance. More encouraging recent research shows that exchange rates revert to their PPP values, but it seems to take many years for this correction to take place. Purchasing power parity is a poor explanation for *short-term* exchange rate movements, and hence for exchange rate volatility, but it holds quite well over the *long run.*[3] This phenomenon, in which exchange rates revert to their fundamental (PPP) value over the long run, is known as *mean reversion* of the real exchange rate.

Going beyond a summary of research results, we provide a quick look at the international monetary environment of the past 26 years (1976–2001). Exhibit 3.2 indicates the simple relationships among inflation rates, interest rates, and exchange rates. Two pairs of countries and their exchange rates are presented: the United States and Japan, and Germany and the United Kingdom. For each year, the figure indicates the inflation differential in percentage terms, the exchange rate movement, and the short-term interest rate differential. Differentials are calculated

---

[2] For surveys of the empirical literatures, see Grossman and Rogoff (1995), Rogoff (1996), Lothian and Taylor (1996), and Lothian (1998).

[3] Tests of PPP have moved from the traditional regression techniques to a cointegration approach. The latter approach states that the exchange rate and the price level series should be cointegrated if the PPP holds as a long-term equilibrium relation. Tests performed in the 1990s provide supportive evidence in favor of long-run PPP. See, among others, Grossman and Rogoff (1995), Mark (1995), Lothian and Taylor (1996), and Cheung and Lai (1998).

EXHIBIT 3.2

Annual Comparison of Exchange Rate Movements, Inflation Differentials, and Interest Rate Differentials, 1976–2001

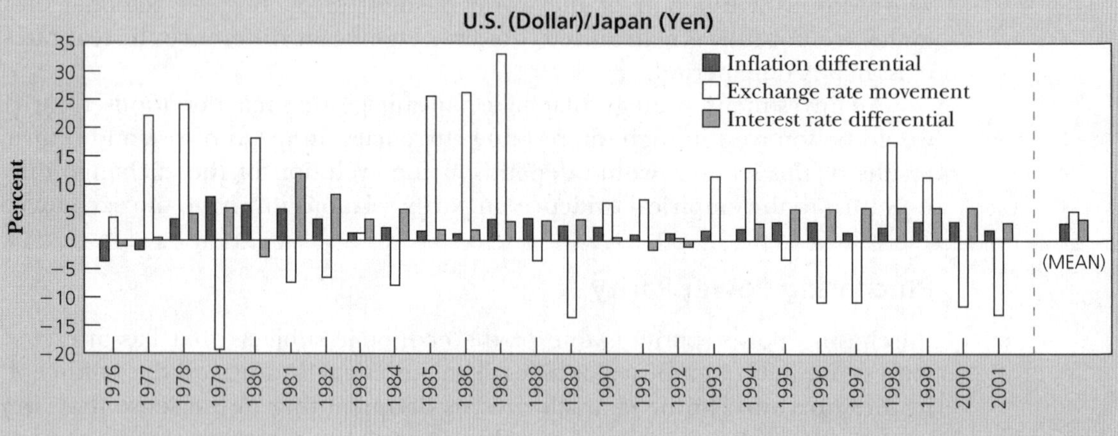

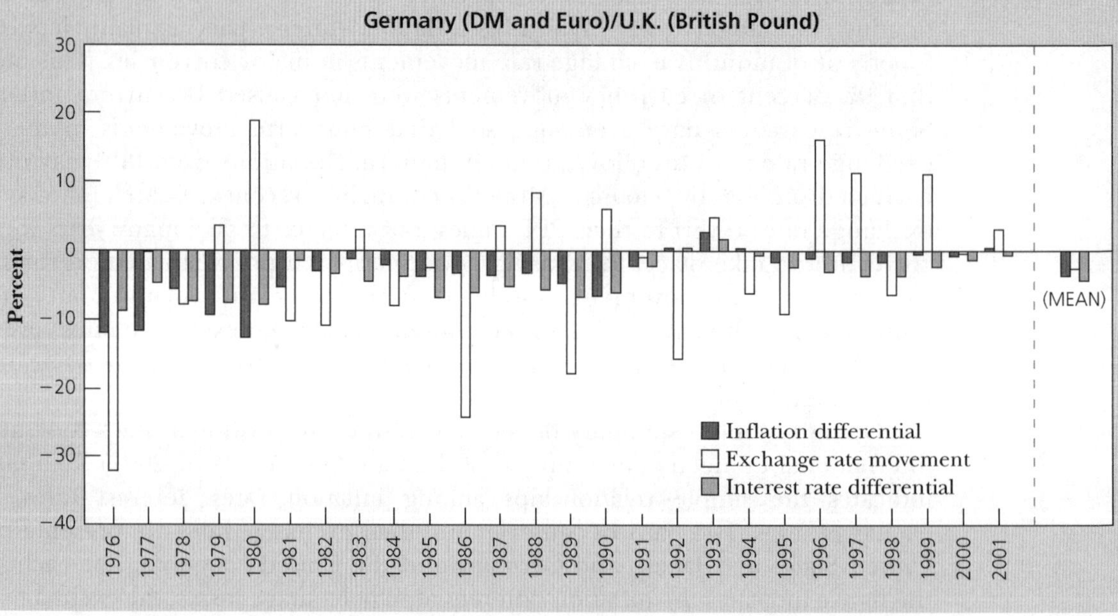

as the value for the first country minus that of the second one. For example, Exhibit 3.2 shows that in 1998, the United States had about 2 percent more inflation than Japan and a higher short-term interest rate (a differential of approximately 5 percent). The exchange rate used is the value of the second country's currency in units of the first country's currency. For example, in Exhibit 3.2, we can track the dollar value of the Japanese yen (¥/$). In 1998, the yen appreciated by some 15 percent relative to the U.S. dollar. In theory, we would expect all three measures to be of the same sign and magnitude: For each year, the three bars should be at the same level, but they typically are not.

If PPP were to hold, exchange rate movements and inflation differentials should be identical. Although the interest rate and inflation differentials tend to be of the same sign and magnitude each year, this is not the case for exchange rate movements and inflation differentials. For many years, the exchange rate has moved in the opposite direction from the inflation differential. Note that this effect is not dollar-specific because it also applies to the euro/British pound exchange rate. For example, Exhibit 3.2 shows that the British pound appreciated strongly relative to the euro in 1999, although inflation was lower in Germany than in the United Kingdom.

PPP is more tenable over the long run, as can be seen from the last bars in Exhibit 3.2 giving the annualized means over the period 1976–2001. The means of the exchange rate movements, the inflation differentials, and the interest rate differentials are fairly similar. Over the whole period, there was more inflation in the United States than in Japan, and more in the U.K. than in Germany; and this should have had exchange rate depreciation implications. In keeping with PPP theory, the dollar depreciated against the yen and the British pound depreciated against the euro (formerly the Deutsche mark). Although the long-run exchange rate movement does not exactly match the inflation differential, this could be caused by measurement error in the inflation rate or by some structural real exchange rate movement.

There are several explanations for why PPP is not verified in the short run:

- *First,* the very measurement of an inflation rate is questionable. Investors throughout the world have different consumption preferences, and a common basket of consumption goods does not exist. In the short run, relative prices of different consumption goods vary extensively with specific influences on specific consumption baskets. Different baskets of goods will exhibit different price increases as the relative prices of the goods change over time. For example, price changes for a haircut or bread in Uruguay do not closely track changes in imported computer prices. Because of differences in imported and exported goods, an inflation rate measured from an index of consumed goods will be different from an inflation rate measured from an index of produced goods. Similarly, nontraded goods enter the national consumption price index, but their prices should have little short-run influence on the exchange rate. As an illustration, the price of sake might double in Japan (thereby affecting the local price index), but the price rise should have little influence on the yen exchange rate; few foreigners consume sake, so its price is not very relevant to the exchange rate, even though it would be included in a domestic price index. In the long run, consumption substitution will take place in Japan to reflect the higher price of sake, and Japanese people may consume more beer or wine.

- *Second,* transfer costs, import taxes and restrictions, and export subsidies may not allow arbitrage in the goods markets to restore PPP. In the long run, however, industries from countries with overvalued currencies will make direct investments in undervalued countries. For example, the U.S. dollar was overvalued in terms of PPP in the early 1980s, which meant that the real price of U.S. goods was high compared with the goods of other countries. Because the U.S. dollar was strong, wages were lower in Europe than in the United States when converted into dollars. U.S. exports were not competitive because of their high prices, which were a result of the exchange rate; similarly, foreign imports to the United States were cheap. Because the situation persisted, many U.S. companies built plants abroad to take advantage of this deviation from PPP. In time, such behavior leads to a restoration of PPP.

- *Third,* many factors other than inflation influence exchange rates. Because physical goods arbitrage is constrained, PPP plays only a small role in the short run; other variables have a major impact on the short-run behavior of exchange rates. Over the long run, economic fundamentals, such as PPP, are restored.

The practical implications of these deviations from PPP are very important. The real returns of an asset as measured by investors from different countries are different. In Chapter 2, we saw that an exchange rate movement can have a dramatic real impact on an investor holding even a foreign risk-free instrument. During June 2002, the U.S. dollar depreciated by 7 percent against the euro. One-month bills in euros and in dollars had the same interest rate of 3 percent (annualized) and annual inflation rates were about 2 percent in both regions. Consider a European investor holding U.S. Treasury bills. Such an investor would have had a real return of minus 6.92 percent (−6.75% return in euros minus 0.17 percent monthly European inflation rate).

Furthermore, uncertainty about the real exchange rate adds uncertainty to a foreign investment. Consider, for example, an investment in an emerging country. Many emerging countries have attempted to maintain a fixed or stable exchange rate with the U.S. dollar despite a much higher inflation rate. This tactic leads to a real appreciation of their currencies. Such overvaluation can persist for a few years, but at some point in time, the bubble will burst and the currency will be forced to devalue. Many examples can be found in the past two decades: the Mexican peso devaluation in 1994, the East Asian crisis of 1997, the Russian ruble devaluation of 1998, and the Argentinean peso devaluation of 2002. Over the long run, exchange rates tend to revert to fundamentals.

Foreign Exchange Expectations

The foreign exchange expectations relation links the expected future exchange rate to the forward rate. In a risk-neutral world, the expected exchange rate movement should be equal to the forward discount/premium, and hence to the interest rate differential between the two currencies.

Exchange rate expectations are not directly observable, so the ex post movements are used instead, assuming that the realized exchange rate movement is equal to its expectation plus a random unpredictable element. Tests of this parity relation focus on two aspects:

- Is the interest rate differential a good predictor of future spot exchange rate movements?
- Is there a currency risk premium in the form of a systematic difference between the spot exchange rate movement and the interest rate differential?

Although complex econometric procedures are often used,[4] an examination of Exhibit 3.2 allows a summary of the main conclusions. The exchange rate is very volatile, so the interest rate differential is a poor forecaster of the exchange rate in the short run. Over the long run (here, 26 years), the foreign exchange expectation relation is reasonably well verified. The mean realized exchange rate movement and interest rate differentials are of the same direction and magnitude. For the dollar/yen and euro/pound, there appears to exist a 1 percent currency risk premium. Of course, the question is whether this risk premium is statistically significant and could have been expected ex ante. Furthermore, it is unlikely that an ex ante currency risk premium stays constant.[5]

In making foreign investments, one should not expect foreign exchange rates to deviate strongly from fundamentals forever. Again, this reversion to fundamentals is most apparent with currencies from emerging countries. Many could achieve maintaining a stable exchange rate with the U.S. dollar, only with high domestic interest rates to induce capital flows to support their currency. At some point, the emerging country cannot defend the fixed exchange rate and a large devaluation takes place. This situation is illustrated for the Korean won in Exhibit 3.3, which gives the annual depreciation of the won relative to the U.S. dollar as well as the short-term interest rate differential between the two countries. From 1991 to 1996, the won had a much higher interest rate than the dollar (an annual differential of several percent), but the exchange rate with the dollar remained stable. In 1997, the Asian crisis hit many currencies in the region and the won was devalued by some 50 percent. Averaging over the 1991–1997 period, we find that the interest rate differential roughly matches the currency depreciation. So, any investor applying the strategy to invest in this high-interest-rate currency would have made a profit for several years and lost all of it in 1997.

The current variability of exchange rates is very large compared with that of interest rates and inflation rates. So, risk must be an important factor in all parity relations involving the expected exchange rate. Any strategy designed to take advantage of real interest rate differentials or of expected exchange rate movements has a very uncertain outcome.

---

[4] See Hodrick (1987), Kaminsky and Peruga (1990), Bekaert and Hodrick (1993), and Baillie and Bollerslev (2000). Other researchers have tested this relation by drawing exchange rate expectations from survey data; see Liu and Maddala (1992) and Cavaglia, Verschoor, and Wolff (1993).

[5] For example, Dumas and Solnik (1995) found evidence of time-varying currency risk premiums.

EXHIBIT 3.3

Korean Won

Depreciation versus Interest Rate Differential (in % per year)

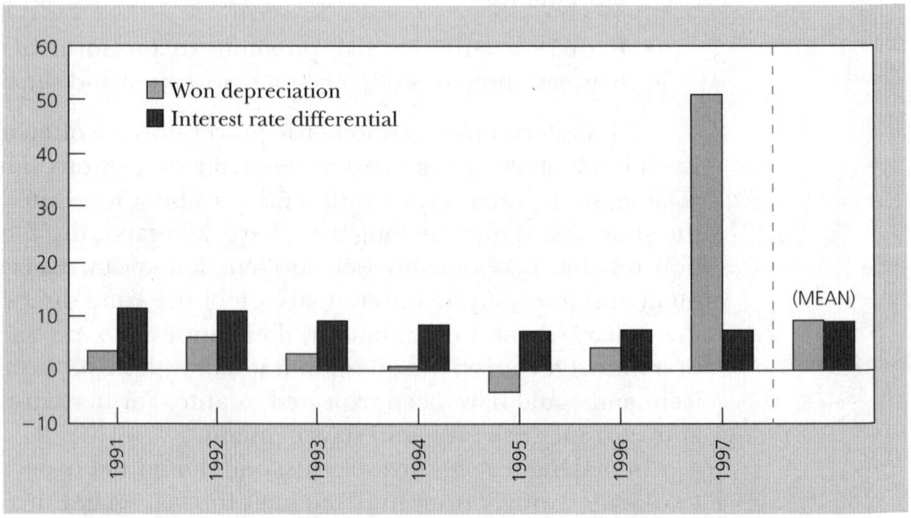

Practical Implications

To summarize the experience of the past decades, exchange rates have been quite volatile year to year. International investors have been faced with currency risk in the short run. Over the long run, this impact becomes smaller because of mean reversion toward fundamentals, but it does not fully disappear. Parity conditions are very useful because they help frame the approach to investing in an international context. The complexity brought by multiple interest rates and currencies requires a simplifying theoretical base. Investors can then take into account empirical evidence to adopt currency-risk hedging strategies and/or formulate expectations about future currency movements.

The empirical findings are both perplexing and exciting. Exchange rates are a matter of concern for all international investors because evidence shows that they do not simply neutralize inflation differentials in real terms. Furthermore, movements do not generally correct interest rate differences between two currencies. Basically, one cannot rely on money markets to correctly assess and neutralize future exchange rate movements, at least in the short run. Exchange rates have a significant influence on returns and risks in a global setting. In the longer run, fundamentals start to prevail. But the horizon to obtain mean reversion might be considered too long for an investment manager.

The empirical evidence gives analysts a chance to improve the performance of a portfolio significantly by forecasting exchange rates correctly, as discussed in the next section. Even over a period of 26 years, exchange rate movements are not fully offset by interest rate differentials, so the currency-hedging decision is meaningful and the question of a currency risk premium needs to be addressed. Exchange rates add a dimension to international investments not encountered in the domestic situation, which makes it all the more important to gain an understanding of the influence of international monetary variables on equity and bond prices and to develop international asset pricing models that explicitly incorporate exchange risk (see Chapter 4).

Exchange Rate Forecasting

Exchange rate forecasting is novel to traditional portfolio investors. Rather than examining companies or industrial sectors, financial analysts must study the relative social, political, and economic situations of several countries. Two methods are actively used to forecast exchange rates. Economic analysis is the usual approach for assessing the fair value, present and future, of foreign exchange rates. However, it is often argued that technical analysis may better explain short-run exchange rate fluctuations. This brings us back to the traditional segmentation of financial analysts into fundamentalists and technicians. Both methods often use quantitative models that make extensive use of computers, as well as qualitative (or judgmental) analysis.

Before proceeding any further, it is important to determine what our naive forecast would be in the absence of any specific model or information. In other words, assuming efficient foreign exchange markets, what is the exchange rate prediction implicit in market quotations? As discussed previously, the forward exchange rate (or spot exchange rate plus the interest rate differential) is the rational, expected value of the future spot exchange rate in a *risk-neutral* world. Suppose the spot exchange rate is €/$ = 1.05 and the dollar and euro annual interest rates are 1.76 percent and 3.39 percent, respectively. The one-year forward exchange rate would then be

$$F = S(1 + r_{€})/(1 + r_{\$}) = 1.05(1.0339/1.0176) = 1.0668$$

Hence, the one-year forward exchange rate would be €1.0668 per dollar.

Arbitrageurs would buy (or sell) currency forward and arbitrage away profit opportunities if this forward exchange rate did not reflect all information available to the market. Note that the international money market does in fact meet most of the technical criteria of an efficient market, at least for the major currencies. A huge volume of quick and almost costless transactions is performed by numerous informed and competent traders. The only restriction on the market might be central bank intervention. On the other hand, central banks may simply be regarded as transactors like any others, although having somewhat different motives. The main upshot of this scenario is that investors should average the same returns on their deposits in every currency because short-term interest rate differentials are expected to offset exchange rate movements.

In a *risk-averse* world, forward exchange rates deviate from the pure expectation value by a risk premium. If the direction and magnitude of this risk premium are hard to estimate and volatile over time, the best market estimate of the future spot exchange rate is still the forward rate.

As mentioned, forward exchange rates are poor indicators of future spot rates because of exchange rate volatility. This does not necessarily mean that a better forecasting model can be found. It may be that frequent unanticipated news has a strong influence on spot exchange rates, making them inherently volatile and unpredictable. Before reviewing the various approaches to foreign exchange forecasting, it is useful to ask whether the foreign exchange market treats information efficiently and whether market participants are rational. These questions seem reasonable in view of the negative comments often made by the press and government officials.

Is the Market Efficient and Rational?

In an efficient market, all information should be immediately reflected in the exchange rates. Rational market traders should base their forecasts on all available information. Consider an information set ϕ_t known at time t; the spot exchange rate for time $t+1$ forecasted, or expected, at time t and based on this information set is usually denoted

$$E(S_{t+1}|\phi_t) \tag{3.1}$$

Finance tends to focus on rates of returns and percentage variations. Using the notations introduced in previous chapters, we have

$$s_{t+1} = (S_{t+1} - S_t)/S_t$$
$$E(s_{t+1}|\phi_t) = [E(S_{t+1}|\phi_t) - S_t]/S_t$$

The percentage forecast error is defined as the percentage deviation of the realized rate at time $t+1$ from the expected rate:

$$e_{t+1} = s_{t+1} - E(s_{t+1}|\phi_t) \tag{3.2}$$

If market participants are rational, the forecast error should be uncorrelated with the information previously available at time t. Deviations from the expected value should be caused only by unpredictable news. Any information already available at time t should be reflected in the forecast and should not explain subsequent deviations from the forecast.

In a *risk-neutral* world, the forward exchange rate should be the best predictor of the future spot rate. It should already incorporate all relevant information available at the time of quotation. Let's denote F_t the forward rate quoted at time t for maturity $t+1$ and f_t its percentage deviation from the spot exchange rate:

$$f_t = (F_t - S_t)/S_t$$

Remember that f_t is also called the forward premium (discount) and is equal, by arbitrage, to the interest differential. We should get

$$F_t = E(S_{t+1}|\phi_t)$$
$$f_t = (F_t - S_t)/S_t = E(s_{t+1}|\phi_t)$$

The forecast error of the exchange rate movement is given by

$$e_{t+1} = s_{t+1} - f_t \tag{3.3}$$

One simple way to test that the foreign exchange market is efficient in processing information, and therefore that the forecast error is uncorrelated with f_t, is to run a regression between the realized exchange rate movement and the forward premium/discount:

$$s_{t+1} = \alpha + \beta f_t + \epsilon_{t+1} \tag{3.4}$$

We should find that α is equal to 0 and that β is equal to 1.

Numerous studies have tested this relation on many currencies and for various time periods.[6] They tend to find that the slope coefficient β is significantly smaller than 1, and sometimes negative. This negative sign is surprising. It means that a successful strategy would be to bet against the forward exchange rate. When a currency quotes with a forward premium, it should depreciate rather than appreciate. Because the forward premium (discount) is equal to the interest rate differential, the currency with the higher interest rate should appreciate. But as shown by Baillie and Bollerslev (2000), the power of these tests is very limited given the volatility in exchange rates and the difficulty in measuring expectations. The return on such investment strategies is highly uncertain.

Another common finding is that the forecast errors appear to be positively correlated over successive periods. In other words, exchange rates follow trends. Again, this is inconsistent with market rationality. It seems that exchange rate movements (or forecast errors) are positively correlated over time for short horizons (one or two years) and start to exhibit negative autocorrelation for long horizons (several years). A possible justification for this finding is that exchange rates tend to exhibit *jumps*. Over short periods that exclude the jump, exchange rates appear to trend, and forecast errors exhibit positive autocorrelation. This phenomenon disappears when the jump is included in the data. Market traders expect this jump but do not know when it will take place. The exchange rate drifts away from its fundamental, or equilibrium, value, and the correction can take several years to materialize but in a brutal fashion. This is sometimes referred to as the *peso problem*. The Mexican peso used to see its real exchange rate against the U.S. dollar appreciate progressively until the Mexican government finally devalued the peso (generally after an election). Such problems are more likely to appear on foreign exchange markets, in which participants try to forecast the policy and timing of monetary authorities, than on other capital markets, such as stock markets. Surveys of foreign exchange expectations formulated by various market participants conducted in New York, London, and Tokyo suggest that expectations extrapolate the recent trend for short horizons and predict a reversal for long horizons.[7]

---

6 See Hodrick (1987), Froot and Thaler (1990), Bekaert and Hodrick (1992), and Baillie and Bollerslev (2000).

7 See Dominguez (1986), Frankel and Froot (1987), and Liu and Maddala (1992).

Another possible explanation for the autocorrelation of forecast errors is the existence of a time-varying risk premium. The forward exchange rate could deviate from the future expected value of the spot exchange rate by a risk premium rp_t, which can change over time:

$$f_t = E(s_{t+1}|\phi_t) + rp_t$$

The percentage forecast error becomes

$$e_{t+1} = s_{t+1} - f_t + rp_t$$

and autocorrelation in forecast errors could come from the time-series properties of the required risk premium. However, the magnitude and volatility of this risk premium would have to be very large to justify the observed phenomenon.[8]

Any test of market efficiency/rationality confronts serious econometric problems. Clearly, exchange rates are not stationary, in the sense that exchange rate movements are not identically independently distributed. Expected returns vary over time in a somewhat predictable fashion, but more work is needed to attempt to model these time-varying expectations: The volatility of an exchange rate is not constant, and researchers have found evidence of GARCH effects (see the appendix to this chapter). Modeling variance is quite difficult, given the existence of infrequent jumps whose timing and magnitude are unknown. Many studies illustrate the econometric difficulties in estimating the foreign exchange risk premium.[9]

It seems fair to say that current empirical research has not solved the exchange rate puzzle. More work is needed to establish rationality and to understand the behavior of exchange rates over time. Hence, attempts to forecast exchange rates seem potentially rewarding.

The Econometric Approach

Advisory services and institutional investors that have developed foreign exchange forecasting tools may use an *econometric* model, a *subjective* approach, or both. An econometric approach implies that a quantitative model of the exchange rate is estimated on past data and used to make predictions. A subjective approach implies that a large number of parameters are taken into account in a subjective, not a quantitative, way. One set of models attempts to deduce theoretical values for current exchange rates. If the values deviate from going market rates, the models assume that the deviation will quickly be corrected by the market. Another set of models assumes that current exchange rates are correctly priced, or in equilibrium, and attempts to forecast rates in the future based on the present and predicted values of other variables.

Econometric models, which are statistical estimations of the economic theories, make it feasible to take complex correlations between variables into account explicitly. Parameters for the models are drawn from historical data. Then, current and

8 See Fama (1984).

9 See Bekaert and Hodrick (1993) and Evans and Lewis (1995).

expected values for causative variables are entered into the model, producing forecasts for exchange rates. Econometric models clearly suffer from two drawbacks. First, most of them rely on predictions for certain key variables (money supply, interest rates) that are not easy to forecast. Second, the structural correlation estimated by the parameters of the equation can change over time, so that even if all causative variables are correctly forecasted, the model can still yield poor exchange rate predictions. In periods when structural changes are rapid compared with the amount of time-series data required to estimate parameters, econometric models are of little help.[10] In these instances, subjective analysis is generally more reliable.

Many econometric forecasts rely on a single equation founded on PPP and equated to an expression containing variables for interest rates, trade balances, and money supply. Other models rely on a large number of simultaneous equations, which no doubt provide a more satisfactory description of international correlations than simplistic, single-equation models. But at the same time, complex models cannot be revised frequently. Moreover, it is time consuming to simulate each scenario, as the amount of input required is very large.

The recent models developed for exchange rate forecasting take the view that an exchange rate is the price of an asset (the currency). This asset market approach implies that the short-term behavior of exchange rates is influenced mostly by news. News appears when economic data or a political statement differs from its predicted value. The time-series properties of the exchange rate are specifically modeled with a focus on time variations in expected returns and volatility. These models seem to fare better than the traditional economic approach.

Several banks and advisory services make their models available worldwide on time-sharing systems. Using terminals with simple telephone modems, subscribers may input their own forecasts for the causative variables and even change parameters in the model equations. In fact, portfolio managers commonly use home or hotel telephones to connect laptops to any one of several wire services that provide information ranging from up-to-date economic forecasts to quoted prices to investment management packages. In periodic reports, econometric forecasts are generally combined with more subjective discussions of the international scene.

Technical Analysis

Technical analysis of exchange rates bases predictions solely on price information. The analysis is technical in the sense that it does not rely on fundamental analysis of the underlying economic determinants of exchange rates, but only on extrapolations of past price trends.[11] Technical analysis looks for the repetition of specific price patterns. Once the start of such a pattern has been detected, it automatically suggests what the short-run behavior of an exchange rate will be.

[10] The failure of econometric models to satisfactorily depict the behavior of the exchange rates is illustrated in Meese and Rogoff (1983) and Huizinga (1987).

[11] For a general description of technical analysis, see Murphy (1999) and Pring (1991); see also Rosenberg (1996).

Technical analysis has long been applied to commodity and stock markets. Its application to the foreign exchange market is a more recent phenomenon, but has attracted a wide and rapidly growing audience. One difference that sets the currency market apart from other markets is that data for trading volume are not available for currencies, so price history is the only source of information. As for economic analysis, technical analysts often use quantitative computer models or subjective analysis based on the study of charts *(chartism).*

Computer models attempt to detect both major trends and critical, or turning, points. These models are often simple and rely on *moving averages, filters,* or *momentum.* The objective of all computer models is to detect when a sustainable trend has begun.

In moving-average models, buy and sell signals are usually triggered when a short-run moving average (SRMA) of past rates crosses a long-run moving average (LRMA). The aim of a moving average is to smooth erratic daily swings of exchange rates in order to signal major trends. An LRMA will always lag behind an SRMA because the LRMA gives a smaller weight to recent movements of exchange rates than an SRMA does. If a currency is moving downward, its SRMA will be below its LRMA. When it starts rising again, as in Exhibit 3.4a, it soon crosses its LRMA, generating a buy signal/(buy dollar). The opposite is true for sell signals.

Filter methods generate buy signals when an exchange rate rises X percent (the filter) above its most recent trough and sell signals when it falls X percent below the previous peak. Again, the idea is to smooth (filter) daily fluctuations in order to detect lasting trends (see Exhibit 3.4b). Momentum models determine the strength of a currency by examining the change in velocity of currency movements. If an exchange rate climbs at increasing speed, a buy signal is issued (see Exhibit 3.4c).

In a sense, these models monitor the derivative (slope) of a time-series graph. Signals are generated when the slope varies significantly.

EXHIBIT 3.4

Computer Methods in Technical Analysis

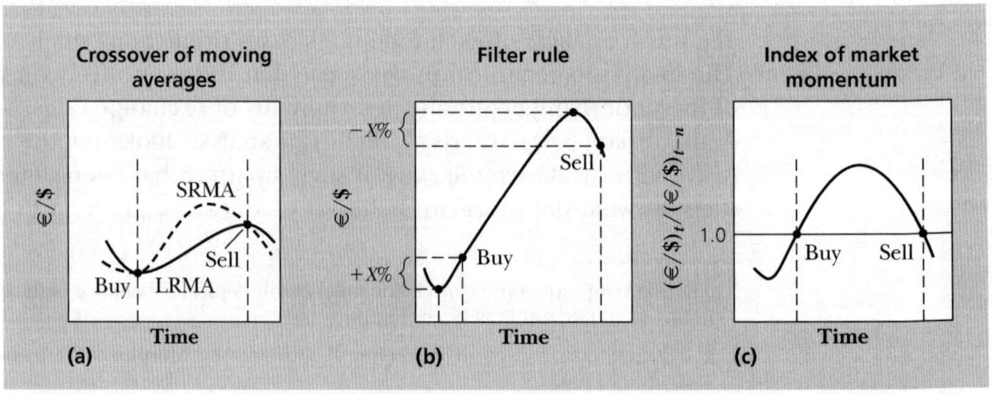

Note that there is a good deal of discretionary judgment inherent in these models. Signals are sensitive to alterations in the filters used, the period lengths used to compute moving averages, and the methods used to compute rates of change in momentum models. More sophisticated statistical models have evolved, some of which are direct applications of statistical models developed for other disciplines, such as physics and seismology. Among them are wave-and-cycle models, chaos theory, and autoregressive integrated moving average (ARIMA) estimations à la Box-Jenkins. Some powerful quantitative methods have been applied to forecast the short-term behavior of foreign exchange rates, such as multivariate vector autoregressive methods, multivariate spectral methods, ARCH models, and nonlinear autoregressive methods. Some of these methods are described in the appendix to this chapter.

Chartism (technical) analysis relies on the interpretation of exchange rate charts. Analysts usually attempt to detect recurrent price formations on bar charts that plot daily price ranges as vertical bars. They also use line charts connecting daily closing prices, or point-and-figure charts, which take into account a series of price movements in the same direction.

Chartists consider numerous price patterns significant. Each pattern is representative of a typical market situation, the outcome of which is usually predictable, thereby giving clear sell or buy signals. The various patterns are interpreted as logical sequences, in various market phases (accumulation, resistance, breakaway, reaction). Colorful terminology is generally used to describe the various patterns, including *flag, pennant, head and shoulder,* and *camel.*

Obviously, chartism is more an art than a science. Its main tenet is that market participants tend to behave in the same way over time when confronted with a similar market environment. This repetition of response is ascribed partly to emotional factors and partly to the regulatory and other constraints imposed on major market participants, such as multinational companies' treasurers, bankers, and central bankers. In other words, guidelines, regulations, and central bank intervention help create repeated and predictable currency market patterns.

Charts are sometimes used to time purchases and sales of currencies when large actors, such as central banks, intervene in the market. With the development of graphics software on microcomputers, many more people now engage in technical analysis. One should be aware that technical models, such as moving averages, are constantly calculated by thousands of investors. As a result, those who use this method rarely beat the market, because so many others use similar models.

Central Bank Intervention

It might seem strange to discuss central bank intervention in a section devoted to foreign exchange forecasting, but the behavior of central bankers is somewhat predictable, and forecasters attempt to factor their market intervention into the forecasts. The central banks are major players in the foreign exchange markets, although their motives are somewhat different from those of most other market participants.[12] Some central banks are renowned for the active management of their foreign currency reserves, but most do not attempt to profit from trading. They try to implement the monetary policy and exchange rate targets defined by their monetary authorities.

In the early 1970s, the Bretton Woods system of pegged exchange rates exploded due to the magnitude of speculative flows and the unreasonable attitude of some governments attempting to defend unrealistic exchange rates. In a semi-fixed exchange rate system, exchange rates must stay within a narrow band of a fixed central parity. When a currency is under too much pressure, the monetary authorities must de(re)value its central parity. Let's assume that because of political and economic fundamentals, the British pound is weak, as was the case in 1967. Speculators can speculate against the pound with little risk. They sell pound forward against dollar. If the Bank of England is successful in defending the parity of the pound, the exchange rate will stay constant, and the speculators will lose nothing, or very little. If the Bank of England exhausts its foreign currency reserves in defending the pound and is forced to devalue, the speculators will pocket the amount of devaluation by buying back the pound at a cheaper price. It is a game in which there can be only one loser: the central bank. Of course, monetary authorities and market forces will lift the interest rates of the weak currencies, but this is a small cost to speculation, given the speed at which it can succeed in forcing a de(re)valuation. In the late 1960s, the amount of capital available for currency speculation became large compared with the amount of official reserves of central banks, and the number of currencies forced to de(re)value became large, leading to large losses for central banks. Within two months, the Dutch guilder was forced to devalue by almost 10 percent and then forced to revalue by a similar amount.

The move to floating exchange rates made this type of speculation against the central banks much more problematic. Unfortunately, monetary authorities tend to forget lessons from the past fairly quickly.[13] Before the introduction of the euro, the *European Monetary System* relied on a collective defense of the central parities by all its members, thereby increasing the amount of reserves usable to defend the parities. Unfortunately for the central banks, the amount of private speculative capital also increased. In 1992 and 1993, several European central banks lost many billions of dollars unsuccessfully defending their currencies against a devaluation relative to the Deutsche mark. Conversely, hedge funds and George Soros became notorious for their profit in currency speculation.

However, speculation against central banks is not an easy game, as illustrated by big losses taken by these same currency hedge funds in early 1994. But it is clear that a lucid analysis of the policy and objectives of a country's monetary authorities can, in some cases, help forecast the short-term behavior of speculation and of the exchange rate. In the face of an uncertain social, political, and even electoral environment, monetary authorities are inclined to defend a currency beyond dangerous

---

12 See Lewis (1995), Baillie and Osterberg (1997), Dominguez (1998), Bekaert and Gray (1998), and Neely and Weller (2001).

13 See Goodhart (1993), Leahy (1995), and Szakmary and Mathur (1997).

EXHIBIT 3.5

An Example of the Impact of News about Central Bank Intervention

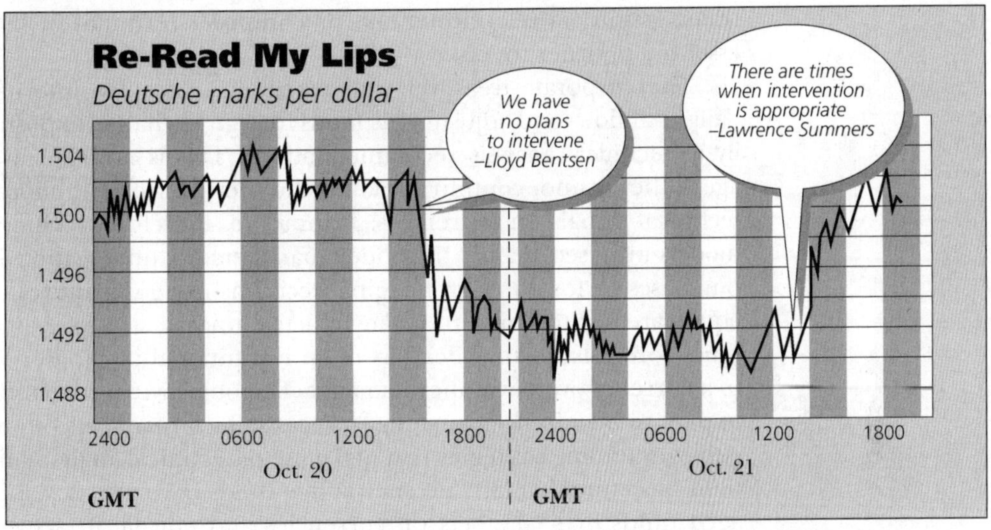

Source: "Bentsen's Dollar Talk. 6 Very Expensive Words," from an article by Alan Friedman, from *International Herald Tribune*. Copyright © 1994 International Herald Tribune. Reproduced with permission of International Herald Tribune.

levels. More generally, the various aspects of central banks' policies should be incorporated in a forecasting model for the exchange rate.

An illustration of the importance of news about official intervention is given in Exhibit 3.5, which tracks the DM/$ exchange rate around October 20, 1994. On October 20, U.S. Treasury Secretary Lloyd Bentsen made a surprise, and imprudent, announcement that the United States had no plans to intervene in the foreign exchange market to defend the dollar, sending the market into a frenzy when the statement appeared on the traders' Reuters screens. The next morning, Treasury Undersecretary Lawrence Summers corrected the statement and suggested that there were times when an intervention was appropriate. The dollar immediately rebounded.

The Use and Performance of Forecasts

Technical analysts closely follow the market and forecast the very near future. Detecting a pattern is beneficial if the market continues to follow that pattern faithfully. But no pattern can be expected to last for more than a few days, possibly weeks; market inefficiencies are corrected too quickly. Indeed, if a technical analyst persuades enough clients to act on her recommendations, prices will move rapidly to a level that rules out additional profits. The more publicity a successful analyst gets, the more quickly the market corrects the inefficiencies she reports. As a result, all systematic black-box models must be continually modified to counter this self-correcting process. A client must react very quickly to a technical recommendation. Unfortunately, there are often time lags between the moment a technical service issues a recommendation, the time it takes to reach the money manager, and the moment it is finally implemented. For this reason, immediate transmission via telephone, fax, or computer terminal of buy and sell signals is essential in order to make a profit.

The corporate treasurer who manages a complex international position with daily cash flows and adjustments in his foreign exchange exposure can respond readily to technical analysis recommendations. This is not the case for portfolio managers; they cannot continually adjust their long-term asset allocations on the basis of technical signals on currencies. In practice, therefore, technical foreign exchange models are used mainly by money managers for timing their investment sales and purchases or for currency-hedging decisions using derivatives. Transaction costs on equity are just too high to make an active trading strategy based on short-term currency forecasts worthwhile. Part of an institutional portfolio is sometimes entrusted to a currency-overlay money manager. The objective of a currency-overlay strategy is, in part, to benefit from currency forecasts. Such managers often resort to short-term currency trading strategies that make use of technical analysis and interpret interventions by central banks. Currency hedge funds have also developed. These are leveraged funds that take bets on currencies and engage in active trading. Banks also trade extensively in currencies for their proprietary accounts. All these traders make use of all the available short-term forecasting techniques described here.

By contrast, long-term economic forecasts for currencies and interest rates are a basic component of the international asset allocation decision. In fact, currency analysis is one of several economic analyses of the international environment that a manager must undertake. Briefly, economic models of exchange rates are commonly used for long-term asset allocation, whereas technical models are more helpful for timing transactions. When the Bank of England conducted a survey among chief foreign exchange dealers based in London, it found that 90 percent of the respondents place some weight on technical analysis when forming views at one or more time horizons.[14] Although technical analysis is used extensively for very short-term forecasts, fundamental economic analysis becomes dominant for longer-term forecasts.

Two questions remain for the user of foreign exchange forecasts: How do we measure the performance of these forecasts, and what is their track record? All methods compare a particular forecast to the forward exchange rate, which is both the implied market forecast and the price at which an investor may contract to try to make a profit based on his or her specific forecast. In order to study the performance of a given forecasting model over a specific time period, we must collect the values for the following series:

Forecasts formulated in t for time $t+n$, $E(S_{t+n}|\phi_t)$

Forward rates quoted in t for time $t+n$, F_t

Spot rates realized in t, S_t and $t+n$, S_{t+n}

---

[14] See Taylor and Allen (1992).

With this set of data in hand, several methods may be used to evaluate the performance of a forecast relative to the forward rate.

A common statistical approach is to compare the forecast errors of the two models (the forecasting model versus the forward rate). The percentage forecast errors (ϵ and e) for each forecast are computed as

$$\epsilon_{t+n} = [S_{t+n} - E(S_{t+n}|\phi_t)]/S_t$$

$$e_{t+n} = [S_{t+n} - F_t]/S_t$$

Average forecasting accuracy is usually measured by the root mean squared error (RMSE). The error is squared because a positive error is no better than a negative one; the squared errors are averaged over all forecasts, and we take the square root of this average to get a number that has the same units as the forecasting errors themselves. A forecasting model is more accurate than the forward rate if it has a smaller RMSE.

This commonly used statistical measure of forecasting accuracy does not satisfy those managers for whom the generation of correct buy and sell signals is an important part of the forecast, even if the magnitude of the expected move is inaccurate. In other words, those managers want to know the number of times the forecast turns out to be on the correct side of the forward exchange rate. The fraction P= correct forecast/total forecasts estimates the probability of making correct forecasts during a given period. If the model has no forecasting ability, P is close to 0.5. If it is unusually accurate, P should be larger than 0.5, and its statistical significance may be measured.

A final method for evaluating forecasting performance is to assume that the money manager systematically buys forward contracts if the forecast is above the forward rate and sells them if the forecast is below the forward rate. The ex post financial return on this strategy is then computed, and the forecasting ability is judged on the basis of the manager's return on the capital invested.

In the 1980s, *Euromoney* provided an annual performance review of major foreign exchange advisory services, using the three methods mentioned previously. Although results vary every year, there is no doubt that exchange rate forecasting is difficult. In some years, advisory services have consistently underperformed the forward exchange rate. As one might expect, the reward for active exchange rate forecasting strategies is potentially large, but so are the risks. Technical models seem to have a slightly better track record, at least in the short run. But those models are too short-term oriented to benefit the international portfolio manager to use systematically.

An illustration of the rather poor performance of forecasters is given in the following summary of the 1984 *Euromoney* survey. The average return is very poor (4.5%), and no single service was able to beat the Treasury bill rate over 1983.

> *Euromoney*'s sixth annual survey of foreign exchange forecasters finds that technical services were once again profitable. But their performance declined in terms of return on capital at risk, from 10.8% in 1982 to 4.5% in 1983. In addition their percentage of correct signals was only 44.9%, worse than the toss of a coin.[15]

---

15 *Euromoney*, August 1984.

As a group, forecasters tend to look at the same variables, use similar methodologies, and come up with forecasts that are often mostly in the same direction. Given the high volatility of exchange rates, it is not surprising to find that they do quite badly as a group in a given year.

However, the long-term record is not that bad. For example, several studies indicate that technical analysis has been able to take advantage of exchange rate trending behavior to generate large returns.[16] Because central banks seem to be consistent losers in the foreign exchange market, with a somewhat predictable trading strategy, one should not be surprised to find that active currency strategies could lead to profits,[17] despite the high risks involved. It also seems possible to model the time variation of expected exchange rate movements in a fashion that can lead, in the long run, to profitable returns on an active asset allocation strategy.

Summary

- The international monetary system evolved from the gold standard to a system of freely floating exchange rates.
- Nevertheless, some currencies of emerging countries are pegged to the dollar, the euro, or the value of a basket of major currencies. The euro is the new common currency of several European countries.
- Parity conditions provide a useful guide to global international investing. But foreign exchange rates are very volatile in the short run. In the longer run they tend to revert to fundamental values.
- Empirical evidence suggests that foreign exchange risk is large and that currency hedging should be seriously considered. It also suggests that currency forecasting could be a fruitful exercise.
- Forecasters resort to technical or economic analysis methods. Technical analysis focuses on the short-run behavior of exchange rates, whereas the economic approach is, by nature, better designed for long-run forecasts. A modeling of central bank intervention sometimes helps to understand the short-term behavior of foreign exchange rates.
- Foreign exchange forecasting is a difficult exercise, and no theory of exchange rate determination can claim to be consistently successful. Some observations have been repeatedly made by forecasters:
  - Exchange rates revert to PPP (real exchange rates are mean-reverting).
  - Exchange rates tend to trend (positive autocorrelation).

[16] Several studies found that technical trading rules can be profitable. See Levich and Thomas (1993a and 1993b), Bilson (1993), Szakmary and Mathur (1997), Lyons (1998), and Neely and Weller (2001).

[17] See Solnik (1993), Glen and Jorion (1993), and Arnott (1999). Strange (1998) shows that currency overlay managers add value.

- Different measures of forecasting ability can be used. The track record of forecasters shows the difficulty of the task.
- The type of method used to forecast exchange rates depends on the user's motivation. A currency hedge fund focuses on short-term movements, while an international asset allocator cares about long-term prospects.

Problems

1. Under a system of exchange rates pegged around official parities, each of the following is a possible remedy for a country facing a balance of payments deficit *except*:
   a. Using its international reserves of gold and convertible currencies.
   b. Adopting tariffs on imports and introducing capital controls.
   c. Applying expansionary macroeconomic policy that drives prices up and interest rates down.
   d. Letting its exchange rate drop within the allowable band around the central parity.

2. In the European Monetary System, a member country was allowed to fluctuate its exchange rates within a band around the fixed parities with other members. In 1993, this system came under severe speculative pressures. Several currencies were pushed down to the limit of their allowed fluctuation margin against the DM; for example, the French franc could not stay within 2.25 percent of its central parity with the DM. One solution would have been to keep the same fluctuation band around the central parity but devalue the parity of the franc against the DM. Instead, the European Union decided to keep the same bilateral parities but widen the allowed fluctuation band to 15 percent on each side of the parity.
   a. What do you think are the advantages and disadvantages of each solution?
   b. Which solution is more likely to prevent currency speculation?

3. Paf is a small country that wishes to control international capital flows. The currency of Paf is the pif. Paf put in place an exchange control whereby all current account transactions can be transferred using the normal exchange rate, but capital account transactions must be transferred at a financial pif rate. In other words, foreigners wishing to invest in assets of Paf must buy them at the financial pif rate, whereas dividends are repatriated at the normal pif rate. The current financial pif rate is 0.8 pif per dollar or 1.25 dollars per financial pif. The financial rate in dollars per pif quotes at a premium of 25 percent over the normal rate.
   a. Assume that the premium of the financial rate stays constant over time. Will a U.S. investor make the same return on investment as a resident of Paf, once the asset is resold?
   b. You hear that the exchange controls may be lifted and that the financial rate may disappear. Would this be good news to an existing foreign investor?
   c. Would the lifting of exchange controls and removal of the financial rate be good news to a new foreign investor?

4. Which of the following statements about the euro is false?
   I. The euro is the sole currency of the Eurozone countries.
   II. The countries in the Eurozone have been limited to the ones that are already in it, and no more countries would be allowed to join it in the future.
   III. The euro has a floating rate against other currencies, such as the U.S. dollar and the Japanese yen.

5. Interest rate parity between two currencies is more likely to be violated when one of the currencies is from a developing market than when both the currencies are from developed markets. Discuss whether or not you agree with this statement.

6. A U.S. institutional investor has invested in a portfolio of stocks in India. The annual inflation rate is 6 percent in India and 2.5 percent in the United States.
   a. If the purchasing power parity holds between the United States and India, by how much should the Indian rupee appreciate or depreciate with respect to the dollar over a year?
   b. Suppose that the annual return on the portfolio is 12 percent in Indian rupees, and the Indian rupee depreciated with respect to the dollar by 5 percent. Also suppose that an Indian institutional investor also held a portfolio with the same composition. Compare the real returns for both investors, and discuss why they do or do not differ from one another.

7. Consider a country whose currency is undervalued as compared to what the PPP relationship indicates. Discuss what is likely to happen in terms of foreign investment and trade, which may help restore PPP in the long run.

8. The spot $:SFr is equal to 1.4723. The three-month interest rates are 1.80 percent for the U.S. dollar (7.2% annualized) and 0.95 percent for the Swiss franc (3.8% annualized). Assuming that the foreign exchange market participants are risk-neutral, what is the implied market prediction for the three-month ahead $:SFr exchange rate?

9. The six-month forward €:$ exchange rate is $0.9976 per €. A major commercial bank has made public a model that it uses to forecast future €:$ spot exchange rates. This model forecasts the spot exchange rate six months later to be $0.9781 per €. Suppose that the market participants believe that this model is quite good, and they all start using this model. What do you think would happen to the spot and forward exchange rates and the six-month interest rates in dollars and euros?

10. Dustin Green likes to invest in the foreign exchange market. After an analysis of the last 10 years of U.S. dollar to British pound exchange rate data, he has come up with his own model to forecast the £:€ exchange rate one year ahead. Based on this model, the forecast for the one-year ahead exchange rate is $1.5315 per £. The spot £:€ is equal to 1.5620. The annual one-year interest rates on the Eurocurrency market are 2 percent in dollars and 4.25 percent in pounds.
    a. What is the one-year forward exchange rate?
    b. If Dustin Green invests based on his model, which currency would he buy forward?
    c. If everyone were to start using Dustin Green's model and follow his transaction, what would happen to the exchange and interest rates?

11. Suppose that the participants in the foreign exchange market know the interest rates for all maturities and have reliable forecasts for inflation rates. If the foreign exchange market is efficient, discuss what is the expected future spot exchange rate if the
    a. market participants are risk-neutral.
    b. market participants are risk-averse.

12. Discuss the dangers of forecasting future spot exchange rates using methods based on trends.

13. Each of the following statements about central banks of countries and foreign exchange markets is true *except*:

a. The central banks are generally major players in the foreign exchange market.
b. Most central banks actively manage their foreign exchange reserves with the purpose of generating trading profits from favorable exchange rate movements.
c. A modeling of central bank intervention in the foreign exchange market sometimes helps to understand the short-term behavior of exchange rates.
d. Central banks may intervene in the foreign exchange market for the implementation of monetary policy and exchange rate targets.

14. Define what is meant by a mean-reverting time series. What does the empirical evidence indicate about exchange rates being mean reverting?

15. What are the problems associated with using econometric models for forecasting exchange rates?

16. For each of the following, indicate whether the individual is more likely to use the econometric approach or technical analysis for foreign exchange forecasting.
a. Manager of a currency hedge fund
b. Manager of an international stock portfolio
c. Currency trader
d. Long-term strategic planner of a corporation

17. Suppose that the three-month forward Swiss franc to dollar rate is SFr1.440 per $. The forecast for the three-month ahead spot exchange rate by Analyst A is SFr1.410 per $ and the forecast by Analyst B is SFr1.580 per $. The actual spot rate realized three months later is SFr1.308 per $.
a. Which of the three forecasts, including the forward rate, is the most accurate?
b. If the spot rate at the time of prediction was SFr1.420 per $, which analyst(s) correctly predicted the appreciation of Swiss franc relative to the dollar?

18. During the early 1990s, *Risk* magazine published exchange rate forecasts provided by 10 of the world's major commercial banks. In one such set of forecasts, Commerzbank and Harris Bank predicted the six-month ahead spot exchange rate to be ¥142 per $ and ¥156 per $, respectively. At the time of prediction, the Japanese yen to dollar spot rate was 145.41. The six-month forward rate was ¥144.697 per $. The actual spot exchange rate realized six months later was ¥148.148 per $.
a. Rank the three forecasts, including the forward rate, based on the forecast error.
b. Which forecast(s) correctly predicted the depreciation of Japanese yen relative to the dollar?
c. David Brock and Brian Lee are speculators who buy and sell currencies forward. David Brock took a position based on Commerzbank's forecast for the yen to dollar exchange rate while Brian Lee took a position based on Harris Bank's forecast. Who turned out to be better off?
d. Discuss whether there is any conflict in your answers to parts (a) and (c).

19. The following table contains Japanese yen to dollar exchange rate data that were published in issues of *Risk* magazine. Each period is three months. *Spot rate* is the actual spot exchange rate prevailing at the start of a period. *Forward rate* is the three-month forward exchange rate prevailing at the start of a period. *Forecast rate* is the forecast made by the Industrial Bank of Japan at the start of a period for the spot exchange rate at the start of the next period (that is, the forecast for three months later). To illustrate, at the beginning of the third period, the actual spot exchange rate was 152.750, the three-month ahead forward rate was 153.600, and the rate forecast by the Industrial Bank for the start of the fourth period was 151. The actual spot exchange rate that was realized at the start of the fourth period was 149.400. Based on the root mean squared error, was the Industrial Bank of Japan able to outperform the forward rate? (Do the calculations for the percentage forecast error.) You are also given that the spot rate realized three months after the last forecast given in the table was 139.25.

Period	Spot Rate	Forward Rate	Forecast Rate
1	143.164	142.511	140
2	144.300	143.968	141
3	152.750	153.600	151
4	149.400	149.400	143
5	129.600	129.700	130
6	129.500	129.800	131

Bibliography

Angel, J. J. "Implications of Chaos for Portfolio Management," *Journal of Investing*, Summer 1994.

Arnott, R. "Tactical Currency Allocation," *Managing Currency Risks in Investment Portfolios*, AIMR Proceedings, 1999.

Baillie, R. T., and Bollerslev, T. "The Forward Premium Anomaly Is Not as Bad as You Think," *Journal of International Money and Finance*, 19(4), August 2000, pp. 471–488.

Baillie, R. T., and Osterberg, W. P. "Why Do Central Banks Intervene?" *Journal of International Money and Finance*, 16(6), December 1997, pp. 909–920.

Bekaert, G., and Gray, S. "Target Zones and Exchange Rates: An Empirical Investigation," *Journal of International Economics*, 1998.

Bekaert, G., and Hodrick, R. J. "Characterizing Predictable Components in Excess Returns on Equity and Foreign Exchange," *Journal of Finance*, June 1992.

———. "On Biases in the Measurement of Foreign Exchange Risk Premiums," *Journal of International Money and Finance*, 12, April 1993, pp. 115–138.

Bilson, I. "Value, Yield and Trend: A Composite Forecasting Approach to Foreign Exchange Trading," in A. Gritlin, ed., *Strategic Currency Investing*, Chicago: Probus, 1993.

Bollerslev, T., Chou, R. Y., and Kroner, K. F. "ARCH Modelling in Finance: A Review of the Theory and Empirical Evidence," *Journal of Econometrics*, 52, 1992.

Box, G. E., and Jenkins, G. M. *Time Series Analysis, Forecasting and Control*, San Francisco: Holden Day, 1994.

Cavaglia, S., Verschoor, W. F., and Wolff, C. P., "Further Evidence on Exchange Rate Expectations," *Journal of International Money and Finance*, 12, February 1993.

Cheung, Y-W., and Lai, K. S. "Parity Reversion in Real Exchange Rates during the Post–Bretton Woods Period," *Journal of International Money and Finance*, 17(4), August 1998, pp. 597–614.

Dominguez, K. M. "Are Foreign Exchange Forecasts Rational? New Evidence from Survey Data," *Economic Letters*, 21, 1986, pp. 277–281.

———. "Central Bank Intervention and Exchange Rate Volatility," *Journal of International Money and Finance,* 17(1), February 1998, pp. 161–190.

Dumas, B., and Solnik, B. "The World Price of Foreign Exchange Risk," *Journal of Finance,* 50(2), June 1995, pp. 445–479.

Engle, R. "Statistical Models for Financial Volatility," *Financial Analysts Journal,* January/February 1993.

Evans, M. D., and Lewis, K. K. "Do Long-Term Swings in the Dollar Affect Estimates of the Risk Premium?" *Review of Financial Studies,* 8(3), Fall 1995, pp. 709–742.

Fama, E. "Forward and Spot Exchange Rates," *Journal of Monetary Economics,* November 1984.

Frankel, J. A., and Froot, K. A. "Using Survey Data to Test Standard Propositions Regarding Exchange Rate Expectations," *American Economic Review,* March 1987.

Frankel, J., and MacArthur, M. A. "Political vs Currency Premia in International Real Interest Differentials: A Study of Forward Rates for 24 Countries," *European Economic Review,* 32, June 1988.

Froot, K. A., and Thaler, R. H. "Anomalies: Foreign Exchange," *Journal of Economic Perspectives,* 4(3), 1990.

Glen, J., and Jorion, P. "Currency Hedging for International Portfolios," *Journal of Finance,* December 1993.

Goodhart, C. A. E. "Central Bank Forex Intervention Assessed in Continuous Time," *Journal of International Money and Finance,* August 1993.

Grossman, G., and Rogoff, K., eds. *Handbook of International Economics,* Volume 3, Amsterdam: North-Holland, 1995.

Hodrick, R. J. *The Empirical Evidence on the Efficiency of Forward Futures Foreign Exchange Market,* Chur, Switzerland: Harwood Academic, 1987.

Huizinga, J. "An Empirical Investigation of the Long-Run Behavior of Real Exchange Rates," in K. Brunner and A. Meltzer, eds., *Carnegie-Rochester Series on Public Policy,* 27, Amsterdam: North-Holland, 1987.

Jorion, P. "On Jump Processes in the Foreign Exchange and Stock Markets," *Review of Financial Studies,* 1, 1989.

Kaminsky, G., and Peruga, R. "Can a Time-Varying Risk Premium Explain Excess Returns in the Forward Market for Foreign Exchange?" *Journal of International Economics,* 28 February, 1990.

Kryzanowski, L., Galler, M., and Wright, D. W. "Using Artificial Network to Pick Stocks," *Financial Analysts Journal,* July/August 1993.

Leahy, M. P. "The Profitability of U.S. Intervention in the Foreign Exchange Market," *Journal of International Money and Finance,* 14(6), December 1995, pp. 823–844.

Levich, R. M., and Thomas, L. "The Merits of Active Currency Risk Management: Evidence from International Bond Portfolios," *Financial Analysts Journal,* 49(5), September/October 1993a, pp. 63–70.

———. "The Significance of Technical Trading-Rule Profits in the Foreign Exchange Market: A Bootstrap Approach," *Journal of International Money and Finance,* 12(5), October 1993b, pp. 451–474.

Lewis, K. L. "Occasional Interventions to Target Rates," *American Economic Review*, September 1995.

Liu, P. C., and Maddala, G. S. "Rationality of Survey Data and Tests for Market Efficiency in the Foreign Exchange Markets," *Journal of International Money and Finance*, August 1992.

Lothian, J. "Some New Stylized Facts of Floating Exchange Rates," *Journal of International Money and Finance*, 17(1), February 1998, pp. 29–40.

Lothian, J., and Taylor, M. "Real Exchange Rate Behavior: The Recent Float from the Perspective of the Past Two Centuries," *Journal of Political Economy*, June 1996, pp. 488–509.

Lyons, R. K. "Profits and Position Control: A Week of FX Dealing," *Journal of International Money and Finance*, 17(1), February 1998, pp. 97–116.

Mark, N. "Exchange Rates and Fundamentals: Evidence on Long-Horizon Predictability," *American Economic Review*, March 1995, pp. 201–218.

Medsker, L., Turban, E., and Trippi, R. "Neural Network Fundamentals for Financial Analysts," *Journal of Investing*, Spring 1993.

Meese, R., and Rogoff, K. "Empirical Exchange Rate Models of the Seventies: Do They Fit Out-of-Sample?" *Journal of International Economics*, February 1983.

Murphy, J. J. *Technical Analysis of the Financial Markets: A Comprehensive Guide to Trading Methods and Applications*, New York: Prentice Hall, 1999.

Neely, C. J., and Weller, P. A., "Technical Analysis and Central Bank Intervention," *Journal of International Money and Finance*, 20(7), December 2001, pp. 949–970.

Peters, E. *Fractal Market Analysis*, New York: Wiley, 1994.

Pring, M. J. *Technical Analysis Explained: The Successful Investor's Guide to Spotting Investment Trends and Turning Points*, New York: McGraw-Hill, 1991.

Rogoff, K. "The Purchasing Power Parity Puzzle," *Journal of Economic Literature*, 34, June 1996, pp. 647–668.

Rosenberg, M. *Currency Forecasting: A Guide to Fundamental and Technical Models of Exchange Rate Determination*, Chicago: Irwin, 1996.

Solnik, B. *Predictable Time-Varying Components of International Asset Returns*, Charlottesville, VA: The Research Foundation of Chartered Financial Analysts, 1993.

Strange, B. "Do Currency Overlay Managers Add Value?" *Pension and Investments*, June 15, 1998.

Szakmary, A. C., and Mathur, I. "Central Bank Intervention and Trading Rule Profits in Foreign Exchange Markets," *Journal of International Money and Finance*, 16(4), August 1997, pp. 513–536.

Taylor, M. P., and Allen, H. "The Use of Technical Analysis in the Foreign Exchange Market," *Journal of International Money and Finance*, June 1992.

Chapter 3 Appendix:

Statistical Supplements on Forecasting Asset Returns

The reader is assumed to have some familiarity with standard statistics. This appendix is intended as a brief but somewhat technical introduction to less conventional statistical models used in forecasting. The basic question is: How can we describe the time behavior of a random variable in a tractable way, that is, in a model whose statistical properties are such that it can easily be estimated from past data and used to forecast the future value of the variable?

Some Notations

Prices move over time in a somewhat random fashion. It is common in finance to focus on the stochastic process followed by the rate of return of an asset, that is, its percentage price movement. Let's introduce some mathematical notations:

r_{t+1}	the rate of return observed at time $t+1$
$E_t(r_{t+1})$	the rate of return *expected* in period t for period $t+1$
e_{t+1}	the deviation of the rate realized in period $t+1$ from its expected value in period t: $e_{t+1} = r_{t+1} - E_t(r_{t+1})$; sometimes called *forecast error* or *shock* or *innovation*
σ^2_{t+1}	the *variance* of the rate of return r_{t+1}; also the variance of e_{t+1}; its square root σ_{t+1} is the standard deviation of returns

The process for the rate of return can be written as

$$r_{t+1} = E_t(r_{t+1}) + e_{t+1} \tag{3.5}$$

where the forecast error e_{t+1} has a zero expected return and a variance σ^2_{t+1}. The variance is equal to

$$\sigma^2_{t+1} = E_t(e^2_{t+1})$$

The variance and expected returns are called *moments* of the probability distribution of the rates of return. The variance is a measure of the *volatility* of the asset.

The notations may seem a bit complicated but are necessary. They stress that the expectation and variance estimates are taken at time t for a return to be realized at time $t + 1$. At this point, we do not assume that expected returns and variances are constant over time. They are assumed to be *conditional* on some set of information available at time t. A more descriptive notation would be

$$E_t(r_{t+1}) = E_t(r_{t+1}|\phi_t)$$

$$\sigma_{t+1}^2 = E_t(e_{t+1}^2|\phi_t)$$

where the notation $|\ \phi_t$ means that the expectation is conditional on an information set ϕ_t known at time t.

Traditional Statistical Models with Constant Moments

The traditional approach to statistical modeling uses models with constant expected returns and variances.

Normal Distribution

The most simple and common statistical model describing the process followed by an asset rate of return is the *normal distribution,* with constant expected return and variance. A normal, or Gaussian, distribution is completely summarized by its mean and variance. The distribution takes the famous bell shape. At each time period $t + 1$, rates of return are assumed to be drawn independently from the same distribution; they are identically independently distributed (i.i.d.). In other words, the rate of return for each time period $t+1$ is independent of what happened in the past and always has the same expected return and variance. We have

$$E_t(r_{t+1}) = E(r) = \text{constant}$$

$$\sigma_{t+1}^2 = \sigma^2 = \text{constant}$$

and

$$r_{t+1} = E(r) + e_{t+1} \tag{3.6}$$

This distribution is *unconditional* in the sense that its expected return and variance are constant through time and not conditional on time or current information.

Let's now see how to empirically estimate the parameters of such a model and use it to forecast. We can look at past data; the expected return is simply estimated as the mean return over the sample. Hence, the best empirical estimate of the future return is the mean return estimated over past data. In the foreign exchange market, the best forecast for a future movement in the exchange rate is its past trend.

Jumps

Some asset prices are likely to exhibit infrequent big *jumps*. For example, exchange rates are periodically devalued or revalued under speculative pressures. The date of the jump is uncertain.

The statistical distribution of daily exchange rate movements could be thought of as a combination of daily normal movements and infrequent jumps.[18] The simplest jump process is a binomial approach, whereby a jump of size J has a probability p to take place at time $t+1$ and a probability $1-p$ not to take place. Hence, the return on date $t+1$ is a random variable λ_{t+1} such that

$$\lambda_{t+1} = \begin{vmatrix} J \text{ with probability } p \\ 0 \text{ with probability } 1-p \end{vmatrix} \tag{3.7}$$

This can lead to so-called Poisson distributions.

Note that both types of distributions—normal and Poisson—are i.i.d. In the simple jump process described, the probability of occurrence of a jump is independent of what happened in the previous periods or independent of current information. Hence, the expected return and the variance are the same for each period. Such a simple statistical jump process is not satisfactory for describing the behavior of exchange rate movements. The probability of a jump in exchange rate is clearly a function of past jumps. If a big jump (e.g., a devaluation) has just taken place, it is unlikely to take place again in the very near future. Also, the magnitude of the jump is uncertain. Unfortunately, complex time-dependent jump processes are untractable from a practical viewpoint.

Traditional Statistical Models with Time-Varying Moments

No theory claims that the expected return on an asset should always stay the same. The assumption that the expected return is constant through time can be relaxed in a number of ways. One way is to assume that past returns influence future returns in a specified manner. Another is to model the influence of a change in the economic environment by stating a linear relation between current observed economic variables and future returns. Still another is to assume that a change in market volatility affects the expected return.

Time-Varying Expected Return: ARIMA

The first approach is to assume that future returns are a function of past returns. A powerful model of time dependence in returns is the *ARIMA (autoregressive integrated moving average)* process. This theory was developed by Box and Jenkins.[19] The basic idea is that the return at time $t+1$ will be affected by past returns in a specified and predictable way. A general ARIMA process can be written as

$$r_{t+1} = a_0 + b_0 r_t + b_1 r_{t-1} + b_2 r_{t-2} + \cdots + c_0 e_t + c_1 e_{t-1} + c_2 e_{t-2} + \cdots + e_{t+1} \tag{3.8}$$

The variance of the innovations e_{t+1} is assumed to be constant.

The terms with the b coefficients are the autoregressive terms. The terms with the c coefficients are the moving-average terms. The *order* of the ARIMA process is the number of lags included on the right-hand side. The number of lags for

---

[18] See, for example, Jorion (1989) and Bekaert and Gray (1998).

[19] See Box and Jenkins (1994).

the moving-average terms and for the autoregressive terms can be different. In Equation 3.8, we stopped detailing the terms at order 3 for both.

One must clearly understand what is known at time t. All past returns, including r_t, have been observed at time t. All innovation terms, including e_t, have also been observed at time t. Hence, and assuming an ARIMA process of order 3, the expectation formulated at time t for the return at time $t+1$ is equal to

$$E_t(r_{t+1}) = a_0 + b_0 r_t + b_1 r_{t-1} + b_2 r_{t-2} + c_0 e_t + c_1 e_{t-1} + c_2 e_{t-2} \tag{3.9}$$

To use this model in forecasting, one would first estimate the c and b coefficients over past data, using standard ARIMA econometric software. The forecast for $t+1$ would then be derived using Equation 3.9.

Expected returns can depend on past returns in ways other than those specified by ARIMA processes. Technical analysis uses a variety of methods, such as filter rules or charts, described in this chapter.

Time-Varying Expected Return: Information Variables

The economic environment changes over time. Clearly, the level of interest rates or the business cycle could affect expectations for future asset returns. A wide body of literature[20] has modeled a linear relation between time-varying expected returns and a set of n observed economic variables Z_t. This can be written as

$$E_t(r_{t+1}) = d_0 + d_1 Z_{1t} + d_2 Z_{2t} + \cdots + d_n Z_{nt} \tag{3.10}$$

The process followed by r_{t+1} can then be written as

$$r_{t+1} = d_0 + d_1 Z_{1t} + d_2 Z_{2t} + \cdots + d_n Z_{nt} + e_{t+1} \tag{3.11}$$

where the variance of innovation e_{t+1} is assumed constant.

It must be stressed that the information variables are known at time t when the forecast of the return for $t+1$ is formulated. The information variables commonly used are the level of interest rates, the spread between short- and long-term interest rates, the interest rate differential between two currencies, and so on.

To use this model in forecasting, one would first estimate the coefficients d's over past data, using a regression technique. The forecast for $t+1$ is obtained by observing the current value Z_t of the information variables and inputting them in Equation 3.10.

Time-Varying Variances: GARCH

Financial market volatility changes over time in a somewhat predictable fashion. This implies that the variance of the returns changes over time in a predictable fashion, conditional on a set of information. To be more precise, the *conditional* variance for period $t+1$ estimated in t, σ_{t+1}^2, depends on the information set available at time t.

[20] A review of the literature can be found in Solnik (1993).

The simplest specification of the conditional variance is the ARCH(p) model (Auto Regressive Conditional Heteroskedastic model), in which the conditional variance is simply a weighted average of p past squared forecast errors:

$$\sigma_{t+1}^2 = \alpha + \beta_1 e_t^2 + \beta_2 e_{t-1}^2 + \cdots + \beta_p e_{t-p+1}^2 \tag{3.12}$$

The order of the ARCH process is the number p of lags included in the equation. A natural generalization is to allow past conditional variance to enter the equation. This is known as *generalized ARCH,* or *GARCH.*[21] The GARCH(p,q) model is written as

$$\sigma_{t+1}^2 = \alpha + \beta_1 e_t^2 + \cdots + \beta_p e_{t-p+1}^2 + \gamma_1 \sigma_t^2 + \cdots + \gamma_q \sigma_{t-q+1}^2 \tag{3.13}$$

The orders of the GARCH process are the number of lags for the squared error terms (p) and for the past variances (q). Most researchers have found that a GARCH(1,1) is generally appropriate for modeling and forecasting the volatility of asset returns. The GARCH(1,1) is written as

$$\sigma_{t+1}^2 = \alpha + \beta_1 e_t^2 + \gamma_1 \sigma_t^2 \tag{3.14}$$

This model means that the current volatility estimate can be deducted from the volatility estimated in the previous period, σ_t^2, modified by the innovation, or shock, e_t^2, just observed. The observation of large shocks leads to an increase in forecasted volatility.

Estimation of the GARCH coefficients requires some specialized econometric software using a so-called maximum-likelihood algorithm. One is sometimes faced with convergence problems in such an algorithm. After the parameters β's and γ's have been estimated, Equation 3.14 can be used to forecast the next period volatility, using the past period volatility and observed shocks.

It is possible to simultaneously model the time variation in expected return and in volatility. For example, the variance of the forecast error in Equation 3.11 could be modeled as a GARCH process, and the conditional variance could be added as an explanatory variable in the conditional expected return. This is known as a GARCH-M process. Numerous variants of GARCH models have been developed.

Nontraditional Models

Numerous models developed in other fields, such as physics and artificial intelligence, have also been applied to forecasting financial returns. Only the most widely quoted of these nonlinear models are briefly described here.

Chaos Theory

Scientists have observed that some mathematical and physical systems that exhibit enormously complicated behavior that appears random are actually generated by some simple nonlinear deterministic models. A *deterministic* model is governed by

[21] A review of GARCH models can be found in Engle (1993) and Bollerslev, Chou, and Kroner (1992).

some mathematical rules that involve no random elements, so that its outcome can be fully described and explained once the rules are known. However, the future behavior is extremely difficult to predict because of the high dependence of these systems on the initial conditions. Such nonlinear deterministic systems, which are highly sensitive to initial conditions, are called *chaotic* systems.[22]

A classic example of chaos is the weather system. The famous "butterfly problem" in weather forecasting states that the wing flapping of a butterfly in a specific spot at a specific time may cause a hurricane several months later in another place. Although weather systems appear to be random, they follow very precise models but are very sensitive to small changes in initial conditions. A reasonable weather forecast for tomorrow can be the same weather as today, but precise forecasts for the weather in 30 days are not possible. Another example of a chaotic system is a random-number generator used on computers. These random numbers are indeed generated by a deterministic system, but they look random for all practical purposes.

Chaos is caused by exact nonlinear mathematical functions but appears to be virtually random, and the next state of the system appears virtually unpredictable. Chaotic systems periodically settle into regular cycles, which leads the observer to believe that the systems are predictable, but they suddenly explode in wild movements. A simple definition of a chaotic system could be a system generated by nonlinear dynamics whereby small differences in starting values can have a very large influence on the time-series dynamics of the variable.

Similarly, financial markets could be chaotic in the sense that financial prices appear to follow random movements, although they follow a set of exact rules. Forecasting returns is extremely difficult, because a minor change in initial conditions can lead to major changes in forecasts. At best, chaos theory could help detect "pockets" of stability that could help the astute forecaster. The estimation of a chaotic system is a difficult empirical exercise that will not be discussed here. It is very difficult, if not impossible, to differentiate between a stochastic process, whereby random shocks affect the financial variable studied, and a deterministic chaotic process whose underlying model is unknown.

Chaotic systems are one class of *nonlinear dynamic* systems. They are related to *fractal* models and other nonlinear dynamic models that will not be discussed here.

Artificial Intelligence, Expert Systems, and Neural Networks

Artificial intelligence attempts to computerize human reasoning. An *expert system* is a simple class of artificial model that attempts to learn from the behavior of market participants and that translates this learning into a set of program rules. In the 1980s, expert systems became quite fashionable in financial markets. They can be used in risk management, trading, and forecasting. The computer program attempts to replicate the *sequential* decision process of interviewed "experts" in the field. An expert system is a computer program that uses a set of rules, procedures,

[22] Most references on chaos theory are very technical. A good introduction to chaos theory and its implications for portfolio management can be found in Angel (1994). See also Peters (1994).

and facts to make inferences to simulate the problem-solving ability of human experts. Although these systems are well adapted to replicate the classic behavior of a portfolio manager or a trader, they have not been very successfully applied to forecasting financial prices. One of the problems with expert systems is that they are sequential processes based on fixed decision rules that need to be adapted continuously. In other words, the market learns more quickly than the expert system designed to mimic the behavior of market participants.

Another approach to artificial intelligence, favored in the 1990s, is constructing programs that mimic the architecture and processing capabilities of the brain. These are known as *artificial neural networks* (ANNs), or, more simply, *neural networks.*[23] Conventional computer programs (like earlier expert systems) process information *sequentially*; the innovation in neural networks is massive *parallel* processing of information, in the sense that, as in a brain, all information is processed simultaneously. A human brain is composed of interconnected neurons. An artificial neural network consists of a set of layers of neurons. Each neuron receives inputs, processes them, and delivers a single output. This output can be an input to another neuron or a final output. The network structures can have different shapes. A typical neural network used in finance would have three layers of 10 to 1,000 neurons.

The development of a neural network requires a vast amount of data, because little a priori theoretical structure is assumed. The data are separated into a *training* set and a *test* set. The training set is used to determine the parameters of the neural network system, and the test set is used to validate, or test, the network. Once the neural network has been validated, it can be used in forecasting. The observed values of the relevant variables are entered as inputs, and the neural network generates a forecast.

Data Mining, Data Snooping, and Model Mining

A word of caution is required after this review of models used in forecasting. All these models used for forecasting are estimated over some past data. Although the models may look attractive over the data sample on which they are estimated, their out-of-sample forecasting performance can be quite poor. The problems come from the fact that researchers report and use only the models that best fit the past data, although they search ("mine") a huge number of possible models.

Data Mining

Data mining refers to the fact that when researchers study a given database long enough, they are likely to find some strong, but spurious, association between some sets of variables. This relation happened by chance over the specific period covered by the data set and is not likely to repeat over the future. A statistician would say that the relation is not stable. There is an obvious selection bias in trying a large

---

[23] A good nontechnical description of neural networks can be found in Medsker, Turban, and Trippi (1993). See also Kryzanowski, Galler, and Wright (1993).

number of models and reporting only the one that yields the best explanatory power in-sample.

For example, let's assume that a regression is performed, over the past 10 years, between the French stock index return and a large number of economic and financial variables from many countries. The researchers attempt to find a combination of any five variables observed at time t that have a good explanatory power for French stock return in the next month (time $t + 1$). By chance, a good explanatory power will be found if the researchers mine across a large number of variables. For example, it could be that the French stock market went up, by chance, in the very months when it rained in Australia. Such a relation found over a past data set would be of little practical help for the future because it is only a statistical artifact of the studied data sample, not a reasonable economic model.

Data Snooping

Data snooping can be defined as using the data mining of other researchers on a similar database. For example, a bank could estimate only one forecasting model, which is quite close to the one published by another researcher after extensive data mining. Data mining is like cheating at an exam by bringing unauthorized notes, whereas data snooping is like looking over your neighbor's shoulder to read his unauthorized notes.

In data snooping you can genuinely claim that you did not personally engage in any data mining and that, hence, your model cannot be guilty of the statistical biases just reported. However, it should be clear that your model is no more likely to work well out-of-sample.

Model Mining

In traditional statistical models, as described earlier, a theoretical model is postulated, and its parameters are estimated over a set of data. The problem of data mining is already present for these traditional econometric models, which clearly expose their underlying theoretical logic. It is more acute for complex systems whose underlying structure is primarily empirical and that need a long data history to be estimated and revised. In artificial intelligence systems, the estimation procedure searches through a huge number of possible model classes. This means that the researcher can also be guilty of *model mining*. It is even less likely that a model that fits well over some past data will do so in the future.

4

International Asset Pricing

LEARNING OUTCOMES

After completing this chapter, you will be able to do the following:

- Explain international market integration and international market segmentation
- Discuss the impediments to international capital mobility
- Discuss the factors that favor international market integration
- Explain the extension of the domestic capital asset pricing model (CAPM) to an international context (the extended CAPM)
- Describe the assumptions needed to justify the extended CAPM
- Determine whether the real exchange rate changes in a period, given the beginning-of-period (nominal) exchange rate, the inflation rates in the period, and the end-of-period (nominal) exchange rate
- Calculate the expected exchange rate and the expected domestic-currency holding period return on a foreign bond (security), given expected and predictable inflation rates for the period, the beginning-of-period nominal exchange rate, and the real exchange rate (assumed to be constant)
- Calculate the end-of-period real exchange rate and the domestic-currency ex post return on a foreign bond (security), given the end-of-period exchange rate, the beginning-of-period real exchange rate, and the inflation rates during the period
- Explain a foreign currency risk premium in terms of interest rate differentials and in terms of forward rates
- Calculate a foreign currency risk premium
- State the risk–pricing relation and the formula for the international capital asset pricing model (ICAPM)
- Calculate the expected returns on a stock, given its world market beta and currency exposure, as well as the appropriate risk-free rates and risk premiums

- Define currency exposure and explain exposures in terms of correlations
- Explain the effect of market segmentation on the ICAPM
- Discuss the likely exchange rate exposure of a company based on a description of its activities and explain the impact of both real and nominal exchange rate changes on the valuation of the company
- Discuss the currency exposures of national economies, equity markets, and bond markets
- Explain the models that relate real exchange rate changes to domestic economic activity

In this chapter, we explore the valuation and portfolio implications of international asset pricing. Several asset-pricing questions arise: What would happen if all investors diversified their portfolios internationally? What asset prices would result from such a market equilibrium? What type of risks would be priced in the marketplace? Would taking foreign currency risk be rewarded, and what would be the optimal currency-hedging policy?

Answers to these questions require some theoretical market equilibrium framework. In this chapter, we review international asset pricing. All asset-pricing theories start from the assumption that markets are efficient, so the first section is devoted to this concept. The second section reviews international asset pricing models. The last section presents some discussion of the relation between exchange rates and asset prices, a central issue in international asset pricing.

Throughout this chapter, we use direct currency quotes expressed as X units of domestic currency per 1 unit of foreign currency.

International Market Efficiency

The notion of an efficient market is central to finance theory. *In an efficient market, any new information would be immediately and fully reflected in prices.* Because all current information is already impounded in the asset price, only news—that is, unanticipated information—could cause a change in price in the future.

Consider why a financial market *quickly*, if not instantaneously, discounts all available information. Any new information will immediately be used by some privileged investors, who will take positions to capitalize on it, thereby making the asset price adjust (almost) instantaneously to this piece of information. For example, a new balance of payments statistic would immediately be used by foreign exchange traders to buy or sell a currency until the foreign exchange rate reached a level considered consistent with the new information. Similarly, investors might use surprise information about a company, such as a new contract or changes in forecasted income, to reap a profit until the stock price reached a level consistent with the news. The adjustment in price would be so rapid that it would not pay to buy information that has already been available to other investors. Hundreds of thousands of expert financial analysts and professional investors throughout the world search for information and make the world markets *close* to fully efficient.

In an efficient market, the typical investor could consider an asset price to reflect its true *fundamental value* at all times. The notion of fundamental value is somewhat philosophical; it means that at each point in time, each asset has an intrinsic value that all investors try to discover. Because the true fundamental value is unknown, the only way to test for market efficiency is to detect whether some specific news is not yet impounded in the asset price and could therefore be used to make some abnormal profit in the future.

All in all, the general consensus is that individual markets across the world are quite efficient, probably due to the intense competition among professional security analysts and managers in each national market. In addition, the number of foreign investors and securities firms using their own financial analysis techniques has increased, helping to make each national market more efficient. Of course, the degree of efficiency is likely to vary among countries, depending on the maturity, liquidity, and degree of regulation of the market. However, investors must be aware that it is not easy to "beat" the market in any developed stock market. This observation also suggests that theoretical asset-pricing models, based on the premise that markets are efficient, are useful guides to investment policy.

Although many national markets may be quite efficient, making it difficult to consistently outperform the local index, the question of international market efficiency still remains. Could active asset allocation among countries consistently outperform the world market index? There is less analyst competition among countries than within a single market. The fundamental issue of international market efficiency is often viewed in terms of international market *integration* or *segmentation.* An integrated world financial market would achieve international efficiency, in the sense that capital flows across markets would instantaneously take advantage of any new information throughout the world. For example, an international investor would not hesitate to move money from Germany to France if she forecasted an election result in France that would improve the competitiveness of French firms against German firms. Similarly, a portfolio manager would arbitrage an Italian chemical stock against a U.S. chemical stock, based on new information on their prospective earnings and market shares. In an efficient, integrated, international market, prices of all assets would be in line with their relative investment values. For example, the market consensus expectation of a prolonged period of outstanding economic growth in one country would be immediately discounted in higher current equity prices and not translate into higher future stock returns once the widely expected superior growth materializes.

The debate over integration versus segmentation involves two somewhat different concepts:

- The first concept has to do with impediments to capital mobility. Are there legal restrictions or other forms of constraints that segment one national market from others?

- The second concept has to do with international asset pricing. Are "similar" securities priced in the same manner on different national markets?

It is sometimes claimed that international markets are not integrated but segmented because of various *impediments to capital mobility*. Although each national market might be efficient, numerous factors might prevent international capital flows from taking advantage of relative mispricing among countries:

- *Psychological barriers*: Unfamiliarity with foreign markets, language, sources of information, and so on might curtail foreign investment.
- *Legal restrictions*: Institutional investors are often constrained in their foreign investments. Also, some national markets regulate foreign investment flowing into or out of the market. Foreign ownership is sometimes constrained in order to avoid loss of national control.
- *Transaction costs*: The costs of foreign investment can be high and greater than for domestic investment. Access to sources of information throughout the world is costly, as are international transaction costs, management fees, and custodial services.
- *Discriminatory taxation*: Foreign investment might be more heavily taxed than domestic investment. Withholding taxes might lead to double taxation.
- *Political risks*: The political risks of foreign investment might dampen enthusiasm for international diversification. This political transfer risk might take the form of a prohibition on repatriation of profits or capital investment from a foreign country. Although the risk is extremely small in the major markets, the associated potential loss is large.
- *Foreign currency risks*: Foreign investments bear the risk of local market movements and unexpected changes in the foreign exchange rate. Foreign currency risk is the risk that the foreign currency *in real terms* will depreciate or the domestic currency will appreciate during the time an investor holds an investment denominated in foreign currency.

All these factors tend to reduce international capital flows and lead to somewhat segmented national markets. This result is most apparent in emerging markets, in which foreign investment restrictions are often severe.

However, international integration requires only a sufficient flow of capital to make the world market efficient and to eliminate relative mispricing among countries. In many countries, private and institutional investors are extensively invested abroad. All major corporations have truly multinational operations; their shares are often listed on several stock exchanges. Large corporations, as well as governments, borrow internationally and quickly take advantage of relative bond mispricing between countries, thereby making the markets more efficient. The flow of foreign investment has grown rapidly over the years; thus, it does not seem that the international markets are fully segmented. What is really important for investors is whether two firms that they regard as similar are priced identically in their respective national markets. To have a meaningful discussion of market segmentation, we must first introduce asset-pricing models.

Asset-Pricing Theory

The Domestic Capital Asset Pricing Model

The value of an asset depends on its discounted anticipated cash flows adjusted for risk. For example, the value of a risk-free bill is equal to the repayment value of the bill discounted at the risk-free interest rate. There is an inverse relation between the price of an asset and its expected return and risk. Modern portfolio theory has proposed models of asset pricing in *fully efficient markets.* All of these models attempt to determine what the expected return should be on an asset in an efficient market given the risk borne by the investor. Market equilibrium requires that the expected return be equal to the risk-free rate plus risk premiums to reward the various sources of risk borne by the investor. The major challenge is to determine the relevant measures of risk, as well as the size of the associated premiums.[1] The *capital asset pricing model (CAPM)* is the first well-known model of market equilibrium. Because the reality of the international market is extremely complex, entailing a huge number of securities and sources of uncertainties, the objective of the model is to provide a simplified view of the world, capturing the major aspects of reality. This simplification is required to allow the formation of operational concepts.

The domestic (standard) CAPM is therefore built on fairly restrictive assumptions regarding investors' preferences. Many of these assumptions can be somewhat relaxed, leading to more complex (and less operational) versions. The assumptions of the standard CAPM are as follows:

- Investors care about risk and return. They are risk-averse and prefer less risk and more expected return.
- A consensus among all investors holds, and everyone agrees about the expected return and risk of all assets.
- Investors care about nominal returns in their domestic currency; for example, U.S. investors care about U.S. dollar returns.
- A risk-free interest rate exists, with unlimited borrowing or lending capacity at this rate.
- There are no transaction costs or taxes.

In the CAPM, all investors determine their demand for each asset by a mean–variance optimization (expected-utility maximization). They optimize a portfolio P made up of a set of assets i. They do so by minimizing the variance of

[1] See Elton, Gruber, Brown and Goetzmann (2006), Reilly and Brown (2006), and Sharpe, Alexander, and Bailey (1999).

the portfolio, σ_p^2, for a selected level of expected return, $E(R_p)$. The selected level of expected return depends on the investor's risk aversion.

The demands from each investor are aggregated and set equal to the supply of assets, their market capitalization. The net supply of borrowing and lending (the risk-free asset) is assumed to be zero.

Two conclusions emerge from the domestic CAPM.

Separation Theorem The *normative* conclusion of the domestic CAPM is that everyone should hold the same portfolio of risky assets, and the optimal combination of risky assets can be separated from the investor's preferences toward risk and return. This portfolio of risky assets must therefore be the *domestic market portfolio,* made up of all assets traded in proportion to their market capitalization. All investors should hold a combination of

- the risk-free asset and
- the market portfolio.

Investors adjust their risk preference by putting some of their money in the risk-free asset (more risk-oriented investors will borrow, instead of lend, at the risk-free interest rate). In other words, investors need only two portfolios to design their investment strategies: a market index fund and the risk-free asset.

Risk-Pricing Relation The *descriptive* conclusion of the CAPM is that the equilibrium expected return of an asset should be equal to the risk-free rate plus a risk premium proportional to the covariance of the asset return with the return on the market portfolio. The notation *beta,* β_i, is used to represent the ratio of the covariance between the asset and the market returns to the variance of the market return; it is the measure of the *sensitivity* of the asset return to market movements. It is sometimes called *market exposure.* The risk–pricing relation of the CAPM for asset i can be written as

$$E(R_i) = R_0 + \beta_i \times RP_m \tag{4.1}$$

where

$E(R_i)$ is the expected return on asset i

$E(R_m)$ is the expected return on the market portfolio

R_0 is the risk-free interest rate

β_i is the sensitivity of asset i to market movements (i.e., market exposure)

RP_m is the market risk premium equal to $E(R_m) - R_0$

Equation 4.1 describes the risk-pricing relation for all assets i. So RP_m and R_0 are constant, whereas $E(R_i)$ and β_i vary, depending on the asset i considered. There is a linear relation between the expected return on all assets and their sensitivity to market movements. This straight line is usually called the *security market line.*

Intuition The type of risk that is relevant to pricing an asset is its sensitivity to market movements, β_i, not its total risk, σ_i^2. To understand the intuitive reason for this result, let's decompose the return on asset i into two components, the market influence and a specific component,

$$R_i = \alpha_i + \beta_i \times R_m + \epsilon_i \tag{4.2}$$

where α_i and β_i are constants and R_i, R_m, and ϵ_i are *stochastic* (meaning that they vary over time in a somewhat unpredictable fashion). The term ϵ_i is specific to asset i and independent of the market return R_m. This equation can easily be estimated as a simple regression of the asset return on the market return; β_i is the slope of the regression. Then the total risk of asset i can be decomposed into its *market* (or *systematic*) *risk* and its *specific* (or *residual*) *risk*:

$$\sigma_i^2 = \beta_i^2 \times \sigma_m^2 + \sigma_\epsilon^2 \tag{4.3}$$

A similar relation applies to any portfolio P. The beta of a portfolio, β_p, is simply the weighted average of the betas of all securities included in the portfolio. As the number of securities included in the portfolio increases, its specific risk decreases. This is because the specific risks of individual securities tend to be independent of each other and tend to cancel each other out. In a well-diversified portfolio, specific risks vanish and the total risk of the portfolio reduces to its market risk σ_m^2:

$$\sigma_p^2 = \beta_p^2 \times \sigma_m^2 \tag{4.4}$$

So the only risk that counts for any investor holding a well-diversified portfolio is market risk.

The average beta of all securities is equal to one (the beta of the market portfolio). Securities with a high beta are more sensitive to the market environment and should provide a higher expected return than securities with a low beta given a positive market risk premium. Investors should care only about the beta of a security, not about its total risk. In an international context, the domestic CAPM implies that all domestic securities would be priced in line with their risk relative to the domestic market. Even if a company has extensive foreign operations, its international risks would not be taken into account specifically.

The simplifying assumptions of any theory, including the CAPM, are never verified exactly in the real world. The empirical question is whether the results are robust. A major problem mentioned by Roll (1977) is that the CAPM requires an exact identification of the market portfolio, including all investable assets. Hence, a proper CAPM should include all world assets in the market portfolio, but this would require a model that accounts for a multicurrency environment.

Asset Returns and Exchange Rate Movements

As we expand the investment universe to include international assets, the currency used to measure returns becomes an issue. For example, a Swiss investor holding the Swiss company Novartis measures value and return in Swiss francs.

A U.S. investor would translate Novartis' value and return into dollars. Consider an investor who uses his domestic currency (DC) to measure return on some securities of a foreign country with a foreign currency (FC). The direct exchange rate between the two currencies is S units of DC for one FC unit. For example, we could have a U.S. investor holding shares of Novartis. The value of Novartis in domestic currency (dollar), V, is equal to its foreign currency (Swiss franc) value, V^{FC}, multiplied by the spot exchange rate, S, expressed in dollars per Swiss franc:[2]

$$V = V^{FC} \times S \tag{4.5}$$

Using Equation 4.5, a simple calculation of return from time 0 to time 1 shows that the DC (dollar) rate of return on an investment in Novartis, $R = (V_1 - V_0)/V_0$, is equal to the FC (Swiss franc) rate of return on Novartis, $R^{FC} = (V_1^{FC} - V_0^{FC})/V_0^{FC}$, plus the percentage exchange rate movement, $s = (S_1 - S_0)/S_0$, plus the cross product of R^{FC} and s. This cross product comes from the fact that the exchange rate movement applies to the original Swiss franc value of Novartis and also to the Swiss franc capital gain (loss), R^{FC}:

$$R = R^{FC} + s + (s \times R^{FC}) \tag{4.6}$$

The last term is of second order and assumed to be very small for short time periods, giving the first-order approximation

$$R = R^{FC} + s \tag{4.7}$$

Alternatively, investors can hedge currency risk in the forward exchange market. The forward exchange rate quoted today for the period-end is F units of DC for 1 unit of FC. A 100 percent hedge would imply selling forward an amount V_1^{FC} of foreign currency. In turn, the investor knows with certainty at the start of the period what exchange rate will be used at the end of the period. So F replaces S_1, and the *hedged* return on the foreign share becomes

$$R = R^{FC} + (F - S_0)/S_0 \tag{4.8}$$

Note that the forward discount/premium $(F - S_0)/S_0$ is fully known at the start of the period.[3]

In terms of expected returns, the DC return on an *unhedged* investment is given by

$$E(R) = E(R^{FC}) + E(s) = E(R^{FC}) + [E(S_1) - S_0]/S_0$$

and the DC expected return on a *hedged* investment is given by

$$E(R) = E(R^{FC}) + (F - S_0)/S_0$$

---

[2] We use the superscript FC when we measure return or value in the foreign currency, but no superscript when we measure return or value in the investor's domestic currency.

[3] Again, Equation 4.8 is a first-order approximation. We can hedge the start-of-period value V_0, but the exact end-of-period value is not known, so the unexpected capital gain (loss) cannot be hedged.

The Domestic CAPM Extended to the International Context

Attempts have been made to justify the use of the domestic CAPM in an international context, in which investors in different countries use different currencies and have different consumption preferences.[4] Such a domestic CAPM extension would involve the domestic rate for the risk-free rate and the market capitalization weighted portfolio of all risky assets in the world for the market portfolio. This domestic CAPM extension can be justified only with the addition of two unreasonable assumptions:

- Investors throughout the world have identical consumption baskets.
- Real prices of consumption goods are identical in every country. In other words, purchasing power parity holds exactly at any point in time.

In this type of perfect world, exchange rates would simply mirror inflation differentials between two countries. Exchange rate uncertainty would be money illusion; it would not matter whether investors used euros or dollars. The exchange rate would be a pure translation-accounting device, and real FC risk would not exist. The real exchange rate is defined as the actual exchange rate multiplied by the ratio of the price levels of the consumption baskets in the two countries. Recall that with direct exchange rates, the relation between the real and nominal exchange rates is

$$X = S \times (P_{FC}/P_{DC}) \tag{4.9}$$

where

X is the real exchange rate (direct quote FC:DC)

S is the nominal exchange rate (direct quote FC:DC)

P_{FC} is the foreign country price level

P_{DC} is the domestic country price level

Real exchange rate movements are defined as movements in the exchange rates that are not explained by the inflation differential between the two countries. We can rewrite Equation 4.9 in terms of percentage changes over a time period (say a year):

$$x = s + I_{FC} - I_{DC} = s - (I_{DC} - I_{FC}) \tag{4.10}$$

where

x and s are the percentage movement in the real and nominal exchange rates

I_{DC} and I_{FC} are the inflation rates in the domestic and foreign countries.

If purchasing power parity holds (see Chapter 2), the real exchange rate is constant ($x = 0\%$), and the nominal exchange rate movement FC:DC is equal to the

[4] See Grauer, Litzenberger, and Stehle (1976).

inflation rate differential (domestic minus foreign inflation). For example, assume that there is a one-month inflation rate of 1 percent in the USA (DC) and 0 percent in Switzerland (FC). For the real exchange rate (dollar value of one Swiss franc) to stay constant over the month, the franc has to appreciate by 1 percent against the dollar ($x = 0\%$, $s = 1\%$). If the franc turned out to appreciate by 5 percent ($s = 5\%$) during that month, then there would be a real appreciation of 4 percent of the franc ($x = 4\%$). Any such real exchange rate movement would violate the assumptions supporting the domestic CAPM extension. To summarize, in the absence of real foreign currency risk, however, the extended CAPM would hold.

Example 4.1 illustrates a constant real exchange rate. Because the real exchange rate is constant in Example 4.1, there is no real foreign currency risk. Note that exchange rate uncertainty due to inflation is generally very small, because inflation rates are highly predictable in the short run, especially relative to equity returns. Predictable inflation rates mean predictable exchange rates if purchasing power parity holds. If purchasing power parity does not hold, *real foreign currency risk* arises even with predictable inflation (see Example 4.2).

International CAPM

Deviations from purchasing power parity can be a major source of exchange rate variation, and consumption preferences can differ among countries. In these cases, the risk that real prices of consumption goods might not be identical in every country is called *real foreign currency risk*, *real exchange rate risk*, or *purchasing power risk*.

EXAMPLE 4.1 CONSTANT REAL EXCHANGE RATE

An investor in his home (domestic) country considers investing in the securities of a foreign country. The direct exchange rate between the two countries is currently two domestic currency (DC) units for one foreign currency (FC) unit. The price level of the typical consumption basket in domestic country relative to the price level of the typical consumption basket in foreign country is also 2 to 1, which means that the real exchange rate is 1 to 1. A year later the inflation rate has been 3 percent in domestic country and 1 percent in foreign country. The foreign currency has appreciated and the exchange rate is now 2.04. What is the new real exchange rate?

SOLUTION

The new real exchange rate is equal to the new nominal exchange rate adjusted by the ratio of the new price levels: $S \times (P_{FC}/P_{DC}) = X$, or $2.04 \times (1.01/2.06) = 1$. The real exchange rate remains constant because the foreign exchange appreciation of 2 percent is equal to the inflation differential between the two countries. As the real exchange rate is fixed, the currencies have fully retained their purchasing power. The appreciation of the nominal exchange rate has no real impact.

EXAMPLE 4.2 *FOREIGN CURRENCY RISK*

An investor in her home (domestic) country would like to expand her portfolio to include one-year bonds in foreign countries. The expected inflation rate in the domestic country is 3 percent and the expected inflation rate in one of the foreign countries is 1 percent. Inflation rates are totally predictable over the next year. The exchange rate between the two countries is currently two DC units for one FC unit. The price level of the typical consumption basket in the domestic country relative to the price level of the typical consumption basket in the foreign country is also 2 to 1. The real exchange rate is 1 to 1. The one-year interest rate is 5 percent in the domestic country and 3 percent in the foreign country. The investor expects the real exchange rate to remain constant over time.

1. What are the expected exchange rate and the expected return on the foreign bond in domestic currency?

A year later the inflation rates have indeed been 3 percent in DC and 1 percent in FC. The foreign exchange rate has been very volatile over the year, and the foreign currency has depreciated with an end-of-year exchange rate of 1.80.

2. What are the real exchange rate at the end of the year and the ex post return on the foreign bond?
3. How would you qualify the risk–return characteristics of this investment?

SOLUTIONS

1. The future exchange rate should be equal to 2.04 DC units per FC unit if the real exchange rate remains constant, corresponding to a 2 percent appreciation of the foreign currency. The expected return on the foreign bond should therefore be approximately 5 percent, the sum of the foreign interest rate and of the currency appreciation, or more precisely $1.03 \times (2.04/2.00) - 1 = 5.06$ percent.
2. Unfortunately, the ex post exchange rate is equal to 1.80 and the real exchange rate has become $S \times (P_{FC}/P_{DC}) = X$, or $1.80 \times (1.01/2.06) = 0.88$. The actual exchange rate movement is not equal to the inflation differential between the two countries, and there is a severe real depreciation of the foreign currency. The ex post return on the foreign bond is negative and equal to $1.03 \times (1.80/2.00) - 1 = -7.3$ percent.
3. This investment had an expected return similar to that of the domestic risk-free rate, but it carried a lot of foreign currency risk. All of the foreign currency risk is real risk, as inflation rates here were predictable. Of course, this foreign currency risk could be hedged.

In real life, daily exchange rate movements are volatile and cannot be simply explained by an adjustment to daily inflation. Because inflation rates are very stable compared with asset returns and exchange rate movements, most if not all of the short-term variability in exchange rates can be referred to as real foreign currency risk. Investors will want to hedge against real foreign currency risk. An *international CAPM* (or *ICAPM*) can be developed under the assumption that nationals of a country care about returns and risks measured in their *domestic currency* (e.g., the U.S. dollar for U.S. investors and the Swiss franc for Swiss investors).[5] All the assumptions of the CAPM still hold. In particular, investors can freely borrow or lend in any currency. Using interest rate parity, investors can therefore freely replicate forward currency contracts to hedge foreign currency risk. It must be stressed that a dollar short-term bill that is risk-free for U.S. investors becomes risky for foreign investors who are concerned with returns in their domestic currency because of foreign currency risk.

Interest Rate Parity It is important here to recall the concept of interest rate parity (IRP). Interest rate parity lies behind the ability to replicate forward currency contracts. In the world of foreign currency risk and the international CAPM, we will encounter foreign currency risk premiums. These premiums will be defined in reference to the movement in the exchange rate implied by parity conditions. In review of IRP, the direct spot exchange rate times one plus the domestic risk-free rate (investing domestically the amount of DC units required to purchase 1 FC unit) equals the direct forward exchange rate times one plus the foreign risk-free rate (exchanging for 1 FC unit now, investing in the foreign country, and repatriating later). Recall that IRP with direct exchange rates is given by

$$F = S(1 + r_{\mathrm{DC}})/(1 + r_{\mathrm{FC}}) \tag{4.11}$$

where

F is the direct forward rate

S is the direct spot rate

r_{DC} is the domestic risk-free rate

r_{FC} is the foreign risk-free rate

As a first-order linear approximation, the percentage forward premium on the exchange rate must equal the domestic risk-free rate minus the foreign risk-free rate, given as

$$(F - S)/S \cong r_{\mathrm{DC}} - r_{\mathrm{FC}} \tag{4.12}$$

The calculation of the forward exchange rate is illustrated in Example 4.3.

Foreign Currency Risk Premiums As a background for the international CAPM, it is also useful to recall the definition of a *foreign currency risk premium.* The risk

---

[5] See Solnik (1974), Sercu (1980), and Adler and Dumas (1983).

EXAMPLE 4.3 INTEREST RATE PARITY

The one-year domestic country risk-free rate of return is 5 percent, and the one-year foreign country rate is 3 percent. The current exchange rate is 2 DC units for 1 FC unit. What is the current level of the forward exchange rate that is implied by these data?

SOLUTION

The investor could invest 2 DC units at the local risk-free rate of $r_{DC} = 5$ percent and would get $2 \times (1 + r_{DC})$ or 2.1 DC units in a year. Alternately, the investor could combine three operations:

- Exchange those 2 DC units at the spot exchange rate S for $2/S = 1$ FC unit.
- Invest this FC unit at the foreign country rate of $r_{FC} = 3$ percent and get 1.03 FC units in a year.
- Sell forward today the proceeds of $1 + r_{FC} = 1.03$ units of FC received in a year at the forward exchange rate of F.

In a year, the investor will therefore receive, with certainty, an amount of DC units equal to

$$(2/S) \times F \times (1 + r_{FC}) \text{ or } F \times 1.03$$

This combination should yield the same result as the first alternative because both are riskless in domestic currency and involve the same investment. Otherwise, an arbitrage will take place. Hence, $F \times 1.03 = 2.1$ and $F = 2.039$, giving our answer that the forward exchange rate is 2.039 DC units per 1 FC unit.

The forward premium can be approximated as the interest rate differential, or a 2 percent premium on the foreign currency. In general, with direct exchange rates, we have

$$F = S \times \frac{1 + r_{DC}}{1 + r_{FC}}$$

premium on any investment is simply equal to its expected return in excess of the domestic risk-free rate:

$$RP = E(R) - R_0$$

Someone investing in a foreign currency will exchange the domestic currency (e.g., U.S. dollar) for the foreign currency (e.g., Swiss franc) and invest it at the foreign risk-free interest rate. So the expected domestic currency return on the foreign currency investment is equal to the foreign risk-free rate plus the expected percentage movement in the exchange rate. The *foreign currency risk premium* is defined as the expected return on an investment minus the domestic currency risk-free rate. Thus, the foreign currency risk premium, denoted as SRP, is equal to the expected

EXAMPLE 4.4 FOREIGN CURRENCY RISK PREMIUM

The one-year risk-free interest rates are 5 percent in DC and 3 percent in FC. The exchange rate between the two countries is currently 2 DC units for 1 FC unit. The expected exchange rate appreciation of FC is 3 percent. What is the foreign currency risk premium?

SOLUTION

Because the interest differential is 2 percent (domestic minus foreign), interest rate parity implies that the forward exchange rate quotes at a premium of approximately 2 percent over the current exchange rate while the expected exchange rate appreciation of FC currency is 3 percent. Therefore, the foreign exchange risk premium is equal to +1 percent (3% − 2%). The expected DC return on the foreign investment is the 3 percent FC risk-free rate plus the 3 percent expected currency appreciation. It is also equal to the 5 percent domestic risk-free rate plus the 1 percent foreign currency risk premium. Note that the hedged investment return is the foreign risk-free rate plus the forward premium, a return of approximately 5 percent. Thus, the expected return on an unhedged foreign investment is 1 percent higher than if hedged against real foreign currency risk. However, hedging removes foreign currency risk.

movement in the exchange rate *minus* the interest rate differential (domestic risk-free rate minus foreign risk-free rate):

$$SRP = E[(S_1 - S_0)/S_0] - (r_{DC} - r_{FC}) = E(s) - (r_{DC} - r_{FC}) \tag{4.13}$$

Substituting for $r_{DC} - r_{FC}$ using the interest rate parity approximation, the risk premium can also be expressed as the difference between the expected exchange rate and the forward rate, in percentage of the current exchange rate: $[E(S_1) - F]/S_0$. The calculation of the foreign currency risk premium is illustrated in Example 4.4.

In the international CAPM, as in the domestic CAPM, all investors determine their demand for each asset by a mean–variance optimization (expected-utility maximization), using their *domestic currency as base currency*. The demand from each investor is aggregated and set equal to the supply of assets, their market capitalization. The net supply of borrowing and lending (the risk-free asset) *in each currency* is assumed to be zero. Two conclusions emerge from this international CAPM.

Separation Theorem The *normative* conclusion is that the optimal investment strategy for any investor is a combination of two portfolios: a risky portfolio common to all investors, and a personalized hedge portfolio used to reduce purchasing power risks. If there is no uncertainty about future inflation rates in any country, the personalized hedge portfolio reduces to the national risk-free asset, and a simpler separation theorem can be demonstrated.[6] All investors should hold a combination of

[6] It has been observed repeatedly that the variability of inflation rates is very small compared with that of exchange rates or asset returns. Therefore, using nominal returns to measure returns is quite reasonable from a practical viewpoint.

- the risk-free asset in their own currency, and
- the world market portfolio optimally hedged against foreign currency risk.

This world market portfolio is the same for each investor and is the only portfolio of risky assets that should be held, partly hedged against foreign currency risk, by any investor. However, it must be stressed that the optimal currency hedge ratio need not be unitary and will generally be different for different assets and currencies.[7] The optimal hedge ratios depend on variables such as differences among countries in relative wealth, foreign investment position, and risk aversion. Unfortunately, these variables cannot be observed or inferred from market data. The international CAPM does not provide simple, clear-cut, operational conclusions about the optimal currency-hedge ratios.

Risk–Pricing Relation The *descriptive* conclusion of the international CAPM is an international equilibrium risk-pricing relation that is more complex than in the domestic CAPM, in which the expected return on any asset is simply a function of its covariance with the domestic market portfolio. In the presence of exchange rate risk, additional risk premiums must be added to the risk–pricing relation to reflect the covariance of the asset with the various exchange rates (the currencies' betas). If there are $k + 1$ currencies, there will be k additional currency risk premiums. Hence, the expected return on an asset depends on the market risk premium plus various foreign currency risk premiums:

$$E(R_i) = R_0 + \beta_{iw} \times RP_w + \gamma_{i1} \times SRP_1 + \gamma_{i2} SRP_2 + \cdots + \gamma_{ik} SRP_k \qquad (4.14)$$

where

R_0 is the domestic currency risk-free interest rate

β_{iw} is the sensitivity of asset i domestic currency returns to market movements (market exposure)

RP_w is the world market risk premium equal to $E(R_w) - R_0$

γ_{i1} to γ_{ik} are the currency exposures, the sensitivities of asset i domestic currency returns to the exchange rate on currencies 1 to k

SRP_1 to SRP_k are the foreign currency risk premiums on currencies 1 to k

In Equation 4.14, all returns are measured in the investor's domestic currency.[8] Equation 4.14 indicates that the foreign investment return in domestic currency

[7] The hedge ratio is the proportion of the value of the portfolio (or component of a portfolio) that is currency hedged.

[8] As stressed by Adler and Dumas (1983), Equation 4.14 applies to returns measured in any base currency. For example, one could choose arbitrarily to measure all returns in U.S. dollars; then Equation 4.14 would apply for dollar returns, and R_0 would be the U.S. risk-free rate. Or one could choose to measure all returns in euros; then Equation 4.14 would apply for euro returns, and R_0 would be the euro risk-free rate.

equals (a) the domestic risk-free rate, plus (b) a world market risk premium, times the asset's sensitivity to the world market, plus (c) foreign currency risk premiums times the investment's currency exposures.

For an asset that is uncorrelated with the various exchange rates or that is optimally hedged against currency risk, the traditional CAPM still applies with its single-market risk premium given as a function of the covariance of the asset with the world market portfolio. So the traditional CAPM applies only to securities or portfolios perfectly hedged against currency risk.[9]

The ICAPM differs from a domestic CAPM in two respects. First, the relevant market risk is world (global) market risk, not domestic market risk. This is not surprising. Second, additional risk premiums are linked to an asset's sensitivity to currency movements. The different currency exposures of individual securities would be reflected in different expected returns.

Intuition on Foreign Currency Risk Premiums in the ICAPM Again, the basic idea is that a risk premium should be earned for taking those risks that cannot be trivially eliminated by a naive diversification of the portfolio. Currency risks will remain in a diversified portfolio because currency movements affect all securities to some extent. One could argue that currency risks could be hedged with forward contracts and, therefore, portfolios need not bear this type of risk.[10] However, a similar argument could be developed for market risk, because futures contracts exist on stock indexes. The basic point is that the world market portfolio has to be held in aggregate, so world market risk has to be borne by investors. Similarly, because the world market portfolio is sensitive to currency risks, these currency risks have to be borne in aggregate.

A question often raised is: Why is there a non-zero currency risk premium? The theoretical answer is that investors from different countries have different net foreign investment positions and different risk aversions. In equilibrium, this will result in positive or negative currency risk premiums. Assume, for example, that Americans invest a lot abroad so that their net foreign investment position is positive while that of foreigners is negative. In other words, Americans have more wealth invested abroad than foreigners have invested in the United States. Also assume that Americans are more risk-averse than foreigners. Then Americans have a larger demand to hedge their foreign currency position (sell foreign currency forward) than foreigners have to hedge their dollar position (sell dollars forward). This imbalance will create, in equilibrium, a currency risk premium on the foreign

9 Note, however, that optimal currency hedging does not mean 100 percent hedging. This is because the value of a foreign asset could be affected by an exchange rate movement. This is detailed in the section on currency exposures. The gammas (γ_{ik}) are sometimes called regression hedge ratios because they can be estimated from a multiple regression of the asset return on the various exchange rate movements.

10 It is sometimes argued that on a forward or futures currency contract there is one seller for each buyer so that the expected return should be zero. This is a flawed argument. If it were true, it would apply to any forward contract. For example, there is one seller for every buyer of an S&P 500 futures contract. Still, the buyer is expected to receive the U.S. equity risk premium, while the seller is expected to lose it.

EXAMPLE 4.5 PAYINGIRECEIVING THE FOREIGN CURRENCY RISK PREMIUM

Suppose Americans are big net investors in a hypothetical country, Arland, and the Arlanders invest little abroad. The Americans have a vast net foreign wealth and are worried about currency risk; hence, they have a strong demand for hedging Arlandian francs into American dollars. The Arlanders have little demand for hedging American dollars because they do not invest much in the United States. The Americans are long in Arlandian stocks, and they can hedge their exposure to the Arlandian franc by selling forward Arlandian francs (buy dollars forward). Arlandians and other speculators buy Arlandian francs forward (sell dollars forward), induced by a positive risk premium on the franc. The one-year risk-free interest rates are 5 percent in the United States and 3 percent in Arland. The exchange rate between the two countries is currently two dollars for one franc. The expected exchange rate appreciation of the Arlandian franc is 3 percent. The expected return on Arlandian stocks is 6 percent in francs.

1. What is the expected return on Arlandian stocks in dollars if there is no currency hedging?
2. What is the expected return on Arlandian stocks in dollars with full currency hedging?
3. What is the foreign currency risk premium on the Arlandian franc, and who pays/receives it?

SOLUTION

1. The expected return on Arlandian stocks in dollars is equal to the expected return in francs, 6 percent, plus the expected currency appreciation of 3 percent, a total expected return of 9 percent.
2. With currency hedging, the forward premium is equal to the interest rate differential of 2 percent. Hence, the expected return on Arlandian stocks, hedged against currency risk, is 8 percent (6 percent plus 2 percent). The expected return is less than for an unhedged investment, but the risk is also less.
3. There is a 1 percent foreign currency risk premium, that is, the difference between the expected currency appreciation of the franc and the forward premium on the franc. This risk premium is "paid" by Americans and "received" by Arlandians. In equilibrium, Americans are willing to pay this currency risk premium to remove currency risks on their net foreign position in Arlandian stocks. Arlandians (and other speculators) are willing to provide that hedge because of the expected return due to the currency risk premium.

currency. Americans will have to pay a currency risk premium on their currency hedge, while foreigners will receive a currency risk premium. This is because the selling pressure on the forward exchange rate will reduce it relative to the expected spot exchange rate. While Americans sell foreign currency forward for hedging motives, foreigners will buy forward to accommodate American needs if induced by a positive expected return, the currency risk premium. Using the dollar as the base currency, the expected exchange rate (in \$ per FC units) for the foreign currency will be larger than the forward rate, and this difference as a percentage of the current exchange rate is a risk premium by definition (see Example 4.5).

Individual assets have different exposures to currencies, and these exposures affect their equilibrium pricing. Foreign currency risk premiums arise from the risk exposures of the average investor. If the average investor is sensitive to the real foreign currency risk of a particular country, he will bid up the price of those stocks that have a low or negative currency exposure (γ). Those are the stocks that are negatively correlated with real foreign currency risk. He is actually paying to hedge and thus accepts a lower expected return as a trade-off for the benefit of reducing real foreign currency risk. This is illustrated in Example 4.6.

EXAMPLE 4.6 INTERNATIONAL ASSET PRICING

You are a European investor considering investing in a foreign country. The world market risk premium is estimated at 5 percent, the foreign currency offers a 1 percent risk premium, and the current risk-free rates are equal to 5 percent in euros and 3 percent in FC units. In other words, you expect the FC unit to appreciate against the euro by an amount equal to the interest rate differential (which is also equal to the expected inflation differential) plus the foreign currency risk premium, or a total of 3 percent. Your broker provides you with some statistics:

	Stock A	Stock B	Stock C	Stock D
World beta	1.0	1.0	1.2	1.4
Currency exposure (γ)	1.0	0.0	0.5	–0.5

1. According to the International CAPM, what should be the expected returns on the four stocks, in euros?
2. Stocks A and B have the same world beta but different expected returns. Give an intuitive explanation for this difference.

SOLUTIONS

1. With one foreign currency and the euro as the base currency, the asset pricing equation of the international CAPM simplifies to

$$E(R_i) = R_0 + \beta_{iw} \times RP_w + \gamma_i \times SRP_{FC}$$

where all returns are measured in euros, RP_w is the risk premium on the world index, and SRP_{FC} is the risk premium on the foreign currency unit, assumed to be the only other currency. If the euro is used as the base currency, then all β's and γ's should be measured using euro returns. Using the exposures (or "sensitivities") given, we get the theoretical expected returns given in the following table. For example, the expected return of Stock A is equal to the euro risk-free rate of 5 percent, plus a world equity risk premium of 5 percent ($1 \times 5\%$), plus a foreign currency risk premium of 1 percent ($1 \times 1\%$).

	Stock A	Stock B	Stock C	Stock D
Theoretical expected return (€)	11.0%	10.0%	11.5%	11.5%

2. Stock A has an expected return of 11 percent, compared with 10 percent for Stock B. The difference is explained by their different exposures to currency movements. The euro value of Stock B is insensitive to unexpected movements in the FC : euro exchange rate. As far as foreign currency risk is concerned, Stock B is less risky than Stock A (currency risk exposure of +1), so its expected return should be different from that of Stock A. Because the currency risk premium is equal to +1 percent, the difference in expected return between Stock A and Stock B should be 1 percent.

Market Imperfections and Segmentation

The international asset pricing relation described applies to all securities only in an integrated world capital market. Financial markets are segmented if securities that have the same risk characteristics, but are listed in two different markets, have different expected returns.

In many countries, various types of institutional investors face severe legal constraints on their international investments. This is often the case with public pension funds or insurance companies that have liabilities denominated in their national currencies and are required to invest in assets denominated in the same currency. The psychological aspects are also important. Investors are much more familiar with their local financial market than with foreign markets. Hence, they feel somewhat uneasy about investing their money in a remote country or an unfamiliar currency.

If currency hedging is not available, either physically or legally, the simple pricing relation breaks down. Furthermore, official restrictions, fear of expropriation, discriminatory taxes, and higher investment costs push domestic investors to underinvest in foreign assets compared with the world market portfolio. The argument for international comparative advantage in imperfect markets might be firm-specific; investors might prefer foreign companies that are not found in other parts of the world (e.g., Club Méditérranée) and avoid companies that are deemed sensitive to national interests (e.g., armament companies) or are located in countries in which foreign interests might be expropriated on short notice.

If all these impediments to international investments are of significant magnitude, buying the market is not a reasonable first-cut strategy. Although it certainly does not mean that investors should avoid foreign investments, the additional costs and risks of foreign investments may cause market segmentation and affect asset pricing.

International asset pricing under various forms of market segmentation, including differential taxes, has been studied, and more complex asset pricing relations have been found.[11] The risk premium has a more complex form than in the traditional international capital asset pricing model. It generally depends on the form of market imperfection, the relative wealth of investors, and parameters of their utility function. However, most forms of market imperfections and constraints to foreign investments cannot be easily incorporated in an equilibrium asset pricing framework. Hence, their precise influence on the resulting optimal portfolio holdings cannot be easily modeled.

Practical Implications

A Global Approach to Equilibrium Pricing

The ICAPM gives useful insights on asset pricing in an efficient world capital market and in the absence of privileged information. It tells us what should be the return on assets if we do not formulate specific forecasts for them; therefore, the ICAPM offers default values from which to start. It also proposes a simplified structure to global asset management—in other words, a *benchmark* or passive investment strategy. It basically tells us "buy the market" optimally hedged against currency risk. The conclusion to buy the market is not truly original, but the recommendations in terms of currency hedging are. We will now study the practical implications of this optimal hedging conclusion and then turn to potential usage of the international asset pricing relation.

More on Currency Hedging The ICAPM concludes that everyone should hold the same risky portfolio, with the same amount of currency hedging. Hence, French and U.S. investors should use the same hedge ratio for their Japanese investments.[12]

Black (1989, 1990) uses this result, derived by Solnik (1974), Sercu (1980), and Adler and Dumas (1983), to suggest the existence of a "universal hedging formula" that every investor should use, independent of nationality and fairly easily estimated. Indeed, everyone hedges the world market portfolio with forward currency contracts, in the same way, because everyone holds the same risky portfolio. The aggregate hedge ratio need not be unity, and Black provides a historical estimate around 0.7. Unfortunately, this universal hedging formula gives only the aggregate dollar amount used to hedge as a proportion of the total dollar value of the world market portfolio of equity. Optimal hedge ratios vary across markets and assets. We also know that

[11] See Black (1974), Subrahmanyam (1975), Stapleton and Subrahmanyam (1977), Stulz (1981), Errunza and Losq (1985, 1989), Eun and Janakiramanan (1986), and Hietla (1989).

[12] It appears that a Japanese investor should also hedge her domestic assets in the same proportion, but hedging yen into yen is totally neutral.

these individual currency hedge ratios are complex, because they depend on such parameters as the covariance structure of assets and currency, the risk aversion of investors from various countries, and investors' relative wealth. Because individual preferences and relative wealth are not observable, the optimal currency hedging policy cannot be deduced from market-observable data. Holding the market portfolio is a practical passive recommendation because we observe market capitalizations and can derive some proxy for the "market." This is not the case for the optimal passive currency hedging policy. To summarize, the ICAPM does not provide simple, clear-cut, operational conclusions about the optimal currency hedge ratios. It is not likely that any reasonable theory could ever produce simple hedging rules.

Equally important, this nice result of a unique aggregate hedge ratio breaks down if, for theoretical or practical purposes, investors do not hold the world market portfolio. For all kinds of reasons, investors tend to underweight foreign assets relative to the world market weights. If a U.S. pension fund puts its 10 percent of foreign assets in a rest-of-the-world index fund, there is no theoretical basis to suggest using the same hedge ratio that should be used if the fund were invested 70 percent in rest-of-the-world assets. Intuitively, the risk diversification benefits brought to the U.S. portfolio by the foreign assets are different in the two cases. A foreign currency risk component may actually lower the total risk of a portfolio with only a small investment in foreign assets (say, 5 percent) because it provides some diversification of the U.S. monetary policy risk. For example, Jorion (1989) conducted an empirical study of optimal asset allocations for a U.S. investor. He concluded that the importance of currency hedging depends on the proportion of foreign assets held in the portfolio and stated that "this question of hedging may not matter so much if the amounts invested in the foreign assets are small, in which case overall portfolio volatility is not appreciably influenced by hedging. Hedging therefore brings no particular benefits in terms of risk reduction . . ." (p. 54). The difference between the risk diversification benefits from small versus large foreign allocations should be even more pronounced if the portfolio of foreign assets is actively managed with country weights that differ markedly from the rest-of-the-world market index.

Hence, currency hedging becomes an individual empirical decision—a function of the portfolio to be hedged—and risk preferences matter. Optimal currency hedging requires the estimation of the currency-risk exposure of each asset (as we discuss later).

In the absence of simple, widely accepted recommendations for a benchmark, simple hedging policy rules with a fixed hedge ratio are commonly adopted. The international benchmark typically used is either fully hedged or unhedged. But several plan sponsors have a 50-percent-hedged benchmark.

Expected Returns Equation 4.14 describes equilibrium asset pricing in fully efficient global markets. It quantifies the risk premiums for each asset. To use this equation, we need to estimate two types of variables:

- The market and currency exposures of each asset
- The risk premiums on the (global) market and on currencies

Estimating a market risk premium is a usual task in asset management. Everyone would agree that it should be positive over the long run. Historical estimates give us an order of magnitude for the future that can be refined by some conceptual forward-looking reasoning.

The task is more difficult for foreign currency risk premiums, which could be positive or negative and unstable over time. For example, a positive foreign currency risk premium on the dollar against the euro implies a negative foreign currency risk premium for the euro against the dollar. Furthermore, the demand for currency hedging is likely to change over time, affecting the risk premiums. For example, individuals and corporations of one country could progressively become large international investors, or conversely reduce their holdings in another country because of political risk or other considerations. These developments would change the magnitude and even the signs of foreign currency risk premiums. Although investors can formulate expectations about currencies over short horizons (say a year), it is harder to do so over the very long run. Hence, asset managers often assume that the risk premiums of all currencies are zero over the very long run, and they use equilibrium pricing relations that include only a market risk premium. A zero long-term foreign currency risk premium assumes that the best predictor of exchange rates is the interest rate differential.[13] This leads to a linear relation between the expected return on assets and the market exposure (β), the *global market line.*

Applications of the ICAPM depend on the investment horizon. An assessment of the *long-term* risk premiums according to the ICAPM is usually undertaken only for asset classes or national markets, not for individual securities, because securities within the same asset class tend to be priced relative to each other and richer risk models are developed for each asset class. The ICAPM is used to anchor expected returns as default values.

An investor who believes that markets are not fully efficient could deviate from the global market line. An illustration of this is Exhibit 4.1, where GIM (Global Investable Market) stands for the world market portfolio of all investable assets. (In the exhibit, risk premium is the expected return in excess of the risk-free return.) Deviations can be explained by several factors:

- The corresponding market or asset class could be felt to be undervalued.
- Its lack of liquidity could justify an additional risk premium.
- Foreign currency risk premiums could be added that translate into a deviation from the global market line.

The determination of the risk premiums will drive the strategic global asset allocation. In the shorter run, the portfolio composition could be revised to reflect changes in the risk premiums and the risk coefficients. This is often called a *tactical*

[13] It is also consistent with an assumption that exchange rates revert to fundamentals in the long run and that foreign currency risk is much smaller in the long run than in the short run, thereby justifying no risk premium.

EXHIBIT 4.1

Example of Relation between Beta and Risk Premiums of Various Asset Classes

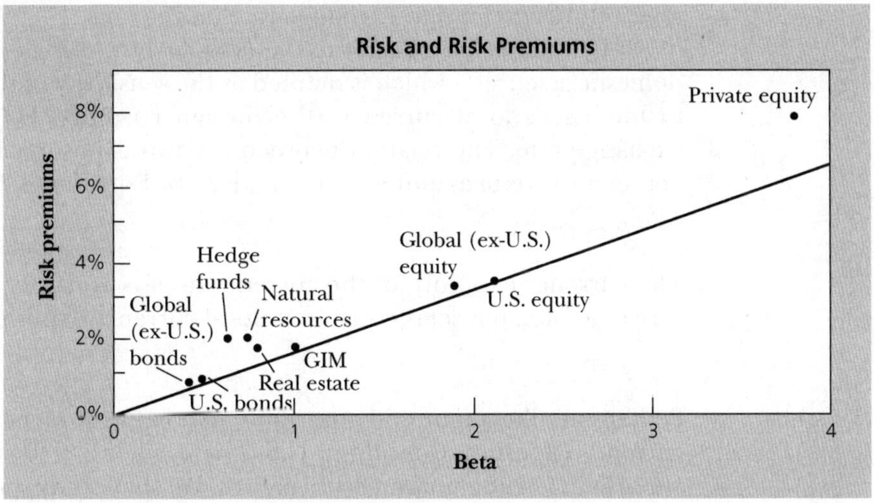

Source: B. Singer, R. Staub, and K. Terhaar, "Asset Allocation: The Alternatives Approach," *Quarterly Focus*, June 30, 2001. Reproduced by permission of UBS.

revision or *tactical asset allocation* (see Chapter 13). In tactical asset allocation, a good appreciation of the risk elements becomes quite important.

Estimating Currency Exposures

The relation between asset returns and exchange rate movements is central to international asset pricing. To benefit from the insights of the ICAPM and knowledge of exchange rate determination, we need to investigate the link between security prices and exchange rates, in theory and in practice. We need to understand what determines the currency exposures of securities, the γ's of Equation 4.14. From a practical standpoint, any investor should be concerned about the reaction of the domestic capital market to international monetary disturbances, such as exchange rate movements. The international investor measures total return as the sum of returns on the assets, in local currencies, plus any currency movements: The investor bears both market and foreign currency risks. Setting aside considerations of portfolio diversification, the reaction of asset prices to fluctuations in currency values is a matter of prime concern for international investors. A major question is whether stocks and bonds provide a hedge against exchange rate movements. We want to get a better economic intuition for the sign and magnitude of the currency exposure γ mentioned in Equation 4.14.

Defining Currency Exposure The currency used to measure the currency exposure of an asset is of great importance. An investor cares about the currency exposure measured in his domestic currency. The *currency exposure* of an asset can be defined as the sensitivity of the asset return, measured in the investor's domestic currency, to a movement in the exchange rate. Just like market β's, currency γ's can be estimated by a regression, namely, a time-series regression of domestic currency asset returns on foreign exchange rate movements.

It is also possible to refer to the *local-currency (foreign currency) exposure* of a non-domestic asset, γ^{FC}, which is defined as the sensitivity of the asset return, measured in the asset's local currency (the foreign currency, FC) to a movement in the exchange rate. The relation between the two exposures follows from the relation between DC returns and FC returns given by Equation 4.7:

$$R = R^{FC} + s$$

The currency exposure of the currency itself is equal to 1. So, the currency exposure of a foreign asset is equal to its local-currency exposure plus 1:

$$\gamma = \gamma^{FC} + 1 \tag{4.15}$$

Perhaps an illustration will contribute to a better understanding of the concept of currency exposure. Consider a U.S. investor holding shares of the Swiss company Novartis, a leading pharmaceutical firm. We shall study various scenarios of the correlation[14] of the price of Novartis stock with the Swiss franc:U.S. dollar exchange rate. Assume a sudden depreciation of the Swiss franc (FC), giving a 1.25 percent loss on the Swiss currency for the U.S. investor (one Swiss franc loses 1.25 percent of its dollar value). The price of Novartis shares may react in different fashions to this exchange rate movement:

- A *zero* correlation between local-currency stock returns and exchange rate movements would mean no systematic reaction to exchange rate adjustments. The immediate rate of return on Novartis shares would tend to be zero for Swiss investors (the Swiss franc price of Novartis does not move) and −1.25 percent for U.S. investors because of the currency translation into U.S. dollars: The dollar value of one share of Novartis drops by 1.25 percent. The local-currency exposure of the Swiss franc price of Novartis is zero ($\gamma^{FC} = 0$), and the investor has a currency exposure of $\gamma = 1$: When the Swiss franc loses 1.25 percent, the investor tends to lose the same amount of 1.25 percent on Novartis in domestic (in this case U.S. dollar) currency.
- A *negative* correlation would mean that the local stock price benefits from a depreciation of the local currency. In other words, the loss on the Swiss currency would be partly offset by a Swiss franc capital gain on the stock price. A perfect currency hedge would be attained if the Swiss franc price of Novartis moved up 1.25 percent. Then the return to a U.S. investor would be zero, because the final dollar price of Novartis would be unchanged. In that case, the local-currency exposure of the Swiss franc price of Novartis is $\gamma^{FC} = -1$,

[14] In this text, we use the convention that *negative* means a correlation in which the local stock price goes up when the local currency depreciates. Also, in this illustration, we assume that the volatility of the stock's local currency return and the volatility of the exchange rate are equal.

and the investor has a currency exposure of $\gamma = 0$: When the Swiss franc loses 1.25 percent, the investor tends to have a zero return on Novartis in domestic currency.

- A *positive* correlation would mean that the local stock price drops in reaction to a depreciation of the local currency. With a perfect positive correlation, for example, Novartis might drop by 1.25 percent with news of the franc depreciation (or go up, following a franc appreciation). The dollar return to a U.S. investor would be −2.5 percent. In this case, foreign asset prices would compound the currency effect and might be considered a bad hedge against currency movement. Here, the currency exposure of the Swiss franc price of Novartis is $\gamma^{FC} = 1$, and the investor has a currency exposure of $\gamma = 2$; when the Swiss franc loses 1.25 percent, the investor tends to lose twice that much on Novartis in domestic currency.

The local currency exposure simply describes the sensitivity of the stock price (measured in local currency) to a change in the value of the local currency. A statistical estimate of the currency exposure can be obtained by a regression between Swiss franc (FC) returns on Novartis and the percentage movements in the SFr:$ exchange rate. If we limit ourselves to one period, the local-currency exposure is simply equal to the return on the Swiss franc price of Novartis during this period divided by percentage movements in the SFr:$ exchange rate:

$$\gamma^{FC} = \frac{R^{FC}}{s}$$

where R^{FC} is the return on the foreign investment in local (foreign) currency and s is the percentage change in the direct exchange rate, $s = (S_1 - S_0)/S_0$.

The currency exposure is equal to

$$\gamma = \frac{R}{s} = \frac{R^{FC} + s}{s} = \gamma^{FC} + 1$$

For example, if the Swiss franc loses 1.25 percent against the dollar (a drop in the dollar value of one Swiss franc, or a negative s) and the Swiss franc price of Novartis goes up by 1.25 percent, the local-currency exposure is $\gamma^{FC} = 1.25/(-1.25) = -1$. In this case, the currency exposure is $\gamma = 0$. If the stock price only goes up by 0.625 percent, the local-currency exposure is $\gamma^{FC} = 0.625/(-1.25) = -0.5$. Hence, the currency exposure is $\gamma = 0.5$.

We now discuss what causes the local-currency exposure to be positive or negative.

Currency Exposure of Individual Companies To the extent that purchasing power parity holds—that is, if exchange rates exactly adjust to inflation differentials—exchange rate movements simply mirror relative inflation and do not add another dimension to the analysis. They have no specific influence on the economy or equity prices beyond that of domestic inflation. But virtually all studies indicate that purchasing power parity does not hold, especially since the advent of floating exchange rates. Short-term shocks to the exchange rate, and hence foreign exchange rate volatility, cannot be explained by an existing inflation differential.

This means that real exchange rate movements (deviations from purchasing power parity) are the relevant variable to study, and the actual effect of real exchange rate movements is large compared with inflation-induced variations. As such, real currency movements may have a significant influence on domestic economies and corporations, and hence, on stock markets.

It might be useful to look at an *individual firm* to examine the influence of a *real exchange appreciation.* Consider a strong real appreciation of the U.S. dollar relative to most currencies, including the Swiss franc, as was the case from 1999 to 2001. Typically, a U.S. tourist had great incentive to spend a skiing vacation in the Swiss Alps, because the dollar purchased much more in terms of accommodations and food in Switzerland. Conversely, Novartis drugs manufactured in Switzerland became highly price-competitive when exported to the United States. The 40 percent *real* appreciation of the U.S. dollar in the early 2000s meant that Novartis could lower its U.S. selling price without reducing its Swiss franc profit margin. The story is only partially true, because the real dollar appreciation raises the cost of some imported goods.

The effect of this real dollar appreciation is the opposite for Merck & Co., an American pharmaceutical company; it gives Merck incentives for establishing plants in countries such as Switzerland, where the company can benefit from lower production costs. Note, however, that the importance of the exchange rate for an individual firm depends on the currency structure of its exports, imports, and financing. For example, a French firm importing U.S. computers financed in U.S. dollars is badly hurt by the real dollar appreciation. Illustrations are provided in Examples 4.7 and 4.8. An interesting analysis of the influence of a currency movement on the value of the firm is provided in Heckman (1985, 1986).

Another argument that would suggest that the local stock market should react favorably to a depreciation of its currency is based on the rapid internationalization of many corporations. Many corporations are now heavy foreign investors. They have operations abroad and directly own foreign companies. As such, these firms should be valued as global portfolios. For example, Novartis derives over 95 percent of its revenue outside of Switzerland. A Swiss franc depreciation should not greatly influence the "real" value of Novartis. If the Swiss franc depreciates, the Swiss franc price of Novartis should increase. Novartis can be seen as a diversified portfolio of assets in foreign currencies. As those currencies appreciate against the franc, the foreign assets should be worth more Swiss francs.

Currency exposures of individual companies could be estimated historically by regressing the company's stock returns on market returns and currency returns.[15] This estimate can be refined by a detailed analysis of the activities and financing of the company, the geographical distribution of its sales and investments, the currency origin of its profits and costs, the currency structure of its debt, and so on.

Currency Exposure of National Economies and Equity Markets In the *macroeconomic* approach, it is widely recognized that economic activity is a major determinant of stock market returns, so the influence of exchange rate movements on domestic economic activity may explain the relation between exchange rate movements and stock returns.

---

[15] See Diermeier and Solnik (2001).

EXAMPLE 4.7 INDIVIDUAL COMPANY RISK EXPOSURE

Two Canadian firms are in quite different businesses:

- Enga manufactures engine parts in Canada for export, and prices are set and paid in U.S. dollars. Production costs are mostly domestic (the labor force) and considered to follow the Canadian inflation rate.
- Klub imports computers from the United States and sells them in Canada to compete with Canadian products.

The market values both at a price–earnings ratio of 10, meaning that the stock price in Canadian currency is equal to 10 times next year's expected earnings. What will happen to the earnings and valuations of the two companies if there is a sudden *real* depreciation of the Canadian dollar? What is likely to happen in the long run? Would your findings be the same if the Canadian dollar depreciation only matched the Canadian–U.S. inflation differential?

SOLUTION

Enga's earnings and stock price, measured in Canadian dollars, should increase because its revenues come from the United States and are worth more in Canadian dollars at the same time that its costs are in Canadian dollars. Enga's revenues in real terms are rising, while its costs are not. Klub faces the opposite situation. Its costs in real terms are rising, while its revenues are not. In the long run, Enga will meet competition from U.S. competitors who will be motivated to build plants in Canada. Klub will be motivated to find Canadian sources for its computers. If the Canadian dollar depreciation only matched the Canadian–U.S. interest rate differential, then the findings would be different. The effects would only be nominal and not real. Real revenues and costs would remain the same.

EXAMPLE 4.8 OIL AND MINING RISK EXPOSURE

In 2001, the South African rand depreciated. South African oil and mining companies sell in dollars but have costs in rand. According to these currency sensitivity factors and given that this was a real depreciation, what should have happened to South African oil and mining company revenues and valuations as a result?

SOLUTION

According to an *Economist* article about the Johannesburg Stock Exchange, "for the past few months the local index has roared. The rand's slump last year helped exporters, and gave a shine to oil and mining companies, which sell in dollars but have costs in rand" (May 18, 2002, p. 71).

Various economic theories have been proposed to explain the influence of real exchange rate movements on domestic economies. The traditional approach can be sketched as follows: A decline in a currency's real exchange rate tends to improve competitiveness, whereas the concomitant deterioration in terms of trade increases the cost of imports, which creates additional domestic inflation and reduces real income and, hence, domestic demand and production. The initial reduction in real gross national product (GNP) caused by a deterioration in the terms of trade should eventually be offset by improved international competitiveness and export demand until purchasing power parity is restored.

A simple example may help to illustrate this phenomenon. Let's assume a sudden 10 percent depreciation of the Swiss franc. Let's also assume that the Swiss trade balance (Swiss exports minus imports) is in deficit. The immediate effect of a 10 percent depreciation of the franc is to make current imports more expensive in terms of francs—if all imports were denominated in foreign currency, the cost of imports would immediately increase by 10 percent. This increase in cost has two major effects. First, the Swiss trade balance deficit measured in francs widens. Although the franc value of exports increases somewhat because part of the export sales are contracted in foreign currency, the percentage of exports denominated in foreign currency is usually smaller than that of imports. Second, the rise in imported goods prices leads to an increase in the domestic price index and imports inflation. Both of these effects are bad for the Swiss economy, and, in a sense, the real wealth is reduced. However, this currency depreciation makes Swiss firms more competitive; they can lower the price of their products by 10 percent in terms of foreign currency without lowering their Swiss franc income. In the long run, this should help increase foreign sales and stimulate the Swiss economy. The reaction of the deficit to the depreciation is often called the J-curve effect because of the J-shape of the trade balance curve as a function of time (see Exhibit 4.2). However, if the economy is slow to improve, this chain of events threatens to become a vicious cycle: The immediate economic activity and trade balance worsens, leading to a further currency depreciation, which in turn may worsen domestic economic conditions, and so on.

The stock market, which immediately discounts the overall influence of an exchange rate movement on the economy, may be positively or negatively affected, depending on whether the short-term or long-term effect dominates. In late 1985, the U.S. dollar was at its highest point, well above its purchasing power parity value. The Group of Five, leading industrialized nations (United States, Japan, United Kingdom, Germany, and France), met at the Plaza Hotel in New York and made the surprising announcement that they would coordinate their intervention policies to lower the value of the dollar on the foreign exchange market. The reaction to this news was immediate; the dollar fell by 5 percent, and the U.S. stock market rose by more than 1 percent, anticipating that the dollar depreciation would have an overall positive effect on the U.S. economy. In many cases, however, a currency depreciation is not followed by this type of stock market reaction.

A money-demand model has also been proposed.[16] In this model, real growth in the domestic economy leads to increased demand for the domestic currency

---

[16] See, for example, Lucas (1982).

EXHIBIT 4.2
The J-Curve Effect

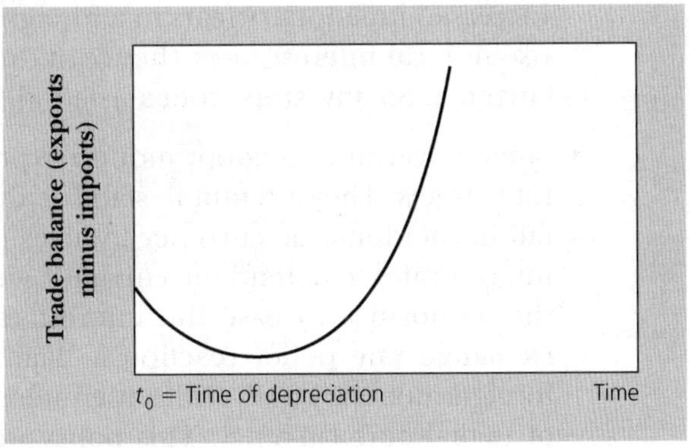

through a traditional money-demand equation. This increase in currency demand induces a rise in the relative value of the domestic currency. Because domestic stock prices are strongly influenced by real growth, this model justifies a positive association between real stock returns and domestic currency appreciation. Although the traditional trade approach suggests that a real exchange rate appreciation tends to reduce the competitiveness of the domestic economy and, therefore, to reduce domestic activity, the money-demand approach leads to the opposite effect: An increase in domestic economic growth leads to a real currency appreciation.

Finally, it is important to stress that the situation of emerging markets is somewhat different from that of developed countries. The economies of emerging countries are usually not very diversified. They rely heavily on foreign investment. A drop in the value of an emerging country's currency is often a signal that the country is running into severe problems. The fate of the currency and of the stock markets is closely linked to the country's economic and political situation. Their correlation is strongly positive. Hence, foreign investors are doubly affected by a drop in the value of the emerging currency: Investors lose not only in the currency translation to their domestic currency, but also in the drop in the local currency value of the emerging stock market.

Currency Exposure of Bonds Because bond prices are directly linked to long-term interest rates, the story for bonds is told by the relation between changes in long-term interest rates and exchange rates. Bond returns are negative when bond yields rise.

There are at least two competing theories about the correlation between bond returns and currency movements:

- It is often stated that a rise in the national real interest rate leads to the appreciation of the home currency, because of international investment flows attracted by the higher real interest rate. This would induce a negative local-currency exposure for bonds (bond prices go down, because of the rise in yields, when the local currency goes up, and vice versa). However, it is important to be careful in differentiating between an interest rate movement caused by a rise in the real rate of interest, as mentioned, and an interest rate movement caused by changes in inflationary expectations (the Fisher effect). Increased inflationary fears in a foreign country could lead to a simultaneous rise in local interest rates (hence, a drop in bond prices) and a drop in the currency. So, investors from abroad will lose doubly.

- Some governments adopt monetary policies that contain foreign exchange rate targets. They attempt to stabilize their home currency's exchange rate. A fall in the domestic currency induces the monetary authorities to raise real interest rates to defend the currency, and a strong domestic currency induces the authorities to ease the interest rate policy. Branson (1984) calls this exchange rate policy reaction a "leaning-against-the-wind" policy, whereby foreign monetary authorities use interest rates to stabilize the exchange rate of their home currency. This policy would induce a positive local-currency exposure for domestic bonds.

Economic versus Accounting Currency Exposure This chapter focuses on economic exposure—the impact of a currency movement on the total return on a foreign investment. Accounting-wise investors often separate the return in local currency and the return on the currency itself. For example, most portfolio accounting systems first value an asset in its local currency and then translate it at the proper exchange rate. So, the local-currency asset return and the currency return will appear as two distinct elements. From an accounting standpoint, currency risk will be measured only by looking at the currency return. For example, consider a U.S. investor holding a foreign stock with little dollar currency exposure, so that the local-currency price tends to offset any depreciation of the foreign currency ($\gamma = 0$). From an economic standpoint, there is little foreign currency exposure: If the foreign currency depreciates by 10 percent, the local-currency stock price will rise by 10 percent, offsetting the depreciation. But from an accounting standpoint, the two returns are treated separately so that a 10 percent currency loss will be reported. If an investor focuses only on this accounting or translation measure of currency risk, then all foreign assets are fully exposed to currency risk.

Tests of the ICAPM

A brief look at investors' portfolio holdings would suggest that a major conclusion of the ICAPM is violated often. Portfolios are strongly biased toward domestic investments. U.S. investors devote almost all of their equity portfolios to U.S. securities, although the theory would have them hold the world market portfolio. French and Poterba (1991), Cooper and Kaplanis (1994), and Tesar and Werner (1995) present evidence of a home preference in portfolio investment and fail to find satisfactory explanations for such a large bias. This does not mean that financial markets are necessarily segmented and that the theory does not provide useful and robust implications regarding the pricing of securities. International capital flows, which are indeed large, could be sufficient to make the markets efficient. The international capital market would be integrated if all securities followed the same international risk-pricing relation outlined here.

Few tests of international market integration and asset pricing models have been performed so far. One problem has been the limited amount of long-term historical data available on international capital markets. Other problems are methodological and affect the testing of any CAPM, whether domestic or international. They have to do with the difficulty of exactly identifying the market portfolio and with the time-varying nature of the expected return and risk measures. The major problem is that any CAPM deals with expected returns, and those are simply not observable. Using past realized returns to proxy expected returns can be very misleading.

A test of the ICAPM investigates whether cross-sectional differences in expected returns among securities are explained by the various risk exposures, β and γ's, as described in Equation 4.14. Empirical researchers have explored several questions:

- Is currency risk priced?
- Is domestic market risk priced beyond global market risk (segmentation)?
- Are other firms' attributes priced beyond global market risk?

Is Currency Risk Priced? In *unconditional* tests, researchers assume that expected returns and risk measures are constant over time. This approach will not be detailed here. In *conditional* tests, expected returns and risk measures are allowed to vary in some specified way. Dumas and Solnik (1995) modeled the time variation in expected return and risk. They found that significant currency risk premiums exist, and they rejected a model that would exclude currency risk factors. De Santis and Gérard (1998) found strong support for a specification of the ICAPM that includes both market risk and currency risk. They stress the importance of a conditional approach allowing variation in market and currency risk premiums. In terms of asset management, this conclusion would encourage tactical revisions in the global asset allocation.

Segmentation Other researchers focus on market segmentation but exclude currency risk from their analysis. The approach is to test an alternative model, including both global risk factors and country-specific factors. If the ICAPM holds, those country-specific factors should not be priced. Bekaert and Harvey (1995) allowed conditionally expected returns in any country to be affected by their exposure to the world market portfolio (beta) *and* by the variance of the country's returns. In a perfectly integrated market, only the beta counts. In segmented markets, the country's variance is a more relevant measure of risk. Bekaert and Harvey looked at emerging markets and allowed the degree of market integration to change over time. They found evidence that many emerging markets were segmented in their early years but have become more integrated to the global market. However, several markets show signs of segmentation, which is not too surprising for most of the emerging markets. De Santis and Gérard (1997) focused on the major equity markets and introduced as country-specific factors the country's variance plus a constant to accommodate other forms of segmentation, such as differences in taxation. They concluded: "To summarize, we find that expected excess returns are positively related to their conditional covariance with a world-wide portfolio, whereas country specific risk is not priced" (p. 1901). These studies, however, suffer from the deficiency that currency factors are not introduced in the test.

Other Attributes In a domestic or international CAPM, attributes of a firm that are not linked to the risk factors outlined here should not be priced. In a domestic framework, Fama and French (1992, 1996) find that some attributes of a firm provide a much better explanation of the differences in return among U.S. firms than their beta. For example, "value" stocks (as measured by ratios such as book-to-market value or earnings-to-price) outperform "growth" stocks. This leads to a rejection of the CAPM. Numerous criticisms have been leveled at this conclusion (see Kothari, Shanken, and Sloan, 1995). Fama and French (1998) extend their analysis to international data. They find that value stocks outperform growth stocks in 12 out of 13 major markets. Value stocks are more likely to go bankrupt than are growth stocks, and Fama and French interpret these results in terms of financial distress. They claim that financial distress is a risk that is not well captured by the standard ICAPM, and that it should be added as a factor to explain stock pricing. On the other hand, Ferson and Harvey (1998) find that the book-to-market value ratio of a firm is strongly related to its world market risk exposure. A fruitful direction of research is to refine the analysis of risk by looking at the underlying economic risk factors, rather than by summarizing all the risk information in a single beta.

Current empirical evidence is still fragmentary, and the results are likely to evolve as the world financial markets are increasingly liberalized and transaction costs are driven down. A summary of current research tends to support the conclusion that assets are priced in an integrated global financial market. The evidence is sufficiently strong to justify using the ICAPM as an anchor in structuring global portfolios. However, the evidence can be somewhat different for emerging and smaller markets, in which constraints are still serious.

Summary

- International markets are integrated if they are efficient in the sense that securities with the same risk characteristics have the same expected return wherever in the world they are traded.
- International markets are segmented if they are inefficient in the sense that securities with the same risk characteristics sell at different exchange-rate-adjusted prices in different countries, thus violating the law of one price.

- Six impediments to international capital mobility are psychological barriers, legal restrictions, transaction costs, discriminatory taxation, political risks, and foreign exchange risks.
- International integration requires only a sufficient flow of capital to make the world market efficient and to eliminate relative mispricing among countries. Investment and borrowing actions of private and institutional investors, major corporations, and governments quickly take advantage of relative mispricing, thereby making the markets more efficient.
- The expected return on an unhedged foreign investment is

$$E(R) = E(R^{FC}) + E(s)$$

where $E(R)$ is the expected domestic-currency return on the investment, $E(R^{FC})$ is the expected foreign investment return, and $E(s)$ is the expected percentage currency movement.
- The expected return on a hedged foreign investment is

$$E(R) = E(R^{FC}) + (F - S)/S$$

where $E(R)$ is the expected domestic-currency return on the hedged investment, $E(R^{FC})$ is the expected foreign investment return, F is the forward rate, and S is the spot exchange rate. Both F and S are direct quotes.
- The extended CAPM is the domestic CAPM with the domestic rate for the risk-free rate and the market capitalization weighted portfolio of all risky assets in the world for the market portfolio.
- The domestic CAPM extension can be justified only with the usual domestic CAPM assumptions and the addition of two assumptions: Investors throughout the world have identical consumption baskets, and real prices of consumption goods are identical in every country (purchasing power parity holds exactly at any point in time).
- With direct rates, the real exchange rate is the nominal exchange rate times the ratio of the foreign price level to the domestic price level: $X = S \times (P_{FC}/P_{DC})$.
- The real exchange rate changes in a period if the foreign exchange appreciation during the period does not equal the inflation differential between the two countries during the period.
- The expected foreign currency appreciation or depreciation should be approximately equal to the interest rate differential: $E(s) = r_{DC} - r_{FC}$, where s is the percentage change in the price of foreign currency (direct exchange rate).
- A foreign currency risk premium (SRP) is equal to the expected movement in the exchange rate *minus* the interest rate differential (domestic risk-free rate minus foreign risk-free rate): $SRP = E[(S_1 - S_0)/S_0] - (r_{DC} - r_{FC})$.

- A foreign currency risk premium is equal to the difference between the expected exchange rate and the forward rate, in percentage of the current exchange rate: $SRP = [E(S_1) - F]/S_0$.

- The risk-pricing expression for the international CAPM (ICAPM) is that the expected return on an asset i is the sum of the market risk premium plus various currency risk premiums:

$$E(R_i) = R_0 + \beta_{iw} \times RP_w + \gamma_{i1} \times SRP_1 + \gamma_{i2} \times SRP_2 + \cdots + \gamma_{ik} \times SRP_k$$

where β is the world market exposure of the asset and the γ's are the currency exposures, sensitivities of the asset returns to the various exchange rates.

- With one foreign currency, for example, the asset pricing equation of the ICAPM simplifies to

$$E(R_i) = R_0 + \beta_{iw} \times RP_w + \gamma_i \times SRP_{FC}$$

- The international asset pricing relation applies to all securities only in an integrated world capital market with currency hedging available.

- Most forms of market imperfections and constraints to foreign investments cannot be easily incorporated in an equilibrium asset pricing framework.

- A local-currency exposure is the sensitivity of a stock price (measured in local currency) to a change in the value of the local currency. A zero correlation between stock returns and exchange rate movements would mean no systematic reaction to exchange rate adjustments. A negative correlation would mean that the local stock price would benefit from a depreciation of the local currency. A positive correlation would mean that the local stock price would drop in reaction to a depreciation of the local currency.

- For an investor, the currency exposure of a foreign investment is the sensitivity of the stock price (measured in the investor's domestic currency) to a change in the value of the foreign currency. It is equal to one plus the local-currency exposure of the asset.

- The exchange rate exposure for an individual firm depends on the currency structure of its exports, imports, and financing. Generally, for example, an importer is hurt by foreign currency appreciation and an exporter helped. If exchange rate movements only reflect inflation rate differentials, they have no specific influence on the economy or equity prices beyond that of domestic inflation. Real exchange rate movements, however, have an effect on equity prices, depending on currency exposures.

- In the macroeconomic approach, it is widely recognized that economic activity is a major determinant of stock market returns, so the influence of exchange rate movements on domestic economic activity may explain the relation between exchange rate movements and stock returns. On the bond side, a rise in the national real interest rate leads to an appreciation of the domestic currency, because of international investment flows attracted by the higher real interest rate. Domestic bond price declines would accompany domestic currency appreciation.

- The two models of how real exchange rate changes affect domestic economic activity give opposite conclusions. The traditional approach can be sketched as follows: A decline in a currency's real exchange rate tends to improve competitiveness, whereas the concomitant deterioration in terms of trade increases the cost of imports, which creates additional domestic inflation and reduces real income and, hence, domestic demand and production. The initial reduction in real GNP caused by a deterioration in the terms of trade should eventually be offset by improved international competitiveness and export demand until purchasing power parity is restored. In the money-demand model, on the other hand, real growth in the domestic economy leads to increased demand for the domestic currency through a traditional money-demand equation. This increase in currency demand induces a rise in the relative value of the domestic currency. Because domestic stock prices are strongly influenced by real growth, this model justifies a positive association between real stock returns and domestic currency appreciation.

Problems

1. Consider an asset that has a beta of 1.25. If the risk-free rate is 3.25 percent and the market risk premium is 5.5 percent, calculate the expected return on the asset.

2. An asset has a beta of 0.9. The variance of returns on a market index, σ_m^2, is 90. If the variance of returns for the asset is 120, what proportion of the asset's total risk is systematic, and what proportion is residual risk?

3. A portfolio consists of three assets. Asset 1 has a beta of 0.85, Asset 2 has a beta of 1.3, and Asset 3 has a beta of 0.9. Asset 1 has an allocation of 50 percent, while Assets 2 and 3 each have an allocation of 25 percent. The variance of returns on a market index, σ_m^2, is 120. Calculate the variance of portfolio returns, assuming that the specific risk of the portfolio is negligible.

4. A Canadian investor is considering the purchase of U.K. securities. The current exchange rate is Can\$1.46 per pound. Assume that the price level of a typical consumption basket in Canada is 1.46 times the price level of a typical consumption basket in the United Kingdom.
   a. Calculate the real exchange rate.
   b. One year later, price levels in Canada have risen 2 percent, while price levels in the United Kingdom have risen 4 percent. The new exchange rate is Can\$1.4308 per pound. What is the new real exchange rate?
   c. Did the Canadian investor experience a change in the real exchange rate?

5. Consider a U.S. investor who wishes to purchase U.K. securities. The current exchange rate is \$1.80 per pound. Assume that the price level of a typical consumption basket in the United States is three times the price level of a typical consumption basket in the United Kingdom.

a. Calculate the real exchange rate.
b. One year later, price levels in the United States have risen 5 percent, while price levels in the United Kingdom have risen 2 percent. The new exchange rate is \$1.854 per pound. What is the new real exchange rate?
c. Did the U.S. investor experience a change in the real exchange rate?

6. An investor based in the United States wishes to invest in Swiss bonds with a maturity of one year. Suppose that the ratio of the price levels of a typical consumption basket in the United States versus Switzerland is 1 to 1.5 and the current exchange rate is \$0.62 per Swiss franc. The one-year interest rate is 2 percent in the United States and 4.5 percent in Switzerland. Assume that inflation rates are fully predictable, and expected inflation over the next year is 1.5 percent in the United States and 4 percent in Switzerland.
   a. Assuming that real exchange rates remain constant, calculate the real exchange rate, the expected exchange rate in one year, and the expected return over one year on the Swiss bond in U.S. dollar terms.
   b. Now assume that the inflation rate over the one-year period has been 1.5 percent in the United States and 4 percent in Switzerland. Further, assume that the exchange rate at the end of one year is \$0.63 per Swiss franc. Calculate the real exchange rate at the end of one year. What is the return on the Swiss bond investment now? Is the return on the Swiss bond the same as in part (a)? Explain.

7. A portfolio manager based in the United Kingdom is planning to invest in U.S. bonds with a maturity of one year. Assume that the ratio of the price levels of a typical consumption basket in the United Kingdom versus the United States is 1.2 to 1. The current exchange rate is £0.69 per dollar. The one-year interest rate is 1.76 percent in the United States and 4.13 percent in the United Kingdom. Assume that inflation rates are fully predictable, and expected inflation over the next year is 1.5 percent in the United States and 3.75 percent in the United Kingdom.
   a. Assuming that real exchange rates remain constant, calculate the real exchange rate, the expected exchange rate in one year, and the expected return over one year on the U.S. bonds in pounds.
   b. Now assume that the inflation rate over the one-year period has been 1.5 percent in the United States and 3.75 percent in the United Kingdom. Further, assume that the exchange rate at the end of one year is £0.67 per dollar. Calculate the real exchange rate at the end of one year. What is the return on the U.S. bond investment now? Is the return on the U.S. bond the same as in part (a)? Explain.

8. Assume that the Eurozone risk-free interest rate on bonds with one year to maturity is 4.78 percent and the U.S. risk-free interest rate on one-year bonds is 3.15 percent. The current exchange rate is \$0.90 per euro. Assume that the United States is the domestic country.
   a. Calculate the one-year forward exchange rate.
   b. Is the euro trading at forward premium or discount?
   c. Is your answer to part (b) consistent with interest rate parity? Explain.

9. Take the case of a U.S. firm that wishes to invest some funds (U.S. dollars) for a period of one year. The choice is between investing in a U.S. bond with one year to maturity, paying an interest rate of 2.75 percent, and a U.K. bond with one year to maturity, paying an interest rate of 4.25 percent. The current exchange rate is \$1.46 per pound, and the one-year forward exchange rate is \$1.25 per pound. Should the U.S. firm invest in U.S. bonds or in U.K. bonds?

10. Consider a German firm that wishes to invest euro funds for a period of one year. The firm has a choice of investing in a euro bond with one year to maturity, paying an interest rate of 3.35 percent, and a U.S. dollar bond with one year to maturity, paying an interest rate of 2.25 percent. The current exchange rate is €1.12 per U.S. dollar, and the one-year forward exchange rate is €1.25 per U.S dollar. Should the German firm invest in euro bonds or in U.S. dollar bonds?

11. The interest rate on one-year risk-free bonds is 4.25 percent in the United States and 3.75 percent in Switzerland. The current exchange rate is $0.65 per Swiss franc. Suppose that you are a U.S. investor and you expect the Swiss franc to appreciate by 2.75 percent over the next year.
a. Calculate the foreign currency risk premium.
b. Calculate the domestic currency return on the foreign bond, assuming that your currency appreciation expectations are met.

12. Suppose that you are an investor based in Switzerland, and you expect the U.S. dollar to depreciate by 2.75 percent over the next year. The interest rate on one-year risk-free bonds is 5.25 percent in the United States and 2.75 percent in Switzerland. The current exchange rate is SFr1.62 per U.S. dollar.
a. Calculate the foreign currency risk premium from the Swiss investor's viewpoint.
b. Calculate the return on the U.S bond from the Swiss investor's viewpoint, assuming that the Swiss investor's expectations are met.

13. Assume you are a U.S. investor who is considering investments in the French (Stocks A and B) and Swiss (Stocks C and D) stock markets. The world market risk premium is 6 percent. The currency risk premium on the Swiss franc is 1.25 percent, and the currency risk premium on the euro is 2 percent. The interest rate on one-year risk-free bonds is 3.75 percent in the United States. In addition, you are provided with the following information:

Stock	A	B	C	D
Country	France	France	Switzerland	Switzerland
β_w	1	0.90	1	1.5
$\gamma_€$	1	0.80	–0.25	–1.0
γ_{SFr}	–0.25	0.75	1.0	–0.5

a. Calculate the expected return for each of the stocks. The U.S. dollar is the base currency.
b. Explain the differences in the expected returns of the four stocks in terms of β_w, $\gamma_€$, and γ_{SFr}.

14. a. List reasons that an international extension of the CAPM is problematic.
b. In an international extension of the CAPM, why would the optimal portfolio differ from the world market portfolio, as suggested by the traditional CAPM, even if the markets are fully efficient?

15. You are a U.S. investor who is considering investments in the Australian stock market, but you worry about currency risk. You run a regression of the returns on the Australian stock index (in A$) on movements in the Australian dollar exchange rate (U.S.$ per A$) and find a slope of –0.5.
a. What is your currency exposure if you invest in a diversified portfolio of Australian stocks?

b. You invest $10 million in the diversified portfolio, but you fear that the Australian dollar will depreciate by 10 percent relative to the U.S. dollar. How much do you expect to lose because of the currency movement?

16. Consider two French firms listed on the Paris stock market:
- Mega manufactures engine parts in France for export, and the prices are set and paid in dollars. Production costs are mostly domestic (the labor force) and considered to follow the French inflation rate.
- Club imports computers from the United States and sells them in France to compete with French products.

a. What will happen to the earnings of the two companies in the short run if there is a sudden depreciation of the euro (say, 20 percent)?
b. What is the difference between the short-run effect and the long-run adjustments?
c. Would your findings be the same if the euro depreciation were only a progressive adjustment to the United States–Europe inflation differential that reflected the higher European inflation rate?

17. Consider two Australian firms listed on the Sydney stock exchange:
- Company A. Its stock return shows a consistent negative correlation with the euro per A$ exchange rate. The stock price of Company A (in Australian dollars) tends to go up when the Australian dollar depreciates relative to the euro.
- Company B. Its stock return shows a consistent positive correlation with the euro per A$ exchange rate. The stock price of Company B (in Australian dollars) tends to go down when the Australian dollar depreciates relative to the euro.

A European investor wishes to buy Australian stocks but is unsure about whether to invest in Company A or Company B. She is afraid of a depreciation of the Australian dollar. Which of the two investments would offer some protection against a weakening Australian dollar?

18. KoreaCo, a South Korean company, is a worldwide leader in widget (a hypothetical manufactured product) production. Europe is KoreaCo's single largest market.

Assumptions:
- KoreaCo's production capacity is located in South Korea and all of its costs are incurred in Korean won.
- Additions to capacity require a lead time of more than one year.
- KoreaCo borrows only in South Korean won.

a. Describe the effect of a short-term appreciation of the won versus the euro on the profitability of KoreaCo's sales in Europe. Address *only* the effects on KoreaCo unit sales and profit margins.
b. KoreaCo expects the appreciation of the won versus the euro to continue for the long term and is considering two business strategies:
   - Continue to operate production plants solely in South Korea.
   - Shift production equal to current European sales to Europe.

   Explain the effect of each of these strategies on the long-run profitability of KoreaCo's European sales.

19. In 2002, a strong depreciation of the U.S. dollar is expected by some observers over the next two years. Are nondollar bonds a good investment for U.S. investors? Why or why not?

20. As a money manager based in the Netherlands, you are asked to advise a domestic client about investing in foreign bonds to diversify domestic inflation risk. You fear that

the strong economic recovery observed in the Netherlands and elsewhere in the Eurozone—but not yet in the Far East and North America—will feed inflationary expectations in Europe. Try to build a "marketing" case for international bond diversification.

Bibliography

Adler, M., and Dumas, B. "International Portfolio Choice and Corporation Finance: A Synthesis," *Journal of Finance*, June 1983.

Bekaert, G., and Harvey, C. R. "Time-Varying World Market Integration," *Journal of Finance*, 50(2), June 1995, pp. 403–444.

Black, F. "International Capital Market Equilibrium with Investment Barriers," *Journal of Financial Economics*, December 1974.

———. "Universal Hedging: Optimizing Currency Risk and Reward in International Equity Portfolios," *Financial Analysts Journal*, July/August 1989.

———. "Equilibrium Exchange Rate Hedging," *Journal of Finance*, July 1990.

Branson, W. H. "Exchange Rate Policy after a Decade of Floating," in J. Bilson and R. Marston, eds., *Exchange Rate Theory and Practice*, Chicago: University of Chicago Press, 1984.

Cooper, I., and Kaplanis, E. "Home Bias in Equity Portfolios, Inflation Hedging and International Capital Market Equilibrium," *Review of Financial Studies*, Spring 1994.

De Santis, G., and Gérard, B. "International Asset Pricing and Portfolio Diversification with Time-Varying Risk," *Journal of Finance*, 52(5), December 1997, pp. 1881–1912.

———. "How Big Is the Premium for Currency Risk?" *Journal of Financial Economics*, 49(3), September 1998, pp. 375–412.

Diermeier, J. J., and Solnik, B. "Global Pricing of Equity," *Financial Analysts Journal*, July/August 2001.

Dumas, B., and Solnik, B. "The World Price of Foreign Exchange Risk," *Journal of Finance*, June 1995.

Elton, E., Gruber, M., Brown, S., and Goetzmann, W. *Modern Portfolio Theory and Investment Analysis*, New York: Wiley, 2006.

Errunza, V., and Losq, E. "International Asset Pricing under Mild Segmentation: Theory and Test," *Journal of Finance*, 40(1), March 1985.

———. "Capital Flow Controls, International Asset Pricing and Investor's Welfare: A Multi-Country Framework," *Journal of Finance*, September 1989.

Eun, C., and Janakiramanan, S. "A Model of International Asset Pricing with a Constraint on the Foreign Equity Ownership," *Journal of Finance*, September 1986.

Fama, E., and French, K. "The Cross-Section of Expected Stock Returns," *Journal of Finance*, June 1992.

———. "Multifactor Explanations of Asset Pricing Anomalies," *Journal of Finance*, 51(1), March 1996, pp. 54–84.

———. "Value versus Growth: The International Evidence," *Journal of Finance*, 52(6), December 1998, pp. 1975–1999.

Ferson, W. E., and Harvey, C. R. "Fundamental Determinants of National Equity Returns: A Perspective on Conditional Asset Pricing," *Journal of Banking and Finance*, 21, October 1998, pp. 1625–1665.

French, K., and Poterba, J. "Investor Diversification and International Equity Markets," *American Economic Review*, March 1991.

Grauer, F., Litzenberger, R., and Stehle, R. "Sharing Rules and Equilibrium in an International Capital Market under Uncertainty," *Journal of Financial Economics*, June 1976.

Heckman, C. R. "A Financial Model of Foreign Exchange Exposure," *Journal of International Business Studies*, Summer 1985.

———. "Don't Blame Currency Values for Strategic Errors: Protecting Competitive Position by Correctly Assessing Foreign Exchange Exposure," *Midland Corporate Finance Journal*, Fall 1986.

Hietla, P. T. "Asset Pricing in Partially Segmented Markets: Evidence from the Finnish Market," *Journal of Finance*, July 1989.

Jorion, P. "Asset Allocation with Hedged and Unhedged Foreign Stocks and Bonds," *Journal of Portfolio Management*, Summer 1989.

Kothari, S. P., Shanken, J., and Sloan, R. G. "Another Look at the Cross-Section of Expected Stock Returns," *Journal of Finance*, 50(1), March 1995, pp. 185–224.

Lucas, R. "Interest Rates and Currency Prices in a Two-Country World," *Journal of Monetary Economics*, November 1982.

Reilly, F. K., and Brown, K., *Investment Analysis and Portfolio Management*, 7th ed., South-Western, 2006.

Roll, R. "A Critique of the Asset Pricing Theory's Test: On Past and Potential Testability of the Theory," *Journal of Financial Economics*, 4, March 1977.

Sercu, P. "A Generalization of the International Asset Pricing Model," *Revue de l'Association Française de Finance*, June 1980.

Sharpe, W. F., Alexander, G. J., and Bailey, J. V., *Investments*, 6th ed., Englewood Cliffs, NJ: Prentice Hall, 1999.

Solnik, B. "An Equilibrium Model of the International Capital Market," *Journal of Economic Theory*, July/August 1974.

Stapleton, R. C., and Subrahmanyam, M. G. "Market Imperfections, Capital Asset Equilibrium and Corporation Finance," *Journal of Finance*, 32, May 1977.

Stulz, R. "A Model of International Asset Pricing," *Journal of Financial Economics*, 9, December 1981.

Subrahmanyam, M. G. "On the Optimality of International Capital Market Integration," *Journal of Financial Economics*, August 1975.

Tesar, L., and Werner, I. "Home Bias and High Turnover," *Journal of International Money and Finance*, August 1995.

5

Equity: Markets and Instruments

LEARNING OUTCOMES

After completing this chapter, you will be able to do the following:

- Explain the origins of different national market organizations
- Differentiate between an order-driven market and a price-driven market, and discuss the risk and advantages of each
- Discuss the evolution of stock markets worldwide and their differences in terms of size, transaction volumes, and concentration
- Calculate the impact of different national taxes on the return of an international investment
- Explain the relative advantages of various stock indexes
- Explain how indexes are adjusted for free float
- Describe the components of execution costs: commissions and fees, market impact, and opportunity cost
- Explain ways to reduce execution costs, and discuss the advantages and disadvantages of each
- Describe an American Depositary Receipt (ADR) and differentiate the various forms of ADRs in terms of trading and information supplied by the company listed
- Explain why firms choose to be listed abroad
- Calculate the cost trade-off between buying shares listed abroad and buying ADRs
- State the determinants of the value of a closed-end country fund
- Discuss the advantages of exchange-traded funds (ETFs) and explain the pricing of international ETFs in relation to their net asset value
- Discuss the advantages and disadvantages of the various alternatives to direct international investing

This chapter discusses equity markets worldwide and also presents facts and concepts relevant to executing trades in those markets. The financial specialist is often struck by the differences among stock market organizations across the world. Traditionally, national stock markets have not only different legal and physical organizations but also different transaction methodologies. The international investor must have a minimal familiarity with these technical differences because they influence the execution costs of every transaction. After reviewing some statistics on the market size, liquidity, and concentration, we discuss some practical aspects of international investing. These include taxes, market indexes, and the availability of information. A major practical aspect of international investing is the estimation of execution costs in each market. Understanding the determinants and magnitude of overall transaction costs is very important when implementing a global investment strategy. Getting best execution does not reduce to minimizing commissions and fees; market impact must also be estimated. Investment performance depends on the overall execution costs incurred in implementing a strategy. This chapter concludes with a review of alternatives to direct international investing, which involve the purchase of foreign shares listed at home. These alternatives include American Depositary Receipts (ADRs), closed-end country funds, and open-end funds, especially exchange-traded funds (ETFs). Each of these investment vehicles has advantages and disadvantages relative to directly investing on foreign markets.

Market Differences: A Historical Perspective

Financial paper, in the form of debt obligations, has long been traded in Europe, whereas trading in company shares is relatively recent. The Amsterdam Bourse is usually considered the oldest stock market. The first common stock to be publicly traded in the Netherlands was the famous East Indies Trading Company (Verenigde Oost-Indische Compagnie) in the seventeenth century. But organized stock markets really started in the mid to late eighteenth century. In Paris, a stock market was started on a bridge (Pont au Change). In London, the stock market originated in a tavern; churches and open-air markets were also used as stock markets on the Continent. For example, the Amsterdam Bourse spent some time in the Oude-Kerk (Old Church) and later in the Nieuwe-Kerk (New Church). Most of these European exchanges became recognized as separate markets and were regulated around 1800. The same holds for the United States. However, stock exchanges in Japan and other countries in Asia and most of the Americas are more recent creations.

Historical and cultural differences explain most of the significant differences in stock-trading practices around the world. Rather than engage in a detailed analysis of each national market, this section looks at the major differences in terms of

Jan R. Squires, CFA, and Philip J. Young, CFA, provided important suggestions for this chapter.

market structures and trading procedures. Many of these differences are being eliminated, but some historical perspective helps gain a better understanding of the current working of those stock markets.

Historical Differences in Market Organization

Each stock exchange (bourse) has its own unique characteristics and legal organization, but broadly speaking, all exchanges have evolved from one of three market organization types.

Private Bourses Private stock exchange corporations are founded by private individuals and entities for the purpose of securities trading. Several private stock exchanges may compete within the same country, as in the United States, Japan, and Canada. In other countries, one leading exchange has emerged through either attrition or absorption of its competitors. Although these bourses are private, they are not free of public regulation, but the mix of self-regulation and government supervision is oriented more toward self-regulation than in the public bourses. Historically, these private bourses developed in the British sphere of influence.

Public Bourses The public bourse market structure has its origin in the legislative work of Napoleon I, the French emperor. He designed the *bourse* to be a public institution, with brokers appointed by the government and enjoying a monopoly over all transactions. Commissions are fixed by the state. Brokerage firms are private, but their number is fixed and new brokers are proposed to the state for nomination by the brokers' association. The Paris Bourse followed this model until 1990. Stock exchanges organized under the authority of the state were found in the sphere of influence of Napoleon I: Belgium, France, Spain, Italy, Greece, and some Latin American countries. Most have moved toward a private bourse model.

Bankers' Bourses In some countries, banks are the major, or even the only, securities traders. In Germany, the Banking Act granted a brokerage monopoly to banks. Bankers' bourses were found in the German sphere of influence: Austria, Switzerland, Scandinavia, and the Netherlands. Bankers' bourses may be either private or semipublic organizations, but their chief function is to provide a convenient place for banks to meet. Sometimes trading takes place directly between banks without involving the official bourse at all. Government regulation is imposed both on the bourse itself and directly on the banks. Bankers' bourses suffered from potential conflicts of interests, and more trading transparency was required by international investors. Most bankers' bourses moved to a private bourse model in the 1990s to allow foreign financial intermediaries to become brokers.

Historical Differences in Trading Procedures

Apart from legal structure, numerous other historical differences are found in the operation of national stock markets. The most important differences are in the trading procedures.

Cash Versus Forward Markets In most markets, stocks are traded on a cash basis, and transactions must be settled within a few days (typically three business days after the transaction). To allow more leveraged investment, margin trading is available on most cash markets. In *margin trading*, the investor borrows money (or shares) from a broker to finance a transaction. This is still a cash market transaction, and trade settlement takes place in three days; however, a third party steps in to lend money (shares) to the buyer (seller) to honor a cash transaction commitment.

In contrast, some stock markets were organized as a forward market. This was the case for London and Paris, as well as some markets in Latin America and Asia. In Paris, the settlement date was the end of the month for all transactions made during the month (London settled accounts every two weeks). To simplify the clearing operations, all transactions were settled at the end of the month on the settlement day. This is a periodic settlement system. Of course, a deposit is required to guarantee a position, as on most forward markets. Moreover, the transaction price is fixed at the time of the transaction and remains at this value even if the market price has changed substantially by the settlement time. Settling all accounts once a month greatly simplifies the security clearing system, but it also opens the door to short-term speculation and to frequent misconceptions on the part of foreign investors who are unfamiliar with the technique. Although most forward markets (including London and Paris) have moved to a cash market, they usually have institutionalized procedures to allow investors to trade forward, if desired.

Price-Driven Versus Order-Driven Markets U.S. investors are accustomed to a *continuous* market, whereby transactions take place all day and *market makers* (also called *dealers*) ensure market liquidity at virtually any point in time. The market maker quotes both a *bid* price (the price at which the dealer offers to buy the security) and an *ask* price (the price at which the dealer offers to sell the security). The ask price is sometimes called the *offer price.* These quotes are firm commitments by the market maker to transact at those prices for a specified transaction size. The customer will turn to the market maker who provides the best quote. Of course, market makers adjust their quotes continuously to reflect supply and demand for the security as well as their own inventory. This type of market is often referred to as a *dealer market.* It is also known as a *price-driven* market (or *quote-driven* market), because market makers publicly post their bid–ask prices to induce orders. For example, NASDAQ is a dealer market.[1]

---

[1] The New York Stock Exchange (NYSE) has a unique system in which each stock is allocated to one specialist who acts both as a dealer and as an auctioneer. As a dealer, a specialist posts bid and ask quotes and uses his or her own capital to buy or sell securities (under strict regulations). As an auctioneer, a specialist maintains the order book of all orders that are submitted.

In many other markets and countries, however, active market makers do not exist, and the supply and demand for securities are matched directly in an *auction market.* Because the quantities demanded and supplied are a function of the transaction price, a price will exist that equilibrates demand and supply. In a traditional auction market, liquidity requires that an asset be traded only once or a few times per day. This is known as a *call auction* or *fixing* procedure, whereby orders are batched together in an order book until the auction when they are executed at a single price that equilibrates demand and supply. This auction price maximizes trade volume. In the past, many stock markets used an open *criée* (outcry) system in which brokers would negotiate loudly until a price was found that would equilibrate buy and sell orders (quietness is restored). All these stock markets have moved to computerized trading systems in which buy-and-sell orders are entered on the computer trading system, which matches them directly. An auction market is also known as an *order-driven market* because all traders publicly post their orders, and the transaction price is the result of the equilibrium of supply and demand. Although a single call auction provides excellent liquidity at one point in time, it makes trading at other times difficult. Hence, the market- making function is being developed on all call auction markets (e.g., Paris, Tokyo, or Frankfurt) to allow the possibility of trading throughout the day.

Automation on the Major Stock Exchanges

Trading on a floor where participants noisily meet is increasingly being replaced by computerized trading. Automation allows more efficient handling of orders, especially a large number of small orders. Competition across national stock exchanges and the increased volume of trading hastened the adoption of computerized systems, including price quotation, order routing, and automatic order matching. The design of the automated systems reflects the historical and cultural heritage of the national market. Automated trading systems have followed two different paths, depending on whether the traditional market organization was dominated by dealers making the market or by brokers acting as agents in an auction system.

Price-Driven and Order-Driven Systems The U.S. NASDAQ is a typical *price-driven* system. The automated system posts firm quotes by market makers. There is no centralized book of *limit orders.* When posting a quote, the market maker does not know what trades it will generate. In a price-driven system, a market maker is placing the equivalent of limit orders: a buy limit order representing his bid and a sell limit order representing his ask.

At the other extreme, auction markets, such as Paris, Frankfurt, or Tokyo (and most other markets), have put in place electronic order-driven systems. The computer stores all orders, which become public knowledge. All limit orders that have not been executed are stored in a central order book. A new order is immediately matched with the book of orders previously submitted (see Example 5.1). The central limit order book is the hub of these automated systems. Viewing all standing orders, a trader

EXAMPLE 5.1 ORDER-DRIVEN MARKET

LVMH (Moët Hennesy Louis Vuitton) is a French firm listed on the Paris Bourse. You can access the central limit order book directly on the Internet and find the following information (the limit prices for sell orders are ask prices and those for buy orders are bid prices):

Sell Orders		Buy Orders	
Quantity	Limit	Limit	Quantity
1,000	58	49	2,000
3,000	54	48	500
1,000	52	47	1,000
1,000	51	46	2,000
500	50	44	10,000

You wish to buy 1,000 shares and enter a market order to buy those shares. A market order will be executed against the best matching order. At what price will you buy the shares?

SOLUTION

Unless a new sell order is entered at a price below 51 before your order is executed, you will buy 500 shares at 50 and 500 shares at 51.

knows exactly what trades will be executed if she enters a new order. Market makers provide liquidity by entering limit buy-and-sell orders in the order book. The highest limit bid and the lowest limit offer act as the bid and ask prices in a price-driven market.

To improve liquidity, most order-driven markets have retained periodic call auctions. There is a fixing at the opening of the market, where all orders that arrived before opening are stored and the opening price is set through a call auction.[2] In Frankfurt, call auctions take place periodically throughout the day, at prespecified times other than opening and closing. At the time of the call auction, the continuous trading of the stock on XETRA is interrupted. (XETRA is a trading platform that includes all stocks on the Deutsche Boerse.) In a *pretrading* phase, traders can submit limit and market orders, which are accumulated in the order book. At auction time, orders are automatically crossed (matched) at a price that maximizes the volume of trading. In Tokyo, a call auction system, called *itayose,* is used to establish prices at the start of the morning and afternoon sessions (the market closes for lunch). During the sessions, a continuous auction is used for new orders. This auction system, called *zaraba,* is an order-matching method and does not require the intervention of a market maker.

The NYSE has developed a hybrid market that integrates traditional floor trading with electronic auction trading. The electronic system allows the order to find the best transaction price on the NYSE or elsewhere.

[2] On the NYSE, the opening price is determined through a call auction.

Advantages and Risks of Each System Automation brings many improvements in the speed and costs of trading. An order-driven system requires little human intervention and is therefore less costly to run. Cost considerations have pushed all markets in this direction. Only some U.S. stock markets have retained a price-driven model. Markets with lesser transaction volumes have found it more efficient to adopt order-driven electronic trading systems. For example, London had a price-driven market with competitive market makers. Cost-efficiency considerations caused it to move to an automated order-driven system called SETS (Stock Exchange Electronic Trading Service) at the end of the twentieth century.[3] Market makers enter their bid-and-ask quotes directly in the order book in the form of limit orders. Most emerging stock markets have adopted an order-driven electronic trading system.

The cost of running the trading system, however, is only one component of the transaction cost borne by investors. Investors try to get the best execution price for each trade. This raises the question: Which market structure provides the best liquidity and lowest execution costs? Theoretical and experimental research suggests that the market design affects trader behavior, transaction prices, and market efficiency. In real life, the answer depends on the market environment, and there is no clear-cut conclusion. An electronic auction market is cheaper to operate, but that could be at the expense of liquidity—hence, trading could be more costly because of overall execution costs, including price impact.[4] Domowitz (2001) suggests that the public dissemination of the electronic order book in order-driven markets allows traders to monitor liquidity and provide liquidity at a lower cost than in price-driven markets.

A drawback of electronic order-driven systems is their inability to execute large trades. In the absence of active market makers, trading a *block* (a large transaction) on an automated order-driven system is difficult. Because of the lack of depth in the market, it may take a long time before the block is traded. This will leave the trader who discloses the block on the system fully exposed to the risk that new information might hurt him unless he continuously updates the limit on the block order. This is the risk of being "picked off"—that is, having an order accepted at a price no longer desired by the trader at the time of the transaction. Blocks are generally traded away from the automated system. This is often called *upstairs trading*. Order-driven systems have developed in part because they are much cheaper to operate than traditional dealers' markets. However, market makers are still needed for trading large blocks.

Another drawback of a continuous order-driven system, in the absence of developed market making, is the danger in placing *market orders* (i.e., orders with no price limits). In the absence of competitive market makers providing liquidity, a sell market order will be immediately crossed with the highest buy limit order, which could be very far from the lowest sell limit order. The Tokyo Stock Exchange

---

[3] Smaller and many foreign companies, however, are traded on an automated price-driven system called SEAQ (Stock Exchange Automated Quotation System).

[4] Conrad, Johnson, and Wahal (2004) find some evidence that realized execution costs are lower on electronic trading systems for U.S. stocks. Using data up to 2000, Huang (2002) finds that electronic communication network quoted spreads are smaller than dealer spreads for NASDAQ stocks. However, the period of study was prior to the U.S. adoption of decimal quotations, which reduced spreads markedly.

has a special procedure to limit this risk. Other markets are trying to implement rules protecting market orders. This is typically true for less active stocks, in which market making would help provide liquidity.

Any automated trading system exposes one party to transparency risk. It forces one side of the transaction to expose itself first and, therefore, run the risk of being picked off. In all cases, a limit order gives a free trading option to other market participants. In an order-driven market, the trader who submits the order implicitly gives the free option to the rest of the market. In a price-driven market, it is the dealer posting a firm quote who gives this free option, as shown in Example 5.2. Of course, the option holder depends on the dealer to deliver in a non-automated system, and "backing away" (reneging) can be a problem.

EXAMPLE 5.2 EXPOSITION RISK IN TWO TYPES OF MARKETS

LVMH is traded on the Paris Bourse, and the last transaction was at 50 euros per share. An investor entered on the French electronic trading system NSC (Nouveau Système Cotation) a limit order to sell LVMH shares at 51 euros while the market price was 50.

LVMH is also traded as an ADR on NASDAQ. One ADR represents one-fifth of an LVMH French share (so 5 ADRs equal 1 LVMH share). The exchange rate is one dollar per euro, and the ADR price is quoted by a market maker at 10–10.20. Assume that the exchange rate remains constant over time.

Suppose that favorable information suddenly arrives that justifies a higher price for LVMH—say, 55 euros. Who are the parties exposed to losses on the Paris Bourse and on NASDAQ if they do not react immediately?

SOLUTION

- On the Paris Bourse, informed market participants have an option worth four euros per share, and the investor who has a standing order in the electronic order book gets picked off (the informed participant can buy at 51 euros a share now worth 55 euros).
- On NASDAQ, the market maker posts a firm bid–ask quote for LVMH of 10–10.20 for the dollar ADR, which is equivalent for the French share of LVMH quoted in euros to a quote of 50–51. Under the same scenario, informed market participants suddenly get a free option worth 0.8 dollar per ADR or four euros per French share (they can buy at 10.2 dollars from the market maker a share now worth 11 dollars). In a price-driven market, dealers run the risk of being picked off.

The danger of automation is that market liquidity may be reduced because dealers (in a price-driven system) or public investors (in an order-driven system) may be less willing to publicly place limit orders.

Electronic Communication Networks and Electronic Crossing Networks (ECNs) Some electronic trading systems have developed alongside official exchanges. They tend to be privately owned and offer trading on stocks of one market or of a region. Electronic communication networks and electronic crossing networks are both often called ECNs, although they are quite different.

Electronic communication networks are order-driven systems, in which the limit order book plays a central role as previously described. Many of them coexist in the United States. Virt-x is a pan-European ECN specialized in blue chips.

Electronic crossing networks are different systems. These crossing systems anonymously match the buy and sell orders of a pool of participants, generally institutional investors and broker-dealers (see Example 5.3). Participants enter market orders,[5] which are crossed at prespecified times (once or a few times every day) at prices determined in the primary market for the security. The trade price is the mid-market quote, the midpoint between the bid and the ask, observed on the primary market at the prespecified time. POSIT is a major electronic crossing network in the United States, but there are many others in the United States, Asia, and Europe.

EXAMPLE 5.3 CROSSING

Market orders for LVMH have been entered on a crossing network for European shares. There is one order from Participant A to buy 100,000 shares, one order from Participant B to sell 50,000 shares, and one order from Participant C to sell 70,000 shares. Assume that orders were entered in that chronological order and that the network gives priority to the oldest orders. At the time specified for the crossing session, LVMH transacts at 51 euros on the Paris Bourse, its primary market.

1. What trades would take place on the crossing network?
2. Assume now that all the orders are AON (all or nothing), meaning that the whole block has to be traded at the same price. What trades would take place?

SOLUTION

1. A total of 100,000 shares would be exchanged at 51 euros. Participant A would buy 100,000. Participants B and C would sell 50,000. Participant B's order has priority, so Participant C's order would not be executed entirely (20,000 shares remain unsold).
2. There is no way that the AON condition could be achieved for the three orders, so, no trade would take place.

---

[5] Participants also can specify various constraints on their orders.

Crossing networks present two advantages for large orders of institutional investors:

- *Low transaction costs*: The trade is executed at mid-market prices, so there is no market impact or bid–ask spread, even for large trades.
- *Anonymity*: The identity of the buyers and sellers, and the magnitude of their order, will not be revealed, so there is little exposure risk.

On the other hand, crossing networks have a distinct disadvantage:

- *No trading immediacy*: The trader must wait until the crossing session time to execute a trade, and the trade takes place only if there are offsetting orders entered by other participants. Only a small proportion of orders are executed at each crossing session. The order has to wait in the system or needs to be worked through other market mechanisms.

Basically, electronic crossing networks allow a substantial reduction in execution cost for large trades, to the detriment of immediacy.

Cross-Border Alliances of Stock Exchanges Fragmentation of national stock markets, especially the smaller ones, is a hindrance to international investors, who often think in terms of regions rather than individual countries. Periodically, plans for cross-border mergers of national stock exchanges are drafted. But most of these projects collapse, in part because the cultural heritage of different trading, legal, and regulatory systems make it very difficult to harmonize trading systems. The canceled merger between the London Stock Exchange and the Deutsche Boerse is a vivid example. As of 2007, Euronext was the only successful merger between Paris, Amsterdam, Brussels, and Lisbon. But the process of rapprochement between bourses accelerated in the mid 2000s. OMX progressively became the trading platform of most Nordic and Baltic exchanges. As of 2007, OMX includes the Copenhagen, Helsinki, Iceland, Stockholm, Tallinn, Riga, and Vilnius stock exchanges. Euronext and the NYSE merged in 2007; in the same year, Deutsche Boerse purchased 5 percent of the Bombay Stock Exchanges, and the Tokyo Stock Exchange announced alliances with the NYSE and the London Stock Exchange. The process of consolidation among stock exchanges is likely to continue. As we shall see later, stock markets also internationalize by listing shares of foreign companies.

A related hindrance is the fragmentation of settlement systems. The multiplicity of national settlement systems adds to the cost of international investing. But a consolidation of settlement systems is taking place, especially in Europe. A common depository and counterparty platform has been developed around Euronext and Euroclear, the international securities clearinghouse. So, trades in several European stock markets, as well as international bonds, use the same system, Clearnet. Another platform, Clearstream, has been created around the Deutsche Boerse from the former international securities clearinghouse, Cedel.

Some Statistics

Market Size

Relative national market capitalizations give some indication of the importance of each country for global investors. Market-capitalization weights are used in the commonly used global benchmarks; hence, market sizes guide global investment strategies.

Developed and emerging markets are usually classified in two different asset classes. Although they are somewhat arbitrary, and some countries have been moved from the status of emerging to developed in the recent past, these classifications are still widely used by investors. In the statistics given below, we adopt the widely used classification of Morgan Stanley Capital International.

Developed Markets The U.S. stock exchanges are the largest exchanges in the world. It is worth noting that the U.S. capital market is very large compared to the U.S. economy. The U.S. stock market capitalization (cap) is much larger than the annual U.S. gross domestic product (GDP). Britain also has a market cap almost double its GDP, but the corresponding figure for France or Germany is below 80 percent. This difference between the United States and continental Europe has several explanations. Most U.S. firms prefer to go public, whereas in France, as well as in the rest of Europe, tradition calls for maintaining private ownership as much as possible. In many European countries, corporations are undercapitalized and rely heavily on bank financing. Germany is a typical example because banks finance corporations extensively, thereby reducing the need for outside equity capital. In Europe, banks tend to provide corporations with all financial services, assisting them in both their commercial needs and their long-term debt and equity financing. In contrast to banks in the United States, it is common for European banks to own shares of their client companies. U.S. companies, especially small- and medium-sized ones, tend to go public and raise capital in the marketplace, thereby increasing the public stock market cap. In other countries, many large firms are still government-owned and therefore are not listed on the capital markets. In France, for example, portions of the telecommunication, arms manufacturing, banking, and transportation industries are partly owned by the government. Countries such as France, Italy, and Germany progressively evolve along the U.S. model, and their weights in a global index are likely to rise.

The size of the world stock market has grown dramatically since the 1970s, passing the $50 trillion mark at the end of 2000. It has multiplied by approximately 50 since the early 1970s. Developed markets had a total market cap of some $44 trillion at the end of 2006, while emerging markets cap reached $6.8 trillion. The market sizes of the largest developed stock markets (with market cap of $1 trillion or more in 2006) are given in Exhibit 5.1. Japan, the United Kingdom, and Euronext have the largest markets outside of the United States. Currency movements induce changes in the total size and geographical breakdown of the world market. A drop in the value of the dollar reduces the market share of U.S. stocks; the dollar value

EXHIBIT 5.1

Market Sizes of Developed Markets *Billions of U.S. dollars, end of 2006*

NYSE	15,421
Japan	4,614
NASDAQ	3,865
United Kingdom	3,794
Euronext	3,708
Hong Kong, China	1,715
Canada	1,701
Germany	1,638
Spain	1,323
Switzerland	1,212
OMX Nordic Exchange	1,123
Australia	1,096
Italy	1,027
Others	1,636
Total	**43,872**

Source: World Federation of Exchanges.

of non-U.S. stocks increases by the amount of the dollar depreciation, assuming that the stocks' values in domestic currency do not change and that the dollar value of U.S. stocks stays constant. The share of U.S. markets decreased from almost two-thirds of the world market cap in 1972 to only one-third by the early 1990s. It moved back up to over 50 percent after 2000, partly because of a big drop in Asian markets. At the end of 2006 it stood at 45 percent of developed market cap and 39 percent of total world market cap. Meanwhile, the shares of European and Asian markets in total world market cap are roughly equal at 30 percent.

The figure for Japan is somewhat inflated by the practice of cross-holding of stocks among publicly traded Japanese companies and financial institutions (*mochiai*). A similar feature can be found in South Korea, where companies within large conglomerates (*chaebols*) are linked with extensive equity cross-holding. Index providers are trying to adjust the market cap weights used in the index. This is part of the so-called free-float adjustment, which attempts to eliminate the effects of cross-holdings, as illustrated in Example 5.4.

Emerging Markets The 1980s saw the emergence and rapid growth of stock markets in many developing countries. In Africa, stock markets opened in Egypt, Morocco, and the Ivory Coast, but with limited growth. Growth has been somewhat faster in Latin America, especially in Brazil and Mexico. The most spectacular change, however, has been witnessed in Asia. Stock markets have grown rapidly in China, India, Indonesia, Malaysia, Thailand, South Korea, and Taiwan (China).

EXAMPLE 5.4 EXAMPLE OF ADJUSTMENT FOR CROSS-HOLDING

Three companies belong to a group and are listed on the stock exchange:

- Company A owns 30 percent of Company B.
- Company B owns 20 percent of Company C.
- Company C owns 10 percent of Company A.

Each company has a total market cap of 100 million.

You wish to adjust for cross-holding to reflect the weights of these companies in a market cap–weighted index. What adjustment would you make to reflect the free float?

SOLUTION

The apparent market cap of these three companies taken together is 300 million. But because of their cross-holding, there is some double counting. The usual free-float adjustment would be to retain only the portion that is not owned by other companies within the group. Hence, the adjusted market capitalization is:

$$90 + 70 + 80 = 240\,\text{million}$$

EXHIBIT 5.2

Sizes of Emerging Markets *Billion of U.S. dollars, end of 2006*

China	1,146	Turkey	162
Korea	834	Israel	162
India	819	Poland	149
South Africa	711	Thailand	140
Brazil	710	Indonesia	139
Taiwan, China	595	Egypt	93
Mexico	348	Other Europe/Africa/Middle East	114
Malaysia	236	Other Latin America	150
Chile	174	Other Asia	81
		Total	**6,763**

Source: World Federation of Exchanges.

The emerging market crisis of 1997 stopped that growth, but growth picked up again in 2002. We see in Exhibit 5.2 that the total capitalization of emerging markets represents over 13 percent of the world stock market cap at the end of 2006.

Liquidity

Transaction volume gives indications on the liquidity of each market. In a liquid market, investors can be more active and design various arbitrage strategies. Some markets are large via their market cap, and hence their weight in a global index, but with little turnover. Illiquidity tends to imply higher transaction costs. Investors measuring performance relative to a global benchmark will tend to be more passive on such illiquid markets.

Exhibit 5.3 gives the turnover ratio of major markets computed as the ratio of the annual transaction volume to the market cap at year-end 2006. This is a simple indicator of the liquidity on each market. It is sometimes called *share turnover velocity*. Depending on market activity, these figures can vary widely from one year to the next, but it is apparent that some national markets are more active than others. The ranking of countries based on the volume of transactions differs slightly from that based on market cap.

In fact, the turnover ratio varies significantly over time. For example, the transaction volume in Japan soared in the late 1980s to surpass that of the NYSE, and the Japanese turnover ratio became a multiple of the U.S. ratio, but it dropped dramatically in the 1990s. Therefore, comparison of national market liquidity based on this variable could lead to different conclusions, depending on the years observed.

In addition, the transaction volume on some emerging markets is very large relative to their size. Transaction volumes in Korea or Taiwan (China) are sometimes

EXHIBIT 5.3

Annual Turnover on Major Stock Markets

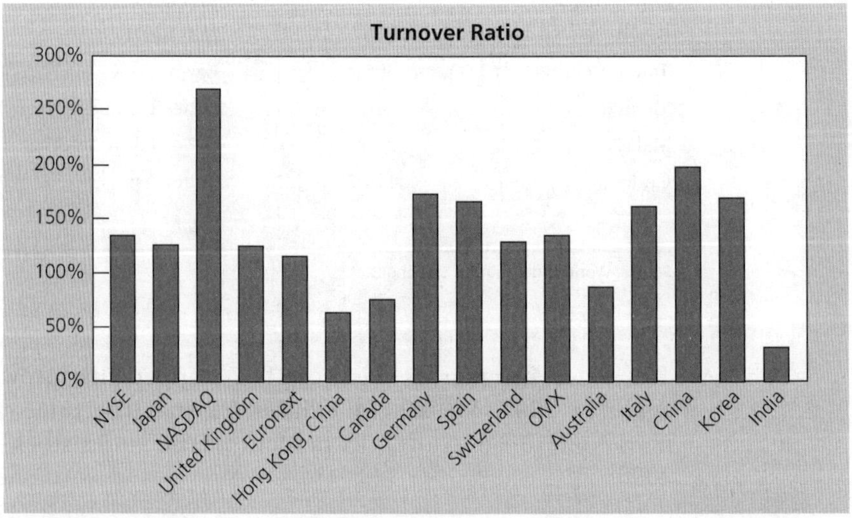

Source: World Federation of Exchanges.

larger than that of any developed market except the United States. But this is not the case for many other emerging markets that are quite illiquid.

Concentration

Another informative statistic is the degree of concentration of the market cap found in the major markets. It is important that investors know whether a national market is made up of a diversity of firms or concentrated in a few large firms. Institutional investors are reluctant to invest in small firms, fearing that they offer poor liquidity. Also, it is easier for the investor to track the performance of a market index, which is usually market cap–weighted, if it is dominated by a few large issues. On the other hand, a market dominated by a few large firms provides fewer opportunities for risk diversification and active portfolio strategies.

As shown in Exhibit 5.4, the NYSE and Tokyo Stock Exchange are diverse markets in which the top ten firms represent less than 20 percent of total market cap. In the United States, the largest firm represents less than 3 percent of the capitalization for the NYSE. At the other end of the spectrum, the top ten Swiss multinational firms account for some 70 percent of the Swiss stock exchange. Nokia is larger than the sum of all other Finnish firms.

Some Practical Aspects

A few practical aspects must be taken into account when investing abroad.

EXHIBIT 5.4

Share of the Ten Largest Listed Companies in the National Market Capitalization

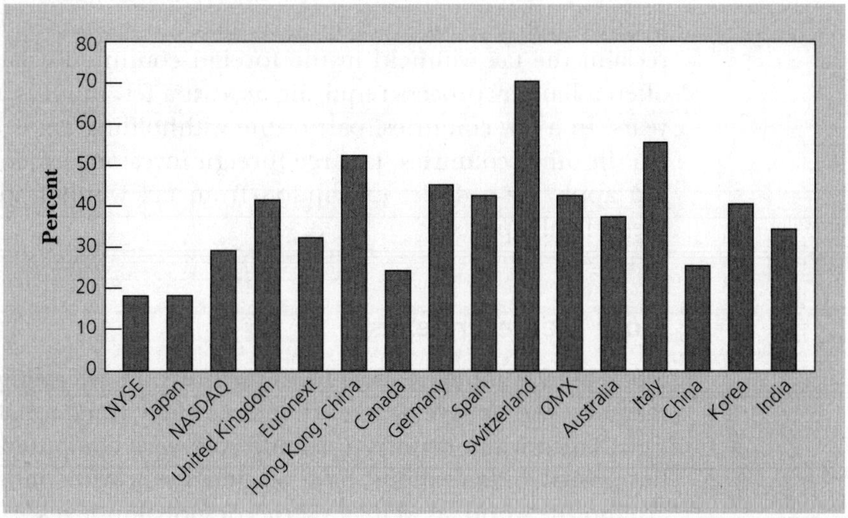

Source: World Federation of Exchanges.

Tax Aspects

Taxes can add to the cost of international investment. Foreign investments may be taxed in two locations: the investor's country and the investment's country. Taxes are applied in any of three areas: transactions, capital gains, and income (dividends, etc.).

Some countries impose a tax on transactions. The United Kingdom has retained a stamp tax of 0.5 percent on purchases of domestic securities (but not on sales). Most countries have eliminated, or drastically reduced, such transaction taxes. In countries where brokers charge a commission rather than trade on net prices, a tax proportional to the commission is sometimes charged. For example, France levies a 19.6 percent value-added tax (VAT) on commissions (not on the transaction value), just as on any service. Market makers are usually exempted from these taxes when they trade for their own accounts.

Capital gains are normally taxed where the investor resides, regardless of the national origin of the investment. In other words, domestic and international investments are taxed the same way.

Income on foreign stocks is paid from the legal entity of one country to a resident of another country. This transaction often poses a conflict of jurisdiction, because both countries may want to impose a tax on that income. The international convention on taxing income is to make certain that taxes are paid by the investor in at least one country, which is why withholding taxes are levied on dividend payments. Because many investors are also taxed on income received in their country of residence, double taxation can result from this practice but is avoided through a network of international tax treaties. An investor receives a dividend net of withholding tax plus a tax credit from the foreign government. The investor's country of residence imposes its tax on the gross foreign dividends, but the amount of this tax is reduced by the withholding tax credit. In other words, the foreign tax credit is applied against the home taxes. Tax rules change frequently, but the typical withholding tax rate is 15 percent of dividends.

To a tax-free investor, such as a pension fund, this tax credit is worthless because the investor does not pay taxes at home. In this case, the investor can reclaim the tax withheld in the foreign country. Reclaiming a withholding tax is often a lengthy process requiring at least a few months and even up to a couple of years. In a few countries, part of the withholding tax is kept by the country of origin. In other countries, tax-free foreign investors, especially public pension funds, can apply for a direct exemption from tax withholding. Example 5.5 illustrates these fiscal aspects.

Stock Market Indexes

Stock market indexes allow us to measure the average performance of a national market. One or several market indexes may track a national market at any given time. Historically, country stock indexes were computed by the local stock market, but global organizations have started to provide indexes for national markets around the world, as well as a series of global indexes.

EXAMPLE 5.5 EXAMPLE OF TAX ADJUSTMENTS

A U.S. investor buys 100 shares of Heineken listed in Amsterdam for 40 euros. She goes through a U.S. broker, and the current exchange rate is 1 euro = 1.1 U.S. dollars. Her total cost is $4,400, or $44 per share of Heineken (40 × 1.1 $ per €). Three months later, a gross dividend of €2 is paid (15 percent withholding tax), and she decides to sell the Heineken shares. Each share is now worth 38 euros, and the current exchange rate is euro = 1.2 U.S. dollars because the euro has sharply risen against the dollar. The same exchange rate applied on the dividend payment date. What are the cash flows received in U.S. dollars?

SOLUTION

The cash flows are as follows:

Dividend Payment Minus Withholding Tax ($/€ = 1.2)

	Net Dividend	Tax Credit
In euros per share	1.70	0.30
In dollars per share	2.04	0.36
Net in dollars (100 shares)	204	36

Sale of Heineken Shares ($/€ = 1.2)

In euros per share	38
In dollars per share	45.6
Net in dollars (100 shares)	4560

Our investor has made a capital gain of $160 ($4,560 – $4,400), which will be taxed in the United States at the U.S. capital gains tax rate. She will also declare a total gross dividend of $240 as income, which will be taxed at her income tax rate. She can deduct from her income tax a tax credit of $36, however, thanks to the United States–Netherlands tax treaty.

Domestic Stock Indexes Domestic investors usually prefer indexes that are calculated and published locally. Most of these are broadly based, market value–weighted indexes. Each company is assigned an index weight proportional to its market cap. Market value–weighted indexes are true market portfolio indexes in the sense that when the index portfolio is held by an investor, it truly represents movements in the market. This is not true of equal-weighted indexes, such as the U.S. Dow Jones 30 Industrial Average (DJIA) or the Japanese Nikkei 225 Stock Average. The DJIA adds up the stock price of 30 corporations. Each company is assigned an index weight proportional to its market price, when computing the index percentage price movement. For example, the return on a share with a price of $100 will have ten times more importance than the return on a share with a price of $10. So the weighting method is quite artificial. Not only is the DJIA narrowly based, but also its composition is somewhat arbitrary; for example, IBM was removed from the index in the 1970s because its price was too high compared with the other 29 corporations. Many stock exchanges have introduced indexes based on a small number of large stocks. There are two reasons for this trend toward narrow-based indexes. First, investors like to get instantaneous information and market movements by accessing Internet or information providers such as Reuters or Bloomberg. Meaningful market indicators must be computed using the most actively traded stocks, not those that trade infrequently. Second, exchanges have introduced *derivatives* (futures, options) on these stock indexes. Dealers in those derivative markets prefer to have an index that is based on a small number of actively traded stocks. Such an index makes it much easier to hedge their derivatives exposure in the cash stock market. Most stock indexes published do not include dividends, although some countries also report dividend-adjusted indexes.

Because some stocks are listed on several exchanges, some companies appear in different national indexes. For example, the S&P 500 used to include some very large non-U.S. companies.

Global Stock Indexes Morgan Stanley Capital International (MSCI) has published international market cap–weighted indexes since 1970. MSCI now publishes country indexes for all developed as well as numerous emerging markets, in addition to a variety of regional and global indexes. The World index includes only developed markets, while the All Country World index includes both developed and emerging markets. The MSCI index of non-U.S. stock markets has been extensively used as a benchmark of foreign equity portfolios by U.S. investors; it is called the *index EAFE* (for Europe, Australasia, Far East). Besides market cap–weighted indexes, MSCI also publishes indexes with various weighting schemes (e.g., GDP weights) and with full currency hedging. Global industry and style indexes are also available.

FTSE, created as a joint venture of the *Financial Times* and the London Stock Exchange, has published international indexes since 1987. The most important international indexes are the World index, the Europe index, the Pacific Basin index, and the Europe and Pacific index. Country indexes are provided for developed and emerging markets, as well as numerous industrial and regional indexes. Global industry indexes are available.

Other series of global indexes are also available. Dow Jones publishes, in collaboration with Wilshire Associates, a series of global indexes called the Dow Jones Wilshire Global Index that covers developed and emerging markets. The series includes country and industry indexes calculated daily. S&P publishes an S&P Global 1200 index of developed markets as well as various subindexes, including the S&P 350 Europe index, intended to be the European counterpart of the S&P 500.

The introduction of the euro has created intensive competition among index suppliers. They all try to provide a European index that will be used as a benchmark by global money managers. Besides the well-established indexes of MSCI and FTSE,

Dow Jones has launched a series of European indexes in collaboration with the French, German, and Swiss stock exchanges, which are named DJ STOXX. The EURO DJ STOXX 50 is a widely used index of Eurozone blue chips (countries having adopted the euro). Other international blue-chip indexes are published by Dow Jones.

Emerging market indexes are available from the index providers mentioned previously/(MSCI, FTSE, Dow Jones, S&P). In the past the International Finance Corporation (IFC) of the World Bank published popular emerging market indexes. Standard and Poor's acquired its emerging market database and now performs the calculation of various S&P/IFC indexes. The Global index series (S&P/IFCG) is the broadest possible indicator of market movements, and the coverage exceeds 75 percent of local market capitalizations. Weights are adjusted for government and cross-holdings. The Investable index series (S&P/IFCI) is designed to represent the market that is legally and practically available to foreign investors. The Frontier index series tracks small and illiquid markets.

All these global indexes are widely used by international money managers for asset allocation decisions and performance measurements (benchmarks). They differ in terms of coverage and weights. Hence, these global indexes can have significant differences in performance. Besides deciding on which company and country should be included in the respective indexes, the provider must decide on the market-cap weights to be used. Because of cross-holding, government ownership, and/or regulations applying to foreign investors, the amount of market value available to foreign investors (the free float) can differ significantly from the market cap that can be obtained by multiplying the number of shares issued by their market price. Most indexes now perform an adjustment so that the weight of each security represents its free float.

Not all indexes are intended as investable benchmarks tracking an overall market. Specific European indexes have been launched, on which derivatives can be traded. They must comprise a small number of highly liquid stocks, so that market makers in the derivatives can easily hedge their exposure on the stock markets. The DJ Euro Stoxx 50 (50 leading Eurozone stocks) and the FTSE Eurotop 100 (100 leading European stocks) are European indexes on which futures, options, and ETFs are traded.

Which Index to Use? Local indexes are widely used by domestic investors. Private investors often prefer these indexes over country indexes of international providers, such as MSCI or FTSE, for several reasons:

- In most cases, the local indexes have been used for several decades.
- Local indexes are used for derivative contracts (futures, options) traded in that country.
- Local indexes are calculated immediately and are available at the same time as stock market quotations on all electronic price services.
- Local indexes are available every morning in all the newspapers throughout the world.

- The risk of error in prices and capital adjustment is possibly minimized in local indexes by the fact that all calculations are done locally, with excellent information available on the spot.

Institutional investors, on the other hand, prefer to use the MSCI, FTSE, or other international indexes for the following reasons:

- The institutional investors do not need up-to-the-minute indexes.
- The indexes on all stock markets are available in a central location, whereas local indexes must be drawn from several locations.
- All international indexes are calculated in a single consistent manner, allowing for direct comparisons between markets.
- MSCI and FTSE provide global or regional indexes (World, Europe, EAFE), which international money managers need to measure overall performance.
- They also provide indexes that include dividends.

The choice of index is important. In any given year, the performance between two indexes for the same stock market can differ by as much as several percentage points.

Information

The information available from different countries and companies varies in quality. Accounting standards differ across countries (see Chapter 6), but most developed countries are now enforcing accounting standards of increased quality. Under the pressure of international investors, companies are learning that they must report accurate information on their accounts and prospects in a timely fashion. The situation can be worse for smaller firms in countries where there is less tradition of information transparency, and it can become worrisome in some emerging markets.

In some emerging countries, the earnings forecasts announced by companies that become publicly listed are totally unverifiable. A notable case is China. The rapid move from a centrally planned economy to a socialist market economy system means that the notion of accounting at the firm level is a new concept. State-owned companies have been listed on Chinese or foreign stock exchanges but have no tradition of having separate accounts, and therefore they have problems trying to identify earnings to shareholders during a given time period. It is equally difficult to assess who is the legal owner of some of the assets of a Chinese firm; the state, the province, and the municipality all lay some claim on existing firms' assets, and legal property titles do not exist historically. Shanghai Petrochemical Co., for example, was the largest company to be introduced on the NYSE in 1993. Its value is clearly a function of its properties and equipment. A letter from America Appraisal Hong Kong Ltd., included in the 1993 listing prospectus, illustrates that reliable information on companies from emerging markets is sometimes difficult to get:

> We have relied to a considerable extent on information provided by you. . . . As all the properties are situated in the People's Republic of China, we have not searched the original documents to verify ownership. . . . All dimensions, measurements and areas are approximate. We have inspected the exterior and, when possible, the interior of all the properties valued. However, no structural survey has been made and we are therefore unable to report as to whether the properties are or not free of rot, infestation or any other structural defects.

Given the uncertainty about a company's information, it is not surprising that its valuation is a matter of highly subjective judgment. The uncertainty surrounding companies' information is damaging. Most emerging markets trade at low price–earnings ratios compared with developed markets with similar or lesser growth potential. Local authorities and the management of listed firms have come to realize that stricter standards must be applied to the timely release of reliable information. Many countries are adopting accounting standards that conform to the International Accounting Standards or U.S. *generally accepted accounting principles (GAAP),* but progress in their implementation can only be slow.

Execution Costs

The importance of execution costs, also referred to as *transaction costs,* is sometimes overlooked in portfolio management. These costs vary among countries and should be taken into account in active global investment strategies. Execution costs can reduce the expected return and diversification benefits of an international strategy. The difference in return between a paper portfolio and a managed portfolio can be significant. In theory, forecasted costs should be subtracted from expected return before implementing any active strategies. This is all the more important when investing in high-cost countries such as emerging countries. Portfolio managers must gain a good understanding of the determinants of execution costs and should develop some ability to measure them for trades worldwide.

A manager should try to get the best execution for each trade. *Best execution* refers to executing client transactions so that total cost is most favorable to the client under the particular circumstances at the time. Best execution is an objective even though it is difficult to quantify. Execution costs take many forms, some explicit and easily measurable, others implicit and more difficult to measure.

Components of Execution Costs

Costs can be listed in decreasing reliability of estimation, as described in the following three sections.

Commissions, Fees, and Taxes Commissions paid to brokers are generally negotiated. They depend on the characteristics of the trade (market, liquidity of the stock, size of the order, etc.) and of the market mechanism used (see next section).

Some additional fees are generally paid to compensate for various services, including post-trade settlement costs. As discussed, some taxes are also levied in various countries.

The payment of commissions to brokers often allows access to the broker's research and other services. Therefore, some of the cost is an indirect way to obtain various services beyond direct trading execution. In theory, one should separate the direct dealing cost component and the cost of other services provided ("soft dollars").

All these costs are explicit and easily measurable, but getting the best execution is not equivalent to minimizing commissions and fees.

Market Impact Executing a transaction will generally have an impact on the price of the security traded. Market impact can be defined as the difference between the actual execution price and the market price that would have prevailed had the manager not sought to trade the security. For example, an order to buy that is large relative to the normal transaction volume in that security will move the price up, at least temporarily. So, one must estimate the market impact of any trade.

In a price-driven system, the bid–ask spread is a major component of the market impact.[6] However, a bid–ask spread is generally quoted for a maximum number of shares that the market maker is willing to trade and is adjusted upward for large transactions, so a large order will move quoted prices. When investing directly on an order-driven market, there is no bid–ask quote and the market impact has to be estimated from market data. Measuring the overall price impact is a difficult exercise because the price that would have prevailed if the transaction had not taken place, the benchmark price, is not observable. A traditional method to estimate this benchmark price is to compute the volume-weighted average price (VWAP) on the day of the transaction. The idea is that an average of the prices before and after the transaction is an unbiased estimate of the benchmark price. The VWAP method is further discussed below. Market impact is measured as the percentage difference between the execution price and this benchmark price. It must be stressed that the market impact is highly dependent on the order size, market liquidity for the security traded, and the speed of execution desired by the investor. Institutional investors often trade securities in order sizes which are a significant percentage, and even multiple, of the typical daily trading volume for that security. Hence, the market impact for institutional trades can be high, especially if the investor requires immediacy of trading.

Opportunity Cost The costs mentioned in the preceding section are incurred on an executed trade. But there is also an opportunity cost in case of nonexecution. This opportunity cost can be defined as the loss (or gain) incurred as the result of delay in

---

[6] This is also the case when transacting on an order-driven market but asking the broker for a firm bid–ask quotation.

completion of, or failure to complete in full, a transaction following an initial decision to trade. Opportunity costs can be significant for investors using crossing networks or order-driven systems, in which the risk of nonexecution or partial execution is significant. On any market, it could take hours or days to execute a large trade, and the opportunity cost can be significant in case of an adverse market movement over that period (for example, a price rise in the case of a buy order). Because of this opportunity cost, an active manager is reluctant to complete a trade over a long time period. The information on which the manager bases his trading decision could be quickly reflected in market prices, that is, before the trade is completed. Furthermore, there is a risk of information leakage, whereby the progressive price movement caused by the large order reveals that some trader possesses useful information; this can even be more pronounced if the trader's anonymity is not preserved. Anonymity is very important for large active fund managers. If it becomes known that a large active asset manager starts buying or selling some specific shares, other participants will immediately imitate on the assumption that the manager has some superior analysis or information or that the manager will continue buying or selling. The slower an order is completed, the higher the potential opportunity cost. But trading a large order with immediacy induces high market impact. So there is a trade-off between market impact and opportunity cost.

Estimation and Uses of Execution Costs

Deregulation and increased globalization of all stock markets has led to a global trend toward negotiated commissions. Market impact has also been reduced because of the improvement in trading mechanisms and liquidity on most markets. This does not alleviate the need for measurement of execution costs. Some surveys provide estimates of the average cost of a trade in various markets. Other methods, reviewed below, attempt to measure ex-post execution costs on a trade by trade basis. All these measures allow us to derive estimates of expected execution costs that can affect investment strategies.

Global Surveys Several global surveys of execution costs are available. These give market averages for a typical trade in each country. Various studies come up with different estimates. Exhibit 5.5 reports some cost estimates for trading in the shares on major developed and emerging stock markets obtained from Barclays Global Investors. Market impact is measured at half the bid–ask spread plus price impact for a typical small transaction; the impact would be larger for a large transaction. Trading in non-U.S. securities tends to be somewhat more expensive than trading in U.S. securities. But trading in some European markets, notably France, the Netherlands, Spain, and Germany, tends to be cheaper than in the United States. The execution cost on U.K. securities is large on the buy side (0.76%) because of the stamp tax levied on purchases; it is much lower on sales (0.26%). Trading on emerging markets incurs large execution costs, often close to 1 percent; these costs can significantly affect the return on a portfolio invested in emerging markets.

EXHIBIT 5.5
Execution Costs in Basis Points

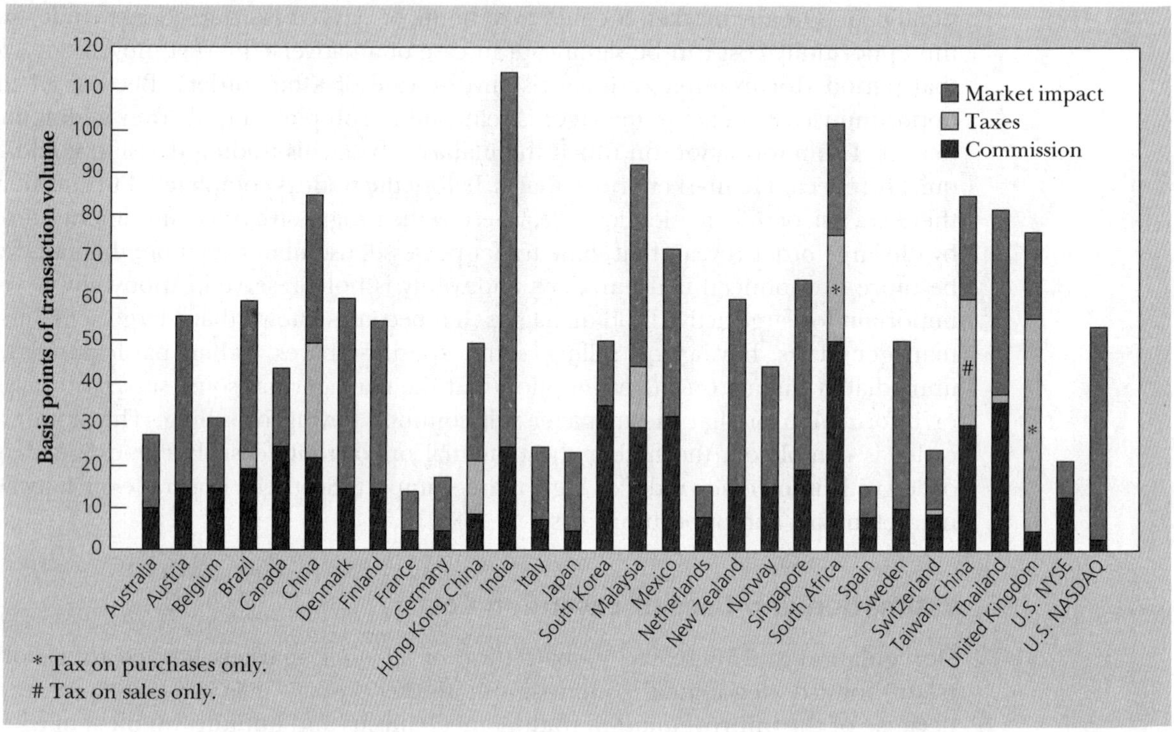

Source: Barclays Global Investors, 2002.

Of course, the total execution cost is a function of the size of the transaction and the market depth. The average execution costs for buying a $10 million slice of an EAFE portfolio is estimated to be 0.36 percent by Barclays Global Investors (0.25% to sell). The same cost is 0.63 percent for a $1 billion slice (0.53% to sell). Execution costs for a large trade in a single stock can be considerably higher than the figures reported here for a diversified EAFE basket of stocks, for which the magnitude of a trade in each stock is rather small.

Detailed Measures: VWAP As mentioned above, a traditional method to estimate the ex-post execution costs for a trade is to compute the volume-weighted average price (VWAP) on the day of the transaction. The difference between the actual trade price and this benchmark price is an indication of execution costs. The idea is that an average of the prices before and after the transaction is an unbiased estimate of the benchmark price.

Unfortunately, this method tends to understate the true market price impact of a trade that represents a significant proportion of the day's trading volume. Another criticism is that this method fails to reflect another hidden cost, namely, opportunity cost. For example, suppose that a manager wishes to buy 100,000 shares of a stock in the belief that its price will rise in the near future. An immediate purchase will result in a transaction price that will be significantly higher than the daily VWAP. Spreading the trade over ten days would result in daily transaction prices which will be closer to their daily VWAP. However, if the expected price appreciation takes place very quickly, the manager will miss taking full advantage of the initial prediction. The opportunity cost is large and not reflected by the VWAP methodology.

The daily VWAP method has been adapted to measure the VWAP over longer time intervals to better reflect the impact of opportunity costs.

Detailed Measures: Implementation Shortfall A somewhat different approach to measure ex-post costs is the *implementation shortfall.* The implementation shortfall is the difference between the value of the executed portfolio (or share position) and the value of the same portfolio at the time the trading decision was made. This analysis does not require the use of market data on transaction prices and volumes over the period surrounding the executed transaction. The implementation shortfall measures the impact of the trade as well as the impact of intervening market events until the transaction is completed. While opportunity cost is captured, general market movements caused by other factors are also captured. This shortfall can be adjusted for general market movements by subtracting the return on some broad market index over the measurement period.

Using Expected Execution Costs Estimates of ex-post execution costs can be used to judge whether best execution has been achieved. They also allow us to formulate expectations for execution costs on various types of prospective trades. Indeed, some sophisticated execution cost models have been developed.

Active international strategies should factor forecasted execution costs into their expected return estimates. For example, a manager who desires to sell German stocks and replace them with French stocks should estimate whether the expected return overweighs the execution costs incurred in the buy-and-sell transactions. More generally, execution costs are a drag on returns. To see how execution costs should be taken into account to calculate net expected returns, let's consider a strategy with the following features:

- $E(R)$ is the annual expected return on a strategy before execution costs.
- Execution costs are measured (in percentage) as the average cost of a round trip trade (purchase and sale) on the portfolio.
- The annual turnover ratio is the percentage of the portfolio that is traded during the year; it is commonly measured as the lesser of purchases or sales for a year divided by the average market value of the portfolio during that year.

Then the annual expected return net of execution costs is measured as

$$\text{Net expected return} = E(R) - \text{Turnover ratio} \times \text{Execution costs}$$

EXAMPLE 5.6 EXAMPLE OF THE IMPACT OF EXECUTION COSTS

An asset manager follows an active international asset allocation strategy. The average execution cost for a buy or a sell order is forecasted at 0.5 percent. On average, the manager turns the portfolio over 1.5 times a year. The annual expected return before transaction costs is 10 percent. What is the annual expected return net of execution costs?

SOLUTION

On the average, the portfolio is turned over 1.5 times. The average execution cost for a simultaneous purchase and sale of securities is 1 percent (0.5% for a buy and 0.5% for a sale). Hence, the net expected return is equal to

$$E(R) - \text{Turnover ratio} \times \text{Execution costs} = 10\% - 1.5 \times 1\% = 8.5\%$$

The calculation is illustrated in Example 5.6. Clearly, the impact of execution costs on returns depends on the level of activity of the account and the markets in which the account is invested.

Some Approaches to Reducing Execution Costs

International investment strategies can be costly, especially for large portfolios. Several approaches can be used to reduce execution costs. Let's take the example of a tactical asset allocation approach, whereby a fund manager decides to reduce the exposure to a country or a region. This would require the sale of a large number of stocks from that region. Rather than trading stock by stock, the manager could engage in *program trading*, in which the manager offers simultaneously a basket of securities for sale. The manager would require a quote from the broker for the whole basket. For the other counterparty, such large trades are often deemed as less risky than a large trade for a single stock because it is clear that they are not motivated by useful information on a specific company; hence, the bid–ask spread quoted could be smaller. There is less risk for the counterparty making a firm quote.

When engaging in a large trade—that is, a trade size that is beyond the normal trade size for which dealers give a standard bid–ask spread, or one that will result in significant market impact—a manager can try to get the best execution through a variety of trading techniques:

- *Internal crossing*: The manager will attempt to cross the order with an opposite order for another client of the firm.

  —The *advantage* is that this is the trading method that minimizes costs.

  —The *disadvantage* is that few managers can use this technique because having offsetting orders among clients is rare. There is also a problem in setting the transaction price. One must be sure to determine the price that would have been obtained in the marketplace and not privilege one client at the expense of another. Internal crossing is mostly applied by very large asset management firms specialized in passive strategies, such as index funds. For example, it could be the case that one client wants to reduce its exposure to European stocks, while another is in the process of building a global portfolio, including European stocks. Active managers would have a difficult time justifying selling shares of one company for a client, based on some forecast or model, and at the same time buying shares of the same company for another client.

- *External crossing*: The manager sends the order to an electronic crossing network, as described above.

  —The *advantage* is that execution costs are very low and anonymity is assured.

  —The *disadvantage* is that it can take a very long time before an opposite order is entered on the crossing network and the trade is executed. Often orders have to be redirected to another trading venue. A large block is less likely to be swiftly crossed than a small order, as it is unlikely that another party will happen to be interested in an opposite transaction of that magnitude. The speed of execution is a clear disadvantage of this technique, which is exposed to opportunity cost.

- *Principal trade*: The manager trades through a dealer who guarantees full execution at a specified discount/premium to the prevailing price. The dealer acts as a principal because she commits to taking the opposite side of the order at a firm price.

  —The *advantage* is that trading immediacy is assured and opportunity cost minimized.

  —The *disadvantage* is that the overall execution costs can be quite large. The principal broker commits some of its capital to complete the trade, often buying or selling shares on its own account. A principal dealer must maintain, and finance, an inventory of shares. Hence the dealer has to charge a "rent" for its capital, which increases execution costs. Anonymity cannot be assured, but this is not important as the trade is executed in full and immediately.

- *Agency trade*: The fund manager negotiates a competitive commission rate and selects a broker on the basis of his ability to reduce total execution costs. In turn the broker will "work" the order to try to get the best price for the manager. In a way, the search for best execution is delegated to the broker. The broker acts as an agent because he does not act as the counterparty on its own account but executes the order with another client.

  —The *advantage* is that the fund manager expects to achieve best execution by relying on the quality of the broker, who is compensated by a commission. This often leads to a compromise between opportunity cost and market impact.

—The potential *disdvantage* is that the commission paid could be too large for the quality of service provided. Also, anonymity cannot be assured.

- *Use of dealer "indications of interest" (IOI)*: Some other party might have a wish to engage in an opposite trade for a stock or basket of stocks. Polling IOIs from various dealers helps to identify possible pools of liquidity.

  —The *advantage* is that the fund manager can hope to achieve low execution costs by finding some opposite trading interest.

  —The *disadvantage* is that this search for liquidity among numerous dealers reveals publicly an interest in the security. Even if the anonymity of the investor is preserved, the trading interest is not.[7] It also slows trading speed. This technique is best suited for informationless trading by passive managers.

- *Use of futures*: There is an opportunity cost associated with the delay in execution of a large trade. The fund manager could use futures to monitor the position while the trade is progressively executed. For example, a manager whose tactical asset allocation decision is to reduce the French exposure on a large portfolio, because of the fear of a sudden drop in the French stock market, could immediately sell futures on the CAC, the French stock index. The manager will progressively sell the French stocks in the portfolio with low execution costs, while simultaneously reducing his position in futures.

  —An *advantage* is the reduction in the opportunity cost component of execution costs.

  —A *disadvantage* is the additional source of risk if the price of the security traded is not strongly correlated to that of the futures contract. Use of futures is well suited for building positions in diversified portfolios of stocks, with a high correlation between the price of the futures contract and that of the portfolio traded. But it is not well suited for trading in a single security, where the correlation with a stock index futures contract is not so large. So adding a futures position does little to eliminate the opportunity cost for that specific security while adding a new source of risk (the futures price volatility).

Several services, and asset management firms, provide models of expected execution costs. These can also be used as a benchmark when executing a trade. Looking at deviations from the forecasted cost model over a number of trades allows one to review the quality of execution of a broker and of various trading techniques. Choosing a venue to get best execution is basically searching for liquidity. It is a difficult task that depends on the type of trade and implies trade-offs that depend on several parameters, such as the following:

---

[7] Investors can ask for IOI on a basket of securities to hide their interest in a specific security.

- *Desire for confidentiality*: An active manager looking for alphas (i.e., betting on the misvaluation of some securities) will be very sensitive to the confidentiality of trades, while a passive manager will be less sensitive.
- *Desire for urgency*: An active manager looking for alphas will be very sensitive to the speed of transaction, while a passive manager will be a bit less sensitive.
- *Size of transaction*: The larger the transaction relative to the typical daily transaction volume, the higher the market impact.

Finally, fund managers often pay commissions to get additional services such as broker or third-party research (soft dollars). A detailed analysis of execution costs should unbundle these additional services, so that a broker charging a commission is not unduly penalized relative to other trading venues.

In the United Kingdom, the Myners report has prompted managers to focus on minimizing execution costs. A similar focus can be found in the United States. The need to invest in a sophisticated cost-reduction program[8] depends on the type of portfolio strategy followed. Passive index-linked strategies tend to incur lower execution costs than active stock-picking strategies because they trade on diversified baskets of securities. But execution cost is an important component of the performance of a manager attempting to closely track an index.[9] Saving a few basis points in execution costs is worth the effort, given the typical size of a passive portfolio. Also, index-linked basket trades are typically repetitive and more easily modeled.

On the other hand, in an active stock-picking strategy, trades are generally not repetitive. A pairwise trade, for example, buying an undervalued French oil company and selling an overvalued British one has unique characteristics. Such trades are not repetitive, and their costs are difficult to model ex ante. A focus on execution costs will usually mean finding the broker offering the best execution for this type of trade.

Investing in Foreign Shares Listed at Home

Investors need not go abroad to diversify internationally. We shall discuss several ways to accomplish this.

Global Shares and American Depositary Receipts

Some companies are listed on several stock markets around the world. Multinational firms, such as Royal Dutch/Shell or BP, are traded on more than a dozen markets.

---

[8] Such a program is quite costly in terms of human resources, data management, and modeling.

[9] This is true not only for a purely indexed strategy but also for any strategy that promises a small alpha while closely tracking a preassigned index (enhanced indexing).

Motivation for Multiple Listing

Foreign companies have a variety of reasons for being listed on several national stock markets, in spite of the additional costs involved:

- Multiple listing gives them more access to foreign ownership, allowing a better diversification of their capital and access to a larger amount of funds than is available from smaller domestic equity markets. For example, numerous firms combine an initial listing on the NYSE with a public offering of new shares in their home market.
- Diversified ownership in turn reduces the risk of a domestic takeover.
- Foreign listing raises the profile of a firm in foreign markets, enabling it to raise financing more easily both on the national level and abroad, and is good advertising for its product brands.
- Some companies from emerging countries, especially from remote countries, find multiple listing particularly attractive. Listing abroad allows access to a wider capital base and increases the business visibility of the firm. Chinese companies provide a good illustration of this opportunity. Foreign listing is the way to raise new capital abroad. The advantage for non-Chinese investors is that it is easier, and sometimes cheaper, to buy shares on a well-known, developed market. The currency of quotation for shares listed in the United States is the dollar, dividends are paid in dollars, and information in English is provided.

A danger of foreign listing may be the increased volatility of the firm's stock due to a stronger response in foreign versus domestic markets to domestic economic news. Bad political and economic (domestic) news in the Scandinavian countries, for example, has frequently been followed by an immediate negative impact from shares cross-listed on foreign markets. Scandinavian shareholders display less volatile behavior than foreign investors for two reasons: They are not as shaken by bad domestic news, and they tend to keep their capital invested at home anyhow (home bias).

Foreign Listing and ADRs

The procedure for admitting foreign stocks to a local market varies; in some markets, the regulations are quite lenient. For example, in 1986 the Quebec Securities Act allowed a foreign company to list in Montreal simply by meeting the same regulatory requirements as those in the foreign company's jurisdiction. In other markets, foreign companies must abide by the same rules as domestic companies. For instance, non-U.S. companies wanting to be listed on U.S. stock exchanges must satisfy the requirements of both the exchange and the U.S. Securities and Exchange Commission. Although this SEC regulation offers some protection to the U.S. investor, it imposes substantial dual-listing costs on non-U.S. companies, which must produce frequent reports in English.

In the United States and a few other countries, trading takes place in negotiable certificates representing ownership of shares of the foreign company. In the United States, trading is in *Amercian Depositary Receipts (ADRs).* Under this arrangement foreign shares are deposited with a U.S. bank, which in turn issues ADRs in the name of the foreign company. To avoid unusual share prices, ADRs may represent a combination of several foreign shares. For example, Japanese shares are often priced at only a few yen per share. They are therefore combined into lots of 100 or more so that their value is more like that of a typical U.S. share. Conversely, some ADRs represent a fraction of the original share. For example, the NASDAQ ADR of LVMH, the French luxury-goods firm, represents one-fifth of a French share.

The United States is the country of preference for foreign listing, with some 450 foreign companies traded on the NYSE and a similar number on the NASDAQ. The total turnover of foreign companies represents over 10 percent of the NYSE transaction volume. Foreign companies can be traded in several different ways in the United States.

An ADR program created without the company's involvement is usually called an *unsponsored* ADR. These over-the-counter (OTC) shares are traded through *pink sheets,* electronic bulletin boards, or an electronic trading system called PORTAL. An ADR program created with the assistance of the foreign company is called a *sponsored* ADR. Sponsored ADRs are often classified at three levels:

- *Level I*: The company does not comply with SEC registration and reporting requirements, and the shares can be traded only on the OTC market (but not NASDAQ).
- *Level II*: The company registers with the SEC and complies with its reporting requirements. The shares can be listed on an official U.S. stock exchange (NYSE, ASE) or NASDAQ.
- *Level III*: The company's ADRs are traded on a U.S. stock exchange or NASDAQ and the company may raise capital in the United States through a public offering of the ADRs.

A nonregistered (Level I) company can also raise capital in the United States, but it must be done through a private placement under rule 144A. A drawback of this type of private placement is that only certain private investors and qualified institutional buyers (QIBs) can participate. The retail sector is excluded. Furthermore, liquidity of ADRs on the OTC market is not good. The cost of being registered with the SEC (Levels II and III) is the public reporting that must be performed. The foreign company must file a Form 20-F annually. If domestic statements using national accounting standards are presented as primary statements on Form 20-F, the company must provide a reconciliation of earnings and shareholder equity under domestic and U.S. GAAP. This implies that the company must supply all information necessary to comply with U.S. GAAP. Furthermore, the stock exchanges require timely disclosure of various information, including quarterly accounting statements. Some national accounting practices can very easily be reconciled with U.S. practices. For example, the SEC considers that Canadian accounting practices are similar to U.S. practices and accepts Canadian statements; Canadian firms are not required to go through an ADR program; they can simply list their shares on a U.S. stock exchange. Many companies from Bermuda, the Cayman Islands, the Netherlands Antilles, Hong Kong (China), or Israel simply use the U.S. GAAP statements as their primary financial statements, so they do not even need to provide reconciliation data. At the other extreme, German and Swiss firms have been very reluctant to list shares in the United States because of the difficulty of reconciling U.S. and German or Swiss accounting practices and the detailed information that these firms are not accustomed to disclosing. German and Swiss have tended to smooth reported earnings by using various hidden reserves.

Some firms have issued Global Depositary Receipts (GDRs) that are simultaneously listed on several national markets. These GDRs give the firms access to a larger base to raise new capital. Several Japanese and Chinese firms have seized this opportunity.

When Daimler Benz merged with Chrysler, it decided to become listed on both the Deutsche Bourse and the NYSE. The *same* DaimlerChrysler share is traded on both exchanges, in euros in Frankfurt and in dollars in New York. This is exactly the same share, often called a "global share," that is traded on both exchanges (not an ADR), so an investor can buy shares in Frankfurt and sell them in New York. This would not be possible with an ADR that must go through a difficult conversion process. To make this dual trading possible, several legal and regulatory constraints have to be overcome, besides the accounting harmonization discussed previously. The Sarbanes-Oxley Act of 2002 introduced additional compliance requirements on foreign cross-listed companies. There is considerable discussion about whether the costs of compliance outweigh the benefits of cross-listing.

London is another market with trading of depositary receipts, as well as very active trading of foreign stocks. Foreign companies can list their shares, and the listings can be in all major currencies. The motivation for trading in London is to reduce transaction costs by avoiding some taxes or high commissions charged on the home market and to benefit from the liquidity provided by highly professional market makers based in London. Hong Kong has seen many initial public offerings by mainland Chinese companies. Their shares are referred to as H-shares.

Valuation of ADRs Multiple listing implies that the share values of a company are linked on several exchanges. One company should sell at the same share price all over the world, once adjustments for exchange rates and transactions costs have been made. Arbitrage among markets ensures that this is so. An important question is: What is the dominant force affecting the stock price of a multiple-listed company? In a dominant–satellite market relationship the home market is the dominant force, and the price in the foreign market (the satellite) simply adjusts to the home market price. This is clearly the case for many dual-listed stocks of which only a very small proportion of capitalization is traded abroad. For most ADRs, the price quoted by market makers is simply the home price of the share adjusted by the exchange rate. But, because the ADR market is less liquid, a large bid–ask spread is added. A fairly large discrepancy in prices between the home and foreign market can be observed because the arbitrage costs between the ADR and the original share can be sizable. The answer is less obvious, however, for a few large European, Chinese, and South American companies that have a very active market in other countries (especially the United States). The volume of trading of a few European multinationals is sometimes bigger in New York, Hong Kong, and London than on their home market. This situation also applies to a few Latin American firms and to many of the GDRs.

The influence of time zones should also be noted. Because stock trading takes place at different times around the world, U.S. stocks listed on the Paris Bourse are traded before the opening of the U.S. markets. Their French prices reflect not only the previous close in New York and the current exchange rate, but also anticipation about the current day's new price, based on new information released following the U.S. close.

Advantages/Disadvantages ADRs allow an easy and direct investment in some foreign firms. Although buying ADRs is an attractive alternative for retail investors, it is usually more costly than a direct purchase abroad for a large investor. On the other hand, some ADRs issued by companies from emerging countries tend to have larger trading volumes in New York than in their home markets, and the execution costs are lower in New York. Whereas the small investor may find it more convenient to trade in foreign shares listed on the home market, the large investor may often find the primary market of overseas companies to be more liquid and cheaper. In all cases, price levels, transaction costs, taxes, and administrative costs should be major determinants of whichever market the investor chooses. This is illustrated in Example 5.7.

Another disadvantage of ADRs is that only a limited number of companies have issued ADRs, and they represent only a small proportion of foreign market capitalization. They tend to be large companies in each country, so they do not offer full international diversification benefits.

Closed-End Country Funds

Closed-end country funds have been created for many countries, especially emerging countries.

Definition and Motivation A *closed-end fund* is an investment vehicle that buys stocks in the market; in turn, shares of the closed-end fund are traded in the stock market at a price determined by supply and demand for that fund. The number of shares of the fund usually remains fixed, and shares cannot be redeemed but are only traded in the stock market. The fund's market price can differ from the value of the assets held in its portfolio, which is called the *net asset value (NAV)*. The *premium* on the fund is the difference between the fund market price and its NAV:

$$\text{Fund market price} = \text{NAV} + \text{Premium}$$

EXAMPLE 5.7 EXAMPLE OF PRICE ARBITRAGE

DaimlerChrysler shares are listed in Frankfurt (XETRA) and on the NYSE. You are a German investor with a large portfolio of German and international stocks. You just bought 10,000 shares in Frankfurt at 51 euros per share. In addition, your broker charges a 0.25 percent commission. At the same time, a U.S. broker quotes DaimlerChrysler traded on the NYSE at 44.70–44.90 dollars, net of commissions. The exchange rate quoted in dollar per euro is 0.8800–0.8820 net. So you can buy one euro for 0.8820 dollar and sell one euro for 0.8800 dollar. Would it have been better to buy the shares in New York rather than in Frankfurt, knowing that these are the same global shares?

SOLUTION

Let's compute the euro purchase price of one share listed on the NYSE. You would buy the shares from the broker at 44.90 dollars. To pay for this purchase, you would need to exchange euros for dollars (sell euros, buy dollars) at the rate of 0.8800 dollar per euro. The net purchase cost per share in euros is

$$44.90/0.88 = 51.0227 \text{ euros}$$

The cost of purchasing shares directly in Frankfurt is the purchase price plus the 0.25 percent commission:

$$51 \times 1.0025 = 51.1275 \text{ euros}$$

You would have saved 0.1048 euro per share, or 1,048 euros for the 10,000 shares. Of course, you would end up with shares delivered in New York, but they could be held in custody with the rest of your U.S. stock portfolio.

The premium is often expressed as a *percentage of the NAV* and is usually called a discount when negative. The situation is quite different for a portfolio directly entrusted to a portfolio manager or for an open-end fund, such as a mutual fund. There, the value of the portfolio or fund is, by definition, equal to the market value of the invested assets (the NAV). The advantage of a closed-end fund for the investment manager is that she does not have to worry about redemptions; once a closed-end fund is initially subscribed, the investment manager keeps the money under management. This vehicle is well suited to investing in emerging markets, because the manager does not face redemption demands and can invest in the long term without liquidity concerns. The disadvantage for the closed-end shareholder is the uncertainty in the premium, as will be discussed later.

A *country fund* (e.g., the Korea Fund) is a closed-end fund whose assets consist primarily of stocks of the country for which the fund is named (e.g., stocks of Korean companies). Numerous country funds are listed in the United States, the United Kingdom, and major stock markets.

The motivation for investing in those country funds is twofold. First, they offer a simple way to access the local market and benefit from international diversification.

For example, country funds invested in Italy, Spain, Australia, the United Kingdom, or Germany can be purchased in the United States. These funds invested in developed markets are of interest primarily to private investors, who find an easy way to hold a diversified portfolio of that country. Country funds are simply managed portfolios specializing in stocks of a specific country. The case for country funds investing in emerging markets is more compelling, because the alternative of investing directly in emerging markets is a more difficult process. Furthermore, some countries (e.g., Brazil, India, and Korea) traditionally restricted foreign investment. Country funds, approved by the local government, are a way to overcome foreign investment restrictions. So, foreign investment restriction is a second motivation for the creation and use of some of these country funds. The International Finance Corporation (IFC) of the World Bank has been instrumental in the launching of country funds in small emerging markets.

The Pricing of Country Funds The price of a country fund is seldom equal to its NAV. Some funds trade at a substantial premium or discount from their NAV, posing problems for investors. The change in market price of a country fund is equal to the change in NAV plus the change in the premium (discount). If the premium decreases or the discount widens, the return on the fund will be less than the return on underlying assets making up the portfolio.

Some country funds provide a unique way to invest in emerging countries with foreign investment restrictions. When these foreign investment restrictions are binding, one would expect the country fund to sell at a premium over its NAV; see Bonser-Neal et al. (1990) or Eun, Janakiramanan, and Senbet (1995). The premium should be equal to the amount that investors are willing to pay to circumvent the restriction. Indeed, funds invested in India, Korea, Taiwan (China), or Brazil have generally sold at a steep but volatile premium. Emerging countries are progressively liberalizing foreign access to their financial markets. When the lifting of a foreign investment restriction is announced, the premium on a local-country fund should drop, as local shares will be more widely available to foreign investors. This drop in premium is a risk associated with investing in these country funds. It can only be hoped that the local market will respond favorably to the prospect of attracting more foreign investors and that a rise in NAV will compensate for a drop in the fund's premium. The liberalization in Brazil and Korea has indeed led to large drops in the premium of closed-end funds invested in those countries.

The volatility in the value of the premium can add volatility to that of the underlying assets. Historically, premiums on country funds have been very volatile. Johnson, Schneeweiss, and Dinning (1993) studied a sample of country funds listed in the United States and invested either in developed markets or in emerging markets. They measured the U.S. dollar volatilities of the fund, the fund's NAV, and the local underlying stock index (e.g., the Korean index for the Korean Fund). For emerging-country funds, the volatility of the fund was about 30 percent more than that of its NAV, and 10 percent more than that of the local stock index. This additional volatility might be a necessary cost to bear when few other alternatives are open. Because these markets are becoming much more accessible, the attraction of country funds is reduced.

EXAMPLE 5.8 EXAMPLE OF MOVEMENTS IN PREMIUM

Paf is an emerging country with severe foreign investment restrictions but an active stock market open mostly to local investors. The exchange rate of the pif, the local currency, with the U.S. dollar remains fixed at $:Pif = 1. A closed-end country fund, called Paf Country Fund, has been approved by Paf. Its net asset value is 100 dollars. It trades in New York with a premium of 30 percent.

1. Give some intuitive explanations for this positive premium.
2. Paf unexpectedly announces that it will lift all foreign investment restrictions, which has two effects. First, stock prices in Paf go up by 20 percent because of the expectation of massive foreign investment attracted by the growth opportunities in Paf. Second, the premium on the Paf Country Fund drops to zero. Is this scenario reasonable? What would be your total gain (loss) on the shares of Paf Country Fund?

SOLUTION

1. There is no alternative to investing in the closed-end fund for foreign investors. Foreign investors may find Paf shares so attractive from a risk–return viewpoint that they compete and bid up the price.
2. The scenario is reasonable. The net result can be calculated for 100 dollars of original NAV. Before the lifting of restrictions, the fund was worth 130 dollars for 100 dollars of NAV. After the lifting of restrictions, the NAV moves up to 120 dollars and the fund is now worth its NAV, or 120 dollars. The rate of return for the foreign investor is

$$\frac{120 - 130}{130} = -7.7\%$$

For developed-country funds, Johnson et al. (1993) found that the volatility of a fund was almost twice as large as that of its NAV or of the local stock index. To avoid the additional volatility of closed-end country funds invested in developed markets, investors can buy open-end funds or buy a portfolio directly on the foreign market. These portfolios will always be valued at their NAV, without premium or discount. It can be argued that the large discount observed on many developed-country funds simply reflects large management fees[10] and the lack of liquidity of the market for the fund's shares.

Another interesting feature of the pricing of country closed-end funds listed in the United States is the fact that a fund's value is often strongly correlated with the U.S. stock market and reacts only slowly to changes in the fundamentals (i.e., changes in the NAV). Both phenomena are inconsistent with market efficiency. For

[10] Indeed, Bekaert and Urias (1999) suggest that closed-end funds are not an attractive substitute for direct investment in foreign stock markets, even for most emerging markets.

example, a Korean fund is a portfolio of Korean stocks; its value should not be affected by movements in the U.S. stock market (beyond the normal correlation between Korea and the United States). Many behavioral finance explanations are provided, including over- and underreaction to news, investor demand, and investor "sentiment." Klibanoff, Lamont, and Wizman (1998) provide an interesting study that focuses on the "salience" of news. They show that, although the elasticity of the fund's price to news is less than one, it is much higher when the news appears on the front page of the *New York Times*. So, investors will react quickly only to salient news.

Advantages/Disadvantages Closed-end funds allow investors access to a portfolio invested in some foreign region. The portfolio is generally better diversified than a collection of a few ADRs of that region.

The previous discussion of costs and volatility suggests, however, that buying closed-end funds is an inferior substitute for direct investment in foreign stock markets, even for most emerging markets.

Open-End Funds

An open-end mutual fund is publicly offered and its shares can be purchased and redeemed at the NAV of the assets owned by the fund. Although an *open-end fund* is attractive from the shareholders' viewpoint, it would be risky for the fund manager if investors could redeem shares at a known NAV (which the manager might not be able to realize if he needs to liquidate assets to meet redemptions). Typically investors must announce their decision to buy/redeem their shares before the NAV is calculated. For example, investors must notify their decision before noon, and the NAV is calculated at the end of the day. For open-end funds invested in foreign shares, the lag between notification and determination of the NAV that will be used to execute the transaction can be a couple of days. A large bid–ask spread on the fund's price can also be imposed. The efficiency improvements in many emerging markets have allowed managers to offer open-end funds on the most liquid markets. Open-end funds are now offered not only for individual countries but also for regions or international industries. Many of these funds take the form of index funds tracking an international index of developed or emerging market. Most new international open-end funds now take the form of ETFs.

Exchange Traded Funds

Exchange traded funds (*ETFs*) trade on a stock market like shares of any individual company. They can be traded at any time during market hours and can be sold short or margined. But ETFs are shares of a portfolio, not of an individual company. ETFs are generally designed to closely track the performance of a specific index. ETFs on the indexes of several individual, developed stock markets, as well as on many international indexes, are listed on all major stock markets. ETFs on some emerging markets, or international emerging indexes, are also offered. So, they can be used for international diversification strategies. ETFs have been an exceptional commercial success in the early 2000s. ETFs are offered by the large asset management firms that specialize in indexing. Other financial institutions offer ETFs under their name by subcontracting with these specialists.

Definition and Motivation An ETF is an open-end fund with special characteristics (see Gastineau, 2001). ETFs have a management cost advantage over traditional mutual funds because there is no shareholder accounting at the fund level. ETFs are traded like common stocks. A major feature is the redemption in-kind process. Creation/redemption units are created in large multiples of individual ETF shares, for example, 50,000 shares. These units are available to exchange specialists (*authorized participants*) who will generally act as market makers for the individual shares. If an authorized participant decides to redeem ETF shares, it will do so by exchanging the redemption unit for a portfolio of stocks held by the fund and used to track the index. The fund publishes the portfolio that it is willing to accept for in-kind transactions. As opposed to traditional open-end funds, the in-kind redemption means that no capital gain will be realized in the fund's portfolio on redemption. If the redemption is in cash, a traditional fund may have to sell stocks held in the fund's portfolio. If their price has appreciated, the fund will realize a capital gain and the tax burden will have to be passed to all existing fund shareholders. This is not the case with ETFs. As in any open-end fund, though, individual ETF shareholders[11] can require in-cash redemption based on the NAV. Redemption in cash by individual ETF shareholders is discouraged in two ways:

- Redemption is based on the NAV computed one or a couple of days after the shareholder commits to redemption. So, the redemption value is unknown when the investor decides to redeem.
- A large fee is assessed on in-cash redemptions.

It is more advantageous for individual ETF shareholders to sell their shares on the market than to redeem them in cash. The sale can take place immediately based on observed share prices at a low cost. Arbitrage by authorized participants ensures that the listed price is close to the fund's NAV.[12] Authorized participants maintain a market in the ETF share by posting bid and ask prices with a narrow spread, or by entering buy-and-sell limit orders in an electronic order book. The transaction costs of ETFs can be estimated as the sum of the commission charged by the broker plus half this bid–ask spread.

International ETFs have distinguishing features. An ETF indexed on some less-liquid emerging market is bound to have high bid–ask spreads. Managing an ETF on a broad international index, such as EAFE, means holding stock from numerous countries with different custodial arrangements and time zones. Again, the bid–ask spreads are likely to be larger than for *plain-vanilla* ETFs. But the size of

[11] But authorized participants commit to redeem only in kind.

[12] The fund publishes an indicative intraday NAV every 15 seconds; it is available on major data providers, such as Bloomberg, Reuters, or Telekurs.

the ETF is an important factor influencing costs. The effect of non-overlapping time zones should be taken into account when comparing the ETF price with its NAV. Consider the example of an ETF on a Japanese stock index, traded in New York. During Wall Street opening hours, the Tokyo stock market is closed. The NAV available in the morning in the United States is based on the closing prices in Tokyo several hours before New York opens. Except for currency fluctuations, the NAV will remain unchanged as Tokyo is closed throughout the New York trading session. However, the ETF price will be affected by expectations about future stock prices in Tokyo, so it could differ significantly from the official NAV. This is not an inefficiency and there are no arbitrage opportunities, because the NAV is stale and does not correspond to current market pricing (see Example 5.9).

EXAMPLE 5.9 ETF PRICING

An ETF is indexed on a Japanese stock index and is listed in New York. Its NAV is computed based on closing prices in Tokyo. When it is 9 A.M. in New York, it is already 11 P.M. in Tokyo on the same day. The NAV based on Tokyo closing prices is 10,000 yen. The exchange rate at 9 A.M. EST is 1 dollar = 100 yen.

1. What is the dollar NAV of this ETF at the opening of trading in New York?
2. When New York closes at 4 P.M. EST, Tokyo is still closed (6 A.M. local time), but the exchange rate is now 99 yen per dollar. What is the dollar NAV at closing time?
3. Bad international news hit after the Tokyo closing. European and U.S. stock markets dropped by 5 percent. Should the ETF price have remained at its NAV? Assuming that the Tokyo market is strongly correlated with the U.S. market (at least for this type of international news), give an estimate of the ETF price at the New York closing.

SOLUTION

1. The dollar NAV is \$100 (= 10,000/100).
2. The closing dollar NAV is \$101.01 (= 10,000/99)
3. The price of the ETF should reflect expectations that the Tokyo stock index will drop in reaction to the news, so its price should be below the NAV computed on past closing prices in Tokyo. If the markets are strongly correlated, we could estimate that Tokyo will also drop by 5 percent. Hence, we should have an estimated market value for the dollar NAV equal to

   $$10{,}000 \times (1-0.05)/99 = \$95.96$$

   This is an estimate of the current price of the ETF. It will trade at a 5 percent discount from its "official" NAV.

Advantages/Disadvantages ETFs are attractive to individual investors because they offer the benefits of international diversification with excellent liquidity at a low cost. They are also designed to be tax efficient. ETFs are useful in an international portfolio strategy. They can be purchased in the home market while offering a diversified play on a foreign market or region. They are well designed to be used in active asset allocation. On the other hand, they usually are designed to match a benchmark and will not provide active return above that benchmark. To add active return, investors can combine them with the direct purchase of specific companies or ADRs.

For large institutional investors, the alternative is to invest directly in an indexed, or actively managed, international portfolio; the cost structure could be less and the tax situation equivalent or better.

Summary

- Stock exchanges throughout the world evolved from three models: private bourses, public bourses, and bankers' bourses.
- Trading procedures differ in order-driven and price-driven markets. In a price-driven market, market makers stand ready to buy or sell at posted prices (bid and ask prices). In an order-driven market, all buy-and-sell orders are entered in a central order book and a new order is immediately matched with the book of limit orders previously submitted. Each system presents advantages and risks for traders and customers.
- Electronic communication and crossing networks (ECNs) have developed alongside official stock exchanges. Electronic crossing networks match anonymously buy-and-sell orders submitted by institutional investors and broker-dealers at prespecified times and at prices determined in the primary market for the security. The trade is made at the midpoint between the bid and ask prices of the primary market, so there is no market impact or bid–ask spread even for large orders. But there is also no trading immediacy.
- The relative market capitalization of national equity markets has changed dramatically over time. The share of the U.S. equity markets moved from two-thirds of the world market in the early 1970s to only one-third by the early 1990s, when Japan had about the same market size as the United States. In 2007, U.S. equity markets represented some 40 percent of the world market cap, with Europe and Asia accounting for approximately 30 percent each.
- Numerous stock indexes are available to track country and regional markets and measure performance. They can be domestic stock indexes computed locally, such as the U.S. Dow Jones Industrial Average or the Japanese Nikkei

225 stocks average. They can be global stock indexes computed by a global organization, such as MSCI, FTSE, DJ, or S&P.

- Many practical aspects must be taken into account in global equity investing: market concentration, liquidity, tax aspects, and transaction costs.
- Asset managers should try to get the best execution for each trade. Execution costs include several components: commissions and fees, market impact, and opportunity cost. Although commissions and fees are easy to measure, this is less true for market impact and opportunity cost. A transaction has an impact on the price of the security traded, so market impact can be a significant component of execution cost.
- To optimize global asset management, one should forecast the execution cost of trading in the various markets. Several global surveys of execution costs are available, but the actual cost depends on the transaction size and the market depth for the specific trade. Various trading techniques allow reduction of execution costs.
- It is possible to get some of the benefits of international diversification by investing solely in securities or funds listed at home:
  - Some companies have their shares traded on foreign exchanges; these are called ADRs in the United States. Unfortunately, the number of foreign-listed companies is small, and the price of these ADRs is sometimes unattractive. A few companies offer global shares listed and traded simultaneously in several stock markets.
  - Some closed-end funds specialize in investing in foreign stock markets. The market price of these country funds often differs from their net asset value by a large premium (or discount). The uncertainty concerning this premium adds to investment risk.
  - Exchange traded funds (ETFs) are special open-end funds that trade on a stock market like shares of individual companies. Their design has made them very successful. The most popular ETFs track some country or regional stock indexes.

Problems

1. Which of the following statements about stock markets is not true?

I. Many of the stock markets are organized as private bourses.

II. On most markets, stocks are traded on a cash basis, and transactions are settled within a two- to five-day period.

III. The central electronic limit order book is the hub of those automated markets that are price-driven.

IV. An auction market, such as the Paris Bourse, is also known as an order-driven market.

2. The central limit order book of Air Liquide, a French firm that trades on the Paris Bourse, is currently as follows:

Sell Orders		Buy Orders	
Quantity	**Limit**	**Limit**	**Quantity**
500	151	145	500
2,000	150	143	2,000
1,000	149	142	1,000
500	147	141	2,000
500	146	140	1,000

   a. Vincent Jacquet wishes to buy 1,500 shares and enters a market order to buy those shares. At what price will Jacquet buy the shares?
   b. Suppose Vincent Jacquet had instead wanted to sell 1,000 shares of Air Liquide that he already had in his investment portfolio. At what price will he sell those shares?

3. *Business Objects* trades on the Paris Bourse as ordinary shares and on the NASDAQ as American Depositary Receipts (ADRs). One ADR of *Business Objects* corresponds to one share on the Paris Bourse. Suppose the last transaction of *Business Objects* on the Paris Bourse was at €25. An investor then entered on the French electronic trading system a limit order to purchase *Business Objects* shares at €24. The ADR price quoted by a NASDAQ dealer is \$23.90–24.45. The exchange rate is \$0.96/€. Suppose that some unfavorable information suddenly arrives that suggests that a lower price of *Business Objects* shares at €21 would be fair. Assuming that the exchange rate has not changed, discuss which parties stand to lose on the Paris Bourse and on NASDAQ?

4. It is often argued that automated order-driven trading systems must provide special arrangements for small trades (which are often market orders) as well as for block trades. Advance some explanations for this argument.

5. Which of the following statements about electronic communication and crossing networks (ECNs) is/are true?
   I. Electronic communication networks are order-driven systems, in which the limit order book plays a central role.
   II. Electronic crossing networks anonymously match buy-and-sell orders by a pool of participants, generally institutional investors and broker-dealers.
   III. In an ECN, a trade takes place only during a crossing session time and only if there are offsetting orders entered by other participants.

6. Consider a European electronic crossing network that runs six crosses daily, that is, the orders are matched six times a day. This network allows a participant to specify several constraints, such as price and minimum fill. Suppose that all the orders submitted to this network for the shares of Christian Dior are good for day (GFD); that is, any unfulfilled part of an order is automatically resubmitted to subsequent crossing sessions duing the day.
   a. The following orders are on the network for the shares of Christian Dior at the time of the first crossing session of the day. The most recent trading price of Christian Dior at the Paris Bourse is €37.
      - Participant A: a market order to buy 100,000 shares
      - Participant B: a market order to sell 50,000 shares
      - Participant C: a market order to sell 150,000 shares, with a minimum fill of 125,000 shares
      - Participant D: an order to buy 20,000 shares at €36

Discuss what trades would take place on the crossing network and what orders would remain unfulfilled.

b. The following new orders are submitted to the next crossing session. The most recent trading price of Christian Dior at the Paris Bourse is €38.
   - Participant E: a market order to buy 150,000 shares
   - Participant F: A market order to sell 50,000 shares

Discuss what trades would take place on the crossing network in this crossing session and what orders would remain unfulfilled.

7. The U.S. stock market capitalization is larger relative to U.S. GDP than is the case in most European countries for all the following reasons *except*:

a. A greater proportion of firms in Europe is nationalized.
b. European banks cannot own shares of stock of their client firms.
c. Many European companies rely heavily on bank financing.
d. Privately held companies are a tradition in Europe.

8. Standard & Poor's announced in 2001 that it was considering integrating free-float adjustments to its existing practices for the S&P Australian index. It said that it would use a measure called Investable Weight Factor (IWF) to reflect a company's free float. A full free-floated company will have an IWF of 100 percent. For others, the IWF will be adjusted downward by subtracting the percentage of shares that are not freely available for trade. Now consider three Australian manufacturing companies: Alpha, Beta, and Gamma. Alpha owns 5 percent each of Beta and Gamma. Gamma owns 15 percent of Beta. Taking into account the cross-holdings, what will be the IWF of each company?

9. Four companies belong to a group and are listed on a stock exchange. The cross-holdings of these companies are as follows:

- Company A owns 20 percent of Company B and 10 percent of Company C.
- Company B owns 15 percent of Company C.
- Company C owns 10 percent of Company A, 10 percent of Company B, and 5 percent of Company D.
- Company D has no ownership in any of the other three companies.

Each company has a market capitalization of $50 million. You wish to adjust for cross-holding in determining the weights of these companies in a free-float market capitalization–weighted index.

a. What are the market capitalizations of each company after adjustment to reflect free float?
b. What would be the total adjusted market cap of the four companies?

10. The shares of Volkswagen trade on the Frankfurt stock exchange. A U.S. investor purchased 1,000 shares of Volkswagen at €56.91 each, when the exchange rate was €:$ = 0.9790–0.9795. Three months later, the investor received a dividend of €0.50 per share, and the investor decided to sell the shares at the then prevailing price of €61.10 per share. The exchange rate was €:$ = 0.9810–0.9815. The dividend withholding tax rate in Germany is 15% and there is a tax treaty between the United States and Germany to avoid double taxation.

a. How much did the U.S. investor receive in dividends in dollars, net of tax?
b. What were the capital gains from the purchase and sale of Volkswagen shares?
c. How would the dividend income be declared by the investor on a U.S. tax return, and what tax credit would he receive?

11. The shares of Microsoft were trading on NASDAQ on January 1 at \$41. A Swedish investor purchased 100 shares of Microsoft at that price. The Swedish kroner to dollar exchange rate then was \$:Skr = 9.4173–9.4188. One year later, the investor received a dividend of \$2 per share, and the investor then sold the shares at a price of \$51 per share. The exchange rate at that time was \$:Skr = 9.8710–9.8750. The dividend withholding tax rate in the United States is 15 percent and there is a tax treaty between the United States and Sweden that allows the U.S. withholding tax to be used as a tax credit in Sweden. Suppose the Swedish investor is taxed at 50 percent on income and 15 percent on capital gains, and ignore any commissions on purchase and sale of shares.

a. What is the gross rate of return on the investment, in dollars?
b. What is the gross rate of return on the investment, in kroners?
c. What is the rate of return on the investment, in kroners, net of taxes?

12. Which of the following statements best characterizes the taxation of returns on international investments in an investor's country and the country where the investment is made?

a. Capital gains normally are taxed only by the country where the investment is made.
b. Tax-exempt investors normally must pay taxes to the country where the investment is made.
c. Investors in domestic common stock normally avoid double taxation on dividend income by receiving a tax credit for taxes paid to the country where the investment is made.
d. The investor's country normally withholds taxes on dividends payments.

13. A U.S. institutional investor would like to purchase 10,000 shares of Lafarge. Lafarge is a French firm that trades on the Paris Bourse, the London stock exchange, and the NYSE as an ADR. At the NYSE, one depositary receipt is equivalent to one-fourth of a Lafarge share. The U.S. investor asks its brokers to quote net prices, without any commissions, in the three trading venues. There is no stamp tax in London on foreign shares listed there. The stock quotes are as follows:

New York	\$24.07–24.37
London	£66.31–67.17
Paris	€99.40–100.30

The exchange rate quotes from banks are as follows:

£:\$ 1.4575–1.4580

€:\$ 0.9691–0.9695

Compare the dollar costs of purchasing 10,000 shares, or its equivalent, in New York, London, and Paris.

14. The chief financial executive of a German firm is considering raising capital in the United States by cross-listing her firm on the NYSE as an ADR and having a public offering. However, she has some concerns about this. Discuss what you think some of these concerns might be.

15. A U.S. institutional investor would like to buy 10,000 shares of British Polythene Industries. This U.K. firm trades on the London stock exchange, but not on the NYSE or NASDAQ. A U.K.-based broker of the investor quotes the price as £3.45–3.60, with a commission of 0.10 percent of the transaction value. There is a 0.50 percent U.K. securities transaction tax on purchase. The exchange rate quoted by a bank is £:$ = 1.5005–1.5010. What would be the total cost in dollars?

16. A French institutional investor wishes to decrease its exposure to Taiwan (China). It is interested in selling 20,000 shares of a particular Taiwanese firm that is currently in its portfolio. This firm trades on the Taiwan Stock Exchange. A Taiwan-based broker quotes the Taiwan dollar (TW$) price of the shares of this firm as 150.35–150.75, with a commission of 0.10 percent of the transaction value. The Taiwan Stock Exchange charges a tax of 0.30 percent of the value traded from the seller. A bank is quoting the TW$ to € exchange rate as 32.8675–32.8800. How many euros will the French institutional investor receive on selling the shares?

17. Which of the following statements is/are true about stock indexes?

I. Compared with the equal-weighted indexes, market value–weighted indexes are better representative of movements in the market.

II. Many of the global indexes, such as those provided by MSCI and S&P, are widely used by international money managers for asset allocation decisions and performance measurements.

III. It is possible that, in any given year, the performance between two indexes for the same stock market can differ significantly, by as much as several percentage points.

18. In 1996, a group of securities called the World Equity Benchmark Shares (WEBS) started trading on the American Stock Exchange. WEBS for a country is a passively managed ETF indexed on the MSCI country benchmark index for that country. All else equal, what do you think would be the effect of the launch of WEBS for a country on the premium or discount of the closed-end country fund for that country?

19. Consider a closed-end country fund that trades in the United States. Suppose that country decides to impose restrictions on investments by foreigners in that country. All other things constant, what do you think would be the effect of these international investment restrictions on the price–net asset value ratio of the closed-end fund for that country?

20. A U.S. institutional investor with a large portfolio of U.S. and international stocks wants to add 20,000 shares of DaimlerChrysler to its portfolio. DaimlerChrysler trades as the same global share on several exchanges in the world. A U.S. broker quotes the NYSE price of DaimlerChrysler as $43.45–43.65, net of commissions. The institutional investor is also considering purchasing shares in Germany, where the offer price quoted for DaimlerChrysler's shares on the Frankfurt stock exchange (XETRA) is €44.95, with a 0.10 percent commission to be paid on the transaction value. Which of the two alternatives is better for the investor? How much would be the total saving by using the better of the two alternatives? The exchange rate is €:$ 0.9705–0.9710.

21. Consider a U.K. index fund that trades on a U.S. exchange. This fund is indexed on a British stock index based on several stocks that trade on the London stock exchange. The different time zones of the U.K. and the U.S. markets result in four distinct time periods in a 24-hour period: (a) a 6-hour time period prior to the U.S. open, when the market in London is open but the market in the United States is not; (b) a 2-hour period between 9:30 A.M. and 11:30 A.M. in New York, when both London and New York markets are open; (c) a 4.5-hour time period between 11:30 A.M. and 4:00 P.M. in New

York, when the New York market is open but the London market is not; (d) the subsequent period when both markets are closed. For each of these time periods, discuss how British pound NAV and the U.S. dollar price of the fund would fluctuate.

Bibliography

Bekaert G., and Urias, M. S. "Is There a Free Lunch in Emerging Market Equities?" *Journal of Portfolio Management*, 1999.

Bonser-Neal, C., Brauer, G., Neal, R., and Wheatley, S. "International Investment Restrictions and Closed-End Country Fund Prices," *Journal of Finance*, June 1990.

Conrad, J., Johnson, K. M., and Wahal, S. "Institutional Trading Costs and Alternative Trading Systems," *Journal of Financial Economics*, April 2004.

Domowitz, I. "Liquidity, Transaction Costs and Reintermediation in Electronic Market," Penn State Working Paper, April 2001.

Eun, C., Janakiramanan, S., and Senbet, L.W. "The Design and Pricing of Country Funds under Market Segmentation," presented at the AFA annual meetings, January 1995.

Gastineau, G. L., "Exchange-Traded Funds: An Introduction," *Journal of Portfolio Management*, Spring 2001.

Huang, R. "The Quality of ECN and Nasdaq Market Maker Quotes," *Journal of Finance*, 57 (3), June 2002.

Johnson, G., Schneeweiss, T., and Dinning, W. "Closed-End Country Funds: Exchange Rate and Investment Risk," *Financial Analysts Journal*, November/December 1993.

Klibanoff, P., Lamont, O., and Wizman, T. A. "Investor Reaction to Salient News in Closed-End Country Funds," *Journal of Finance*, 53(2), April 1998, pp. 673–699.

6

Equity: Concepts and Techniques

LEARNING OUTCOMES

After completing this chapter, you will be able to do the following:

- Discuss the major differences in national accounting standards
- Discuss off-balance-sheet assets and liabilities such as special purpose entities
- Discuss how to analyze the accounting treatment of employee stock option compensation
- Demonstrate how neoclassical growth theory and endogenous growth theory can be used to explain trends in economic growth
- Demonstrate how to conduct a global industry analysis by analyzing return potential and risk characteristics
- Demonstrate how to conduct global financial analysis, including DuPont analysis
- Discuss the role of market efficiency in individual stock valuation
- Discuss franchise value and the growth process
- Demonstrate how to analyze the effects of inflation for valuation purposes
- Discuss multifactor models as applied in the global context

Thomas R. Robinson, CPA, CFA, made significant contributions to the accounting material in this chapter.

Investing in foreign stocks poses at least two types of problems: First, the portfolio manager must gain sufficient familiarity with the operations, trading mechanisms, costs, and constraints of foreign markets. This issue was addressed in Chapter 5. Second, the portfolio manager's investment approach must be global; that is, his method of analyzing and selecting stocks should be part of an optimal worldwide investment strategy. The conceptual and technical aspects of this analysis are discussed in this chapter. Chapter 13 is devoted to designing a global international asset allocation strategy.

To structure their analysis of expected return and risk of stocks, investors must start from a view of the world. What are the worldwide factors affecting stock prices? In an open-economy world, companies should be valued relative to their global competitors; hence, global industry analysis is of primary importance. Before conducting such an analysis, it is important to understand the differences in national accounting standards that affect the raw information used. Then the important aspects of global industry analysis can be studied with data adjusted for comparability across countries. Global industry analysis of expected returns and risks leads naturally to a discussion of risk factor models used to structure global portfolios and manage their risk.

Approaching International Analysis

There is nothing unique to financial analysis in an international context. Analysts must already take foreign variables into account in evaluating domestic firms. After all, product markets in which many domestic industrial companies compete are international.

Large domestic firms tend to export extensively and head a network of foreign subsidiaries. These companies must be analyzed as global firms, not purely domestic ones. In many sectors, the competition is fully global. The methods and data required to analyze international manufacturers are quite similar. In brief, research on a company should produce two pieces of information:

- *Expected return*: The *expected return* on an investment can be measured by a rate of return, including potential price appreciation, over some time period, or by some other quantified form of buy-or-sell recommendation.

- *Risk exposure*: Risk sensitivity, or risk exposure, measures how much a company's value responds to certain key factors, such as economic activity, energy costs, interest rates, currency volatility, and general market conditions. Risk analysis enables a manager or investment policy committee to simulate the performance of an investment in different scenarios. It also helps the manager design more diversified portfolios.

The overall purpose of analysis is to find securities with superior expected returns, given current (or foreseeable) domestic and international risks.

Quantifying the analysis facilitates a consistent global approach to international investment. This is all the more desirable when the parameters that must be considered are numerous and their interrelationships are complex. Although qualitative analysis seems easier to conduct in some institutions than in others, it must be carefully structured so that it is consistent for every security, and provides an estimation of the reaction of security prices to various risk factors.

The Information Problem

Information on foreign firms is often difficult to obtain; once obtained, it is often difficult to interpret and analyze using domestic methods. It is no wonder, then, that comparisons of similar figures for foreign firms are often misleading.

In the United States, companies publish their quarterly earnings, which are publicly available within just a couple of weeks after the close of the quarter. The 10-K reports are particularly useful for trend analysis and intercompany comparisons. Moreover, these reports are available on computerized databases. In contrast, certain European and Asian firms publish their earnings only once a year and with a considerable reporting time lag. French companies, for example, follow this pattern and don't actually publish their official earnings until two to six months after the end of their fiscal years. As a result, official earnings figures are outdated before they become public. To remedy this lack of information, most corporations with significant foreign ownership have begun announcing quarterly or semiannual earnings estimates a short time after the close of the quarter. This is true worldwide for large international corporations. These corporations also follow the U.S. practice of issuing "warnings" as soon as some bad news is likely to affect earnings. The format and reliability of these announcements vary from firm to firm, but overall, they help investors get better financial information more quickly. As do U.S. firms, British firms publish detailed financial information frequently. Similarly, Japanese firms have begun publishing U.S.-style financial statements, though sometimes only once a year.

Other problems arise from the language and presentation of the financial reports. Many reports are available only in a company's domestic language. Whereas multinational firms tend to publish both in their domestic language and in English, many smaller but nevertheless attractive firms do not. In general, financial reports vary widely from country to country in format, degree of detail, and reliability of the information disclosed. Therefore, additional information must sometimes be obtained directly from the company. Differences in national accounting standards are discussed later in this chapter.

As international investment has grown, brokers, banks, and information services have, fortunately, started to provide more financial data to meet investors' needs. In fact, today, many large global brokerage houses and banks provide analysts' guides covering companies from a large number of countries. The guides include information ranging from summary balance sheet and income statement information to growth forecasts, expected returns on equity investments, and risk measures, such as betas, which are discussed later. The reports are usually available in both the domestic language and English. Similarly, several data services, such as Bloomberg, Reuters, Thomson Financial, Factset, and Moody's, are extending their international coverage on companies and currently feature summary financial information on an increasing number of international corporations. Some financial firms, such as Thomson First Call, have specialized in collecting earnings forecasts from financial analysts worldwide. They provide a service giving the individual analyst's forecast for most large companies listed on the major stock exchanges of the world. They also calculate a consensus forecast, as well as various other global statistics.

Despite these developments, to get the most timely information possible, financial analysts may have to visit international corporations. This, of course, is a time-consuming and expensive process. Moreover, the information obtained is often not homogeneous across companies and countries. The next section reviews differences in international accounting standards.

A Vision of the World

A major challenge faced by all investment organizations is structuring their international research efforts. Their choice of method depends on what they believe are the major factors influencing stock returns. The objective of security analysis is to detect relative misvaluation, that is, investments that are preferable to other *comparable* investments. That is why sectoral analysis is so important. A financial analyst should be assigned the study of securities that belong to the same sector, that is, that are influenced by the *same* common factors and that can therefore be directly compared. The first task, though, is defining these sectors, or common factors. For example, one can reasonably claim that all oil companies belong to the same sector. Another sector would be French common stocks, which are all influenced by national factors. An alternative would be all high-technology companies across the world, which should be influenced by similar worldwide industrial factors. In a homogeneous sector, research should detect securities that are underpriced or overpriced relative to the others.

A first step for an organization to structure its global equity investment requires that it adhere to some vision of the world regarding the dominant factors affecting stock returns. Traditionally, investment organizations use one of three major approaches to international research, depending on their vision of the world:

- If a portfolio manager believes that the value of companies worldwide is affected primarily by global industrial factors, her research effort should be structured according to industrial sectors. This means that companies are valued relative to others within the same industry, for example, the chemical industry. Naturally, financial analysts who use this approach are specialists in particular industrial sectors.
- If a portfolio manager believes that all securities in a national stock market are influenced primarily by domestic factors, her research effort should be structured on a country-by-country or region-by-region basis. The most important

investment decision in this approach is how to allocate assets among countries or regions. Thereafter, securities are given a relative valuation within each national market.

- If a portfolio manager believes that some particular attributes of firms are valued worldwide, she will engage in *style investing*. For example, *value stocks* (corporations with a low stock market price compared with their book value) could be preferred to *growth stocks* (corporations with a high stock market price compared with their book value).

In general, an organization must structure its investment process based on some vision of the major common factors influencing stock returns worldwide.

Differences in National Accounting Standards

In this chapter, we develop a top-down approach to global equity investing. We examine country and industry analysis before moving to equity security analysis. Global industry financial analysis examines each company in the industry against the industry average. Plots of one financial ratio against another can show the relative location of individual companies within the industry. To carry out such analysis, we must first know something about the differences in national accounting standards so that we can adjust ratios to make them comparable. For example, discounted cash flow analysis (DCF) and compound annual growth rates (CAGR) in cash flows must be based on comparable data to be meaningful

In global industry financial analysis, the pattern is to contrast the financial ratios of individual firms against the same ratios for industry averages. The analyst will encounter and possibly need to adjust such ratios as enterprise value (EV) to earnings before interest, taxes, depreciation, and amortization (EBIDTA), return on equity (ROE), and the book value multiple of price to book value per share (BV). In practice, one also sees such ratios as price to net asset value (NAV), EV to capital employed (CE), return on capital employed (ROCE), and value added margin. *Capital employed* is usually defined as equity plus long-term debt.[1] *Net asset value* is usually defined on a per-share basis as equity minus goodwill. *Value added margin* is ROCE minus the weighted average cost of capital (WACC). Such ratios are detailed later.

With an understanding of differences in national accounting standards, the analyst will be prepared to evaluate companies from around the world within the context of global industry. After discussing these differences, we will return to global industry analysis.

Today all companies compete globally. Capital markets of developed countries are well integrated, and international capital flows react quickly to any perceived mispricing. Hence, companies tend to be priced relative to their global competitors, and it is for this reason that this chapter focuses on global industry analysis.

---

[1] See Temple (2002) for definitions.

Companies and investors have become more global. Mergers and acquisitions often occur on a global basis. Further, it is not unusual for a company to have its shares listed on multiple exchanges. Similarly, investors often seek to diversify their holdings and take advantage of opportunities across national borders. This globalization of financial markets creates challenges for investors, creditors, and other users of financial statements. Comparing financial statements of companies located in different countries can be a difficult task. Different countries may employ different accounting principles, and even where the same accounting methods are used, currency, cultural, institutional, political, and tax differences can make between-country comparisons of accounting numbers hazardous and misleading.

For example, the treatment of depreciation and extraordinary items varies greatly among countries, so that net income of a company located in one country might be different from that of a similarly performing company located in another country, even after adjustment for differences in currency. This disparity is partly the result of different national tax incentives and the creation of *secret* or *hidden reserves* (provisions) in certain countries. German and Swiss firms (among others), for example, have been known to stretch the definition of a liability; that is, they tend to overestimate contingent liabilities and future uncertainties when compared with other firms. The provisions for these liabilities reduce income in the current year, but increase income in later years when the provisions are reduced. This practice can have a smoothing impact on earnings and mask the underlying variability or riskiness of business operations.

Similarly, German and Swiss firms allow goodwill resulting from acquisitions to be deducted from equity immediately, bypassing the income statement and resulting in reporting the balance sheet based on book value, not on actual transaction prices. Similar idiosyncrasies often make comparisons of Japanese and U.S. earnings figures or accounting ratios meaningless. As a result, many large Japanese companies publish secondary financial statements in English that conform to the U.S. generally accepted accounting principles (GAAP). But even when we examine these statements, we find that financial ratios differ markedly between the two countries. For example, financial *leverage* is high in Japan compared with the United States, and coverage ratios are poor. But this does not necessarily mean that Japanese firms are more risky than their U.S. counterparts, only that the relationship between banks and their client corporations is different than in the United States.

With increasing globalization there has been a movement toward convergence of accounting standards internationally. In spite of this movement, there are still differences in existing accounting standards that must be considered by investors.

Historical Setting

Each country follows a set of accounting principles that are usually prepared by the accounting profession and the national authorities. These sets of accounting principles are sometimes called national GAAP. Two distinct models can describe the preparation of these national accounting principles:

- In the Anglo-American model, accounting rules have historically been set in standards prepared by a well-established, influential accounting profession.
- In the Continental model, used by countries in Continental Europe and Japan, accounting rules have been set in a codified law system; governmental bodies write the law, and the accounting profession is less influential than in the Anglo-American model.

Anglo-American countries typically report financial statements intended to give a true and fair view of the firm's financial position. Hence, there can be large differences between accounting statements, the intent of which is to give a fair representation of the firm's financial position, and tax statements, the intent of which is to reflect the various tax provisions used to calculate the amount of income tax owed. Many other countries (France, Germany, Italy, and Japan, for example) have a tradition that the reported financial statements and earnings conform to the method used to determine taxable income. This implies that financial statements were geared to satisfy legal and tax provisions and may not give a true and fair view of the firm. This confusion between tax and financial reporting is slowly disappearing under the pressure of international harmonization, as noted in the next section.

International Harmonization of Accounting Practices

Investors, creditors, and other users of financial statements have exerted pressure to harmonize national accounting principles. The International Accounting Standards Committee (IASC) was set up in 1973 by leading professional accounting organizations in nine countries: Australia, Canada, France, Germany, Japan, Mexico, the Netherlands, the United Kingdom and Ireland, and the United States. Over time, additional countries became members of the IASC. In 1974 the IASC issued its first international accounting standard (IAS), the Disclosure of Accounting Policies. In 2001, the IASC was renamed the International Accounting Standards Board (IASB), and we will use this name hereafter.

The IASB publishes both International Accounting Standards (IAS) and International Financial Reporting Standards (IFRS). The twenty-nine standards IAS adopted in 2001 form the body of the accounting standard and are periodically updated. Since 2002, new standards published by the IASB have taken the form of IFRS. Detailed interpretations of some of these IFRS are published by the International Financial Reporting Standards Interpretation Committee (IFRIC) of the IASB. A list of these standards, as of early 2007, is given in Exhibit 6.1 Given the numerous appellations (IAS, IFR, IFRIC), the set of standards edicted by the IASB is usually simply referred to as IFRS, as we will do here. Although the IASB is able to propose international accounting standards, it does not have the authority to require companies to follow these standards. Without a mechanism to compel companies to

EXHIBIT 6.1

List of IFRS and IAS as of March 2007

IFRS	
IFRS 1	First-time Adoption of International Financial Reporting Standards
IFRS 2	Share-based Payment
IFRS 3	Business Combinations
IFRS 4	Insurance Contracts
IFRS 5	Non-current Assets Held for Sale and Discontinued Operations
IFRS 6	Exploration for and evaluation of Mineral Resources
IFRS 7	Financial Instruments: Disclosures
IFRS 8	Operating Segments
IAS	
IAS 1	Presentation of Financial Statements
IAS 2	Inventories
IAS 7	Cash Flow Statements
IAS 8	Accounting Policies, Changes in Accounting Estimates and Errors
IAS 10	Events After the Balance Sheet Date
IAS 11	Construction Contracts
IAS 12	Income Taxes
IAS 16	Property, Plant and Equipment
IAS 17	Leases
IAS 18	Revenue
IAS 19	Employee Benefits
IAS 20	Accounting for Government Grants and Disclosure of Government Assistance
IAS 21	The Effects of Changes in Foreign Exchange Rates
IAS 23	Borrowing Costs
IAS 24	Related Party Disclosures
IAS 26	Accounting and Reporting by Retirement Benefit Plans
IAS 27	Consolidated and Separate Financial Statements
IAS 28	Investments in Associates
IAS 29	Financial Reporting in Hyperinflationary Economies
IAS 31	Interests in Joint Ventures
IAS 32	Financial Instruments: Presentation
IAS 33	Earnings per Share
IAS 34	Interim Financial Reporting
IAS 36	Impairment of Assets
IAS 37	Provisions, Contingent Liabilities and Contingent Assets
IAS 38	Intangible Assets
IAS 39	Financial Instruments: Recognition and Measurement
IAS 40	Investment Property
IAS 41	Agriculture

use IFRS and enforce the standards, harmonization is not easily achievable. In 2000, the International Organization of Securities Commissions (IOSCO) endorsed the existing IAS. IOSCO is an important organization whose members are the agencies regulating securities markets in all countries. IOSCO's objectives are to promote high standards of regulation in order to maintain just, efficient, and sound markets. In 2005 IOSCO encouraged its members to accept financial statements prepared under the IFRS in filings for cross-border listings and new offerings, with additional reconciliation or disclosure as necessary to meet national standards.

These two international organizations, one representative of the accounting profession (private sector) and the other of government regulators, play an important role in moving toward global harmonization of disclosure requirements and accounting practices. This goal is all the more important for multinational corporations that wish to raise capital globally. They need to be able to present their accounts in a single format wherever they want to be listed or raise capital. Of particular importance is the attitude of the United States toward international accounting standards. Convergence of the U.S. GAAP and IFRS is a desirable but difficult goal. A topic under discussion is to allow foreign firms listed on a U.S. stock exchange to publish accounts according to IFRS rather than asking them to provide earnings statements calculated according to the U.S. GAAP.

The IASB also received the support of the *World Bank.* A large number of emerging countries have adopted the IFRS as a basis for their accounting standards. In some cases national standards are virtually word-for-word IFRS, while in some others there are slight differences. Australia, Hong Kong and New Zealand have basically adopted the IFRS. In 2006, Canada decided to incorporate IRFS into Canadian GAAP within five years. Other developed countries are taking convergence steps. In 2005, the Accounting Standards Board of Japan decided to work on the convergence of Japanese GAAP with IFRS. In countries where national accounting standards are still different from IFRS, many corporations voluntarily use IFRS in their financial reporting. For example, most of the leading industrial companies in Switzerland voluntarily report their accounts according to international accounting standards.

A major step toward the worldwide acceptance of IFRS has been the decision by the European Union (*EU*) to adopt them. In countries where accounting rules are governed by law, specific legislation is required to allow for the use of other accounting standards. The harmonization of European accounting principles has come mostly through *Directives* published by the EU. These EU Directives are drafted by the EU Commission, and member states' parliaments must adapt the national law to conform to these Directives. The EU also issues *Regulations*, which have the force of law without requiring formal transposition into national legislation. In 2002, the EU issued a Regulation requiring listed companies to prepare their consolidated financial statements in accordance with IAS from 2005 onward. Endorsement and implementation of the IFRS by all members of the EU can be a lengthy process that requires translation into all national laws or regulations. But by March 2007, the EU Commission had voted to endorse all IAS and IFRS published to date, with one carve-out from IAS 39, Financial Instruments: Recognition and Measurement, relevant only for financial institutions. As of 2007, IFRS applies to the 27 EU members, plus members of the European Economic Area (Iceland, Liechtenstein, and Norway). EU listed companies are now required to perform their financial reporting according to IFRS, but this is not yet the case for unlisted companies, although most countries now permit IFRS for consolidated statements. In most Continental European countries, the national GAAP is codified in a law with a tax focus. But the trend is clearly to separate the financial reporting objective from the tax calculation objective.

While most countries are adopting IFRS, the United States retains the U.S. GAAP. The U.S. Securities and Exchange Commission (SEC) requests that all foreign firms listed on a public stock exchange in the United States, including NASDAQ, provide financial reports according to the U.S. GAAP (10-K reports) or provide all necessary reconciliation information (20-F reports). Strong efforts are devoted by financial reporting standard setters on both sides to achieve convergence of the two sets of standards. The U.S. GAAP are prepared by the U.S. Financial Accounting Standards Board (FASB) in consultations with various bodies, including the SEC. In October 2002, the FASB and the IASB formalized their commitment to the convergence of their standards by issuing a memorandum of understanding (commonly referred to as the *Norwalk agreement*). The two boards pledged to use their best efforts to

- make their existing financial reporting standards fully compatible as soon as is practicable, and
- coordinate their future work programs to ensure that once achieved, compatibility is maintained.

Compatible does not mean word-for-word identical standards; rather, it means that there are no significant differences between the two sets of standards. In February 2006, the IASB and the FASB released a "road map" that identified short- and long-term convergence projects. The objective is to remove the need for IFRS reconciliation requirements by 2009.

The road to global cooperation is never easy, and it will take time before full harmonization of financial reporting is achieved, especially between the United States and other countries.

Differences in Global Standards

Financial reporting standards are evolving rapidly, at least for listed companies. Historical financial information for these companies, or that available for unlisted companies, is based on national GAAP that can differ markedly from IFRS. In many countries adopting the IFRS there were huge differences between the existing national GAAP and the new IFRS. For example, generous provisions could be taken in Germany and Switzerland for all types of general risks. In good times, German firms build provisions to reduce earnings growth; in bad times, they draw on these provisions to boost reported earnings. Adoption of IFRS by listed companies greatly reduces the leeway for provisioning.

But the major differences that remain are between IFRS and U.S. GAAP, and we will focus on those. A complete presentation of accounting standards is beyond the scope of this book. The full text of standards can be obtained from the International Accounting Standards Board and the Financial Accounting Standards Board.[2] Many of the differences in reporting are progressively eliminated.

The differences can be highlighted by looking at the reconciliation statements (20-F reports) that are provided by foreign firms listed in the United States. Ernst & Young surveyed 130 major foreign firms in 2006.[3] IFRS are new standards with transitional provisions for first-time adoption, that is, when a company adopts IFRS for the first time. A considerable number of reconciling differences may arise as a result of the first-time adoption rules in IFRS 1, First-time Adoption of International Financial Reporting Standards. A company preparing an IFRS-to-U.S. GAAP reconciliation is required to apply U.S. standards as if it had always applied those standards. Conversely, IFRS 1 provides first-time adopters with a number of exemptions from full retrospective application. In some cases these rules permit a first-time adopter to base IFRS information on measurements under its previous GAAP. Hence, some of the reconciling items may reflect differences between a first-time adopter's previous GAAP and U.S. GAAP rather than differences between IFRS and U.S. GAAP. The impact of IFRS 1 will decline over time as companies accumulate years of reporting under IFRS. In 2006, the major differences that needed reconciliation were in the following areas:

- Consolidation methods
- Business combinations
- Foreign currency translation
- Intangible assets
- Impairment
- Capitalization of borrowing costs
- Financial instruments—recognition and measurement
- Financial instruments—shareholders' equity
- Financial instruments—derivatives and hedge accounting
- Leasing
- Provisions and contingencies
- Revenue recognition
- Share-based payments
- Pensions and post-retirement benefits

---

[2] See www.iasb.org and www.fasb.org. Detailed information and comparisons of various standards are also provided by the Web sites of major accounting firms, for example, www.iasplus.com.

[3] "Towards Convergence: A Survey of IFRS to US GAAP Differences," Ernst & Young, 2006.

A technical discussion of these differences is beyond the scope of this book. Furthermore, the IASB and FASB are working on convergence of the reporting standards, and most differences will disappear in financial statements by 2010. A few illustrations of major points in mid-2000 are nevertheless useful:

- Consolidation under IFRS and U.S. GAAP can lead to some differences. IFRS bases the consolidation of subsidiaries in terms of "control," either through voting rights or through power to govern. U.S. GAAP distinguishes between a *voting interest* model and a *variable interest* model. There can be significant differences for minority interest and joint ventures. The Enron collapse, for example, illustrated the importance of accounting for *special purpose entities (SPEs)*, sometimes referred to as off-balance-sheet arrangements. The ability of firms to avoid consolidation of SPE has often enabled them to keep large amounts of liabilities off the balance sheet, to the detriment of investors and creditors alike. Under IAS 27, SPEs are consolidated if controlled. In the United States, pre-Enron accounting standards did not provide an accurate picture of the relationships between the parent companies and their SPEs, leaving plenty of leeway to avoid consolidation. In December 2003, the FASB issued a revised interpretation known as FIN 46(R), Consolidation of Variable Interest Entities, which enlarges the scope of SPE consolidation. There are still cases, however, where a SPE would be consolidated under IFRS but not under U.S. GAAP. Further convergence is planned.

CONCEPTS IN ACTION *RULES SET FOR BIG CHANGE*

Millions of Dollars of Debt Could Be Brought Back on to Companies' Balance Sheets

Among the many consequences of the collapse of Enron has been a new focus by regulators on how companies account for off-balance-sheet transactions.

Enron's swift demise raised questions over its complex web of off-balance-sheet transactions, leading the U.S.'s Financial Standards Accounting Board to consider new rules governing special purpose entities (SPEs). The changes could result in millions of dollars of debt being brought back on to corporate balance sheets, and represent a significant challenge for the rapidly developing structured finance market. SPEs are used for a wide range of financial transactions because they isolate assets from the financial fortunes of companies that own them.

SPEs can be organized in a variety of forms, such as trusts or corporations, but usually have no full-time employees or operating business. They can be used for different activities, including acquiring financial assets, property or equipment, and as a vehicle for raising funds from investors by issuing stock or other securities.

Depending on the type of SPE, its assets and liabilities may not appear in the financial statements of the entity that created it. . . .

Source: Jenny Wiggins, "Special Purpose Entities," *Financial Times,* October 7, 2002, p. 4. From *Financial Times.*

- Under U.S. GAAP, investments are reported at historical cost (acquisition cost less depreciation and impairment), except for some financial instruments revalued to fair value. Under IFRS, intangible assets, property plant and equipment (PPE), and investment property may be revalued to *fair value.* Derivatives, biological assets, and some financial securities must be fair valued.
- Share-based payments have been the object of heated debate in the United States. *Employee stock options* represent potential earnings dilution to existing shareholders. As a form of employee compensation, these stock options should be treated as expenses from an economic perspective. Under IFRS 2, Share-based Payment, the fair value of employee share offers (stock options) are recorded immediately in personnel costs, with an adjustment to equity. So share options are treated as expenses. Under U.S. GAAP, many companies were accounting for share-based payments under the intrinsic value method in accordance with APB 25, Accounting for Stock Issued to Employees. The *intrinsic value* of an option is simply the difference between the market value of the share minus the *strike price* or *exercise price* indicated in the option. If the stock price is below the exercise price when the option is granted, the intrinsic value is nil. In December 2004, the FASB published FAS 123(R), Accounting for Stock-Based Compensation, which supersedes APB 25. It requires the application of a fair value option pricing model to determine the value of the option to be expensed. As of 2007, there are still some slight technical differences between IFRS and U.S. GAAP in terms of timing principles, namely, the valuation of options that are granted but not yet vested (i.e., they cannot yet be exercised by the employee). There exist different option pricing models that can be used (mainly the *Black-Scholes model* and the binomial model) and different calculation assumptions can lead to very different fair values. Hence, the expense reported by a company can be more or less conservative. An illustration of option expensing is given in Example 6.1.

The Effects of Accounting Principles on Earnings and Stock Prices

The same company using different national accounting standards could report different earnings. Some accounting standards are more conservative than others, in the sense that they lead to smaller reported earnings. Several comparative studies have attempted to measure the relative conservativeness of national standards. For example, Radebaugh and Gray (1997) conclude that U.S. accounting principles are significantly more conservative than U.K. accounting principles but significantly less conservative than Japanese and Continental European accounting principles. If the United States' earnings are arbitrarily scaled at 100, Japanese earnings would scale at 66, German earnings at 87, French earnings at 97, and British earnings at 125. These national accounting principles also affect the reported book value of equity. Now that most countries are adopting IFRS for listed companies, the differences are going to be much smaller. The reconciliation statements (Form 20-F) that are provided by foreign firms listed in the United States still show some differences in

EXAMPLE 6.1 EMPLOYEE STOCK OPTIONS

A company has 100,000 shares outstanding at $100 per share. To its senior management, the company granted employee stock options on 5,000 shares. The options can be exercised at a price of $105 any time during the next five years. For five years, the employees thus have the right but not the obligation to purchase shares at the $105 price, regardless of the prevailing market price of the stock. Using price volatility estimates for the stock, a standard Black-Scholes valuation model gives an estimated value of $20 per share option. Without expensing the options, the company's pretax earnings per share are reported as $1 million/100,000 = $10 per share. What would they have been if they had been expensed?

SOLUTION

The expense is 5000 × $20 = $100,000.

The pretax income per share would be ($1,000,000 − $100,000)/100,000 = $9 per share.

reported net profit and book value between IFRS and U.S. GAAP. Part of these differences are caused by first-time adoption of IFRS by some of these firms, but significant discrepancies in reported numbers are caused by existing differences between the two reporting systems.

Price–earnings (P/E) ratios are of great interest to international investors, who tend to compare the P/E ratios of companies in the same industrial sector across the world. The P/E ratio divides the market price of a share by its current or estimated annual earnings. Japanese companies have traditionally traded at high P/E ratios in comparison with U.S. companies. For comparison purposes, these P/E ratios should be adjusted because of the accounting differences in reporting earnings. They also should be adjusted to reflect the fact that Japanese firms tend to report nonconsolidated statements despite the extent of cross-holding. For example, if Company A owns 20 percent of the shares of Company B, it will include in its own earnings only the dividend paid by Company B, not a proportion of Company B's earnings. In the P/E ratio of Company A, the stock price reflects the value of the holding of shares of Company B, but the earnings do not reflect the earnings of Company B. For all these reasons, French and Poterba (1991) claim that the average 1989 Japanese P/E ratio should be adjusted from 53.7 to 32.6. Again, these differences are likely to be reduced in the near future as Japanese GAAP evolves toward IFRS in requiring consolidation of controlled subsidiaries.

All investment managers regard accounting harmonization as a good thing.[4] But they stress the importance of the quality and timeliness of the information

[4] See a survey of European fund managers conducted by PriceWaterhouseCoopers/Ipsos MORI: *IFRS—The European Investors' View*, February 2006.

disclosed. Indeed, the quality and speed of information disclosure are of paramount importance to investors. Restating the same information in a different accounting standard does not address the issue of the quality of the information disclosed or the firm's future prospects. Investment managers deciding to include a specific stock in a portfolio need to do more than simply look at past accounting data.

Global Industry Analysis

The valuation of a common stock is usually conducted in several steps. A company belongs to a global industry and is based in a country; hence, country and industry analysis are necessary. Companies compete against global players within their industry, so studying a company within its global industry is the primary approach to stock valuation.

With the knowledge that financial ratios from different international companies are difficult to compare, the analyst still faces the task of looking forward. What conditions in the industry prevail, and how are companies likely to compete in the future?

Within the framework of industrial organization, this section outlines the most important elements that should be looked at when conducting a company analysis in a global setting. We begin with a general introduction to country analysis to provide a starting point for the analysis of the company and industry.

Country Analysis

Companies tend to favor some countries in their business activities: They target some countries for their sales and base their production in only a few countries. Hence, country analysis is of importance in studying a company. In each country, economists try to monitor a large number of economic, social, and political variables, such as the following:

- Anticipated real growth
- Monetary policy
- Fiscal policy (including fiscal incentives for investments)
- Wage and employment rigidities
- Competitiveness
- Social and political situations
- Investment climate

In the long run, real economic growth is probably the major influence on a national stock market. Economists focus on economic growth at two horizons:

- Business cycle
- Long-term sustainable growth

What are favorable country conditions for equity investment? There can be favorable business cycle conditions as well as favorable long-term sustainable growth conditions. If the favorable conditions are a consensus view, however, they will already be priced in the equity markets. The analyst must find a way of discerning these conditions before others do.

A high long-term sustainable growth rate in gross domestic product (GDP) is favorable, because this translates into high long-term profits and stock returns. In creating GDP and productivity growth rate expectations, the analyst will undoubtedly examine the country's savings rate, investment rate, and total factor productivity (TFP). TFP measures the efficiency with which the economy converts capital and labor into goods and services. Increased investment rates due to technical progress will increase rates of return, but the savings and investment rates themselves must be closely analyzed. A country's investments reflect replacement and capacity expansion and influence future productivity gains. If the ratio of investment to GDP is low, then the investments are largely replacement investments; whereas a high rate suggests that capacity expansion is under way.[5] Further, a positive correlation between investment rates and subsequent GDP growth rates cannot be taken for granted because there are other factors to consider.

The main factors that interact with the country's investment rate to affect GDP growth are the rate of growth in employment, work hours, educational levels, technological improvement, business climate, political stability, and the public or private nature of the investment. A higher long-term growth in the work force will lead to higher GDP growth just as a reduction in work hours will lead to less GDP growth. Increasing skills in the work force complement technological advances as they will both lead to higher GDP growth. A business climate of more privatization and reduced regulation is conducive to more investment. Attractive investment opportunities will also lead to more investment, although an increased propensity to invest can depress rates of return. Political stability will reduce the risk and hence increase the attractiveness of investments. Finally, private investments are more likely to be made with maximal return on equity as the objective and hence lead to higher GDP growth.

In the short term, business cycle conditions can be favorable for investments, but business cycle turning points are so difficult to predict that such predictions should cause the analyst to make investment recommendations to only slightly adjust portfolio. Business cycles represent a complex control system with many causes and interacting private and governmental decisions. For example, companies invest in plant and equipment and build inventories based on expected demand but face the reality that actual demand does not continuously meet expectations.

[5] See Calverley (2003), p.11.

Although an investor would benefit from buying stocks at the trough of a business cycle and bonds at the peak, such perfect market timing is virtually impossible, and one might better take the approach of ignoring the country's business cycle and concentrate rather on its long-term sustainable growth rate in GDP. Nevertheless, even limited prescient ability can lead to informed adjustments to portfolio holdings. Calverley (2003, pp. 15–19) classifies the business cycle stages and attractive investment opportunities as follows:

- *Recovery*: The economy picks up from its slowdown or recession. Good investments to have are the country's cyclical stocks and commodities, followed by riskier assets as the recovery takes hold.
- *Early upswing*: Confidence is up and the economy is gaining some momentum. Good investments to have are the country's stocks and also commercial and residential property.
- *Late upswing*: Boom mentality has taken hold. This is not usually a good time to buy the country's stocks. The country's commodity and property prices will also be peaking. This is the time to purchase the country's bonds (yields are high) and interest-rate-sensitive stocks.
- *Economy slows or goes into recession*: The economy is declining. Good investments to have are the country's bonds, which will rally (because of a drop in market interest rates), and its interest-rate-sensitive stocks.
- *Recession*: Monetary policy will be eased but there will be a lag before recovery. Particularly toward the end of the recession, good investments to make are the country's stocks and commodities.

Inflation is generally associated with the late upswing, and deflation is possible in a recession. Inflation effects on equity valuation are analyzed later in this chapter.

Business Cycle Synchronization Stock market performance is clearly related to the business cycle and economic growth.[6] National business cycles are not fully synchronized. This lack of synchronization makes country analysis all the more important. For example, the United States witnessed a strong economic recovery in 1992, Britain started to enjoy strong economic growth in 1993, and the European continent only started to recover in 1995, but Japan's economy was still stagnant.

However, economies are becoming increasingly integrated. Growth of major economies is, in part, exported abroad. For example, growth in the United States can sustain the activity of an exporting European firm even if demand by European consumers is stagnant. But rigidities in a national economy can prevent it from quickly joining growth in a world business cycle. Studies of rigidities are important here.

---

[6] See Canova and De Nicolo (1995). An analysis of the business cycle is provided in Reilly and Brown (2006).

What are the business cycle synchronization implications for equity valuation? Although national economies are becoming increasingly integrated with a world economy, there are so many economic variables involved that the chances of full synchronization are extremely remote. For example, within the European Union, tensions arise because governments are not free to pursue domestic and fiscal economic policies to deal with their own domestic business cycles. The experience of the 1990s and early 2000s is that the economies of Continental Europe, Japan, the United Kingdom, and the United States had markedly different GDP growth rates and entered various stages of the business cycle at different times. Recalling that any correlation less than unity supports diversification benefits, the lack of perfect business cycle synchronization is an a priori argument in favor of international diversification. If long-term GDP growth and business cycles were perfectly synchronized among countries, then one would expect a high degree of correlation between markets, especially in periods of crisis. In making investment asset-allocation decisions, one must always consider long-term expected returns, variances, and correlations. In the long term, international diversification will always be advantageous until national economies are expected to be perfectly synchronized around the world. It is difficult to imagine such a possibility. Expected returns and expected standard deviations will differ among countries with unsynchronized short-term business cycles and long-term GDP growth rates, even though investors may follow the crowd in their short-term reactions to crises.

Further considerations in the divergence between countries come from a consideration of growth clubs. Baumol (1986) examined three convergence growth clubs (clubs of countries converging to a similar steady state in terms of income per capita): western industrialized countries, centrally planned economies, and less developed countries. Regardless of the number of growth clubs, one can expect within-group convergence but intergroup divergence in TFP and income per capita. The degree of business cycle synchronicity also varies over time depending on the pattern of regional shocks and changes in economies' propagation mechanisms.

Growth Theory Growth theory is a branch of economics that examines the role of countries in value creation. The output of a country is measured by gross domestic product (GDP), and growth theory attempts to explain the rate of GDP growth in different countries. For two countries with equal risk, portfolio managers will want to overweight the country with sustainable expected long-term GDP growth. The inputs considered are labor, capital, and productivity. In addition to labor and capital, there are also human capital and natural resources. Increases in educational levels can lead to an increase in labor skills, and discoveries of natural resources can lead to resource-based growth. Two competing economic theories attempt to shed light on the sustainable long-term growth rate of a nation.

Neoclassical growth theory assumes that the marginal productivity of capital declines as more capital is added. This is the traditional case in economics with diminishing marginal returns to input factors. *Endogenous growth theory* assumes that the marginal productivity of capital does not necessarily decline as capital is added. Technological advances and improved education of the labor force can lead to efficiency gains. Any one firm faces diminishing returns, but endogenous growth theory assumes that externalities arise when a firm develops a new technology. Thus, one firm's technical breakthrough begets another's breakthrough, perhaps through imitation. In this case, the marginal product of capital does not decline with increasing capital per capita.

In growth theory, *steady state* is defined as the condition of no change in capital per capita. This comes about when the savings rate times GDP per capita just matches the investment required to maintain the amount of capital per capita. The rate of growth in the population plus the yearly depreciation in equipment gives a replacement rate to be multiplied by the amount of capital per capita, and this multiplication yields the investment required to maintain the amount of capital per capita.

Neoclassical growth theory predicts that the long-term level of GDP depends on the country's savings rate, but the long-term growth rate in GDP does not depend on the savings rate. This is because a steady state is reached, and this steady state is reached because additions to the capital stock provide smaller and smaller increases to GDP and consequently to savings (the savings rate times GDP). In the context of endogenous growth theory, steady state may never be reached because the ability to avoid a decline in the marginal product of capital means there is no necessary decline in savings as capital is increased. Thus, endogenous growth theory predicts that the long-term growth rate in GDP depends on the savings rate.

Neoclassical growth theory suggests that countries above steady state will slow to steady state and countries below steady state will have their growth speed up. Thus, there will be convergence in the case of countries that have similar steady states. Endogenous growth theory, however, maintains that technological progress is not exogenous but rather depends on research and development and the generation of ideas. Essentially, the productivity term in the production function does not grow exogenously at a constant rate as specified in neoclassical growth theory. Rather, the rate of change in the productivity term depends on the stock of innovations to date and the number of researchers at work on innovations.

Equity valuation implications are different for countries experiencing neoclassical versus endogenous growth. If a country is experiencing neoclassical growth and its savings rate increases, there would be an increase in dividends as the new level of GDP is reached, but not an increase in the dividend growth rate. For a country experiencing endogenous growth with cascading breakthroughs, however, there would be an increase in both dividends and the dividend growth rate.

In an open world economy, it is important to ascertain whether growth is caused by an increased mobilization of inputs or by efficiency gains. Input-driven growth is necessarily limited. For example, many developing countries have witnessed high growth rates because of capital flows from abroad, but they face diminishing returns in the absence of productivity gains. National sustainable growth rates require careful examination.

The Limitation of the Country Concept in Financial Analysis The distinction between countries and companies is misleading in some respects. Both types of economic entities produce and market a portfolio of products. Indeed, some companies are bigger in economic size than some countries.

Many companies compete globally. The national location of their headquarters is not a determinant variable. Many multinational corporations realize most of their sales and profits in foreign countries. So, an analysis of the economic situation of the country of their headquarters is not of great importance. In Chapter 5, we showed that many national stock markets are dominated by a few multinationals. For example, Nokia market capitalization is larger than the sum of that of all other Finnish firms. The top ten Swiss multinational firms account for more than 70 percent of the Swiss stock exchange. But these companies do most of their business outside of their home country, so their valuation should be based on the global competition they face in their industry, not on the state of their home economy.

Industry Analysis: Return Expectation Elements

To achieve excess equity returns on a risk-adjusted basis, an investor must find companies that can earn return on equity (ROE) above the required rate of return and do this on a sustained basis. For this reason, global industry analysis centers on an examination of sources of growth and sustainability of competitive advantage. Growth must be distinguished from level. A high profit level may yield high current cash flows for valuation purposes, but there is also the question of how these cash flows will grow. Continued reinvestment opportunities in positive net present value investment opportunities will create growth. Curtailment of research and development expenditures may yield high current cash flows at the expense of future growth.

An analyst valuing a company within its global industry should study several key elements. Following are some important conceptual issues.

Demand Analysis Value analysis begins with an examination of demand conditions. The concepts of complements and substitutes help, but demand analysis is quite complex. Usually, surveys of demand as well as explanatory regressions are used to try to estimate demand. Demand is the target for all capacity, location, inventory, and production decisions. Often, the analyst tries to find a leading indicator to help give some forecast of demand.

In the global context, *demand* means *worldwide demand.* One cannot simply define the automobile market as a domestic market. A starting point, then, is a set of forecasts of global and country-specific GDP figures. The analyst will want to estimate the sensitivity of sales to global and national GDP changes.

Country analysis is important for demand analysis because most companies tend to focus on specific regions. Many European car manufacturers tend to sell and produce outside of Europe, but the European car market is their primary market. An increase in demand for cars in Europe will affect these companies more than it will affect Japanese car producers.

Value Creation Sources of value come from using inputs to produce outputs in the value chain. The *value chain* is the set of transformations in moving from raw materials to product or service delivery. This chain can involve many companies and countries, some providing raw materials, some producing intermediate goods, some producing finished consumer goods, and some delivering finished goods to the consumer. From the point of view of an intermediate goods producer, basic raw materials are considered to be *upstream* in the value chain, and transformations closer to the consumer are considered *downstream.*

Within the value chain, each transformation adds value. Value chain analysis can be used to determine how much value is added at each step. Indeed, some countries have a value-added tax (VAT). The value added at each transformation stage is partly a function of four major factors:

- *The learning (experience) curve*: As companies produce more output, they gain experience, so that the cost per unit produced declines.
- *Economies of scale*: As a company expands, its fixed costs may be spread over a larger output, and average costs decline over a range of output.
- *Economies of scope*: As a company produces related products, experience and reputation with one product may spill over to another product.
- *Network externalities*: Some products and services gain value as more consumers use them, so that they are able to share something popular.

Equity valuation implications come from an analysis of the industry's value chain and each company's strategy to exploit current and future profit opportunities within the chain. For company managers, Christensen, Raynor, and Verlinden (2001) recommend a strategy of predicting profit migration within the industry's value chain. For example, they break the computer industry down into value chain stages: equipment, materials, components, product design, assembly, operating system, application software, sales and distribution, and field service. In the early days of the computer industry, vertically integrated manufacturers delivered the entire value chain. The advent of the personal computer led to specialization within each stage, and profits migrated to stages such as components and operating systems. For the analyst also, the strategy of predicting dividends and dividend growth rates must be based on profit migration in the value chain. The risk can be gauged from the degree of competition within the stage—the more the competition, the more the risk. The ability of companies to compete at each stage will be enhanced by their learning curve progress, economies of scale or scope, and network externalities.

Christensen et al. also point out that industries often evolve from vertical integration to disintegration. If an industry becomes too fragmented, however, consolidation pressures will come from resource bottlenecks as well as the continuing search for economies of scale. During the industry's life cycle, tension between disintegration and consolidation will require the company and the analyst to constantly monitor company positions in the profit migration cycle.

Industry Life Cycle Traditionally, the industry life cycle is broken down into stages from pioneering development to decline. Of course, one must be careful in industry definition. If railroads were defined as an *industry*, we would see a global industry life cycle. Defining the industry as transportation provides a different picture. In any case, industry life cycles are normally categorized by rates of growth in sales. The stages of growth can clearly vary in length:

1. Pioneering development is the first stage, and has a low but slowly increasing industry sales growth rate. Substantial development costs and acceptance by only early adopters can lead to low profit margins.
2. Rapid accelerating growth is the second stage, and the industry sales growth rate is still modest but is rapidly increasing. High profit margins are possible because firms from outside the new industry may face barriers to entering the newly established markets.
3. Mature growth is the third stage and has a high but more modestly increasing industry sales growth rate. The entry of competitors lowers profit margins, but the return on equity is high.

One would expect that somewhere in stage 2 or 3 the industry sales growth rate would move above the GDP growth rate in the economy.

4. Stabilization and market maturity is the fourth stage and has a high but only slowly increasing sales growth rate. The sales growth rate has not yet begun to decline, but increasing capacity and competition may cause returns on equity to decline to the level of average returns on equity in the economy.
5. Deceleration of growth and decline is the fifth stage, with a decreasing sales growth rate. At this stage, the industry may experience overcapacity, and profit margins may be completely eroded.

One would expect that somewhere in stage 5, the industry sales growth rate would fall back to the GDP growth rate and then decline below it. (This cannot happen in stage 4, where the sales growth is still increasing.) The position of an industry in its life cycle should be judged on a global basis.

Competition Structure One of the first steps in analyzing an industry is the determination of the amount of industry concentration. If the industry is fragmented, many firms compete, and the theories of competition and product differentiation are most applicable. With more concentration and fewer firms in the industry, oligopolistic competition and game theories become more important. Finally, the case of one firm is the case in which the theory of monopoly applies.

In analyzing industry concentration, two methods are normally used. One method is the N firm concentration ratio: the combined market share of the largest N firms in the industry. For example, a market in which the three largest firms have a combined share of 80 percent would indicate largely oligopolistic competition. A related but more precise measure is the *Herfindahl index* (H), the sum of the squared market shares of the firms in the industry. Letting M_i be the market share of an individual firm, the index is $H = M_1^2 + M_2^2 + \ldots + M_N^2$.

If two firms have a 15 percent market share each and one has a 70 percent market share, $H = 0.15^2 + 0.15^2 + 0.7^2 = 0.535$.

The Herfindahl index has a value that is always smaller than one. A small index indicates a competitive industry with no dominant players. If all firms have an equal share, $H = N(1/N^2) = 1/N$, and the reciprocal of the index shows the number of firms in the industry. When the firms have unequal shares, the reciprocal of the index indicates the "equivalent" number of firms in the industry. Using our example above, we find that the market structure is equivalent to having 1.87 firms of the same size:

$$\frac{1}{H} = \frac{1}{(0.15^2 + 0.15^2 + 0.70^2)} = \frac{1}{0.535} = 1.87$$

One can classify the competition structure of the industry according to this ratio.

In practice, the equity analyst will see both the *N* firm concentration ratio and the Herfindahl index. The analyst is searching for indicators of the likely degree of cooperation versus competition within the industry. Although the balance between cooperation and competition is dynamic and changing, the higher the *N* firm concentration ratio and the higher the Herfindahl index, the less likely it is that there is cut-throat competition and the more likely it is that companies will cooperate.

The advantage of the *N* firm concentration ratio is that it provides an intuitive sense of industry competition. If the analyst knows that the seven largest firms have a combined share of less than 15 percent, he or she immediately knows that the industry is extremely fragmented and thus more risky because of competitive pressures and the likely lack of cooperation.

The Hefindahl index has the advantage of greater discrimination because it reflects all firms in the industry and it gives greater weight to the companies with larger market shares. An *H* below 0.1 indicates an unconcentrated industry, an *H* of 0.1 to 0.18 indicates moderate concentration, and an *H* above 0.18 indicates high concentration. A high Herfindahl index can also indicate the presence of a market leader with a higher share than others, another indication of likely coordination as the leader might impose discipline on the industry.

Suppose the analyst is comparing two industries:

Market Shares in Industry A	**Market Shares in Industry B**
One firm has 45%	Four firms have 15% each
Three firms have 5% each	Four firms have 10% each
Ten firms have 4% each	
Four firm concentration ratio is 60%	Four firm concentration ratio is 60%
Herfindahl index is 0.23	Herfindahl index is 0.13

Even though the four firm concentration ratios are the same for both industries, the Herfindahl index indicates that industry A is highly concentrated, but industry B is only moderately concentrated.

Competitive Advantage In his book *The Competitive Advantage of Nations*,[7] Michael Porter used the notions of economic geography that different locations have different competitive advantages. Some national factors can lead to a competitive advantage:

- Factor conditions such as human capital, perhaps measured by years of schooling
- Demand conditions such as the size and growth of the domestic market
- Related supplier and support industries such as the computer software industry to support the hardware industry
- Strategy, structure, and rivalry such as the corporate governance, management practices, and the financial climate

Competitive Strategies A competitive strategy is a set of actions that a firm is taking to optimize its future competitive position. In *Competitive Advantage*, Porter distinguishes three generic competitive strategies:[8]

- *Cost leadership*: The firm seeks to be the low-cost producer in its industry.
- *Differentiation*: The firm seeks to provide product benefits that other firms do not provide.
- *Focus*: The firm targets a niche with either a cost or a benefit (differentiation) focus.

Equity valuation analysis in large part is analysis of the probability of success of company strategies. Analysts will consider the company's commitment to a strategy as well as the likely responses of its competitors. Is the company a tough competitor that is likely to survive a war of attrition? Is it likely that a Nash equilibrium will hold, in which each company adopts a strategy to leave itself with the best outcome regardless of the competitor's strategy and, by doing this, causes a reduction in the size of the total reward to both?

Co-opetition and the Value Net *Co-opetition* refers to cooperation along the value chain and is an application of game theory. Brandenberger and Nalebuff developed the concept of the value net as the set of participants involved in producing value along the value chain: the suppliers, customers, competitors, and firms producing complementary goods and services.[9] Although these participants compete with each other, they can also cooperate to produce mutually beneficial outcomes. In this respect, co-opetition is an application of cooperative game theory.

---

7 Porter (1998b)

8 Porter (1998a).

9 Brandenberger and Nalebuff (1996).

In the context of equity valuation, co-opetition analysis is an important element of risk analysis. Cooperating participants in a good economy may become staunch competitors in a poor economy. If a company's abnormal profits depend on co-opetition, those profits are riskier than if they are the result of a purely competitive environment. In a good economy, a company may outsource some of its production to cooperating value net participants who may build capabilities based on lucrative long-term contracts. In a poor economy, however, no new contracts may be forthcoming.

Sector Rotation Many commercial providers sell reports on the relative performance of industries or sectors over the business cycle, and sector rotation is a popular investment-timing strategy. Some investors put more weight on industries entering a profitable portion of their role in the business cycle. Certainly industries behave differently over the business cycle. Because consumer cyclical industries (durables and nondurables) correlate highly with the economy as a whole, these industries do well in the early and middle growth portion of the business cycle. Defensive consumer staples (necessities) maintain their profitability during recessions. Nevertheless, a successful sector rotation strategy depends on an intensive analysis of the industry and faces many pitfalls. An upturn in the economy and the demand for industry products does not automatically mean an increase in profits, because factors such as the status of industry capacity, the competitive structure, the lead time to increase capacity, and the general supply/demand conditions in the industry also have an impact on profits.

Indicators of the various stages of the business cycle are complex. We have already seen that different sectors—for example, cyclical sectors—will do well at various stages of the business cycle. Again, the five stages are

- *Recovery*: The economy picks up from its slowdown or recession.
- *Early upswing*: Confidence is up and the economy is gaining some momentum.
- *Late upswing*: Boom mentality has taken hold.
- *Economy slows or goes into recession*: The economy is declining.
- *Recession*: Monetary policy will be eased but there will be a lag before recovery.

Industry Analysis: Risk Elements

To achieve excess equity returns on a risk-adjusted basis, investors must be able to distinguish sources of risk in the investments they make. For example, an increase in ROE may be attributable solely to an increase in leverage (gearing). This increased leverage raises the financial risk and hence the required rate of return; the increased ROE then does not yield an excess risk-adjusted return. Although return expectations can be established by evaluating firm strategies within the industry, the analyst must always examine the risk that the strategy may be flawed or that assumptions about competition and co-opetition may hold only in a good economic environment. What seems to be an attractive strategy in good times can turn into a very dangerous one in bad times. The risks can differ widely, not only between firms in the same industry but also across industries. Some industries are more sensitive to technological change and the business cycle than are others. So, the outlined growth factors that affect return expectations should also be taken into account to assess industry risk.

Ultimately, firms that follow high-risk strategies in an industry that is also risky will have a higher ex ante stock market risk, and this fact should be incorporated in expected risk measures. Ex post, this stock market risk will eventually be measured by looking at volatility and covariance measures.

Market Competition Microeconomics[10] examines the various types of competition in markets. The question is always to look at price versus average cost. Particularly with oligopolies and monopolies, game theory helps to discern the likely success or failure of corporate strategies. Preservation of competitive position and competitive advantage often involves entry-deterring or exit-promoting strategies. *Limit pricing* is pricing below average cost to deter entry. Similarly, *holding excess capacity* can deter entry. *Predatory pricing* is pricing below average cost to drive others out of the industry. Any valuation of an individual company must examine the strategy contest in which companies in the industry are engaged. Risks are always present that the company's strategy will not sustain its competitive advantage.

Value Chain Competition In producing goods and services of value, companies compete not just in markets, but also along the value chain. Suppliers can choose to compete rather than simply cooperate with the intermediate company. Labor, for example, may want some of the profit that a company is earning. In lean times labor may make concessions, but in good times labor may want a larger share of the profits. Buyers may organize to wrest some of the profit from the company.

A major issue in value chain analysis is whether labor is unionized. Japanese automobile companies producing in the United States face lower production costs because of their ability to employ non-unionized workers. Union relations are a major factor in valuing airline companies worldwide.

Suppliers of commodity raw materials have less ability to squeeze profits out of a downstream company than do suppliers of differentiated intermediate products. Companies may manage their value chain competition by vertically integrating (buying upstream or downstream) or, for example, by including labor in their ownership structure.

Co-opetition risks are presented by the possibility that the company's supply may be held up or that its distributors may find other sources of products and services. Suppose a firm acts as a broker between producers and distributors and outsources

[10] See Besanko, Dranove, and Shanley (2007).

its distribution services by selling long-term distribution contracts to producers, thus also keeping distributors happy. Because of the low fixed costs involved in brokering, this business strategy should make the firm less sensitive to recession than a distribution company with heavy fixed costs. But what if producers are unwilling to enter long-term distribution contracts during a recession?

In his book, Porter (1998a) discussed five industry forces, as well as the generic competitive strategies mentioned earlier. Porter's so-called five forces analysis can be seen as an examination of the risks involved in the value chain. Oster (1999) provides a useful analysis of the five forces, and we show her insights as bulleted points below. In some cases, we slightly modify or extend them.

Rivalry Intensity This is the degree of competition among companies in the industry. For example, airline competition is more intense now with more carriers and open skies agreements between countries than in the days of heavier regulation with fewer carriers limited to domestic companies. Coordination can make rivalry much less intense. The analyst must be alert for possible changes in coordination and rivalry intensity that are not yet reflected in equity prices.

- Intense rivalry among firms in an industry reduces average profitability.
- In an industry in which coordination yields excess profits (prices exceed marginal costs), there are market share incentives for individual companies to "shade" (slightly cut) prices as they weigh the benefits and costs of coordination versus shading.
- Large numbers of companies in a market reduce coordination opportunities.
- Rivalry is generally more intense when the major companies are all similarly sized and no one large company can impose discipline on the industry.
- Generally, coordination is easier if companies in the market are similar. All gravitate to a mutually agreeable focal point, the solution that similar companies will naturally discern.
- Industries that have substantial specific assets (which cannot be used for other purposes) exhibit high barriers to exit and intensified rivalry.
- Variability in demand creates more rivalry within an industry. For example, high fixed costs and cyclical demand create capacity mismatches and price cutting from excess capacity.

Substitutes This is the threat of products or services that are substitutes for the products or services of the industry. For example, teleconferencing is a substitute for travel. The analyst must be alert for possible changes in substitutes that are not yet reflected in equity prices.

- Substitute products constrain the ability of firms in the industry to raise their prices substantially.

- Industries without excess capacity or intense rivalry can present attractive investment opportunities; but substitute products can reduce the attraction by constraining the ability of firms in the industry to substantially raise their prices.

Buyer Power This is the bargaining power of buyers of the producer's products or services. For example, car rental agencies have more bargaining power with automobile manufacturers than have individual consumers. The analyst must be alert for possible changes in buyer power that are not yet reflected in equity prices.

- The larger the number of buyers and the smaller their individual purchases, the less the bargaining power.
- Standardization of products increases buyer power because consumers can easily switch between suppliers.
- If buyers can integrate backwards, they can increase their bargaining power because they would cut out the supplier if they choose to integrate.
- Greater buyer power makes an equity investment in the producer less attractive because of lower profit margins.

Supplier Power This is the bargaining power of suppliers to the producers. For example, traditional aircraft manufacturers lost supplier power when niche players entered the market and began producing short-haul jets. The analyst must be alert for possible changes in supplier power that are not yet reflected in equity prices.

- The more suppliers there are for the industry, the less is the supplier power.
- Standardized raw materials (commodities) reduce supplier power because the supplier has no differentiation or quality advantage.
- If buyers can integrate backwards, this reduces supplier power because the buyer would cut out the supplier if it chooses to integrate.
- Greater supplier power makes an equity investment in the producer less attractive because of the possibility of a squeeze on profits.

New Entrants This is the threat of new entrants into the industry. For example, a European consortium entered the aircraft manufacturing industry and has become a major company now competing globally. In addition, a Brazilian and a Canadian company have entered the short-haul aircraft market. The analyst must be alert for possible changes in new entrant threats that are not yet reflected in equity prices.

- The higher the payoffs, the more likely will be the entry, all else equal.
- Barriers to entry are industry characteristics which reduce the rate of entry below that needed to remove excess profits.

- Expectations of incumbent reactions influence entry.
- Exit costs influence the rate of entry.
- All else equal, the larger the volume needed to reach minimal unit costs, the greater the difference between pre- and post-entry price (the increase in industry capacity would drive down prices), and thus the less likely entry is to occur.
- The steeper the cost curve, the less likely is entry at a smaller volume than the minimal unit cost volume.
- Long-term survival at a smaller than minimal unit cost volume requires an offsetting factor to permit a company to charge a price premium. Product differentiation and a monopoly in location are two possible offsets.
- Excess capacity deters entry by increasing the credibility of price-cutting as an entry response by incumbents.
- Occasional actions that are unprofitable in the short run can increase a company's credibility for price cutting to deter entry, giving an entry-deterring reputation as a tough incumbent.
- An incumbent contract to meet the price of any responsible rival can deter entry.
- Patents and licenses can prevent free entry from eliminating excess profits in an industry. They deter entry.
- Learning curve effects can deter entry unless new entrants can appropriate the experience of the incumbents. For example, Boeing learned about metal fatigue from the British experience of accidents with the Comet, the first commercial jet airliner.
- Pioneering brands can dominate the industry and deter entry when network externalities exist and when consumers find it costly to make product mistakes.
- High exit costs discourage entry. A primary determinant of high exit costs is asset specificity and the irreversibility of capital investments.

After presenting the insights above, Oster follows up with an excellent presentation of many related topics: strategic groups within industries, competition in global markets, issues of organizational structure and design, competitive advantage, corporate diversification, and the effect of rival behavior. Indeed, industry analysis is a complex subject as the analyst attempts to deduce the valuation implications of corporate strategies.

Government Participation Governments subsidies to companies can seed companies in the early stages and can also give companies an unfair advantage in steady state. There is extra uncertainty for a company competing head to head with one subsidized by its home country. Governments also participate by supporting their domestic country stock prices in one way or another. This creates uncertainty about future policy in addition to the normal risk associated with cash flows.

Governments participate indirectly by their involvement in the social contract. In the United States, automobile companies bear the costs of defined benefit pension funds. Japanese automobile companies do not bear these costs because of government-sponsored pension schemes. Some European governments dealt with the possibility of increased unemployment by shortening the work week to keep employment spread out. Such government policy may make a European company less competitive.

Governments control competition. Open-skies laws allow foreign airlines to operate between domestic cities. Closed-skies laws in the past prevented Canadian carriers from operating between U.S. cities. Closed-skies laws have also been a factor in the Eurozone. Risks are presented by the uncertainty involved in trying to predict government policy.

Risks and Covariance Investors care about stock market risk, that is, the uncertainty about future stock prices. Risk is usually viewed at two levels. The total risk of a company or an industry is the first level of risk, and it is usually measured by the *standard deviation of return* (that is, stock returns) of that company or industry. But part of this risk can be diversified away in a portfolio. So, the second level of risk is measured by the covariance with the aggregate economy, which tells how the returns of a company vary with global market indexes. Although this risk is usually measured by the beta from regressions of company returns against market returns, it is useful to note those beta changes over time as a function of business cycle conditions and shifting competition within the industry.

When analyzing an industry, the analyst is faced with a continuing challenge of determining diversifiable versus nondiversifiable risk. Because future cash flow and return covariance must be predicted in order to estimate the firm and industry's beta, simple reliance on past regressions is not sufficient. Part of the risk from a strategy failure or a change from co-opetition to competition may be firm-specific and diversifiable. At the same time, part of the risk may be nondiversifiable, because it involves fundamental shifts in industry structure.

In order to manage a global equity portfolio, the risk of a company is usually summarized by its exposure to various risk factors. The last section of this chapter is devoted to global risk factor models.

Equity Analysis

Because it should be forward looking, equity analysis needs to be carried out within the context of the country and the industry. Reasonable prediction of cash flows and risk is required to provide useful inputs to the valuation process.

Industry Valuation or Country Valuation A frequently asked question is whether a company should primarily be valued relative to the global industry to which it belongs or relative to other national companies listed on its home stock market. Indeed, many corporations are now very active abroad and, even at home, face worldwide competition. So, there are really two aspects to this question:

- Should the *financial analysis* of a company be conducted within its global industry?
- Do the stock prices of companies within the same global industry move together worldwide, so that the *relative valuation* of a company's equity should be conducted within the global industry rather than within its home stock market?

The answer to the first question is a clear yes. Prospective earnings of a company should be estimated taking into account the competition it is facing. In most cases, this competition is international as well as domestic. Most large corporations derive a significant amount of their cash flows from foreign sales and operations, so their competition is truly global.

The answer to the second question raised is less obvious. At a given point in time, different industries face different growth prospects, and that is true worldwide. Furthermore, different industries exhibit different sensitivities to unexpected changes in worldwide economic conditions. This implies that the stock market valuation should differ across industries. Some industries, such as electronic components or health care, have large P/E and P/BV ratios while other industries, such as energy and materials, have low P/E and P/BV ratios. The major question related to the importance of industry factors in stock prices, however, is whether a company has more in common with other companies in the same global industry than with other companies in the same country. By "more in common," we mean that its stock price tends to move together with that of other companies, and to be influenced by similar events. Before presenting some empirical evidence on the relative importance of country and industry factor in stock pricing, let's stress some caveats:

- Any industry classification is open to questions. MSCI, S&P, FTSE, and Dow Jones produce global industry indexes with different industry classification systems. The number of industry groups identified differs. It is not easy to assign each company to a single industry group. Some industry activities are clearly identified (e.g., producing automobiles), but others are not so clear-cut. It is not unusual to see the same company assigned to different industry groups by different classification systems. Some large corporations have diversified activities that cut across industry groups. Standard and Poor's and MSCI have recently designed a common Global Industry Classification Standard (GICS). The GICS system consists of four levels of detail: 10 sectors, 23 industry groupings, 59 industries, and 122 subindustries. At the most specific level of detail, an individual company is assigned to a single GICS subindustry, according to the definition of its principal business activity determined by S&P and MSCI. The hierarchical nature of the GICS structure will automatically assign the company's industry, industry group, and sector. There are currently over 25,000 companies globally that have been classified.

- The answer could be industry-specific. Some industries are truly global (e.g., oil companies), while others are less so (e.g., leisure and tourism). However, competition is becoming global in most, if not all, industries. For example, travel agencies have become regional, if not global, through a wave of mergers and acquisitions. Supermarket chains now cover many continents, and many retailers capitalize on their brand names globally.
- The answer could be period-specific. There could be periods in which global industry factors dominate, and other periods in which national factors are more important (desynchronized business cycles).
- The answer could be company-specific. Some companies in an industry group have truly international activities with extensive global competition, while others are mostly domestic in all respects. Small Swiss commercial banks with offices located only in one province (canton) of Switzerland have little in common with large global banks (even Crédit Suisse or UBS).
- Even if industry factors dominate, two opposing forces could be at play.[11] A worldwide growth in the demand for goods produced could benefit all players within the industry. However, competition also means that if one major player is highly successful, it will be at the expense of other major players in the industry. For example, Japanese car manufacturers could grow by extensively exporting to the United States, but it will be at the expense of U.S. car manufacturers. The stock price of Nissan would therefore be negatively correlated with that of GM or Ford.

Despite these caveats, all empirical studies find that industry factors have grown in importance in stock price valuation.[12] Global industry factors tend now to dominate country factors, but country factors are still significant. Companies should be valued relative to their industry, but country factors should not be neglected, particularly when conducting a risk analysis.

Two industry valuation approaches are traditionally used: ratio analysis and discounted cash flow models.

Global Financial Ratio Analysis As already mentioned, global industry financial analysis examines each company in the industry against the industry average. One well-accepted approach to this type of analysis is the DuPont model. (It may be better to think of this as an *approach* of decomposing return ratios, but this approach is usually called the DuPont model.) The basic technique of the DuPont model is to explain ROE or return on assets (ROA) in terms of its contributing elements. For example, we will see that ROA can be explained in terms of net profit margin and asset turnover. The analysis begins with five contributing elements, and these elements appear in several variations, depending on what most interests the analyst. The five elements reflect the financial and operating portions of the income statement as linked to the

[11] See Griffin and Stulz (2001).

[12] See, for example, Cavaglia, Brightman, and Aked (2000) and Hopkins and Miller (2001).

assets on the balance sheet and the equity supporting those assets. In the analysis here, past performance is being examined. Because income is a flow earned over a period of time, but the balance sheet reflects a balance (stock) at only one point in time, economists would calculate the flow (e.g., net income) over an average (e.g., the average of beginning and ending assets). The typical decompostion of ROE is given by

$$\frac{\text{NI}}{\text{EBT}} \times \frac{\text{EBT}}{\text{EBIT}} \times \frac{\text{EBIT}}{\text{Sales}} \times \frac{\text{Sales}}{\text{Assets}} \times \frac{\text{Assets}}{\text{Equity}} = \frac{\text{NI}}{\text{Equity}}$$

where

NI is net income

EBT is earnings before taxes

NI/EBT is 1 minus the tax rate, or the tax retention rate with a maximum value of 1.0 if there were no taxes (lower values imply higher tax burden)

EBIT is earnings before interest and taxes, or operating income

EBT/EBIT is interest burden, with a maximum value of 1.0 if there are no interest payments (lower values imply greater debt burden)

EBIT/Sales is operating margin

Sales/Assets is asset turnover ratio (a measure of efficiency in the use of assets)

Assets/Equity is leverage (higher values imply greater use of debt)

NI/Equity is return on equity (ROE)

The analyst would then compare each firm ratio with the comparable ratio for the industry. Does the firm have a higher operating margin than the industry's? If the company has a higher ROE than the industry ROE, is this higher-than-average ROE due to leverage, or is it due to more operations management–oriented ratios, such as operating margin or asset turnover?

Depending on the analyst's focus, the ratios can be combined in different ways. What is essential in DuPont analysis is the specification of the question of interest rather than the question of whether the model has five, three, or two factors.

We can collapse the first three ratios into the net profit margin (NI/sales) to leave

$$\text{ROE} = \text{Net profit margin} \times \text{Asset turnover} \times \text{Leverage}$$

We could also combine the first three ratios and include the fourth ratio to yield a return on assets breakdown:

$$\text{ROA} = \frac{\text{NI}}{\text{Assets}} = \text{Net profit margin} \times \text{Asset turnover}$$

Without combining the first three ratios, we could also have a four-ratio ROA breakdown (tax retention rate × interest burden × operating margin × asset turnover). Also, we could explore a two-ratio ROE explanation by using ROA × leverage.

In all of this analysis, a global comparison of ratios of different companies in the same industry should take into account national valuation specificities. Due to national accounting differences detailed previously, earnings figures should sometimes be reconciled to make comparisons meaningful.

In addition to understanding how the financial statements are decomposed for DuPont analysis, it is important to maintain some context of what the analyst is trying to accomplish. The DuPont model was developed in 1919 to dissect (analyze) performance as due to such factors as operating efficiency and asset utilization. Of course, this dissection depends on the financial statements, so the link to underlying economics is not direct. Nevertheless, a comparison of companies within an industry and companies across time can serve as a starting point for the analyst to ask more questions.

Because simple DuPont analysis is surely reflected in security prices, the analyst invariably digs deeper into the questions raised by the analysis and maintains a focus on the future. Beyond its service as a starting point for asking questions, DuPont analysis also serves as a framework for making forecasts. But Soliman (2004) refers to the lack of forecasting ability available in the standard forecasting models. These models assume that DuPont ratios revert to the economy-wide mean. He proposes and successfully tests an approach assuming reversion to an industry-wide rather than economy-wide mean for profit margin and asset turnover ratios, using the time series for each of these. Example 6.2 illustrates an application of DuPont analysis.

The Role of Market Efficiency in Individual Stock Valuation The notion of an efficient market is central to finance theory and is important for valuing securities. Generally, the question in company analysis is whether a security is priced correctly, and if it is not, for how long will it be mispriced. In an efficient market,

EXAMPLE 6.2 DUPONT ANALYSIS COMPARISON OF TWO COMPANIES

Consider two representative companies in an industry. The return on equity for the two companies, A and B, is 15 percent and 7 percent, respectively. Company B has a superior net profit margin but inferior ROE. Despite Company A's advantages in operating margin (16%) and tax rate (40%), Company B's much lower interest burden (30%) translates into a distinct advantage in net profit margin (4%).

Ratio	DuPont Analysis	A	B
1	NI/EBT = one minus tax rate	0.60	0.50
2	EBT/EBIT = one minus interest burden	0.19	0.70
3	EBIT/Sales = operating margin	0.16	0.12
4	Net Profit margin = $1 \times 2 \times 3$	0.02	0.04
5	Sales/Assets = asset turnover = efficiency	0.60	0.70
6	Assets/Equity = leverage	14.00	2.50
7	ROE = $4 \times 5 \times 6$	0.15	0.07

Nevertheless, a raw comparison of ROE is dramatically in favor of Company A (15%), although Company B has the advantage in net profit margin (4%) and efficiency (0.70). Company A's interest burden of 81 percent tells the story of more leverage with a 14 to 1 ratio of assets to equity. Leverage means volatility and a question of the required return on equity. Which company will have the higher beta?

SOLUTION:

Company A should have a much larger beta. Company A is highly leveraged so its return on equity is likely to be much more volatile than that of Company B. Its return on equity will be higher than that of Company B in good times, but will be much lower in bad times.

any new information would be immediately and fully reflected in prices. Because all current information is already impounded in the asset price, only news (unanticipated information) could cause a change in price in the future.

An efficient financial market quickly, if not instantaneously, discounts all available information. Any new information will immediately be used by some privileged investors, who will take positions to capitalize on it, thereby making the asset price adjust (almost) instantaneously to this piece of information. For example, a new balance of payments statistic would immediately be used by foreign exchange traders to buy or sell a currency until the foreign exchange rate reached a level considered consistent with the new information. Similarly, investors might use surprise information about a company, such as a new contract or changes in forecasted income, to reap a profit until the stock price reached a level consistent with the news. The adjustment in price would be so rapid it would not pay to buy information that has already been available to other investors. Hundreds of thousands of expert financial analysts and professional investors throughout the world search for information and make the world markets close to fully efficient.

In a perfectly efficient market, the typical investor could consider an asset price to reflect its true *fundamental value* at all times. The notion of fundamental value is somewhat philosophical; it means that at each point in time, each asset has an intrinsic value that all investors try to discover. Nevertheless, the analyst tries to find mispriced securities by choosing from a variety of valuation models and by carefully researching the inputs for the model. In this research, forecasting cash flows and risk is critical.

Valuation Models Investors often rely on some form of a discounted cash flow analysis (DCF) for estimating the intrinsic value of a stock investment. This is simply a *present value* model, where the intrinsic value of an asset at time zero, P_0, is determined by the stream of cash flows it generates for the investor. This price is also called the *justified price* because it is the value that is "justified" by the forecasted cash flows. In a dividend discount model (DDM), the stock market price is set equal to the stream of forecasted dividends D discounted at the required rate of return r:

$$P_0 = \frac{D_1}{1+r} + \frac{D_2}{(1+r)^2} + \frac{D_3}{(1+r)^3} \cdots \tag{6.1}$$

Financial analysts take great care in forecasting future earnings and hence, dividends.

A simple version of the DDM assumes that dividends will grow indefinitely at a constant compounded annual growth rate (CAGR), g. Hence, Equation 6.1 becomes

$$P_0 = \frac{D_1}{1+r} + \frac{D_1(1+g)}{(1+r)^2} + \frac{D_1(1+g)^2}{(1+r)^3} \cdots$$

or

$$P_0 = \frac{D_1}{r-g} \tag{6.2}$$

Analysts forecast earnings, and a payout ratio is applied to transform earnings into dividends. Under the assumption of a constant earnings payout ratio, we find

$$P_0 = \frac{E_1(1-b)}{r-g} \tag{6.3}$$

where

P_0 is the justified or intrinsic price at time 0 (now)

E_1 is next year's earnings

b is the earnings retention ratio

$1-b$ is the earnings payout ratio

r is the required rate of return on the stock

g is the growth rate of earnings

Note that Equation 6.3 requires that the growth rate g remain constant indefinitely and that it must be less than the required rate of return r. Take the example of a German corporation whose next annual earnings are expected to be €20 per share, with a constant growth rate of 5 percent per year, and with a 50 percent payout ratio. Hence, the next-year dividend is expected to be €10. Let's further assume that the required rate of return for an investment in such a corporation is 10 percent, which can be decomposed into a 6 percent risk-free rate plus a 4 percent risk premium. Then the firm's value is equal to

$$P_0 = \frac{10}{0.10-0.05} = €200$$

The intrinsic price-to-earnings (P/E) ratio is defined as P_0/E_1. The intrinsic P/E of this corporation, using prospective earnings, is equal to

$$P/E = \frac{1-b}{r-g} = \frac{0.50}{0.10-0.05} = 10$$

A drop in the risk-free interest rate would lead to an increase in the P/E and in the stock price. For example, if the risk-free rate drops to 5 percent and everything else remains unchanged, a direct application of the formula indicates that the P/E will move up to 12.5 and the stock price to €250.

A more realistic DDM approach is to decompose the future in three phases. In the near future (e.g., the next two years), earnings are forecasted individually. In the second phase (e.g., years 3 to 5), a general growth rate of the company's earnings is estimated. In the final stage, the growth rate in earnings is assumed to revert to some sustainable growth rate.[13]

A final step required by this approach is to estimate the normal rate of return required on such an investment. This rate is equal to the risk-free interest rate plus a risk premium that reflects the relevant risks of this investment. Relevant risks refer to risks that should be priced by the market.

Franchise Value and the Growth Process Given the risk of the company's forecasted cash flows, a key determinant of value is the growth rate in cash flows. The growth rate depends on relevant country GDP growth rates, the industry growth rates, and the company's sustainable competitive advantage within the industry. Regardless of the valuation model used, some analysis of the growth-rate input is useful. Using the DDM as a representative model, Leibowitz and Kogelman (2000) developed the *franchise value* method and separated the intrinsic P/E value of a corporation into a tangible P/E value (the no-growth or zero-earnings retention P/E value of existing business) and the franchise P/E value (derived from prospective new investments). The franchise P/E value is related to the *present value of growth opportunities* (PVGO) in the traditional breakdown of intrinsic value into the no-growth value per share and the present value of growth opportunities. In that breakdown, the no-growth value per share is the value of the company if it were to distribute all its earnings in dividends, creating a perpetuity valued at E_1/r, where E_1 is next year's earnings and r is the required rate of return on the company's equity. Using the DDM and the company's actual payout ratio to generate an intrinsic value per share, P_0, the present value of growth opportunities must be the difference between intrinsic value and the no-growth value per share, $P_0 - E_1/r$.

The franchise value approach focuses on the intrinsic P/E rather than on the intrinsic value P_0; thus, the franchise value P/E is $PVGO/E_1$. In the franchise value approach, however, the franchise value P/E is further broken down into the *franchise factor* and the *growth factor*. The growth factor captures the present value of the opportunities for productive new investments, and the franchise factor is meant to capture the return levels associated with those new investments. The *sales-driven franchise value* has been developed to deal with multinational corporations that do business globally (see Leibowitz, 1997, 1998).

---

13 A detailed analysis of the use of DDM in companies' valuation is provided in Stowe et al. (2002).

The separation of franchise P/E value into a franchise factor and a growth factor permits a direct examination of the response of the intrinsic P/E to ROE.[14] This factor helps an investor determine the response of the P/E to the ROE expected to be achieved by the company. It focuses on the sustainable growth rate of earnings per share. Earnings per share will grow from one period to the next because reinvested earnings will earn the rate of ROE. So the company's sustainable growth rate is equal to the retention rate b multiplied by ROE: $g = b \times \text{ROE}$. Substituting into Equation 6.3 the sustainable growth rate calculation for g, we get the intrinsic price:

$$P_0 = \frac{E_1(1-b)}{r - b \times \text{ROE}}$$

and converting to an intrinsic P/E ratio,

$$\frac{P_0}{E_1} = \frac{(1-b)}{r - b \times \text{ROE}}$$

Now, multiplying through by r/r yields

$$\frac{P_0}{E_1} = \frac{1}{r}\left[\frac{r(1-b)}{r - b \times \text{ROE}}\right]$$

$$= \frac{1}{r}\left[\frac{r - r \times b}{r - \text{ROE} \times b}\right]$$

and arbitrarily adding and subtracting $\text{ROE} \times b$ in the numerator,

$$\frac{P_0}{E_1} = \frac{1}{r}\left[\frac{r - r \times b + \text{ROE} \times b - \text{ROE} \times b}{r - \text{ROE} \times b}\right]$$

$$= \frac{1}{r}\left[\frac{r - \text{ROE} \times b + \text{ROE} \times b - r \times b}{r - \text{ROE} \times b}\right]$$

or

$$\frac{P_0}{E_1} = \frac{1}{r}\left[1 + \frac{b(\text{ROE} - r)}{r - \text{ROE} \times b}\right] \tag{6.4}$$

This P_0/E_1 equation[15] is extremely useful because we can use it to examine the effects of different values of b and of the difference between ROE and r, that is, $\text{ROE} - r$. Two interesting results can be found. First, if $\text{ROE} = r$, the intrinsic P_0/E_1 equals $1/r$ regardless of b, the earnings retention ratio. Second, if $b = 0$, the intrinsic P_0/E_1 equals $1/r$ regardless of whether ROE is greater than r. These two results have an intuitive explanation:

- When the return on equity is exactly equal to the required rate of return ($\text{ROE} = r$), there is no *added* value in retaining earnings for additional

[14] The model is derived here under the assumptions of a constant growth rate g, a constant earnings retention rate b, and a constant ROE. It can accommodate more complex assumptions about the pattern of growth.

[15] Note that in all equations, E_1 refers to estimated (future) earnings, not past earnings. This is also the case in derivations in Leibowitz and Kogelman (2000).

investments rather than distributing them to shareholders. A company with ROE = r has no franchise value potential because its return on equity is just what the market requires, but no more.

- An earnings retention ratio of zero ($b = 0$) means that the company distributes all its earnings, so equity per share stays constant. There is no growth of equity, and the stream of future earnings will be a perpetuity because the rate of return on equity (ROE) remains constant. The value of a share is given by discounting a perpetuity of E_1 at a rate r; hence the $P_0/E_1 = 1/r$ result. Of course, the total equity of the company could grow by issuing new shares, but there will be no growth of earnings per existing share. There is potential franchise value in the company with ROE > r, but because the company does not reinvest earnings at this superior rate of return, existing shareholders do not capture this potential.

In general, there is a franchise value created for existing shareholders if the company can reinvest past earnings ($b > 0$) at a rate of return (ROE) higher than the market-required rate r.

Examining Equation 6.4 further, we return to the intrinsic value version. We can transform Equation 6.4 by multiplying and dividing by ROE and replacing $b \times$ ROE by g:

$$\frac{P_0}{E_1} = \frac{1}{r}\left[1 + \frac{\text{ROE} \times b \times (\text{ROE} - r)}{\text{ROE} \times (r - \text{ROE} \times b)}\right] = \frac{1}{r} + \frac{g \times (\text{ROE} - r)}{r \times \text{ROE} \times (r - g)}$$

and simplify it as

$$\frac{P_0}{E_1} = \frac{1}{r} + \left(\frac{\text{ROE} - r}{\text{ROE} \times r}\right)\left(\frac{g}{r - g}\right)$$

$$\frac{P_0}{E_1} = \frac{1}{r} + \text{FF} \times \text{G} \tag{6.5}$$

where the franchise factor is FF = (ROE − r)/(ROE × r) or $1/r - 1/\text{ROE}$ and the growth factor is $\text{G} = g/(r - g)$.

The growth factor is the ratio of the present value of future increases in the book value (BV) of equity to the current BV of equity. If the current BV of equity is B_0, then next year's increment to BV is gB_0. With a constant growth rate in BV increments, these increments can be treated as a growing perpetuity with a present value of $gB_0/(r - g)$. Because the present value of the BV increments is to be given as a ratio to the most recent BV, the growth factor is then given as $g/(r - g)$.

The franchise factor stems from the fact that a firm has a competitive advantage allowing it to generate a rate of return (ROE) greater than the rate of return normally required by investors for this type of risk, r. If the franchise factor is positive, it gives the rate of response of the intrinsic P_0/E_1 ratio to the growth factor. The growth factor G will be high if the firm can sustain a growth rate that is high relative to r.

Consider a pharmaceutical firm with some attractive new drugs with large commercial interest. Its ROE will be high relative to the rate of return required by investors for pharmaceutical stocks. Hence, it has a large positive franchise factor FF. If it continues to make productive new investments (G positive), such a firm can continue to generate a return on equity well above the rate of return required by the stock market, and thus it has a large positive franchise value. On the other hand, if the pharmaceutical company's sustainable growth rate is small because of a low earnings retention rate b, then G will be small and so will the franchise value, even though the franchise factor is large. For a firm with less franchise potential and ROE possibilities only equal to the company's required rate of return ($r = \text{ROE}$), the franchise factor is zero and the intrinsic P_0/E_1 is simply $1/r$, regardless of the earnings retention ratio. Example 6.3 illustrates the calculation of the franchise value.

The Effects of Inflation on Stock Prices Because inflation rates vary around the world and over time, it is important to consider the effects of inflation on stock prices. To do this, we begin at the obvious place—earnings. After examining the effects of inflation on reported earnings, we discuss an inflation flow-through model.[16]

Because historical costs are used in accounting, inflation has a distorting effect on reported earnings. These effects show up primarily in replacement, inventories, and borrowing costs. Replacement must be made at inflated costs, but depreciation is recorded at historical cost—hence, reported earnings based on depreciation as

EXAMPLE 6.3 FRANCHISE VALUE

A company can generate an ROE of 15 percent and has an earnings retention ratio of 0.60. Next year's earnings are projected at $100 million. If the required rate of return for the company is 12 percent, what are the company's tangible P/E value, franchise factor, growth factor, and franchise P/E value?

SOLUTION

The company's tangible P/E value is $1/r = 1/0.12 = 8.33$.

The company's franchise factor is $1/r - 1/\text{ROE} = 1/0.12 - 1/0.15 = 1.67$.

Because the company's sustainable growth rate is $0.6 \times 0.15 = 0.09$, the company's growth factor is $g/(r - g) = 0.09/(0.12 - 0.09) = 3$.

The company's franchise P/E value is the franchise factor times the growth factor, $1.67 \times 3 = 5.01$.

Because its tangible P/E value is 8.33 and its franchise P/E value is 5.01, the company's intrinsic P/E is 13.34. Note that the intrinsic P/E calculated directly is $P/E = (1 - b)/(r - g) = 0.4/(0.12 - 0.09) = 13.33$. Thus, the franchise value method breaks this P/E into its basic components.

[16] For example, see Leibowitz and Kogelman (2000).

an estimate of replacement costs gives an overstatement of earnings. Similarly, a first-in, first-out (FIFO) inventory accounting system leads to an understatement of inventory costs and an overstatement of reported earnings. Unlike replacement and inventory distortions, borrowing costs at historical rates cause an understatement of reported earnings. Inflation causes borrowing costs to increase, but nominal interest costs do not reflect the increase. Finally, capital gains taxes reflect an inflation tax because the base for the capital gains tax is historical cost.

To analyze the effects of inflation on the valuation process, analysts try to determine what part of inflation flows through to a firm's earnings. A full-flow-through firm has earnings that fully reflect inflation. Thus, any inflation cost increases must be getting passed along to consumers.

In an inflationary environment, consider a firm that would otherwise have no growth in earnings, a zero earnings retention ratio, and full-inflation flow-through. So, earnings only grow because of the inflation rate I, assumed constant over time. For example, we have

$$E_1 = E_0 \times (1 + I)$$

By discounting this stream of inflation-growing earnings at the required rate r, we find that the intrinsic value of such a firm would then be

$$P_0 = \frac{E_1}{r - I} = E_0\left(\frac{1 + I}{r - I}\right) \quad (6.6)$$

where

P_0 is the intrinsic value

E_0 is the initial earnings level

I is the annual inflation rate

r is the nominal required rate of return

Let's now consider a company with a partial inflation flow-through of λ percent, so that earnings are only inflated at a rate λI:

$$E_1 = E_0(1 + \lambda I)$$

By discounting this stream of earnings at the nominal required rate r, we find

$$P_0 = E_0 \times \frac{1 + \lambda I}{r - \lambda I} \quad (6.7)$$

If we introduce the real required rate of return $\rho = r - I$, we get

$$P_0 = E_0 \times \frac{1 + \lambda I}{\rho + (1 - \lambda)I} = \frac{E_1}{\rho + (1 - \lambda)I}$$

The intrinsic P/E using prospective earnings is now equal to

$$P_0/E_1 = \frac{1}{\rho + (1 - \lambda)I} \quad (6.8)$$

From Equation 6.8 we can see that the higher the inflation flow-through rate, the higher the price of the company. Indeed, a company that cannot pass inflation through its earnings is penalized. Thus, the P/E ratio ranges from a high of $1/\rho$ to a low of $1/r$. For example, assume a real required rate of return of 6 percent and an inflation rate of 4 percent. Exhibit 6.2 shows the P/E of the company with different flow-through rates. With a full-flow-through rate ($\lambda = 100\%$), the P/E is equal to $1/\rho = 1/0.06 = 16.67$. The ratio drops to 12.5 if the company can pass only 50 percent of inflation through its earnings. If the company cannot pass through any inflation ($\lambda = 0$), its earnings remain constant, and the P/E ratio is equal to $1/(\rho + I) = 1/r = 10$. The higher the inflation rate, the more negative the influence on the stock price if full inflation pass-through cannot be achieved. Example 6.4 illustrates the influence of inflation on the P/E of two companies.

This observation is important if we compare similar companies in different countries experiencing different inflation rates. A company operating in a high-inflation environment will be penalized if it cannot pass through inflation.

The Inflation-like Effects of Currency Movements on Stock Prices A currency movement is a monetary variable that affects stock valuation in a fashion similar to the inflation variable. Just as some companies cannot fully pass inflation through their earnings, they cannot fully pass exchange rate movements either. Consider an importing firm faced with a sudden depreciation of the home currency. The products it imports suddenly become more expensive in terms of the home currency. If this price increase can be passed through to customers, earnings will not suffer from the currency adjustment. But this is often not the case. First, the price increase will tend to reduce demand for these imported products. Second, locally produced goods will become more attractive than imported goods, and some substitution will take place.

The currency exposure of individual companies was discussed in Chapter 4. Currency exposure depends on such factors as each particular company's production cycle, the competitive structure of its product market, and the company's financing structure.

EXHIBIT 6.2

Inflation Effects on P/E

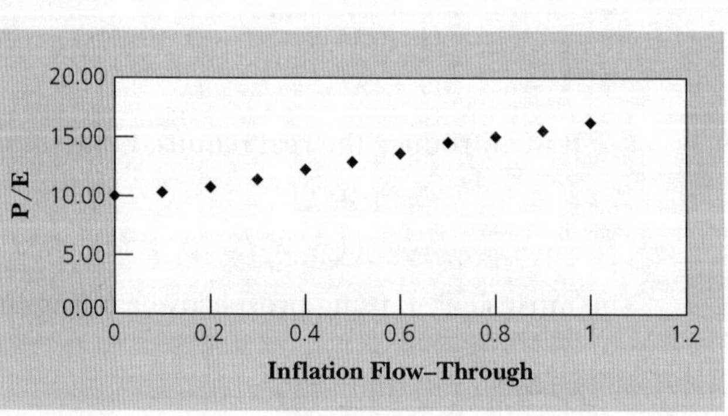

EXAMPLE 6.4 INFLATION

Consider two companies in the same line of business, but with mostly domestic operations. Company A is based in a country with no inflation. Company B is based in a country with a 4 percent inflation rate. There is no real growth in earnings for both companies. The real rate of return required by global investors for this type of stock investment is 6 percent. Company B can pass only 80 percent of inflation through its earnings. What should be the P/E of the two companies?

SOLUTION

The nominal required rate of return for Company A is equal to the real rate because there is no inflation: $r = \rho = 6$ percent. Earnings are constant, and the P/E is equal to

$$P/E(A) = 1/\rho = 1/0.06 = 16.67$$

There is a 4 percent inflation rate in the country of Company B. Its earnings will be inflated only at a rate of $\lambda I = 80 \text{ percent} \times 4 \text{ percent} = 3.2$ percent. The P/E of company B will be

$$P/E(B) = \frac{1}{6\% + (20\%) \times 4\%} = \frac{1}{6.8\%} = 14.71$$

In the inflationary environment, Company B's earnings cannot grow as fast as inflation. Penalized by inflation and its inability to pass along inflation, Company B's P/E ratio is below that of Company A.

Global Risk Factors in Security Returns

The analysis of an individual company can require a detailed review of various strategic risk elements that are difficult to quantify precisely. However, a portfolio manager needs to summarize the information on a large number of securities into a few statistics that help construct a portfolio and manage its risk. To structure a portfolio properly, a manager must have a clear understanding of the main factors influencing the return on a security and of the risk exposures of each security.

Global equilibrium pricing was discussed in Chapter 4. We showed that the risk premium of a security should be proportional to the covariance (or beta) of the security's return with the world market return; this is the world market risk of a security. In Chapter 13 we show how to use this theory to derive long-term expected returns for asset classes. However, the world market risk of a security is the result of the exposure to many sources of risk that can be detailed in factor models. Factor models allow a better understanding of the risks that affect stock returns in the short run and allow the risk management of a portfolio.

Risk-Factor Model: Industry and Country Factors

A factor model, where R is the rate of return on the security, may be written mathematically as

$$R = \alpha + \beta_1 f_1 + \beta_2 f_2 + \cdots + \beta_k f_k + \epsilon \tag{6.9}$$

where

R is the rate of return on a security

α is a constant

$f_1 \cdots f_k$ are the k factors common to all securities

$\beta_1 \cdots \beta_k$ represent the sensitivity, or risk exposure, of this security to each factor

ϵ is a random term specific to this security

The ϵ is the source of idiosyncratic or diversifiable risk for the security, and $\beta_1 \ldots \beta_k$ represent the risk exposure of this security to each factor. The betas vary among securities. Some stocks may be highly sensitive to certain factors and much less sensitive to others, and vice versa.

A global risk-factor model would use industry and country as factors. The degree of granularity can be adapted; for example, one could use global sector factors, global industry factors, or regional industry factors. The geographical factors could be a list of regions (e.g., Europe) or of individual countries.

The factors are measured as the return on some index portfolio representative of the factor ("mimicking portfolios"). For example, the oil industry factor could be proxied by the return on a global stock index of oil firms. Various statistical techniques can be used to optimize the factor structure.

The determination of the risk-factor exposures can follow one of two techniques or a combination of the two:

- The exposure can be assessed a priori by using information on the company studied. This usually leads to a 0/1 exposure. For example, the oil company Total would have a unitary exposure to the oil industry factor and zero exposures to all other industry factors, because it is an oil company.
- The exposure can be estimated using a multiple regression approach. The exposures would then be the estimated betas in a time-series regression.

The question of currency should be addressed. A global risk-factor model can be written in some arbitrary currency (e.g., the U.S. dollar). It also can be written in currency-hedged terms. If companies are reacting differently to currency movements, currencies could be added as risk factors. For example, an exporting firm could be influenced negatively by an appreciation of its currency, while the reverse would be true for an importing firm. These currency exposures could be cancelled if the company adopts a currency-hedging policy in its business operations.

Other Risk Factors: Styles

Other factors influence the stock price behavior of companies worldwide. As mentioned, many researchers believe that the future performance of a stock also depends on other attributes of a company that have not been discussed so far. Among many others, three attributes have been researched extensively:

- *Value* stocks do not behave like *growth* stocks. A value stock is a company whose stock price is "cheap" in relation to its book value, or in relation to the cash flows it generates (low stock price compared with its earnings, cash flows, or dividends). A growth stock has the opposite attribute, implying that the stock price capitalizes growth in future earnings. This is known as the *value effect.*
- *Small* firms do not exhibit the same stock price behavior as *large* firms. The size of a firm is measured by its stock market capitalization. This is known as the *size effect.*
- In the short run, winners tend to repeat. In other words, stocks that have performed well (or badly) in the recent past, say in the past six months, will tend to be winners (or losers) in the next six months. This is known as the *momentum, success,* or *relative strength effect.*

The observation of these effects, or factors, has led to the development of *style investing,* in which portfolios are structured to favor some of these attributes (e.g., value stocks).

Risk-factor models often incorporate style factors in which the factors are proxied by some mimicking portfolio (e.g., long in value stocks and short in growth stocks). A security's exposure is either measured a priori by using some information on the company, by a regression technique, or by a combination of the two techniques.

Although this style approach has been extensively used in the United States, there is some practical difficulty in applying it in a global setting. This is best illustrated by looking at the size factor. An Austrian company that is regarded as "large" in Austria would be regarded as medium-sized in Europe and probably as small according to U.S. standards. To construct a global size factor, one must make assumptions on how to measure relative size. Different risk-factor models use different criteria.

Other Risk Factors: Macroeconomic

Factors are postulated a priori as sources of risk that are common to all companies. This clearly leads us to some macroeconomic variables that affect the economics of all firms, as well as the behavior of stock market participants who price those firms.

Selecting a set of *macroeconomic factors* is as much an art as a science. These factors must be logical choices, easy to interpret, robust over time, and able to explain a significant percentage of variation in stock returns. Some macroeconomic variables are logical candidates as factors but suffer from serious measurement error or long publication lags. For example, the evolution in industrial production is a logical candidate, but it is difficult to get timely, good-quality, reliable data. The technique is to use as factor proxies the returns on mimicking portfolios that are most strongly correlated with the economic variable.

Burmeister, Roll, and Ross (1994) propose a set of five factors.[17] These five factors, listed here, apply to domestic U.S. stocks:

- *Confidence factor* (f_1): This factor is measured by the difference in return on risky corporate bonds and on government bonds. The *default risk* premium required by the market to compensate for the risk of default on corporate bonds is measured as the spread between the yields on risky corporate bonds and government bonds. A decrease in the default-risk spread will give a higher return on corporate bonds and implies an improvement in the investors' confidence level. Hence, confidence risk focuses on the willingness of investors to undertake risky investments. Most stocks have a positive exposure to the confidence factor ($\beta_1 > 0$), so their prices tend to rise when the confidence factor is positive ($f_1 > 0$). The underlying idea is that in periods when investors are becoming more sensitive to risks (less confident with $f_1 < 0$), they require a higher premium on risky corporate bonds, compared with government bonds. They also require a higher risk premium on risky stocks and will bid their prices down, inducing a negative stock-price movement.
- *Time horizon factor* (f_2): This factor is measured as the difference between the return on a 20-year government bond and a 1-month Treasury bill. A positive difference in return is caused by a decrease in the term spread (long minus short interest rates). This is a signal that investors require a lesser premium to hold long-term investments. Growth stocks are more exposed (higher β_2) to time horizon risk than income stocks. The underlying idea is to view the stock price as the discounted stream of its future cash flows. The present value of growth stocks is determined by the long-term prospects of growing earnings while current earnings are relatively weak (high P/E ratio). An increase in the market-required discount rate will penalize the price of growth stocks more than the price of value stocks.
- *Inflation factor* (f_3): This factor is measured as the difference between the actual inflation for a month and its expected value, computed the month before, using an econometric inflation model. An unexpected increase in inflation tends to be bad for most stocks ($\beta_3 < 0$), so they have a negative exposure to this inflation surprise ($f_3 > 0$). Luxury goods stocks tend to be most sensitive to inflation risk, whereas firms in the sectors of foods,

[17] Earlier, Chen, Roll, and Ross (1986) had identified four factors for the U.S. equity market as (a) growth rate in industrial production, (b) unexpected inflation, (c) slope of the yield curve (the difference between long- and short-term interest rates), and (d) changes in the attitude toward risk as proxied by changes in the pricing of default risk implicit in the difference between yields on Aaa and Baa corporate bonds.

cosmetics, or tires are less sensitive to inflation risk. Real estate holdings typically benefit from increased inflation.

- *Business cycle factor* (f_4): This factor is measured by the monthly variation in a business activity index. Business cycle risk comes from unanticipated changes in the level of real activity. The business cycle factor is positive ($f_4 > 0$) when the expected real growth rate of the economy has increased. Most firms have a positive exposure to business cycle risk ($\beta_4 > 0$). Retail stores are more exposed to business cycle risk than are utility companies because their business activity (sales) is much more sensitive to recession or expansion.
- *Market-timing factor* (f_5): This factor is measured by the part of the S&P 500 total return that is not explained by the first four factors. It captures the global movements in the market that are not explained by the four macroeconomic factors. The inclusion of this market-timing factor makes the capital asset pricing model (CAPM) a special case of this approach. If all relevant macroeconomic factors had been included, it would not be necessary to add this market-timing factor.

A common criticism of this approach is that the risk exposures (betas) have to be estimated statistically from past data and may not be stable over time. Even the factor proxies (mimicking portfolios) have to be constructed using statistical optimization, and the procedure could yield unstable proxies.

Practical Use of Factor Models

Risk-factor models are used in risk management and in selecting stocks. A major application is the analysis of the risk profile of portfolios. The exposure of the portfolio to the various factors is the weighted average of the exposures of the stocks making up the portfolio. A manager can estimate the risks taken and the exposure of the portfolio to the various sources of risk. If some specific stock index is assigned as a benchmark to measure performance, the manager can analyze the risks of deviations from the benchmark. This helps the manager identify and quantify the bets and risks that are taken in the portfolio.

Managers can also use factor models to tilt the portfolio along some factor bets. Assume, for example, that a manager believes that the economy is going to grow at a faster rate than generally forecasted, leading to some inflationary pressure. The manager will tend to increase the portfolio exposure to business risk but reduce its exposure to inflation risk. This could also lead the manager to take some industry bets and invest in small companies.

We have seen that companies operate globally and compete within an industry. As background to the following concept in action, it is useful to look at key financial ratios and beta for General Motors (http://finance.yahoo.com/q/ks?s=GM) and Toyota (http://finance.yahoo.com/q/ks?s=TM).

CONCEPTS IN ACTION *DETROIT BEGINS SPRING IN A FOG*

Housing, Gas Prices Crimp Big Three's March Sales; Toyota Reaches a Record

Detroit's Big Three auto makers face worsening economic headwinds as they head into the crucial spring selling season, threatening their efforts to stem sales declines.

General Motors Corp., Ford Motor Co. and DaimlerChrysler AG's Chrysler Group have suffered year-over-year sales drops as they work to restructure and wean themselves off lower-margin sales to daily rental fleets. Yesterday, the Big Three posted sales declines for March, while Toyota Motor Corp.'s sales rose 11.7%, making it the Japanese auto maker's best sales month ever.

Now, auto makers must contend with a run-up in fuel prices and a weakening housing market. Both could undermine sales and force cash-sapping production cuts and incentives. GM cut its second-quarter production forecast by 15,000 vehicles, to 1.16 million, and several auto makers indicated incentives like low interest rates and rebates on many vehicles would remain.

Auto makers sold 1.5 million cars and trucks last month, translating into an annual sales rate of 16.3 million, according to Autodata Corp. Auto makers are hoping the industry will end the year selling around 16.5 million, roughly flat with last year.

GM's sales declined 4% to 345,418 vehicles in March from a year earlier, according to Autodata. Truck sales fell 8%. But GM said declines in fleet sales overshadowed relatively strong retail sales, with the new Chevrolet Silverado pickup, GMC Sierra and Acadia, and Saturn Outlook exceeding expectations.

"We're very content with sales for the month," said Paul Ballew, GM's top sales analyst, adding that GM had "a terrific first quarter on full-size pickups." Sales of those pickup trucks rose 8.2% in the first quarter, he said. Even so, March Silverado sales were off 5.2% from February, according to Autodata, a hiccup as GM ramps up introduction of the new truck.

Ford's sales dropped 9% to 263,441 vehicles, a trend the company's top sales analyst, George Pipas, has warned will continue as the auto maker restructures and recalibrates its mix of cars and trucks.

Ford has adjusted its business close to a 50–50 split between trucks and passenger cars, Mr. Pipas said, whereas just three years ago it tilted toward 70% trucks. Ford trumpeted a 37% increase from February in sales of its new Edge—a sport-utility vehicle known as a crossover because it is built on a car platform—but sales of the auto maker's best-selling F-Series pickups dropped 15%. Mr. Pipas said Ford may consider a production increase during this year's second half, depending on economic conditions.

DaimlerChrysler's sales dipped 4% to 228,077 vehicles in March. A 4.6% drop at the unprofitable Chrysler Group, which many investors want DaimlerChrysler to sell, offset a 1% gain at Mercedes-Benz.

GM said incentive spending rose slightly from last year, while Ford said its spending remained steady. A March truck incentive that offered a free Hemi engine upgrade helped Chrysler's Dodge pickup sales. In April, Chrysler will launch a nationwide minivan incentive that includes offers of a free DVD system on top of consumer cash as high as $4,000. Chrysler is sticking it out in the minivan segment while its domestic rivals retrench.

Toyota's sales totaled 242,675 vehicles, boosted by robust sales of hybrid gasoline-electric vehicles. Toyota has been offering discounts on the Prius hybrid and is expected to roll out new discount offers for April.

The average retail price of gasoline in the U.S. climbed to $2.70 a gallon as of Monday, according to the Energy Department, 12 cents higher than the same time last year. That's bad news for GM, Ford and Chrysler, whose best-selling vehicles are fuel-thirsty pickup trucks and SUVs.

Still, Ford's Mr. Pipas said he is less worried that rising gasoline prices will substantially change what consumers want. Now, he worries about the effect on auto sales generally, as more pain at the pump saps consumers' spending power. "The more money they're spending on [gasoline], the less they have for other things," Mr. Pipas said in an interview. "I really think that's the biggest factor."

Moreover, softness in the housing market threatens future sales. Depreciating homes deprive consumers of equity to finance car purchases, and economists worry the rise in subprime-mortgage defaults could spill to other parts of the economy, perhaps causing auto lenders to tighten standards, which would make it harder for consumers to buy new cars. So far, a noticeable spillover hasn't occurred.

Overall, the largest auto markets continue to present challenges. Retail sales—considered the best gauge of consumer demand—dropped 17% in California and 11% in Florida through the first 10 weeks of the year, according to CNW Marketing Research. U.S. car makers suffered declines amid slower conditions in those markets while sales for Toyota and Honda were closer to flat.

Source: Mike Spector, Terry Kosdrosky, and John D. Stoll, *The Wall Street Journal*, April 4, 2007, p. A3.

Summary

- Differences in national accounting standards used to be significant. But most countries, except the United States, are moving toward adopting the International Financial Reporting Standards (IFRS)
- U.S. GAAP and IFRS are converging, but they can yield somewhat different values for the reported earnings and book equity of specific companies.
- From an economic perspective, employee stock option compensation should be treated as an expense, with the options valued by an option-pricing model.
- Neoclassical growth theory predicts that the long-term level of GDP depends on the country's savings rate, but the long-term growth rate in GDP does not depend on the savings rate. Endogenous growth theory predicts that the long-term growth rate in GDP depends on the savings rate.

- A global industry analysis should examine return potential evidenced by demand analysis, value creation, industry life cycle, competition structure, competitive advantage, competitive strategies, co-opetition and the value net, and sector rotation. The analysis also should examine risk elements evidenced by market competition, value chain competition, government participation, and cash flow covariance.
- Global financial analysis involves comparing company ratios with global industry averages. In this context, DuPont analysis uses various combinations of the tax retention, debt burden, operating margin, asset turnover, and leverage ratios.
- The role of market efficiency in individual asset valuation is to equate fundamental value with asset valuation so that the analyst searches for mispricing or market inefficiency.
- Franchise value is the present value of growth opportunities divided by next year's earnings. The intrinsic P_0/E_1 ratio equals $1/r$ plus the franchise value, where r is the nominal required return on the stock. The franchise value is further divided into a franchise factor (FF) and a growth factor (G) to give $P_0/E_1 = 1/r + \text{FF} \times \text{G}$.
- To analyze the effects of inflation for valuation purposes, the analyst must recognize the distorting effects of historical inventory and borrowing costs on reported earnings, as well as recognize the inflation tax reflected in capital gains taxes. Further, the analyst must estimate the degree of inflation flow-through, λ.
- With earnings that are constant except for inflation, I as the inflation rate, r as the required nominal return on the stock, and ρ as the required real return on the stock, the P/E ratio can be estimated as $P_0/E_1 = 1/(\rho + (1 - \lambda)I)$.
- Multifactor models can be used in the analysis of the risk profile of portfolios. The exposure of a portfolio to the various factors is the weighted average of the exposures of the stocks making up the portfolio.

Problems

1. Explain why a corporation can have a stock market price well above its accounting book value.
2. The accounting and fiscal standards of countries allow corporations to build general provisions (or "hidden reserves") in anticipation of foreseen or unpredictable expenses. How would this practice affect the book value of a corporation and its ratio of market price to book value?
3. Discuss some of the reasons the earnings of German firms tend to be understated compared with the earnings of U.S. firms.
4. Consider a firm that has given stock options on 20,000 shares to its senior executives. These call options can be exercised at a price of $22 anytime during the next three

years. The firm has a total of 500,000 shares outstanding, and the current price is $20 per share. The firm's net income before taxes is $2 million.

a. What would be the firm's pretax earnings per share if the options are not expensed?
b. Under certain assumptions, the Black–Scholes model valued the options given by the firm to its executives at $4 per share option. What would be the firm's pretax earnings per share if the options are expensed accordingly?
c. Under somewhat different assumptions, the Black-Scholes model valued the options at $5.25 per share option. What would be the firm's pretax earnings per share if the options are expensed based on this valuation?

5. Japanese companies tend to belong to groups (*keiretsu*) and to hold shares of one another. Because these cross-holdings are minority interest, they tend not to be consolidated in published financial statements. To study the impact of this tradition on published earnings, consider the following simplified example:

   Company A owns 10 percent of Company B; the initial investment was 10 million yen. Company B owns 20 percent of Company A; the initial investment was also 10 million yen. Both companies value their minority interests at historical cost. The annual net income of Company A was 10 million yen. The annual net income of Company B was 30 million yen. Assume that the two companies do not pay any dividends. The current stock market values are 200 million yen for Company A and 450 million yen for Company B.

   a. Restate the earnings of the two companies, using the equity method of consolidation. Remember that the share of the minority-interest earning is consolidated on a one-line basis, proportionate to the share of equity owned by the parent.
   b. Calculate the P/E ratios, based on nonconsolidated and consolidated earnings. How does the nonconsolidation of earnings affect the P/E ratios?

6. The annual revenues (in billion dollars) in financial year 2001 for the top five players in the global media and entertainment industry are given in the following table. The top five corporations in this industry include three U.S.-based corporations (AOL Time Warner, Walt Disney, and Viacom), one French corporation (Vivendi Universal), and one Australian corporation (News Corporation). The revenue indicated for Vivendi Universal does not include the revenue from its environmental business. Assume that the total worldwide revenue of all firms in this industry was $250 billion.

Company	**Revenue**
AOL Time Warner	38
Walt Disney	25
Vivendi Universal	25
Viacom	23
News Corporation	13

   a. Compute the three-firm and five-firm concentration ratios.
   b. Compute the three-firm and five-firm Herfindahl indexes.
   c. Make a simplistic assumption that in addition to the five corporations mentioned in the table, there are 40 other companies in this industry with an equal share of the remaining market. Compute the Herfindahl index for the overall industry.
   d. Suppose there were not 40, but only 10 other companies in the industry with an equal share of the remaining market. Compute the Herfindahl index for the overall industry.
   e. Interpret your answers to parts (c) and (d) in terms of the competition structure of the industry.

7. News Corporation is headquartered in Australia, and its main activities include television entertainment, films, cable, and publishing.
   a. Collect any relevant information that you may need, and discuss whether an analyst should do the valuation of News Corporation primarily relative to the global media and entertainment industry or relative to other companies based in Australia.
   b. One of the competitors of News Corporation is Vivendi Universal, a firm headquartered in France. Should an analyst be concerned in comparing financial ratios of News Corporation with those of Vivendi Universal?

8. You are given the following data about Walt Disney and News Corporation, two of the major corporations in the media and entertainment industry. The data are for the end of the financial year 1999, and are in US$ millions. Though News Corporation is based in Australia, it also trades on the NYSE, and its data in the following table, like those for Walt Disney, are according to the U.S. GAAP.

	Walt Disney	**News Corporation**
Sales	23,402	14,395
EBIT	3,035	1,819
EBT	2,314	1,212
NI	1,300	719
Assets	43,679	35,681
Equity	20,975	16,374

   a. Compute the ROE for Walt Disney and News Corporation.
   b. Use the DuPont model to analyze the difference in ROE between the two companies, identifying the elements that primarily cause this difference.

9. In the past 20 years, the best-performing stock markets have been found in countries with the highest economic growth rates. Should the current growth rate guide you in choosing stock markets if the world capital market is efficient?

10. Consider a French company that pays out 70 percent of its earnings. Its next annual earnings are expected to be €4 per share. The required return for the company is 12 percent. In the past, the company's compound annual growth rate (CAGR) has been 1.25 times the world's GDP growth rate. It is expected that the world's GDP growth rate will be 2.8 percent p.a. in the future. Assuming that the firm's earnings will continue to grow forever at 1.25 times the world's projected growth rate, compute the intrinsic value of the company's stock and its intrinsic P/E ratio.

11. Consider a company that pays out all its earnings. The required return for the firm is 13 percent.
   a. Compute the intrinsic P/E value of the company if its ROE is 15 percent.
   b. Compute the intrinsic P/E value of the company if its ROE is 20 percent.
   c. Discuss why your answers to parts (a) and (b) differ or do not differ from one another.
   d. Suppose that the company's ROE is 13 percent. Compute its intrinsic P/E value.
   e. Would the answer to part (d) change if the company retained half of its earnings instead of paying all of them out? Discuss why or why not.

12. Consider a firm with a ROE of 12 percent. The earnings next year are projected at $50 million, and the firm's earnings retention ratio is 0.70. The required return for the firm is 10 percent. Compute the following for the firm:
    i. Franchise factor
    ii. Growth factor
    iii. Franchise P/E value
    iv. Tangible P/E value
    v. Intrinsic P/E value

13. Consider a firm for which the nominal required rate of return is 8 percent. The rate of inflation is 3 percent. Compute the P/E ratio of the firm under the following situations:
    i. The firm has a full inflation flow-through.
    ii. The firm can pass only 40 percent of inflation through its earnings.
    iii. The firm cannot pass any inflation through its earnings.

    What pattern do you observe from your answers to items (i) through (iii)?

14. Company B and Company U are in the same line of business. Company B is based in Brazil, where inflation during the past few years has averaged about 9 percent. Company U is based in the United States, where the inflation during the past few years has averaged about 2.5 percent. The real rate of return required by global investors for investing in stocks such as B and U is 8 percent. Neither B nor U has any real growth in earnings, and both of them can pass only 60 percent of inflation through their earnings. What should be the P/E of the two companies? What can you say based on a comparison of the P/E for the two companies?

15. Omega, Inc., is based in Brazil, and most of its operations are domestic. During the period 1995–99, the firm has not had any real growth in earnings. The annual inflation in Brazil during this period is given in the following table:

Year	Inflation (%)
1995	22.0
1996	9.1
1997	4.3
1998	2.5
1999	8.4

Source: International Monetary Fund.

The real rate of return required by global investors for investing in stocks such as Omega, Inc., is 7 percent.
    a. Compute the P/E for Omega in each of the years if it can completely pass inflation through its earnings.
    b. Compute the P/E for Omega in each of the years if it can pass only 50 percent of inflation through its earnings.
    c. What conclusion can you draw about the effect of inflation on the stock price?

16. Consider a French company that exports French goods to the United States. What effect will a sudden appreciation of the euro relative to the dollar have on the P/E ratio of the French company? Discuss the effect under both the possibilities—the company being able to completely pass through the euro appreciation to its customers and the company being unable to completely pass through the euro appreciation to its customers.

17. Using the five macroeconomic factors described in the text, you outline the factor exposures of two stocks as follows:

Factor	Stock A	Stock B
Confidence	0.2	0.6
Time horizon	0.6	0.8
Inflation	−0.1	−0.5
Business cycle	4.0	2.0
Market timing	1.0	0.7

a. What would be the factor exposures of a portfolio invested half in stock A and half in stock B?

b. Contrary to general forecasts, you expect strong economic growth with a slight increase in inflation. Which stock should you overweigh in your portfolio?

18. Here is some return information on firms of various sizes and their price-to-book (value) ratios. Based on this information, what can you tell about the *size* and *value* style factors?

Stock	Size	P/BV	Return (%)
A	Huge	High	4
B	Huge	Low	6
C	Medium	High	9
D	Medium	Low	12
E	Small	High	13
F	Small	Low	15

19. You are analyzing whether the difference in returns on stocks of a particular country can be explained by two common factors, with a linear-factor model. Your candidates for the two factors are changes in interest rates and changes in the approval rating of the country's president, as measured by polls. The following table gives the interest rate, the percentage of people approving the president's performance, and the prices of three stocks (A, B, and C) for the past 10 periods.

	Interest	Approval		Price of Stock	
Period	Rate (%)	(%)	A	B	C
1	7.3	47	22.57	24.43	25.02
2	5.2	52	19.90	12.53	13.81
3	5.5	51	15.46	17.42	19.17
4	7.2	49	21.62	24.70	23.24
5	5.4	68	14.51	16.43	18.79
6	5.2	49	12.16	11.56	14.66
7	7.5	72	25.54	24.73	28.68
8	7.6	45	25.83	28.12	21.47
9	5.3	47	13.04	14.71	16.43
10	5.1	67	11.18	12.44	12.50

Try to assess whether the two factors have an influence on stock returns. To do so, estimate the factor exposures for each of the three stocks by doing a time-series regression for the return on each stock against the changes in the two factors.

20. You are a U.S. investor considering investing in Switzerland. The world market risk premium is estimated at 5 percent, the Swiss franc offers a 1 percent risk premium, and the current risk-free rates are equal to 4 percent in dollars and 3 percent in francs. In other words, you expect the Swiss franc to appreciate against the dollar by an amount equal to the interest rate differential plus the currency risk premium, or a total of 2 percent. You believe that the following equilibrium model (ICAPM) is appropriate for your investment analysis:

$$E(R_i) = R_f + \beta_1 \times RP_w + \beta_2 \times RP_{SFr}$$

where all returns are measured in dollars, RP_w is the risk premium on the world index, and RP_{SFr} is the risk premium on the Swiss franc. Your broker provides you with the following estimates and forecasted returns.

	Stock A	Stock B	Stock C	Stock D
Forecasted return (in francs)	0.08	0.09	0.11	0.07
World beta (β_1)	1	1	1.2	1.4
Dollar currency exposure (β_2)	1	0	0.5	−0.5

a. What should be the expected dollar returns on the four stocks, according to the ICAPM?
b. Which stocks would you recommend buying or selling?

Bibliography

Baumol, W. "Productivity Growth, Convergence, and Welfare: What the Long-Run Data Show," *American Economic Review*, 76(5), December 1986, pp. 1072–1085.

Besanko, D., Dranove, D., and Shanley, M. *Economics of Strategy*, 4th edition, New York: Wiley, 2007.

Blumenthal, R.G. "'Tis the Gift to Be Simple: Why the 80-Year-Old DuPont Model Still Has Fans," *CFO Magazine*, January 1998.

Brandenberger, A., and Nalebuff, B. *Co-opetition*, New York: Currency-Doubleday, 1996.

Burmeister, E., Roll, R., and Ross, S. "A Practitioner's Guide to Arbitrage Pricing Theory," in *A Practitioner's Guide to Factor Models*, Charlottesville, VA: The Research Foundation of the ICFA, 1994.

Calverley, J. *The Investor's Guide to Economic Fundamentals*, Chichester, West Sussex: Wiley, 2003.

Canova, F., and De Nicolo, G. "Stock Returns and Real Activity: A Structural Approach," *European Economic Review*, 39, 1995, pp. 981–1019.

Cavaglia, S., Brightman, C., and Aked, M. "On the Increasing Importance of Industry Factors," *Financial Analysts Journal*, 56(5), September/October 2000.

Chen, N., Roll, R., and Ross, S. "Economic Forces and the Stock Market," *Journal of Business*, September 1986.

Christensen, C., Raynor, M., and Verlinden, M. "Skate to Where the Money Will Be," *Harvard Business Review*, November 2001, pp. 72–81.

French, K. R., and Poterba, J. M. "Were Japanese Stock Prices Too High?" *Journal of Financial Economics*, October 1991.

Griffin, J. M., and Stulz, R. "International Competition and Exchange Rate Shocks: A Cross-Country Industry Analysis of Stock Returns," *Review of Financial Studies*, 14, 2001, pp. 215–241.

Hopkins, P., and Miller, H. *Country, Sector, and Company Factors in Global Portfolios*, Charlottesville, VA: The Research Foundation of AIMR, 2001.

Jones, C. I. *Introduction to Economic Growth*, 2nd ed., Norton, New York, 2002.

Leibowitz, M. L. "Franchise Margins and the Sales-Driven Franchise Value," *Financial Analysts Journal*, 53(6), November/December 1997, pp. 43–53.

Leibowitz, M. L. "Franchise Valuation under Q-Type Competition," *Financial Analysts Journal*, 54(6), November/December 1998, pp. 62–74.

Leibowitz, M. L., and Kogelman, S. *Franchise Value and the Price/Earnings Ratio*, The Research Foundation of AIMR, 2000.

Oster, S. M. *Modern Competitive Analysis*, New York: Oxford University Press, 1999.

Porter, M. E. *Competitive Advantage: Creating and Sustaining Superior Performance*, New York: Free Press, 1998a.

———. *The Competitive Advantage of Nations*, New York: Free Press, 1998b.

Radebaugh, L. H., and Gray, S. J. *International Accounting and Multinational Enterprises*, New York: Wiley, 1997.

Reilly, F. K., and Brown, K. C. *Investment Analysis and Portfolio Management*, 8th ed., Mason, OH: Thomson South Western, 2006.

Romer, P. The Origins of Endogenous Growth, *Journal of Economic Perspectives*, 8, Winter 1994, pp. 3–22.

Soliman, Mark T. "Using Industry-Adjusted DuPont Analysis to Predict Future Profitability," Working Paper, Stanford University, February 2004.

Stowe, J., Robinson, T., Pinto, J., and McLeavey, D. *Analysis of Equity Investments: Valuation*, Charlottesville, Va: Association for Investment Management and Research, 2002.

Temple, P. *Magic Numbers: The 33 Key Ratios That Every Investor Should Know*, Hoboken, NJ: Wiley, 2002.

7

Global Bond Investing

LEARNING OUTCOMES

After completing this chapter, you will be able to do the following:

- Discuss the difference between domestic bonds, foreign bonds, and international bonds
- Describe the various stages of an international bond issue
- Describe the various ways to invest in bonds from emerging countries
- Describe a Brady bond
- Define bond quotation and day count conventions across the world
- Describe the basic valuation method for straight fixed-rate bonds
- Define a yield curve based on zero-coupon bonds
- Describe and contrast the various methods used to report a yield to maturity (simple yield, annual yield, semiannual yield)
- Define the duration, or interest sensitivity, of a bond
- Compute the expected excess return (risk premium) on a domestic bond as the sum of the yield spread over the cash rate plus the duration-adjusted expected yield movement
- Define the three components of the quality spread (expected loss component, credit-risk premium, liquidity premium)
- Compare yield curves in various currencies
- Define the implied forward exchange rate from yield curves in different currencies
- Conduct an exchange rate break-even analysis
- Explain the various sources of return and risk from an international bond
- Compute the return on a foreign-currency bond

- Compute the return on a foreign bond, hedged against currency risk
- Compute the expected excess return (risk premium) on a foreign-currency bond, hedged and not hedged against currency risk
- Recommend and justify whether to hedge a bond market investment
- Discuss the various stages of international bond portfolio management
- Describe and analyze a floating-rate note (FRN) and explain why an FRN is not always priced at par
- Describe the characteristics and valuation of straight FRNs, bull FRNs, bear FRNs, dual-currency bonds, and currency-option bonds, and the motivation for their issuance
- Describe and analyze collateralized debt obligations (CDOs).

Global bond investment is both technical and difficult because of the vast diversity of markets, instruments, and currencies offered. Terminology and conventions vary from one market to the next, as do trading methods and costs. For example, yields to maturity are computed on an annual basis on the international bond market but on a semiannual basis on the U.S. market. And the Japanese sometimes use a simple-interest method to calculate yield to maturity rather than the usual compound-interest method. Moreover, instruments vary in these markets from straight bonds and floating-rate notes denominated in various currencies to bonds with numerous, and often exotic, option clauses.

This chapter first presents some statistics on the various *bond* markets. It then outlines the major differences among markets and describes the international bond market. After a brief reminder on bond valuation, the chapter discusses multicurrency bond portfolio management. The last section reviews more exotic bonds. It introduces floating-rate bonds and various structured notes found on the international bond market. It also describes collateralized debt obligations.

The Global Bond Market

The Various Segments

Debt certificates have been traded internationally for several centuries. Kings and emperors borrowed heavily to finance wars. Bankers from neutral countries assisted in arranging the necessary financing, thereby creating a market in debentures (bonds). The Rothschilds, for example, became famous for supporting the British war effort against Napoleon I through their European family network. As a matter of fact, organized trading in domestic and foreign debentures took place well before the start of any equity market.

Although debt financing has always been international in nature, there is still no unified global bond market. Instead, the global bond market is divided into three broad groups: *domestic bonds, foreign bonds,* and *international bonds.*

- Domestic bonds are issued locally by a domestic borrower and are usually denominated in the local currency.
- Foreign bonds are issued on a local market by a foreign borrower and are usually denominated in the local currency. Foreign bond issues and trading are under the supervision of local market authorities.
- International bonds are underwritten by a multinational syndicate of banks and are placed mainly in countries other than the one in whose currency the bond is denominated. These bonds are not traded on a specific national bond market.

Domestic bonds make up the bulk of a national bond market. Different issuers belong to different market segments: government, semigovernment, and corporate. In many countries, local corporations and government agencies have issued asset-backed securities. These are debt securities backed by some assets typically used as collateral—for example, other loans such as mortgages.

Foreign bonds issued on national markets have existed for a long time. They often have colorful names, such as *Yankee* bonds (in the United States), *Samurai* bonds (in Japan), *Rembrandt* bonds (in the Netherlands), *Matador* bonds (in Spain), *Caravela* bonds (in Portugal), or *Bulldog* bonds (in the United Kingdom).

Because many non-U.S. firms have financing needs in U.S. dollars, they have a strong incentive to issue bonds in New York. But these bonds must satisfy the disclosure requirements of the U.S. Securities and Exchange Commission (SEC). This can be a costly process for non-U.S. corporations that use accounting standards different from U.S. GAAP. In 1963, the United States imposed an Interest Equalization Tax (IET) on foreign securities held by U.S. investors. The tax forced non-U.S. corporations to pay a higher interest rate in order to attract U.S. investors. A few years later, the Federal Reserve Board restricted the financing of foreign direct investment by U.S. corporations. These measures, taken to support the dollar, made the U.S. bond market less attractive to foreign borrowers and simultaneously created a need for offshore financing of U.S. corporate foreign activities. This led to the development of the *international bond* market, known as the Eurobond market. Because of the Glass-Steagall Act, U.S. commercial banks were prevented from issuing and dealing in bonds. Such restrictions did not apply to their offshore activities, and foreign subsidiaries of U.S. commercial banks became very active on the Eurobond market. The repeal of the IET in 1974 and the partial relaxation of the Glass-Steagall Act, as well as various measures to attract foreign borrowers and issuers on the U.S. domestic market, did not slow the growth of the international bond market. More important, the international bond market came to be recognized by borrowers and investors alike as an efficient, low-cost, and most innovative market.

In 1999, all bonds denominated in one of the former currencies of Euroland were translated into euros. For example, all French government bonds denominated in French francs became bonds denominated in euros, using the legacy exchange rate set on January 1, 1999. This denomination could create great confusion between "Eurobonds" and "bonds issued in euros." In other words, a French government bond issued in France is not a Eurobond, although it is a euro bond—that is, a bond denominated in euros. The name *Eurobond* comes from the historical fact that the banks placing the Eurobond are located in Europe. The terminology had to evolve to clear the confusion. The term *international bond* is now used in lieu of *Eurobond*.

Debt issued by companies and governments from emerging countries tends to be considered a separate segment of the market (discussion to follow). Floating-rate notes, issued in euros and dollars, are an important segment of the international bond market, where a variety of more complex bonds can also be found, as we discuss later.

World Market Size

The world bond market comprises both the domestic bond markets and the international market. The size of the world bond market was estimated at $66 trillion at the start of 2007. The world market capitalization of bonds is, therefore, somewhat higher than that of equity. Bonds denominated in dollars currently represent just under half the value of all outstanding bonds. Yen bonds represent a bit less than 20 percent of the world bond market, and bonds denominated in euros, about a quarter. Exhibit 7.1 gives the relative size of the domestic bond markets (total capitalization around $48.7 trillion). Note that the relative share of each currency market depends not only on new issues and repaid bonds but also on exchange rate

EXHIBIT 7.1

Market Capitalization of Domestic Bond Markets
Total $48.7 trillion

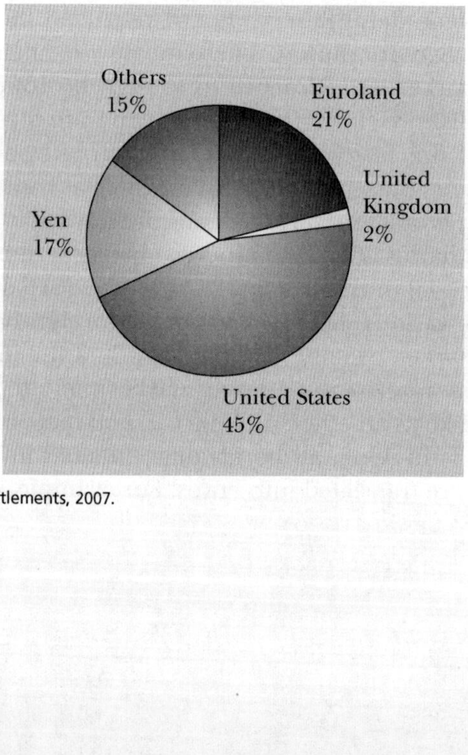

Source: Bank for International Settlements, 2007.

EXHIBIT 7.2

Market Capitalization of International Bonds
Total $17.6 trillion

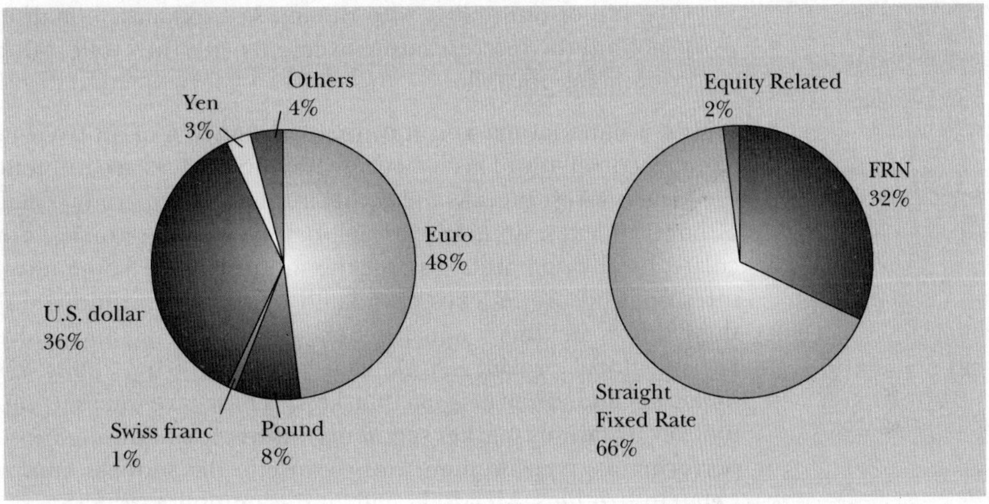

Source: Bank for International Settlements, 2007.

movements. Exhibit 7.2 details the international bond market (total capitalization around $17.6 trillion) by type of instrument and by currency of issuance. The international bond market has grown dramatically in the past few years.

The major types of instruments are straight bonds with fixed coupons, *floating-rate notes (FRNs)* with a coupon indexed on a short-term interest rate, and bonds with some equity feature (e.g., *convertible bond*). The euro is the major currency of issuance on the international bond market, followed by the dollar.

Bond Indexes

Bond indexes used to be less commonly available than stock indexes. However, total-return bond indexes serve many purposes and are increasingly used. A total-return index cumulates the price movement with accrued interest; it is a cumulative index of the total return on a bond portfolio.

These indexes are put to different uses:

- A bond index calculated daily for each bond market allows quick assessment of the direction and magnitude of movements in the market. Such an index must be based on a small but representative sample of actively traded bonds, because many bonds are not traded every day. A single actively traded bond, called a *benchmark bond,* is sometimes used. News services such as the *Financial Times*, Reuters, or Bloomberg publish daily quotes on benchmark bonds representative of each market.

- Total-return bond indexes are also required for measuring the performance of a bond portfolio in a domestic or multicurrency setting. This is usually done monthly or quarterly. One needs an exhaustive index covering all bonds in the market. Because many issues are not liquid and their prices may be old or out of line with the market, exhaustive market indexes tend to lag behind the interest rate movements, but they reflect the current valuation of a market portfolio.

Within a national market, the price movements of all fixed-rate bonds tend to be strongly correlated. This is because all bond prices are influenced by movements in the local interest rate. As for equity indexes, there are two major types of providers of bond indexes: domestic and global. In many countries, domestic providers calculate local bond indexes weekly, monthly, and sometimes daily. International investors find the indexes calculated by these institutions difficult to use because they differ in their construction methodology and calculation frequencies. Several global providers have developed consistent bond indexes for the major domestic and international markets. These are market capitalization–weighted indexes of various market segments and regions. Among those commonly used for performance measurements, one can cite the indexes computed by J.P. Morgan, Lehman Brothers, Merrill Lynch, and Bloomberg/EFFAS.

The International Bond Market

The international bond market is an attractive one to the global investor. It avoids most national regulations and constraints and provides sophisticated instruments geared to various investment objectives. Because of the important role of international bonds in global investment, we will examine in some detail how they are issued and traded.

An example of such a bond issue is presented in Exhibit 7.3. The *tombstone* advertises a bond issued by NKK, a Japanese company. An interesting feature of this bond is that it is a dual-currency bond: It is issued in yen (20 billion), with interest coupons fixed in yen (8 percent), but its principal repayment is fixed in U.S. dollars ($110,480,000). The underwriting syndicate is listed at the bottom of the tombstone.

In general, several points distinguish an international bond from a domestic bond, and some can be spotted on the *tombstone* in Exhibit 7.3:

- The underwriting syndicate is made up of banks from numerous countries.
- U.S. commercial banks can participate, as well as U.S. investment banks. This would not be the case for a domestic or foreign bond issued on the U.S. market.
- Underwriting banks tend to use subsidiaries established in London or a foreign country with a favorable tax situation. This can be easily recognized by the label appearing at the end of the banks' names listed on the tombstone: *Limited* (Britain or a British Isle), *SA* (usually Luxembourg), and

EXHIBIT 7.3

International Bond Tombstone

These securities have been sold outside the United States of America and Japan. This announcement appears as a matter of record only.

NEW ISSUE

22nd January, 2004

NKK

Nippon Kokan Kabushiki Kaisha

8 per cent. Dual Currency
Yen/U.S. Dollar Bonds Due 2014

Issue Price: 101 per cent. of the Issue Amount

Issue Amount:	**¥20,000,000,000**
Redemption Amount at Maturity:	**U.S.$110,480,000**

Nomura International Limited
Mitsubishi Trust & Banking Corporation (Europe) S.A.
Prudential-Bache Securities International
Yamaichi International (Europe) Limited

Bankers Trust International Limited
Crédit Lyonnais
Credit Suisse First Boston Limited
Dresdner Bank Aktiengesellschaft
EBC Amro Bank Limited
Fuji International Finance Limited
Generale Bank
Kleinwort, Benson Limited
Lloyds Merchant Bank Limited
Morgan Guaranty Ltd
Morgan Stanley International
Orion Royal Bank Limited
Swiss Bank Corporation International Limited
Union Bank of Switzerland (Securities) Limited
S.G. Warburg & Co., Ltd.

NV (Netherlands or the Dutch Antilles). U.S. commercial banks must use a foreign subsidiary because of U.S. regulations.

- Corporate borrowers sometimes use a subsidiary incorporated in a country with a favorable tax and regulatory treatment. This is done to avoid double taxation or some stamp tax (as is the case in Switzerland). But the guarantee of the mother company is usually granted to the investor.
- The frequency of coupon payments is annual for fixed-rate international bonds, but it is semiannual for U.S. bonds.

The Issuing Syndicate International bonds are sold in a multistage process. The issue is organized by an international bank called the *lead manager.* This bank invites several *comanagers* to form the *management group* (from 5 to 30 banks, usually). For large issues, there may be several lead managers. The managers prepare the issue, set the final conditions of the bond, and select the *underwriters* and *selling group.* One of the managers is appointed as the principal paying agent and fiscal agent. A large portion of the issue is directly subscribed by the management group.

The underwriters are invited to participate in the issue on the basis of their regional placement power. Their number varies from 30 to 300 and comprises international banks from all regions of the world. Together with the management group, the underwriters guarantee final placement of the bonds at a set price to the borrower.

The selling group is responsible for selling the bonds to the public and consists of managers, underwriters, and additional banks with a good selling base. Note that a participant may be, at the same time, manager, underwriter, and seller. Separate fees are paid to compensate for the various services. The total fee ranges from 1 percent to 2.5 percent. Unlike their U.S. counterparts, international underwriters are not obligated to maintain the bond's market price at or above the issue price until the syndicate is disbanded. This means that bonds are often placed at a price below the issue price. There is considerable price discrimination among clients, and selling members may pass along part of their fee to the final buyer of the bond.

The Timetable of a New Issue Unlike national markets, the international bond market has neither *registration formalities* nor *waiting queues.* A new issue may be placed within three weeks. A typical timetable is depicted in Exhibit 7.4.

First, the lead manager gets together with the borrower to discuss the terms of the bond (amount, maturity, fixed or floating rate, and coupon). The terms generally remain provisional until the official offering date. During this period, the lead manager arranges the management syndicate and prepares various documents, one of which is a preliminary prospectus called, at this stage, a *red herring.* On the *announcement day,* the managers send e-mails or faxes describing the proposed bond issue and inviting banks to join the underwriting and selling groups. Potential underwriters are sent the preliminary prospectus. A week or two later, the final terms of the bond are set and the syndicate commits itself to the borrower.

EXHIBIT 7.4

Timetable of a New International Bond Issue

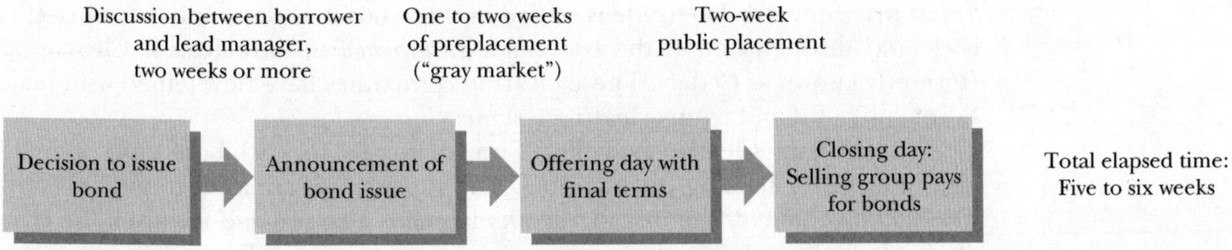

A final prospectus is printed, and the bonds are publicly offered on the *offering day*. At the end of a public placement period of about two weeks, the subscription is closed on the *closing day*, and the bonds are delivered in exchange for cash paid to the borrower. A tombstone is later published in international newspapers to advertise the successful issue and to list the participating banks.

After the closing day, the bonds can be publicly traded. However, bond trading actually takes place well before the closing day. A *gray market* for the bonds starts before the final terms have been set on the offering day; trading is contingent on the final issue price. That is, bonds are traded in the gray market at a premium or discount relative to the future issue price. For example, a quote of *less ¼* means that the bonds are exchanged at a price of 99.25 percent if the future issue price is set at 99.5 percent. This is a form of forward market for bonds that do not yet exist. The gray market is often used by members of the selling group to resell part of their bond allocation at a discount below the issue price, but possibly at a net profit if their fee is large enough.

Dealing in International Bonds The secondary market is truly international and comprises an informal network of market makers and dealers. A market maker quotes a net price to a financial institution in the form of a bid–ask price. No commissions are charged. Although the international bond market has no physical location, most of the bonds are listed on the Luxembourg stock exchange to nominally satisfy the requirement of obtaining a public quotation at least once a year or quarter. However, very few transactions go through the exchange. Instead, bond dealers created an around-the-clock market among financial institutions across the world, forming the *International Capital Market Association (ICMA)*, based in Zurich and London and formerly known as ISMA and AIBD. The geographical composition of the ICMA shows the prominent role of London. But Swiss banks are large investors in the market and the second major force in ICMA.

All market makers and dealers in Eurobonds are part of the ICMA. The ICMA bears some similarities to the U.S. National Association of Securities Dealers (NASD). But, whereas NASD is under the supervision of the SEC, the ICMA is purely self-regulated and is subject to no government intervention.

Clearing System Let's assume that a Scottish investment manager wants to buy $100,000 worth of a specific international bond. The investment manager calls several market makers to get their best quotations and concludes the deal at the lowest price quoted. The trade is settled in three business days, and the transaction is cleared through one of the two major *clearinghouses,* Euroclear or Clearstream (formerly known as Cedel). These clearing companies have now joined with major European bond and equity clearing systems.

Euroclear and Clearstream collect a transaction fee for each book entry, as well as a custody fee for holding the securities. The custody fees are a function of a client's transaction volume: If the member bank maintains a large bond turnover, the custodial fee is nil. Euroclear and Clearstream also provide security lending facilities.

Emerging Markets and Brady Bonds

Investors wishing to buy bonds issued by emerging countries have several alternatives:

- They can directly access the *domestic bond* markets of some emerging countries. These emerging markets have been growing, albeit in an erratic fashion. Various restrictions and liquidity problems reduce the amount available to foreign investors. Latin America dominates the fixed-income market of emerging countries, but some European and Asian markets, such as Turkey, Hungary, the Czech Republic, India, Indonesia, and the Philippines, are also worth mentioning. Most of the bonds traded on emerging markets are *not* investment grade, that is, rated Baa or above by Moody's or BBB or above by Standard & Poor's. This means that they are not eligible for many U.S. institutional investors. These instruments are generally denominated in the local currency and carry the exchange risk of that currency. On the other hand, local governments are less likely to default on these bonds, because they can always print more national currency.
- They can buy *foreign bonds* directly issued by some emerging country or corporation on a major national bond market. The bond is issued in the national currency of that market.
- They can buy *international bonds* issued by emerging countries. Latin American governments and firms represent the largest share of these new issues denominated in U.S. dollars and other major currencies. Major issuers come from Mexico, Argentina, Venezuela, and Brazil.
- They can buy *Brady bonds* on the international capital market. In 1990, the Brady plan allowed emerging countries to transform nonperforming debt into so-called Brady bonds, which are traded on the international bond market.

Brady Bonds: A Historical Perspective In the 1980s, many developing countries were hit hard by the drop in commodity prices and other problems, and they became unable or unwilling to service their loans from international banks. This situation led to an international debt crisis that threatened the international financial system. The emerging-country debt often took the form of bank loans, which are nontradable, as opposed to bonds. Although many emerging countries have not serviced their bank loans, leading to a negotiation to reschedule them, they have usually kept servicing their bond debt. The creditor banks formed the *Paris Club* to negotiate with emerging countries the rescheduling of their debts. A secondary market for nonperforming loans developed in which these loans traded at a steep discount from their par value. The principles of Brady plans, named after U.S. Treasury Secretary Nicholas F. Brady, were implemented from 1990 to provide a satisfactory solution to this debt crisis.

To negotiate its Brady plan, the emerging country must initiate a credible economic reform program that receives approval and funding from the World Bank, the International Monetary Fund (IMF), and regional development banks, such as the Inter-American Development Bank, the African Development Bank, the Asian Development Bank, or the European Bank for Reconstruction and Development. Once the IMF and the World Bank have agreed that the economic reform plan will reduce the risk of new insolvency problems, these organizations provide funding, which can be used in part to provide collateral and guarantees in the debt rescheduling. One advantage for creditors is that they exchange commercial loans for tradable bonds. A Brady plan is basically a debt-reduction program whereby sovereign debt is repackaged into tradable Brady bonds, generally with collateral. Close to 20 countries have issued Brady bonds, including Argentina, Brazil, Bulgaria, Costa Rica, Nigeria, Poland, the Philippines, Uruguay, and Venezuela. These bonds are traded on the international bond market. While many Brady bonds have now been retired, several newly issued bonds have adopted the technical innovations introduced in the structuring of Brady bonds as described below.

International commercial banks, which were most active in lending to emerging countries, are the major market makers on the Brady bond market. The bid–ask spread on these bonds averages 25 basis points and is low relative to that of bonds issued by emerging countries, because the issue size of Brady bonds can be very large and their market is quite active.

Characteristics of Brady Bonds Brady bonds come with a large menu of options, which makes their analysis somewhat complicated. The basic idea is to replace existing government debt with Brady bonds, whose market value is less than the par value of the original debt, but that are more attractive than the original debt because of the guarantees provided and their tradability on the international bond market.

Types of Guarantees Three types of guarantees can be put in place. These guarantees are not available on all types of Brady bonds.

- *Principal collateral*: The U.S. Treasury issues long-term (e.g., 30-year) *zero-coupon bonds* to collaterallize the principal of the Brady bond. The collateral is paid for by a combination of the IMF, the World Bank, and the emerging country. The value of the collateral increases with time and reaches *par value* at maturity of the Brady bond.

- *Rolling-interest guarantee:* The first semiannual coupons (generally three) are guaranteed by securities deposited in escrow with the New York Federal Reserve Bank, to protect the bondholder from interest suspension or default. If an interest payment is missed, the bondholder will receive that interest payment from the escrow account. If the interest payment is made by the emerging country, the interest collateral will be rolled forward to the next interest payments.

- *Value recovery rights:* Some bonds issued by Mexico and Venezuela have attached warrants linked to the price of oil. Investors can get extra interest payments if the oil export receipts of these countries increase over time.

Types of Bonds Two major types of Brady bonds have been issued:

- *Par bonds (PARs):* These can be exchanged dollar for dollar for existing debt. Typically, these bonds have fixed coupons and a long-term maturity (30 years) and are repaid in full on the final maturity. In some cases, the coupon is stepped up progressively over the life of the bond. The debt reduction is obtained by setting a coupon rate on the par value of the bond well below the current market interest rate. In other words, the market value of the bond is well below its face value, because of the low coupon. These bonds are sometimes known as interest-reduction bonds. The difference between the par value of the bond and its market value at issue time can be regarded as the amount of debt forgiveness.

- *Discount bonds (DISCs):* These are exchanged at a discount to the par value of the existing debt but with a "market-rate" coupon. These bonds are sometimes known as principal-reduction bonds. Typically, these bonds have floating-rate coupons (*the London interbank offer rate,* or LIBOR, plus a market-determined spread) and a long maturity (20 years or more).

Other types of Brady bonds can be negotiated:

- *Front-loaded interest-reduction bonds (FLIRBs):* These have low initial coupons that step up to higher levels for a number of years, after which they pay a floating rate.

- *New-money bonds (NMBs) and debt-conversion bonds (DCBs):* These are generally issued together through the new-money option of the Brady plan. This option is designed to give debtholders incentives to invest additional capital in the emerging country. For every dollar of NMB subscribed, the investor can exchange existing debt for DCBs in a ratio stated in the Brady plan (typically $5 of DCBs for each $1 of NMBs). The incentive is provided by making DCBs more attractive than the bonds available in other Brady options.

- *Past-due interest bonds (PDIs):* These are issued in exchange for unpaid past interest. In a way, they pay interest on interest.

This list is not exhaustive, and the option menu of a Brady plan can be quite varied.

Major Differences among Bond Markets

A thorough technical knowledge of the various bond markets reduces investors' trading costs and enhances returns; it also helps investors better understand the risks involved. Because bond markets are still rapidly developing, new types of instruments and issuing techniques appear throughout the world all the time. For this reason, the following description of these markets is bound to become partially outdated over time; it is meant to serve chiefly as a broad overview.

Types of Instruments

The variety of bonds offered to the international or even the domestic investor is amazing, because of the recent development of bonds with variable interest rates and complex optional clauses. Although the U.S. bond market is among the more innovative markets, the international market is surely the most creative of all. Investment bankers from many countries bring their expertise to this unregulated market. Each month, new instruments appear or disappear. The international market's major difference from domestic markets lies in its multicurrency nature. Many international bonds are designed to have cash flows in different currencies (see Example 7.1).

EXAMPLE 7.1 *SWISS FRANC JAPANESE CONVERTIBLE BOND*

Japanese firms have frequently issued Swiss franc–denominated bonds convertible into common shares of a Japanese company. This is a bond issued in Swiss francs, paying a fixed coupon in Swiss francs, and repaid in Swiss francs. But the bond can also be converted into shares of the Japanese issuing company. What are various scenarios that would benefit a buyer of this bond?

SOLUTION

A Swiss investor can benefit from purchasing this bond in any one of three situations:

- A drop in the market interest rate on Swiss franc bonds (as on any straight Swiss franc bond)
- A rise in the price of the company's stock (because the bonds are convertible into stock)
- A rise in the yen relative to the franc (because the bond is convertible into a Japanese yen asset)

A non-Swiss investor would also benefit if the franc appreciates relative to the investor's currency.

Unfortunately, the reverse scenarios would lead to a loss.

In this chapter, we provide a refresher on the analysis of traditional bonds, such as *straight bonds* (fixed-coupon bonds) and floating-rate notes; we also analyze some of the more complex international bonds.

Quotations, Day Count, and Frequency of Coupons

Quotation Bonds are usually quoted on the basis of price plus *accrued interest* in percentage of *face value.*[1] This means that the price is quoted separately (as a percentage of the bond's nominal value) from the percentage coupon accrued from the last coupon date to the trade date. Accrued interest is computed linearly by multiplying the amount of coupon by the ratio of the time since the last coupon payment divided by the coupon period. It is also expressed in percentage of face value. The buyer pays (or the seller receives) both the quoted price of the bond and accrued interest. Thus, the price quoted is "clean" of coupon effect and allows meaningful comparisons between various bonds. This quoted price is often called a *clean price.* Hence, the *full* price P is equal to the sum of the quoted or clean price, Q plus accrued interest AI:

$$P = Q + AI \tag{7.1}$$

Accrued interest is generally calculated as follows:

$$AI = \text{Coupon} \times \frac{\text{Days since last coupon date}}{\text{Days in coupon period}}$$

Example 7.2 illustrates calculation of the full price of a bond.

EXAMPLE 7.2 FULL PRICE AND CLEAN PRICE

The clean price of a Eurobond is quoted at $Q = 95$ percent. The annual coupon is 6 percent, and we are exactly three months from the past coupon payment. What is the full price of the bond?

SOLUTION

$$P = Q + \text{Accrued interest} = 95\% + 90/360 \times 6\% = 96.5\%$$

[1] Unfortunately, this method of quotation is not universal. Convertible bonds, some index-linked bonds, or FRNs in which the coupon is determined ex post (at the end of the coupon period) are quoted with coupons attached. Even some exceptions exist for straight bonds. For example, in the United Kingdom's *gilt* market, the market for U.K. government bonds, an *ex dividend* date, or *ex date,* is set roughly a month before the coupon payment when the bond trades without the next coupon payment. An investor who buys the bond after the ex date but before the payment date does not receive the coupon. Instead, it goes to the previous bondholder. Hence, the full price of the gilt (clean price plus accrued interest) still drops on the ex date as the security holder loses the right to the next coupon.

Coupon Frequency and Day Count Bonds differ internationally by the frequency of their coupon payments and in the way accrued interest is calculated. In the United States, straight bonds usually pay a semiannual coupon equal to half of the annual coupon reported. The day-count method used in accrued interest rate calculations for agency, municipal, corporate and foreign bonds assumes months of 30 days in a year of 360 days. In other words, the basic unit of time measurement is the month; it does not matter if a month is actually 28 or 31 days long. An investor holding a bond for one month receives 30/360, or one-twelfth of the annual coupon (one-sixth of the semiannual coupon). This day-count convention is known as "30/360." The same method is used in Germany, Scandinavia, Switzerland, and the Netherlands. On the other hand, the day count for U.S. Treasury bonds is based on the actual number of days in a year of 365 or 366 days, so that an investor receives accrued interest proportional to the number of days the bond has been held. This day-count convention is known as "actual/actual." Many countries use this actual/actual convention. By contrast, Canada and Japan use a day count based on the actual number of days in a 365-day year (even in years of 366 days).

Straight international bonds usually pay an annual coupon and use the U.S. 30/360 day-count convention, regardless of their currency of denomination, so that a yen or pound bond uses a 30-day month in a 360 day year. On the other hand, international FRNs use actual days in a 360-day year, which is also the convention used for short-term deposits. This follows naturally from the fact that FRN coupons are indexed to short-term interest rates, which follow the "actual/360" day-count convention. Straight international bonds tend to pay annual coupons, whereas FRNs pay quarterly or semiannual coupons. The coupon characteristics of the major bond markets are summarized in Exhibit 7.5.

EXHIBIT 7.5

Coupon Characteristics of Major Bond Markets

Characteristic	United States	U.S. Treasuries	Canada
Usual frequency of coupon	Semiannual	Semiannual	Semiannual
Day count (month/year)	30/360	Actual/actual	Actual/365
Characteristic	**Australia**	**United Kingdom**	**Switzerland**
Usual frequency of coupon	Semiannual	Semiannual	Annual
Day count (month/year)	Actual/actual	Actual/actual	30/360
Characteristic	**Germany**	**Netherlands**	**France**
Usual frequency of coupon	Annual	Annual	Annual
Day count (month/year)	30/360	30/360	Actual/actual
Characteristic	**Japan**	**International Bonds**	**FRNs**
Usual frequency of coupon	Semiannual	Annual	Quarter or semiannual
Day count (month/year)	Actual/365	30/360	Actual/360

Yield to Maturity The issue of yields also needs to be addressed. Most financial institutions around the world calculate and publish *yields to maturity (YTMs)* on individual bonds. These calculations are detailed in the next section, but let's stress that the methods used for this calculation vary among countries, so yields are not directly comparable. Most Europeans, for instance, calculate an annual, and accurate, *actuarial YTM* using the ICMA-recommended formula. U.S. (and often British) institutions publish a semiannual actuarial YTM. For example, a U.S. bond issued at par with 6 percent coupons will pay a coupon of $3 semiannually per $100 of face value and is reported as having a semiannual YTM of 6 percent.

On the other hand, Europeans would quote this bond as having a 6.09 percent (annual) YTM because of the compounding of the two semiannual coupons. Common sense dictates that yields for all maturities and currencies be compared in an identical fashion. The tradition of using semiannual yields is understandably confusing for international investors.[2]

The situation is even worse in Japan, where financial institutions sometimes report YTM based on a simple-interest calculation. The following simple formula shows how this is done:

$$\textit{Simple yield} = \frac{\textit{Coupon}}{\textit{Current price}} + \frac{(100 - \textit{Current price})}{\textit{Current price}} \times \frac{1}{\textit{Years to maturity}} \qquad (7.2)$$

This simple yield is the immediate yield, measured by the coupon over the price, plus the future capital gain or loss amortized over the remaining maturity of the bond. This simple yield understates the true YTM for bonds priced over par and overstates the yield for bonds priced below par. The historical rationale for this approximate formula is the ease of calculation (see Example 7.3).

EXAMPLE 7.3 SIMPLE YIELD CALCULATION

A three-year bond has exactly three years till maturity, and the last coupon has just been paid. The coupon is annual and equal to 6 percent. The bond price is 95 percent. What is its simple yield?

SOLUTION

$$\text{Simple yield} = \frac{6}{95} + \frac{(100 - 95)}{95} \times \frac{1}{3} = 8.07\%$$

Legal and Fiscal Aspects

Bonds are securities issued in either *bearer* or *registered* forms. On the international market, as well as in many European countries, the bearer of a bond is assumed to

[2] The rationale for this method is that it is easy to calculate a yield for a bond issued at par with semiannual coupons. We just multiply the semiannual coupon by 2. However, the use of an annual actuarial yield (with compounding of semiannual yields) makes more sense and allows a direct comparison between instruments and markets.

be its legal owner. In the United States and many other countries, owners must be registered in the issuer's books. Bond registration allows for easier transfer of interest payments and amortization. Coupons are usually paid annually on markets in which bonds are issued in bearer form, reducing the cost associated with coupon payments. Coupons are paid this way on international bonds in all currencies. Bearer bonds provide confidentiality of ownership, which is very important to some investors.

The U.S. Securities Act is typical of government regulations designed to ensure that domestic investors are protected. The act requires that all public issues of securities be registered with the U.S. Securities and Exchange Commission (SEC). Any bond not registered with the SEC cannot be publicly offered to U.S. residents at the time of issue. SEC registration is imposed to ensure that accurate information on bond issues is publicly available. Bonds issued in foreign markets and international bonds do not meet this requirement, but Yankee bonds do because they undergo a simplified SEC registration. No other bonds can be purchased by U.S. residents at the time of issue; they may be purchased only after they are "seasoned" (i.e., traded for some time). Sometimes it is difficult to know when an issue is seasoned; usually three months, but sometimes a longer period, such as nine months, is necessary. U.S. banks can participate in international bond-issuing syndicates only if they institute a procedure guaranteeing that U.S. investors cannot purchase the bonds. This can be difficult because international bonds are issued in bearer form.

Fiscal considerations are important in international investment. Some countries impose withholding taxes on interest paid by their national borrowers. This means that a foreign investor is often taxed twice: once in the borrowing country (withholding tax) and again in the investor's home country through the usual income tax. Tax treaties help by allowing investors to claim the foreign withholding tax as a tax credit at home; nontaxable investors can also reclaim all or part of a withholding tax, but this is a lengthy and costly process. Avoiding double taxation, in fact, was a major impetus behind the development of the international market. And that is why today the official borrower on the international market is usually a subsidiary incorporated in a country with no withholding tax (e.g., the Netherlands Antilles). Of course, the parent company must fully guarantee the interest and principal payments on the bond. Nevertheless, the trend seems to be toward eliminating withholding taxes for foreign investors. To attract foreign investors in their government bonds, most countries eliminated withholding taxes on foreign investment in their domestic bond markets. The United States allowed domestic corporations to borrow directly from foreign investors on international markets without paying a 30 percent withholding tax. This removed the need to borrow through a subsidiary incorporated in the Netherlands Antilles or another tax-free base. Similar regulations already existed in other countries.

The repeal of withholding taxes promotes a greater integration of the international and domestic markets, but not at the expense of the international market. The international market continues to grow despite the removal of these taxes on major national markets.

A Refresher on Bond Valuation

Bond portfolio management[3] requires the use of mathematical techniques. International bond management adds a new dimension to these techniques, namely, a multicurrency strategy. It also implies the analysis of a large variety of unusual bonds, floating-rate notes, currency option bonds, and other instruments.

The following section could appear in any textbook that deals with domestic investment; as such, it is presented only briefly here. It is followed by a more detailed analysis of the techniques used in international portfolio management, especially the comparison of international yield curves, and an analysis of special bonds.

Zero-Coupon Bonds

It is useful to start the analysis with zero-coupon bonds, which are bonds that do not pay a coupon but pay only a fixed cash flow at their maturity.

Yield to Maturity: Zero-Coupon Bonds The theoretical value of a bond is determined by computing the present value of all future cash flows generated by the bond discounted at an appropriate interest rate. Conversely, we can calculate the internal rate of return, or yield to maturity (YTM), of a bond on the basis of its current market price and its promised payments.

For example, a bond that promises a payment of $C_1 = \$100$ one year from now, with a current market value of $P = \$90.91$, has a YTM r_1 given by

$$P = \frac{C_1}{(1 + r_1)} \quad \text{or} \quad 90.91 = \frac{100}{(1 + r_1)}$$

Hence,

$$r_1 = 10\%$$

Similarly, we can use the following formula to compute the YTM of zero-coupon bonds maturing in t years:

$$P = \frac{C_t}{(1 + r_t)^t} \tag{7.3}$$

where r_t is expressed as a yearly interest rate. The term $1/(1 + r_t)^t$ is the discount factor for year t. The YTM is defined as the interest rate at which P dollars should be invested today in order to realize C_t dollars t years from now.

For example, a two-year zero-coupon bond paying $C_2 = \$100$ two years from now and currently selling at a price $P = \$81.16$ has a YTM r_2 given by

$$81.16 = \frac{100}{(1 + r_2)^2}$$

[3] A detailed analysis can be found in Fabozzi (2007).

Hence,

$$r_2 = 11\%$$

Finally, if the price is $P = 32.2$ and maturity $t = 10$ years, we have $r_{10} = 12$ percent.

Prices and Yields All bonds of the same issuer (e.g., government bonds) with the same maturity and other contractual terms must have the same YTM; otherwise, an easy arbitrage would exist. If we know the market YTM for the relevant maturity, we can use Equation 7.3 to derive the price of the bond. For example, assume that the one-year market yield moves from 10 percent to 9 percent; then the price of the one-year zero-coupon bond should move from 90.91 percent to 91.74 percent:

$$P = \frac{C_1}{(1 + r_1)} = \frac{100}{1.09} = 91.74$$

We have an inverse relationship between the market yield and the bond price.

Yield Curves The yields to maturity (YTMs) of two zero-coupon bonds in the same currency but with different maturities are usually different. Graphing the YTMs on bonds with different maturities allows us to draw a *yield curve*. The yield curve shows the YTM computed on a given date as a function of the maturity of the bonds. It provides an estimate of the current term structure of interest rates. To be meaningful, a yield curve must be drawn from bonds with identical characteristics except for their maturity.

The most important yield curve is derived from zero-coupon government bonds. This is a default-free yield curve. Different zero-coupon bonds are represented as points on the hypothetical yield curve in Exhibit 7.6. Although government bonds

EXHIBIT 7.6

Example of a Yield Curve

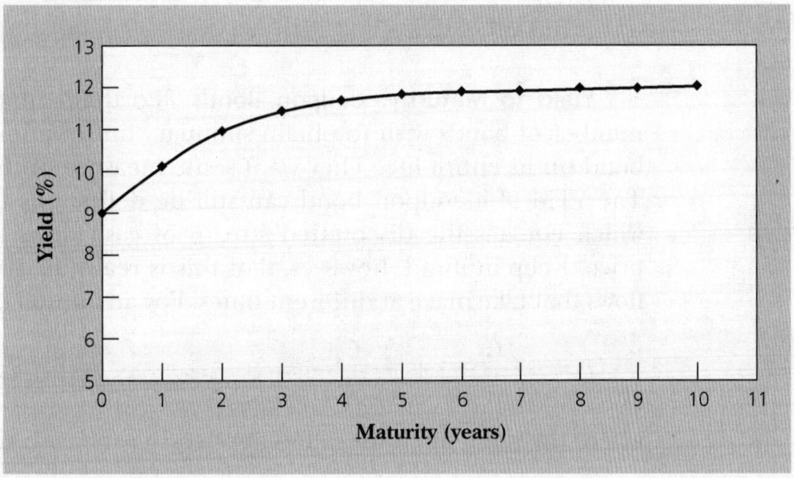

are seldom issued without coupons, a common technique for creating zero-coupon bonds is called *stripping*. In many countries, the government lets bankers strip a government coupon bond: Each cash flow of a given government bond is transformed into a separate bond. So, there are as many zero-coupon bonds as there are coupon payments and final reimbursement. The government zero-coupon yield curve is derived from these strips.

A yield curve can also be calculated from the YTM on government coupon bonds. It is usually derived from bonds trading at, or around, par (100%) and is called the *par yield curve*. As discussed in the next section, the YTM of a coupon bond is really some average interest rate over the life of the bond, so it is preferable to rely on a zero-coupon yield curve for pricing of fixed-income securities. Other yield curves can be drawn for risky bonds—for example, those with an AA quality rating or bonds denominated in foreign currencies.

Bond with Coupons

Most bonds issued pay a periodic coupon.

Valuing a Bond with Coupons The theoretical value of a coupon-paying bond is a little more difficult to assess. It may be considered the present value of a stream of cash flows consisting of each coupon payment and the principal reimbursement. Because the cash flows occur at different times, they should be discounted at the interest rate corresponding to their dates of payment. Accordingly, the coupon to be paid in one year should be discounted at the one-year interest rate on the yield curve. The coupon to be paid in two years should be discounted at the two-year rate, and so forth. In essence, then, a coupon-paying bond is a combination of zero-coupon bonds with different maturities. In general, we will call $C_1, C_2, \ldots, C_n$, the cash flows paid by the bond at times 1, 2, to n. The last cash flow will generally include a coupon and the principal reimbursement. We then have the pricing formula

$$P = \frac{C_1}{(1 + r_1)^1} + \frac{C_2}{(1 + r_2)^2} + \cdots + \frac{C_n}{(1 + r_n)^n} \tag{7.4}$$

Yield to Maturity: Coupon Bonds Portfolio managers dealing with a large number of bonds wish to obtain summary information on the yield promised by a bond on its entire life. They want some measure of the average YTM of the bond. The YTM of a coupon bond can still be defined as the internal rate of return r, which equates the discounted stream of cash flows to the current bond market price. Keep in mind, however, that this is really an average yield provided by cash flows that take place at different times. For an annual coupon bond, the equation is

$$P = \frac{C_1}{(1 + r)^1} + \frac{C_2}{(1 + r)^2} + \cdots + \frac{C_n}{(1 + r)^n} \tag{7.5}$$

where the same discount rate is applied to each cash flow.

In practice, coupons may be paid semiannually or quarterly, and a valuation may be made at any time during the coupon period. This calls for the more general valuation formula to determine YTM:

$$P = \frac{C_{t_1}}{(1+r)^{t_1}} + \frac{C_{t_2}}{(1+r)^{t_2}} + \cdots + \frac{C_{t_n}}{(1+r)^{t_n}} \tag{7.6}$$

where r is the annualized YTM, and t_1, t_2, to t_n are the exact dates on which the cash flows occur, expressed in number of years from the current date. Hence, these dates are usually fractional. For example, consider a bond with a semiannual coupon to be paid three months from now (one-fourth of a year); the next cash flow dates are $t_1 = 0.25$, $t_2 = 0.75$, etc. The cash flows include coupons and principal redemption. Again, P represents the total value of the bond, or *full price* (*dirty price*).

European versus U.S. YTM Equation 7.6 allows us to determine the annual YTM on a bond if we know its cash flows and observe its market value. This is the standard compounding, or actuarial, method that can be used whatever the frequency and dates of coupons. This method is used worldwide except in the United States, where the tradition is to calculate a YTM over a six-month period and multiply it by 2 to report an annualized yield. We call this annualized yield a U.S. YTM or bond-equivalent-basis YTM. Hence, the U.S. YTM or yield is a mixture of an internal rate of return calculation to obtain the semiannual yield, and of a multiplication to transform it into an annualized yield. Bond traders often refer to the *European*, or *ICMA*, method when they use the standard method described in Equation 7.6. They refer to the *U.S.* method when they use the U.S. convention.

This method for computing an annualized semiannual yield r' can be described by the formula

$$P = \frac{C_{t_1}}{(1+r'/2)^{2t_1}} + \frac{C_{t_2}}{(1+r'/2)^{2t_2}} + \cdots + \frac{C_{t_n}}{(1+r'/2)^{2t_n}} \tag{7.7}$$

where r' is the U.S. yield, and the cash flow dates are still expressed in number of years. The logic of Equation 7.7 is to use six months as the unit of time measurement. You can verify that it uses a semiannual yield $r'/2$ to discount the cash flows and that the exponents ($2t_1$, $2t_2$, ..., $2t_n$) are the number of six-month periods from the valuation date. The difference between r' and r comes from the difference between compounding and linearizing semiannual yields to get annual yields. If a semiannual yield of 3 percent is found, the U.S. method will report a yield of $r' = 3 \times 2 = 6$ percent, whereas the European method will report a yield of $(1.03) \times (1.03) - 1 = 6.09$ percent. In general, we have

$$(1 + r) = (1 + r'/2)^2 \tag{7.8}$$

Example 7.4 illustrates calculation of European and U.S. YTMs.

EXAMPLE 7.4 EUROPEAN AND U.S. YTMs

A three-year bond has exactly three years till maturity, and the last coupon has just been paid. The coupon is annual and equal to 6 percent. The bond price is 95 percent. What are its European and U.S. YTMs?

SOLUTION

The European YTM is r, given by the formula

$$95 = \frac{6}{(1+r)^1} + \frac{6}{(1+r)^2} + \frac{106}{(1+r)^3}$$

Using a spreadsheet, we find $r = 7.94$ percent.

The U.S. YTM is r', given by the formula

$$95 = \frac{6}{(1+r'/2)^2} + \frac{6}{(1+r'/2)^4} + \frac{106}{(1+r'/2)^6}$$

Hence, $r' = 7.79$ percent. We verify that $1.0794 = (1 + 7.79\%/2)^2$.

Duration and Interest Rate Sensitivity

There is an inverse relationship between the price of a bond and changes in interest rates. As seen in Equation 7.3, if the bond's cash flows are fixed, the price is solely a function of the market yield. Practitioners usually define *interest rate sensitivity*, or *duration*, as the *approximate percentage price change for a 100 basis points (1 percentage point) change in market yield.* Mathematically, the duration D can be written as

$$\frac{\Delta P}{P} = -D \times \Delta r \tag{7.9}$$

where $\Delta P/P$ is the percentage price change induced by a small variation Δr in yield. The minus sign comes from the fact that bond prices drop when interest rates move up. For example, a bond with a duration of $D = 5$ would tend to decline by 5 basis points ($\Delta P/P = -5$) when yields go up by $\Delta r = 1$ basis point. Hence, duration is a measure of interest risk for a specific bond. Duration allows us to estimate the capital loss induced by an unfavorable interest rate scenario (see Example 7.5). The interest rate sensitivity or risk of a portfolio is the weighted average of the durations of individual bonds.

The Macaulay duration of a standard bond is its weighted-average maturity. This is a time-weighted average, with each date weighted by the present value of the cash flow paid by the bond on that date as a fraction of the bond's price. The price of a bond is a function of its yield to maturity $P(r)$. By computing the first derivative of the bond price $P(r)$ relative to the yield r, it is easy to show that the interest rate sensitivity of a bond is simply its Macaulay duration divided by $1 + r$.

EXAMPLE 7.5 DURATION

You hold a government bond with a duration of 10. Its yield is 5 percent. You expect yields to move up by 10 basis points in the next few minutes. Give a rough estimate of your expected return.

SOLUTION

Given the very short horizon, the only component of return is the expected capital loss:

$$Return = -10 \times 0.1 = -1\%$$

Hence, some authors call it *modified duration*. We simply use the term *duration*, and Equation 7.9 is for duration in this sense.[4] The longer the maturity of a bond, the larger its duration.

Strictly speaking, the duration is a good approximation of the bond price reaction to interest rate movements only for small movements in the general level in interest rates. In other words, it gives a good approximation for the percentage price movements only for small parallel shifts in the yield curve (yields for all maturities move together). For larger movements in yield, the *convexity* (or second derivative) can be introduced. Also note that the duration of a bond changes over time. To summarize, duration is a simple measure of the sensitivity of a bond, or a portfolio of bonds, to a change in interest rates. A more complete approach requires the full valuation of the bond under various interest rate scenarios.

The return on a bond is equal to the yield over the holding period plus any capital gain or losses due to movements in the market yield, $\Delta yield$. Using Equation 7.9, the bond return can be approximated as

$$Return = Yield - D \times (\Delta yield) \tag{7.10}$$

Over a short holding period, the risk-free rate is the short-term interest rate or cash rate. Hence, the return on a bond investment can be expressed as the sum of

- the cash rate,
- the spread of the bond yield over the cash rate, and
- the percentage capital gain/loss due to a movement in yield.

$$Return = Cash\ rate + (Yield - Cash\ rate) - D \times (\Delta yield) \tag{7.11}$$

[4] The exact formula is $D = \frac{1}{(1+r)} \times \frac{\Sigma \frac{tC_t}{(1+r)^t}}{\Sigma \frac{C_t}{(1+r)^t}} = \frac{1}{1+r} \times [Macaulay\ duration]$.

The *expected* return on a bond is equal to the risk-free cash rate plus a *risk premium*:

$$E(return) = Cash\ rate + Risk\ premium \tag{7.12}$$

As seen from Equation 7.11, this risk premium is equal to the sum of

- the spread of the bond yield over the cash rate and
- the percentage gain/loss due to expected yield movements.

Example 7.6 illustrates the calculation of the expected return and risk premium on a domestic bond.

Credit Spreads

Credit risk is an additional source of risk for corporate bonds. The yield required by the market on a corporate issue is a function of the default risk of the bond: The greater the risk, the higher the yield the borrower must pay. This implies that the yield reflects a *credit spread*, or *quality spread*, over the default-free yield. The quality spread for a specific bond captures three components:

- An *expected loss* component. Investors expect that the bond will default with some probability. To compensate for that expected loss, the issuer must pay a spread above the default-free yield. If investors were risk-neutral, they would require only that the expected return on the corporate bond, taking into account the probability of default, be equal to the default-free yield. Example 7.7 illustrates the determination of the credit spread for risk-neutral investors.
- A *credit-risk premium*. Investors are risk-averse and cannot easily diversify the risk of default on bonds. Furthermore, when the economy is in recession, the financial situation of most corporations deteriorates simultaneously. This is,

EXAMPLE 7.6 EXPECTED RETURN ON A DOMESTIC BOND

You hold a government bond with a duration of 10. Its yield is 5 percent, although the cash (one-year) rate is 2 percent. You expect yields to move up by 10 basis points over the year. Give a rough estimate of your expected return. What is the risk premium on this bond?

SOLUTION

The expected return on the year is the sum of the accrued interest plus the expected capital loss stated as a percent:

$$Return = 5\% - 10 \times 0.1 = 4\%$$

This is a rough estimate because the duration is going to move down over the year as the bond's maturity shortens.

The risk premium is obtained by deducting the short-term interest rate:

$$Risk\ premium = 2\%$$

EXAMPLE 7.7 *CREDIT SPREAD ESTIMATION*

A one-year bond is issued by a corporation with a 1 percent probability of default by year end. In case of default, the investor will recover nothing. The one-year yield for default-free bonds is 5 percent. What yield should be required by investors on this corporate bond if they are risk-neutral? What should the credit spread be?

SOLUTION

Let's call y the yield and m the credit spread, so that $y = 5$ percent $+ m$. The bond is issued at 100 percent of par. If the bond defaults (1% probability), the investor gets nothing in a year. In case of no default (99% probability), the investor will get $(100 + y)$ percent. So, the yield should be set on the bond so that its expected payoff is equal to the expected payoff on a risk-free bond (105%):

$$105 = 99\% \times (100 + y) + 1\% \times 0$$

The yield is equal to $y = (105 - 99)/99 = 6.06$ percent. The credit spread is equal to $m = 1.06$ percent.

The spread is above 1 percent, the probability of default, for two reasons. First, the investor loses 105, not 100, in case of default, so the spread must offset both the lost principal and the lost interest. Second, the spread has to be a bit larger because it is paid on bonds only 99 percent of the time.

An investor who is risk-neutral, or who can diversify this risk by holding a large number of bonds issued by different corporations, would be satisfied with this 1.06 percent credit spread. But a risk-averse investor would usually add a risk premium on top, because risk of default tends to be correlated across firms (business cycle risk).

in part, systematic market risk (business cycle risk) as the stock market is also affected. So, investors require a risk premium to compensate for that risk, on top of the expected loss component.

- A *liquidity premium.* Each corporate bond is a bit different from another one, in part because each issuer has some distinctions in quality from other issuers. All domestic government bonds have the same credit quality within their domestic market (e.g., U.S. Treasury in the United States, British gilts in the United Kingdom, or JGB in Japan); there is a vast amount issued and excellent trading liquidity. Because of the lack of liquidity on most corporate issues, investors require a compensation in the form of an additional yield, a liquidity premium. In practice, it is difficult to disentangle the liquidity premium and the credit-risk premium.

International rating agencies (Moody's, Standard & Poor's, Fitch) provide a credit rating for most debt issues traded worldwide. In some countries, local firms provide credit ratings for debt securities issued by domestic firms (e.g., Japan Credit Rating

Agency in Japan or Dominion Bond Rating Service in Canada). These rating agencies play a crucial role in the pricing of debt securities. When a rating agency announces a revision in its rating of a company's debt, the prices of that company's securities are immediately affected, sometimes by a large amount.

On a specific bond market, one can draw yield curves for each credit rating; the credit spread typically increases with maturity. A top-quality issuer will generally not default immediately. It will first be downgraded one or several notches, reflecting an increase in the probability of default. So, in the short run, the credit spread will be affected by the probability of a change in the rating of the corporation. This is usually called *migration* probability, that is, the probability of moving from one credit rating to another. Rating agencies conduct migration studies and annually publish rating migration tables (also called rating transition tables) over some defined time horizons. The *n*-year migration table shows the percentage of issues with a given rating at the start of the year that migrated to another rating at the end of the *n* years. The information in a rating migration table can be used to infer the probability of default. It should be noted that the expected loss on a bond is also affected by recovery rates. In case of default, the debtholder hopes to recover part of the loaned amount.

Multicurrency Approach

International Yield Curve Comparisons

A term structure of interest rates exists for each currency. Investors focus on the default-free yield curve for government bonds. YTMs generally differ across currencies. International interest rate differences are caused by a variety of factors, including differences in national monetary and fiscal policies and inflationary expectations. Furthermore, the interest rate differential for two currencies is not constant over the maturity spectrum.

Government yield curves in April 2007 for U.S. dollar, euro, yen, and British pound bonds are given in Exhibit 7.7. A major feature is that Japanese interest rates are well below those on other markets. For example, the one-year yield is equal to 0.4 percent in Japan and equal to 4.8 percent in the United States.

Clearly, the difference in yield curves between two currencies is caused by foreign exchange expectations. Otherwise, arbitrage would occur between bonds denominated in different currencies. This key relation between interest rate differentials and exchange rate expectations for a given maturity is the subject of our next discussion.

Implied Forward Exchange Rates and Break-Even Analysis The purpose of this section is to introduce the analytical tools that can help a manager choose an optimal investment strategy, given a particular exchange rate and interest rate scenario. The main objective is to determine the implication for exchange rates of

EXHIBIT 7.7

Yield Curves in Different Currencies in 2007

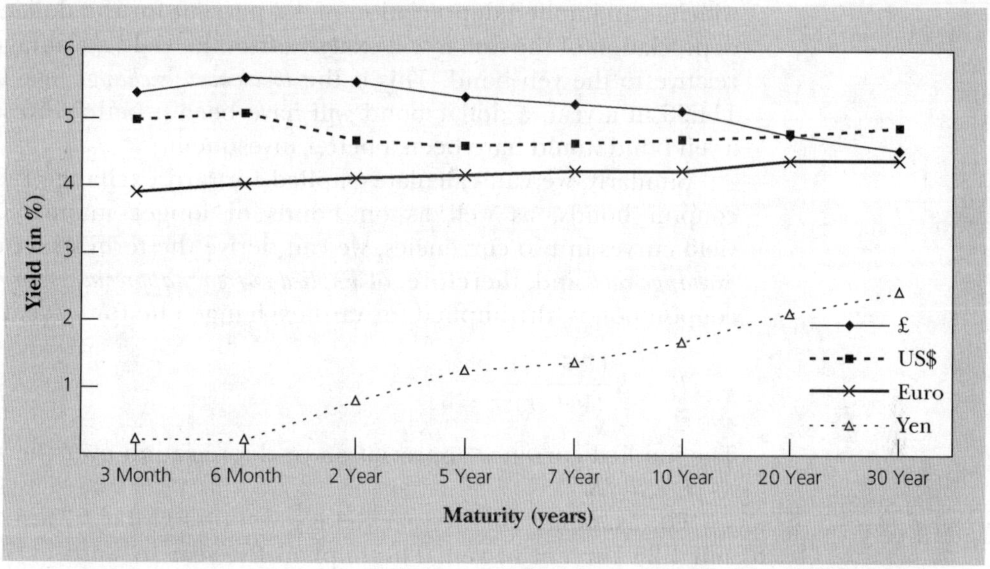

Source: Data from Bloomberg, 2007.

yield differentials on bonds denominated in different currencies but with similar maturities. In other words, how do we compare exchange rate movements and YTM differentials?

A higher yield in one currency is often compensated for, ex post, by a depreciation in this currency and, in turn, an offsetting currency loss on the bond. It is important to know how much currency movement will compensate for the yield differential. Let's first consider a one-year bond with an interest rate r_1 in domestic currency (e.g., U.S. dollar) and r_1^* in foreign currency (e.g., yen). The current exchange rate is S, expressed as the foreign currency value of one unit of a domestic currency (e.g., 120 yen per dollar). One year from now, the exchange rate must move to a level F_1 in order to make the two investments identical (i.e., have the same total return). In Chapter 1, we called F_1 the forward exchange rate. It is expressed as follows:

$$F_1(1 + r_1) = S(1 + r_1^*) \tag{7.13}$$

The implied offsetting currency depreciation is given by

$$\frac{F_1 - S}{S} = \frac{r_1 - r_1^*}{(1 + r_1)}$$

As an illustration, assume that the dollar one-year yield is $r_1 = 4.8$ percent, the yen one-year yield is $r_1^* = 0.4$ percent, and the current exchange rate is $S = 120$ yen per dollar. From Equation 7.13 we see that the forward exchange rate should equal

$$F_1 = S\frac{(1 + r_1^*)}{(1 + r_1)} = 120\frac{1.004}{1.048} = 114.96$$

which is an implied depreciation of 4.2 percent for the dollar. Thus, a 4.2 percent depreciation of the dollar will exactly offset the yield advantage on the dollar bond relative to the yen bond. This is the *break-even exchange rate.* If the dollar is above 114.96 in a year, a dollar bond will have been a better investment; if it is below, a yen bond would have been a better investment.

Similarly, we can calculate implied forward exchange rates on two-year zero-coupon bonds, as well as on bonds of longer maturity. By comparing the yield curves in two currencies, we can derive the term structure of *implied forward exchange rates* and, therefore, of *implied currency appreciation or depreciation.* For zero-coupon bonds, the implied forward exchange rate for a t-year bond is given by

$$F_t = S\frac{(1 + r_t^*)^t}{(1 + r_t)^t} \tag{7.14}$$

The implied currency appreciation or depreciation over the t-year period is equal to $(F_t - S)/S$.

For example, the five-year yields given on Exhibit 7.7 are 4.6 percent in dollars and 1.25 percent in yen. The implied five-year forward exchange rate, or break-even rate, is equal to

$$F_5 = 120\frac{(1.0125)^5}{(1.046)^5} = 101.98$$

which amounts to a 15 percent depreciation of the dollar. These simple calculations assume that we use yield curves for zero-coupon bonds. The formulas are slightly more complicated if we use the par yield curves for coupon bonds, because we must assume that the coupons are reinvested each year or six-month period until final maturity.

Applications The implied forward exchange rate is not a forecast but a break-even point. It provides investors with a yardstick against which to measure their own foreign exchange forecasts. In our hypothetical example, Japanese bond investments are clearly not attractive if we expect a stable dollar relative to the yen.

A more precise scenario analysis can be performed for individual bonds. Consider an investor from the United Kingdom who wants to buy bonds denominated in a foreign currency—say, the euro. Bonds are available on the market, with a variety of coupons and sinking fund provisions. To evaluate them, an investor should posit several scenarios for the British pound/euro exchange rate over time. Actuaries can compute the expected pound return for each bond, given these scenarios, by translating each bond payment at the expected exchange rate on the payment date. For example, a rapid euro appreciation over the next two years, followed by a period of stable exchange rate, would make high-coupon, short-term euro bonds very attractive.

Banks are interested in bonds for both lending and borrowing, and banks often prepare spreadsheets simulating a variety of interest rate and currency scenarios (i.e., one-time depreciation, trends, and combinations) and their influence on bond returns, taking duration into account. A final step is to engage in active currency hedging on bonds.

The Return and Risk on Foreign Bond Investments

The *return* from investing in a foreign bond has three components:

- During the investment period, the bondholder receives the foreign yield.
- A change in the foreign yield (*Δforeign yield*) induces a percentage capital gain/loss on the price of the bond.
- A currency movement induces a currency gain or loss on the position.[5]

$$Return = Foreign\ yield - D \times (\Delta foreign\ yield) + Percentage\ currency\ movement \tag{7.15}$$

Example 7.8 illustrates the calculation of the loss on a foreign-currency bond under an interest rate and currency scenario.

The *risk* on a foreign bond investment has two major sources:

- *Interest rate risk* is the risk that the foreign yields will rise.
- *Currency risk* is the risk that the foreign currency will depreciate.

EXAMPLE 7.8 RETURN ON A FOREIGN CURRENCY BOND

You are British and hold a U.S. Treasury bond with a full price of 100 and a duration of 10. Its yield is 5 percent. The next day, U.S. yields move up by 5 basis points and the dollar depreciates by 1 percent relative to the British pound. Give a rough estimate of your loss in British pounds.

SOLUTION

The dollar price of the bond should drop by

$$\frac{\Delta P}{P} = -D \times \Delta r = -10 \times 0.05\% = -0.5\%$$

On top of that, there will be a currency loss of 1 percent. So, the total loss in pounds is approximately equal to 1.5 percent.

---

[5] The percentage currency gain or loss also applies to the bond return in local currency, but this is a second-order effect.

Of course, the two risks could be somewhat correlated, as discussed in Chapter 4. Furthermore, credit risk should also be taken into account for nongovernment bonds.

As for any investment, the expected return on a foreign bond is equal to the domestic cash rate plus a risk premium. This risk premium equals the sum of

- the spread of the foreign bond yield over the domestic cash rate,
- the percentage capital gain/loss due to an expected foreign yield movement, and
- the expected percentage currency movement.

Currency-Hedging Strategies

Foreign investments can be hedged against currency risk by selling forward currency contracts for an amount equal to the capital invested. Short-term forward contracts, typically up to a few months in maturity, are available for currency hedging. So, the currency hedge is periodically rolled over. By arbitrage (see Chapter 1), the percentage difference (discount or premium) of the forward rate with the current spot rate is equal to the interest rate differential between the two currencies. This is the differential between the two cash rates for the contract maturity. Hence, the return on the hedged bond will be

$$\begin{aligned} \textit{Hedged return} = {} & \textit{Foreign yield} - D \times (\Delta \textit{ foreign yield}) \\ & + \textit{Domestic cash rate} - \textit{Foreign cash rate} \end{aligned} \tag{7.16}$$

Example 7.9 illustrates the calculation of the expected return on a foreign-currency bond hedged against currency risk. By definition, the risk premium is equal to the expected return minus the investor's risk-free rate, the domestic cash rate. Reshuffling terms in Equation 7.16, we find that the risk premium on a foreign bond, hedged against currency risk, is simply equal to the sum of

- the spread of the foreign bond yield over the foreign cash rate, and
- the percentage gain/loss due to an expected foreign yield movement.

Note that this risk premium is exactly the same for a local (foreign) investor in that foreign bond. A local investor would use the foreign cash rate as risk-free rate, but the risk premium stated in Equation 7.12 would be identical. The foreign bond risk premium is just transferred domestically, and currency risk does not play a direct role anymore.

The decision to hedge depends on return and risk considerations. Hedging will turn out to improve return on a foreign bond if the percentage currency movement is less than the cash rate differential (domestic minus foreign); otherwise, hedging will not be advantageous ex post. In other words, if you expect the foreign exchange rate to move below the forward exchange rate, you should hedge; otherwise, you should not hedge. Hedging reduces currency risk, but interest and currency movements are somewhat correlated.

EXAMPLE 7.9 HEDGED RETURN ON A FOREIGN CURRENCY BOND

You are British and hold a U.S. Treasury bond with a full price of 100 and duration of 10. Its yield is 5 percent. The dollar cash rate is 2 percent, and the pound cash rate is 3 percent. You expect U.S. yields to move up by 10 basis points over the year. Give a rough estimate of your expected return if you decide to hedge the currency risk.

SOLUTION

The expected return on the year is equal to the U.S. dollar expected return plus the cash rate differential:

$$\textit{Expected return} = 5\% - (10 \times 0.1) + 3\% - 2\% = 5\%$$

The risk premium in pounds is equal to this expected return minus the British cash rate, or 5 percent − 3 percent = 2 percent. It is also equal to the risk premium on the same U.S. Treasury bond for a U.S. investor: expected return of 4 percent in dollars minus the U.S. cash rate of 2 percent. Hedging improves the expected return if you expect the dollar to appreciate by less than 1 percent. It also eliminates currency risk.

International Portfolio Strategies

Active management of international and global bond portfolios requires both a good technical knowledge of the various domestic and international markets and some ability to forecast interest rates and currencies. The *neutral,* or *normal,* position is dictated by the benchmark chosen for the portfolio. Assuming no forecasting ability, the portfolio will follow the benchmark weights in the major currencies and market segments; deviations from these weights are induced by specific forecasts.

International bond portfolio management includes several steps:

- Benchmark selection
- Bond market selection
- Sector selection/credit selection
- Currency management
- Duration/yield curve management
- Yield enhancement techniques

The choice of a benchmark is often imposed in the mandate set by the client, and it will clearly guide the structure of the portfolio.

Benchmark Selection The benchmark used is some bond index. The benchmark for bonds is open to more discussion than for equity. It depends in part on the investment objective; for example, do we want a global bond portfolio or an international one (e.g., ex-U.S. for a U.S. investor)? But even the logic of using market capitalization weights is open to debate. For equity, market cap weights represent the relative economic importance of corporations throughout the world. For bonds, market cap weights are influenced by the relative national budget deficits. For example, a country with chronic large budget deficits will see its government bonds have a relatively large weight in a global bond index. Do investors want to follow an investment policy favoring lax budget policy? Other questions influence the choice of benchmark:

- What types of issuers should be included? If corporates are included, do we put a threshold on their credit quality (e.g., no junk bonds)? Should we include debt from emerging countries? In other words, do we use a broad index or a narrow one?
- Do we include all countries/currencies, or do we restrict the benchmark to major ones (e.g., G7 countries)?
- Do we allow all maturities, or do we constrain the maturity of bonds included (e.g., only bonds with a long maturity)?
- Is the benchmark unhedged against currency risk, or is it hedged?

Benchmarks selected are usually some of the widely accepted bond indexes discussed. But index providers can also calculate "customized" or "normal" portfolios, as defined by a money manager or a specific client.

Bond Market Selection Managers will differ from national benchmark weights, and over- or underweight some markets based on interest rate and currency forecasts. More than for common stocks, the observation that all bonds issued in a given currency behave similarly tends to justify a *top-down* market/currency approach. For an international investor, the major differences in performance are caused by the selection of currency markets. All fixed-interest bond prices are influenced by changes in interest rates in the respective currencies, as well as the translation in the domestic currency. For example, the dollar performance of all British government bonds is influenced primarily by two factors: movements in British interest rates and movements in the pound/dollar exchange rate. In comparison, the difference in performance within a market segment is relatively small. When investing in international bonds, the volatility of the foreign exchange is often larger than the volatility of the bond market, measured in local currency. This has been observed repeatedly in empirical studies.

Hence, the overweighting of a market is both a bet on changes in local market yields and a bet on the currency. Such a decision must be based on sound economic analysis. Among economic fundamentals that bond managers follow for each country, one can cite the following:

- Monetary and fiscal policy
- Public spending

- Current and forecasted public indebtedness
- Inflationary pressures
- Balance of payments
- International comparison of the real yields
- National productivity and competitiveness
- Cyclical factors
- Political factors

Sector Selection/Credit Selection In many countries and currencies, governments used to be the main issuers. Now, banks and corporations are increasingly borrowing on the bond markets. Within a given currency market (e.g., bonds issued in euros), there are also different segments grouping bonds issued by different types of issuers. Prices on different segments of the same currency market are not fully correlated. Besides the yield curve on government securities, different additional factors affect prices on each segment. The yields on each segment reflect a quality spread over government bonds. The quality spread is influenced by credit risk, liquidity, and possibly some specific institutional and tax aspects. Hence, bond managers tend to over- or underweight some segments based on their forecast of these factors. Commonly used segments within a currency market are the following:

- Government securities
- Regional states and municipalities bonds
- Mortgage-backed and public-loan-backed bonds (e.g., the huge German *Pfandbrief* market)
- Investment-grade corporates
- Junk bonds
- Inflation-indexed bonds
- Emerging-country debt

Currency Management For default-free bonds, there are two main sources of unanticipated excess return: currency and duration-adjusted interest rate movements. The volatility of exchange rates tends to be higher than that of bond prices, so currency management is an important component of active global bond management. Exhibit 7.8 gives the volatility of major bond markets measured in U.S. dollars, in euros, and in local currency. For example, the British bond market has a volatility (annual standard deviation of returns) of 5.4 percent in pounds and 9.3 percent in dollars. The higher volatility for a U.S. investor stems from currency risk.

EXHIBIT 7.8

Volatility of Bond Markets Measured in Local Currency, in U.S. Dollars, and in Euros in % per year, early 2000s, Effas/Bloomberg Indexes

Bond Market	In Local Currency	In Dollars	In Euros
United States	4.8	4.8	10.6
Germany	3.7	10.4	3.7
United Kingdom	5.4	9.3	9.3
Japan	4.2	12.9	12.5

When investing in international bonds, the choice of a market often also implies the choice of a currency. If the manager forecasts a depreciation of a foreign currency, she can reduce the currency exposure by reducing the weight of that market relative to benchmark weights. Alternatively, the manager can retain the same market exposure and hedge the currency risk using forward contracts. Currency management requires a good understanding of the previously developed break-even analysis.

Duration/Yield Curve Management In each currency market, the manager can adjust the duration of the portfolio according to a forecast about changes in the level of interest rates and deformations in the yield curve. The average duration in each market and segment provides an estimate of the portfolio's sensitivity to yield movements. If an increase in yields is expected in one market segment, the manager can trade bonds to reduce the duration of this segment. Another alternative is to retain the same bonds but to reduce the interest rate exposure through various derivatives, such as interest rate futures or swaps.

Yield Enhancement Techniques Numerous techniques are proposed to add value to the performance of the basic strategy. Some specialized trading techniques are used to provide incremental returns with very little risk (e.g., securities lending). These techniques evolve over time and are too specialized to be described here.

Valuation techniques are used to detect the cheapest bonds to buy (undervalued) when the portfolio has to be rebalanced. Spread analysis is often used to assess the relative value of two securities with fairly similar characteristics. This spread analysis can even lead to an arbitrage between two bonds. The idea is very simple. Two bonds with close characteristics should trade at very similar prices and YTM. Each day, a manager computes the spread between the two bond prices and plots them. Because of market inefficiencies, the spread is likely to be high above (or below) its average, or "normal," value at some point in time. This is the time to arbitrage one bond against the other. This spread analysis is conducted in terms of YTM rather than in terms of prices. Other bond portfolio management techniques are more complex and involve instruments such as futures, swaps, or option contracts.

A typical way to enhance return on a bond portfolio is to add securities with higher promised yield, because of the borrower's credit risk. Investors can also obtain higher yields by investing in emerging-country bonds, for which the credit risk stems from the risk that a country will default on its debt servicing. Managers must be aware that the higher yield is a compensation for the risk of default. If this risk materializes, the realized yield on the bond investment can be very bad.

Other bonds have been designed as fairly complicated securities with uncertain cash flows, which offer some plays on interest rate, currencies, or other variables. Some of these more complicated bonds, often called structured notes, are presented in the next section.

To summarize, the investment strategy is based on forecasted scenarios for interest rates, currencies, and quality spreads. Note that exchange rate movements are correlated, to some extent, with interest rate changes so that the two forecasts are not independent. Given the current portfolio, managers can simulate the effect of a scenario on the value of the portfolio. This simulation also suggests which securities to sell and buy, given the forecasted scenario. The three basic inputs are

- changes in the default-free yield curve for each currency,
- changes in quality spreads (e.g., changes in the spread between the domestic and international segments), and
- changes in exchange rates.

Yield enhancement techniques can help individual security selection.

Floating-Rate Notes and Structured Notes

Investment bankers bring domestic expertise from around the world to bear on the international market, and that is why the international market boasts so many sophisticated techniques. This sophistication is evident in the incredible diversity of bonds issued. We will start with plain-vanilla *floating-rate notes* (*FRNs*), which are an important segment of the international market, in euros, dollars, or pounds. We will then study some exotic bonds, involving some currency play, which have been frequently issued. They often take the form of a structured note. A *structured note* is a bond (note) issued with some unusual clause, often an option-like clause. These notes are bonds issued by a name of good credit standing and can therefore be purchased as investment-grade bonds by most institutional investors, even those that are prevented by regulations from dealing in options or futures. Another attraction for investors is that these structured notes offer some long-term options that are not publicly traded. Structured notes are designed for those specific investors wishing to take a bet on some forecasts such as interest rates and currencies. If their forecasts are correct, the yield on the note will be enhanced. In turn, the issuer seems to be basically taking the opposite bet. However, the bank structuring the note proposes to the issuer a hedging structure that will eliminate this risk. The idea is that the issuer should end up, after hedging, with a plain-vanilla bond (with fixed or floating-rate coupons) but at a total cost that is less than the prevailing market conditions for those bonds. To determine the "fair" price of the structured note, the investment bank constructs a replication portfolio using elementary securities (such as plain-vanilla FRNs, straight bonds, swaps, and options). The structured note can be issued at better conditions for the issuer, because it satisfies the needs of some investors. To summarize, structured notes are often used by institutional investors as a vehicle to make a bet within an investment-grade bond structure. On the other side, the issuer will hedge the bet and will end up with a plain-vanilla bond at a reduced all-in cost of funds because investors are willing to accept a lower yield to be able to bet.

Some structured notes offer interest rate plays (see the discussion of bull and bear bonds that follows). Others offer currency play (see the discussion of dual-currency and currency-option bonds that follows). Other structured notes offer a play on some other variables, such as equity or commodity prices. The list of bonds covered in this chapter is not exhaustive; some of them are discussed in the Problems section. For example, inflation-linked bonds can be found in many countries (e.g., the United States, the United Kingdom, and France). The coupons and principal of these bonds are indexed to the local inflation index (usually the local CPI). For example, U.S. Treasury inflation protected securities (TIPS) pay a real yield fixed at time of issue. The principal value is adjusted for CPI on each semiannual coupon payment. So the nominal coupon, equal to the real yield times the CPI-adjusted principal, increases with inflation. At maturity, the CPI-adjusted principal is reimbursed. Inflation-linked bonds attract institutional investors wishing to get a risk-free yield to hedge their liabilities. As these bonds are mostly used by domestic investors to hedge their local-inflation risk, we will not detail them here. Many other types of complex bonds are periodically created.

A *collateralized debt obligation* (*CDO*) is a special type of structured note that allows structuring the credit risk assumed on a portfolio of bonds (see the discussion that follows).

Floating-Rate Notes (FRNs)

FRNs, or *floaters*, are a very active segment of the international bond market. This is explained by the fact that the interbank short-term lending/borrowing market (LIBOR market) is primarily an international market, not a domestic market, even for the U.S. dollar. Because banks lend and borrow short term at a cost closely linked to LIBOR, it is natural that they use the international bond market when they issue long-term bonds with a coupon indexed on LIBOR. FRNs represent a quarter of all international bonds, with issues in euros and dollars playing a dominant role. Major issuers are financial institutions.

Description The clauses used in interest rate indexation are diverse, but plain-vanilla FRNs tend to dominate. FRNs are generally indexed to the London interbank offer rate (LIBOR), which is the short-term deposit rate on Eurocurrencies. This rate is called *Euribor* (Euro interbank offer rate) for euros. The coupon on Eurobond FRNs is generally reset every semester or every quarter. The maturity of the LIBOR chosen as index usually matches the coupon period; for example, FRNs with semiannual coupons are indexed on the six-month LIBOR. The coupon to be paid is determined on the *reset date,* which usually coincides with the previous coupon date. On the reset date, the value of the index (say, the six-month LIBOR) is determined by looking at the quotations of a panel of major banks. The coupon to be paid the next period is then set equal to the LIBOR plus a spread that has been fixed at the time of issue. In other words, the coupon C_t that will be paid at time t is set at time $t-1$ (the previous coupon date) equal to the LIBOR rate i_{t-1} plus a fixed spread m_0:

$$C_t = i_{t-1} + m_0 \tag{7.17}$$

All rates are annualized and quoted in percent. The spread is fixed when the bond is issued and generally remains fixed for the maturity of the bond. For top-quality issuers, the spread is very small, because some of them, such as banks, can easily borrow in the Eurocurrency short-term deposit market at LIBOR. LIBOR is already a short-term rate quoted for top-quality corporate borrowers; it is not a government rate such as the Treasury bill rate. Some FRNs are issued with various mismatches that deviate from the plain-vanilla FRNs described earlier.

Motivation FRN prices behave quite differently from fixed-interest straight bond prices, which adjust to fluctuations in the market interest rate. The price of a straight bond must go down if the market interest rate goes up, in order to maintain a competitive YTM. By contrast, floaters have coupons that adjust to interest rates, so the coupons react to interest rate movements rather than the bond price. This means that FRNs exhibit great price stability when compared with straight bonds.

The motivation for an investor to buy FRNs is to avoid interest rate risk that could lead to a capital loss in case of a rise in interest rates. Investors have a long-term investment with little interest rate risk.

FRNs are generally issued by financial institutions with short-term lending activities. These institutions wish to have long-term resources but want to index the cost of their funds to their revenues. Because revenues on short-term loans are indexed on LIBOR, FRNs achieve this objective.

Valuing FRNs: No Default Risk From a theoretical viewpoint, we may ask why there is any price variability at all on floating-rate bonds. It turns out that there are several major reasons for this price variability. To study the pricing of FRNs, it is useful to look first at the case in which the borrower carries no default risk.

On Reset Date FRN coupons are periodically reset, or rolled over. The rollover may be annual, semiannual, or quarterly. This means that the coupon is fixed at the reset, or rollover, date for the coming period. The first question is to determine the theoretical price of the bond on the reset date, when the previous coupon has just been paid and the new coupon has just been fixed for the coming period. To disentangle the effects, it is useful to start the analysis by assuming that the borrower has, and will have, no default risk and that the index has been chosen as the relevant short-term interest rate for that borrower.[6] For example, assume that an FRN with annual reset[7] is issued by a major bank, which has to pay exactly LIBOR without any spread, in the absence of default risk:

$$C_t = i_{t-1}$$

Remember that all rates and prices are quoted in percent. Under this assumption of no default risk, we can show that the price of the bond should always be 100 percent on reset dates. The argument is recursive. There is a future date when we know the exact value of the bond: This is at maturity T. Right after the last coupon payment, the bond will be reimbursed at 100 percent. Let's now move to the previous reset date $T-1$. We know that the bond contract stipulates that the coupon C_T will be set equal to the one-year LIBOR observed at time $T-1$. Of course, we do not know today (time 0) what this rate will be at $T-1$, but we know that it will be exactly equal, by contractual obligation, to the market rate for a one-year instrument. Hence, a bond with a maturity of one year paying the one-year interest rate must have a price equal to its principal value. This is confirmed by discounting at time $T-1$ the future cash flow received at time T:

$$P_{T-1} = \frac{100\% + C_T}{1 + i_{T-1}} = \frac{1 + i_{T-1}}{1 + i_{T-1}} = 100\%$$

Hence, we now know that the price one period before maturity must be equal to 100. We can apply the same reasoning to the price of the bond at time $T-2$ and so on, until time 0. We have therefore shown that the bond price must be equal to 100 at each reset date.

Between Reset Dates There is no reason, however, for the price to stay constant between reset dates. Once the coupon is fixed on a reset date, the bond tends to behave like a short-term fixed-coupon bond until the next reset date. FRN prices are more volatile just after the reset date, because that is when they have the longest fixed-coupon maturity. FRNs with a semiannual reset tend to be more volatile than FRNs with quarterly reset dates, but both should have stable prices on reset dates. This is illustrated in Exhibit 7.9 for the clean price of a Midland Bank FRN with a semiannual reset and maturing in May 1987. Prices on reset appear as a dot in the illustration. The period is chosen because 1979–1980 was a period of high and extremely volatile interest rates; nevertheless, the FRN price is very close to 100 on reset dates (shown with dots on the graph). Note that in December 1980,

[6] To be precise, the assumption is that it is certain that the bank will retain its AAA credit rating forever and will therefore always be able to borrow at LIBOR.

[7] There is an annual coupon set at one-year LIBOR.

six-month LIBOR climbed suddenly from 15 percent to over 20 percent, just after the coupon on the bond had been reset. This induced a 2 percent drop in the bond price. By contrast, the prices on reset dates are very stable.

Practitioners usually consider that the interest sensitivity to movements in the index interest rate is simply equal to the duration to the next reset date. The price of the FRN between reset dates can be estimated by assuming that it is worth 100 plus the reset coupon at the next coupon date, discounting by the LIBOR rate with maturity equal to the next reset date (see Example 7.10).

In practice, issuers carry some default risk, and a spread over LIBOR is required by the market. This can explain why the prices on reset dates observed in Exhibit 7.9 are not exactly equal to 100.

Valuing FRNs: Default Risk Let's now assume that the issuer carries some default risk, justifying a credit spread as shown in Equation 7.17. The problem is that the credit spread paid by the FRN, m_0, is set at issuance and remains fixed over the whole maturity of the bond. On the other hand, the credit quality of the issuer

EXAMPLE 7.10 VALUING FRNs BETWEEN RESET DATES

A company without default risk has issued a 10-year FRN at LIBOR. The coupon is paid and reset semiannually. It is certain that the issuer will never have default risk and will always be able to borrow at LIBOR. The FRN is issued on November 1, 2007, when the six-month LIBOR is at 5 percent. On May 1, 2008, the six-month LIBOR is at 5.5 percent.

1. What is the coupon paid on May 1, 2008, per $1,000 bond?
2. What is the new value of the coupon set on the bond?
3. On May 2, 2008, the six-month LIBOR has dropped to 5.4 percent. What is the new value of the FRN?

SOLUTION

1. The coupon paid on May 1 was set on November 1 at 5 percent or $25 per $1,000 bond. Remember that rates are quoted on an annual basis, but they apply here to a semester period.
2. The coupon to be paid on November 1, 2008, is set at $27.5.
3. Neglecting that one day has passed, we discount the known future value of the bond on November 1, 2008, at the new six-month LIBOR of 5.4 percent:

$$P = \frac{1{,}000 + 27.5}{(1 + (5.4/2)\%)} = 1{,}000.49$$

To be exact, we should discount with a LIBOR for six months minus one day. To derive the quoted price, we should subtract one day of accrued interest from the full price.

EXHIBIT 7.9

FRNs: The Stability of Reset Date Prices
Midland Bank, May 1987

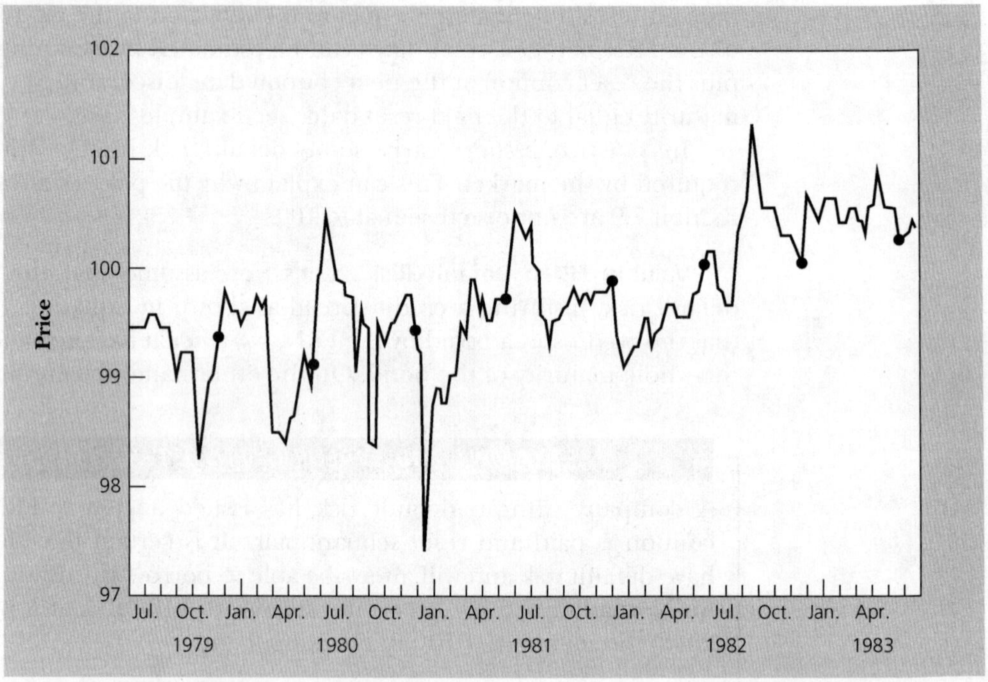

Source: J. Hanna and G. Pariente, *International Bond Market Analysis*, Salomon Brothers, July 1983. Reprinted with permission.

could fluctuate over time causing a change in its credit rating, or the risk premium required by the market for this type of borrower could be changed. The market-required spread at time *t*, m_t, is likely to be different from that at time of issuance, m_0. The market-required spread changes with the perception of credit risk.

Two observations have repeatedly been made on the FRN market:

- FRNs with long maturities tend to sell at a discount relative to those with a short maturity.
- Long-term FRN prices are more volatile than are short-term FRN prices.

Changes in the spread required by the marketplace explain these two observations.

The *first observation* can be explained by the fact that the default-risk premium tends to increase with time to maturity. A 20-year loan to a corporation, rated A, seems more risky than a 3-month loan to the same corporation. The coupon spread on an FRN is fixed over the life of the bond, whereas the market-required spread, which reflects the default-risk premium, tends to decrease as the bond nears maturity. Hence, bond prices, at least on reset dates, should progressively increase. This is observed in Exhibit 7.9. Of course, there is a survival bias, because defaulted bonds disappear from the comparison.

The *second observation* can be explained by unexpected changes in the market-required spread. FRNs are "protected" against movements in LIBOR by their indexation clause, but they are sensitive to variations in the required spread because they pay a spread that is fixed at issuance. Hence, the coupon of an FRN is not fully indexed to the market-required yield, because the interest rate component is indexed but the spread is fixed over the life of the bond. The coupon paid is equal to LIBOR + m_0, while the market requires LIBOR + m_t. If the market-required spread changes over time, the FRN behaves partly like a fixed-coupon bond, precisely because of this feature. And we know that, technically, long-term bonds are more sensitive than are short-term bonds to changes in market yield. By contrast, short-term bonds are repaid sooner, and this drives their price close to par.

This price volatility, induced by the fixity of the spread, is shown in Exhibit 7.10 for the price of a Midland Bank perpetual FRN with semiannual reset at LIBOR plus 0.25 percent (a spread of 25 basis points). The price remained relatively stable until 1987, when an international debt crisis threatened the international financial system. Investors became afraid that banks had made too many bad loans, especially to many emerging countries, which stopped servicing their debts. Lenders shied away from the long-term debts of banks. The required spread for holding FRNs issued by banks increased by 100 basis points within a few weeks. This led to a huge drop in FRN prices, as can be seen in Exhibit 7.10.

FRNs cannot be valued as if they were fixed-coupon bonds. Their future cash flows are uncertain because LIBOR fluctuates over time, and these uncertain cash flows cannot be discounted at risk-free interest rates. The modeling of default risk is a complex issue that requires many assumptions.[8] Nevertheless,

EXHIBIT 7.10

The Impact of a Change in Market-required Spread

Perpetual Midland Bank FRN, LIBOR Plus 0.25 Percent

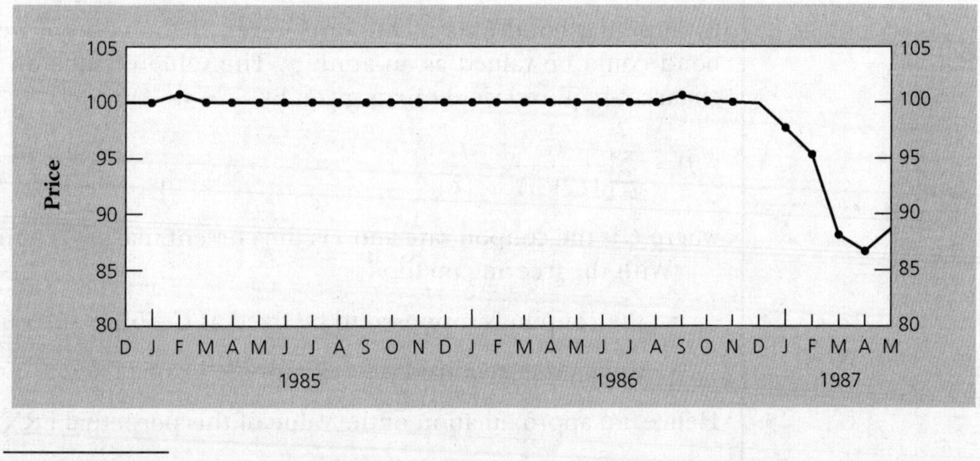

[8] See credit risk analysis in Sundaresan (1997), Duffee (1999), Duffie and Singleton (2003), and Collin-Dufresne, Goldstein, and Martin (2001).

practitioners often try to estimate the impact of a change in spread on the FRN value by resorting to some approximate method. For example, they assume that LIBOR will remain at its current value until maturity ("freezing"). So, they discount the forecasted future cash flows, equal to a "frozen" LIBOR plus the original spread m_0 at a discount rate equal to the frozen LIBOR plus the current market-required spread m_t. This is illustrated in Example 7.11. A variant of this approach is to use forward LIBOR rates implied by the LIBOR yield curve rather than the current LIBOR.

We now turn to some structured notes involving interest rate or currency plays.

Bull FRNs

Description *Bull floating-rate notes* (*bull FRNs*) are bonds that strongly benefit investors if interest rates drop. A typical example is a *reverse* (*inverse*) *floater*, whereby the coupon is set at a fixed rate minus LIBOR. Consider a five-year dollar FRN with a semiannual coupon set at 14 percent minus LIBOR. The coupon cannot be negative, so it has a minimum (floor) of 0 percent, which is attractive to investors if

EXAMPLE 7.11 ESTIMATING THE VALUE OF A FRN WHEN THE REQUIRED SPREAD CHANGES

A perpetual bond is issued by a corporation rated A with an annual coupon set at yearly LIBOR plus a spread of 0.25 percent. Some time later, LIBOR is equal to 5 percent, and the market requires a spread of 0.5 percent for such an A corporation. Give an estimate of the bond value on the reset date using the "freezing" method.

SOLUTION

A perpetual bond pays a coupon forever. If the coupon were fixed at C, the bond could be valued as an annuity. The value of such an annuity, assuming a market-required yield of r, is given by

$$P = \sum_{t=1}^{\infty} \frac{C}{(1+r)^t} = \frac{C}{r}$$

where C is the coupon rate and r is the current market-required rate.

With the freezing method,

- the coupon is supposed to be fixed at $C = 5\% + 0.25\%$, and
- the market-required yield is supposed to be fixed at $r = 5\% + 0.5\%$.

Hence, an approximation of the value of this perpetual FRN is given by

$$P = \frac{5.25}{5.5} = 95.4545\%$$

LIBOR moves over 14 percent.[9] At the time the bond was issued, the yield curve was around 7 percent.

Motivation Let's consider an investor wishing to benefit markedly from a drop in market interest rates ("bullish" on interest rates). He can buy a bull bond. For a straight FRN, the coupon decreases if market interest rates drop and the bond price remains stable. For a straight (fixed-coupon) bond, the coupon remains fixed if market interest rates drop and the bond price increases, so this is an attractive investment. For a bull bond, the coupon increases if interest rates drop, and hence the bond price rises by much more than for a straight bond with fixed coupon, which is very attractive. The properties of various bonds are reproduced in Exhibit 7.11.

Valuation We have seen that straight bonds and FRNs proceed from two different pricing philosophies. So, it is useful to separate the cash flows of a bull bond in two different sets that can be easily priced.

The bull bond could be seen by investors as the sum of three plain-vanilla securities:

- Two straight bonds with a 7 percent coupon
- A short position in a plain-vanilla FRN at LIBOR flat
- A 14 percent cap option on LIBOR

The reader can verify that the cash flows of this replicating portfolio exactly match those of the bull bond, including at time of redemption. It is straightforward to price the three plain-vanilla securities using quoted prices.

The issuer of a bull FRN seldom desires to retain such a coupon structure, but prefers to issue a straight fixed-coupon obligation or a plain-vanilla FRN. In turn, the issuer can hedge and transform this bull bond into a straight fixed-coupon bond by using interest rate swaps. For example, the bull FRN could be transformed into a fixed-coupon obligation by swapping for the face value of the bull FRN to pay floating and receive fixed.[10]

EXHIBIT 7.11

Characteristics of Bonds, Assuming a Drop in Market Interest Rates

	Straight Bond	Straight FRN	Bull FRN	Bear FRN
Coupon	→	↓	↑	↓↓
Price	↑	→	↑↑	↓

[9] In effect, the bull FRN includes a coupon of 14 percent minus LIBOR, as well as a 14 percent cap option on LIBOR (14 percent is the strike price of the cap; see the description of caps in Chapter 10). A cap option pays the difference between LIBOR and the strike of 14 percent, if LIBOR is above 14 percent on a coupon payment date. If LIBOR goes above 14 percent, this cap is activated and offsets the potentially negative coupon.

[10] In addition, the issuer should buy a 14 percent cap option, but its cost is likely to be minimal because the strike price of 14 percent is well above the current interest rate of 7 percent.

Of course, more volatile bull bonds can be created by introducing a higher multiple. For example, one could create a bond with a coupon set at 28 percent − 3 × LIBOR. This bull bond would be equivalent to four straight bonds at 7 percent minus three FRNs at LIBOR flat (plus three caps with a strike of 9.33%).

Bear FRNs

Description *Bear floating-rate notes* (*bear FRNs*) are notes that benefit investors if interest rates rise. Plain-vanilla straight bonds or FRNs do not have that property. An example of a bear bond is a note with a coupon set at twice LIBOR minus 7 percent. Again, the coupon has a floor of 0 percent, which is attractive to the investor if LIBOR goes below 3.5 percent.

Motivation The coupon of the bear bond will increase rapidly with a rise in LIBOR. We know that the price of a plain-vanilla FRN is stable, because its coupon increases parallel to LIBOR. So, the price of a bear bond will rise, because its coupon increases twice as fast as LIBOR.

Valuation Such a bond could be replicated by the investor as a portfolio long two plain-vanilla FRNs and short one straight bond with a coupon of 7 percent.[11] Because the value of the plain-vanilla FRNs should stay at par on reset dates, even if LIBOR moves, the net result is that the portfolio should appreciate if market interest rates rise. In summary, this bear note could be seen by investors as the sum of

- two plain-vanilla FRNs at LIBOR flat,
- a short position in a straight bond (with a coupon of 7 percent), and
- two 3.5 percent floor options on LIBOR.

In turn, the issuer can hedge and transform this bear FRN into a plain-vanilla FRN by simultaneously entering into an interest rate swap to pay fixed and receive floating.[12]

Again, more volatile bear bonds can be created by increasing the multiple. For example, a bear bond could be issued with a coupon set at 4 × LIBOR − 21 percent. This bear bond is equivalent to four FRNs at LIBOR flat minus three straight bonds at 7 percent (plus four floors with a strike price of 5.25%).

Dual-Currency Bonds

Description A *dual-currency bond* is a bond issued with coupons in one currency and principal redemption in another. Exhibit 7.3 gave the tombstone of such a yen/dollar international bond. NKK, a Japanese corporation, issued a 10-year bond for 20 billion yen. During 10 years, it pays an annual coupon of 8 percent in yen, or 1.6 billion yen. Ten years later, it is redeemed in U.S. dollars

[11] Furthermore, the investor gets two floor options with a strike price of 3.5 percent.

[12] The issuer should also buy two 3.5 percent floor options from the bank.

for a total of $110,480,000. The redemption amount in dollars is set so that it is exactly equal to the issue amount using the spot exchange rate prevailing at time of issue, $S_0 = 181.02824$ yen per dollar. Based on historical accounting costs, the bond is thus reimbursed at par.

The fact that the bond is originally subscribed in yen, dollars, or any other currency has no importance. A spot exchange rate transaction can be performed instantaneously at very little cost. What is important is that NKK takes on a series of future obligations in yen (coupons) and in dollars (redemption value). It is a dual-currency bond because future obligations are in two different currencies. Note that there is no option involved in dual-currency bonds, because all of their terms are fixed at issue.

Motivation The motivation for all borrowers to issue any of these fancy bonds is to be able to end up borrowing money in their desired currency but at a lower cost than directly issuing straight bonds in that currency. For example, NKK could swap,[13] at time of issue, the final dollar payment (redemption value) to take place in 10 years into yen. Although having to pay some $110 million seems to carry a lot of currency risk for a Japanese issuer, the obligation can be easily transformed into a pure yen liability. This can be done by selling forward, swapping, the redemption value of $110 million for yen at a known 10-year forward exchange rate. Borrowers are not only Japanese corporations but also non-Japanese entities, such as the U.S. Federal National Mortgage Association (Fannie Mae). Such U.S. issuers simply swap (or hedge on the forward exchange market), at time of issue, the stream of yen coupon payments for a stream of dollar coupon payments, ending up with a pure dollar liability. This type of bond will be attractive if the U.S. company ends up borrowing dollars at a cheaper rate than by issuing directly a U.S. dollar bond.

In the 1990s, many Swiss franc/U.S. dollar dual-currency bonds were issued at a time when Swiss franc yields were low and well below those on dollar bonds. These bonds were issued mostly by non-Swiss corporations.

The motivation of investors to buy these dual-currency bonds relies on institutional features and/or market conditions. We will illustrate those on the previously detailed NKK bond:

- Local investors (e.g., Japanese) are, in part, attracted to the issues by the opportunity for limited currency speculation, only on the principal, that they provided. Those who invested were betting on an appreciation of the dollar. This is a minor motivation, because it can easily be replicated by holding a portfolio of straight bonds issued in the two currencies.
- An institutional feature provided additional motivation, in the case of Japanese institutional investors. These bonds are attractive to Japanese investors because they are considered yen bonds for regulatory purposes, although they are dollar-linked. They allow institutional investors to increase the amount of fixed-income investments in higher-yield currencies.

[13] A description of swaps is provided in Chapter 10.

- On dual-currency bonds, the coupon is paid in a currency for which interest rates are low (e.g., yen or Swiss francs)[14] and reimbursed in a currency (dollar) with high interest rates. As we will see in the valuation section, dual-currency techniques allow investors to receive a higher coupon than would be received on a straight bond in that currency (e.g., yen). So, local investors (e.g., Japanese) are attracted to this type of bond because it announces a high coupon rate in that currency (e.g., yen). This is a major motivation for local retail or institutional investors looking for income.

The bond can be issued at attractive conditions to the issuer (below fair price) because it satisfies the need of a category of investors outlined previously. Issuers often do not wish to carry the currency risk implicit in those bonds. In the NKK example, the bank organizing the issue can offer the Japanese issuer the opportunity to swap the dollar exposure back into yen.

Valuation The value of a yen/dollar dual-currency bond can be broken down into two parts, as follows:

- A stream of fixed coupon payments in yen: The current value of this stream of cash flow is obtained by *discounting at the yen yield curve.*
- A dollar zero-coupon bond for the final dollar principal repayment: The current value of this single cash flow is obtained by *discounting at the dollar yield* of the appropriate maturity.

Given the yield curve in the two currencies, this is a trivial valuation exercise because there is no optional clause involved. Let's decide to value the dual-currency bond in yen. It is the sum of the present value of a yen bond corresponding to the stream of coupons and the present value of a zero-coupon dollar bond corresponding to the principal redemption. This latter dollar value can be transformed into yen at the current spot exchange rate (see Example 7.12).

A dual-currency bond is typically issued in two currencies with very different yield levels. The valuation formula ensures that the fair coupon rate on the dual-currency bond is set in between the two yield levels. For example, the NKK dual-currency bond pays an 8 percent coupon, while the yield on straight yen bonds is much lower. This is attractive to Japanese investors.

At time of issue, investment bankers have to decide the fair coupon rate to set on this dual-currency bond, given current market conditions. Because such bonds are particularly attractive to some categories of investors (see previous section), these investors are willing to subscribe to the bonds at conditions (coupon rate) that are below fair market conditions. This is typical of all of these complex bonds.

---

[14] Of course, the yield curves in various currencies change over time, reducing or enhancing the attraction to use some currency pairs to construct those bonds.

EXAMPLE 7.12 VALUING A DUAL-CURRENCY BOND

Let's consider the NKK bond described in Exhibit 7.3. It promises annual coupons of 8 percent on 20 billion yen and is redeemed in 10 years for $110.48 million. The current spot exchange rate is ¥181.02824 per dollar, so that $110.48 million is exactly equal to ¥20 billion. The yen yield curve is flat at 4 percent, and the dollar yield curve is flat at 12 percent.

1. What is the theoretical value of this dual-currency bond?
2. If the coupon on the bond was set at fair market conditions, what should be its exact value? (A bond is issued at fair market conditions if its coupon is set such that the issue price is equal to its theoretical market value.)

SOLUTION

1. The NKK bond can be valued as the sum of a stream of yen cash flows and a zero-coupon dollar bond. The present value of this dollar zero-coupon bond is then translated into yen at the current spot exchange rate. The total market value in billion yen is *V*:

$$V = \frac{1.6}{(1.04)} + \frac{1.6}{(1.04)^2} + \cdots + \frac{1.6}{(1.04)^{10}} + 181.02824 \times \frac{\$110.48 \text{ million}}{(1.12)^{10}} = ¥19.4169 \text{ billion}$$

An alternative approach to derive the present value of the final dollar cash flow would be to first convert the dollar redemption value at the forward exchange rate *F*, quoted today for a maturity of 10 years. This would yield a fixed amount of yen in 10 years. This amount would be discounted at the yen interest rate:

$$V = \frac{1.6}{(1.04)} + \frac{1.6}{(1.04)^2} + \cdots \frac{1.6}{(1.04)^{10}} + F \times \frac{\$110.48 \text{ million}}{(1.04)^{10}}$$

The two alternatives would yield the same result if $F = S \times (1.04/1.12)^{10}$, which is indeed the theoretical value of the forward exchange rate.

The percentage price is obtained by dividing by the issue amount of 20 billion, obtaining a price *P* of 97.0845 percent.

$$P = \frac{8\%}{(1.04)} + \frac{8\%}{(1.04)^2} + \cdots + \frac{8\%}{(1.04)^{10}} + \frac{100\%}{(1.12)^{10}} = 97.0845\%$$

The bond has been issued below its fair value.

2. To be issued at fair market conditions, the coupon rate should have been set at *x* percent, such that

$$100\% = \frac{x\%}{(1.04)} + \frac{x\%}{(1.04)^2} + \cdots + \frac{x\%}{(1.04)^{10}} + \frac{100\%}{(1.12)^{10}}$$

or $x = 8.36$ percent. This rate is in between the yen and dollar yields on straight bonds.

The dual-currency bond is attractive to some Japanese investors because it pays coupons in yen but has a large yield of 8 percent (compared with 4% for straight yen bonds). These investors are willing to buy this dual-currency bond below fair value.

Currency-Option Bonds

Description A *currency-option bond* is one for which the coupons and/or the principal can be paid in two or more currencies, as chosen by the bondholder. For example, a British company issues a five-year pound/euro bond. Each bond is issued at £100 and is repaid £100 or €160. The annual coupon is £3, or €4.8. This particular option gives the bondholder the right to receive principal and interest payments in either pounds or euros, whichever is more advantageous to the investor. Both the coupon rate and the euro/pound exchange rate are fixed during the life of the bond. The exchange rate of 1.6 euros for a British pound was the market exchange rate at the time of issue. So, this currency-option bond is referred to as a 3 percent (the coupon rate) euro/pound bond. If the euro/pound exchange rate drops in future years (the pound depreciates), investors will naturally prefer to receive their interest payments in euros at that time. For example, if the pound depreciates to 1.2 euros, it is much more attractive to receive a coupon of €4.8 than £3. The €4.8 coupon is then equivalent to $4.8/1.2 = £4$. If the same exchange rate holds at maturity, bondholders will ask to be reimbursed €160, which is equivalent to £133.33.

A currency-option bond benefits the investor, who can always select the stronger currency. On the other hand, the interest rate set at issue is always lower than the yields paid on single-currency straight bonds denominated in *either* currency.[15] For example, the British company should have paid approximately 5 percent on a straight pound bond and 6 percent on a straight euro bond. It should be obvious that the currency option bond must be issued at a coupon below the lower of the two yields if the option clause is to be of any value. For example, suppose for a moment that the coupon on the currency-option bond were set at 5.5 percent. The currency-option bond, then, is always better than a straight pound bond paying 5 percent, because the bondholder can elect to always receive payments in pounds. Furthermore, the currency-option bond gives the option to receive payments in euros if the pound depreciates. Having a yield above that on straight bonds in pounds would be too good to be true.

Motivation Investors select currency-option bonds because they offer a long-term currency play with limited risk. Retail investors can directly buy currency options on some options markets, but the maturity of these options is generally

[15] A call redemption clause usually protects the issuer against a large movement in one of the currencies.

limited to a few months. Institutional investors are often prohibited from directly buying derivatives. On the other hand, currency-option bonds are usually issued by good-quality issuers and are therefore available to institutional investors who are attracted by the implicit currency play. Investors are willing to receive a lower yield in order to get the currency play.

Issuers pay a lower yield than on straight bonds but run currency risk. They might not wish to retain the currency exposure. For example, the British company might wish to issue a straight pound bond. The bank organizing the issue will then sell to the issuer a long-term currency option to exactly offset the currency exposure. If the sum of the low coupon paid on the currency-option bond and the cost of the option purchased from the bank is less than the coupon rate on a straight bond, the currency-option bond is an attractive low-cost alternative to a straight bond. As with any complex bond, this alternative can be made possible only if a particular category of investors is attracted by the special features of the bond that they cannot access directly. Example 7.13 illustrates the valuation of a currency-option bond.

Valuation The value of such a currency-option bond can be broken down into two elements: the value of a straight 3 percent pound bond and the value of an option to swap a 3 percent pound bond for a 3 percent euro bond at a fixed exchange rate of 1.6 €/£. So, the value of this bond is the sum of the value of a straight bond plus the value of currency options. Basically, the issuer is writing the currency options. Of course, the bond value could also be seen as the sum of a straight 3 percent bond in euros plus an option for a £/€ currency swap. The only difficulty in valuing such a bond is the theoretical valuation of the currency options.

Collateralized Debt Obligations (CDOs)

Description A *collateralized debt obligation (CDO)* is a set of structured notes backed by a pool of assets, generally a portfolio of bonds or loans. A bank bundles together a set of bonds and sells the portfolio of bonds to a special purpose vehicle (e.g., a trust). In turn, the special purpose vehicle securitizes the portfolio and issues a set of structured notes called *tranches* or *slices*. Each tranche gets a different claim on the cash flows (coupons and principal) paid by the portfolio of bonds held as collateral by the special purpose vehicle. Exhibit 7.12 illustrates a typical CDO. The collateral portfolio consists of 100 bonds issued by different corporations with varying degrees of default risk. The portfolio has $100 million equally invested in each bond. The average yield on the portfolio is 8 percent. The special purpose vehicle issues four tranches with varying degree of credit risk and different yields. Investors can buy into any of these tranches. The losses arising from defaults on the bonds in the portfolio are distributed to the four tranches as follows:

- Tranche 1 has a principal of $5 million and is responsible for the first 5 percent of losses on the portfolio.
- Tranche 2 has a principal of $10 million and is responsible for the next 10 percent of losses.

EXAMPLE 7.13 VALUING A CURRENCY-OPTION BOND

A company issues a one-year euro/pound currency-option bond with a coupon rate of 3 percent. It is issued for £100, pays a coupon of either £3 or €4.8, and is redeemed for either £100 or €160, at the option of the bondholder. Of course, the bondholder will require payment in euros if the €/£ exchange rate is below 1.6 at maturity of the one-year bond. The current spot exchange rate is €1.6 per pound, and the one-year interest rates are 6 percent in euros and 5 percent in British pounds. A one-year put pound, with a strike price of 1.6 euros per pound, is quoted at £0.015. In other words, investors have to pay a premium of 0.015 pound to get the right to sell one pound at 1.6 euros.

1. What is the fair market value of this currency-option bond?
2. What should have been the fair coupon rate set on this currency-option bond according to market conditions? (A bond is issued at fair market conditions if its coupon is set such that the issue price is equal to its theoretical market value.)

SOLUTION

1. The currency-option bond can be replicated by a straight one-year pound bond redeemed at £100 with a 3 percent coupon plus an option to exchange £103 for €164.8. So, the value of this bond should be equal to the present value of a fixed £103 received in one year plus the value of the currency option:

$$V = \frac{103}{1.05} + 103 \times 0.015 = £99.64$$

The value of the bond is below par.

2. To be issued according to market conditions on the bond and options market, it should have been issued with a coupon rate of x percent, such that

$$\frac{100 \times (1 + x\%)}{1.05} + 100 \times (1 + x\%) \times 0.015 = £100$$

or $x = 3.37\%$

- Tranche 3 has a principal of $10 million and is responsible for the next 10 percent of losses.
- Tranche 4 has a principal of $75 million and is responsible for all remaining losses.

The yields in the exhibit are the rates of interest paid to tranche holders. These rates are paid on the balance of the principal remaining in the tranches after the losses have been paid. Consider the first tranche ("equity," sometimes called

EXHIBIT 7.12

Example of a CDO

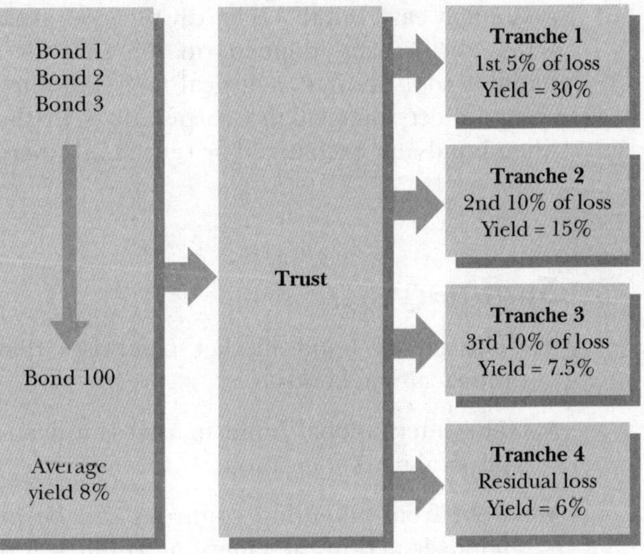

"toxic waste"). Initially, the 30 percent is paid on $5 million, but after the tranche has had to absorb some default in the portfolio, say, a loss of $1 million, the yield is paid only on the remaining balance, say, $4 million. Tranche 1 is quite risky, and in a five-year deal it could be wiped out; hence its name *toxic waste.* By contrast, the senior tranche 4 is usually rated AAA and is unlikely to have to bear any losses.

CDOs using a portfolio of actual bonds as collateral are called *cash CDOs* or *cash flow CDOs.* Synthetic CDOs use derivatives (credit default swaps) rather than actual bonds as collateral. They have become very common but are not detailed here.

Motivation A CDO is a structured product that allows creating securities with widely different credit risk characteristics. It caters to the risk desires of various investors. For example, an investor who believes that the economy will do well in the future and that few firms will default could invest in the more risky tranches (tranches 1 and 2 in Exhibit 7.12). If the assumption is correct, the investor will obtain a large yield. A CDO could focus on a specific sector (e.g., car manufacturers) and hence allow bets on the future of that industry. On the other hand, the most secure tranche (e.g., tranche 4) allows some investors to obtain a near riskless structured note at a yield that could be higher than that on government bonds. The credit risk is very low because the collateral portfolio is well diversified across issuers, and the structure of the CDO means that there is only a tiny chance of defaults reaching that tranche.

Valuation Valuing a CDO is really valuing whether the yields paid on the various tranches are "fair" given their credit risk. This is a difficult exercise.

Without getting into details, let's just say that fair valuation depends on the correlation of defaults across the various issuers in the collateral portfolio. If the probabilities of default for each bond were independent, valuation would be reasonably easy. But this is hardly the case, as defaults could be correlated within or across sectors and depend on the state of the economy. Hence, the analysis requires sophisticated statistical tools. Another problem could arise when special events affect some of the corporations in the collateral portfolio, for example, when bonds are exchanged or retired in a merger or acquisition.

Summary

- The global bond market comprises domestic bonds, foreign bonds, and international bonds.
- The international bond market is a dynamic international market without a physical market location.
- Debt from emerging countries can be purchased in many forms: domestic bonds issued in the emerging country, foreign bonds issued on a major bond market, international bonds, and Brady bonds.
- Bonds from emerging countries have often been restructured into Brady bonds to make them attractive to global investors.
- Bonds are quoted in the form of a clean price net of accrued interest. So, the full price (or value) of a bond is the sum of its clean price plus accrued interest. The day-count conventions to calculate accrued interest vary across markets and instruments.
- The yield curve based on zero-coupon government bonds is the central tool for valuing individual bonds in each currency.
- For each bond, it is common practice to report its yield to maturity (YTM), which is an average promised yield over the life of the bond. However, the convention used to calculate this YTM varies across markets. The simple yield used to be reported in Japan, and sometimes still is. Europeans tend to use an actuarial annual YTM, by discounting the bond cash flows at an annual rate. In the United States, YTM is calculated by discounting the bond cash flows at a semiannual rate and multiplying the result by 2 to report an annualized rate.
- Practitioners usually define interest rate sensitivity, or duration, as the approximate percentage price change for a 100-basis-point (1%) change in market yield. Duration provides a good approximation of the reaction of a bond price to small movements in market interest rates.
- The return on a domestic bond is the sum of the yield over the holding period plus any capital gain/loss caused by a movement in the market yield.

- The expected return on a domestic bond is the sum of the cash rate (the risk-free rate) plus a risk premium. This expected excess return, or risk premium, is the sum of the yield spread over the cash rate plus the duration-adjusted expected yield movement.
- Corporate bonds provide a yield equal to the yield on government bonds with similar duration plus a credit spread. This credit spread can be decomposed as the sum of an expected loss component, a credit-risk premium, and a liquidity premium.
- A multicurrency approach to bond management starts from a comparison of yield curves in each currency. Comparing the yield curves in two currencies allows one to calculate an implied forward exchange rate (or break-even exchange rate) between the two currencies. It is the future exchange rate that would make it equivalent, ex post, to invest in bonds of both currencies. The investor's forecast of future exchange rates has to be compared with this implied forward rate.
- The *return* from investing in a foreign bond has three components:
  - During the investment period, the bondholder receives the foreign yield.
  - A change in the foreign yield (Δ*foreign yield*) induces a percentage capital gain/loss on the price of the bond.
  - A currency movement induces a currency gain or loss on the position.
- The *risk* from investing in a foreign bond has two major components:
  - *Interest rate risk:* the risk that the foreign yield will rise
  - *Currency risk:* the risk that the foreign currency will depreciate
- The expected return on a foreign bond is equal to the domestic cash rate plus a risk premium. This risk premium equals the sum of
  - the spread of the foreign bond yield over the domestic cash rate,
  - the percentage capital gain/loss due to an expected foreign yield movement, and
  - the expected percentage currency movement.
- Currency hedging allows one to remove currency risk. The risk premium on a foreign bond hedged against currency risk is simply equal to its risk premium in its local currency.
- Global bond portfolio management includes several stages. First, a benchmark has to be chosen. Then, a bond manager tries to outperfom the benchmark by combining various strategies: bond market selection, sector selection/credit selection, currency management, duration/yield curve management, and yield enhancement techniques.
- Because currency is a major source of return and risk in global bond management, special attention should be devoted to the currency dimension.
- Floating-rate notes (FRNs) are a major segment of the bond market. Their valuation proceeds from a logic that is quite different from that of straight fixed-rate

bonds. In the absence of default risk, an FRN should be priced at par on the reset dates. Between reset dates, its value could fluctuate slightly in case of a movement in market interest rates, because the coupon is fixed until the next reset date. In the presence of default risk, the value of an FRN can move if the market-required credit spread becomes different from the spread that has been set at time of issue.

- Various complex bonds, often called structured notes, are issued on the international market. A *structured note* is a bond (note) issued with some unusual clause, often an option-like clause. These notes are bonds issued by a name of good credit standing and can therefore be purchased as investment-grade bonds by most institutional investors, even those that are prevented by regulations from dealing in options or futures. Structured notes are designed for specific investors wishing to take a bet on some forecasts. If the forecasts are correct, the yield on the note will be enhanced.
- The issuer will usually hedge the unusual risks (bets) of a structured note and end up with a plain-vanilla bond at a low cost.
- Some bonds offer plays on interest rates (bull and bear FRNs). Others offer play on currencies (dual-currency bonds, currency-option bonds).
- A collateralized debt obligation (CDO) is a structured product that allows creating securities with widely different credit risk characteristics.

Problems

1. Which of the following is the most appropriate term for the bonds issued in the United States by a European corporation and denominated in U.S. dollars?
   a. Domestic bonds
   b. Foreign bonds
   c. International bonds
   d. European bonds

2. Which of the following statements about the global bond market are true?
   I. Bonds issued in the United States by a non-U.S. corporation must satisfy the disclosure requirements of the U.S. Securities and Exchange Commission.
   II. Two bond indexes of the same market tend to be highly correlated, even if their composition is somewhat different.
   III. It is not necessary that a bond be denominated in euros for it to be termed an international bond.

3. An international bank loaned money to an emerging country a few years ago. Because of the nonpayment of interest due on this loan, the bank is now negotiating with the borrower to exchange the loan for Brady bonds. The Brady bonds that would be issued would be either par bonds or discount bonds, with the same time to maturity.
   a. Would both types of bonds, par and discount, provide debt reduction to the emerging country?

b. Would both types of bonds, par and discount, have a lower coupon amount than the original?
c. Of the two types of bonds being considered, which one would have a lower coupon amount?

4. Consider a newly issued dollar/yen dual-currency bond. This bond is issued in yen. The coupons are paid in yen and the principal will be repaid in dollars. The market price of this bond is quoted in yen. Discuss what would happen to the market price of this dual-currency bond in the following situations:
   a. The market interest rate on yen bonds drops significantly.
   b. The dollar drops in value relative to the yen.
   c. The market interest rate on dollar bonds drops significantly.

5. A European corporation has issued bonds with a par value of SFr 1,000 and an annual coupon of 5 percent. The last coupon on these bonds was paid four months ago, and their current clean price is 90 percent.
   a. If these bonds are international bonds, what is their full price?
   b. Would your answer to part (a) be different if the bonds were not international bonds but were issued in the Swiss domestic bond market?

6. a. Compute the yield to maturity (YTM) of a zero-coupon bond with nine years to maturity and currently selling at 45 percent.
   b. Compute the YTM of a perpetual bond with an annual coupon of € 6 and currently selling at €108.

7. a. Consider a bond issued at par. The annual coupon is 8 percent and frequency of coupon is semiannual. How would the YTM of this bond be reported in most of the European markets?
   b. The market price of a two-year bond with annual coupon is 103 percent of its nominal value. The annual coupon to be paid in exactly one year is 6 percent. Compute its
      i. YTM (European method), and
      ii. YTM (U.S. method).

8. Bonds A and B are two straight yen-denominated international bonds, with the same maturity of four years and the same YTM of 9 percent. Bond A has an annual coupon of 11 percent and is accordingly priced at 106.48 percent. Bond B has an annual coupon of 7 percent and is accordingly priced at 93.52 percent.
   a. Compute the simple yield for each of these bonds, as reported sometimes by financial institutions in Japan.
   b. What does your answer to part (a) indicate about the potential biases in using the simple yield?

9. You hold a bond with nine years until maturity, a YTM of 4 percent, and a duration of 7.5. The cash (one-year) rate is 2.5 percent.
   a. In the next few minutes, you expect the market yield to go up by 5 basis points. What is the bond's expected percentage price change, and your expected return, over the next few minutes?
   b. Over the next year, you expect the market yield to go down by 30 basis points. For this period, estimate the following:
      i. The bond's expected price change
      ii. Your expected return
      iii. The bond's risk premium

10. a. Discuss the statement that it is easy to estimate the credit spread of a corporate bond because it could be done by simply comparing the bond's YTM with that of a Treasury bond that has identical cash flows.

b. There is a 0.5 percent probability of default by the year-end on a one-year bond issued at par by a particular corporation. If the corporation defaults, the investor will get nothing. Assume that a default-free bond exists with identical cash flows and liquidity, and the one-year yield on this bond is 4 percent. What yield should be required by risk-neutral investors on the corporate bond? What should the credit spread be?

11. An investor is considering investing in one-year zero-coupon bonds. She is thinking of investing in either a British-pound-denominated bond with a yield of 5.2 percent or a euro-denominated bond with a yield of 4.5 percent. The current exchange rate is €1.5408 per £.

a. What exchange rate one year later is the break-even exchange rate, which would make the pound and euro investments equally good?

b. Which investment would have turned out to be better if the actual exchange rate one year later is €1.4120 per £?

12. A French investor has purchased bonds denominated in Swiss francs that have been issued by a Swiss corporation with a mediocre credit rating. Which of the following is a source of risk for this investment?

a. Interest rate risk on Swiss francs
b. Currency risk
c. Credit risk
d. a and b only
e. a, b, and c

13. A Swiss investor has purchased a U.S. Treasury bond priced at 100. Its yield is 4.5 percent, and the investor expects the U.S. yields to move down by 15 basis points over the year. The duration of the bond is 6. The Swiss franc cash rate is 1 percent and the dollar cash rate is 2 percent. The one-year forward exchange rate is SFr1.4600 per $.

a. The Swiss investor has come up with his own model to forecast the SFr per $ exchange rate one year ahead. This model forecasts the one-year ahead exchange rate to be SFr1.3500 per $. Based on this forecast, should the Swiss investor hedge the currency risk of his investment using a forward contract?

b. If the Swiss investor decides to hedge using a forward contract, give a rough estimate of his expected return.

c. Verify for the hedged investment that the risk premium in Swiss francs is the same as the risk premium on the same U.S. Treasury bond for a U.S. investor.

14. In determining the composition of an international bond portfolio, the decision regarding the weights of different national markets/currencies is more critical than the decision regarding the weights of different bonds within a national market/currency. Discuss why you agree or disagree with this statement.

15. A company without default risk has issued a perpetual dollar FRN at LIBOR. The coupon is paid and reset semiannually. It is certain that the issuer will never have default risk and will always be able to borrow at LIBOR. The FRN is issued on March 1, 2007, when the six-month LIBOR is at 5 percent. The dollar yield curve on September 1, 2007, and December 1, 2007, is as follows:

	September 1, 2007 (%)	December 1, 2007 (%)
One month	4.25	4.00
Three months	4.50	4.25
Six months	4.75	4.50
Twelve months	5.00	4.75

a. What is the coupon paid on September 1, 2007, per $1,000 FRN?
b. What is the new value of the coupon set on the FRN on September 1, 2007?
c. What is the new value of the FRN on December 1, 2007?

16. A company rated A has issued a perpetual dollar FRN. The FRN has a semiannual coupon set at six-month LIBOR plus a spread of 0.5 percent. Six months later, LIBOR is equal to 6 percent, and the market-required spread for an A-rated corporation has moved up to 1 percent. Give an estimate of the value of the FRN on the reset date using the freezing method.

17. The yield curves on the dollar and yen are flat at 7 percent and 3 percent per year, respectively. An investment banker is considering issuing a dollar/yen dual-currency bond for ¥150 million. This bond would pay the coupons in yen, and the principal would be repaid in dollars. The bond will make a principal payment of $1.36 million in two years, with interest paid in years 1 and 2. The spot exchange rate is ¥110.29 per $.
a. What should the coupon rate be if the bond is issued at fair market conditions—that is, if the issue price is equal to its theoretical market value?
b. If the actual coupon rate is 6 percent, compute the percentage price.

18. The current dollar yield curve on the international bond market is flat at 6.5 percent for AAA-rated borrowers. A French company of AA standing can issue straight and plain-vanilla FRN dollar bonds at the following conditions:
- Bond A: Straight bond. Five-year straight-dollar bond with a semiannual coupon of 6.75 percent.
- Bond B: Plain-vanilla FRN. Five-year dollar FRN with a semiannual coupon set at LIBOR plus 0.25 percent and a cap of 13 percent. The cap means that the coupon rate is limited at 13 percent, even if the LIBOR passes 12.75 percent.

An investment banker proposes to the French company the option of issuing bull and/or bear FRNs at the following conditions:
- Bond C: Bull FRN. Five-year FRN with a semiannual coupon set at 12.75 percent–LIBOR.
- Bond D: Bear FRN. Five-year FRN with a semiannual coupon set at 2 × LIBOR – 6.5 percent.

The coupons on the bull and bear FRNs cannot be negative. The coupon on the bear FRN is set with a cap of 19 percent.

Assume that LIBOR can never be below 3.25 percent or above 12.75 percent.
a. By comparing the net coupon per bond for the following combination to that of a straight Eurobond, show that it would be more attractive to the French company to issue the bull and/or bear FRNs than the straight Eurobond.
   i. Issue 2 bull FRNs + 1 bear FRN.
   ii. Issue 1 plain-vanilla FRN (bond B) + 1 bull FRN.

b. By comparing the net coupon per bond for the combination of 1 straight bond (bond A) + 1 bear FRN, show that it would be more attractive to the French company to issue the bull and/or bear FRNs than the plain-vanilla FRN.

19. An investment banker is considering the issue of a one-year Australian dollar/U.S. dollar currency-option bond. The currency-option bond is to be issued in A$ (A$1,000), and the interest and principal are to be repaid in A$ or US$ at the option of the bondholder. The principal repaid would be either A$1,000 or US$549.45. The current spot exchange rate is A$1.82 per US$. The current one-year market interest rates are 8 percent in A$ and 5 percent in US$. A one-year put option on the A$, with a strike price of A$1.82 per US$, is quoted at 2 U.S. cents; this is an option to sell one A$ for 1/US$1.82.

a. What should be the fair coupon rate set on this currency-option bond, according to market conditions?
b. What is the value of the bond if it is issued at a coupon of 3.4 percent?

20. A French bank offers an investment product ("guaranteed bond with stock market participation") that has been extremely successful with European retail investors. This is a two-year bond with a zero coupon. However, there is an attractive clause at maturity. The bondholder will get full principal payment plus the percentage capital appreciation on the French CAC stock index between the date of issuance and maturity, if this capital appreciation is positive. So, a bondholder investing 100 will get, at maturity, either 100 (if the CAC index went down over the two years) or 100 plus the percentage gain of the index (if the CAC index went up over the two years).

a. Assume that the stock market is expected to go up by 20 percent over the two years. What is the expected annual yield on the bond?
b. At time of issue, the euro yield curve was flat at 6 percent. A two-year at-the-money call on the CAC index was quoted at 11 percent of the index value. What was the fair value of the bond at issuance?

Bibliography

Collin-Dufresne, P., Goldstein, R. S., and Martin, J. S. "The Determinants of Credit Spread Changes," *Journal of Finance*, December 2001.

Duffee, G. R. "Estimating the Price of Default Risk," *Review of Financial Studies*, 12, 1999, pp. 197–226.

Duffie D., and Singleton, K. J. *Credit Risk: Pricing, Measurement and Management*, Princeton, NJ: Princeton University Press, 2003.

Fabozzi, F. J. *Fixed Income Analysis* (*CFA Institute Investment Series*), Hoboken, NJ: John Wiley & Sons, 2007.

Sundaresan, S. M. *Fixed Income Markets and their Derivatives*, Mason, OH: Thomson: Southwestern, 1997.

8 Alternative Investments

LEARNING OUTCOMES

After completing this chapter, you will be able to do the following:

- Discuss the general features of alternative investments and distinguish between alternative assets and alternative strategies
- Distinguish between an open-end and a closed-end fund and between a load and a no-load fund
- Explain how the net asset value of a fund is calculated
- Explain the nature of various fees charged by mutual funds
- Distinguish between style, sector, index, global, and stable value strategies in equity investment
- Distinguish between exchange traded funds (ETFs), traditional mutual funds, and closed-end funds
- Explain the advantages and risks of ETFs
- Discuss the characteristics of real estate as an investable asset class
- Describe the various approaches to the valuation of real estate
- Calculate the net operating income from a real estate investment
- Calculate the value of a property under the cost, sales comparison, and income approaches
- Calculate the after-tax cash flow, net present value, and yield of a real estate investment
- Outline the various stages in venture capital investing
- Discuss the various types of private equity investments
- Discuss venture capital investment characteristics as well as the challenges to venture performance measurement
- Calculate the net present value of a venture capital project given its possible payoffs and its conditional failure probabilities

---

Jot Yau, CFA, made contributions to the exchange traded and hedge funds sections of this chapter.

- Discuss the descriptive accuracy of the term *hedge fund* and define hedge fund in terms of objectives, legal structure, and fee structure
- Calculate the return of a hedge fund, given an absolute return scenario and the fund's fee structure
- Discuss the various types of hedge funds
- Discuss the benefits and drawbacks to fund of funds investing
- Discuss the leverage and unique risks of hedge funds
- Discuss the performance of hedge funds and the biases present in hedge fund performance measurement
- Identify the possible presence of survivorship bias in a hedge fund data base
- Explain how the legal environment affects the valuation of closely held companies
- Discuss alternative valuation methods for closely held companies; and distinguish between the bases for the discounts and premiums for these companies
- Discuss distressed securities investing and the similarities between venture capital investing and distressed securities investing
- Discuss the role of commodities as a vehicle for investing in production and consumption
- Explain the role of commodity trading advisors (CTAs) and the role of managed futures in commodity investing
- Discuss the sources of return on a collateralized commodity futures position
- Discuss the motivation for investing in commodities, commodity derivatives, and commodity-linked securities
- Explain how to manage risk for managed futures

Alternative investments complement stocks, bonds, and other traditional financial instruments traded on international financial markets. There is a large variety of alternative investments, and the list evolves over time. Both alternative assets (such as real estate) and alternative strategies (hedge funds) are classified as alternative investments. Alternative investments generally have lower liquidity, sell in less efficient markets, and require a longer time horizon than publicly traded stocks and bonds. Sharpe, Alexander, and Bailey (1999) provide a nice summary of the common features of alternative investments:

- Illiquidity
- Difficulty in determining current market values
- Limited historical risk and return data
- Extensive investment analysis required

When present, liquidity can make alternative investments, such as real estate, attractive; but are there cases in which the general illiquidity of alternative investments can be attractive? Alternative investments beckon investors to areas of the market where alpha[1] is more likely to be found than in more liquid and efficient markets. Illiquidity, limited information, and less efficiency do not suit all investors but can be attractive features to those looking for likely places to add value through investment expertise.

Terhaar, Staub, and Singer (2003) discuss two additional features of alternative investments:

- A liquidity premium compensates the investor for the investor's inability to continuously rebalance the alternative investments in the portfolio.
- A segmentation premium compensates investors for the risk of alternative assets that, by nature, are generally not priced in a fully integrated global market.

It is difficult to give a broad characterization of alternative investments, but they are often equity investments in some nonpublicly traded asset. In some cases, however, they may look more like an investment strategy than an asset class. Whatever the nature of alternative investments, specialized intermediaries often link the investor to the investments. Whether the investor invests directly or through an intermediary, he must know the investment's characteristics. In the case of investing through an intermediary, he must make sure that the incentive structure for any intermediary suits his investor needs.

Finally, alternative investments can be characterized as raising unique legal and tax considerations. A financial advisor would coordinate with an attorney and a tax accountant before recommending any specific real estate investment. Also, many forms of alternative investments involve special legal structures that avoid some taxes (exchange traded funds) or avoid some regulations (hedge funds).

Before getting into alternative investments per se, it is useful to first review investment companies.

Investment Companies

Investment companies are financial intermediaries that earn fees to pool and invest investors' funds, giving the investors rights to a proportional share of the pooled fund performance. Both managed and unmanaged companies pool investor funds in this manner. Unmanaged investment companies (unit investment trusts in the United States) hold a fixed portfolio of investments (often tax exempt) for the life of the company and usually stand ready to redeem the investor's shares at market value. Managed investment companies are classified according to whether or not they stand ready to redeem investor shares. *Open-end funds* operated by

[1] *Alpha* is risk-adjusted return in excess of the required rate of return, but, more colloquially, stands for positive excess risk-adjusted return, the goal of active managers.

investment companies (mutual funds) offer this redemption feature, but *closed-end funds* do not. Closed-end investment companies issue shares that are then traded in the secondary markets.

Valuing Investment Company Shares

The basis for valuing investment company shares is *net asset value (NAV)*, the per-share value of the investment company's assets minus its liabilities. Liabilities may come from fees owed to investment managers, for example. Share value equals NAV for unmanaged and open-end investment companies because they stand ready to redeem their shares at NAV. The price of a closed-end investment company's shares is determined in the secondary markets in which they trade, and, consequently, can be at a premium or discount to NAV.

Fund Management Fees

Investment companies charge fees, some as one-time charges and some as annual charges. By setting an initial selling price above the NAV, the unmanaged company charges a fee for the effort of setting up the fund. For managed funds, loads are simply sales commissions charged at purchase (*front-end load*) as a percentage of the investment. A redemption fee (*back-end load*) is a charge to exit the fund. Redemption fees discourage quick trading turnover and are often set up so that the fees decline the longer the shares are held (in this case, the fees are sometimes called *contingent deferred sales charges*). Loads and redemption fees provide sales incentives but not portfolio management performance incentives.

Annual charges are composed of operating expenses including management fees, administrative expenses, and continuing distribution fees (12b-1 fees in the United States). The ratio of operating expenses to average assets is often referred to as the fund's "expense ratio." Distribution fees are fees paid back to the party that arranged the initial sale of the shares and are thus another type of sales incentive fee. Only management fees can be considered a portfolio management incentive fee. Example 8.1 illustrates the effects of investment company fees on fund performance.

Investment Strategies

Investment companies primarily invest in equity. Investment strategies can be characterized as style, sector, index, global, or stable value strategies. Style strategies focus on the underlying characteristics common to certain investments. Growth is a different style than value, and large capitalization investing is a different style than small stock investing. A growth strategy may focus on high price-to-earnings stocks, and a value strategy on low price-to-earnings stocks. Clearly, there are many styles.[2] A sector investment fund focuses on a particular industry. An index fund tracks an

---

[2] See, for example, Richard Bernstein, *Style Investing*, Wiley, 1995, and Richard Michaud, *Investment Styles, Market Anomalies, and Global Stock Selection*, The Research Foundation of AIMR, 1999.

EXAMPLE 8.1 INVESTMENT COMPANY FEES: EFFECTS ON PERFORMANCE

An investor is considering the purchase of TriGroup International Equity Fund (TRIEF) for her portfolio. Like many U.S.-based mutual funds today, TRIEF has more than one class of shares. Although all classes hold the same portfolio of securities, each class has a different expense structure. This particular mutual fund has three classes of shares, A, B, and C. The expenses of these classes are summarized in the following table:

Expense Comparison for Three Classes of TRIEF

	Class A	Class B*	Class C
Sales charge (load) on purchases	3%	None	None
Deferred sales charge (load) on redemptions	None	5% in the first year, declining by 1 percentage point each year thereafter	1% for the initial two years
Annual expenses:			
Distribution fee	0.25%	0.50%	0.50%
Management fee	0.75%	0.75%	0.75%
Other expenses	0.25%	0.25%	0.25%
	1.25%	1.50%	1.50%

*Class B shares automatically convert to Class A shares 72 months (6 years) after purchase, reducing future annual expenses.

The time horizon associated with the investor's objective in purchasing TRIEF is six years. She expects equity investments with risk characteristics similar to TRIEF to earn 8 percent per year, and she decides to make her selection of fund share class based on an assumed 8 percent return each year, gross of any of the expenses given in the preceding table.

A. Based on only the information provided here, determine the class of shares that is most appropriate for this investor. Assume that expense percentages given will be constant at the given values. Assume that the deferred sales charges are computed on the basis of NAV.

B. Suppose that, as a result of an unforeseen liquidity need, the investor needs to liquidate her investment at the end of the first year. Assume an 8 percent rate of return has been earned. Determine the relative performance of the three fund classes, and interpret the results.

C. Based on your answers to A and B, discuss the appropriateness of these share classes as it relates to an investor's time horizon, for example, a one-, six-, and ten-year horizon.

SOLUTION

A. To address this question, we compute the terminal value of $1 invested at the end of year 6. The share class with the highest terminal value, net of all expenses, would be the most appropriate for this investor, as all classes are based on the same portfolio and thus have the same portfolio risk characteristics.

Class A. $1 \times (1 - 0.03) = \$0.97$ is the amount available for investment at $t = 0$, after paying the front-end sales charge. Because this amount grows at 8 percent for six years, reduced by annual expenses of 0.0125, the terminal value per \$1 invested after six years is $\$0.97 \times 1.08^6 \times (1 - 0.0125)^6 = \$1.4274$.

Class B. After six years, \$1 invested grows to $\$1 \times 1.08^6 \times (1 - 0.015)^6 = \$1.4493$. According to the table, the deferred sales charge disappears after year 5; therefore, the terminal value is \$1.4493.

Class C. After six years, \$1 invested grows to $\$1 \times 1.08^6 \times (1 - 0.015)^6 = \$1.4493$. There is no deferred sales charge in the sixth year, so \$1.4493 is the terminal value.

In summary, the ranking by terminal value after six years is Class B and Class C (\$1.4493), followed by Class A (\$1.4274). Class B or Class C appears to be the most appropriate for this investor with a six-year horizon.

B. For Class A shares, the terminal value per \$1 invested is $\$0.97 \times 1.08 \times (1 - 0.0125) = \$1.0345$. For Class B shares, it is $\$1 \times 1.08 \times (1 - 0.015) \times (1 - 0.05) = \$1.0106$, reflecting a 5 percent redemption charge; for Class C shares, it is $\$1 \times 1.08 \times (1 - 0.015) \times (1 - 0.01) = \$1.0532$, reflecting a 1 percent redemption charge. Thus, the ranking is Class C (\$1.0532), Class A (\$1.0345), and Class B (\$1.0106).

C. Although Class B is appropriate given a six-year investment horizon, it is a costly choice if the fund shares need to be liquidated soon after investment. That eventuality would need to be assessed by the investor we are discussing. Class B, like Class A, is more attractive the longer the holding period, in general. Because Class C has higher annual expenses than Class A and Class B (after six years), it becomes less attractive the longer the holding period, in general.

After 10 years Class B shares would return $\$1 \times 1.08^{10} \times (1 - 0.015)^6 \times (1 - 0.0125)^4 = \$1.8750$, reflecting conversion to Class A after six years. Class C would return $\$1 \times 1.08^{10} \times (1 - 0.0150)^{10} = \$1.8561$. Class A shares would return the smallest amount, $\$0.97 \times 1.08^{10} \times (1 - 0.0125)^{10} = \$1.8466$. Though Class A underperforms Class C for a ten-year investment horizon, one could verify that Class A outperforms Class C for an investment horizon of 13 years or more. Also, in practice, the sales charge for Class A shares may be lower for purchases over certain sizes, making them more attractive in such comparisons.

index. In the simplest implementation, the fund owns the securities in the index in exactly the same proportion as the market value weights of those securities in the index. A global fund includes securities from around the world and might keep portfolio weights similar to world market capitalization weights. An international fund is one that does not include the home country's securities, whereas a global fund includes the securities from the home country. A stable value fund invests in securities such as short-term fixed income instruments and guaranteed investment contracts which are guaranteed by the issuing insurance company and pay principal and a set rate of interest.

Exchange Traded Funds

Exchange traded funds (ETFs) are index-based investment products that allow investors to buy or sell exposure to an index through a single financial instrument. ETFs are funds that trade on a stock market like shares of any individual companies. Gastineau (2001) gives a good introduction to ETFs. They can be traded at any time during market hours and can be sold short or margined. But they are shares of a portfolio, not of an individual company. They represent shares of ownership in either open-end funds or unit investment trusts that hold portfolios of stocks or bonds in custody, which are designed to track the price and yield performance of their underlying indexes—broad market, sector/industry, single country/region (multiple countries), or fixed income. Although many investors regard ETFs simply as a form of diversified equity investment, their novelty and legal specificity suggested their inclusion in this chapter.

Recent Developments of ETFs ETFs first appeared as TIP 35 (Toronto Index Participation Fund) in Canada in 1989, and they appeared in the United States in 1993 with the introduction of Standard & Poor's 500 (S&P 500) Depositary Receipts (SPDRs or "spiders"). The first Asian ETF, the Hong Kong Tracker Fund, was launched in 1999. The first ETF launched in Europe, Euro STOXX 50, did not appear until 2000. Japan did not trade ETFs until 2001, when eight were listed. Today, most national stock exchanges list some ETFs. Their popularity has grown so quickly that they have become one of the most successful financial products of the decade.

As of 2007, several hundred ETFs were listed in the United States with total assets of around $500 billion. Leading ETF providers are Barclays Global Investors and State Street Global Advisors. Several hundred ETFs are also listed outside the United States. Listings of multiple ETFs on the same underlying index are common in Europe. European ETFs generally are structured according to the European Commission's 2001 Undertakings for Collective Investment in Transferable Securities (UCITS) III directive, which is considered by many managers to be more flexible than the fund guidelines of the U.S. Investment Company Act of 1940. As a result, a number of new strategies in ETF investments—including commodities, long leveraged, short leveraged, and private equity—have been introduced in Europe within the past several years.

ETF Structure The usual ETF structure adopted worldwide is that of open-end funds with special characteristics, such as the "in-kind" process for creation and redemption of shares described subsequently (see Gastineau, 2001). Details of the legal structure vary depending on the country where the ETF is incorporated. In the United States, ETFs have adopted three different legal structures:

- *Managed investment companies* are open-ended investment companies registered under the Investment Company Act of 1940. They offer the most flexible ETF structure. The index can be tracked using various techniques, such as holding only a sample of the underlying securities in the index, lending of securities, and trading in derivatives. Dividends paid on the securities can be immediately reinvested in the fund. Sector SPDRs, iShares, and WEBS (World Equity Benchmark Shares) use this legal structure.
- *Unit investment trusts (UITs)* are also registered investment companies, but they operate under more constraints because they do not have a manager per se (but trustees). UITs are required to be fully invested in all underlying securities forming the index and must hold dividends received on securities in cash until the ETF pays a dividend to shareholders. This could result in a slight cash drag on performance. UITs are not permitted to lend securities and do not generally use derivatives. S&P 500 SPDR, Midcap 400 SPDR, and NASDAQ-100 QQQ ("qubes," trading symbol QQQQ) use this legal structure.
- *Grantor trusts* are not registered investment companies. Accordingly, owning a grantor trust is substantially similar to holding a basket of securities. A grantor trust often takes the form of an *American Depositary Receipt (ADR)* and trades as such. Because a grantor trust is fully invested in the basket of securities, no investment discretion is exercised by the trust. This is basically an unmanaged (and unregistered) investment company with a limited life. The trust passes all dividends on the underlying securities to shareholders as soon as practicable. Securities lending and use of derivatives are generally not practiced. HOLDRs (Holding Company Depository Receipts) use this legal structure. Grantor trusts are a structure that allows investors to indirectly own an unmanaged basket of stocks rather than tracking an index, and some do not classify them as ETFs.

We will now introduce the unique "in-kind" creation and redemption process used by open-end and UIT ETFs. This in-kind process is a major distinguishing feature of ETFs. Creation/redemption units are created in large multiples of individual ETF shares, for example, 50,000 shares. These units are available to exchange specialists (*authorized participants* or *creation agents*) that are authorized by the fund and who will generally act as market makers on the individual ETF shares. The fund publishes the index tracking portfolio that it is willing to accept for in-kind transactions. When there is excess demand for ETF shares, an authorized participant will create a *creation unit* (a large block of ETF shares) by depositing with the trustee of the fund the specified portfolio of stocks used to track the index. In return, the authorized participant will receive ETF shares that can be sold to investors on the stock market. The redemption process is the same but in reverse.

EXHIBIT 8.1

Creation/Redemption Process of Exchange Traded Funds

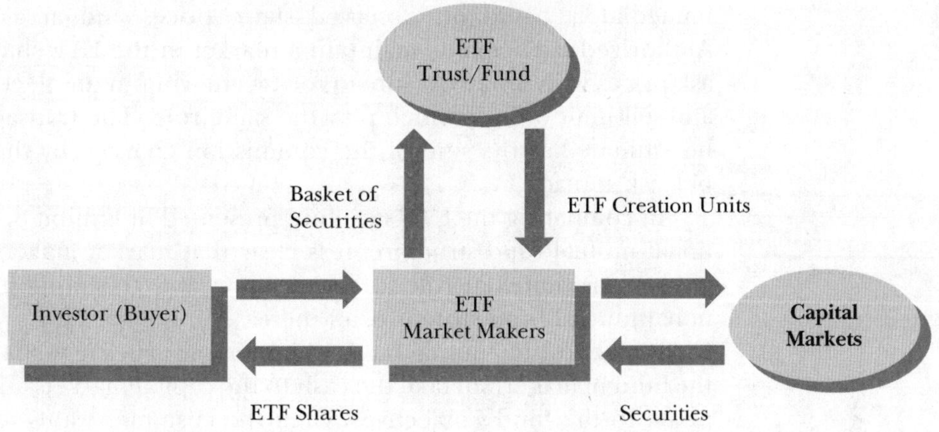

If there is an excess number of ETF shares sold by investors, an authorized participant will decide to redeem ETF shares; it will do so by exchanging with the fund a *redemption unit* (a large block of ETF shares) for a portfolio of stocks held by the fund and used to track the index. Exhibit 8.1 depicts the ETF structure and the creation/redemption process.

As opposed to traditional open-end funds, the in-kind redemption means that no capital gain will be realized in the fund's portfolio on redemption. If the redemption were in cash, the fund would have to sell stocks held in the fund's portfolio. If their price had appreciated, the fund would realize a capital gain, and the tax burden would have to be passed to all existing fund shareholders. This is not the case with ETFs. This in-kind transfer for redemptions does not create a tax burden for the remaining ETF shareholders under current U.S. tax law, unlike the capital gains distributions on traditional mutual fund shareholders that could result from the sale of securities to meet redemption demand.[3] As in any open-end fund, individual ETF shareholders[4] can require in-cash redemption based on the NAV. Redemption in cash by individual ETF shareholders is discouraged in two ways:

- Redemption is based on the NAV computed a couple of days after the shareholder commits to redemption. So, the redemption value is unknown when the investor decides to redeem. This is a common feature of mutual funds.
- A large fee is assessed on in-cash redemptions.

[3] There are situations in which capital gains distributions are generated for the ETF, such as capital gains resulting from selling securities directly to the capital markets due to an index reconstitution. Thus, zero capital gains distributions are not guaranteed.

[4] But authorized participants commit to redeem only in kind.

It is more advantageous for individual shareholders to sell their shares on the market than to redeem them in cash. Arbitrage[5] by authorized participants ensures that the listed price is close to the fund's NAV, and the sale can take place immediately based on observed share prices and at a low transaction cost. Authorized participants maintain a market in the ETF share by posting bid-and-ask prices with a narrow spread, or by entering in an electronic order book buy-and-sell limit orders, which play the same role. The transaction cost of ETFs can be estimated as the sum of the commission charged by the broker plus half this bid–ask spread.

In comparing the ETF structure presented in Exhibit 8.1 with that of the traditional mutual fund structure, it is clear that market makers in the ETF structure play an instrumental role in the creation and redemption process. In the traditional mutual fund structure, an increase in demand for the shares of the mutual fund is met by the mutual fund, which simply issues new shares to the investor, and the fund manager will take the cash to the capital markets and buy securities appropriate to the fund's objective. When the customer wants to sell the mutual fund shares, the fund manager may need to raise cash by selling securities back to the capital markets. In contrast, when a customer wants to buy ETF shares, the order is not directed to the fund but to the market makers on the exchange. The market maker will exchange ETF shares for cash with the customer (via broker/dealer) and, when necessary, replenish the supply of ETFs through the creation process outlined earlier.

Advantages/Disadvantages of ETFs ETFs are used by a wide spectrum of investors, both individual and institutional, in a wide variety of investment strategies. This is because ETFs have the following advantages:

- Diversification can be obtained easily with a single ETF transaction. With equity-oriented ETFs, investors can gain instant exposure to different market capitalizations, style (value or growth), sector or industries, or countries or geographic regions. With fixed income ETFs, they can gain exposure to different maturity segments and bond market sectors. Thus, ETFs provide a convenient way to diversify.
- Although ETFs represent interests in a portfolio of securities, they trade similarly to a stock on an organized exchange. For example, ETFs can be sold short and also bought on margin.
- ETFs trade throughout the whole trading day at market prices that are updated continuously, rather than only trading once a day at closing market prices, as do the traditional open-end mutual funds.
- For many ETFs, there exist futures and options contracts on the same index, which is convenient for risk management.

[5] ETFs usually publish an indicative intraday NAV every 15 seconds that is available from major data providers.

- Portfolio holdings of ETFs are transparent. The ETF sponsor publishes the constituents of the fund on a daily basis. This should closely resemble the constituents of the underlying index. This is in contrast to other funds, for which the manager publishes only the list of assets in the fund from time to time.
- ETFs are cost effective. There are no load fees. Moreover, because the ETFs are passively managed, the expense ratio (which includes management fee for open-end funds, trustee fee for UITs, and custody fee for HOLDRs) can be kept low relative to actively managed funds. The expense ratio is comparable to that of an index mutual fund. For example, management fee can be as low as 8 basis points for the most successful U.S. ETFs, and up to 90 basis points for sector and international products (Mussavian and Hirsch, 2002). ETFs have a cost advantage over traditional mutual funds because there is no shareholder accounting at the fund level.
- ETFs have an advantage over closed-end index funds because their structure can prevent a significant premium/discount. Although supply and demand determine the market price of an ETF just like any other security, arbitrage helps keep the traded price of an ETF much more in line with its underlying value. By simultaneously buying (or selling) the ETF basket of securities and selling (or buying) the ETF shares in the secondary market, and creating (or redeeming) ETF shares to be delivered against the sale, market makers can capture the price discrepancy and make an arbitrage profit. Thus, UIT and open-end ETFs have the capability to avoid trading at large premiums and discounts to the NAVs. This is in contrast to closed-end index funds, which offer a fixed supply of shares, and as demand changes, they frequently trade at appreciable discounts from—and sometimes premiums to—their NAVs.
- The exposure to capital gains distribution taxes is lower than for traditional funds, so the consequences of other shareholders' redemptions are limited. As mentioned, capital gains resulting from in-kind transfer for redemptions do not create a tax burden for the remaining ETF shareholders. For this reason, capital gains tax liability is expected to be lower for ETF shareholders than for mutual fund shareholders.
- Dividends are reinvested immediately for open-end ETFs (but not for UIT ETFs), whereas for index mutual funds, timing of dividend reinvestment varies.

However, ETFs are not necessarily the most efficient alternative for investing in a market segment.

- In many countries, actively traded ETFs track a narrow-based market index, including only stocks with large market capitalization. So, no ETF is available for mid or low market-cap stocks. This is not the case in the United States, where a variety of ETF products trade actively.

- Many investors do not require the intraday trading opportunity provided by ETFs, because they have a long investment horizon.
- Some ETFs do not have large trading volumes and the bid–ask spread can be quite large. For example, some U.S. ETFs based on some sector indexes or on some foreign indexes (e.g., emerging markets) do not trade actively, and directly investing in a managed fund can be a less costly alternative, especially for large investors. Sector and international ETFs have an expense ratio that can be substantial (close to 1 percent) compared with that of a managed portfolio.
- For large institutional investors, the alternative to international ETFs is to invest directly in an indexed, or actively managed, international portfolio; the costs could be less, and the tax situation equivalent or better.

Types of ETFs ETFs can be grouped by investment category, based on their investment target (broad domestic market index, style, sector/industry, country or region). For a given investment target, ETFs can be created based on different indexes of the same market, as well as by different sponsors. The number of ETFs keeps growing, and the diversity of investment targets increases, although not all ETFs launched are successful. We cite only some notable examples under each of the following categories:

- *Broad domestic market index:* In many countries, the most active ETFs are those launched on the major local stock index. Hong Kong Tracker Fund was the first ETF listed in Asia and the largest ever IPO in Asia excluding Japan. In Japan, Nikkei 225 and TOPIX ETFs have amassed significant assets under management, and there are several competing sponsors offering ETFs on the same indexes. In Europe, ETFs based on the French CAC 40 index and the German DAX 30 index are by far the most actively traded. In the United States, there are many market indexes followed by investors, so there are many competing ETFs; the most notable examples in this category include S&P 500 Depositary Receipts, iShares S&P 500, NASDAQ-100 QQQ and DIA (Diamonds Trust Series tracking the Dow Jones index). There are also ETFs based on very broad U.S. market indexes, such as the Russell 1000, Russell 3000, or Wilshire 5000 indexes. It is fair to say that ETFs based on local market indexes now exist in most countries, including in many emerging countries.
- *Style:* Some ETFs track a specific investment style, namely, value and growth. These ETFs are based on value and growth indexes developed by several index providers. This type of ETF is primarily found in the United States because investors from other countries are less accustomed to style investing, but there are some pan-European and Japanese style ETFs. There also exist ETFs specialized by market capitalization (large, mid, and small cap).
- *Sector or industry:* Some ETFs track a sector index or invest in baskets of stocks from specific industry sectors, including consumer, cyclicals, energy, financial,

health care, industrials, insurance, materials, media, staples, technology, telecommunications, transportation, and utilities. Some ETFs specialize on a narrow sector or industry. For example, some ETFs track indexes of traded U.S. real estate investment trusts (REITs). Sector and industry ETFs can be found in the United States, Europe, and Japan. Many European funds track pan-European or global-sector indexes. In the United States, industry HOLDRs offer a series of investment portfolios that are based not on an index but on a basket of 20 to 50 companies in the same industry.

- *Foreign country or region (multiple countries):* A fast-growing segment of the ETF market is funds tracking foreign-country indexes and regional indexes. In the United States, for example, iShares are indexed to several developed and emerging equity markets as well as to international indexes such as MSCI Europe and EAFE. International ETFs now represent a significant segment of ETFs offered in the United States. Country and regional ETFs have also been launched in Europe and Asia. Again, several sponsors are sometimes competing for products on the same international indexes.

- *Fixed income:* This category is a recent addition to the universe of ETFs, and mostly in the United States. These have had less success than equity ETFs so far.

- *Commodity:* ETFs have been introduced on some commodities, such as precious metals, and on some broad-based commodity index such as the GSCI.

- *Actively managed funds:* Some providers have introduced "active" ETFs in Europe. As of 2007 U.S. listing of active ETFs was also considered by several providers. While relying on the traditional design of ETF products, active ETFs do not intend to passively replicate the performance of an index but rely on active management of the portfolio to manage the risk/return profile. A challenge to actively manage an ETF using some proprietary model is the required daily transparence of ETFs. Active managers do not want to divulge their holdings for fear of being "front-run" by the market. The cost and tax advantage of an ETF structure would also be reduced.

As stressed in Chapter 5, international ETFs have distinguishing features. An ETF indexed on some less-liquid emerging market is bound to have high bid–ask spreads. Managing an ETF on a broad international index means holding stocks from numerous countries with different custodial arrangement and time zones. Again, the bid–ask spreads are bound to be larger than for *plain-vanilla* ETFs. But the size (assets under management) of the ETF is an important factor influencing costs. The effect of non-overlapping time zones should be taken into account when comparing the ETF price and its NAV. Take the example of an ETF on a Japanese stock index, traded in New York. During Wall Street opening hours, the Tokyo stock market is closed. The NAV available in the morning in the United States is based on the closing prices in Tokyo several hours before New York opened. Except for currency fluctuations, the NAV will remain unchanged because Tokyo is closed throughout the New York trading session. However, the ETF price will be affected by expectations about future stock prices in Tokyo, so it could differ significantly from the official NAV. This is not an inefficiency and there are no arbitrage opportunities because the NAV is stale and does not correspond to current market pricing.

Risks in ETFs Listed next are the major risks faced by ETFs. They, however, do not affect all ETFs to the same extent. For example, market risk, trading risk, and tracking error risk affect all ETFs, while sector risk, currency risk, and country risk may affect sector and country ETFs. Likewise, derivatives risk affects only those funds that employ derivatives in their investment strategies. In addition, different ETFs may face risks that are unique to the fund (not discussed in this chapter).

- *Market risk:* ETF shareholders are subject to risks similar to those of holders of other diversified portfolios. The NAV of the ETF will change with changes in the market index tracked by the fund.
- *Asset class/sector risk:* Some ETFs invest in some market segment. The returns from the type of securities in which an ETF invests may underperform returns from the general securities markets or different asset classes. For example, the performance of a sector ETF may be susceptible to any single economic, market, political, or regulatory occurrence. Thus, a sector ETF also may be adversely affected by the performance of that specific sector or group of industries on which it is based. This risk is directly implied by the investment strategy offered by the fund.
- *Trading risk:* Although an ETF is designed to make it likely that it will trade close to its NAV, impediments to the securities markets may result in trading prices that differ, sometimes significantly, from NAV. Moreover, there is no assurance that an active trading market will always exist for the ETF on the exchange, so the bid–ask spread can be large for some ETFs. The overall depth and liquidity of the secondary market also may fluctuate.
- *Tracking error risk:* Although ETFs are designed to provide investment results that generally correspond to the price and yield performance of their respective underlying indexes, the funds/trusts may not be able to exactly replicate the performance of the indexes because of fund/trust expenses and other factors. Tracking risk comes from trading risk (the ETF market price deviates from its NAV), but also from the fact that the ETF NAV differs from the index value.
- *Derivatives risk:* ETFs that invest in index futures contracts and other derivatives to track an index are subject to additional risks that accrue to derivatives, for example, counterparty credit risk and higher leverage.
- *Currency risk and country risk:* ETFs that are based on international indexes may involve risk of capital loss from unfavorable fluctuations in currency values or from economic and political instability in other nations. ETFs invested

in emerging markets bear greater risk of market shutdown and of the imposition of capital controls than those typically found in a developed market. Country risk also includes the risk of expropriation. It could be that foreign investors are discriminated against, so that the return of an ETF will significantly underperform the local market index return achieved by a local investor.

Applications of ETFs ETFs can be used in a wide variety of investment strategies. Following are some suggested popular applications:

- *Implementing asset allocation:* ETFs can be used to effect asset allocation among baskets of stocks and bonds at either the strategic or the tactical level.
- *Diversifying sector/industry exposure:* ETFs on broad market indexes can be used to diversify away the sector- or industry-specific event risks borne in an otherwise undiversified portfolio. Such ETF exposure is a natural complement to an investment strategy of holding only a few attractive stocks.
- *Gaining exposure to international markets:* Money managers can quickly and easily purchase ETFs for instant and extensive international exposure to a single country or multiple countries within a geographic region, compared with the expense and difficulty of assembling a portfolio of foreign securities.
- *Equitizing cash:* By investing in ETFs, money managers can put idle cash to work temporarily while determining where to invest for the longer term. For example, a fund manager using the Nikkei 225 as its benchmark could invest cash inflows into one of the ETFs tied to this benchmark before he decides which stocks to buy. This can minimize cash drag or benchmark risk. It is a convenient alternative to buying futures contract on the market index.
- *Managing cash flows:* Investment managers can take advantage of ETFs' liquidity during periods of cash inflows and outflows. A portfolio manager can establish a position in an ETF that corresponds to the portfolio's benchmark or investment strategy, investing inflows into the ETF and liquidating the position as needed to meet redemptions or invest in specific stocks or bonds.
- *Completing overall investment strategy:* Fund or money managers can use ETFs to quickly establish or increase exposure to an industry or sector to "fill holes" in an overall investment strategy.
- *Bridging transitions in fund management:* Pension plan assets can often lie dormant during times of investment manager appointments, replacements, or shifts. Institutions can use ETFs as a cost-effective method to keep assets invested in the interim.
- *Managing portfolio risk:* Because ETFs can be sold short in a declining equity market (or rising interest rate market for fixed-income ETFs), portfolio managers can use ETFs to hedge overall portfolio risk or sector/industry exposure.

- *Applying relative value, long/short strategies:* Institutions can take advantage of ETF features to apply long/short strategies aimed at increasing returns. For example, an institution can establish a long position in a broad market, country, sector, style, or bond index expected to outperform while shorting an index expected to underperform. Doubling the size of the long position versus the short position can leverage the total position. Market makers can use ETFs to exploit price discrepancies between ETFs, the underlying index, the futures, and/or options.

Real Estate

Real estate is usually considered to be buildings and buildable land, including offices, industrial warehouses, multifamily buildings, and retail space. Real estate is a form of tangible asset, one that can be touched and seen, as opposed to financial claims that are recorded as pieces of paper. Other forms of tangible assets are available for investment purposes. These include natural resources, timber, containers, artwork, and many others. We will focus on real estate, which is by far the most common form of investment in tangible assets.

Real estate as an investment has several unique characteristics as well as several characteristics common to other types of investments. Even the definition of real estate isolates it as a unique investment. Real estate is an immovable asset—land (earth surface) and the permanently attached improvements to it. Graaskamp defines real estate as artificially delineated space with a fourth dimension of time referenced to a fixed point on the face of the earth.[6] This astrophysical definition stresses the idea that ownership rights to earth areas can be divided up not only in the three dimensions of space, but also in a time dimension, as well as divided up among investors. One plot of land with its building can be divided into above ground (e.g., buildings) and below ground (e.g., minerals), into areas within the building (e.g., rooms), and into periods of time (timesharing). Different investors can own the different divisions. Many classifications can be adopted for real estate. Real estate can be classified by usage (office space, multifamily housing, retail space) and location. It can also be classified into four quadrants by form of ownership, public or private, and by form of financing, debt or equity.[7] Clearly, it is not possible to adopt a simple classification of real estate because this asset class covers so many different investment products.

Real estate is an important investment category. In many countries, domestic real estate is a common investment vehicle for pension funds and life insurance companies. It is not uncommon to have private European investors owning and renting directly a few real estate units, such as houses, condominium apartments, or parking spaces. But there are some obstacles for institutions and individuals

[6] Jarchow (1991), p. 42.

[7] See, for example, Hudson-Wilson (2001).

wishing to invest in foreign real estate. First, it is difficult to monitor properties located abroad. Second, taxes, paperwork, and unforeseen risks may make foreign real estate investment impractical on a large scale, although investments can be made through specialized managers in the countries of interest. To be sure, private deals can be arranged for special projects, but these are well beyond the scope of this book. There is, however, a definite trend toward the development of negotiable forms for real property interest. In many countries, pooled funds have been created with the specific purpose of real estate investment. Mortgage-backed Eurobonds are rapidly growing in popularity. Many institutional investors, especially in Europe, have started to invest in international real estate. The time may not be too far off when real estate will be a normal component of international investment strategies.

Forms of Real Estate Investment

There are several forms of real estate investment: free and clear equity, leveraged equity, mortgages, and aggregation vehicles.

Free and Clear Equity *Free and clear equity,* sometimes called *fee simple,* refers to full ownership rights for an indefinite period of time, giving the owner the right, for example, to lease the property to tenants and resell the property at will. This is straightforward purchase of some real estate property.

Leveraged Equity *Leveraged equity* refers to the same ownership rights but subject to debt (a promissory note) and a pledge (mortgage) to hand over real estate ownership rights if the loan terms are not met. A mortgage is a pledge of real estate ownership rights to another party as security for debt owed to that party. Thus, leveraged equity involves equity ownership plus a debt and a requirement to transfer ownership of the equity in case of default on the debt. The debt and the mortgage are usually packaged together into a mortgage loan.

Mortgages Mortgages (or more precisely, *mortgage loans*) themselves are another real estate investment vehicle, representing a type of debt investment. Investing in a mortgage provides the investor with a stream of bondlike payments. These payments include net interest, net of mortgage servicing fees, and a scheduled repayment of principal. This is a form of real estate investment because the creditor may end up owning the property being mortgaged. Mortgage loans often include a clause of early repayment (at a cost) at the option of the debtor. So, the debtholder may also receive excess principal repayments, called mortgage prepayments. These prepayments produce uncertainty in the amount and timing of mortgage cash flows.

To diversify risks, a typical investor does not invest in one mortgage, but in securities issued against a pool of mortgages. An intermediary buys a pool of mortgages and then issues securities backed by the mortgages, but with the securities passing through the net mortgage payments to the investors.

Aggregation Vehicles *Aggregation vehicles* aggregate investors and serve the purpose of giving investors collective access to real estate investments. *Real estate limited partnerships* (*RELPs*) allow investors (the limited partners) to participate in real estate projects while preserving limited liability (the initial investment) and leaving management to the general partners who are real estate experts. *Commingled funds* are pools of capital created largely by like-minded institutional investors organized together by an intermediary to invest chiefly in real estate investment projects. The investors share in the investment rewards according to the amount of capital they invest. Commingled funds can be either open or closed end. Closed-end funds have a set termination date, typically allow no new investors after initiation of the fund, and typically buy and hold a real estate portfolio for the life of the fund, with no reinvestment as sales occur. By contrast, open-end funds have indefinite lives, accept new investors, and revise their real estate portfolios over time. Finally, *real estate investment trusts* (*REITs*) are a type of closed-end investment company. They issue shares that are traded on a stock market, and they invest in various types of real estate. Thus, they aggregate individual investors and provide them easy access to real estate and diversification within real estate. Of course, the risk and return characteristics of REITs depend on the type of investment they make. Mortgage REITs, which invest primarily in mortgages, are more akin to a bond investment, while equity REITs, which invest primarily in commercial or residential properties using leverage, are more akin to an investment in leveraged equity real estate. The shares of REITs trade freely on the stock market, so they are liquid investments, but their share price can trade at a discount (or premium) to the NAV of the properties in their portfolio.

Valuation Approaches

Real estate assets are quite different from securities traded on a financial market: "Because the real estate market is not an auction market offering divisible shares in every property, and information flows in the market are complex, these features place a premium on investment judgment. Managers who want to own some of IBM simply buy some shares. Managers who want to participate in the returns on, say, a $300 million office building must take a significant position in the property."[8] Following are some characteristics of real estate as an investable asset class:

- Properties are immovable, basically indivisible, and unique assets, as contrasted to fungible (perfectly interchangeable) and divisible assets such as currencies. Though unique, even art is movable and thus not as unique as real estate.
- Properties are only approximately comparable to other properties.
- Properties are generally illiquid, due to their immobility and indivisibility.
- There is no national, or international, auction market for properties. Hence, the "market" value of a given property is difficult to assess.

[8] Firstenberg, Ross, and Zisler (1988).

- Transaction costs and management fees for real estate investments are high.
- Real estate markets suffer inefficiencies because of the nature of real estate itself and because information is not freely available.

Valuation of real estate focuses on intrinsic value just as does the valuation of any asset. In real estate, the term *appraisal* is used for the process of estimating the market and the investment value of the property. The market value estimate is independent of the particular investor, but the investment value depends on the particular use that the investor plans for the property.

To estimate a property's value, a real estate appraiser generally uses one of three approaches or a combination of the approaches. The approaches are the cost approach, the sales comparison approach, and the income approach. An investor can further take into account her specific tax situation to value the property using a discounted after-tax cash flow approach. These four approaches are used worldwide.

The Cost Approach The cost approach is analogous to the use of replacement cost of total assets in the calculation of Tobin's Q for equity valuation. What would it cost to replace the building in its present form? Of course, an estimate of the land value must be added to the building replacement cost estimate. The replacement cost approach is relatively easy to implement because it is based on current construction costs, but it suffers from severe limitations. First, an appraisal of the land value is required and that is not always an easy task. Second, the market value of an existing property could differ markedly from its construction cost. An office building could be very valuable because it has some prestigious and stable tenants that pay high rents, not because of the value of the construction. Conversely, an office building in poor condition, with a large vacancy rate and in a bad neighborhood, could be worth much less than its replacement cost.

The Sales Comparison Approach The sales comparison approach is similar to the "price multiple comparables" approach in equity valuation. Market value is estimated relative to a benchmark value. The benchmark value may be the market price of a similar property, or the average or median value of the market prices of similar properties, in transactions made near the time of the appraisal. The benchmark-based estimate needs to be adjusted for changing market conditions, the possibility that the benchmark itself is mispriced, and the unique features of the property relative to the benchmark. Properties with comparable characteristics might not have traded recently.

One formal variation of the sales comparison approach is the method of *hedonic price estimation*. In this method, the major characteristics of a property that can affect its value are identified. The characteristics of a residential property that are relevant to its value can be the age of the building, its size, its location, its vacancy rate, its amenities, and so on. Individual properties are given a quantitative rating for each of the characteristics. For example, location could be ranked from 1 (very bad) to 10 (very good). The sales price for all recent transactions of the properties in the benchmark are then regressed on their characteristics ratings. This is a regression in which there is one observation for each transaction. The dependent (left-hand side) variable is the transaction price, and the independent (right-hand side) variables are the ratings for each of the characteristics. The estimated slope coefficients are the valuation of each characteristic in the transaction price. The result is a benchmark monetary value associated with each characteristic's rating. It is then possible to estimate the selling price of a specific property by taking into account its rating on each feature (see Example 8.2). Although this has become a standard technique in residential property appraisal, it has also been applied to income producing property.[9]

EXAMPLE 8.2 SALES COMPARISON APPROACH: HEDONIC PRICE MODEL

A real estate company has prepared a simple hedonic model to value houses in a specific area. Here is a summary list of the house's characteristics that can affect pricing:

- The number of main rooms
- The surface area of the garden
- The presence of a swimming pool
- The distance to a shopping center

A statistical analysis of a large number of recent transactions in the area allowed the company to estimate the following slope coefficients:

Characteristics	Units	Slope Coefficient in Pounds per Unit
Number of rooms	Number	20,000
Surface area of the garden	Square feet	5
Swimming pool	0 or 1	20,000
Distance to shopping center	In miles	−10,000

A typical house in the area has five main rooms, a garden of 10,000 square feet, a swimming pool, and a distance of one mile to the nearest shopping center. The transaction price for a typical house was £160,000.

You wish to value a house that has seven rooms, a garden of 10,000 square feet, a swimming pool, and a distance of two miles to the nearest shopping center. What is the appraisal value based on this sales comparison approach of hedonic price estimation?

SOLUTION

The appraised value is given by the equation

$$\text{Value} = 20{,}000 \times (\#\ \text{Rooms}) + 5 \times (\text{Garden surface}) + 20{,}000 \times (\text{Pool}) - 10{,}000 \times (\text{Distance to shopping center})$$

[9] See Söderberg (2002), pp. 157–180.

$$= 20{,}000 \times 7 + 5 \times 10{,}000 + 20{,}000 \times 1 - 10{,}000 \times 2$$
$$= £190{,}000$$

This specific house has an appraised value of £190,000. Compared to the typical house in the area, it has two more rooms but is one mile farther from the nearest shopping center.

The Income Approach The income approach to real estate valuation values property using a perpetuity discount type of model. The perpetuity is the annual net operating income (NOI). This perpetual stream is discounted at a market required rate of return (the market capitalization or cap rate). NOI is gross potential income minus expenses, which include estimated vacancy and collection losses, insurance, taxes, utilities, and repairs and maintenance. Technically, the market cap rate is the rate used by the market in recent transactions to capitalize future income into a present market value. For a constant and perpetual stream of annual NOI, we have

$$\text{Appraisal price} = \frac{\text{NOI}}{\text{Market cap rate}}$$

And the market cap rate is calculated on the benchmark transactions as

$$\text{Market cap rate} = \frac{\text{Benchmark NOI}}{\text{Benchmark transaction price}}$$

Benchmark may refer to a single comparable property or the median or mean of several comparable properties, with any appropriate adjustments. A numerical illustration is presented in Example 8.3.

It must be stressed that the income approach makes the simplifying assumption of a constant and perpetual amount of annual income. The income approach can also be adjusted for the special cases of a constant growth rate in rentals or a constant growth rate in rentals coupled with long-term leases. Valuation with a constant growth rate in rentals parallels the constant growth dividend discount model. Inflation could make NOI grow at the inflation rate over time. As long as inflation can be passed through, it will not affect valuation, because the market cap rate also incorporates the inflation rate. In the long-term lease case, the growth in rentals is not fully reflected in the NOI growth rate. The rent remains fixed over the term of the lease, while costs grow at the inflation rate. This is analogous to the inflation pass-through question raised in equity valuation (see Chapter 6). If expected inflation will cause operating expenses to rise, how much of the inflation can the owner pass through to the tenants? Longer lease terms delay the pass-through. Another limitation of this approach is that all calculations are performed before tax.

EXAMPLE 8.3 THE INCOME APPROACH

An investor wants to evaluate an apartment complex using the income approach. Recent sales in the area consist of an office building and an apartment complex. He gathers the following data on the apartment complex, as well as on recent sales in the area. All income items are on an annual basis. According to the income approach, what is the value of the apartment complex?

	Apartment Investment under Consideration	Office Building Recently Sold	Apartment Complex Recently Sold
Gross potential rental income	$120,000		
Estimated vacancy and collection losses	6%		
Insurance and taxes	$10,000		
Utilities	$7,000		
Repairs and maintenance	$12,000		
Depreciation	$14,000		
Interest on proposed financing	$11,000		
Net operating income		$300,000	$60,000
Sales price		$2,000,000	$500,000

SOLUTION

The NOI for the apartment complex is gross potential rental income minus estimated vacancy and collection costs minus insurance and taxes minus utilities minus repairs and maintenance.

$$\text{NOI} = 120{,}000 - 0.06 \times 120{,}000 - 10{,}000 - 7{,}000 - 12{,}000 = 83{,}800$$

The other apartment complex is the comparable property, and that has a capitalization rate of

$$\text{NOI}/(\text{Transaction price}) = 60{,}000/500{,}000 = 0.12$$

Applying this cap rate to the apartment complex under consideration gives an appraisal price of

$$\text{NOI}/(\text{Cap rate}) = 83{,}800/0.12 = \$698{,}333$$

Note that we do not use the financing costs to determine the NOI, because we wish to appraise the value of the property independently of its financing. Neither do we subtract depreciation. The implicit assumption is that repairs and maintenance will allow the investor to keep the building in good condition forever.

The Discounted After-Tax Cash Flow Approach Supplementing the cost, sales comparison, and income approach used for market value appraisals, the discounted after-tax cash flow approach is a check on investment valuation. If the investor can deduct depreciation and any interest payments from NOI, then the investor's after-tax cash flows depend on the investor's marginal tax rate. Hence, the value of a property for a specific investor depends on the investor's marginal tax rate. Once these cash flows and after-tax proceeds from future property disposition are estimated, the net present value of the property to an equity investor is obtained as the present value of the cash flows, discounted at the investor's required rate of return on equity, minus the amount of equity required to make the investment.

For an equity investment to be worthwhile, its expected net present value must be positive. Alternatively, the investment's yield (internal rate of return) should exceed the investor's required rate of return. A numerical illustration is presented in Example 8.4.

EXAMPLE 8.4 THE DISCOUNTED CASH FLOW APPROACH

An analyst is assigned the task of evaluating a real estate investment project. The purchase price is $700,000, which is financed 20 percent by equity and 80 percent by a mortgage loan at a 10 percent pretax interest rate. According to the applicable country's tax rules, the interest on real estate financing for this project is tax deductible. The mortgage loan has a long maturity and level annual payments of $59,404. This includes interest payments on the remaining principal at a 10 percent interest rate and a variable principal repayment that steps up with time. The analyst calculated NOI in the first year to be $83,800. NOI is expected to grow at a rate of 5 percent every year.

The analyst faces the following valuation tasks: determining the first year's after-tax cash flow, determining interim after-tax cash flows, determining the final year's after-tax cash flow, and calculating two measures of the project's profitability, the investment's net present value (NPV) and the investment's yield (internal rate of return).

i. Determine the first year's after-tax cash flow using the following data:

Net operating income (NOI) for first year	$83,800
Straight-line depreciation	$18,700
Mortgage payment	$59,404
Purchase price	$700,000
80% financing at a 10% interest rate	
NOI growth rate	5%
Marginal income tax rate	31%

ii. Determine the second year's after-tax cash flow, using the preceding table and with a growth rate of 5% in NOI.

iii. The property is sold at the end of the fifth year. Determine the after-tax cash flow for that property sale year, using the following data (the after-tax cash flow without property sale has been calculated as previously).

After-tax cash flow without property sale	$33,546
Straight-line depreciation	$18,700
Mortgage payment	$59,404
Cumulative mortgage principal repayments by end of fifth year	$20,783
Purchase price	$700,000
80% financing at 10% interest rate	
NOI growth factor	5%
Marginal income tax rate	31%
Capital gains tax rate	20%
Forecasted sales price	$875,000
Property sales expense as a percentage of sales price	6%

Use the information below to answer Parts iv and v.

The following data summarize the after-tax cash flows for all five years of the project's life (the table includes the results we have calculated previously for years 1, 2, and 5, as well as results for years 3 and 4):

Year	**1**	**2**	**3**	**4**	**5**
Cash flow	21,575	24,361	27,280	30,339	273,629

The analyst now turns to evaluating whether the project should be undertaken. She estimates the required rate of return for an equity investment in projects of similar risk as 16 percent. The purchase price for the property is $700,000. The financing plan calls for 80 percent debt financing, so the equity investment is only $140,000. The investor's cost of equity for projects with this level of risk is 16 percent, but a sensitivity analysis on cost of equity helps provide some perspective for the analyst. She decides to conduct a sensitivity analysis, calculating the present value of the year 1 to year 5 after-tax cash flows using a range of discount rates other than 16 percent; the results appear in the following table:

Discount Rate	**Present Value**
0.10	$250,867
0.14	$216,161
0.18	$187,637
0.22	$164,012
0.26	$144,303
0.30	$127,747
0.34	$113,750

iv. Determine the real estate project's NPV, using the analyst's required rate of return, and make a purchase recommendation based only on this analysis.

v. Determine an approximate yield for the real estate project, and make a purchase recommendation based only on this analysis.

SOLUTION TO i

Because interest is tax deductible here, calculate the first year's interest, and then calculate after-tax net income. The amount borrowed is $560,000 = 700,000 × 0.8. The first year's interest at 10 percent is then $56,000 = 0.1 × $560,000. After-tax net income is then ($83,800 − $18,700 − $56,000) × (1 − 0.31) = $6,279.

To get after-tax cash flow from after-tax net income, depreciation must be added and the principal repayment component of the $59,404 mortgage payment must be subtracted. The principal repayment is the mortgage payment minus the interest payment, or $3,404 = $59,404 − $56,000. Thus, the after-tax cash flow is $21,575 = $6,279 + $18,700 − $3,404.

SOLUTION TO ii

First we calculate the new NOI, equal to $87,990 = $83,800 × (1.05).

Second, we calculate after-tax net income. We need to calculate the second year's interest payment on the mortgage balance after the first year's payment. This mortgage balance is the original principal balance minus the first year's principal repayment, or $556,596. The interest on this balance is then $55,660. After-tax net income is then ($87,990 − $18,700 − $55,660) × (1 − 0.31) = $9,405.

Third, the second year's principal repayment is the mortgage payment minus the interest payment, or $3,744 = $59,404 − $55,660.

Finally, then calculate the second year's after-tax cash flow, which equals the second year's after-tax net income plus depreciation minus the principal repayment, or $24,361 = $9,405 + $18,700 − $3,744.

SOLUTION TO iii

The after-tax cash flow for the property sale year is equal to the sum of the after-tax cash flow without the property sale plus the after-tax cash flow from the property sale. When a property is sold, the outstanding mortgage principal balance (the outstanding mortgage, for short) must be paid to the lender. In the following calculations, we incorporate that effect into the after-tax cash flow from the property sale.

To begin, we calculate the capital gains on the sale of the property. To do that, first determine the ending book value as the original purchase price minus five years' worth of depreciation, or $606,500 = $700,000 − 5 × $18,700. The net sale price is equal to the forecasted sale price, $875,000, minus sales expenses of 6 percent, or $52,500. Capital gains taxes are paid on the difference between the net sales price and the book value, or a difference of \$216,000 = (\$875,000 − \$52,500) − \$606,500. The capital gains taxes are then \$43,200 = 0.2 × \$216,000. The after-tax cash flow from the property sale is then the net sales price minus the outstanding mortgage minus the capital gains taxes. The outstanding mortgage is the original mortgage minus five years' worth of principal repayments, or \$539,217 = \$560,000 − \$20,783. Thus the after-tax cash flow from the property sale is \$240,083 = (\$875,000 − \$52,500) − \$539,217 − \$43,200. The after-tax cash flow for the property sale year is then \$273,629 = \$33,546 + \$240,083.

SOLUTION TO iv

At a cost of equity of 16 percent, the present value of the cash flow is \$201,215 = \$21,575/1.16 + \$24,361/1.16^2 + \$27,280/1.16^3 + \$30,339/1.16^4 + \$273,629/1.16^5. The investment requires equity of \$140,000 = 0.2 × \$700,000. Thus, the NPV is \$61,215 = \$201,215 − \$140,000. The analyst recommends this investment because it has a positive NPV.

SOLUTION TO v

We can address the question using the results of the analyst's sensitivity analysis. The yield or internal rate of return is the discount rate that makes the project's NPV equal to zero. The yield must be between 26 percent and 30 percent because discounting at 26 percent gives a present value (\$144,303) that is larger than the initial investment (of \$140,000), or a positive NPV, while discounting at 30 percent gives a present value (\$127,747) that is smaller than the initial investment, or a negative NPV. Consequently, the project's yield must lie between 26 percent and 30 percent. Actually, the internal rate of return of this project is slightly below 27 percent. The analyst recommends the investment because the investment's yield exceeds the investor's required rate of return (16 percent).

Real Estate in a Portfolio Context

Some real estate indexes have been developed to attempt to measure the average return on real estate investment. Good-quality indexes with a long-term historical record exist in the United States and United Kingdom, but they are more recent in other countries. There are also global real estate indexes.

Real estate returns consist of income and capital gain or loss. The income on a property can usually be measured in a straightforward fashion. The value appreciation is more difficult to assess. The most common method is to use changes in *appraised* value. Appraisal of each property is conducted by specialists fairly infrequently (typically once a year). Appraisals are generally based on the approaches discussed previously. In practice, appraisal prices exhibit remarkable inertia. The value of a real estate portfolio is further smoothed because properties are appraised infrequently, so their prices remain constant between appraisals.

The major U.S. real estate index based on appraisal values is the National Council of Real Estate Investment Fiduciaries (NCREIF) property index, or NPI. This is a quarterly index, starting in 1978 and broken down by regions and property types.

Another method of measuring price appreciation is to use a reference to REITs. The total return on a REIT is made up of the income paid to shareholders as well as the stock market appreciation of the REIT share price. Various REIT indexes are used to proxy the average total return on real estate investments. REIT indexes are easy to construct because they are simply some weighted average of market-traded shares. The major REIT indexes are as follows:

- The National Association of Real Estate Investment Trusts (NAREIT), a monthly index of over 100 REITs, starting in 1972
- REIT indexes published by various institutions, for example, Dow Jones Wilshire or MSCI

For all the REIT indexes mentioned above, one can access a global index, broken down by regions or individual countries.

Appraisal based indexes and REIT stock market indexes provide very different performance and risk characteristics for real estate. Appraisal-based indexes are much less volatile than REIT indexes. For example, Goetzmann and Ibbotson (1990) found that a REIT index had an annual standard deviation of 15.4 percent, comparable to that of the S&P 500 index but six times larger than that of an appraisal-based index of 2.6 percent. Furthermore, appraisal-based indexes and REIT indexes have very little correlation. Appraisal-based indexes exhibit persistent returns (returns are correlated over time), showing the inertia in appraisals. REIT indexes are strongly correlated with the rest of the stock market.

In summary, real estate returns can be calculated using either appraisal indexes or REIT indexes. Appraisals do not provide continuous price data, and they do not provide market prices but only market price estimates. REIT indexes provide continuous market prices of REITs but not of the underlying real estate. Thus, they reflect the amount of leverage used in the REITs. Therefore neither approach to calculating returns is entirely satisfactory. In any case, the issue in investment is one of forecasting returns, standard deviations, and correlations. For example, in analyzing a particular real estate project, an investor would supplement cash flow forecasts and discounted cash flow analysis with considerations of how the project's cash flows will covary with his existing portfolio. An individual investor will not receive diversification benefits from a real estate project whose returns are highly correlated with his own business employment income.

A few studies have looked at real estate from a global viewpoint. These studies examine the proposed portfolio benefits of real estate, risk reduction (through diversification), and inflation protection. These studies involve either appraisal-based real estate indexes or returns on publicly traded real companies such as REITs. Eichholtz (1996) looked at the diversification benefits of real estate shares quoted in many countries. He found that international diversification strongly reduces the risk of a real estate portfolio. The argument seems even stronger than for international equity diversification because the international correlation of real estate appears lower than that of equity. Hoesli, Lekander, and Witkiewicz (2004) confirm that international diversification is useful within a real estate portfolio. They also show that real estate provides a useful element of diversification within a portfolio of stocks and bonds. Their study uses appraisal-based indexes, with their well-known smoothing characteristic, although they attempt to correct for it. However, Mull and Soenen (1997) showed that REITs are strongly correlated with other U.S. stocks, so that foreign investors who buy U.S. REITs do not gain a large diversification benefit beyond the U.S. stock market exposure. Quan and Titman (1997) studied commercial real estate values in 17 countries where property values and rents are calculated using an appraisal-based approach. Commercial real estate prices and stock prices are both affected by the general level of economic activity, so they should be correlated. Pooling their international data, Quan and Titman did find that the relation between stock returns and changes in real estate values is strong. Two other statistical properties of real estate prices are worth mentioning. Liu, Hartzell, and Hoesli (1997) looked at real estate securities traded on seven national stock markets and concluded that their correlation with inflation is low, so they do not provide a good hedge against inflation. Furthermore, there is a general finding that real estate prices tend to react negatively to interest rate levels and changes.

Although research studies have not provided overwhelming evidence to support the risk reduction and inflation protection benefits of real estate, such studies are always limited by the use of either appraisal indexes or REIT indexes. Judgment is needed in assessing the impact of real estate on a portfolio. First, what are the projected cash flows and what are the predicted covariances of the cash flows with the current portfolio? Second, what are the inflation pass-through characteristics of the real estate investment?

Private Equity

Private equity investing has grown rapidly in the 2000s. *Private equity* is a broad term that commonly refers to an equity investment in a potentially successful company or asset not publicly traded on capital market. *Private equity investments* are equity investments that are not traded on exchanges. Institutional and individual investors usually invest in private equity through limited partnerships, which allow investors (the limited partners) to participate in a portfolio of private equity projects while preserving limited liability (the initial investment) and leaving management to the general partners, who are private equity experts. General partners often get involved in the management of the companies they invest in. Typically, the general partners are associated with a firm that specializes in private equity or with the private equity department of a financial institution. The limited partnership is often called the fund, and the general partners are sometimes designated as the management company (although at times that is a separate company affiliated with the general partner). Funds of funds are also offered that pool investments in several private equity funds. There are several overlapping categories of private equity investing. The three main categories are described below.

Venture capital is one of the main categories of private equity investing and the most traditional one. Venture capital investments are private equity investments in business ventures from idea stage through expansion of a company already producing and selling a product and through preparation for exit from the investment via buyout or initial public offering. Venture capital investing may be done at several stages along the way, but eventual exit is a primary consideration. By its very nature, such investing requires a horizon of several years and the willingness to accept several failures for every success in the venture capital portfolio: The possibly enormous return on the winning venture must compensate for many likely failed ventures. Venture capital is detailed below.

Leveraged buyout investing has become the largest category of private equity. Buyout investors typically take a majority control in acquired companies, as opposed to venture capitalists who only take a minority interest. These companies are established, ongoing concerns and are often publicly traded on some exchange. In buyouts, investors put up an equity stake, typically between 20 and 40 percent of the total purchase price, and borrow the rest; hence the term *leveraged.* After acquisition, the purchased company is taken private. The private equity firm gets involved in the management of the acquired company and takes steps to increase its value. The objective is to resell the acquired company, or part of it, within a few years at a higher price. The sale is done privately or through an *initial public offering (IPO).* A *management buyout* (*MBO*) is a special form of leveraged buyout in which the managers of the acquired company become large investors in the company after its privatization. Large buyouts of public companies can exceed $10 billion and make news headlines. But there are also numerous deals involving "middle market" companies that enter the portfolio of companies held by a private equity fund. The leveraged buyout market has become global; private equity firms from many nationalities invest all over the world, including in emerging countries. While the concept of leveraged buyout investing is simple, success primarily depends on the ability of the managers to restructure the portfolio companies to extract value when they are taken private.

Distressed investing, also called *special situations* or *vulture investing,* refers to investing in the equity and debt of companies in financial distress. Because the private equity firm typically buys out the distressed company, there is some overlap with the previous category. But debtholders have a priority claim over equity holders, so any improvement in the company's situation will first accrue to debtholders. The concept is to invest in operationally sound, financially distressed companies and to reorganize them. A further discussion of distressed investing is provided later in the chapter.

It must be stressed that hedge funds (described on page 351) have also ventured into private equity, especially in buyouts of small companies and distressed-debt investing. While most hedge funds shy away from taking control of companies and restructuring them, instead focusing on somewhat liquid financial investments, many experts predict that the move into private equity is a natural progression for hedge funds, so the line between private equity funds and hedge funds will get blurred.

The rest of this section is devoted to venture capital, which is the original form of private equity investment. The success of buyouts and distress investing relies on the restructuring of the acquired companies, a topic beyond the scope of this book.

Stages of Venture Capital Investing

Schilit (1996) provides a good review of the various stages of venture capital investing. Several rounds of financing take place, and these can be characterized by where they occur in the development of the venture itself. Here, Schilit's classification review is adapted and blended with other common industry terminology.[10] Each stage of financing is matched by investments, so that aggregate investment activity is often reported by the amount in different stage funds.

1. *Seed-stage* financing is capital provided for a business idea. The capital generally supports product development and market research.
2. *Early stage* financing is capital provided for companies moving into operation and before commercial manufacturing and sales have occurred.
   - *Start-up* is capital provided for companies just moving into operation but without any commercial product or service sales. The capital generally supports product development and initial marketing.
   - *First-stage* financing is capital provided to initiate commercial manufacturing and sales.
3. *Formative-stage* financing includes seed stage and early stage.
4. *Later-stage* financing is capital provided after commercial manufacturing and sales have begun but before any initial public offering.
   - *Second-stage* financing refers to capital used for initial expansion of a company already producing and selling a product but perhaps not yet profitably.
   - *Third-stage* financing is capital provided for major expansion, such as physical plant expansion, product improvement, or a major marketing campaign.
   - *Mezzanine* (bridge) financing is capital provided to prepare for the step of going public and represents the bridge between the expanding company and the initial public offering (IPO).

Expansion-stage financing includes second and third stage. *Balanced-stage* financing is a term used to refer to all the stages, seed through mezzanine.

10 See, for example, Thomson Venture Economics, the National Venture Capital Association (in the United States), the European Venture Capital Association, and the British Venture Capital Association.

Investment Characteristics

Venture capital investing has several characteristics, some of which are common to alternative investing in general, but many of which are unique:

- *Illiquidity:* Venture capital investments do not provide an easy or short-term path for cashing out. Liquidation or divestment of each venture within a portfolio is dependent on the success of the fund manager in creating a buy-out or IPO opportunity. One particular risk is that inexperienced venture fund managers will "grandstand" and bring ventures to the market too early, especially when the IPO market is good. Conversely, a poor IPO market may mean that otherwise successful ventures may afford no immediate path to liquidity.
- *Long-term commitment required:* Venture capital requires a long-term commitment because of the time lag to liquidity. If the average investor is averse to illiquidity, there will be a liquidity risk premium on venture capital. Thus, an investor with a longer than average time horizon can expect to profit from this liquidity risk premium. It is not surprising that university endowments (with their long horizons) have sought venture capital vehicles.
- *Difficulty in determining current market values:* Because there is no continuous trading of the investments within a venture fund portfolio, there is no objective way of determining the current market value of the portfolio. This poses a problem for reporting the market value exposure of the current venture capital portion of an investor's portfolio.
- *Limited historical risk and return data:* Because there is no continuous market in venture capital, historical risk and return data have limitations.
- *Limited information:* Because entrepreneurs operate in previously uncharted territory, there is little information on which to base estimates of cash flows or the probability of success of their ventures.
- *Entrepreneurial/management mismatches:* Although surely profit motivated, some entrepreneurs may be more wedded to the success of their favorite idea than to the financial success of the venture. During the early life of a firm, there are also two major problems that may arise. First, the entrepreneur may not be a good manager, so the existence or creation of a good management team is critical. Second, rapid growth produces a change in the type of managerial expertise required, so that entrepreneurs/managers who can succeed with small ventures need the ability to adapt to the different demands of larger companies, or the investors must be in a position to replace them.
- *Fund manager incentive mismatches:* Fund managers may be rewarded by size of their fund rather than by performance of their fund. Investors interested in performance must look for fund managers whose incentives are aligned with theirs.

- *Lack of knowledge of how many competitors exist:* Because entrepreneurs operate in uncharted territory, there is often little way for them or for analysts to know how many other entrepreneurs are developing substitute ideas or products at the same time. Thus, competitive analysis for venture capital investments is even more difficult than for investments in established companies in established industries.

- *Vintage cycles:* Some years are better than others. Both entry and exit are factors here. If too many entrepreneurial firms enter at the prompt of increased venture capital availability, the economics of perfect competition will prevail and returns will be weak. On the exit side, poor financial market conditions can cause venture capital to dry up, and perhaps some firms that could be successful will not find the financing needed for their success. Thus, some years provide better firm planting and growing conditions than others.

- *Extensive operations analysis and advice may be required:* More than financial engineering skill is required of fund managers. Venture capital investments require extensive investment analysis, but they also require extensive operating management experience. Thus, a venture capital manager who can add value will be the one who has both financial and operating experience, and knowledge of the emerging industry in which the entrepreneur is operating. The venture capital manager must be able to act as both a financial and an operations management consultant to the venture. Reflecting David Swensen's philosophy[11] at the Yale Endowment, the investor is well advised to choose a fund manager who knows the business and can add value.

Types of Liquidation/Divestment[12]

Exit strategies are critical for venture capital investing. The main types of liquidation/divestment are trade sales, IPOs followed by the sale of quoted equity, and write-offs. Trade sales are sales or mergers of the private company for cash or stock of the acquirer. An IPO is the initial issuance of shares registered for public trading. Shares are distributed to the private equity investors who can sell them in the marketplace only after the expiration of a lock-up period. (In rare cases, a sale or merger of the private company follows the IPO.) Write-offs are voluntary liquidations that may or may not produce any proceeds. In addition to the main types of liquidation, there are cases of bankruptcy as well as the situation in which the founder/entrepreneur buys out the outside venture capital investors and takes the company back to a privately held company without institutional shareholders.

Participating in a venture capital fund, investors get distributions of public stock or cash from realized venture capital investments. The fund may require additional investments (drawdowns) from limited partners and may make cash or

[11] See pages 17 and 18 in Lerner (2000).

[12] This section has benefited from correspondence with Dean Takahashi.

share distributions at random times during the life of the fund. Investors might also be able to sell their interests if they can find a buyer. Also, at the end of the fund's life, there are often illiquid, barely alive companies ("living dead") that are transferred to a liquidating vehicle with minimal fees. A very few funds have an evergreen type of structure, which rolls old fund investments into a new fund that has new cash commitments.

Valuation and Performance Measurement

In the venture capital area, valuation and performance measurement is a difficult exercise. This is true at the level of a single venture project, but also at the level of an investment in a venture capital fund.

Valuation and Project Risk Valuing a prospective venture capital project is a challenging task. Although some valuation methods can be applied, quantifying future cash flows is difficult. Investing in a particular venture capital project is motivated by an anticipated large payoff at time of exit. But many projects will fail along the way. In addition to the normal risk of equity investments, the particular risk of venture capital stems from the increased uncertainty created by possibly inexperienced entrepreneurs with innovative products or product ideas and uncertain time to success, even if successful. Some of the unique risks of venture capital projects come from their investment characteristics, as described. Of course, the risk of a portfolio of venture capital investments is less than the risk of any individual venture project, because of risk diversification.

So, there are three main parameters that enter into valuing a venture capital project:

- An assessment of the expected payoff at time of exit, if the venture is successful
- An assessment of the time it will take to exit the venture successfully
- An assessment of the probability of failure

This is illustrated in Example 8.5.

The payoff structure of actual projects is generally more complex than that of Example 8.5. Practitioners may use a multiple-scenario approach to valuation. In this approach, payoffs are simulated under each scenario (from optimistic to pessimistic) and weighted by the probability of occurrence of the scenario.

Performance Measurement Investors in a venture capital fund need to evaluate the performance of their investment not only at time of liquidation but also during the life of their investment. This is usually done by calculating an internal rate of return based on cash flows since inception and the end-of-period valuation of the unliquidated remaining holdings (residual value or net asset value). The European Private Equity and Venture Capital Association (www.evca.com), the British Private Equity and Venture Capital Association (www.bvca.co.uk), and CFA Institute have valuation guidelines bearing on this.

EXAMPLE 8.5 VENTURE CAPITAL VALUATION AND RISK

An investor estimates that investing $1 million in a particular venture capital project will pay $16 million at the end of seven years if it succeeds; however, she realizes that the project may fail at any time between now and the end of seven years. The investor is considering an equity investment in the project and her cost of equity for a project with this level of risk is 18 percent. In the following table are the investor's estimates of some probabilities of failure for the project. First, 0.25 is the probability of failure in year 1. For year 2, 0.25 is the probability that the project fails in the second year, given that it has survived through year 1. For year 3, 0.20 is the probability that the project fails, given that it has survived through year 2, and so forth.

Year	1	2	3	4	5	6	7
Failure probability	0.25	0.22	0.20	0.20	0.20	0.20	0.20

i. Determine the probability that the project survives to the end of the seventh year.

ii. Determine the expected NPV of the project.

iii. Make a recommendation.

SOLUTION

i. The probability that the project survives to the end of the first year is (1 – 0.25) = 1 minus the probability of failure in the first year; the probability that it survives to the end of the second year is the product of the probability it survives the first year times the probability it survives the second year, or (1 – 0.25) (1 – 0.22). Using this pattern, the probability that the firm survives to the end of the seventh year is (1 – 0.25) (1 – 0.22) $(1 - 0.20)^5 = (0.75)\ (0.78)\ (0.80)^5 = 0.192$ or 19.2%.

ii. The NPV of the project, given that it survives to the end of the seventh year and thus earns $16 million, equals $4.02 million = –$1 million + $16 million/$1.18^7$. The NPV of project given that it fails is –$1 million. Thus, the project's expected NPV is a probability-weighted average of these two amounts, or (0.192) ($4.02 million) + (0.808) (–$1 million) = –$36,160.

iii. Based on its negative NPV, the recommendation is to decline the investment.

There are several challenges to performance measurement in the venture capital area. Lerner (2000) points these out in a discussion of future directions for an endowment fund:

- The difficulty in determining precise valuations. Venture capital funds do not have market prices to value their holdings, so they use some arbitrary technique to value their portfolios of ongoing projects. For example, some managers apply an average internal rate of return to the historical investment costs of their ongoing projects. Of course, the actual exit value is used at the time of exit of a project, or a zero value is used if a project failed.

- The lack of meaningful benchmarks against which fund manager and investment success can be measured.
- The long-term nature of any reliable performance feedback in the venture capital asset class.

Hedge Funds and Absolute Return Strategies

The early 1990s saw the explosive development of *hedge funds*. Even though the attraction of these funds was tempered by many huge losses suffered in 1994 and 1998, the hedge fund industry continued to prosper. The assets under management of hedge funds passed the $2 trillion mark in 2007, and the number of hedge funds was estimated to be over 13,000 in mid-2007.[13] The growth in the past few years has been explosive. On the global scene, the asset base of hedge funds managed in the United States tends to dominate, but many hedge fund managers are based in Europe (especially London) and Asia is starting to develop a hedge fund industry.

Although wealthy individual investors have been the traditional client bases of hedge funds, institutional investors, especially endowments and foundations, have started to invest en masse. We start this section by describing the different types of hedge funds available, including funds of funds. A discussion of the leverage and unique risk characteristics of hedge funds will complete this description. Hedge funds follow strategies that promise a large absolute return and deserve a close investigation of the actual performance and risk of those strategies. We therefore present the case for investing in hedge funds in some detail, but we also provide the caveats.

Definition of Hedge Funds

Objective It is difficult to provide a general definition of hedge funds. The original concept of a hedge fund was to offer plays *against* the markets, using short selling, futures, and other derivative products. Today, funds using the hedge fund appellation follow all kinds of strategies and cannot be considered a homogeneous asset class. Some funds are highly leveraged; others are not. Some engage in hedging activities; others do not. Some focus on making macroeconomic bets on commodities, currencies, interest rates, and so on. Some are mostly "technical" funds trying to take advantage of the mispricing of some securities within their

[13] See *www.HedgeFund.net*.

market. Futures funds belong to the world of hedge funds. In fact, the common denominator of hedge funds is not their investment strategy but the *search for absolute returns.*

Money management has progressively moved toward a focus on performance *relative to preassigned benchmarks.* An institutional money manager's performance is generally evaluated relative to some market index that is assigned as a mandate. In turn, these benchmarks guide (some would say unduly constrain) the money manager's investment policy. The risk of deviating from the performance of the benchmark has become huge, given all of the publicity surrounding relative performance in a very competitive money management industry. The development of hedge funds can be seen as a reaction against this trend, with the search for absolute return in all directions. In practice, this means that hedge funds might have more appropriately been termed *isolation funds.* They generally try to isolate specific bets for the purpose of generating alpha. One can infer the particular bet from each hedge fund position. Hedge fund managers seek freedom to achieve high absolute returns and wish to be rewarded for their performance. These objectives are apparent in the legal organization and the fee structure of hedge funds. These two aspects are probably the only uniform characteristics of hedge funds.

Legal Structure Hedge funds are typically set up as a *limited partnership, limited liability corporation* (in the United States), or *offshore corporation.* These legal structures allow the fund manager to take short and long positions in any asset, to use all kinds of derivatives, and to leverage the fund without restrictions.

Hedge funds based in the United States most often take the form of a limited partnership organized under section 3(c)(1) or section 3(c)(7) of the Investment Company Act of 1940, thereby gaining exemption from registration with the U.S. Securities and Exchange Commission (SEC) and therefore from most SEC regulations.[14] Investment in a hedge fund, whatever its legal structure, is a security for purposes of the Securities Act of 1933. In order to avoid the registration requirements of the Securities Act with respect to the sale of their securities, hedge funds generally rely on the private offering exemption in section 4(2) of that act and on the safe harbor contained in Regulation D promulgated thereunder. Section 4(2) exempts from registration securities sold without any "public offering." As a practical matter, this means that there can be no communication (electronic or otherwise) that could be viewed as a general solicitation or advertisement. Under section 3(c)(1) of the Investment Company Act, the fund is limited to no more than 100 partners. In practice, those investors must be "accredited investors,"[15] although up to 35 partners could be unaccredited. Under section 3(c)(7) of the Investment Company Act, the

---

[14] Congress enacted the Investment Advisers Act of 1940 ("Advisers Act") in conjunction with the Investment Company Act of 1940.

[15] An accredited investor under the Securities Act of 1933 is an individual with a net worth in excess of $1 million or an annual income in excess of $200,000, or an entity with total assets of $5 million or more. This standard was enacted in 1982 and is being upgraded. The SEC proposed in 2007 to add the requirement that investors own at least $2.5 million in investments (excluding the personal residence and some other personal assets). This addition applies only to new investors.

fund is limited to no more than 499 investors, who must be "qualified purchasers".[16] As of early 2006, the SEC imposed much stricter rules that prompted many hedge funds to register with the SEC as investment advisers. But this new rule was struck down by a federal appeals court in June 2006. Rather than imposing stricter registration requirements, the SEC then decided to propose a new anti-fraud rule under the Investment Advisers Act, which applies to all investment advisers regardless of their registration status. Advisers to funds (or other pooled investment vehicles) are prohibited from making false, misleading, or deceptive statements or acts. The effect of the proposed anti-fraud rule would be to permit the SEC to bring enforcement actions against advisers that violate the rule. While hedge funds remain under light regulation throughout the world, some countries are pushing for tighter regulation; Germany has been the most vocal proponent of tighter regulations.

Given the small number of partners, a minimum investment is typically several hundred thousand dollars. Institutional investors can become partners. U.S. hedge funds are typically incorporated in a "fund-friendly" state such as Delaware.

Offshore funds have also proved to be an attractive legal structure. These are incorporated in locations such as the British Virgin Islands, the Cayman Islands, Bermuda, or other locations attractive from a fiscal and legal point of view. A hedge fund might consider using "feeders" (vehicles that have an ownership interest in the hedge fund) that enable it to solicit funds from investors in every imaginable tax and legal domain—one feeder for ordinary U.S. investors, another for tax-free pensions, another for Japanese who want their profits hedged in yen, and still another for European institutions, which invest only in shares that are listed on an exchange (e.g., a dummy listing on the Irish Stock Exchange). These feeders don't keep the money; they are used as paper conduits that channel the money to a central fund, typically a Cayman Islands partnership.

Fee Structure The manager is compensated through a *base management fee* based on the value of assets under management (at one time as much as 2 to 3 percent, now more typically 1 percent of the asset base) plus an *incentive fee* proportional to the realized profits (ranging from 15 percent to 30 percent, typically 20 percent of total profits).[17] The base fee is paid whatever the performance of the fund. The incentive fee cannot be negative, so a negative return on the funds implies a zero incentive fee. The incentive fee is sometimes applied to profits measured above a risk-free rate applied to the assets. In other words, the hedge fund return has to be greater than the risk-free rate before the incentive fee is activated. The fee structure sometimes includes a "high-water mark" stating that following a year in which the fund declined in value, the hedge fund would first have to recover those losses before any incentive fee would be paid. Example 8.6 shows the effect of a hedge fund's fee structure on its net return.

[16] A qualified purchaser (or qualified investor) is an individual with at least $5 million in investments or an entity with at least $25 million in investments.

[17] Besides the management and incentive fees that all hedge funds charge their clients, some hedge funds may charge other fees, such as surrender fees, ticket charges, and financing fees.

EXAMPLE 8.6 HEDGE FUND FEE

A hedge fund has an annual 1 percent base management fee plus a 20 percent incentive fee applied to profits above the risk-free rate, taken to be the Treasury bill rate. Hence, the incentive fee is applied to annual profits after deduction of the Treasury bill rate applied to the amount of assets under management at the start of the year. The gross return during the year is 40 percent. What is the net return (the return after fees) for an investor if the risk-free rate is 5 percent?

SOLUTION

$$\text{Fee} = 1\% + 20\% \times (40\% - 5\%) = 8\%$$

$$\text{Net return} = 40\% - 8\% = 32\%$$

Classification

Hedge funds have become quite global, as evidenced by the wide array of global investments used by these hedge funds and the international diversity of their client base. Some classifications of hedge funds by investment strategy is provided in the media and by hedge funds databases. These classifications are somewhat arbitrary, exhibit a large degree of overlap, and differ extensively across sources. Following is one possible classification system:

- *Long/short funds* are the traditional types of hedge funds, taking short and long bets in common stocks. They vary their short and long exposures according to forecasts, use leverage, and now operate on numerous markets throughout the world. These funds often maintain net positive or negative market exposures, so they are not necessarily market neutral. In fact, a subgroup within this category is funds that have a systematic short bias, known as dedicated short funds or short-seller funds. Long/short funds represent a large amount of hedge fund assets. An illustration is presented in Example 8.7.
- *Market-neutral funds* are a form of long/short funds that attempt to be hedged against a general market movement. They take bets on valuation differences of individual securities within some market segment. This could involve simultaneous long and short positions in closely related securities with a zero net exposure to the market itself. A market-neutral long-short portfolio is constructed so that the total value of the positions held long equals the total value of the positions sold short (dollar neutrality) and so that the total sensitivity of the long positions equals and offsets the total sensitivity of the short positions (beta neutrality). The long position would be in stocks considered undervalued, and the short position would be in stocks considered overvalued. Leverage is generally used, so that the investment in the long position (or the short position) is a multiple of the hedge fund equity. Another alternative is to use derivatives to hedge market risk. For example, a manager could buy some bond deemed to be underpriced with a simultaneous short position in bond futures or other fixed-income derivatives. This type of fund is sometimes called a fixed-income arbitrage fund. Other types

EXAMPLE 8.7 LONG/SHORT MARKET-NEUTRAL STRATEGY

A hedge fund has a capital of $10 million and invests in a market-neutral long/short strategy on the British equity market. Shares can be borrowed from a primary broker with a cash margin deposit equal to 18 percent of the value of the shares. No additional costs are charged to borrow the shares. The hedge fund has drawn up a list of shares regarded as undervalued (list A) and a list of shares regarded as overvalued (list B). The hedge fund expects that shares in list A will outperform the British index by 5 percent over the year, while shares in list B will underperform the British index by 5 percent over the year. The hedge fund wishes to retain a cash cushion of $1 million for unforeseen events. What specific investment actions would you suggest?

SOLUTION

The hedge fund would sell short shares from list B and use the proceeds to buy shares from list A for an equal amount such that the overall beta of the portfolio with respect to the market equals zero. Some capital needs to be invested in the margin deposit. The hedge funds could take long/short positions for $50 million:

- Keep $1 million in cash.
- Deposit $9 million in margin.
- Borrow $25 million of shares from list B from a broker, and sell those shares short.
- Use the sale proceeds to buy $25 million worth of shares from list A.

The positions in shares from lists A and B are established so that the portfolio's beta is zero. Also, note that the invested assets of $50 million equals $9 million divided by 0.18. The ratio of invested assets to equity capital is roughly 5:1.

If expectations materialize, the return for investors in the hedge fund will be high. The long/short portfolio of shares should have a gain over the year of 10 percent on $50 million, whatever the movement in the general market index. This $5 million gain will translate into an annual return before fees of 50 percent on the invested capital of $10 million. This calculation does not take into account the return on invested cash ($1 million) and assumes that the dividends on long positions will offset dividends on short positions.

of arbitrage make use of complex securities with option-like clauses, such as convertibles, warrants, or collateralized mortgage obligations (CMOs). Among the various techniques used by market-neutral funds are the following:

- Equity long/short
- Fixed-income arbitrage

- Pairs trading
- Warrant arbitrage
- Mortgage arbitrage
- Convertible bond arbitrage
- Closed-end fund arbitrage
- Statistical arbitrage

It must be stressed that despite their labels ("arbitrage," "neutral"), these funds are not riskless because hedges can never be perfect. Loss can be incurred if the model used is imperfect, and it can be high because hedge funds tend to be highly leveraged.

- *Global macro funds* take bets on the direction of a market, a currency, an interest rate, a commodity, or any macroeconomic variable. These funds tend to be highly leveraged and make extensive use of derivatives. There are many subgroups in this category, including the following:
    - *Futures funds* (or *managed futures funds*) are commodity pools that include commodity trading advisor funds (CTAs). They take bets on directional moves in the positions they hold (long and short) in a single asset class, such as currency, fixed income, or commodities, and tend to use many actively traded futures contracts.
    - *Emerging-market funds* primarily take bets on all types of securities in emerging markets. The securities markets in these economies are typically less efficient and less liquid than those in developed markets. There typically is not an organized lending market for securities, so it is difficult to sell short most issues. Emerging market investments tend to be fairly volatile and greatly influenced by economic and political factors.
- *Event-driven funds* take bets on some event specific to a company or a security. Typically the events are special situations or opportunities to capitalize on price fluctuations. These include the following, among others:
    - *Distressed securities funds:* The manager invests in the debt and/or equity of companies having financial difficulty. Such companies are generally in bankruptcy reorganization or are emerging from reorganization or appear likely to declare bankruptcy in the near future. Because of their distressed situations, the manager can buy such companies' securities at deeply discounted prices. The manager stands to make money should the company successfully reorganize and return to profitability. The manager may take short positions in companies whose situations he believes will worsen, rather than improve, in the short term.
    - *Risk arbitrage in mergers and acquisitions:* Before the effective date of a merger, the stock of the acquired company will typically sell at a discount

to its acquisition value as officially announced. A hedge fund manager simultaneously buys stock in a company being acquired and sells stock in its acquirers. Even though a merger has been accepted by the board of directors of the two companies, there is always a chance that the merger will not go through, possibly because of objections by regulatory authorities. This is a reason for the existence of the discount. If the takeover falls through, fund managers can be left with large losses. An illustration is presented in Example 8.8.

Funds of Funds

Funds of funds (*FOF*) have been created to allow easier access to small investors, but also to institutional investors. An FOF is open to investors and, in turn, invests in a selection of hedge funds. If an FOF has a large client base, it can invest large sums

EXAMPLE 8.8 MERGER RISK ARBITRAGE AND LONG/SHORT MARKET-NEUTRAL STRATEGY

A merger has been announced between a French company A and a German company B. A will acquire B by offering one share of A for two shares of B. Shares of B were trading in a €15 to €20 range prior to the merger announcement. Shares of B currently trade at €24, while shares of A trade at €50. The merger has been approved by both boards of directors but is awaiting ratification by all shareholders (which is extremely likely) and approval by the EU commission (there is a slight risk of non-approval because the combined company has a large European market share in some products). How could a hedge fund take advantage of the situation? What arc the risks?

SOLUTION

The hedge fund should construct a hedged position whereby it buys two shares of B for every share of A that it sells short. Because the proceeds of the short sale of one share of A (€50) can be used to buy two shares of B (€48), the position can be highly leveraged. Of course, the cost of securities lending and margin deposit should also be taken into account. When the merger is completed, the hedge fund will make a profit of approximately two euros for each share of A.

The risk is that the merger will fall through. If it does, the stock price of B will drop sharply, because it was to be acquired at a price well above its premerger market value. If the stock price of A also falls, it should be by less than for B, resulting in an overall loss. The stock price of A might also rise, adding to the loss related to the position in B. That would mean a sizable loss for the hedge fund.

of money in each hedge fund. With their attractive benefits, FOFs have grown rapidly and now hold more than a third of all hedge fund assets. An FOF provides investors with several benefits:

- *Retailing:* Typically, a single hedge fund requires an investment of one to several hundred thousand dollars or euros. For the same amount, an investor can get exposure to a large number of hedge funds.
- *Access:* FOF managers may be able to offer investments in successful hedge funds that are closed to individual investors because the maximum number of investors has been reached. As long-time investors, they may have "old" money invested with funds that have been closed to new investment. They are also privileged clients that will have priority in buying shares of individual investors who cash out from the hedge fund for personal reasons.
- *Diversification:* An FOF allows investors to diversify the risk of a single hedge fund. The good performance of a single hedge fund could be due to specific market conditions prevailing in the past. An FOF can diversify across several types of hedge funds that may have good performance in different market conditions.
- *Expertise:* The manager of the FOF is supposed to have expertise in finding reliable and good-quality hedge funds in a world where information on the investment strategies of hedge funds is difficult to obtain. Selecting the right hedge fund and strategy requires a large database and intimate knowledge of strategies, and their advantages and potential pitfalls.
- *Due diligence process:* The due diligence (both at the outset and ongoing) that has to be performed by an institutional investor when selecting a hedge fund is highly specialized and time consuming, given the secretive nature of hedge funds and their complex investment strategies. An FOF may be better equipped to perform this due diligence than is a typical institutional investor.

However, there are drawbacks with an FOF:

- *Fee:* The fee charged by its manager is in addition to that charged by each hedge fund. The total fee can be quite hefty.
- *Performance:* Individual hedge funds are mostly selected by the FOF on the basis of past performance, which in practice often gives little indication of future performance. Biases of the existing databases on hedge funds used by FOFs in their selection process are described subsequently. There is little evidence of persistence in the performance delivered by FOFs.
- *Diversification is a double-edged sword:* Blending a high expected return hedge fund with many others for risk reduction purposes means that the overall FOF expected return will be lowered by this diversification. But the fees paid are still very high.

Leverage and Unique Risks of Hedge Funds

Prior to discussing the performance of hedge funds, we review the use of leverage by hedge funds and the unique risks for hedge funds. Some people regard the use of leverage as one of the main sources of risk for hedge funds, while others maintain that proper use of leverage with appropriate risk management benefits hedge fund investors. In addition, risks that are unique to hedge funds may make hedge funds look unduly risky. Thus, we can usefully discuss hedge funds' risks prior to presenting their historical track record.

Use of Leverage One of the common characteristics of hedge funds is their use of leverage as part of their trading strategy, although some hedge funds do not use leverage at all. For certain strategies (such as arbitrage strategies), leverage is essential because the arbitrage return is so small that leverage is needed for amplifying the profit. However, leverage is a double-edged sword that also magnifies losses on the downside. In this traditional sense, leveraged investments are more aggressive than those without leverage, and to some people, this may mean high risk.

Leverage in hedge funds often runs from 2:1 to 10:1 (depending on the type of assets held and strategies used) and can run higher than 100:1 [e.g., at one point in time, a well-known hedge fund, Long Term Capital Managment or LTCM, had leverage that stood over 500:1 (Lhabitant, 2002)]. Thus, some hedge funds may specifically limit the leverage they will employ in the limited partnership agreement so that hedge fund managers are legally bound by that limit. Within the limit, however, hedge fund managers have considerable flexibility.

In general, hedge fund managers can create leverage in trading by

- borrowing external funds to invest more or sell short more than the equity capital they put in,
- borrowing through a brokerage margin account, and
- using financial instruments and derivatives that require posting margins (typically a fraction of the full value of the position) in lieu of trading in the cash securities that require full payment.

Unique Risks of Hedge Funds In addition to market and trading risks in different markets, hedge funds face the following unique risks:

- *Liquidity risk:* The liquidity risk is common to all investors who trade in illiquid or thin markets. However, the lack of liquidity under extreme market conditions can cause irreversible damage to hedge funds whose strategies rely on the presence of liquidity in specific markets. For example, the demise of LTCM was attributed to the unexpected absence of normal liquidity.
- *Pricing risk:* Hedge funds often invest in complex securities traded over-the-counter. Pricing securities that trade infrequently is a difficult task, especially in periods of high volatility. Broker-dealers tend to adopt an extremely

conservative pricing policy to protect themselves in periods of high volatility. The marking-to-market (margin calls) of positions based on these prices can create severe cash needs for hedge funds, even if the funds do not try to liquidate their positions. For example, it is widely believed that the cash drain of marking-to-market positions based on brokers' conservative pricing of derivatives compounded the problems of LTCM.

- *Counterparty credit risk:* Because hedge funds deal with broker-dealers in most transactions—from buying securities on margin to mortgage trading—counterparty credit risk can arise from many sources. Thus, hedge funds face significant counterparty risk.
- *Settlement risk:* Settlement risk refers to the failure to deliver the specified security or money by one of the parties to the transaction on the settlement day.
- *Short squeeze risk:* A short squeeze arises when short sellers must buy in their positions at rising prices, for example because owners of the borrowed stock demand their shares back. Because some hedge fund strategies require short selling (e.g., long/short strategies), this risk can affect fund performance significantly.
- *Financing squeeze:* If a hedge fund has reached or is near its borrowing capacity, its ability to borrow cash is constrained. Margin calls and marking position to market might result in a cash need for the fund. This risk puts the hedge fund in a vulnerable position when it is forced to reduce the levered positions, say, in an illiquid market at substantial losses, in order to stop the leverage from rising. If the hedge fund were able to borrow more cash, these substantial losses could be avoided.

Hedge Funds Universe and Indexes

Hedge funds are not publicly offered or listed. Hence, information must be obtained directly from each hedge fund or through data providers who specialize in collecting data on some universe of hedge funds and funds of funds. Data providers also publish hedge fund indexes. The performance of these indexes is widely disseminated and is used to build the case for investing in hedge funds. Indexes also allow a comparison of the performance of specific hedge funds to competitors.

Indexes A number of indexes track the hedge fund industry. Specialized hedge fund firms (such as Hedge Fund Research, Van Hedge, Hennessee, Greenwich), banks (such as Credit Suisse/Tremont,[18] ABN AMRO EurekaHedge), index providers (such as MSCI, S&P, FTSE), and even educational institutions (CISDM, EDHEC) offer dedicated hedge fund indexes.[19] These indexes are also

[18] As of 2007, the Credit Suisse/Tremont indexes are based on the TASS database that is managed by Tremont but owned and distributed by Lipper.

[19] The launching dates of these indexes differ. Some were launched in the 1990s, others in the 2000s. In some cases, the historical value of the index was back-calculated to an earlier date, with the risk of including only surviving hedge funds and biasing the performance upward.

broken down in subindexes for various classifications of hedge funds according to investment strategy, but the classifications vary across providers.

Some indexes are equal-weighted, while others are weighted by the assets under management for each fund. One reason for using equal weights is that hedge funds are reluctant to provide information on their size. But asset-weighted indexes are more representative of the performance of money invested in hedge funds. Some are audited and have a transparent composition, but others are not. The criteria for inclusion vary; in many cases, all that is required is that the hedge fund volunteers to be included in the database used for the index construction. Any database only includes a number of the existing hedge funds; furthermore, most providers build their hedge fund indexes from a selection of the funds in their database. For any month, the performance reported by the various index providers can vary widely.

Investable indexes are created from funds that can be actually bought and sold by investors, the so-called open funds. Investability is an attractive property for an index because it makes the index more relevant to the choices truly available to investors. Several providers publish investable indexes that use various eligibility criteria to include specific hedge funds in the index. Typically, the hedge fund should be accepting new investments and redemption should have no lock-up period; however, such indexes do not represent the total universe of hedge funds and may underrepresent the more successful managers, who may not find the requirements for inclusion in the index attractive. Funds of funds have been created to track these investable indexes.

Biases Investors should exercise caution when using the historical track record of hedge funds in reaching asset allocation decisions. The hedge fund industry does not adhere to rigorous performance presentation standards. Biases in historical performance data can make it difficult to interpret hedge fund performance; past winners may also not repeat. The performance data from hedge fund databases and indexes suffer from serious biases:

- *Self-selection bias:* Hedge fund managers themselves decide whether they want to be included in a database. Managers who have funds with an unimpressive track record will not wish to have that information exposed.
- *Backfilling bias:* When a hedge fund enters a database, it brings with it its track record. Only hedge funds with good track records enter the database, creating a positive bias in past performance in the database. Ibbotson and Chen (2006) studied the TASS database from 1995 to 2006 and estimate that excluding backfilled data reduces the average annual return by some 350 basis points. Reliable index providers have recently taken steps to minimize backfill bias.
- *Survivorship bias:* In the investment industry, unsuccessful funds and managers tend to disappear over time. Only successful ones search for new clients and present their track records. This trend creates a survivor bias. The problem is acute because hedge funds often do not have to comply with performance

presentation standards. It is not uncommon to see hedge fund managers present the track records of only their successful funds, omitting those that have been closed. If a fund begins to perform poorly, perhaps even starting to go out of business, it may stop reporting its performance entirely, thus inflating the reported average performance. Hedge fund indexes and databases may include only funds that have survived; funds with bad performance disappear and are removed from the database that is used by investors to select among existing funds. Most academic studies suggest that survivorship bias overstates return by 200 to 400 basis points per year. Malkiel and Saha (2005) studied the TASS database from 1996 to 2003 and estimated the average annual bias in performance to be 442 basis points. A similar survivorship bias exists for equity mutual funds, but it is smaller because the attrition rate of mutual funds is much smaller that the hedge fund attrition rate (on the order of 8 to 15 percent per year, on average). Reliable hedge fund indexes are now much less susceptible to survivorship bias as defunct hedge funds are kept in the database; however, funds that simply stop reporting still pose a problem.

Hedge funds risk measures are also affected by biases:

- *Smoothed pricing of infrequently traded assets*: Some assets trade infrequently. This is the case for many alternative assets that are not exchange-traded, such as real estate or private equity. This is also the case for illiquid exchange-traded securities or OTC instruments often used by hedge funds. Because prices used are often not up-to-date market prices but estimates of fair value, their volatility is reduced (*smoothing effect*). The infrequent nature of price updates for alternative investments induces serial correlation of returns and a downward bias to the measured risk of the assets. In addition, correlations of alternative investment returns with conventional equity and fixed income returns, and correlations among the alternative investments, are often artificially low simply because of the smoothing effect and the absence of market-observable returns. The bias can be large, so the true risk is much larger than the reported estimates. As suggested by Asness, Krail, and Liew (2001), Lo (2002) and Getmansky, Lo, and Mei (2004), the correction requires taking serial correlation of return into account. This will lead to an increase in the estimated standard deviation and a decrease in the Sharpe ratio commonly used to measure risk-adjusted performance. After adjusting for serial correlation, Lo (2002) finds estimates that differ from the naive Sharpe ratio estimator by as much as 70 percent. Some hedge funds purport to be market neutral (i.e., funds with relatively small market betas), but Asness, Krail, and Liew (2001) show that including both contemporaneous and lagged market returns as regressors and summing the coefficients yields significantly higher market exposure.
- *Option-like investment strategies:* Traditional risk measures used in performance appraisal assume that portfolio returns are drawn from normal, or at least symmetric, distributions. Standard deviation (and hence the Sharpe ratio) is a good estimate of risk if the return distributions are close to normal. As shown in Malkiel and Saha (2005), distributions of hedge funds return tend

to deviate strongly from normality (with high kurtosis, or "fat" tails, and negative skewness). Many investment strategies followed by hedge funds have some option-like features that violate the normal distributional assumptions. For example, hedge funds following so-called arbitrage strategies will generally make a small profit when asset prices converge to their estimated fair value, but they run the risk of a huge loss if their arbitrage model fails. Standard deviation or traditional value-at-risk (VaR) measures understate the true risk of losses, and the Sharpe ratio can be an inappropriate performance measure, even after correcting for smoothed pricing.

- *Fee structure and gaming:* It is also important to remember the high fees charged by hedge funds, typically a fixed fee of 1 percent plus an incentive fee of 20 percent of the total return, if positive. This compensation structure is option-like. Clearly, fund managers are paid to take risks. One can argue that they have strong incentives to take a huge amount of risk if their recent performance has been bad. However, one can also argue that because of the high-water mark provision, hedge fund managers may not want to ruin their chance to stage a comeback by taking more risk as their performance diminishes. In either case, past risk measures may be misleading for forecasting future performance and risk for a fund that has performed badly in the recent past.

To summarize, investors need to exercise caution in interpreting the reported performance of hedge funds (see Example 8.9). Furthermore, the risks in hedge fund investments are easily underestimated.

The Case for Investing in Hedge Funds

Hedge funds are attractive because of their risk and performance characteristics. Proponents stress that the unique value of hedge funds is their ability to produce attractive risk-adjusted returns, independent of broad market trends. Most types of hedge funds seek positive returns regardless of market conditions. This approach differs from traditional funds that take only long positions in the markets and therefore have returns that are strongly correlated with the market in which they invest. For example, most equity hedge fund strategies (long/short, market neutral, merger arbitrage, etc.) are designed to have limited correlation with the equity market; thus, they may not fully capture the upside potential during equity bull markets, but they aim to generate positive returns and preserve capital during equity bear markets. Hedge funds aim at providing "good" returns in all stock market phases. Furthermore, hedge funds cover a wide diversity of investment strategies in a variety of instruments and markets; such investment strategies are not available within traditional asset classes. Hence, as a group, reflected in a broad hedge fund index, hedge funds offer attractive risk diversification benefits to traditional investments, so hedge funds are often marketed as an attractive asset class.[20]

[20] Some are hesitant to call hedge funds an asset class because of their heterogeneity, but we will keep the appellation for lack of a better term.

EXAMPLE 8.9 BIASES IN REPORTED PERFORMANCE

A manager without any expertise has decided to launch five long/short hedge funds with some seed money. The investment strategies of the five funds are quite different. Actually, the investment strategy of fund A is just the opposite of that of fund E. After a couple of years, some funds have performed well and some badly, as could be expected by pure chance. The annualized standard deviation is 10 percent, and the annual risk-free rate is 3 percent. The manager decides to close funds A, B, and C and to enter funds D and E in a well-known hedge fund database. The marketing pitch of the manager is that the funds have superior performance (Sharpe ratio of 1.7 and 2.7). What do you think?

Fund Name	Mean Annual Return	Standard Deviation	Sharpe Ratio
Fund A	−30%	10%	−3.3
Fund B	−20%	10%	−2.3
Fund C	0%	10%	−0.3
Fund D	+20%	10%	1.7
Fund E	+30%	10%	2.7

SOLUTION

The performance on the funds is purely random; however, only the good-performing funds are included in the hedge fund database. The performance reported for a selection of funds is misleading. There is obvious survivorship and self-selection bias. Similarly, the performance of the hedge fund index is biased upward and misleading.

Asset Class Many suggest that investors should allocate part of their assets to hedge funds, even in a passive way. The usual argument in favor of hedge funds as an asset class is illustrated in Exhibit 8.2, which gives risk and performance estimates for a variety of indexes over the period January 1994 to December 2006. All calculations are conducted in U.S. dollars. The first is the Credit Suisse/Tremont hedge fund index, a broad index of all hedge funds. Next is the MSCI World equity index, followed by the U.S., European, and Japanese equity indexes. The last column is the Lehman Global Aggregate bond index. The first observation is that the volatility of the broad hedged fund index, measured by the standard deviation of returns, is considerably smaller than that of the global equity market (7.7% instead of 13.4%). Another interesting parameter is the correlation with the global equity index. The correlation of the global hedge fund index with the equity market is 0.5. It is clearly positive but far from one, suggesting excellent diversification benefits. Part of the explanation for a low correlation comes from the fact that hedge funds do not experience big negative return or drawdown in periods when the equity market drops, as was the case from 2001 to 2003. Estimating correlation

EXHIBIT 8.2

Performance and Risk Characteristics of Various Market Indexes
January 1994–December 2006, in U.S. dollars

	Credit Suisse/Tremont Hedge Fund Index	MSCI World Index	S&P 500	DJ EURO STOXX	TOPIX	Lehman Global Aggregate
Average annualized return	10.9%	7.2%	10.9%	12.2%	1.2%	6.1%
Annualized volatility (standard deviation)	7.7%	13.4%	14.3%	17.7%	16.8%	5.1%
Correlation with MSCI World index	0.5	1.0	0.9	0.9	0.5	0.1
Beta with MSCI World index	0.3	1.0	1.0	1.1	0.7	–
Sharpe ratio	0.9	0.2	0.5	0.5	(0.2)	0.4

Source: Credit Suisse/Tremont Hedge Fund Index, www.hedgeindex.com, February 2007.

over shorter periods, the correlation between hedge fund returns and equity returns tends to decrease in periods of bear markets and increase in periods of bull markets (see Lo, 2002). For example, the correlation increased drastically in the bull market period of 2003 to 2006. Again, hedge fund marketers would argue that the diversification benefits of hedge funds are less needed in periods of booming equity markets but badly needed in periods of falling markets. The last row gives the Sharpe ratio, namely, the average return in excess of the U.S. 90-day Treasury bill rate divided by the standard deviation. The Sharpe ratio for the broad hedge fund index (0.9) is superior to that of all the other asset classes. While the empirical case for allocating investments to the hedge funds asset class is impressive, one should not forget the statistical caveats mentioned above: the performance and risk estimates of hedge funds indexes suffer from some bias.

Individual Funds Within the universe of hedge funds, individual funds can follow vastly different investment strategies using different instruments and markets. Some strategies and managers can deliver outstanding performance. Investors often wish to go beyond a passive allocation to the hedge fund class and find top-performing hedge funds. The fee structure and flexibility of hedge funds attract talented fund managers. Someone having an outstanding investment idea can apply it in a hedge fund with few constraints. The investment idea can be leveraged to generate high returns for investors and for the manager. So, the search for an attractive hedge fund is based in part on the perceived talent of the manager to generate superior performance. The hedge fund class is different from traditional asset classes in many respects, including the fact that there is an enormous dispersion in returns of individual hedge funds. Malkiel and Saha (2005) stress, "The cross-sectional variation and the range of individual hedge fund returns are far greater than they are for traditional asset classes.

Investors in hedge funds take on a substantial risk of selecting a dismally performing fund or, worse, a failing one" (p. 87). Of course, investors take this risk in the hope of finding top-performing hedge funds.

Performance of individual hedge funds can come from many sources, but two primary sources of return on a specific fund are the selection of market exposures (often called beta) and the skill in constructing strategies or selecting securities (often called alpha). When a fund takes some market exposure (beta), its performance is partly attributable to its exposure to market movements. If a fund were totally market neutral, it would have no beta. Part of the performance (alpha) also comes from the good (bad) skill of the manager in implementing the strategy with a given market exposure. Take the example of a U.S. equity long/short fund with a market exposure (beta) of 0.3, or 30 percent, relative to the U.S. equity market. If the equity market goes up (down), the market exposure will have a positive (negative) contribution to the fund return. However, the manager could have skills in selecting individual securities, say an alpha of 5 percent per year, that induce a positive return in any market environment, on top of the market exposure contribution. Investors must try to disentangle the two effects (beta and alpha) in attributing performance of a hedge fund. Investors sometimes use multifactor market models to estimate the fund's exposures (betas) to various market factors. Performing such a calculation for individual hedge funds is a difficult task because of data availability and because hedge funds tend to follow nonlinear strategies implying that the betas vary considerably over time.

Some argue that it is not worth paying the large fees of hedge funds for simply taking some market exposures that can be replicated at a very low cost. Hence, some replication funds ("clones") have been created with risk market exposures similar to various hedge fund indexes. They offer risk diversification benefits that are somewhat similar to those of hedge funds, without their high management fee. But they cannot deliver any of the alpha that is promised by individual hedge funds.

Closely Held Companies and Inactively Traded Securities

Investments in closely held companies and inactively traded securities require analysis of legal, financial, and ownership considerations with account taken of the effects of illiquidity. *Closely held companies* are those that are not publicly traded. *Inactively traded securities* are securities of companies that are infrequently traded; they generally do not trade on major exchanges. Illiquidity, limited information availability, and minority ownership issues are common to such companies.

Legal Environment

Closely held companies may be organized in various legal forms, such as special tax-advantaged corporations (subchapter S corporations in the United States), regular corporations, general partnerships, limited partnerships, and sole proprietorships. These forms have tax implications, as well as ownership differences, for the investor. Ownership is a bundle of rights, and these rights differ, depending on the business form. Because valuations can be required to provide evidence in litigation—for example, minority shareholder claims—much case law defines terms such as *intrinsic value, fundamental value,* and *fair value.* These definitions may vary in different jurisdictions. Even what is judged as evidence for a valuation can vary. There has long been a tension between the theory of value as based on projected cash flows and the acceptance of the *hard* evidence of recent cash flows. In a real sense, then, valuation of closely held and inactively traded securities requires extensive knowledge of the law and the purposes of the valuation.[21]

Valuation Alternatives

The basic types of valuation are the cost approach, the comparables approach, and the income approach.

The Cost Approach This approach attempts to determine what it would cost to replace the company's assets in their present form.

The Comparables Approach In the company comparison approach, market value is estimated relative to a benchmark value. The benchmark value may be the market price of a similar but actively traded company, or the average or median value of the market prices of similar companies, in transactions made near the time of the appraisal. The benchmark-based estimate needs to be adjusted for changing market conditions, the possibility that the benchmark itself is mispriced, and the unique features of the company relative to the benchmark. Companies with comparable characteristics might not have traded recently.

The Income Approach For business valuation, Pratt, Reilly, and Schweihs (2000) essentially define the income approach as one of appropriately discounting any anticipated future economic income stream.

Bases for Discounts/Premiums

Because closely held companies and inactively traded securities are illiquid, some discount must be made for that illiquidity. For infrequently traded stocks, share prices should reflect a liquidity discount compensating investors for illiquidity in the market for the shares. Shares of closely held companies lack a public market (lack marketability) and so their valuation should reflect a marketability discount to account for the extra return investors should require on those shares. In addition to a discount for lack of marketability for a closely held company, the analyst may also need to apply a discount for minority interest, or a premium for control. The minority interest discount is applied if the interest will not be able to influence corporate strategy and other business decisions. To estimate a marketability discount, minority discount, or control premium, the analyst must carefully define the amount or base to which the discount or premium should be applied.

[21] See Pratt, Reilly, and Schweihs (2000) for an extensive treatment of the analysis and appraisal of closely held companies.

To estimate a marketability discount for a closely held company, the analyst identifies a publicly traded comparable company with a liquid market. The comparable's market value of equity is the base to which the marketability discount is applied.

To estimate a minority interest discount for a company, the base is an estimate of that company's value of equity inclusive of the value arising from ownership of all rights of control. To estimate a control premium, the base is an estimate of that company's value of equity not reflecting control (the value of equity from a minority shareholder perspective).

Distressed Securities/Bankruptcies

Distressed securities are securities of companies that have filed or are close to filing for bankruptcy court protection, or that are seeking out-of-court debt restructuring to avoid bankruptcy. The legal framework of bankruptcy proceedings differs across countries. In the United States, two types of bankruptcy protection are available: protection for liquidation (called Chapter 7) and protection for reorganization (called Chapter 11). Valuation of such securities requires legal, operational, and financial analysis.

To understand distressed securities, one must appreciate the inherent divergence of interests between the stockholders and bondholders of a company. Stockholders own the successful company, but bondholders have a prior claim to the assets of the bankrupt company. In reorganizations, bondholders' prior claim can allow them to negotiate for ownership in the postbankruptcy company, thus diluting the original shareholders' claims. Investing in distressed securities, then, usually means investing in distressed company bonds with a view toward equity ownership in the eventually reconstituted company. In this regard, such investments have characteristics somewhat similar to those of venture capital investing. For example, they are illiquid and require a long horizon, as well as intense investor participation in guiding the venture to a successful outcome. Another similarity, though, is the possibility of mispricing. Hooke (1998) reports on the disappointment of some traditional distressed-securities investors that these investments are attracting attention and efficient prices; but he suggests that business volatility and high leverage will guarantee many problem companies with inevitable value discrepancies (mispricing).

Distressed-security investing may be viewed as the ultimate in value investing. A distressed company with low enterprise value (EV) to earnings before interest, taxes, depreciation, and amortization (EBITDA) will attract the attention of an investor looking for positive, postrestructuring cash flows. The primary question for any distressed security is the question of the distress source. Is the company operationally sound but financially hampered by too much gearing (leverage), or is the company weak operationally? If the company is weak operationally, is it a candidate to be turned around by cost cutting and improvement in the business cycle or else by new management and/or a new competitive strategy? Distressed-security investing requires intense industry analysis, as well as analysis of business strategies and of the management team that will conduct the restructuring.

Commodity Markets and Commodity Derivatives

Commodities present an unusual investment alternative. Investing in commodities complements the investment opportunities offered by shares of corporations that extensively use those commodities in their production process. Investing directly in agricultural products and other commodities gives the investor a share in the commodity components of the country's production and consumption. Money managers and average investors, however, usually prefer commodity derivatives (financial instruments that derive their value from the value of the underlying commodity) rather than commodities themselves. The average investor does not want to store grains, cattle, crude oil, or metals. There are several indirect ways to invest in commodities:

- *Futures contracts*: A commodity futures contract is a standardized, exchange-traded agreement between two parties in which the buyer agrees to buy a commodity from the seller at a future date at a price agreed upon today.
- Bonds indexed on some commodity price.
- Stocks of companies producing the commodity.

Investing in commodity futures is the most common strategy. Commodity trading advisers (CTAs) offer *managed futures funds* that take positions in exchange-traded derivatives on commodities and financials.[22]

Commodity Futures

Futures contracts are the easiest and cheapest way to invest in commodities. Commodities can be grouped into three major categories:

- *Agricultural products*, including fibers (wool, cotton), grains (wheat, corn, soybeans), food (coffee, cocoa, orange juice), and livestock (cattle, hogs, pork bellies). These are often called soft commodities by professionals.
- *Energy*, including crude oil, heating oil, and natural gas
- *Metals*, such as copper, aluminum, gold, silver, and platinum

Numerous commodity indexes have been developed. Some traditional indexes are broadly based, with a global economic perspective; they aim to track the evolution of input prices. Other indexes have been developed as *investable* indexes. They

[22] See Jaeger (2002), p. 18.

are based on the most liquid commodity futures contracts, so they can easily be replicated by taking positions in individual commodities. For example, the Goldman Sachs Commodity Index (GSCI) is a world-production weighted index of 24 commodities with liquid futures contracts. The composition and weights of the GSCI are periodically revised. Futures contracts on the GSCI trade in Chicago. The composition and weights of the various commodity indexes differ widely, and so do their performances.

Motivation and Investment Vehicles

Commodities are sometimes treated as an asset class because they represent a direct participation in the real economy. The motivation for investing in commodities ranges from the diversification benefits achievable by a passive investor to the speculative profits sought by an *active* investor. The design of the investment vehicle used reflects these different motivations.

Passive Investment A passive investor would buy commodities for their risk-diversification benefits. A passive investor would typically invest through a collateralized position in a futures contract (see Example 8.10). Many banks and money managers offer collateralized futures funds based on one of the investable commodity indexes. A collateralized position in futures is a portfolio in which an investor takes a long position in futures for a given amount of underlying value and simultaneously invests the same amount in government securities, such as Treasury bills. The various investable indexes and collateralized futures indexes are published both in excess-return and total-return form. The indexes reported assume that the *total return* on the index is continuously reinvested. The *excess return* is the return above the risk-free rate. The total return is the risk-free rate plus the excess return.

EXAMPLE 8.10 COLLATERALIZED FUTURES

Assume that the futures price is currently $100. If $100 million is added to the fund, the manager will take a long position in the futures contract for $100 million of underlying value and simultaneously buy $100 million worth of Treasury bills (part of this will be deposited as margin). If the futures price drops to $95 the next day, the futures position will be marked to market, and the manager will have to sell $5 million of the Treasury bills to cover the loss. Conversely, if the futures price rises to $105, the manager will receive a marked-to-market profit of $5 million, which will be invested in additional Treasury bills. Discuss the sources of total return from such an investment.

SOLUTION

The total return on the collateralized futures position comes from the change in futures price and the interest income on the Treasury bills.

Generally, the volatility of commodity futures is higher than that of domestic or international equity, but commodities tend to have a low to negative correlation with stock and bond returns and a desirable positive correlation with inflation. Looking at the period from 1959 to 2004, Gorton and Rouwenhorst (2006) find that commodities have an average return comparable to stocks and a low to negative correlation with stocks and bonds. While stocks and bonds are negatively correlated with unexpected inflation, commodity prices tend to be positively correlated with unexpected inflation—an attractive feature. However, Erb and Harvey (2006) point out that over the period 1969–2004 there is a wide dispersion of results across individual commodities, so all conclusions on performance and risk of commodities strongly depend on the composition and weighting scheme of the commodity index used. For example, energy-related commodities offer the best hedge against inflation, but precious metals have not provided an inflation hedge over the period under study. Furthermore, the excellent long-term performance of some commodity indexes requires a word of caution. The commodities and weights selected to enter indexes reflect a selection bias when they include data from time periods prior to the initiation of the index, which biases any back-calculated performance. Index providers are now careful to avoid this bias.

Active Investment

Besides making inflation bets, another motivation for investing in commodities is their link to economic growth. In periods of rapid economic growth, commodities are in strong demand to satisfy production needs, and their prices tend to go up. Because of productivity gains, the prices of finished goods are unlikely to rise as fast as those of raw materials. This suggests an active management strategy in which specific commodities are bought and sold at various times. Managed futures are proposed by a large number of institutions.

As with any investments, the risk-and-return characteristics of managed futures must be analyzed carefully. Schneeweis (2002) discusses the proposed attraction of managed futures: the possibility of positive returns in months when the market does well and in the months when it does poorly. Jaeger (2002) proposes several principles for the risk management of managed futures portfolios:

- Diversification
- Liquidity monitoring, because diversification into a larger universe of contracts can include illiquid contracts
- Volatility dependent allocation where the weight of the different contracts in the portfolio is determined by their historical or implied volatility
- Quantitative risk management techniques such as value at risk (VaR) and stress tests
- Risk budgeting on various aggregation levels to detect undesired risk concentrations

- Limits on leverage
- Use of derivatives to hedge any unwanted currency risk
- Care in model selection with respect to data mining, in and out of sample performance, and adequate performance adjustments for risk

The Example of Gold

Gold has always played a special role in investments. It is a commodity traded worldwide, but more important, it has been regarded by many Europeans and Asians as the ultimate store of value. It is considered an international monetary asset that offers protection in case of a major disruption. Central banks and many investors regard gold as a monetary asset because it has been the core of domestic and international monetary systems for many centuries. This section focuses on gold investment because of the historical importance of gold in investment strategies, and as an example of a real asset investment. Of course, precious stones, stamps, or paintings could also be profitable long-term investments, but they usually require high transaction costs; moreover, each stone or painting is in a sense unique, which reduces its marketability. Gold is offered in a wide variety of investment vehicles that can be used in passive or active strategies. Gold-linked investments include gold bullion, coins, bonds, mining equity, futures, and options on gold and on mining equity or bonds.

The Motivation for Investing in Gold The traditional role of gold as the ultimate hedge and store of value is well known. For centuries, Europeans and Asians alike have regarded gold as the best possible protection against inflation and social, political, or economic crises because it can easily be traded worldwide at any time, and its real value increases during crises. Europeans and others who have suffered revolutions, invasions, and periods of hyperinflation need no correlation coefficients to be convinced of this attractive portfolio hedge characteristic. For example, gold kept its real value during the U.S. stock market crash from 1929 to 1932 and the London Stock Exchange collapse in equity and bonds from 1973 to 1975. Furthermore, the central role gold has played in domestic and international monetary systems for thousands of years makes it, in part, a monetary asset with exceptional liquidity. Other real assets, such as diamonds or stamps, do not have this characteristic.

In general, gold often allows investors to diversify against the kinds of risks that affect all stock markets simultaneously. For example, in 1973 and 1974, the price of bullion tripled when stock markets worldwide dropped dramatically during the oil crisis; the NYSE dropped approximately 50 percent.

A theoretical comment is in order here. In modern portfolio theory, a small or negative beta implies that the expected return on gold should be small. For example, a negative beta caused by a negative correlation between gold and the market portfolio implies that in the capital asset pricing model (CAPM) framework, the expected return on gold should be less than the risk-free interest rate. Indeed, it can be claimed that we should expect a modest long-term performance in gold and a greater return on the other assets in the portfolio; however, gold assets will reduce the risk of the portfolio in the event of adverse economic conditions. The question for a prudent portfolio manager, then, is whether these hedge benefits are worth the implicit cost she must pay in the form of a smaller expected long-term return for a small part of the portfolio.

Gold Price Determinants The following material is intended to indicate the kind of information and methods that analysts and investment managers use to analyze real asset investments. Commodities other than gold could also serve as examples.

Gold is a tangible international asset in limited supply. Gold can be extracted at a cost but cannot be produced artificially. Although gold is immune to the effects of weather, water, and oxygen, it suffers from human habits. The tradition of hiding gold treasures in the ground is consistent with the observation that gold is the ultimate physical store of value during major disruptions such as civil unrest, coup d'état, and war. During World War II, most Europeans dug a hole in their gardens or cellars to hide their gold holdings. Part of this hidden gold is never recovered if the owner dies. Most of the gold used in dentistry also disappears with the owner. Despite these losses, the stock of gold keeps slowly increasing with the amount extracted.

In a sense, the price of gold should be easy to forecast: The product is well defined. The supply sources are well identified, and reserves can be reasonably estimated. The major demands are clearly identified: carat jewelry, industrial needs, coins, and investment.

Supply and demand clearly determine the price of gold. It is therefore necessary to study the various components of supply and demand to forecast the price of gold. A different model may be required for each component. For example, Western mine production is affected by technological considerations, South African extraction policy, and political situations in sensitive countries. Russia's gold sales depend on that country's need for hard currencies. Official sales may also be induced by monetary and balance of payments problems. Industrial demand depends on technological innovation and the discovery of cheaper substitutes. Jewelry demand is sensitive to short-term gold price movements, as well as fashion; the investment motivation is often present in jewelry purchases. Investment demand for bullion and coins is a component of the total demand affecting gold price but is also determined by expectations of future price movements.

So, although gold is a single, well-identified, extensively researched product, its analysis and valuation is not a simple exercise. This difficulty may add another dimension to gold's mystical attraction.

Commodity-Linked Securities

Holding commodities provides no income, so the sole return to the owner is through price increase. Investors can select securities that are linked to some commodity prices and also provide some income. This can be an attractive alternative for investors who wish to, or must, hold financial investments rather than real assets. The two major types of commodity-linked securities are bonds and equity. The indexation clause is explicit for commodity-linked bonds but implicit for equity. Again, we focus on the example of gold.

Commodity-Linked Bonds There are many examples of commodity-linked bonds in the world capital markets. In periods of high inflation, governments have often been forced to offer loans with coupons or principal indexed to either the price of a specific good or a global inflation index. Inflation-indexed gilts became popular in the United Kingdom during the 1980s. The capital and coupons of these bonds are indexed to British retail prices.

In 1997, the U.S. Treasury started to offer Inflation-Indexed Securities, also known as Treasury Inflation Protected Securities (TIPS). The first such security was a 10-year bond, issued with a real yield of 3.45 percent. The principal value is adjusted for changes in the consumer price index (CPI) on each semiannual coupon payment date. So, the nominal coupon, equal to the real yield times the CPI-adjusted principal, increases with inflation. At maturity, the CPI-adjusted principal is reimbursed. In the United States, some government agencies, municipalities, and corporations have also issued inflation-indexed bonds. Often, the inflation adjustment to the principal is paid out immediately rather than at final maturity. This structure has been adopted because seeing their nominal credit exposure on nongovernment issues accumulate automatically over time worried investors.

Several countries have issued inflation-indexed bonds (United Kingdom, France, Sweden, Canada, etc.), and corporations and governments have issued bonds indexed to a variety of specific prices, such as oil prices. Gold bonds, and bonds with warrants on gold, have been an attractive alternative to holding gold ingots.

Commodity-Linked Equity The value of some companies is directly affected by commodity prices. This is clearly the case with the so-called energy companies. For example, companies in the oil and gas industries are affected by the evolution of oil prices. The link between commodity prices and stock prices is more evident for small, undiversified companies that specialize in one type of activity, for example, oil and gas exploration and production. However, large oil companies tend to be quite diversified across activities and the link between commodity prices and stock prices is weaker. An integrated exploration, production, and refining company will be less affected by oil price increases than a company operating in only one of the industry segments.

Gold mining companies are another example of commodity-linked equity. Gold mining shares differ from commodity-linked bonds in that the indexation clause is not fixed by contract but depends on mining economics. In fact, the mining industry is probably the simplest activity to describe in a valuation model. The economics of mining can be described by a simple discounted cash flow model. The principal relationship in the model is the cost structure of the mine as measured by the ratio of costs to revenues. The cost to remove an ounce or a gram of gold from so-called storage and refine it depends on several factors: technology, wage rates, power rates, and the grade and depth of the mine. Revenues depend on the world price of gold. Any movement in the market price of gold will directly affect the cash flows of a mine and therefore its market value; the higher the ratio of costs to revenues, the more sensitive will be the cash flows to gold price movements. However, note that the correlation between gold mine share prices and the price of gold is far from perfect. Gold mine values are influenced by factors other than gold prices; for example, social and political factors have strongly affected South African share prices over time.

Summary

- Alternative investments usually involve illiquidity, difficulty in the determination of current market values, limited historical risk and return data, the requirement for extensive investment analysis, a liquidity risk premium, and a segmentation risk premium. Alternative assets are assets not traded on exchanges. Alternative strategies are strategies that mostly use traded assets for the purpose of isolating bets and generating alpha.
- An open-end fund stands ready to redeem investor shares at market value, but a closed-end fund does not. A load fund has sales commission charges, and a no-load fund does not. Sales fees may also appear in annual distribution fees.
- The net asset value of a fund is calculated as the per-share value of the investment company's assets minus liabilities.
- Mutual funds may charge several different fees: Loads and redemption fees provide sales incentives; distribution and operating fees are annual fees; the part of the operating fee that is allocated to the fund manager can be considered an investment performance incentive.
- An exchange traded fund (ETF) is a special type of fund that tracks some market index but that is traded on a stock market like any common share.
- A mutual fund's purchases and sales of stocks held in the fund lead to taxable gains at the level of the fund, but this is not the case for an ETF because of its in-kind creation and redemption process.
- The advantages of ETFs are diversification, trading similarly to a stock, management of their risk augmented by futures and options contracts on them, transparency, cost effectiveness, avoidance of significant premiums or discounts to NAV, tax savings from payment of in-kind redemption, and immediate dividend reinvestment for open-end ETFs. The disadvantages are these: only a narrow-based market index is tracked in some countries; intraday trading opportunity is not important for long-horizon investors; large bid–ask spreads on some ETFs; and possibly better cost structures and tax advantages to direct index investing for large institutions.

- Some characteristics of real estate as an investable asset class are that each property is immovable, basically indivisible, and unique; real estate is not directly comparable to other properties; it is illiquid; and it is bought and sold intermittently in a generally local marketplace, with high transaction costs and market inefficiencies.
- The main approaches to real estate valuation are the cost approach, the sales comparison approach, the income approach, and the discounted after-tax cash flow approach.
- The net operating income from a real estate investment is gross potential income minus expenses, which include estimated vacancy and collection costs, insurance, taxes, utilities, and repairs and maintenance.
- The value of a property can be calculated as the cost to replace the building in its present form in the cost approach; an adjusted value from a benchmark of comparable sales in the sales comparison approach; a hedonic price estimate from a regression model in the sales comparison approach; and capitalized net operating income in the income approach.
- The net present value of a property to an equity investor is obtained as the present value of the after-tax cash flows, discounted at the investor's required rate of return on equity, minus the amount of equity required to make the investment.
- The three main categories of private equity are venture capital, leveraged buyouts, and distressed investing.
- Venture capital investing is done in many stages from seed through mezzanine.
- Venture capital investment characteristics include illiquidity, long-term commitment, difficulty in determining current market values, limited historical risk and return data, limited information, entrepreneurial/management mismatches, fund manager incentive mismatches, lack of knowledge of how many competitors exist, vintage cycles, and the requirement for extensive operations analysis and advice. The challenges to venture capital performance measurement are the difficulty in determining precise valuations, the lack of meaningful benchmarks, and the long-term nature of any performance feedback.
- The expected net present value of a venture capital project with a single terminal payoff and a single initial investment can be calculated, given its possible payoff and its conditional failure probabilities, as the present value of the expected payoff minus the required initial investment.
- The term *hedge fund* is not fully descriptive because the hedged position is generally designed to isolate a bet rather than to reduce risk. Hedge funds can be defined as funds that seek absolute returns; have a legal structure avoiding some government regulations; and have option-like fees, including a base management fee and an incentive fee proportional to realized profits.
- The net performance of a hedge fund can be calculated by subtracting its fees from its gross performance.

- Hedge funds can be categorized in a variety of ways: long/short, market neutral, global macro, event driven, convertible arbitrage, fixed-income arbitrage.
- The advantages of fund of funds (FOF) investing are availability to the small investor, the fact that access to funds is closed to new investors, diversification, managerial expertise, and a due diligence process. The disadvantages of FOF investing are high fees, little evidence of persistent performance, and the absolute return loss through diversification.
- High leverage is often present in hedge funds as part of the trading strategy and is an essential part of some strategies in which the arbitrage return is so small that leverage is needed to amplify the profit. The unique risks of hedge funds are liquidity risk, pricing risk, counterparty credit risk, settlement risk, short squeeze risk, and financing squeeze risk.
- In terms of performance, hedge funds are generally viewed as delivering a good return in both up and down markets. The net return on hedge fund indexes tends to be attractive, with a lower standard deviation of return than equity investments, a Sharpe ratio that is higher than that of equity investments, and a low correlation with conventional investments. The biases present in hedge fund performance and risk reporting include self-selection bias, backfilling bias, survivorship bias, smoothed pricing on infrequently traded assets, option-like investment strategies, and fee structure–induced gaming.
- For closely held companies and inactively traded securities, a discount is used for lack of liquidity, for lack of marketability, and for a minority interest, but a control premium is added for controlling ownership. The base for the marketability discount is the market value of equity for a comparable publicly traded company.
- Distressed-securities investing usually means investing in distressed company bonds with a view to equity ownership in the eventually reconstituted company. Such investments are similar to venture capital investments because they are illiquid, they require a long investment horizon, they require intense investor participation/consulting, and they offer the possibility of alpha because of mispricing.
- As a vehicle for investing in production and consumption, commodities complement the investment opportunities offered by shares of corporations that extensively use these as raw materials in their production processes. Investing directly in agricultural products and other commodities gives the investor exposure to the commodity components of the country's production and consumption.
- Commodity trading advisors (CTAs) offer managed futures funds that take positions in exchange traded derivatives on commodities and financials.
- The return on a collateralized futures position comes from the change in the futures price plus the interest income on risk-free government securities.

- The motivation for investing in commodities, commodity derivatives, and commodity-linked securities is that they may have negative correlation with stock and bond returns and a desirable positive correlation with inflation. In the case of commodity-linked securities, the investor can receive some income rather than depending solely on commodity price changes.
- The risk of managed futures can be managed through diversification, liquidity monitoring, volatility dependent allocation, quantitative techniques such as VaR, risk budgeting on various aggregation levels, limits on leverage, use of derivatives, and care in model selection.

Problems

Use the following information for Problems 1 and 2: Global Leveraged Equity Fund (GLEF) has three classes of shares, each holding the same portfolio of securities but having a different expense structure. The following table summarizes the expenses of these classes of shares.

Expense Comparison for Four Classes of GLEF

	Class A	Class B*	Class C
Sales charge (load) on purchases	5%	None	None
Deferred sales charge (load) on redemptions	None	4% in the first year, declining by 1% each year thereafter	1% for the initial 2 years only
Annual expenses:			
Distribution fee	0.25%	0.50%	0.50%
Management fee	0.50%	0.50%	0.50%
Other expenses	0.50%	0.50%	0.50%
	1.25%	1.50%	1.50%

*Class B shares automatically convert to Class A shares 72 months (6 years) after purchase.

Assume that expense percentages given will be constant at the given values. Assume that the deferred sales charges are computed on the basis of NAV.

An investor is considering the purchase of GLEF shares. The investor expects equity investments with risk characteristics similar to GLEF to earn 9 percent per year. He decides to make his selection of fund share class based on an assumed 9 percent return each year, gross of any of the expenses given in the preceding table.

1. Decide which class of shares of GLEF is best for the investor if he plans to liquidate his investment toward the end of
   a. Year 1
   b. Year 3
   c. Year 5
   d. Year 15

2. You have analyzed the relative performance of different classes of GLEF shares for liquidation in several years. Specifically, you have looked at liquidation in years 1, 3, 5, and 15. Your results are as follows. (The > symbol implies that the class preceding the sign performs better than the class following and the = symbol implies equal performance of the two classes.)

- Liquidation in year 1: Class C > Class B > Class A
- Liquidation in year 3: Class C > Class B > Class A
- Liquidation in year 5: Class B = Class C > Class A
- Liquidation in year 15: Class B > Class C > Class A

Provide an intuitive explanation for the pattern of relative performance that you observe.

3. Using the price data for several houses recently sold in a particular area, a real estate firm has identified the main characteristics that affect the prices of houses in that area. The characteristics identified include the living area, the number of bathrooms, whether the house has a fireplace, and how old the house is. The estimated slope coefficient for each of these characteristics and the constant term are as follows:

Characteristic	Units	Coefficient in Euros per Unit
Intercept	—	140,000
Living area	Square meters	210
Number of bathrooms	Number	10,000
Fireplace	0 or 1	15,000
Age of the house	Years	−6,000

Use these above estimates to value a five-year-old house with a living area of 500 square meters, three bathrooms, and a fireplace.

4. A real estate firm is evaluating an office building using the income approach. The real estate firm has compiled the following information for the office building. All information is on an annual basis.

Gross potential rental income	$350,000
Estimated vacancy and collection losses*	4%
Insurance and taxes	$26,000
Utilities	$18,000
Repairs and maintenance	$23,000
Depreciation	$40,000
Interest on proposed financing	$18,000

*As a percentage of gross potential rental income

There have been two recent sales of office buildings in the area. The first building had a net operating income of $500,000 and was sold at $4 million. The second building had a net operating income of $225,000 and was sold at $1.6 million.

a. Compute the net operating income for the office building to be valued.
b. Use the income approach to compute the appraisal price of the office building.

5. An analyst is evaluating a real estate investment project using the discounted cash flow approach. The purchase price is $3 million, which is financed 15 percent by equity and 85 percent by a mortgage loan. It is expected that the property will be sold in five years. The analyst has estimated the following after-tax cash flows during the first four years of the real estate investment project.

Year	1	2	3	4
Cash flow	$60,000	$75,000	$91,000	$108,000

For the fifth year, that is, the year when the property would be sold by the investor, the after-tax cash flow without the property sale is estimated to be $126,000 and the after-tax cash flow from the property sale is estimated to be $710,000.

Compute the NPV of this project. State whether the investor should undertake the project. The investor's cost of equity for projects with level of risk comparable to this real estate investment project is 18 percent.

6. An investment firm is evaluating a real estate investment project, using the discounted cash flow approach. The purchase price is $1.5 million, which is financed 20 percent by equity and 80 percent by a mortgage loan at a 9 percent pre-tax interest rate. The mortgage loan has a long maturity and constant annual payments of $120,000. This includes interest payments on the remaining principal at a 9 percent interest rate and a variable principal repayment that steps up with time. The net operating income (NOI) in the first year is estimated to be $170,000. NOI is expected to grow at a rate of 4 percent every year. The interest on real estate financing for the project is tax deductible. The marginal income tax rate for the investment firm is 30 percent. Using straight-line depreciation, the annual depreciation of the property is $37,500.
   a. Compute the after-tax cash flows in years 1, 2, and 3 of the project.
   b. It is expected that the property will be sold at the end of three years. The projected sale price is $1.72 million. The property's sales expenses are 6.5 percent of the sale price. The capital gains tax rate is 20 percent. Compute the after-tax cash flow from the property sale in year 3.
   c. The investor's cost of equity for projects with level of risk comparable to this real estate investment project is 19 percent. Recommend whether to invest in the project or not, based on the NPV of the project.

7. Would you suggest using real estate appraisal-based indexes in a global portfolio optimization?

8. Suppose the estimated correlation matrix of the Wilshire 5000 U.S. stock index and two real estate indexes, the Federal Russell Company index (FRC) and the National Association of Real Estate Investment Trusts (NAREIT) is as follows:

	Wilshire 5000	NAREIT	FRC
Wilshire 5000	1.00	0.79	0.18
NAREIT	0.79	1.00	0.02
FRC	0.18	0.02	1.00

Based on this matrix, compare the expected price behavior of the two real estate indexes.

9. An investor is evaluating a venture capital project that will require an investment of $1.4 million. The investor estimates that she will be able to exit the venture successfully in eight years. She also estimates that there is an 80 percent chance that the venture will not survive until the end of the eighth year. If the venture does survive until then, it is equally likely that the payoff at the time of exit will be either $25 million or $35 million. The investor is considering an equity investment in the project, and her cost of equity for a project with similar risk is 20 percent.
   a. Compute the NPV of the venture capital project.
   b. Recommend whether to accept or reject the project.

10. VenCap, Inc. is a venture capital financier. It estimates that investing £4.5 million in a particular venture capital project can return £60 million at the end of six years if it succeeds; however, it realizes that the project may fail at any time between now and the end of six years. The following table has VenCap's estimates of probabilities

of failure for the project. First, 0.28 is the probability of failure in year 1. The probability that the project fails in the second year, given that it has survived through year 1, is 0.25. The probability that the project fails in the third year, given that it has survived through year 2, is 0.22, and so forth. VenCap is considering an equity investment in the project, and its cost of equity for a project with this level of risk is 22 percent.

Year	**1**	**2**	**3**	**4**	**5**	**6**
Failure probability	0.28	0.25	0.22	0.18	0.18	0.10

Compute the expected net present value of the venture capital project and recommend whether VenCap should accept or reject the project.

11. Consider a hedge fund that has an annual fee structure of 1.5 percent base management fee plus a 15 percent incentive fee applied to profits above the risk-free rate. If the risk-free rate is 5.5 percent, compute the net percentage return for an investor if the gross return during the year is
a. 35%
b. 5%
c. −6%

12. A hedge fund currently has assets of $2 billion. The annual fee structure of this fund consists of a fixed fee of 1 percent of portfolio assets plus a 20 percent incentive fee. The fund applies the incentive fee to the gross return each year in excess of the portfolio's previous high-water mark, which is the maximum portfolio value since the inception of the fund. The maximum value the fund has achieved so far since its inception was a little more than a year ago when its value was $2.1 billion. Compute the fee that the manager would earn in dollars if the return on the fund this year turns out to be
a. 29%
b. 4.5%
c. −1.8%

13. Consider a hedge fund whose annual fee structure has a fixed fee and an incentive fee with a high-water mark provision. The fund manager earns an incentive fee only if the fund is above the high-water mark of the maximum portfolio value since the inception of the fund. Discuss the positive and negative implications of the high-water mark provision for the investors of the hedge fund.

14. A hedge fund has compiled a list of French firms that it believes will outperform the overall French stock market by 7 percent over the year. It also has compiled a list of French firms that it believes will underperform the overall French stock market by 7 percent. The hedge fund wants to invest in a market-neutral long/short strategy on the French stock market. It has a capital of €25 million for this purpose. However, it would like to retain a cash cushion of €1 million for unforeseen events. The hedge fund can borrow shares from a primary broker with a cash margin deposit equal to 20 percent of the value of the shares. No additional costs are charged to borrow the shares.
a. Outline the strategy for the hedge fund.
b. Compute the return on the hedge fund's capital of €25 million if the returns on both lists of stocks are as expected. Ignore the return on invested cash of €1 million, and assume that dividends on the long stocks will offset dividends on the short stocks.

15. The shares of an Italian firm have been trading earlier around €6. Recently, a Spanish firm entered into talks with the Italian firm to acquire it. The Spanish firm offered two of its shares for every three shares of the Italian firm. The boards of directors of both firms have approved the merger, and ratification by shareholders is expected soon. The shares of the Spanish firm are currently trading at €12.50, and the shares of the Italian firm are trading at €8.
    a. Should the shares of the Italian firm trade at a discount? Explain.
    b. What position do you think a hedge fund that specializes in risk arbitrage in mergers and acquisitions will take in the two firms? Assume that the hedge fund's position will involve 250,000 shares of the Italian firm.
    c. It turns out that the European Union commission does not approve the merger because it fears that the merged firm will have a monopolistic position in its industry. After this announcement, the shares of the Italian firm fell to €6.10 each. The shares of the Spanish firm are still trading at €12.50 each. Discuss the consequences for the hedge fund. Ignore the cost of securities lending and margins deposit.

16. Global group manages hedge funds and has three hedge funds invested in the stock market of a particular emerging country. These three hedge funds have very different investment strategies. As expected, the 2007 returns on the three funds were quite different. Over the year 2007, an index based on the overall stock market of the emerging country went up by 20 percent. Here are the performances of the three funds before management fees set at 15 percent of gross profits:

Fund	**Gross Return**
A	50%
B	20%
C	−10%

    At year end, most clients had left fund C, and Global group closed this fund. At the start of 2008, Global group launched an aggressive publicity campaign among portfolio managers, stressing the remarkable return on fund A. If potential clients asked whether the firm had other hedge funds invested in the particular emerging market, it mentioned the only other fund, fund B, and claimed that the group's average gross performance during 2008 was 35 percent.
    a. Compare the average gross return and the average net return on the three hedge funds with the percentage increase in the stock market index.
    b. Comment on the publicity campaign launched by Global group.

17. An analyst is examining the performance of hedge funds. He looks at the 90 hedge funds that are in existence today and notes that the average annual return on these funds during the last 10 years is 25.17 percent. The standard deviation of these returns is 17.43 percent and the Sharpe ratio is 1.15. The analyst also observes that the average of the annual returns on a stock market index during the last 10 years is 14.83 percent. The standard deviation of these returns is 11.87 percent and the Sharpe ratio is 0.81. The analyst concludes that the hedge funds have substantially outperformed the stock market index. Discuss why the comparison by the analyst could be misleading.

18. Consider the four major commodities traded on a commodity futures exchange today (year 10). The following table lists the average annualized price movements from year 1 to year 10, as well as the production volumes, expressed in the local currency unit, today (year 10) and ten years ago (year 1).

Commodity	Average Return	Annual Production Year 1	Annual Production Year 10
A	20%	10	50
B	20%	5	20
C	−10%	50	10
D	0%	35	20

The futures exchange has now decided to create a commodity index based on the four commodities, with weights equal to their current relative importance in economic production. These indexes are back-calculated till year 1 using today's weights.

a. Would such an index give unbiased indications over the past 10 years?
b. What suggestions do you have regarding weights that can be used to back-calculate the indexes?

19. The beta of gold relative to the market portfolio is −0.3. The risk-free rate is 7 percent, and the market risk premium is 4 percent.

a. What is the expected return on gold based on the capital asset pricing model (CAPM)?
b. Give an intuitive explanation for the magnitude of the expected return on gold.

Bibliography

Asness, C., Krail, R., and Liew, J. "Do Hedge Funds Hedge?" *Journal of Portfolio Management*, Fall 2001.

Eichholtz, P. M. A. "Does International Diversification Work Better for Real Estate Than for Stocks and Bonds?" *Financial Analysts Journal*, January/February 1996.

Erb, C. B., and Harvey, C. R., "Strategic and Tactical Value of Commodities Futures," *Financial Analysts Journal*, 62(2), March/April 2006.

Firstenberg, P. M., Ross, S. A., and Zisler, R. C. "Real Estate: The Whole Story," *Journal of Portfolio Management*, Spring 1988.

Gastineau, G. L., "Exchange-Traded Funds: An Introduction," *Journal of Portfolio Management*, Spring 2001.

Getmansky, M., Lo, A., and Mei, S., "Sifting Through the Wreckage: Lessons from Recent Hedge-Fund Liquidations," *Journal of Investment Management*, 2(4), 2004.

Goetzmann, W. N., and Ibbotson, R. G. "The Performance of Real Estate as an Asset Class," *Journal of Applied Corporate Finance*, Fall 1990.

Gorton, G., and Rouwenhorst, K. G., "Facts and Fantasies About Commodity Futures," *Financial Analysts Journal*, 62(2), March/April 2006.

Hoesli, M., Lekander, J., and Witkiewicz, W., "International Evidence on Real Estate as a Portfolio Diversifier," *Journal of Real Estate Research*, 26(2), 2004.

Hooke, J. C. *Security Analysis on Wall Street*, New York: John Wiley & Sons, 1998.

Hudson-Wilson, S. "Why Real Estate?" *Journal of Portfolio Management*, 28(1), Fall 2001.

Ibbotson, R., and Chen, P., "The A, B, Cs of Hedge Funds: Alphas, Betas, and Costs," Yale ICF Working Paper No. 06-10, September 2006.

Jaeger, L. *Managing Risk in Alternative Investment Strategies*, London: Prentice Hall, 2002.

Jarchow, S. P. *Graaskamp on Real Estate,* Washington, DC: Urban Land Institute, 1991.

Lerner, J. *Venture Capital and Private Equity,* New York: John Wiley & Sons, 2000.

Lhabitant, F. *Hedge Funds: Myths and Limits,* New York: John Wiley & Sons, 2002.

Liu, C., Hartzell, D. J., and Hoesli, M. "International Evidence on Real Estate Securities as an Inflation Hedge," *Real Estate Economics,* 25(2), Summer 1997, pp. 193–233.

Lo, A., "The Statistics of Sharpe Ratios." *Financial Analysts Journal,* 58(4), July/August 2002.

———. *The Dynamics of The Hedge Fund Industry,* Research Foundation of the CFA Institute, 2005.

Malkiel, B., and Saha, A. "Hedge Funds: Risk and Return," *Financial Analysts Journal,* 61(6), November/December 2005.

Mull, S. R., and Soenen, L. A. "U.S. REITs as an Asset Class in International Investment Portfolios," *Financial Analysts Journal,* March/April 1997.

Mussavian, M., and Hirsch, J. "European Exchange-Traded Funds: An Overview," *Journal of Alternative Investments,* 5(2), Fall 2002, pp. 63–77.

Pratt, S. P., Reilly, R. F., and Schweihs, R. P. *Valuing a Business,* 4th ed., Chicago: Irwin, 2000.

Quan, D. C., and Titman, S. "Commercial Real Estate Prices and Stock Market Returns: An International Analysis," *Financial Analysts Journal,* May/June 1997.

Schilit, W. K. "Venture Catalysts or Vulture Capitalists?" *Journal of Investing,* Fall 1996.

Schneeweis, T. "Managed Futures," in D. R. Jobman, Ed., *The Handbook of Alternative Investments,* New York: John Wiley & Sons, 2002.

Schwartz, E. "The Pricing of Commodity-Linked Bonds," *Journal of Finance,* May 1982.

Sharpe, W. F., Alexander, G. J., and Bailey, J. V. *Investments,* 6th ed., Upper Saddle River, NJ: Prentice-Hall, 1999.

Söderberg, B. "A Note on the Hedonic Model Specification for Income Properties," in K. Wang and M. L. Wolverton, Eds., *Real Estate Valuation Theory,* Boston: Kluwer Academic, 2002.

Terhaar, K., Staub, R., and Singer, B. "The Appropriate Policy Allocation for Alternative Investments," *Journal of Portfolio Management,* Spring 2003.

9

The Case for International Diversification

LEARNING OUTCOMES

After completing this chapter, you will be able to do the following:

- Discuss why investors should consider constructing global portfolios
- Compare the relative size of the U.S. market with other global stock and bond markets
- Discuss the changes in risk that occur when investors add international securities to their portfolios and calculate the expected return and standard deviation for a two-asset portfolio containing a domestic asset and a foreign asset
- Demonstrate how changes in currency exchange rates can affect the returns that investors earn on foreign security investments
- Demonstrate how changes in currency exchange rates can affect the risk that investors bear on foreign security investments
- Explain the effect of international diversification on the efficient frontier by comparing a frontier that includes foreign investments with one that does not
- Discuss the factors that cause equity market correlations across countries to be relatively low
- Discuss the factors that cause bond market correlations across countries to be relatively low
- Discuss the influence of time differences between countries on the correlation of daily returns
- Discuss the reasons for an increased Sharpe ratio with international investing and explain why this increase could be simultaneously true for investors of different countries
- Illustrate the potential risk–return impact of adding bonds to a global asset allocation
- Discuss patterns of global equity returns and global market correlations for different market environments

- Discuss the reasons that currency risk may only slightly magnify the volatility of foreign currency–denominated investments
- Explain the increasing correlation argument against international diversification and discuss the factors leading to increased correlations
- Evaluate the implication of non-normal return distributions and changes in volatility for the usual case in favor of global risk diversification
- Explain the country-specific outperformance argument against international diversification
- Discuss the barriers to international investing
- Discuss the pitfalls in estimating correlations during volatile periods
- Explain why international performance opportunities have increased over time
- Distinguish between global investing and international diversification
- Discuss the potential benefits of investing in emerging markets
- Evaluate the historical performance of emerging equity markets
- Discuss the return volatility, return correlation, and expected return characteristics that result from including emerging-market securities in a portfolio
- Discuss the importance of currency issues in emerging-market investing
- Describe the concept of investability in emerging markets
- Discuss the segmentation versus integration characteristics of emerging markets

International portfolio investment has long been a tradition in many European countries, but it is a more recent practice in North America.[1] There is now a strong trend toward international diversification in all countries, however, especially among U.S. institutional investors, such as corporate and public pension funds. In the early 1970s, U.S. pension funds basically held no foreign assets; the percentage of foreign assets approached 20 percent of total assets by 2006. British institutional investors hold more than 25 percent of their assets in non-British securities. Some Dutch pension funds have more than half of their assets invested abroad. Recently, private investors have joined the trend toward global investment.

Indeed, the mere size of foreign markets justifies international diversification, even for U.S. investors. At the end of 2006, the world stock market capitalization was around $25 trillion. The U.S. stock market accounted for roughly half of the world market. The growth of the world stock market since the early 1970s has been remarkable. In 1974, the New York Stock Exchange was the only significant market in the world, representing 60 percent of a world market capitalization of less than

[1] The terminology varies across countries. Americans use the word *international* to refer to non-U.S. investments and *global* to refer to U.S. plus non-U.S. investments. Other English-speaking nationals tend to use the word *foreign* to refer to nondomestic investments and *international* to refer to domestic plus foreign investments. We use the U.S. terminology.

$1 trillion.[2] As shown in Exhibit 9.1, the size of the world market multiplied by a factor of 50 in the next 32 years, and the share of U.S. equity moved from 60 percent to less than 30 percent in 1988 and back to 40 percent by the end of 2006. The Asia–Pacific region, which made up one-third of the world stock market in the early 1990s, shrank to 25 percent at the end of 2006. Europe makes up one-third of the world market. The world market capitalization of bonds, domestic and international, was around $66 trillion at the end of 2006. U.S. dollar bonds accounted for roughly 45 percent of the world bond market, while yen bonds accounted for somewhat less than 20 percent and bonds denominated in European currencies accounted for some 30 percent.

In a fully efficient, integrated, global capital market, buying the world market portfolio would be the natural passive strategy. In theory, an American investor should hold half of the portfolio in international securities. But, even if one does not believe in a perfect, integrated world market, the case for diversifying in international securities is strong. The basic argument in favor of international diversification is that foreign investments allow investors to reduce the total risk of the portfolio, while offering additional profit potential. By expanding the investment opportunity set, international diversification helps to improve the risk-adjusted performance of a portfolio.

EXHIBIT 9.1

Stock Market Capitalization

Developed Markets to 2000; all Markets from 2002

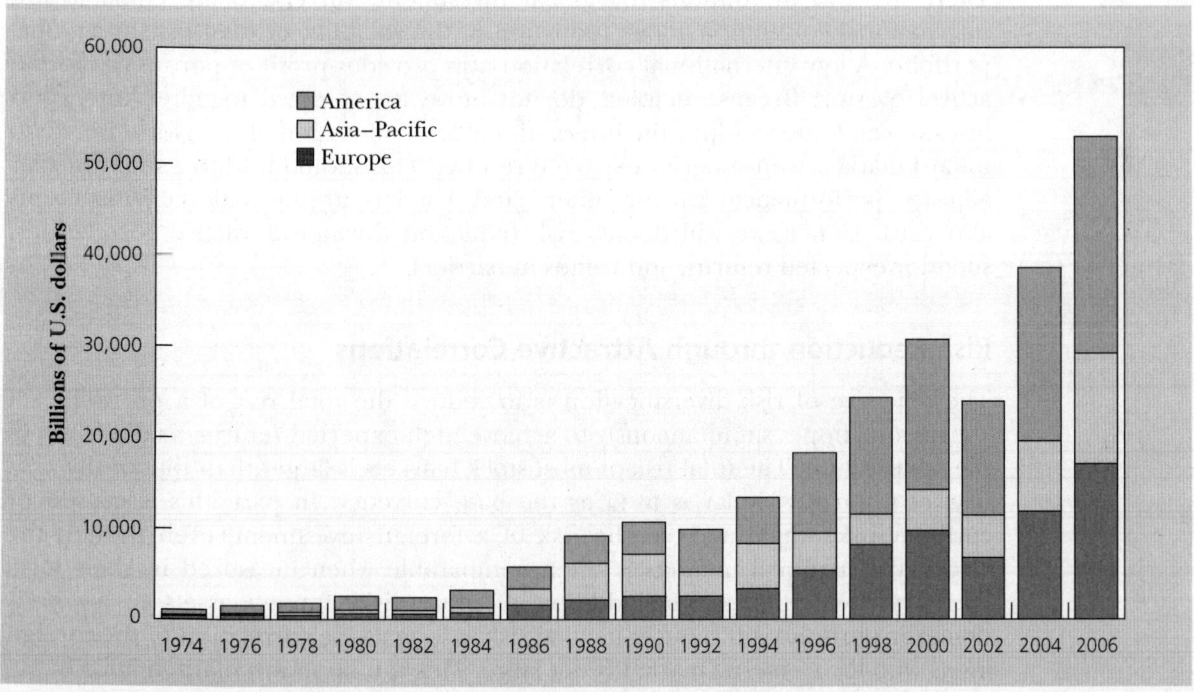

Source: Data from World Federation of Stock Exchanges.

[2] At that time, Solnik (1974) presented the case for international diversification to U.S. pension plans that had zero overseas investments.

Domestic securities tend to move up and down together because they are similarly affected by domestic conditions, such as monetary announcements, movements in interest rates, budget deficits, and national growth. This creates a definite positive correlation among nearly all stocks traded in the same national equity market. The correlation applies equally to bonds; bond prices on the same national market are very strongly correlated. Investors have searched for methods to spread their risks and diversify away the national market risk. In their variety, foreign capital markets provide good potential for diversification beyond domestic instruments and markets.

This chapter presents the advantages and disadvantages of international investing. It focuses on equity investments but also refers to bond investments. The first section presents the traditional case for international diversification. However, this case has been criticized recently because of an increase in international correlations, especially in periods of high market volatility. The second section reviews these criticisms. The third section revisits the benefits of a global approach in light of the recent changes in the global economic landscape. The last section presents the case for investing in emerging markets.

The Traditional Case for International Diversification

There are two motivations for global investment. All else being equal, a low international correlation allows reduction of the volatility, or total risk, of a global portfolio. A low international correlation also provides profit opportunities for an active investor: Because markets do not move up or down together, an expert investor can hope to adjust the international asset allocation of the global portfolio toward markets with superior expected returns. This should lead to a superior risk-adjusted performance. On the other hand, barriers to international investments also exist. Hence, we will discuss risk reduction through attractive correlations, superior expected returns, and trends in barriers.

Risk Reduction through Attractive Correlations

The objective of risk diversification is to reduce the total risk of a portfolio. Of course, one hopes simultaneously to achieve high expected returns, as discussed in the next section. The total risk of most stock markets is larger than that of the U.S. market when the dollar is used as the base currency. In part, this is caused by currency risk, which adds to the risk of a foreign investment, even though the volatility of national markets is often comparable when measured in their local currency.[3] Nevertheless, the addition of more risky foreign assets to a purely domestic portfolio still reduces its total risk as long as the correlation of the foreign assets with the domestic market is not large. This can be shown mathematically.

[3] Similarly, the volatility of the U.S. stock market would look larger than that of the French stock market when returns are measured in euros.

Let's consider a portfolio partly invested in domestic assets (e.g., a U.S. stock index for a U.S. investor) and partly invested in foreign assets (e.g., a French stock index). The proportions invested in each asset class is denoted w_d for domestic assets and w_f for foreign assets; they sum to 100 percent. The returns are denoted R_p for the portfolio, R_d for the domestic assets, and R_f for the foreign assets. All returns are measured in the base currency (e.g., the U.S. dollar for a U.S. investor). So, the return on foreign assets is subject to currency risk. The domestic and foreign assets have standard deviations denoted σ_d and σ_f, respectively. The total risk of the portfolio is its standard deviation σ_p. The correlation between the two asset classes is denoted $\rho_{d,f}$. Remember that the variance of the portfolio is the square of its standard deviation, and that the covariance between the two asset classes is given by

$$cov_{d,f} = \rho_{d,f}\,\sigma_d\,\sigma_f$$

First, note that the expected return on the portfolio is simply equal to the average expected return on the two asset classes:

$$E(R_p) = w_d\,E(R_d) + w_f\,E(R_f) \tag{9.1}$$

A well-known mathematical result is that the variance of the portfolio is equal to

$$\sigma_p^2 = w_d^2\sigma_d^2 + w_f^2\sigma_f^2 + 2w_d\,w_f\,cov_{d,f}$$

or

$$\sigma_p^2 = w_d^2\sigma_d^2 + w_f^2\sigma_f^2 + 2w_d\,w_f\,\rho_{d,f}\,\sigma_d\,\sigma_f$$

The standard deviation is simply equal to the square root:

$$\sigma_p = (w_d^2\,\sigma_d^2 + w_f^2\,\sigma_f^2 + 2w_d\,w_f\,\rho_{d,f}\,\sigma_d\,\sigma_f)^{1/2} \tag{9.2}$$

The portfolio's total risk σ_p will always be *less* than the average of the two standard deviations: $w_d\,\sigma_d + w_f\,\sigma_f$. The only case in which it will be equal is when the correlation[4] is exactly equal to 1.0 (perfect correlation between the two assets). Otherwise diversification benefits will show, and the lower the correlation, the bigger the risk reduction (see Example 9.1).

Currency Considerations The return and risk of an asset depend on the currency used. For example, the return and risk of a French asset will be different if measured in the euro or in the dollar. The dollar value of the asset is equal to its euro value multiplied by the exchange rate (number of dollars per euro):

$$V^{\$} = V \times S$$

where V and $V^{\$}$ are, respectively, the values in the local currency (euro) and in the dollar, and S is the exchange rate (number of dollars per euro). The rate of return in dollars from time 0 to time 1 is given by

[4] A correlation coefficient between two random variables lies between +1.0 and −1.0. A coefficient of 1.0 means that the two markets go up and down in identical cycles, whereas a coefficient of −1.0 means that they are exactly countercyclical. For more details, see DeFusco et al. (2001).

$$r^{\$} = \frac{V_1^{\$} - V_0^{\$}}{V_0^{\$}} = \frac{V_1S_1 - V_0S_0}{V_0S_0} = \frac{V_1 - V_0}{V_0} + \frac{S_1 - S_0}{S_0} + \frac{V_1 - V_0}{V_0} \times \frac{S_1 - S_0}{S_0}$$

$$r^{\$} = r + s + (r \times s)$$

where r is the return in local currency, $r^{\$}$ is the return in dollars, and s is the percentage exchange rate movement.[5]

EXAMPLE 9.1 INTERNATIONAL RISK DIVERSIFICATION BENEFITS

Assume that the domestic and foreign assets have standard deviations of $\sigma_d = 15$ percent and $\sigma_f = 17$ percent, respectively, with a correlation of $\rho_{d,f} = 0.4$.

1. What is the standard deviation of a portfolio equally invested in domestic and foreign assets?
2. What is the standard deviation of a portfolio with a 40 percent investment in the foreign asset?
3. What is the standard deviation of a portfolio equally invested in domestic and foreign assets if the correlation is 0.5? What if the correlation is 0.8?

SOLUTIONS

1. The variance of the total portfolio equally invested ($w_d = w_f = 50\%$) in both assets, σ_p^2, is given by

$$\sigma_p^2 = 0.5^2[\sigma_d^2 + \sigma_f^2 + (2\rho_{df}\,\sigma_d\,\sigma_f)]$$

$$\sigma_p^2 = 0.5^2[225 + 289 + (2 \times 0.4 \times 255)] = 179.5$$

Hence, the standard deviation σ_p is given by $\sqrt{179.5}$, or 13.4 percent, which is significantly less than that of the domestic asset. Since one can diversify in several foreign markets, the total risk of the portfolio could be further reduced.

2. The risk reduction depends on the percentage invested in each asset. A portfolio invested 60 percent in the domestic asset and 40 percent in the foreign asset has a variance given by

$$\sigma_p^2 = (0.6^2 \times \sigma_d^2) + (0.4^2 \times \sigma_f^2) + (2 \times 0.4 \times 0.6 \times \rho_{d,f}\sigma_d\sigma_f)$$
$$= 176.2$$

The standard deviation is $\sigma_p = 13.27$ percent, and this is the lowest-risk portfolio.

3. The risk reduction also depends on the level of correlation. If the correlation is 0.5 instead of 0.4, the risk of the portfolio equally invested becomes $\sigma_p = 13.87$ percent. If the correlation is 0.8, the risk of the portfolio equally invested becomes $\sigma_p = 15.18$ percent. The risk of the portfolio increases with the level of correlation.

[5] If a dividend or coupon is paid in period 1, it will be included in V_1.

For example, if the return on a French asset is 5 percent in euros and the euro appreciates by 1 percent, the return in dollars is 6.05 percent. This is slightly different from the sum of the euro return and of the currency movement, because the currency appreciation applies not only to the original capital, but also to the capital gain. This cross product is equal to 5% × 1% = 0.05 percent.

It is easy to compare the risks of an asset measured in different currencies. To simplify notations, it is usually assumed that the cross product $r \times s$ is small relative to r and s and can be ignored for risk calculations. Hence, the variance of the dollar return is simply equal to the variance of the sum of the local currency return and the exchange rate movement:

$$var(r^{\$}) = var(r + s) = var(r) + var(s) + 2cov(r,s)$$

or

$$\sigma_f^2 = \sigma^2 + \sigma_s^2 + 2\rho\sigma\sigma_s$$

where σ_f^2 is the variance of the foreign asset measured in dollars, σ^2 is its variance in local currency, σ_s^2 is the variance of the exchange rate (number of dollars per local currency), and ρ is the correlation between the asset return, in local currency, and the exchange rate movement. As the correlation is never greater than 1.0, the asset and currency risks are not additive, and we have

$$\sigma_f \leq \sigma + \sigma_s$$

The difference between σ_f and σ is called the contribution of currency risk (see Example 9.2).

In this chapter, we assume that we measure all returns and risk in the currency of the investor, namely, the U.S. dollar. The issue of currency hedging is discussed in other chapters.

EXAMPLE 9.2 CURRENCY RISK CONTRIBUTION

Suppose that we have a foreign investment with the following characteristics:

$$\sigma = 15.5\% \quad \sigma_s = 7\% \quad \rho = 0$$

What is the risk in domestic currency and the contribution of currency risk?

SOLUTION

We have

$$\sigma_f^2 = \sigma^2 + \sigma_s^2 + 0 = (15.5)^2 + (7.0)^2 = 289.25$$

Hence, the standard deviation σ_f is given by $\sqrt{289.25}$, or 17 percent. Note that this number is well below the sum of the risk of the asset measured in the local currency ($\sigma = 15.5\%$) and the risk of the currency ($\sigma_s = 7\%$). Currency risk increases the asset risk only from 15.5 percent in the local currency to 17 percent in domestic currency. Hence, the difference between σ_f and σ is the contribution of currency risk, here $\sigma_f - \sigma = 1.5$ percent.

Efficient Portfolios A portfolio is mean–variance efficient if it has the highest level of expected return for a given level of risk.[6] The set of all *efficient portfolios* is called the *efficient frontier*. The simple calculation for two assets is illustrated in Example 9.3.

Of course, one can invest in many different domestic and international assets. Combining all domestic stocks in an efficient mean–variance fashion, we derive the domestic efficient frontier represented in Exhibit 9.3. Combining all domestic and

EXAMPLE 9.3 RISK-RETURN TRADE-OFF OF INTERNATIONALLY DIVERSIFIED PORTFOLIOS

Assume that the domestic and foreign assets have standard deviations of $\sigma_d =$ 15 percent and $\sigma_f =$ 17 percent, respectively, with a correlation of $\rho_{d,f} = 0.4$. The expected returns of the domestic and foreign assets are equal, respectively, to $E(R_d) = 10$ percent and $E(R_f) = 12$ percent. Draw the set of all portfolios combining these two assets with positive weights in a risk–return graph.

SOLUTION

We can use Equations 9.1 and 9.2 to derive the set of portfolios invested in various proportions in the two assets. Their representation in a risk–return graph is given in Exhibit 9.2, in which D and F represent the domestic and foreign assets, respectively.

EXHIBIT 9.2

Risk–Return Trade-off of Internationally Diversified Portfolios

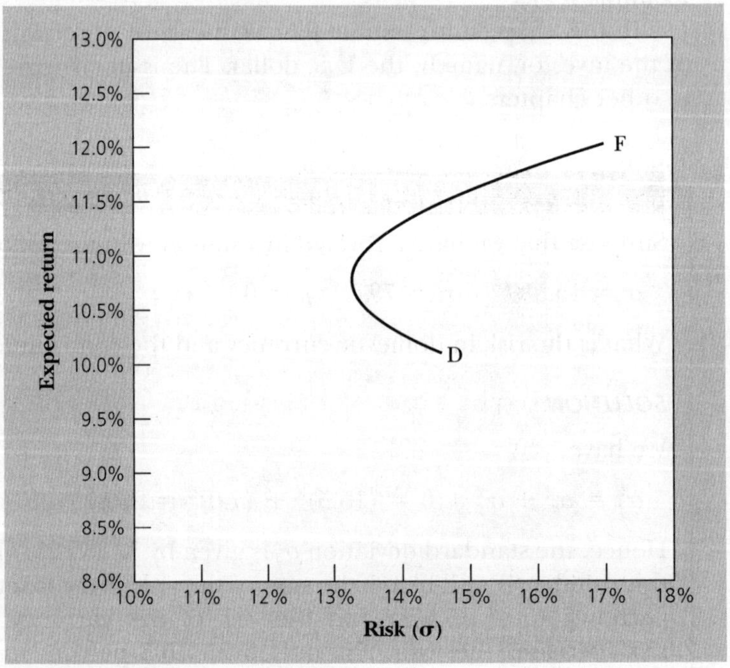

[6] See DeFusco et al. (2007).

EXHIBIT 9.3

Risk–Return Trade-off of Internationally Diversified versus Domestic-Only Portfolios

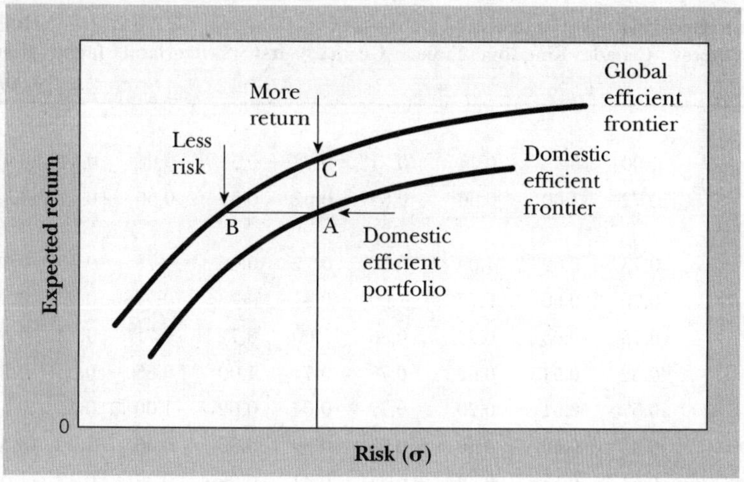

international stocks in an efficient mean–variance fashion, we derive the global mean–variance-efficient frontier represented on the same exhibit. The global efficient frontier is to the left of the domestic efficient frontier, showing the increased return opportunities and risk diversification benefits brought by the enlarged investment universe. For example, portfolio A is on the domestic efficient frontier. Portfolio B on the global efficient frontier has the same return but less risk than portfolio A; portfolio C on the global efficient frontier has the same risk but more return than portfolio A.

A prerequisite for this argument is that the various capital markets of the world have somewhat independent price behaviors. If the Paris Bourse and the London Stock Exchange moved in parallel with the U.S. market, diversification opportunities would not exist. So, we start by an empirical investigation of the level of international correlation.

The correlations between various stock and bond markets are systematically monitored by major international money managers. Although the correlation coefficients between markets vary over time, they are always far from unity. For the portfolio manager, this means that there is ample room for successful risk diversification. Following is a discussion of some recently estimated correlations, as illustration. Correlation estimates change somewhat over time, and the issue of stability in the correlation is discussed in the next sections of this chapter.

Equity Exhibit 9.4 gives the correlations across selected national stock markets with returns measured in two different currencies over the 10-year period from May 1997 to May 2007. The bottom left part of the matrix gives the correlation when all returns are measured in U.S. dollars. The top right part of the matrix gives the correlation when the foreign investments are fully hedged against currency risk; in other words, the foreign currency is assumed to be sold forward

EXHIBIT 9.4

Correlation of Stock Markets, 1997–2007

Monthly returns in U.S. dollars (bottom left) and currency hedged (top right)

	United States	Canada	United Kingdom	France	Germany	Italy	Switzerland	Japan	Hong Kong, China	Europe	EAFE	World	Emerging Markets
United States	1.00	0.73	0.74	0.71	0.73	0.55	0.66	0.41	0.51	0.77	0.77	0.91	0.67
Canada	0.72	1.00	0.60	0.65	0.61	0.51	0.56	0.47	0.54	0.67	0.70	0.77	0.70
United Kingdom	0.73	0.62	1.00	0.76	0.72	0.66	0.73	0.40	0.46	0.86	0.83	0.82	0.59
France	0.70	0.66	0.77	1.00	0.87	0.78	0.77	0.45	0.39	0.91	0.88	0.83	0.59
Germany	0.73	0.63	0.73	0.86	1.00	0.72	0.71	0.42	0.39	0.88	0.85	0.83	0.61
Italy	0.52	0.51	0.62	0.78	0.71	1.00	0.65	0.36	0.26	0.80	0.75	0.68	0.50
Switzerland	0.57	0.51	0.70	0.72	0.64	0.62	1.00	0.45	0.37	0.81	0.80	0.76	0.54
Japan	0.43	0.50	0.40	0.35	0.30	0.23	0.40	1.00	0.31	0.47	0.66	0.56	0.56
Hong Kong, China	0.51	0.55	0.48	0.41	0.41	0.28	0.37	0.43	1.00	0.45	0.50	0.54	0.66
Europe	0.76	0.69	0.86	0.91	0.88	0.78	0.78	0.40	0.48	1.00	0.92	0.88	0.65
EAFE	0.76	0.74	0.83	0.85	0.81	0.70	0.76	0.65	0.57	0.90	1.00	0.90	0.72
World	0.91	0.78	0.81	0.81	0.81	0.64	0.69	0.56	0.57	0.87	0.90	1.00	0.74
Emerging Markets	0.66	0.72	0.58	0.60	0.62	0.49	0.47	0.52	0.68	0.65	0.73	0.74	1.00

for an amount equal to that of the foreign stock investment. Let's first examine the correlations when no currency hedging is undertaken (U.S. dollar returns).

For example, Exhibit 9.4 indicates that the correlation between the Japanese and U.S. stock markets is 0.43. The square of this correlation coefficient, usually called R-square or R^2, indicates the percentage of common variance between the two markets. Note that the *R*-square is simply the square of the correlation ρ. Here only 19 percent ($R^2 = 0.44^2$) of stock price movements are common to the Japanese and U.S. markets.[7] Note that on average, the common variance between the U.S. and other markets is less than 50 percent (average ρ on the order of 0.7). The correlation of the U.S. market with Canada and major European markets is stronger than with Japan, with a typical percentage of common variance around 50 percent (ρ around 0.7). Other groups of countries are also highly correlated, indicating strong regional links. Germany and France tend to have high correlations because their economies are interrelated. Conversely, Japan shows little correlation with European or U.S. markets. This result confirms that the Japanese business cycle has been somewhat disconnected from the rest of the world.

[7] An R^2 of 19 percent may be interpreted as follows: 19 percent of the Japanese stock price movements are the result of influences common to the U.S. stock market. In other words, 81 percent of the price movements are independent of U.S. market influences.

The last four rows and columns in Exhibit 9.4 give the correlation of each national market with four international indexes calculated by Morgan Stanley Capital International. The first three indexes refer to developed stock markets. The Europe index is made up of stock markets from Europe. The Europe, Australasia, and Far East (EAFE) index is the non-U.S. world index and is made up of stock markets from those parts of the world. The World index is a market capitalization–weighted index of all the major stock markets of the world. The Emerging Markets index is a cap-weighted index of emerging stock markets. The correlation of the U.S. market with the EAFE index is 0.76. Therefore, the overall common variance between U.S. and non-U.S. stock indexes is 58 percent ($R^2 = 0.76^2 = 58\%$). This implies that any well-diversified portfolio of non-U.S. stocks provides an attractive risk-diversification vehicle for a domestic U.S. portfolio. The same conclusion, that foreign stocks provide attractive risk-diversification benefits to a domestic stock portfolio, holds true from any other national viewpoint.

The correlation of the U.S. stock market with the world index is much larger ($R^2 = 0.91^2 = 83\%$) than it is for the EAFE index. But this should not be surprising, since the U.S. market accounts for a significant share of the world market.

In general, the low correlation across countries offers risk diversification and return opportunities. It allows naive investors to spread risk, since some foreign markets are likely to go up when others go down. This also provides opportunities for expert international investors to time the markets by buying those markets that they expect to go up and neglecting the bearish ones.

The degree of independence of a stock market is directly linked to the independence of a nation's economy and governmental policies. To some extent, common world factors affect expected cash flows of all firms and therefore their stock prices. However, purely national or regional factors seem to play an important role in asset prices, leading to sizable differences in the degrees of independence between markets. It is clear that constraints and regulations imposed by national governments, technological specialization, independent fiscal and monetary policies, and cultural and sociological differences all contribute to the degree of a capital market's independence. On the other hand, when there are closer economic and government policies, as among the euro countries, one observes more commonality in capital market behavior. In any case, the covariation between markets is still far from unity, leaving ample opportunities for risk diversification.

The last row/column of Exhibit 9.4 reports the correlation with a diversified index of emerging markets. Emerging markets present a positive but rather low correlation with developed markets; the correlation with the U.S. stock market is 0.66. The case for diversifying into emerging markets is discussed in the last section of this chapter.

Let's now examine the correlation across stock markets when full currency hedging is undertaken. The correlation coefficients in the top right part of the matrix are very similar to the U.S. dollar correlations. For example, the correlation between the U.S. and Japanese markets decresases slightly to 0.41, but some other

EXHIBIT 9.5

Correlation of Bond Markets, January 1992–January 2002
Monthly Returns in U.S. Dollars (bottom left) and Currency Hedged (top right)

	United States	Canada	United Kingdom	France	Germany	Italy	Switzerland	Netherlands	Japan	U.S. Equity
United States	1.00	0.64	0.51	0.49	0.55	0.33	0.37	0.57	0.23	0.19
Canada	0.49	1.00	0.47	0.37	0.36	0.28	0.23	0.38	0.16	0.26
United Kingdom	0.49	0.30	1.00	0.68	0.74	0.50	0.51	0.75	0.05	0.19
France	0.38	0.11	0.61	1.00	0.85	0.71	0.63	0.83	0.09	0.09
Germany	0.40	0.13	0.62	0.92	1.00	0.58	0.68	0.94	0.25	0.07
Italy	0.27	0.23	0.54	0.61	0.53	1.00	0.34	0.57	0.08	0.21
Switzerland	0.32	0.05	0.50	0.88	0.89	0.43	1.00	0.71	0.24	−0.05
Netherlands	0.40	0.14	0.59	0.96	0.96	0.55	0.90	1.00	0.24	0.12
Japan	0.17	0.06	0.23	0.42	0.46	0.12	0.50	0.48	1.00	−0.09
U.S. Equity	0.19	0.41	0.17	−0.01	0.00	0.08	−0.14	0.01	0.11	1.00

correlations are slightly higher. There is little difference between stock market correlations when we look at hedged and unhedged returns.

Bonds Similar conclusions can be reached for bonds, as can be seen in Exhibit 9.5, which is presented in a fashion similar to that of Exhibit 9.4, but for a different time period. Let's first look at the correlation of the various bond markets when returns are all expressed in U.S. dollars (the bottom left part of the exhibit). For example, the correlation of U.S. dollar returns of U.S. and French bonds is only 0.38, or an average percentage of common variance of less than 15 percent (the square of 0.38). The correlation of U.S. bonds with every foreign bond market is below 0.50. Canadian dollar bonds are most strongly correlated with U.S. dollar bonds. In general, long-term return variations are not highly correlated across countries.

Regional blocs do appear. European bond markets tend to be quite correlated. This is especially true of countries from the Eurozone, because a common currency was progressively introduced over the period under study. The Eurozone bond markets now exhibit a correlation close to 1.0 for government bonds.

The general observation is that national monetary/budget policies are not fully synchronized. For example, the growing U.S. budget deficit in the mid-1980s, associated with high U.S. interest rates and a rapid weakening of the dollar, was not matched in other countries. The relative independence of national monetary/budget policies, influencing both currency and interest rate movements, leads to a surprisingly low correlation of U.S. dollar returns on the U.S. and foreign bond markets. Hence, foreign bonds allow investors to diversify the risks associated with domestic monetary/budget policies.

Finally, the last asset class in Exhibit 9.5 is U.S. equity. The correlation of foreign bonds with the U.S. stock market is quite small. This is not surprising, given the independence between U.S. and foreign national economic and monetary policies. Foreign bonds offer excellent diversification benefits to a U.S. stock portfolio manager.

Let us now examine the correlation across bond markets when full currency hedging is undertaken. The correlation coefficients in the top right part of the matrix are somewhat different from the U.S. dollar correlations. This is because there exists a correlation between currency movements and bond yield movements (and hence bond returns), as discussed in Chapter 4. For example, some countries practice a "leaning against the wind" policy, whereby they raise their interest rates to defend their currencies. So the correlation of two national bond markets would be different if we look at hedged returns or at currency-adjusted returns.

Leads and Lags So far, we have talked about the contemporaneous correlation across markets taking place when an event or factor affects two or more markets simultaneously. Some investigators have attempted to find leads or lags between markets. For example, they studied whether a bear market in February on Wall Street would lead to a drop in prices on other national markets in March. No evidence of a systematic delayed reaction of one national market to another has ever been found, except for daily returns, as outlined later. The existence of such simple market inefficiencies is, indeed, unlikely, because it would be easy to exploit them to make an abnormal profit.

One must take into account the time differences around the world, however, before assessing whether a given national market leads or lags other markets. The stock exchanges in New York and Tokyo are not open at the same time. If important news hits New York prices on a Tuesday, it will affect Tokyo prices on Wednesday. If important news hits London prices on a Tuesday, it will affect New York prices the same day, because New York generally lags London by five hours. Indeed, when it is Tuesday noon in New York, it is already Tuesday 17:00 (or 5 P.M.) local time in London and Wednesday 02:00 (or 2 A.M.) in Tokyo.[8] The opening and closing times of the three major stock markets are depicted in Exhibit 9.6, in which

EXHIBIT 9.6

Stock Exchange Trade Hours in Greenwich Mean Time (GMT) and Eastern Standard Time (EST) Clocks

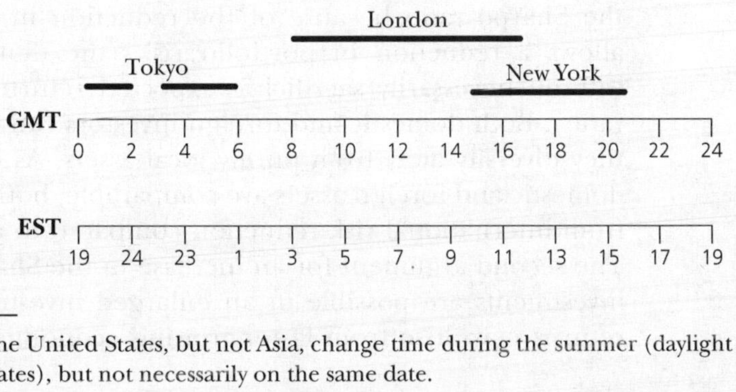

[8] Europe and the United States, but not Asia, change time during the summer (daylight savings time in the United States), but not necessarily on the same date.

the trading hours are indicated using both the universal GMT (Greenwich Mean Time) and the American EST (Eastern Standard Time). It can be seen that New York and Tokyo official trading hours never overlap. London and New York trading hours generally overlap for two hours. If the markets are efficient, international news should affect all markets around the globe simultaneously, with markets closed at that hour reflecting the news immediately on opening. For example, if important news is revealed after noon EST, it can be impounded in Japanese and British stock prices only the next day; because of the time differences involved, we should not be surprised to find a lagging correlation of Tokyo and London with New York when returns are measured from closing price to closing price. This lagged correlation can be explained by the difference in time zones, not by some international market inefficiency that could be exploited to make a profit. This effect gets drastically reduced when looking at correlation of longer-period return, for example, monthly returns.

Portfolio Return Performance

We have devoted so much attention to the risk-reduction benefits of international investment because risk diversification is the most established and frequently invoked argument in favor of foreign investment, justifying foreign investment even to the naive investor. However, risk reduction is not the sole motive for international investment. Indeed, mere risk reduction could more easily be achieved by simply investing part of one's assets in domestic risk-free bills. Unfortunately, although the inclusion of risk-free bills lowers the portfolio risk, it also lowers expected return. In the traditional framework of the capital asset pricing model (CAPM), the expected return on a security is equal to the risk-free rate plus a risk premium. In an efficient market, reducing the risk level of a portfolio by adding less-risky investments implies reducing its expected return. International diversification, however, implies no reduction in expected return. Such diversification lowers risk by eliminating nonsystematic volatility without sacrificing expected return. A traditional way to evaluate a portfolio's risk-adjusted performance is to evaluate its *Sharpe ratio.* This is the ratio of the return on a portfolio, in excess of the risk-free rate, divided by its standard deviation (see Example 9.4). Money managers attempt to maximize this Sharpe ratio, which gives the excess return per unit of risk. Global investing should increase the Sharpe ratio because of the reduction in risk. Investing in foreign assets allows a reduction in portfolio risk (the denominator of the Sharpe ratio) without necessarily sacrificing expected return (the numerator of the Sharpe ratio). Both domestic and foreign investors can see their Sharpe ratio increase if they diversify away from purely local assets. As long as the expected returns on domestic and foreign assets are comparable, both types of investors would benefit from international risk reduction compared to a portfolio of purely local assets. The second argument for an increase in the Sharpe ratio is that more profitable investments are possible in an enlarged investment universe. Higher expected returns may arise from faster-growing economies and firms located around the

EXAMPLE 9.4 INTERNATIONAL DIVERSIFICATION AND THE SHARPE RATIO

Assume that the domestic and foreign assets have standard deviations of $\sigma_d =$ 15 percent and $\sigma_f = 17$ percent, respectively, with a correlation of $\rho_{d,f} = 0.4$. The risk-free rate is equal to 4 percent in both countries.

1. The expected returns of the domestic and foreign assets are both equal to 10 percent: $E(R_d) = E(R_f) = 10$ percent. Calculate the Sharpe ratios for the domestic asset, the foreign asset, and an internationally diversified portfolio equally invested in the domestic and foreign assets. What do you conclude?

2. Assume now that the expected return on the foreign asset is higher than on the domestic asset, $E(R_d) = 10$ percent but $E(R_f) = 12$ percent. Calculate the Sharpe ratio for an internationally diversified portfolio equally invested in the domestic and foreign assets, and compare your findings to those in question 1.

SOLUTION

1. The domestic asset has an expected return of 10 percent and a standard deviation of 15 percent. For this asset,

$$\text{Sharpe ratio} = \frac{E(R) - \text{Risk-free rate}}{\sigma} = \frac{10\% - 4\%}{15\%} = 0.4$$

The foreign asset has a Sharpe ratio of $\frac{10\% - 4\%}{17\%} = 0.353$

A portfolio equally invested in the domestic and foreign asset has an expected return of 10 percent and a standard deviation σ_p given by

$$\sigma_p^2 = 0.5^2[\sigma_d^2 + \sigma_f^2 + (2\,\rho_{d,f}\sigma_d\sigma_f)]$$

$$\sigma_p^2 = 0.5^2[225 + 289 + (2 \times 0.4 \times 255)] = 179.5$$

Hence, the standard deviation σ_p is given by $\sqrt{179.5}$, or 13.4 percent. The Sharpe ratio of the portfolio is equal to

$$\text{Sharpe ratio} = \frac{E(R_p) - \text{Risk-free rate}}{\sigma_p} = \frac{10\% - 4\%}{13.4\%} = 0.448$$

The foreign asset has a lower Sharpe ratio than the domestic asset because it has the same expected return but a larger standard deviation. However, the equally weighted portfolio benefits from risk diversification and a lower standard deviation. Hence, its Sharpe ratio is better than the ratios of both the domestic and the foreign assets.

2. A portfolio equally invested in the domestic and foreign asset has an expected return of 11 percent ($0.5 \times 10\% + 0.5 \times 12\% = 11\%$). Hence,

the Sharpe ratio is equal to (11% − 4%) / 13.4% = 0.522. The portfolio's Sharpe ratio is now better than that of the domestic asset (0.4), both because of risk-diversification benefits and because of the superior expected return of the foreign asset [new Sharpe ratio of (12% − 4%)/17% = 0.471].

world, or simply from currency gains. These advantages can be obtained by optimizing the global asset allocation.

An Ex Post Example It is easy to derive the global asset allocation that would have been optimal from a risk–return viewpoint over some past period, but the results depend on the period selected. To illustrate such an analysis, Exhibit 9.7 shows optimal global stock allocations for different risk levels and for a U.S. investor, as reported by Odier and Solnik (1993). This is the efficient frontier based on returns for the period 1980–1990. No investment constraints other than no short selling are applied; results do not reflect any currency hedging. The mean annual return is given

EXHIBIT 9.7

Efficient Frontier for Stocks (U.S. dollar, 1980–1990)

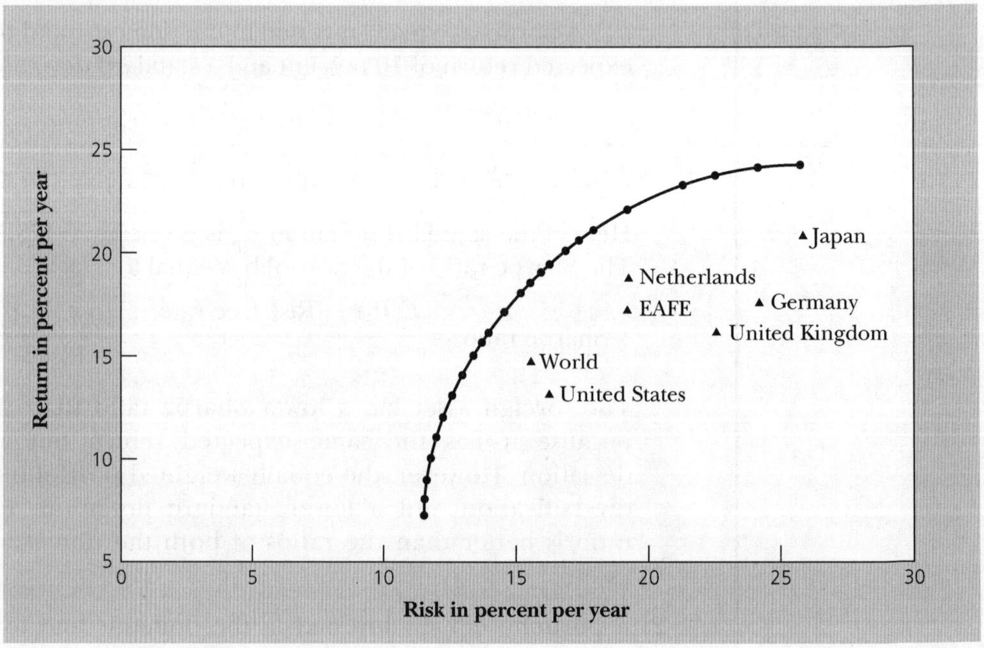

Source: P. Odier and B. Solnik. Adapted from "Lessons for International Asset Allocation," *Financial Analysis Journal*, March/April 1993. Copyright © 2007 CFA Institute. All Rights Reserved.

on the Y axis, and the asset volatility (standard deviation) is given on the X axis. Each asset or portfolio is represented by one point on the graph (a few selected markets are plotted on the graph). The U.S. stock market has a risk of 16.2 percent and an annualized total return of 13.3 percent. Other stock markets are more volatile, partly because of currency risk. By combining the various national stock markets, we get diversified portfolios whose returns and risks can be calculated, because we know the returns and covariances of all the assets. Investors select asset allocations that lie on the efficient frontier depicted in Exhibit 9.7. The best achievable risk–return tradeoffs—the optimal asset allocations—lie on the efficient frontier.

As Exhibit 9.7 shows, international diversification of a pure U.S. stock portfolio would greatly enhance returns without a large increase in risk. A global stock portfolio with the same risk level as the purely U.S. stock portfolio (16.2% per year) would achieve an annualized total return above 19 percent, compared with 13.3 percent for the U.S. portfolio.

Can bonds help improve the risk-adjusted performance of globally diversified portfolios? The question here is not whether investors should prefer portfolios made up solely of bonds or solely of stocks, but whether bonds should be added to a stock portfolio in a global investment strategy. Exhibit 9.8 gives the efficient frontier for a global asset allocation allowing for bonds and stocks, foreign and domestic. To keep the exhibit readable, we did not plot individual bond and stock markets, but only the U.S. bond and stock indexes, as well as the world stock index. Their relative positions are consistent with theory. U.S. bonds have a lower risk and a lower return. Over the long run, riskier stock investments are compensated by a risk premium. The global asset allocations on the efficient frontier strongly dominate U.S. investments. The global efficient asset allocation with a return equal to that of the U.S. stock market (13.3% per year) has a risk equal to only half that of the U.S. stock market. Conversely, a global efficient allocation with the same risk as the U.S. stock market outperforms the U.S. stock market by 8 percent per year. Similarly, any domestic U.S. stock/bond strategy is strongly dominated by a global stock/bond strategy. A domestic portfolio of U.S. stocks and bonds tends to have half the return of that on a global efficient allocation with the same risk level. Adding foreign bonds in a global asset allocation can be attractive from a risk–return viewpoint because of their low correlation with domestic bond and stock investments, as outlined previously.

Exhibit 9.8 also shows the global efficient frontier for stocks only (same as Exhibit 9.7) as well as the efficient international frontier for bonds only. Clearly, stocks offer a strong contribution to a bond portfolio in terms of risk–return tradeoff; the bond-only efficient frontier is also dominated by a global strategy.

Exhibit 9.9 shows the efficient frontier for Japanese, German, and British investors. All calculations are performed in the respective national currencies. Conclusions similar to those developed earlier can be reached when we take the viewpoint of investors from different countries of the world. The benefits of global investing can hold from all national viewpoints simultaneously. The expanded investment universe (from domestic to global) offers potentials for risk diversification and return improvement, and hence an improvement in the Sharpe ratio for all investors.

EXHIBIT 9.8

Global Efficient Frontier for Stocks and Bonds (U.S. dollar, 1980–1990)

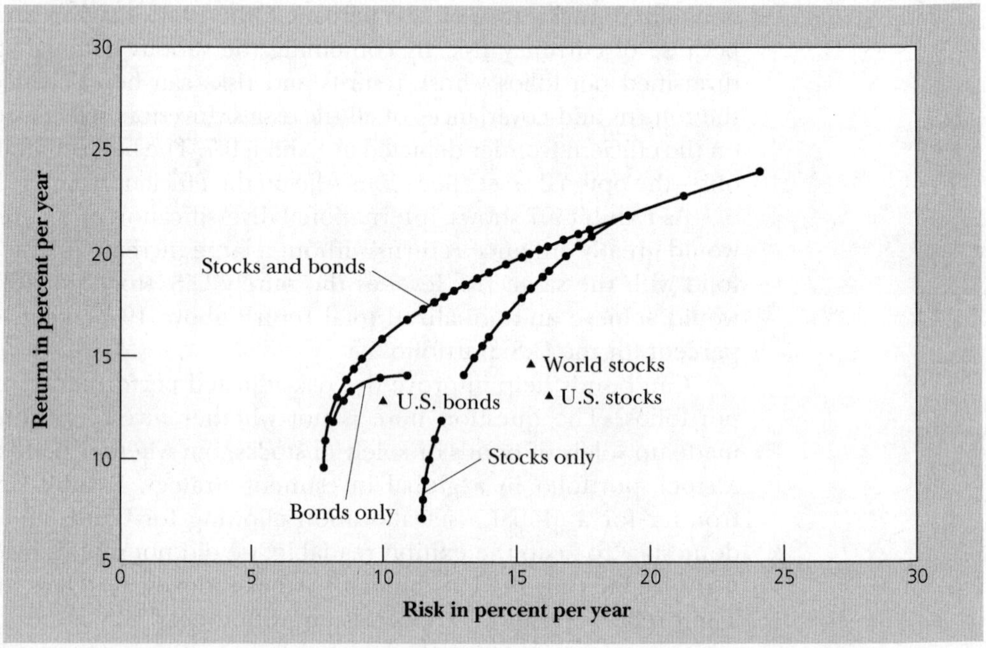

Source: P. Odier and B. Solnik. Adapted from "Lessons for International Asset Allocation," *Financial Analysis Journal*, March/April 1993.

The potential profits are large, but optimizing them requires some forecasting skills. A major question is how much of the potential can be achieved through superior management skills. Even if only 20 percent of the profits could be reaped, global-asset allocation would seem to be very valuable in risk–return terms. It is, of course, quite difficult to know in advance what these optimal asset allocations will be. Therefore, all we can conclude is that the opportunities for increased risk-adjusted returns are sizable and that the performance gap between optimal global asset allocations and a simple world index fund is potentially quite wide. Whether any money manager has sufficient expertise to realize most, or even part, of this performance differential is yet another question.

Different Market Environments It is important to stress that the expected benefits of global investing in terms of risk and return of a portfolio are different. Because of the low (less than 1.0) correlation across different national assets, the volatility of a portfolio is *less* than the average volatility of its components. Risks get partly diversified away. This international risk reduction appears from any currency viewpoint. However, the return on a diversified portfolio is exactly *equal* to the average return of its components. By definition, the return on the world index is

EXHIBIT 9.9

Global Efficient Frontiers for Non-U.S. Investors

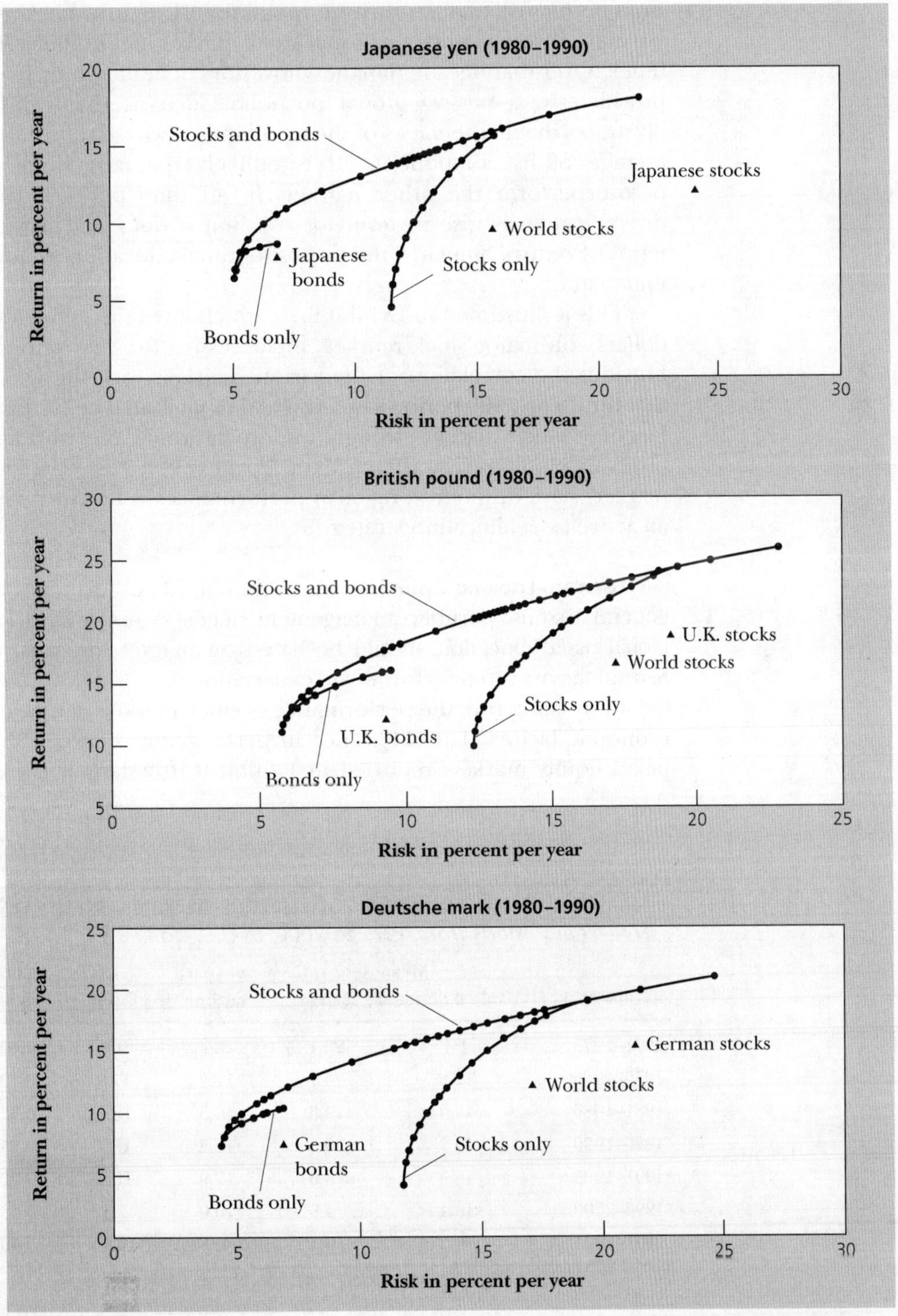

the average return of all national markets. In other words, some countries will outperform the world index, whereas others will underperform the world index. Although international diversification has looked attractive from 1980 to 1990 from both a risk and a return viewpoint for a U.S. investor, this is not the case for a Japanese investor, whose national stock market had higher returns than the world index. Over that decade, Japanese investors benefited only from the risk reduction provided by a passive global portfolio, such as the world index. Again, this illustrates the mathematics of the world index, whose return is exactly the weighted average of its components. It is unlikely that any single market will under- or overperform the other markets in all time periods. Hence, passive global diversification is wise in terms of risk, but it does not provide a "free lunch" in terms of return. Similarly, the ex post optimal allocation will depend on the period under study.

This is illustrated in Exhibit 9.10, which gives the mean annual return (in U.S. dollars) on major stock markets in successive five-year periods. Exhibit 9.10 also provides the correlation of the various markets with the U.S. stock market. Note that the 1990–2000 period saw a reversal of perfomance for Japanese investors. The Japanese stock market strongly underperformed the world index. International diversification was very attractive for Japanese investors. The fact that national stock markets have different long-term performances is not surprising and could justify an active asset allocation strategy.

Forward-Looking Optimization Although ex post exercises yield some interesting general lessons, portfolio management needs to be forward looking. An adequate global asset allocation should be based on market forecasts, not on past returns. Several factors can help formulate expectations.

In the long run, the performance of stock markets can be explained by national economic factors. The difference in performance between the U.S., Europe, and Japan equity markets reported in Exhibit 9.10 is largely the result of differences

EXHIBIT 9.10

Mean Return and Correlation of Selected Markets with the U.S. Equity Market
Five-Year Periods from 1971 to 2000, in U.S. Dollars

	Mean Return (in % per year)				Correlation with U.S. Equity		
5-Year Period	United States	Japan	Europe	EAFE	Japan	Europe	EAFE
1971–1975	1.4	22.1	5.5	9.8	0.40	0.61	0.59
1976–1980	12.3	20.7	12.2	17.0	0.12	0.28	0.36
1981–1985	15.0	19.3	16.3	16.8	0.32	0.49	0.46
1986–1990	12.7	20.6	18.2	18.7	0.25	0.64	0.44
1991–1995	16.9	5.6	12.9	10.1	0.22	0.65	0.47
1996–2000	18.4	−4.6	16.0	7.6	0.48	0.62	0.66
2001–2005	−0.2	6.4	4.0	4.8	0.40	0.87	0.85

EXHIBIT 9.11

Real Growth Rate (GDP Growth) of Selected Regions
Ten-Year Periods from 1971 to 2000

GDP Growth	United States	Japan	Europe	OECD
1971–1980	2.76%	4.51%	2.95%	3.13%
1981–1990	2.48%	4.15%	2.34%	2.71%
1991–2000	3.40%	1.30%	2.50%	2.30%

in real growth rates. This can be seen in Exhibit 9.11, which gives the mean annual growth rate in GDP for successive 10-year periods for the United States, Japan, Europe, and the average of all OECD countries. For example, real growth was much higher in Japan than in the United States in the 1970s and 1980s, and much lower in the 1990s. The stock markets' performance followed the same pattern.

Economic flexibility is also an important factor in investment performance, which may explain differences between past and future performances among emerging countries. Wage and employment rigidity is bad for the national economy. In countries such as France, Canada, and Sweden, corporations have a difficult time adjusting to slowing activity; on the other hand, they do not take full advantage of growth opportunities because they are reluctant to hire new employees, whom they cannot fire if activity slows.

Economic forecasting is a useful exercise, but it should be stressed that scenarios that are widely expected to take place should already be impounded in current asset prices. For example, if a Country X is widely expected to experience higher economic growth than other countries, that fact should be reflected in higher stock prices in Country X. If future growth develops according to expectations, there is no reason to have higher future returns for stocks of Country X. So, investors forecasting economic growth rates must take into account the market consensus about future growth rates.

It should be stressed that there is no guarantee that the past will repeat itself. Indeed, over any given period, one national market is bound to outperform the other, and if an investor had perfect foresight, the best strategy would be to invest solely in the top-performing market, or even in the top-performing security in that market. But because of the great uncertainty of forecasts, it is always better to spread risk in the fund by diversifying globally across markets with comparable expected returns. This ensures a favorable risk–return trade-off or, in the jargon of theory, higher risk-adjusted expected returns. If managers believe that they have some relative forecasting ability, they will engage in active investment strategies that reap the benefits of international risk diversification while focusing on preferred markets. For example, a U.S. investor may concentrate on U.S. and European stocks if she is bullish on those markets and may avoid Japan for political or currency reasons.

Some emerging economies offer attractive investment opportunities. The local risks (volatility, liquidity, political environment) are higher, as illustrated by numerous crises, but the expected profit is large. Furthermore, those risks get partly diversified away in a global portfolio. Hence, emerging markets and alternative investments can have a positive contribution in terms of risk–return trade-offs.

Currency Risk Not a Barrier to International Investment

Currency fluctuations affect both the total return and the volatility of any foreign currency–denominated investment. From time to time, in fact, the effects of currency fluctuations on the investment return may exceed that of capital gain or income, especially over short periods of time. Empirical studies indicate that currency risk, as measured by the standard deviation of the exchange rate movement, is smaller than the risk of the corresponding stock market (roughly half). On the other hand, currency risk is often larger than the risk (in local currency) of the corresponding bond market (roughly twice). In a global portfolio, the depreciation of one currency is often offset by the appreciation of another. Indeed, several points are worth mentioning regarding currency risk.

First, market and currency risks are not additive. This would be true only if the two were perfectly correlated. In fact, there is only a weak, and sometimes negative, correlation between currency and market movements. This point was stressed in the previous section. In Example 9.2, the exchange rate standard deviation is 7 percent compared with a local-currency standard deviation of 15.5 percent for the foreign stock. However, the contribution of currency risk to total risk is only 1.5 percentage points. So, currency risk adds only some 10 percent (1.5 percent as a fraction of 15.5 percent) to the risk of a foreign asset. This is a typical figure.

The correlation between changes in the exchange rate and the asset price is an important element in assessing the contribution of currency risk. The lower the correlation, the smaller the contribution of currency risk to total risk.

Second, the exchange risk of an investment may be hedged for major currencies by selling futures or forward currency contracts, buying put currency options, or even borrowing foreign currency to finance the investment. So, currency risk can easily be eliminated in international investment strategies. But currencies can also provide some attractive profit opportunities.

Third, the contribution of currency risk should be measured for the total portfolio rather than for individual markets or securities, because part of that risk gets diversified away by the mix of currencies represented in the portfolio. As stressed by Jorion (1989), the contribution of currency risk to the total risk of a portfolio that includes only a small proportion of foreign assets (say, 5 percent) is insignificant. The contribution of currency risk is larger if one holds the world market portfolio and, hence, a large share of foreign assets. Actually holding some foreign-currency assets can provide some diversification to domestic fiscal and monetary risks. A lax domestic monetary policy can be bad for domestic asset prices and lead to a home-currency depreciation. Foreign currencies help diversify that risk.

Fourth, the contribution of currency risk decreases with the length of the investment horizon. As shown in Chapters 2 and 3, exchange rates tend to revert to fundamentals over the long run (mean reversion). Hence, an investor with a long time horizon should care less about currency risk than should an investor who is concerned about monthly fluctuations in the portfolio's value. Froot (1993) shows that currency risk can disappear over very long term horizons (over one or several decades).

The Case against International Diversification

Several impediments to international portfolio investing are often mentioned. First, the case for international diversification presented earlier has been attacked on the basis that it strongly overstates the risk benefits of international investing. Second, skeptics also look at the historical performance of their domestic market relative to other foreign markets. Third, there are numerous physical barriers to international investing.

Increase in Correlations

It is often argued that the benefits of international diversification are overstated because markets tend to be more synchronized than suggested previously. There is no reason for the correlation between two equity markets to remain constant over a long period of time. Indeed, it has been observed that international correlations have trended upward over the past decade. It has also been observed that international correlation increases in periods of high market volatility.

Correlations Have Increased over Time Economies and financial markets are becoming increasingly integrated, leading to an increase in international correlation of asset prices. Economic and financial globalization observed at the turn of the millennium can be witnessed in many areas.

- Capital markets are being deregulated and opened to foreign players. Markets that used to be segmented are moving toward global integration.
- Capital mobility has increased, especially among developed countries. International capital flows have dramatically increased since the 1950s. The success of international investing means that foreign institutional investors, such as pension funds, are now major players on most domestic markets.
- National economies are opening up to free trade, in part under the pressure of the World Trade Organization and of regional agreements such as NAFTA, ASEAN, and the European Union. Hence, national economies are becoming more synchronized.
- As the economic environment becomes global, corporations become increasingly global in their operations. They achieve this global strategy through increased exports, international organic growth, and foreign acquisitions. A simple indicator is provided by the amount of cross-border mergers and

EXHIBIT 9.12

Value of Cross-Border M&As, 1987–2005

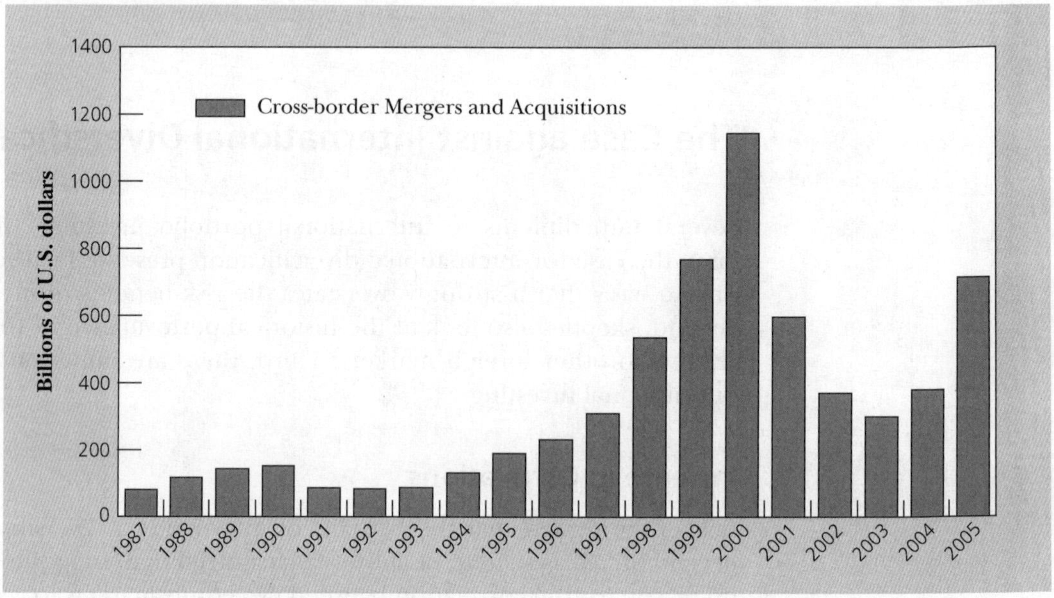

Source: United Nations Conference on Trade and Development (UNCTAD).

acquisitions (M&As) shown in Exhibit 9.12. The amount of cross-border M&As has risen dramatically in the past twenty years. Cross-border M&As were few in the early 1990s, but they have become an increasing proportion of total M&As. While the economic slowdown and bear equity market of the early 2000s has slowed down M&As, the share of cross-border M&As among total M&As has steadily risen since 2003.

As corporations become more global, it is not surprising to see the correlation between their stock prices increase. The legal nationality of a corporation becomes less important. As a firm competes globally and derives a significant part of its cash flows from abroad, its value is affected by global factors, not primarily by the location of its headquarters. Hence, it is not surprising to find that country factors become less important and that the correlation among national stock markets tends to increase.

International correlations move over time, as can be seen in Exhibit 9.10. Correlation is high in periods when global shocks affect all countries (e.g., the oil shock of the early 1970s) and lower in other periods. However, Exhibit 9.10 suggests that the correlation between the U.S. and other stock markets has been trending upward since 1975.

Goetzmann, Li, and Rouwenhorst (2001) examined the correlation structure of the major world equity markets from the late nineteenth century until the end of

2000. They found that correlations varied considerably through time, with peaks in the late nineteenth century, the Great Depression, and the late twentieth century. They concluded that the current diversification benefits to global investing were relatively low compared with the rest of capital market history, because correlation was at a high point.

Correlation Increases When Markets Are Volatile A major criticism addressed to the mean–variance framework used to present the case for international diversification is that it assumes "normality." In statistical terms, all returns are supposed to have a "joint multivariate normal distribution." In real life, returns are not exactly drawn from normal probability tables with constant correlations across assets. Three deviations from market "normality" are most often mentioned:

- Distributions of returns tend to have fat tails (leptokurtic distribution). In other words, the occurrence of large positive or negative returns is more frequent than expected under normal distributions.[9]
- Market volatility varies over time, but volatility is "contagious." In other words, high volatility in the U.S. stock market tends to be associated with high volatility in foreign stock markets, as well as in other financial markets (bond, currency).
- The correlation across markets increases dramatically in periods of high volatility, for example, during major market events such as the October 1987 crash.

The fact that there are fat tails or that volatility tends to move up or down together on all markets is not a direct attack on global risk diversification. It simply says that a static mean–variance analysis is a simplified view of the world and that more sophisticated quantitative methods could be used; it does not negate the advantage of international risk reduction. Correlation moves over time[10] for obvious reasons. There are tranquil periods during which domestic factors dominate and markets are not strongly correlated across countries. There are times during which global shocks affect simultaneously all economies and business cycles move in sync. The oil shock of 1974 provides an example, as shown in Exhibit 9.10, and the correlation measured from 1971 to 1975 was much higher than in the next five years. The correlation estimated over a long period of time

[9] See, for example, Longin (1996).

[10] Longin and Solnik (1995) studied the eight major stock markets from 1960 to 1990, using a GARCH methodology. They rejected the hypothesis that correlation is constant and found a modest but significant increase in international correlation over this 30-year period. Goetzmann, Li, and Rouwenhorst (2001) studied the correlation of the stock markets of France, Germany, the United Kingdom, and the United States from 1870 to 2000. They split the data into six periods based on historical events such as world wars. They found that the correlation structure differed significantly among many of the six time periods.

is simply an average over these various market cycles. For reasons mentioned previously, correlation of developed stock markets tends to increase slowly over time. But what is really troubling is that correlation seems to increase dramatically in periods of crises, so that the benefits of international risk diversification disappear when they are most needed. This phenomenon is sometimes referred to as *correlation breakdown.*

If all markets crash when your domestic market is crashing, there is little risk benefit to being internationally diversified. While it might be beneficial in "normal" times, it becomes useless in the exceptional times when there is a huge loss on domestic investments. And remember that fat tails mean that the occurrence of such crashes is more frequent than expected under "normality."

This concept is illustrated in Exhibit 9.13, which is reproduced from Bookstaber (1997). In one day of October 1987, the U.S. stock market crashed by some 20 percent, or about 20 times its historical daily standard deviation. The British, Japanese, and German markets dropped between 8 and 15 times their normal standard deviations. Other bond and currency market indicators also witnessed large declines.

Implications of such correlation breakdowns extend well beyond international portfolio diversification. If they occur, correlation breakdowns would render very inefficient any hedging operations based on correlations, or betas, estimated over long-term historical data.

EXHIBIT 9.13

1987 U.S. Stock Market Crash
One-Day Movement in Units of "Normal" Daily Standard Deviations

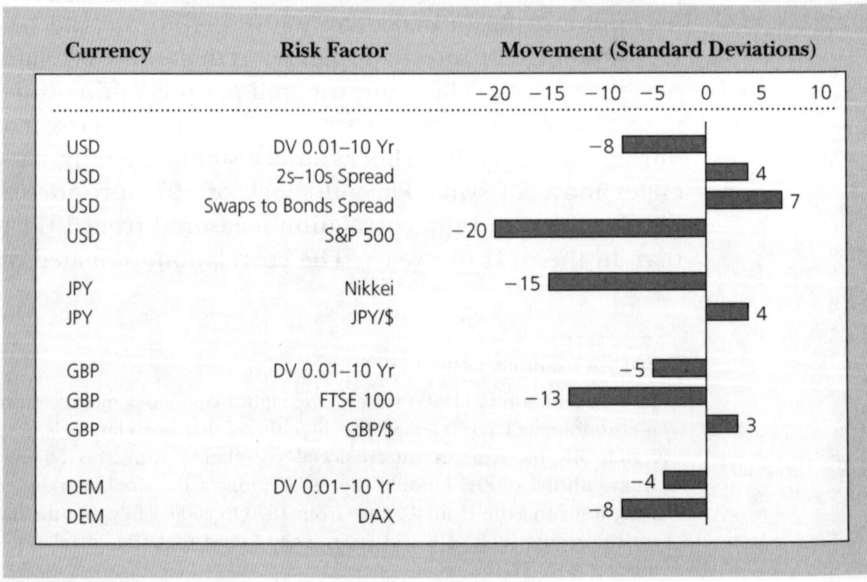

Source: Bookstaber (1997).

Past Performance Is a Good Indicator of Future Performance

Another criticism of international investing is country-specific, as it is typically formulated by investors whose markets have enjoyed a prolonged period of good performance. Skeptics point to the fact that, in recent periods, their domestic markets have generated greater returns than most other markets, and hence that there is no need for international investments in the future. As can be seen in Exhibit 9.10, the Japanese equity market had a superb performance relative to the rest of the world in the 1970s and 1980s. International investing was not in favor in Japan in 1990. A similar attitude has been adopted recently in the United States: U.S. equity yielded greater returns than overseas equity markets, especially Japan, in the 1990s and early 2000s. After a few years of poor performance of their foreign investments relative to domestic equities, U.S. investors were less inclined toward international investing.[11] But that has changed again since 2000, as the U.S. equity market has been strongly outperformed by international markets.

Simply extrapolating past performance to forecast future expected returns is questionable. It is unlikely that one country will always outperform all others, just as one domestic sector is unlikely to continually outperform all other domestic sectors. It could be that one economy is deemed to be more efficient than others, but this should be reflected in higher equity prices. Let's assume, for example, that the U.S. economy is indeed more flexible and competitive than all others in the foreseeable future. In a global context, in which foreign investors extensively invest in the United States and vice versa, this forecast should be discounted today in higher U.S. equity prices. If investors share the vision that the U.S. economy will be superior to other economies forever, that forecast should be reflected immediately into higher U.S. stock prices today, not by higher future returns forever. Future outperformance of U.S. stocks must be caused by "surprise," the unexpected news that the U.S. economy is doing even better than expected. To justify continuing outperformance in the future, we must go from positive surprise to positive surprise.

Barriers to International Investments

The relative size of foreign capital markets would justify extensive foreign investment by investors of any nationality. Empirical studies build a strong case for international diversification. However, international investment, although rapidly growing, is still not widespread in several countries and is certainly far from what it should be according to the world market portfolio weights. This conservative behavior may be explained by the prevalence of potential barriers to foreign investment.

Familiarity with Foreign Markets Culture differences are a major impediment to foreign investment. Investors are often unfamiliar with foreign cultures and markets. They feel uneasy about the way business is done in other countries:

[11] See, for example, Joel Chernoff, "International Investments May Not Decrease Risk after All," *Pensions and Investments*, January 7, 2002.

the trading procedures, the way reports are presented, different languages, different time zones, and so on. Many investors, especially Americans, feel more comfortable investing in domestic corporations. In turn, these local corporations provide some international exposure through their exports, foreign subsidiaries, or acquisitions of foreign corporations. Foreign markets and corporations are perceived as more risky simply because they are unfamiliar.

Political Risk Some countries run the risk of being politically unstable. Many emerging markets have periodically suffered from political, economic, or monetary crises that badly affected the value of local investments. For example, a currency crisis could curtail the dollar value of local investments. Simply looking at a statistical measure of risk based on recent-past stock-price behavior can be misleading and underestimate the risk of a crisis. A statistician would say that the distribution of return on such investments is not "normal" and that the standard deviation of return is not a good proxy of the risk borne.

Market Efficiency A first question in market efficiency is that of *liquidity*. Some markets are very small; others have many issues traded in large volume. Of course, some issues on the major markets, as well as some of the smaller national markets, trade on little volume. Large institutional investors may wish to be careful and invest only a small part of their portfolios in these small-capitalization, less-liquid shares. Indeed, it may be difficult to get out of some national markets on a large scale. An excellent performance on a local index may not translate into a similarly good performance on a specific portfolio because of the share price drop when liquidating the portfolio. Another liquidity risk is the imposition of capital controls on foreign portfolio investments. Such capital control prevents the sale of a portfolio of foreign assets and the repatriation of proceeds. This has never happened on any of the major capital markets of the world; the cost of such a political decision would be very high for any government because it would reduce its borrowing capacity on the international capital market. However, it is a definite risk for investments in many emerging countries. Such capital controls may be imposed in an extreme financial or political crisis, and international money managers need to carefully monitor a few high-risk countries.

In some countries, especially emerging countries, corporations do not provide *timely and reliable information* on their activity and prospects. Foreign investors tend to avoid such corporations. The rapid growth in international investing has put intense pressure on these corporations to live up to the transparency that is the norm in major developed markets.

Another issue in market efficiency is *price manipulation* and *insider trading*. If foreign markets were too affected by these problems, a manager would probably not run the risk of investing in these markets to benefit the domestic speculators. Many studies have established that all major stock markets are nearly efficient in the usual sense. Some countries, however, have historically been quite lax in terms of price manipulation, insider trading, and corporate governance. In some countries, majority stockholders can take advantage of their controlling interest to the detriment of minority stockholders.[12] The globalization of financial markets leads to a rapid improvement in national regulations to control this type of behavior. Some U.S. pension plans, notably CalPERS, have been very active in inciting corporations worldwide to improve their corporate governance.

Regulations In some countries, regulations constrain the amount of foreign investment that can be undertaken by local investors. For example, institutional investors are sometimes constrained on the proportion of foreign assets they can hold in their portfolios. Such quotas can be found in some European countries and even among U.S. public pension plans.

Some countries limit the amount of foreign ownership in their national corporations. This is typically the case for emerging countries, which tend to limit foreign ownership to a maximum percentage of the capital of each firm. This is also the case for some developed countries. For example, Swiss corporations tend to issue special shares to foreign owners, and these shares trade at a premium over those available solely to Swiss nationals. Again, the trend is toward progressive removal of these constraints. For example, the European Union prohibits any ownership discrimination among its members. Such constraints are rarely found for bond investments. All governments are happy to have foreign investors subscribe to their bond issues, financing their budget deficit. Conversely, they often force their national institutional investors to hold domestic bonds. This limits the scope of international investing by these institutional investors.

Transaction Costs The transaction costs of international investments can be higher than those of domestic investments. It is difficult to calculate the average transaction cost on a typical trade. A first component of transaction costs is the brokerage commission, and it varies in the way it is charged (fixed or negotiable commission, variable schedule, or part of the bid–ask spread). However, brokerage commissions on stocks tend to be low in the United States (typically 0.10% for large transactions) and higher in some foreign countries (ranging from 0.10% to 1.0%). In a few countries, commissions are fixed, and a stamp tax applies. However, the deregulation of capital markets is lowering these commissions worldwide. A large component of transaction costs is the price impact of a trade. For example, a large buy order will raise the price. This is a function of the size of the order. Liquidity can be limited on many national stock markets, inducing high transaction costs. However, this effect is present in any country. For example, transaction costs on the NASDAQ can be large, because of the limited liquidity on most issues. Some estimates of the overall transaction costs on the major stock markets are provided in Chapter 5.

It is even more difficult to quote a so-called average commission for bonds. On most of the major bond markets (including the international bond market), prices are quoted net, so that the commissions have to be inferred from the bid–ask spread, which depends on the volume of transactions on a specific bond. In general, commissions on bonds tend to be very low on all markets.

---

12 See, for example, the case of Italy in Zingales (1994).

Custody costs tend to add to the costs of international investments. Custody costs tend to be higher for international investments because here, investors engage in a two-level custodial arrangement, in which a master custodian deals with a network of subcustodians in every country. Higher costs are also incurred because of the necessity of a multicurrency system of accounting, reporting, and cash flow collection. Some countries have a very inexpensive and efficient centralized custodial system with a single clearinghouse, and local costs tend to be less than in the United States. However, the need for the international network may raise the annual cost to more than 0.10 percent of assets.

Management fees charged by international money managers tend to be higher than those charged by domestic money managers. This is justified by the higher costs borne by the money managers for various services:

- International database subscriptions
- Data collection
- Research
- The international accounting system
- Communication costs (international telephone, computer links, and travel)

Management fees for foreign portfolios typically run a few basis points higher than fees on similar domestic portfolios. Some investors believe that they can limit costs by simply buying foreign firms listed on their domestic markets (called American Depositary Receipts, or ADRs, in the United States; see Chapter 5). Although this may be a practical alternative for the private investor, it is a questionable strategy for larger investors. A growing number of companies have multiple listings, but these companies tend to be large multinational firms that provide fewer foreign diversification benefits than a typical foreign firm. Also, the foreign share price of a corporation (e.g., the U.S. dollar ADR price of a French firm) is often determined by its domestic market price adjusted by the exchange rate. When a large order to buy an ADR is received, brokers will generally arbitrage between the prices in New York and the local market. This means that on most ADRs, the execution will be made at a high price compared with the local price (adjusted for the exchange rate). The commission seems low, but the market impact on the price tends to be high. It is often in the best interest of a large customer to deal on the primary market, where there is the largest transaction volume for the shares. However, there are significant exceptions. Several Dutch and British companies have a very large transaction volume on U.S. markets.

Taxes Withholding taxes exist on most stock markets. The country where a corporation is headquartered generally withholds an income tax on the dividends paid by the corporation. This tax can usually be reclaimed after several months; this time lag creates an opportunity cost. In a very few cases, part of the tax is completely lost, according to the tax treaty between the two countries. Alternatively, a taxable investor may claim the amount as a tax credit in his home country, but this is not possible for a nontaxable investor, such as a pension plan. However, the withholding tax (generally 15%) applies only to the dividend yield. For a yield of 2 percent, a total loss of withholding tax on common stocks would imply a 0.30 percent reduction in performance. There are also a few countries (e.g., Australia and France) where investors benefit from some tax credit for the tax that the local corporation has paid on its profits distributed as dividends. This tax credit is usually not available to nonresidents. Withholding taxes have been progressively eliminated on bonds.

Currency Risk As discussed, currency risk can be a major cause of the higher volatility of foreign assets, but is often overstated. Furthermore, it is a risk that need not be borne, because it can be hedged with derivatives. Nevertheless, currency hedging leads to additional administrative and trading costs.

Conclusions Altogether, foreign investment may not seem more costly for a resident from a high-cost country, such as Switzerland, but it is clearly more expensive for a U.S. resident. For a U.S. investor, a ballpark estimate of the increase in total costs (management fee, taxes, commissions, custody) is on the order of 0.10 percent to 0.50 percent for stocks[13] and 0 percent to 0.20 percent for bonds. The difference would be less for a passively managed fund. These figures are still small compared with the risk–return advantage of foreign investment, as presented in the first part of this chapter. However, they could explain why an investor would want to overweigh the domestic component of the portfolio compared with the world market portfolio weights. Information and transaction costs, differential taxes, and sometimes political or transfer risk give a comparative advantage to the domestic investor on the home market. This does not imply that foreign investment should be avoided altogether.

The Case for International Diversification Revisited

Many of the barriers to global investing are disappearing because of the market liberalization induced by global investors. For example, on many days, trading by foreign investors on European equity markets dominates trading by local investors. The global equity landscape has changed dramatically in past decades. Some of the attacks on global diversification are faulty because they are based on poor statistical analysis. More importantly, the scope of international investing has changed, and investors should adapt accordingly.

Pitfalls in Estimating Correlation During Volatile Periods

In the presence of positive correlation between two markets, we would expect that a large market drop (rise) in one country be associated with a large market drop (rise) in the other country, even if the correlation remains constant. The question

[13] See Chapter 5 for more details.

is whether the simultaneous movements are so large that they indicate that correlation is truly increasing in crisis periods. Before concluding on the basis of casual observations, we need to address some econometric issues in correlation estimation. The correlation coefficient is a complex parameter whose statistical properties are not well understood. The conclusion of a correlation breakdown is derived by estimating the correlation in periods of high volatility of returns. This is called *conditioning* correlation on high volatility. Unfortunately, many authors have shown that this is a biased sampling estimate of the true correlation.[14] An example can illustrate this argument. Suppose that two markets have a constant joint-normal distribution of returns with a constant correlation of 0.50. Let's now estimate what would be the sampling correlation if we focus only on volatile observations. For example, suppose that we split the sample in two fractiles (50%) based on the absolute return of one market. The first sample is made of "small" returns, the second of "large" returns (positive or negative). Under the assumption of normality with constant correlation, the estimated *conditional correlation* of small returns is 0.21 and the conditional correlation of large returns is 0.62, even though the true correlation is constant and equal to 0.50. This result can easily be replicated by a simulation on a spreadsheet. If we focus only on the 5 percent most volatile observations, the estimated correlation jumps to 0.81. Still, the true market correlation has not changed. So, the apparent shift in correlation is spurious.

Loretan and English (2000) use a correct statistical procedure to study the correlation of equities, bonds, and foreign exchange during various periods of market turbulence. They conclude that "a significant portion of shifts of correlations over time—including those that occurred in the fall of 1998—may reflect nothing more than the predictable effect of differences in sample volatilities on measured correlation, rather than breaks in the data-generating process for asset returns." In other words, the apparent observation that correlation increases in periods of market turbulence is simply an observation that market volatility has increased, but the true correlation remains constant. Forbes and Rigobon (2002) also study numerous crisis periods, including the October 1987 stock market crash. They conclude that "tests for contagion based on cross-market correlation coefficient are problematic due to the bias introduced by changing volatility in market returns (i.e. heteroskedasticity)." They propose an adjustment for this heteroskedasticity bias and find that correlation does not increase significantly in periods of crisis. To summarize, the conclusion that correlation increases in periods of crisis seems to be simply a statistical bias due to faulty econometrics.

Previous results are based on the volatility of asset returns, with no distinction made between bear and bull markets. Longin and Solnik (2001) find that measured correlations behave as expected under the theory of constant correlation in the presence of large positive shocks, but tend to increase in the presence of large negative shocks. So, there still is some evidence that the international correlation of equity markets increases in periods of market distress, but the evidence is not as strong as suggested by some practitioners. Simply graphing the conditional correlation estimated

[14] See Boyer, Gibson, and Loretan (1999); Loretan and English (2000); and Forbes and Rigobon (2002).

over moving windows of 52 weeks or 200 days can be very misleading, because correlation estimates are biased upward or downward, depending on the volatility of market returns. This bias begs for correction. In reality, the true correlation is much more stable than implied by a casual visual inspection of the graph. Furthermore, Ang and Bekaert (2002) introduce an asset allocation model with different correlation regimes (normal and volatile periods), and they show that the existence of increased correlation in bear markets has only a small influence on the optimal global asset allocation.

To compute a correlation coefficient, one resorts to a time-series estimation over a rather long period, assuming that the distribution of returns stays the same over the estimation period. Overlapping data have been used to study the changes in correlations; this is a poor method to study changes in correlation over time. An alternative is to look at the cross-sectional dispersion of country market returns at any given point of time. If the markets move quite independently, there should be a large dispersion of returns across national markets in any given day, week, or month. Conversely, if the markets move together, all returns should be closely bunched together. Solnik and Roulet (2000) suggest the cross-sectional standard deviation of returns as a simple measure of dispersion to study the correlation of markets.

Expanded Investment Universe and Performance Opportunities

International correlation among developed equity markets is expected to increase over time for reasons outlined earlier. Economies and markets are becoming increasingly integrated, as corporations pursue global strategies. However, the secular increase can only be slow. In some periods, global factors dominate, but this temporary phenomenon should not to be confused with a secular trend. The rise and demise of the technology, media, and telecommunications sector in late 1990s was a worldwide phenomenon. Business cycles are increasingly synchronized, but there still exist vast regional and national differences. To take the late 1990s as an example, most of Asia was in a prolonged recession while the United States was booming. Even within the European Union, the economic performance differs widely among countries. The three leading economies, France, Germany, and the United Kingdom, demonstrated big differences in the timing and intensity of their economic growth.

As major markets become intertwined, new investment opportunities emerge. In the early 1960s, there were only a couple of developed equity markets in the world. Countries like France, Germany, or Japan could be regarded as risky taken in isolation, but they provided diversification benefits to a U.S. or British investor. At the time, they had all the characteristics of emerging markets. Markets in Italy, Spain, Scandinavia, or Hong Kong progressively emerged a few years later. Many national stock markets, which were viewed as "outlandish" thirty years ago, have become "mainstream." But new markets are emerging. Associated with the slow increase in correlation of developed markets is the expansion of the investment universe. This is a natural evolutionary process. As stressed by Goetzmann, Li, and Rouwenhorst (2001), periods of globalization imply both an increase in correlation among developed markets and the emergence of new markets. The investment opportunity set enlarges, thereby offering additional international diversification benefits.

The question of global investing also should be put in a broader context. Although stock markets have become more mature and integrated, the investment universe has greatly expanded beyond equity. The case for global diversification now applies to a wide range of asset classes beyond foreign stock markets. These include emerging stock markets, foreign bonds, and alternative investments such as high-yield bonds, currency, global real estate, private equity, and various arbitrage strategies.

Global Investing Rather Than International Diversification

In the 1990s, the traditional approach to international diversification was based on the premise that country factors were the dominant factors affecting all stocks of a country. Investors were diversifying across country factors, and each stock was assigned to a country based on the location of its headquarters. The investment process was to adopt a two-step process:

- First, decide on a country allocation
- Second, select securities within countries

Today we can observe that companies compete in global industries and have extensive foreign operations. This simple process breaks down in a world where the nationality of a firm becomes fuzzy and industries cut across countries.

Global Industry Factors With increased globalization, industry factors are growing in importance, while country factors see their influence reduced. Numerous studies[15] show that industry factors have a growing influence on stock returns relative to country-specific factors. For example, Exhibit 9.14 displays the pure factor return correlation that considers the country and industry effects independent of each other. The lower the correlation, the larger the risk–benefit diversification. In the early 1990s, countries were less correlated than industries, and country diversification brought great risk diversification benefits. It is clear that there is still benefit from country diversification in the 2000s, but that the benefits from industry diversification, in the form of declining correlation, have become prominent. Increasingly, corporations are focusing on their core business in worldwide fashion rather than spreading domestically across many business lines. For example, Ford, DaimlerChrysler, Renault, and Toyota belong to the same car manufacturing industry and are, to some extent, affected by the same industry factor. All of them have activities in many countries. For example, Daimler-Benz, a German firm, acquired Chrysler, an American firm, while Renault, a French firm, linked with Nissan, a Japanese firm. Ford has many subsidiaries and brand names worldwide.

Regional and Country Factors But regional factors are still present. When car sales are buoyant in France, there is a much bigger impact on Renault than on Ford. Diermeier and Solnik (2001) showed that the stock valuation of corporations

[15] See Cavaglia, Brightman, and Aked (2000); Baca, Garbe, and Weiss (2000); and Gérard, Hillion, and de Roon (2002).

EXHIBIT 9.14

Average Correlation of Countries and of Industries

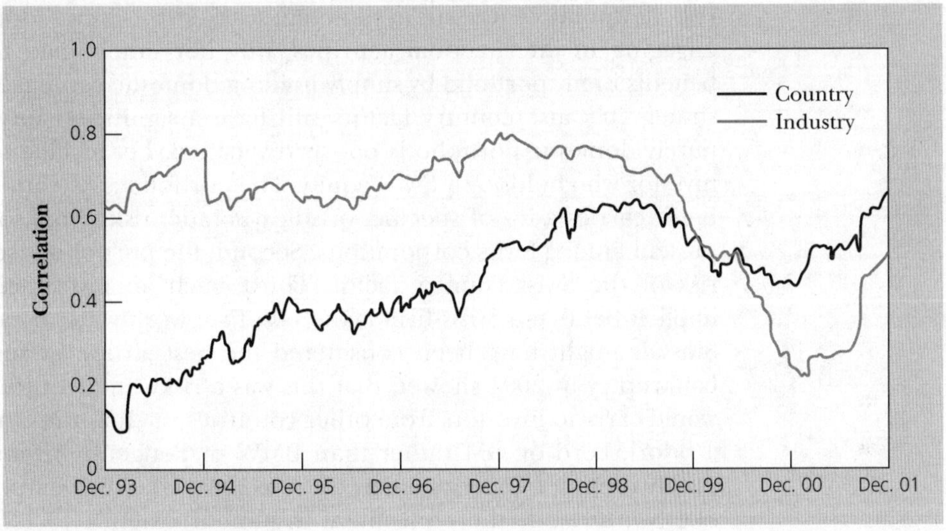

Source: UBS Global Asset Management.

reflects the geograpical distribution of their activities. For example, a corporation like Toyota, which has extensive activities in Japan and in the United States, is strongly influenced by both country factors. So, the picture is quite complex because from a market valuation perspective, we cannot simply use the location of the corporation's headquarters to define its nationality. When we talk about country factors, we should take into account the geographical distribution of activities. The more international the corporation is, the less it is sensitive to purely domestic country factors. This is illustrated in Example 9.5.

EXAMPLE 9.5 COUNTRY AND INDUSTRY EXPOSURES

Ford and Honda are two companies in the car manufacturing industry, deriving, respectively, 19 percent and 9 percent of their revenues in Europe. Lehman and Nomura are two companies in the financial services industry, deriving, respectively, 7 percent and 42 percent of their revenues in Europe.

You are bullish about the European economy and neutral about the Japanese and U.S. economies. You are bullish about the financial services industry. Which stock would you overweight in your portfolio?

SOLUTION

You should overweight Nomura. It is a Japanese company but with extensive operations in Europe (42% of revenues) which will enable it to capitalize on European economic growth. Lehman is also in the financial services industry but has small operations in Europe.

Why Still Diversify Internationally? Even if industry factors have become increasingly important and corporations are becoming more international, it would be wrong to assume that investing purely at home is a wise strategy from a risk viewpoint. A question sometimes asked is, "Since domestic companies are engaging in international activities, why not simply gain the risk diversification benefits in my portfolio by simply holding domestic companies?" This is not a good strategy because country factors still have a significant influence, and because a purely domestic portfolio is poorly diversified. Let us take the example of a Swiss investor who holds only Swiss equity. The portfolio is, to some extent, international, but it carries a lot of specific, or idiosyncratic, risk. First, some industries are not present among Swiss corporations. Second, the portfolio is still very exposed to the risk of the Swiss country factor. Third, such an investment strategy makes the implicit bet that a Swiss firm is the best firm worldwide in each industry. Although Swissair might have been considered the best airline by some Swiss investors, its bankruptcy in 2001 showed that this was a risky, undiversified bet. This argument would carry to investors from other countries, such as the United States. Why favor, a priori, Ford or GM rather than BMW or Peugeot? Although the riskiness of a purely domestic strategy seems obvious if we take the viewpoint of a small country like Switzerland, the conceptual argument extends to large countries like the United States.

Global Investing In a way, the investment world is more complex than it was years ago with segmented national equity markets. It will probably be years before we have a single, fully integrated, global equity market. In this light, the analysis of the individual firm and its diversity becomes more critical. To some extent, the analysis should still be country-specific: Country factors are still significant and many firms are still primarily domestic in their activities. It must also be industry-specific and firm-specific.

Globalization gives more importance to industries and individual companies and less to countries. It implies that investors should be more global in their investment approach, from research to portfolio construction. Even for a purely domestic portfolio, analysts must research the global product market of the domestic companies and their international competition. In global portfolio construction, a cross-country, cross-industry approach is required to capture the full risk benefits of international diversification, and this is rarely practiced. More fundamentally, it seems increasingly harder to justify a "nationalistic" approach to equity investment, with a separation of domestic versus foreign investments. In a world where financial markets have become very integrated across borders and where corporations pursue global strategies, investment managers should respond with truly global financial analysis and portfolio construction. Industries cut across national boundaries, and factors that affect stock pricing are global. The question is no longer "Should I put 20 percent of my assets abroad?" but rather "How can I afford not to be global in all aspects of my investment management approach?"

The Case for Emerging Markets

The Basic Case

Emerging economies offer attractive investment opportunities. The local risks (volatility, liquidity, and political risk) are higher, as illustrated by numerous crises, but the expected profit is large. Exhibit 9.15 plots the value of the MSCI indexes of developed stock markets ("World") and of emerging stock markets ("Emerging") over the period December 1987 to December 2006. Although the higher volatility of emerging markets is apparent, they also had a significantly larger return over the long run. Both indexes are based at 100 at the end of 1987. Although the higher volatility of emerging markets is apparent, they also had a significantly larger return over the long run. While most emerging markets were still in their infancy, they had an excellent performance in the early 1980s. As shown in Exhibit 9.15, the excellent performance continued until the mid-1990s. The Emerging index rose from 100 in December 1987 to approximately 700 in September 1994, while the World index rose to only 180. In late 1994, Mexico suffered a severe financial crisis that partly spread to other equity markets in Latin America: The Emerging index dropped to 520 within six months (loss of 25%), but it quickly recovered and reached a new peak in July 1997 at about 720. In late 1997, several emerging Asian countries got into severe currency and economic troubles: The Emerging index dropped to 320

EXHIBIT 9.15

Performance of World Developed Markets and Emerging Markets

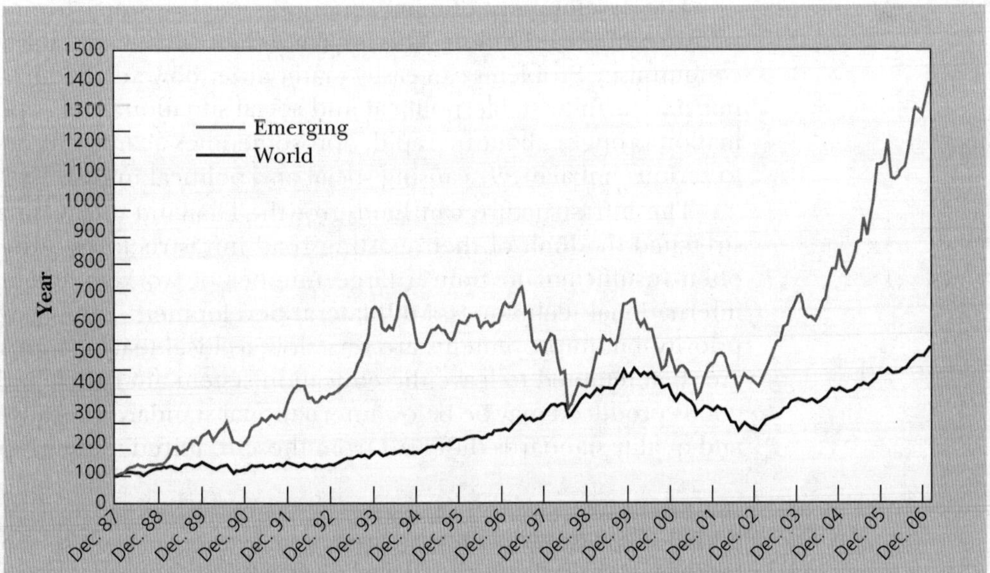

by August 1998 (a yearly loss of some 50%). By March 2000, the Emerging index was up again around 680 (a gain of over 200%). But emerging markets followed the world bear market after 2000 and dropped again. The rebound from 2002 to mid-2007 has been spectacular. From 1987 to May 2007, the geometric mean returns in U.S. dollars are 8.9 percent per year for the World index and 14.5 percent per year for the Emerging index; however, the volatility (annualized standard deviation) is 13.8 percent for the World index and 22.6 percent for the Emerging index.

Emerging markets also present a positive but moderate correlation with developed markets; the correlation with the world index of developed markets from 1987 to 2007 was 0.64, and R^2 of only 41 percent. Because of the low correlation[16] between emerging and developed markets, the risks of investing in emerging markets get partly diversified away in a global portfolio. Hence, emerging markets can have a positive contribution in terms of risk–return trade-offs. Let's review the main factors affecting expected returns and risks that should be taken into account when including emerging markets in a global asset allocation.

Volatility, Correlations, and Currency Risk

Volatility The volatility of emerging markets is much larger than that of developed markets (see Bekaert, Erb, Harvey, and Viskanta [1998]). Furthermore, the distribution of returns is not symmetric, and the probability of a shock (a large price movement) is higher than would be the case if the distribution of returns were normal. This finding implies that the standard deviation is not a sufficient measure of market risk. Investment risk in emerging economies often comes from the possibility of a crisis.

The development of many emerging markets stems from the winds of political reform and liberalization. This is clearly the case in Central Europe since the fall of communism. Problems can easily materialize, however. Some emerging countries do not have a fully stable political and social situation. The explosive social transformation brought about by rapid, and sometimes anarchic, economic growth can lead to serious imbalances, causing social and political unrest.

The infrastructure can limit growth. Thailand and China, for example, have stretched the limit of their existing road infrastructures. Education structures are often insufficient to train a large number of workers and managers in modern international techniques. Multilateral development banks have made education a priority, but improvements are very slow, as local teachers must first be trained but are then tempted to leave the education system after their training. The quality of goods produced may be below international standards because of a lack of training and quality standards different from those required in developed countries.

---

[16] The correlation, however, is still generally positive. One should not be surprised to find that in some periods when developed markets drop, emerging markets also drop, and by a large amount because of their high volatility. This happened in 2000. In other periods, an appreciation of emerging markets can offset a loss in developed markets.

Corruption is a rampant problem everywhere but may be more so in some emerging countries. Family ownership tends to favor family and friends at the detriment of other stockholders, especially foreign ones. Links between politicians and companies' managers sometimes go beyond what would be in the best interest of stockholders. The banking sector is sometimes poorly regulated, unsupervised, undercapitalized for the lending risks assumed, and lacking in the sophistication required by modern financial operations.

Correlation International correlation tends to increase in periods of crises, and emerging markets are subject to periodic large crises. Patel and Sankar (1998) find that crises on emerging markets tend to be more prolonged than crises on developed markets, and tend to spread to all emerging markets in the region. It is often the case, however, that a crisis affecting one emerging country does not spread to other emerging countries, especially outside its region. This is the case when the crisis is caused primarily by domestic political problems; many examples can be found in the recent past. An emerging market boom or crisis does not necessarily spread to developed markets, explaining the rather low correlation between developed and emerging markets. Spread depends on whether the factors creating the boom or crisis are primarily local or global.

Currency Risk Another observation is the correlation between stock and currency returns. Developed markets sometimes exhibit a negative correlation with the value of their currencies. Namely, the local stock market tends to appreciate when the value of the local currency depreciates; the argument is based on an improvement in the international competitiveness of the local firms. This is not the case for emerging stock markets. Both the stock market and the currency are affected by the state of the economy. In periods of crisis, both drop significantly. For example, the Korean won lost more than 50 percent of its value in 1997, and the Seoul stock market also dropped. Both went up significantly in 1998, when the Korean situation showed some encouraging signs. Numerous similar examples could be found in Asia or Latin America. This positive correlation means that foreign investors suffer doubly from currency risk in emerging markets.

Portfolio Return Performance

Emerging markets have a vocation to become developed markets. To emerge, an equity market has to move from an embryonic stage to that of a truly active market attracting international investors. If successful, the market will grow, become more mature, and reach the stage of becoming a developed market. This process should lead to high returns. Clearly, a major argument for investing in emerging economies is their prospective economic growth. Portfolio managers want to find countries that will exhibit in the future the type of growth witnessed by Japan between the 1960s and the 1980s. Most analysts expect emerging economies to grow at a higher rate than developed nations, given the liberalization of international trade. Arguments frequently mentioned are lower labor costs, lower level of unionization and social rigidities, delocalization of production by high-cost developed countries, and rapid growth in domestic demand. The arrival of foreign capital helps those countries develop at a rapid pace and to compete on the world goods market. The transition to a more democratic political system with less corruption, more efficient regulation of the financial industry and other sectors, promotion of free enterprise, and application of the rule of law should strongly benefit local stock markets. Some specific factors could also affect the local stock markets. For example, pension funds have recently been created in many Latin American countries and are likely to invest heavily in their local stock markets. Many countries are pursuing an active program of privatization, and more local firms are attracted by the financing potential of stock markets. Under pressure from international investors, emerging markets are becoming more efficient, providing more rigorous research on companies and progressively applying stricter standards of market supervision. Accounting standards that conform with international accounting standards (IFRS) have been adopted in most countries and are being progressively implemented. Most of these markets have automated their trading and settlement procedures, using computer software tested on developed markets. High returns can be expected in emerging economies that are successful in achieving this transition.

Investability of Emerging Markets

Foreign investors face restrictions when investing on many emerging markets. Although many emerging countries are very liberal toward foreign capital, investability is somewhat restricted in other countries. Restrictions can take many forms:

- *Foreign ownership* can be limited to a maximum percentage of the equity capital of companies listed on the emerging market. This limit can be zero for "strategic" companies, and a fixed percentage for all other companies.[17]
- *Free float* is often small because the local government is the primary owner of many companies. Even though the total market cap of a company looks large, the float available to foreign or domestic private investing is limited.
- *Repatriation of income or capital* can be somewhat constrained. Such capital flows have been liberalized in most emerging countries, but controls are periodically applied in periods of severe crisis. For example, this happened in Malaysia during the 1997 crisis.
- *Discriminatory taxes* are sometimes applied to foreign investors, although this is becoming exceptional.
- *Foreign currency restrictions* are sometimes applied. For example, China applied a dual-currency system for residents and for foreign investors.

[17] Similar restrictions apply, to a much smaller extent, in developed markets. For example, U.S. companies in the defense or transportation industries have foreign ownership constraints.

- *Authorized investors* are the only investors allowed to invest in some emerging countries (e.g., India). These authorized foreign investors are typically institutional investors, not private ones.

The pace of liberalization of emerging markets is rapid, and investability regulations are undergoing continual change. However, there is always the risk of an imposition of constraints in periods of crisis.

Another major problem with investing in emerging markets is the lack of *liquidity.* Any sizable transaction can have a very large price impact. So, there could be a significant performance difference between a "paper" portfolio, such as a passive index, and an actual portfolio.

Providers of emerging-market stock indexes have tried to reflect the investability of markets by constructing "investable" or "free" indexes. In building global emerging-market indexes, foreign ownership restrictions and free float strongly affect the weight of a given emerging country in the index.

Segmentation versus Integration Issue

In integrated markets, assets with identical risk should command identical return, regardless of location. In segmented markets, the expected returns on similar assets from different countries should not be related. In practice, emerging markets are somewhat segmented from the international market. Segmented asset pricing is attractive to the global investor. It implies that assets are mispriced relative to their "international" value. Harvey (1995) and Erb, Harvey, and Viskanta (1998) found evidence to reject the hypothesis that emerging stock markets are priced as if they were integrated in the world market. Returns on local companies are strongly influenced by domestic variables rather than by global variables, and domestic risk is priced, not global risks. As emerging markets are increasingly liberalized, this conclusion is likely to change. In a segmented market, expected asset return should be proportional to local risks. The local volatility is much higher than the contribution of the asset to the world market risk (its beta), which is what should matter in integrated asset pricing. So, expected returns in segmented markets should also be higher.

Despite all the problems of emerging economies, which create higher investment risks, emerging stock markets are an attractive asset allocation opportunity. Again, the idea is that investors should be willing to buy emerging markets, which are inherently very volatile, because some of them are likely to produce very high returns. Altogether, the contribution of emerging markets to the total risk of the global portfolio is not very large because of their low correlation with developed markets.

Summary

- International investing reduces risk because the correlations between country markets are less than 1.0. For a two-asset portfolio of domestic and foreign assets, the expected portfolio return is the weighted average of the domestic expected return and the foreign expected return. The standard deviation is the square root of the quantity: the weight squared times the variance of the domestic asset plus the weight squared times the variance of the foreign asset plus twice the product of the weights times the correlation times the standard deviations of the two assets.

- The domestic rate of return on a foreign asset is the rate of return of that asset in the foreign currency plus the rate of return on the exchange rate plus the product of the rate of return in the foreign currency times the rate of return on the exchange rate. The variance of the domestic rate of return is approximately the variance of the local return plus the variance of the exchange rate return plus twice the covariance of the local return and exchange rate return.
- International diversification provides an efficient frontier that dominates the domestic-only efficient frontier because the domestic-only frontier is more constrained.
- The factors causing equity market correlations across countries to be relatively low are the independence of different nations' economies and government policies, technological specialization, independent fiscal and monetary policies, and cultural and sociological differences.
- The factors causing bond market correlations across countries to be relatively low are the differences in national monetary and budgetary policies.
- No evidence has been found of a systematic delayed reaction of one national market to another, except for daily returns as a result of time differences around the world.
- An increased Sharpe ratio from international investing is possible because of risk reduction and the increase in profitable investment opportunities in an enlarged investment universe.
- Currency risk may only slightly magnify the volatility of foreign currency–denominated investments, because market and currency risks are not additive, exchange risk can be hedged, the contribution of currency risk should be measured for the total portfolio, and the contribution of currency risk decreases with the time horizon. Currency risk is relatively more important for bond investments than equity investments.
- The increase in correlations between national markets reduces diversification benefits. This increase is due to such factors as deregulation, capital mobility, free trade, and the globalization of corporations.
- The country-specific argument against international diversification arises during periods when the domestic market does better than most other markets, leading some to say that there is no need for international investments in the future because the domestic market is outperforming.

- The potential physical barriers to international investing include lack of familiarity with foreign markets, political risk, lack of market efficiency, regulations, transaction costs, taxes, and currency risks.
- The pitfall in estimating correlations during volatile periods is that correlations conditioned on part of a sample are biased. The apparent observation that correlation increases in periods of market turbulence can simply be an observation that market turbulence has increased but the true correlation has remained constant.
- International performance opportunities have increased over time because many markets are moving from the emerging to the developing category.
- International diversification refers to diversifying internationally because correlations between country markets are less than 1.0. As the industry factor becomes more important relative to the country factor, global investing refers to investing in the best companies, wherever they are located in the world, and recognizing that these companies will also be investing worldwide.
- Compared with developed markets, emerging markets exhibit higher volatility than developed markets, with asymmetric return distributions and increasing international correlations in times of crises, but they also exhibit higher return opportunities because of the early growth stages of their economies.
- In contrast to developed economies, emerging markets exhibit positive correlations between the local stock market and the currency; that is, when they do poorly, both the local stock market and the currency do poorly together.
- The investability in emerging markets is constrained by various regulations and liquidity problems.
- Emerging markets tend to be somewhat segmented, and mispricing is evident.

Problems

1. The estimated volatility of a domestic asset is $\sigma_d = 15$ percent (annualized standard deviation of returns). A foreign asset has a volatility of $\sigma_f = 18$ percent, and a correlation of $\rho = 0.5$ with the domestic asset. What is the volatility of a portfolio invested 80 percent in the domestic asset and 20 percent in the foreign asset?
2. You are given the expected return and standard deviation of Asset 1 and Asset 2:

$$E(R_1) = 10\%, \sigma_1 = 10\%$$
$$E(R_2) = 14\%, \sigma_2 = 16\%$$

The correlation between the two assets is $\rho = 0.2$.

a. Calculate the expected return and risk of portfolios invested in the following proportions:

Asset 1	Asset 2
100%	0%
80%	20%
60%	40%
50%	50%
40%	60%
20%	80%
0%	100%

b. Use the expected return and risk calculations for all the portfolios to plot an expected return–risk graph.

3. Consider the following information on the expected return and risk of two assets:

$$E(R_1) = 10\%, \sigma_1 = 14\%$$

$$E(R_2) = 16\%, \sigma_2 = 16\%$$

a. Calculate the expected return and risk of portfolios invested in the following proportions listed. Assume a correlation of $\rho = 0.5$.

Asset 1	Asset 2
100%	0%
80%	20%
60%	40%
50%	50%
40%	60%
20%	80%
0%	100%

Use the expected return and risk calculations for all the portfolios to plot the efficient frontier.

b. Repeat part (a), assuming $\rho = -1$, $\rho = 0$, and $\rho = +1$.

c. Looking at the four graphs you have just drawn for parts (a) and (b), what do you conclude about the importance of correlation in risk reduction?

4. The standard deviation of a foreign asset in local currency is $\sigma = 8.5$ percent, and the standard deviation of the exchange rate is $\sigma_s = 5.5$ percent.

a. If the correlation between the asset return, in local currency, and the exchange rate movement is $\rho = 0$, calculate the amount of risk that can be attributed to currency risk.

b. If the correlation between the asset return, in local currency, and the exchange rate movement is $\rho = 0.25$, calculate the amount of risk that can be attributed to currency risk.

c. If the correlation between the asset return, in local currency, and the exchange rate movement is $\rho = -0.45$, calculate the amount of risk that can be attributed to currency risk.

d. What is the impact of the level of correlation between the asset return in local currency and the exchange rate movement on the risk of a foreign asset measured in dollars?

5. Assume that the domestic volatility (standard deviation) of the German stock market (in euros) is 18.2 percent. The volatility of the euro against the U.S. dollar is 11.7 percent.

a. What would the dollar volatility of the German stock market be for a U.S. investor if the correlation between the stock market returns and exchange rate movements were zero?

b. Suppose the dollar volatility of the German stock market is 20.4 percent. What can you conclude about the correlation between German stock market movements and exchange rate movements?

6. Assume that the domestic volatility (standard deviation) of the German bond market (in euros) is 5.5 percent. The volatility of the euro against the U.S. dollar is 11.7 percent.
   a. What would the dollar volatility of the German market be for a U.S. investor if the correlation between the bond market returns and exchange rate movements were zero?
   b. Suppose the dollar volatility of the German bond market is 13.6 percent. What can you conclude about the correlation between German bond market movements and exchange rate movements? What might explain this correlation?

7. Indicate whether the following statement is correct, and explain your reasoning: "The best diversification vehicle is an asset with high volatility and low correlation with the portfolio."

8. a. Exhibit 9.4 provides correlations of stock markets (currency hedged). Which markets are most correlated, and which are the least correlated with Germany? Provide some explanations for the differences in correlations.
   b. Once again, consider the correlations in Exhibit 9.4. Which markets are most correlated, and which are the least correlated with the United States? Provide some explanations for the differences in correlations.

9. Consider the correlations (in U.S. dollars) of worldwide bond markets presented in Exhibit 9.5. Explain the reasons for the correlations observed between the United States and other countries, and indicate the motivations for diversifying a U.S. dollar bond portfolio into foreign-currency bonds.

10. Explain whether there are any benefits to adding bonds to a stock portfolio in a global investment strategy.

11. What factors can be used to explain differences in the long-run performance of equity markets of different countries?

12. Is currency risk a barrier to international investment?

13. It is often claimed that financial markets are becoming increasingly integrated worldwide. Advance some reasons for this trend.

14. Studies of international financial markets have documented a phenomenon referred to as *correlation breakdown*. Explain what is meant by this term. What are the implications of correlation breakdown for global portfolio strategy?

15. Despite strong arguments in favor of international diversification, international portfolio investment is still not widespread in many countries. One reason for this is the presence of barriers to international investment. List and explain the various barriers to international investment.

16. The traditional approach to global investing was a two-step procedure, in which the first decision was country allocation and the second decision was to select industries and stocks within countries. Is this approach still valid, or have changes in international markets called this two-step approach into question?

17. Risk in developed financial markets is typically measured by the standard deviation of returns. Is the standard deviation a sufficient measure of risk in emerging markets? Explain your answer.

18. Emerging markets are often perceived to be very risky investment propositions. Provide some arguments in favor of investing in emerging markets.

19. TMP has been experiencing increasing demand from its institutional clients for information and assistance related to international investments. Recognizing that this is an area of growing importance, the firm has hired an experienced analyst/portfolio manager specializing in international equities and market strategies. Her first assignment is to represent TMP before a client company's investment committee to discuss the possibility of changing their present "U.S. securities only" investment approach to one including international investments. She is told that the committee wants a presentation that fully and objectively examines the basic, substantive considerations on which the committee should focus attention, including both theory and evidence. The company's pension plan has no legal or other barriers to adoption of an international approach, and no non-U.S. liabilities currently exist.

a. Identify and briefly discuss three reasons for adding international securities to the pension portfolio and three problems associated with such an approach.
b. Assume that the committee has adopted a policy to include international securities in its pension portfolio. Identify and briefly discuss three additional policy-level investment decisions the committee must make before management selection and actual implementation can begin.

20. The HFS Trustees have solicited input from three consultants concerning the risks and rewards of an allocation to international equities. Two of them strongly favor such action, while the third consultant commented as follows:

> The risk reduction benefits of international investing have been significantly overstated. Recent studies relating to the cross-country correlation structure of equity returns during different market phases cast serious doubt on the ability of international investing to reduce risk, especially in situations in which risk reduction is needed the most.

a. Describe the behavior of the cross-country equity return correlations to which the consultant is referring. Explain how that behavior may diminish the ability of international investing to reduce risk in the short run.
b. Assume the consultant's assertion is correct. Explain why it might still be more efficient on a risk/reward basis to invest internationally rather than only domestically in the long run.

Bibliography

Ang, A., and Bekaert, G. "International Asset Allocation with Regime Shifts," *Review of Financial Studies*, 15(4), Winter 2002.

Baca, S., Garbe, B., and Weiss, R. "The Rise of Sector Effects in Major Equity Markets," *Financial Analysts Journal*, 56(5), September/October 2000.

Bekaert, G., Erb, C. B., Harvey, C. R., and Viskanta, T. E. "Distributional Characteristics of Emerging Market Returns and Asset Allocation," *Journal of Portfolio Management*, Winter 1998.

Bookstaber, R. "Global Risk Management: Are We Missing the Point?" *Journal of Portfolio Management*, Spring 1997.

Boyer, B., Gibson, M. S., and Loretan, M. "Pitfalls in Tests for Changes in Correlations," Working Paper 597R, Federal Reserve Board, International Finance Division, 1999.

Cavaglia, S., Brightman, C., and Aked, M. "On the Increasing Importance of Industry Factors," *Financial Analysts Journal*, 56(5), September/October 2000.

DeFusco, R. A., McLeavey, D., Pinto, R., and Runkle, D. *Quantitative Methods for Investment Analysis*, 2nd Ed., Hoboken, NJ: John Wiley & Sons, 2007.

Diermeier, J., and Solnik, B. "Global Pricing of Equity," *Financial Analysts Journal*, July/August 2001.

Erb, C. B., Harvey, C. R., and Viskanta, T. E. *Country Risk in Global Financial Management*, Charlottesville, VA: The Research Foundation of the IFCA, 1998.

Forbes, K., and Rigobon, R. "No Contagion, Only Interdependence: Measuring Stock Market Co-movements," *Journal of Finance*, October 2002.

Froot, K. A. "Currency Hedging over Long Horizons," NBER Working Paper No. 4355, May 1993.

Gérard, B., Hillion, P., and de Roon, F. "International Portfolio Diversification: Industrial Structure, Country and Currency Effects Revisited," Working Paper, 2002.

Goetzmann, W., Li, L., and Rouwenhorst, G. "Long-Term Global Market Correlation," Working Paper, 2001.

Harvey, C. R. "Predictable Risk and Return in Emerging Markets," *Review of Financial Studies*, 8(3), Fall 1995.

Jorion, P. "Asset Allocation with Hedged and Unhedged Foreign Stocks and Bonds," *Journal of Portfolio Management*, Summer 1989.

Longin, F., "The Asymptotic Distribution of Extreme Stock Market Returns," *Journal of Business*, 63, 1996.

Longin, F., and Solnik, B. "Is the International Correlation of Equity Returns Constant: 1960–1990?" *Journal of International Money and Finance*, February 1995.

———."Extreme Correlation of International Equity Returns," *Journal of Finance*, April 2001.

Loretan, M., and English, W. B. "Evaluation 'Correlation Breakdowns' during Periods of Market Volatility," in *International Financial Markets and the Implications for Monetary and Financial Stability*, Bank for International Settlements, Basel, Switzerland, 2000.

Odier, P., and Solnik, B. "Lessons for International Asset Allocation," *Financial Analysts Journal*, March/April 1993.

Patel, S. A., and Sankar, A. "Crises in Developed and Emerging Stock Markets," *Financial Analysts Journal*, November/December 1998.

Solnik, B. "Why Not Diversify Internationally Rather Than Domestically?" *Financial Analysts Journal*, July/August 1974.

Solnik, B., and Roulet, J. "Dispersion as Cross-Sectional Correlation," *Financial Analysts Journal*, January/February 2000.

Zingales, L. "The Value of the Voting Right: A Study of the Milan Stock Exchange Experience," *Review of Financial Studies*, 7, 1994.

10

Derivatives: Risk Management with Speculation, Hedging, and Risk Transfer

LEARNING OUTCOMES

After completing this chapter, you will be able to do the following:

- Describe the similarities and differences between a forward and a futures contract
- Explain how forward and futures contracts are valued by arbitrage
- Discuss various uses of forward and futures contracts
- Describe various hedging strategies
- Describe a swap and detail various types of swaps commonly used
- Calculate the value of a currency swap and an interest rate swap
- Explain the importance of credit risk in swap valuation
- Illustrate the use of a swap to transfer some comparative advantage and to manage long-term exposure to interest rate and currency risk
- Describe an option and detail various types of options commonly found
- Explain the principles of options valuation
- Discuss various uses of options in speculation, insurance of a portfolio, and the construction of structured notes

Investments based on some underlying asset are often known as derivatives. The capital invested is less than the price of the underlying asset, offering financial leverage and allowing investors to multiply the rate of return on the underlying asset. Because of this leverage, derivatives may be used either to take better advantage of a specific profit opportunity or to hedge a portfolio against a specific risk.

Derivatives can be traded on an organized exchange, which is usually the case for futures and options. Other types of derivatives exist in the form of private contracts between two parties, such as forwards and swaps. Once signed, these contracts are not easily traded. This chapter presents a review of major derivatives (forwards and futures, swaps, options) and focuses on their use in investment management. The coverage of each derivative type is structured along the following sequence: a discussion of some basic principles, a review of the different instruments, an analysis of valuation of this derivative type, and a discussion of its use in investment management. Chapter 11 is devoted to currency risk management, and we will use concepts from this chapter on derivatives.

Forward and Futures

Forward contracts have existed for many centuries. They are simply a commitment to buy or sell goods at a future date and price specified at time of contracting.

The Principles of a Forward and a Futures Contract

Definition In both a *forward* contract and a *futures* contract, all terms of a goods exchange are arranged on one day, but the physical delivery takes place at a later date (the delivery date). More precisely, a forward or futures contract is a commitment to purchase or deliver a specified quantity of the underlying asset on a designated date in the future for a price determined competitively when the contract is transacted. A forward contract is a private agreement between two parties, and nothing happens between the contracting date and the delivery date. On the other hand, a futures contract is traded on an organized exchange, and the mechanics are a bit complex.

Let's consider the British pound futures traded on the Chicago Mercantile Exchange (CME). Contracts on the exchange specify delivery of 62,500 British pounds; all futures prices traded in the United States are quoted in dollars per unit of the second currency, in this case dollars per pound. On February 18, an investor could have bought a futures contract for delivery next March at a price of $1.6350 per pound. This means that the buyer of the futures contract was obliged to buy 62,500 pounds in March from the seller of the contract, who likewise was obliged to sell to the buyer. Exchanges offer contracts with different delivery months: On the CME, currency futures are traded with delivery months in March, June, September, and December.

A *futures contract* is simply a commitment to buy or sell. There is no money exchanged when the contract is signed. To ensure that each party fulfills its commitment, therefore, some form of deposit is required. This is called the *margin deposit.* The exchanges set a minimum margin for each contract. In fact, two types of margins are required: When the client first enters a contract, an *initial margin* must be posted. The initial margin on the British pound contract was $1,080 for one 62,500 pounds contract. The *maintenance margin* is the minimum level below which the margin is not allowed to fall once losses on the contract value have been taken into account. The maintenance margin was $800 for the British pound contract. The maintenance margin is typically 70 percent to 80 percent of the initial margin, but it is often equal to the initial margin on non-U.S. futures exchanges. Margins are usually deposited in the form of cash, but brokers often allow large customers to use interest-bearing securities, such as Treasury bills, as deposits. In that case, there is no opportunity cost associated with a futures contract investment, because the margin position continues earning interest.

Futures prices fluctuate every day and even every instant. Therefore, all contract positions are *marked to market* at the end of every day. If net price movements induce a gain on the position from the previous day, the customer immediately receives cash in the amount of this gain. Conversely, if there is a loss, the customer must cover the loss. As soon as a customer's account falls below the maintenance margin, the customer receives a margin call to reconstitute the initial margin. If this is not done immediately, the broker will close the position on the market. The following example illustrates how this works.

Assume that an investor buys a March contract in British pounds at \$1.6350 per pound on February 18 and puts up an initial cash margin of \$1,080. The maintenance margin is \$800. The next day, the futures price drops to \$1.6250, and the position is marked to market. The investor loses \$0.0100 per pound, or \$625 per contract. This amount is debited from the investor's cash position, which is reduced to \$455, now less than the maintenance margin. The investor receives a margin call for \$625 to reconstitute the initial margin to \$1,080. Investors receive a margin call only when their margin falls below the maintenance margin, but then they must deposit cash to reconstitute the initial margin (not the maintenance margin). The next day, the futures price rises to \$1.6400 per pound, and the investor's cash account is credited \$937.50 [$(1.6400 - 1.6250) \times 62{,}500$]. The cash account now has a balance of \$2,017.50, and the investor may draw up to \$937.50 from the account. An investor short in the futures contract has the opposite cash flows.

Margins are set by the exchange, subject to periodic revision. The margin is determined by looking at the risk of a given contract. However, the risk on a portfolio of futures positions is not equal to the sum of the risks on each position. For example, an investor who is long in a March contract and short in a June contract should not be required to post twice the initial margin on a single contract. The CME developed a margin system known as SPAN (Standard Portfolio Analysis of Risk), which has been progressively adopted by most major exchanges throughout the world. SPAN calculates margin requirements on the basis of overall portfolio risk.

The procedure of marking to market implies that all potential profits and losses are immediately realized. This is a major difference between futures and forward contracts. In effect, futures contracts are canceled every day and replaced by new contracts with a delivery price equal to the new futures price, that is, the settlement price at the end of the day.

Market Organization: Futures versus Forward Contracts Like futures contracts, forward contracts are made in advance of delivery. But a *forward contract* is a private agreement between two parties made *over-the-counter* (*OTC*). A forward contract cannot be resold because there is no secondary market for it. For the same reason, forward contracts cannot be marked to market, and the investor has to wait for the delivery date to realize the profit or loss on the position. The margin is set initially and usually never revised. This could lead to fairly large initial margins in order to cover default risk over the life of the contract. In practice, the margin is often set at zero for good-quality parties.

Futures contracts have succeeded because they are standardized. A clearinghouse handles the two sides of a transaction. For any transaction, two contracts are written: one between the buyer and the clearinghouse and one between the clearinghouse and the seller. Through this procedure, all contracts are standardized in terms of a specific counterparty, as well as size and delivery date. To cancel a position, the investor simply has to reverse the trades by selling contracts previously bought or buying back contracts previously sold. This practice creates a highly liquid market in standardized contracts. Forward contracts do not offer the same liquidity because all contracts are different in terms of size, delivery date, and name of the other contracting party. Even if a reverse trade were possible in the forward market (and it would require an identical amount and delivery date), the investor would have to carry both contracts until the delivery date because both are private commitments with two different parties. The reverse trade locks in the profit (or loss) on the initial contract, but this profit (or loss) will be realized only on the delivery date. Of course, the contract could also be renegotiated with the original counterparty with some side payment reflecting current market conditions, but this is usually a costly process because the counterparty does not have to oblige. Exhibit 10.1 summarizes the major differences between the two types of markets.

It should be stressed that, contrary to forward contracts, futures contracts are seldom used to take physical delivery. These contracts are used to hedge, or take advantage of, price movements rather than to delay the sale or purchase of goods. Most investors reverse their position in the futures market before the contract expires.

Futures contracts have become successful relative to forward contracts because their various mechanisms (marking to market, and the clearinghouse as the

EXHIBIT 10.1

Major Differences between Forward and Futures Contracts

Forward Contracts	Futures Contracts
1. Customized contracts in terms of size and delivery dates.	1. Standardized contracts in terms of size and delivery dates.
2. Private contracts between two parties.	2. Standardized contract between a customer and a clearinghouse.
3. Difficult to reverse a contract.	3. Contract may be freely traded on the market.
4. Profit or loss on a position is realized only on the delivery date.	4. All contracts are marked to market; profits and losses are realized immediately.
5. Margins are set once, on the day of the initial transaction.	5. Margins must be maintained to reflect price movements.

counterparty on each contract) basically eliminate default risk. Developed forward markets have prospered only for contracts in which the volume of transactions is large and involves market participants of top credit quality. This is the case for forward oil transactions, in which oil companies are active players. This is also the case for the interbank forward exchange rate market described in Chapter 1. The forward currency market is a wholesale market in which huge positions are taken at extremely low transaction costs. The futures currency market is more of a retail market, although arbitrage between the two markets aligns prices.

The Different Instruments

Currencies The interbank foreign exchange market is usually considered the largest market for forward and futures transactions in currencies. This forward market is closely linked to that of Eurocurrency deposits because of the technical relationship between forward exchange rates and interest rate differentials between two currencies. It is also very large and efficient and boasts minimal transaction costs for normal transactions (several millions). Moreover, the market is open around the clock, with participants throughout the world.

As mentioned, forward contracts are not standardized, and there is no organized secondary market. Forward contracts are usually negotiated on the interbank market with maturities of 1, 2, 3, 6, or 12 months. Because the length of the contracts rather than the delivery date is fixed, each day a new contract is traded on the market. For example, someone buying a 1-month contract on June 2 with maturity July 1 cannot resell it on June 6 because 1-month contracts traded on this day expire on July 5.

To assist a customer, a bank may propose a forward contract tailored to the customer's needs and charge a large commission for this service, because the bank cannot take an exactly offsetting position in the interbank market. Thus, a bank could propose on June 6 a forward contract with a maturity of 25 days expiring on July 1. The *currency swaps* described later in this chapter are also a form of forward exchange rate contract. They involve swapping at a fixed exchange rate a series of cash flows denominated in one currency for a series of cash flows denominated in another currency. This swap may be regarded as a package, or strip, of forward currency contracts where the payments on the contracts are matched to the cash flow dates of the swap. This currency swap market allows for long-term currency hedging. The forward and futures markets cover contracts ranging from one month to several months, whereas swaps extend this range to 10 years.

The CME actively trades futures contracts in many currencies. The CME also offers cross-rate contracts not involving the U.S. dollar, for example, a euro/British pound contract.[1] As shown in Exhibit 10.2, all prices are expressed in U.S. dollars per unit of foreign currency. An investor could have bought, on February 18, a Swiss franc contract with a March delivery wherein he would agree to buy 125,000

[1] However, quotations and costs reflect the lower liquidity of these cross-rate contracts.

Swiss francs in March for a price of 0.7049 dollars per Swiss franc (latest price). If the Swiss franc appreciates and goes above 0.7049 dollars by March, the buyer will make a profit; if the Swiss franc depreciates, the buyer will take a loss.

The currency futures quotations shown in Exhibit 10.2 illustrate the type of information available in the international financial press. For example, note the futures prices for the Swiss franc contracts. The size of the contract is 125,000 Swiss francs. All contract prices are given per unit of goods traded, that is, one Swiss franc. The March contract opened at 0.7060 dollars per Swiss franc and closed, or settled, at 0.7049. The *high* and *low* prices of the day were 0.7080 and 0.7041 dollars. The *change* gives the price change from the settlement price on the previous day. The settlement price is also the price used for the marking-to-market procedure. Someone who had bought one March Swiss franc contract at the close of February 17 at 0.7048 would have gained $12.50 on February 18 (SFr125,000 × $0.0001/SFr). Someone who had sold one contract on February 17 would have lost $12.50 on February 18. The *estimated volume* is the number of contracts traded during that day, and the *open interest* is the number of contracts outstanding.

The advantage of currency futures is that the investor may transact in small amounts for reasonable transaction costs. Moreover, the market is very liquid. An investor may engage in active currency exposure management, because clearing procedures permit covering positions at any time by reverse transactions in the futures contracts. In addition, the procedure of marking to market allows an investor to realize a profit or a loss immediately rather than having to wait until

EXHIBIT 10.2

Quotations for Currency Futures, February 18

	Open	Latest	Change	High	Low	Estimated volume	Open Interest
JAPANESE YEN FUTURES (CME) Yen 12.5m per Yen 100							
Mar	0.8425	0.8364	−0.0059	0.8473	0.8361	40,254	69,382
Jun	0.8560	0.8467	−0.0057	0.8560	0.8462	273	5,239
Sep	—	0.8629	—	—	—	4	1,494
STERLING FUTURES (CME) £62,500 per £							
Mar	1.6350	1.6320	−0.0020	1.6378	1.6316	5,283	54,485
Jun	1.6330	1.6316	−0.0018	1.6348	1.6310	42	1,884
Sep	—	1.6330	−0.0006	1.6340	1.6330	26	230
SWISS FRANC FUTURES (CME) SFr125,000 per SFr							
Mar	0.7060	0.7049	+0.0001	0.7080	0.7041	7,880	55,689
Jun	0.7108	0.7115	+0.0001	0.7118	0.7108	89	530
Sep	—	0.7184	+0.0005	0.7184	—	3	269

Source: *Financial Times*, February 19, 1999

delivery. On the CME, there is physical delivery of currency at expiration of the contract. But reverse trades are often made to cancel the position before the delivery date.

Commodities There has always been a need for futures markets in commodities with volatile spot prices. Farmers and harvest buyers have long used futures markets to hedge price risks arising from climatic conditions. A large variety of commodities are now traded on futures markets throughout the world: perishable goods, such as soybeans or live cattle; metals, such as copper, silver, and gold; energy sources, such as oil. For each commodity, the quality and quantity of the product traded are precisely specified, as are the locations and conditions of delivery. Some contracts on commodity indexes are also traded (Goldman Sachs Commodity Index futures on the CME).

Interest Rate Futures The most actively traded futures contracts in the world are interest rate futures,[2] such as Eurodollar or U.S. Treasury bonds contracts. Commercial banks and money managers use these futures to hedge their interest rate exposure, that is, to protect their portfolios of loans, investments, or borrowing against adverse movements in interest rates. Speculators use them as leveraged investments, based on their forecasts of movements in interest rates.

Organized markets for interest rate futures exist for instruments in several currencies. All countries with an active bond market have developed a futures market for long-term bonds and short-term paper. Active U.S. dollar markets exist in 3-month U.S. Treasury bills, in Eurodollar deposits (3-month LIBOR), and in Treasury bonds for long-term rates. Other futures contracts have been introduced for certificates of deposit (CDs), fed funds (bank reserves at the Federal Reserve), 5- and 10-year Treasury bonds, municipal bonds, and inflation-linked bonds. Similarly, all national futures markets offer, at least, a contract on their three-month interest rate and long-term government bond. The introduction of the euro led to a consolidation among European futures exchanges, with the domination of EUREX (Germany– Switzerland) and Euronext-LIFFE (United Kingdom, France, Netherlands, and Belgium).

Short-Term Deposits The quotation method used for these contracts is difficult to understand but tends to be similar among countries. Quotations for Euribor[3] interest rate futures are given in Exhibit 10.3. Contracts on short-term instruments are quoted at a discount from 100 percent. At delivery, the contract price equals 100 percent minus the interest rate of the underlying instrument. For example, three-month Euribor contracts are denominated in units of €1 million; the price is quoted in points of 100 percent. For this reason, the March contract in Exhibit 10.3

[2] *Interest rate swaps* are described later in this chapter. They are akin to periodic interest rate forward contracts. As mentioned, they may be considered long-term packages of forward contracts.

[3] Euribor (euro interbank offer rate) is the short-term interest rate in euros on the international market. It is equivalent to the LIBOR (London interbank offer rate) for the U.S. dollar.

EXHIBIT 10.3

Quotations for Interest Rate Futures, February 18

THREE-MONTH EURIBOR FUTURES (LIFFE) € 1m, 100 – rate

	Open	Sett Price	Change	High	Low	Estimated Volume	Open Interest
Mar	96.985	96.980	−0.005	96.995	96.960	38,244	146,771
Jun	97.085	97.085	+0.005	97.100	97.070	29,048	134,205
Sep	97.115	97.115	+0.005	97.130	97.095	19,978	91,904
Dec	96.870	96.850	—	96.870	96.845	6,087	86,886

NOTIONAL U.K. GILT FUTURES (LIFFE) £100,000, 100ths of 100%

	Open	Latest	Change	High	Low	Estimated Volume	Open Interest
Mar	117.27	116.98	−0.07	117.40	116.82	45,227	89,090
Jun	118.17	118.00	—	118.39	117.95	2,581	6,963

Source: Financial Times, February 19, 1999

is quoted at 96.980 percent (settlement price) on the Euronext-LIFFE. The price of 96.98 percent is linked to a forward interest rate on three-month Euribor deposits of 3.02 percent (100 − 96.98). If the three-month interest rate at delivery is less than 3.02 percent, the buyer of the contract at 96.98 percent will make a profit.

This quotation method is drawn from the Treasury bill market. However, further calculations are required to derive the profit or loss on such a futures position, because the interest rates for three-month instruments are quoted on an annualized basis. The true interest (not annualized) paid on a three-month instrument is equal to the annualized rate divided by 4. Therefore, the profit or loss on one unit of a Euribor contract (or any other three-month financial contract) equals the futures price variation divided by 4. The total gain or loss on one three-month contract is therefore equal to

$$\text{Gain (loss)} = \left(\frac{\text{Futures price variation}}{4}\right) \times \text{Size of contract} \tag{10.1}$$

Assume that in March the Euribor interest rate drops to 2 percent on the delivery date. The futures price will be 98 percent on that date. The profit to the buyer of one contract is

$$\text{Gain} = \left(\frac{98\% - 96.98\%}{4}\right) \times €1 \text{ million} = €2{,}550$$

The same quotation technique is used for Treasury bills and other short-term interest rate contracts.

Bonds The quotation method for contracts on long-term instruments is quite different. The contract is usually defined in reference to a theoretical bond of well-defined characteristics, usually called a *notional bond.* For example, the British bond contract traded on the Euronext-LIFFE is defined in reference to a long-term gilt (U.K. government bond) with a 6 percent (notional) yield. The notional bond is a theoretical bond; it does not exist in real life. Contract specifications, including delivery conditions, are a bit technical and are detailed in Exhibit 10.4. For the

EXHIBIT 10.4

Bond Contracts Specifications (*U.S. Illustration in Italics*)

The *notional bond* is a theoretical bond, which does not exist in real life and is assumed to be "refreshed" every day, that is, priced as a newly issued bond (without accrued interest). Its main feature is its *notional yield*, the coupon rate on the bond.

Because the notional bond does not exist, we need to specify which bond can be delivered at maturity of the contract in lieu of the notional bond, and what are the conditions of delivery. If the seller of a contract wants to physically deliver a bond, the seller can do so with any bond belonging to a list of bonds published by the exchange.

For example, the U.S. Treasury bond contracts traded on the Chicago Board of Trade are defined in reference to a notional Treasury bond with a 6 percent notional yield. The contract is to deliver 100,000 U.S. dollars of par value of any U.S. Treasury bond that has a minimum life of 15 years and is noncallable over that period.

However, the futures price quoted applies strictly to the notional *6 percent coupon* bond. The price received by the seller of the futures contract who delivers a specific bond at maturity of the contract is equal to the settlement price of the notional bond futures adjusted by a *conversion factor* that takes into account the different characteristics in terms of coupon and maturity of the bond delivered (for example, a high-coupon security is worth more than a comparable low-coupon bond). The conversion factor equals the theoretical price of the delivered bond obtained by discounting its cash flows at the notional yield, on the maturity date of the futures contract. Note that bonds with coupons in excess of the notional yield have conversion factors greater than one (i.e., 100 percent). Bonds with coupons below the notional yield have conversion factors less than one. Actually, bonds are quoted on the basis of their clean price. So, the total present value of a bond (PV) is equal to its clean price quoted plus the accrued interest, which is equal to the proportion of the coupon accrued since the last payment date. Hence, the conversion factor[4] for each deliverable bond is calculated for the maturity date of the contract and is equal to the present value of the bond (discounted at the notional yield) minus accrued interest. For a given deliverable bond B, we have

$$\text{Conversion factor}_B = \text{PV}_B(@\ \text{Notional yield}) - \text{Accrued interest}_B$$

On delivery date, the seller of the futures contract selects a bond to deliver, and delivers a quantity of par value of this delivered bond equal to the contract size (*$100,000 of par value for U.S. contracts*). The buyer of the futures contract will receive this quantity of delivered bonds and pay an *invoice price* equal to the futures settlement price times the contract size times the conversion factor of this specific delivered bond.

[4] Each futures exchange publishes a list of all deliverable bonds and a list of their conversion factors calculated on the maturity date of each available futures contract.

Furthermore, the invoice paid by the buyer is adjusted for accrued interest on the delivered bond.

$$\text{Invoice} = (\text{Futures price} \times \text{Conversion factor}_B + \text{Accrued interest}_B) \times \text{Contract size}$$

At each point in time, some bonds will be cheaper to deliver than others; their market price is low compared to the invoice price received on delivery. Futures prices tend to correlate most closely with the price of the *cheapest-to-deliver* security. This is because the seller of the futures contract, who decides on the bond to be physically delivered at maturity, will naturally select the cheapest to deliver.[5]

purpose of most investors, it is sufficient to know that bond futures contracts are based on a specific bond.

Exhibit 10.3 also shows the quotations for futures contracts on U.K. gilts. The contract size is £100,000 of par value (or nominal value) of the bond. Quotations are expressed in hundredths of 100 percent, that is, in points and basis points. The quotation is in percentage of the par value of the bond. For example, the March contract of U.K. gilts settled at 116.98 percent on February 18. The change from the previous day's settlement price was −0.07 percent.

The gain or loss[6] is simply equal to the futures price variation, in percent, times the size of the contract:

$$\text{Gain(loss)} = (\text{Futures price variation}) \times \text{Size of contract} \qquad (10.2)$$

In this illustration, the loss taken by the holder of one U.K. gilt contract from the previous trading day is equal to

$$\text{Gain} = -0.07\% \times £100{,}000 = -£70$$

Stock Futures Futures are traded on stock indexes and on single stocks.

Stock Index Futures Stock index contracts are linked to a published stock index. The contract size is a multiple of the index. For example, the dollar size of the S&P 500

[5] The design of these bond futures contracts may seem unduly complicated. An alternative would have been to write a contract on a single benchmark bond. Because the market capitalization of any single bond is rather small, this creates liquidity problems and opens up the possibility of price manipulation. By increasing the number of deliverable bonds, this market manipulation becomes very difficult. Assume for a moment that the yield curve is flat and equal to the notional yield, for example, 6 percent for U.S. bonds. Then it can be easily verified that the futures price will be 100 percent and that all bonds will be equally desirable for delivery because their quoted clean price is simply equal to their conversion factor. This is not the case when the yield curve is not flat at 6 percent, but the contract mechanism ensures that other bonds will replace the cheapest-to-deliver bond if its price is manipulated.

[6] Because of the inverse relationship between the long-term interest rate and the market price of a bond, the buyer of a bond contract gains if the interest rate drops (the bond price rises) and loses if the interest rate rises.

contracts traded on the CME is \$250 times the S&P 500 index. The gain (loss) on a stock index futures is calculated by applying the multiple to the futures price variation:

$$\text{Gain (loss)} = \text{Futures price variation} \times \text{Contract value multiple} \qquad (10.3)$$

A characteristic of stock index futures is that the underlying asset, the stock index, does not exist physically as a financial asset. As a result, all final settlements take place in cash rather than by delivery of a good or security. On the delivery date, the buyer of a stock index contract receives the difference between the calculated value of the index and the previous futures price. The procedure works as if the contract were marked to market on the last day, with the final futures price replaced by the stock index value. The cash delivery procedure avoids most of the transaction costs involved in buying and selling a large number of stocks. The calculation of gains on a stock index contract is illustrated in Example 10.1.

Numerous stock index contracts are available in the United States and all major countries. These indexes are sometimes broadly based, as is the S&P 500, to allow for broad participation in the market. They are useful to manage the risk of well-diversified portfolios. More often, these indexes are based on a small number of actively traded stocks. For example, the Euro STOXX 50 contract traded on Eurex tracks the most active European stocks. A narrowly based index has two advantages. First, it is based on stocks that trade frequently, so it gives better indications on instantaneous movements in the market. Second, it allows derivatives professionals to hedge their futures positions with opposite transactions in the cash market more easily and cheaply, hence providing good liquidity to the futures market.

Single Stock Futures Futures contracts on a single stock are traded in some countries, but with limited success. This is a convenient way to buy a stock on margin or short sell it. OneChicago (a joint venture of the Chicago Board of Trade, Chicago Mercantile Exchange, and Chicago Board of Options Exchange) started trading U.S. single stock futures in late 2002. In other countries, specific mechanisms are provided for forward purchase or sale of single stocks. In the United Kingdom, a *contract for difference (CFD)* is a contract between an investor and a broker. The investor will receive (or pay) the difference between the price of the

EXAMPLE 10.1 STOCK INDEX CONTRACT

The December futures contract of the Australian ASX index quotes at 4,050. The multiple is 25 Australian dollars (A\$). The next day, this contract quotes at 4,070. What is the gain for an investor long in one contract?

SOLUTION

The gain in Australian dollars for the holder of one contract is equal to

$$\text{Gain} = (4{,}070 - 4{,}050) \times \text{A\$}25 = \text{A\$}500$$

underlying share when it closed the contract and its price when it opened it. It is a nontraded single stock futures contract.

Forward and Futures Valuation

Valuation models for forward and futures[7] attempt to explain the difference between the current spot price S and the futures price F quoted today for delivery at a future date.

Profit and Loss at Expiration At expiration, the futures price converges to the spot price. Hence, the payoff structure is very simple: For each increase of one cent in the spot price at expiration, there will be an additional one-cent profit for the buyer of the futures. The profit and loss structure of a forward or futures that is held until expiration is shown in Exhibit 10.5. F is the futures price per unit of underlying asset at time of contracting, and the profit at expiration depends on the asset spot price at expiration. Exhibits 10.5a and b show the profit structures for long and short positions in the futures. The link between profit on the futures and the spot price at delivery is a straight line of slope 1. The slope is −1 for the seller of a futures. This feature makes it easy to derive an arbitrage value for the futures.

The Basis A futures price equals the spot price at delivery, though not during the life of the contract. The difference between the two prices is called the *basis*:

$$\text{Basis} = \text{Futures price} - \text{Spot price} = F - S \tag{10.4}$$

EXHIBIT 10.5

Profits and Losses from Buying ("Long") and Selling ("Short") a Futures Contract

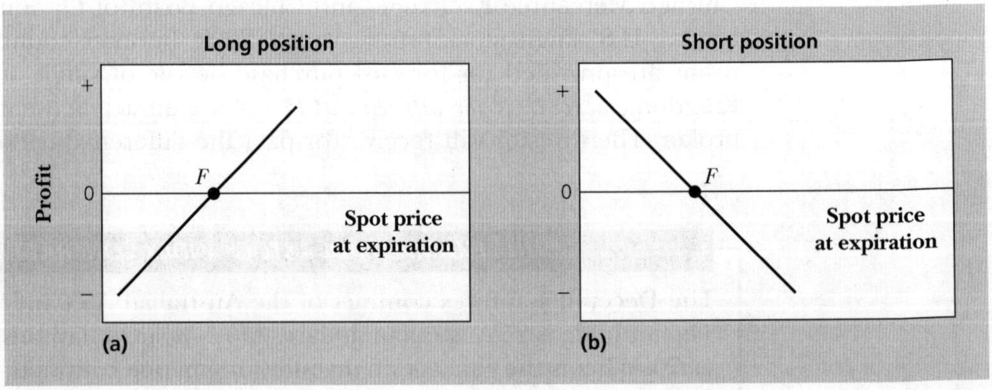

7 Theoretical prices for forwards are easier to derive than for futures because there are no intermediate cash flows until expiration of the contract caused by the marking-to-market procedure. But the usual practice, adopted in this chapter, is to value futures as if they were forwards with the full profit or loss realized at expiration. As discussed later, the theoretical difference between the two prices is sufficiently small to be ignored in practice.

The basis is often expressed as a percentage of the spot price (discount or premium):

$$\text{Percentage basis} = \frac{F - S}{S} \tag{10.4'}$$

Futures valuation models determine a theoretical value for the basis. The bases for perishable goods depend on complex factors that are often difficult to forecast, including harvesting cycles and expected crop sizes. But the bases for financial contracts, such as currencies, interest rates, stock indexes, and gold, depend on much simpler factors.

The theoretical value of the basis is constrained by the existence of profitable riskless arbitrage between the futures and the spot markets for the asset. Arbitrage takes place to eliminate this profit opportunity. Hence, an arbitrage value of the futures is determined within transaction costs.

This is often referred to as a *cash-and-carry arbitrage,* and the basis is sometimes referred to, in percentage of the spot price, as the *cost of carry* of the arbitrage. We will take the example of a currency futures.

Currency Futures A futures pricing argument was developed in Chapter 1. It has been shown that the futures exchange rate cannot differ from the spot exchange rate adjusted by the interest rate differential in the two currencies.

Let's suppose that the current spot exchange rate S is €/$ = 0.80, that the U.S. dollar one-year interest rate is $r_{\$} = 10$ percent, and that the euro one year interest rate is $r_{€} = 14$ percent. Then the one-year futures rate F has to be equal to 0.82909. To illustrate again how the arbitrage works, let's suppose for a moment that the futures rate is only €/$ = 0.81. Then the following (riskless) arbitrage would be possible:

Borrow $1 and transfer it into euros on the spot market:	€0.800
Invest the euros for a year at 14 percent with an income of	€0.112
	€0.912
Sell a futures contract to repatriate enough of these euros to cover the dollars borrowed plus the financing cost, that is, $1.10. At delivery, $1.10 will be obtained for € 0.81 × 1.10	−€ 0.891
The € net profit is	€ 0.021

This is a certain profit, with no invested capital. Arbitrage will take place until this profit opportunity disappears and the futures rate is such that

$$F = S(1 + r_{€})/(1 + r_{\$}) \tag{10.5}$$

or

$$(F - S)/S = (r_{€} - r_{\$})/(1 + r_{\$})$$

In the example, the futures rate must be equal to €0.82909/$. The cost of carry, in percentage of the spot rate, $(F - S)/S$, is linked to the interest differential.[8]

[8] The contract is quoted in dollars, and the percentage basis is equal to the present value of the interest rate differential.

Of course, bid-and-ask quotes on the spot and interest rates should be used, as in Chapter 1, to derive theoretical bid-and-ask quotes for the currency futures.

Other Futures Contracts A similar arbitrage reasoning holds for other contracts. If the futures price is too high relative to the current spot price, the following arbitrage can be undertaken:

- Borrow money to buy spot.
- Simultaneously sell the futures.
- While carrying the spot asset, some income might be received.
- At maturity of the futures contract, use the spot to deliver on the futures contract.

The reverse arbitrage will be done if the futures price is too low relative to the spot price.

At equilibrium, the percentage basis should be equal to the carrying cost. For example, the percentage basis (cost of carry) of a stock index futures should be linked to the differential between the interest rate involved in financing the spot purchase of shares and the dividends received on the shares held (but not on the futures).

Calculations are a bit more difficult for a futures contract on bonds. The spot position taken in the arbitrage should involve the cheapest-to-deliver bond and use its conversion factor. The calculation for a futures contract on a short-term interest rate is also a bit more difficult.

Forward and Futures The pricing relations just described should hold more exactly for forward than for futures contracts because forward contracts have a fixed margin that is not revised over the life of the contract. So far, we have assumed that the initial margin was deposited in the form of interest-bearing securities, so that there was no financing cost for this margin. However, futures contracts are marked to market, so that any loss on the futures position must be paid for and financed. This financing cost is uncertain because it depends on the future price variation. Also, the interest rate used to finance this margin may vary over time. It has been shown that futures and forward prices should be equal if the interest rates are constant over the life of the contract. If interest rates are uncertain, the correlation of interest rate and asset price movements will induce a theoretical difference between forward and futures prices, but the impact will be quite small for contracts that last only a few weeks.[9]

Other futures contract quirks affect futures pricing. For example, many contracts traded in the United States can be delivered within a few days before expiration, so that the exact maturity of the contract is uncertain. Bond contracts traded

---

[9] Cornell and Reiganum (1981) studied the relation between forward and futures exchange rates and found no significant differences. Most authors conclude that forward and futures prices should be empirically very close.

on the Chicago Board of Trade have an implied put option, or *wild card play.* The seller may choose to deliver securities on any day during the delivery month. The invoice price is based on the futures settlement price at the close of trading (around 2:00 P.M.). But the seller has until 8:00 P.M. the same day to decide whether to deliver, during which time the bonds continue to be traded in the cash market. If bond prices drop sharply between 2:00 and 8:00 P.M., the seller may buy cheap bonds in the cash market, bonds that can be used to deliver at the settlement price fixed at 2:00 P.M. Of course, this option held by the seller affects futures pricing[10] and lowers the value of the futures contract.

Use of Forward and Futures

Forward and futures contracts can be used to speculate on the underlying asset because of their leverage. But their major use in investment management is hedging.

Speculation The leverage provided by futures contracts allows investors to capitalize on some market forecast without much capital investment. This can be achieved by buying or selling futures, depending on the direction of the forecast. For example, someone who believes that the stock market will drop can sell stock index futures. Someone who believes that the Swiss franc will rise in value against the dollar could buy Swiss franc futures. Although the rate of return on the invested capital (the margin) can be large, so can the loss if the forecast is proved wrong. Remember that the profit/loss structure outlined in Exhibit 10.5 is symmetric. Prudence, as well as regulation, usually prevents institutional investors from engaging in outright speculation.

Hedging: Basic Principles Leveraged securities allow hedging of specific risks with minimal capital investment. It is customary to distinguish between two types of hedge:

- *Long hedge:* A long or anticipatory hedge generally involves buying futures contracts in anticipation of a spot purchase (see Example 10.2).
- *Short hedge:* A short hedge involves selling futures contracts to cover the risk on a position in the spot market. This is the most common use of hedging in investment management and is the focus of this section.

Hedging the risk of an individual asset is easy if futures contracts on that specific asset exist. However, futures contracts do not exist for every asset, so somewhat imperfect hedging strategies have to be designed. This problem is all the more important in portfolios with an international asset allocation and numerous sources of risk.

As an illustration, let's consider a Swiss manager worried about the British bond part of her portfolio. The manager might fear an increase in British interest rates, while forecasting a strong British pound relative to the Swiss franc. This would lead the manager to selectively hedge against the British interest rate risk,

---

[10] See Fleming and Whaley (1994).

EXAMPLE 10.2 A LONG HEDGE

A British asset manager manages a global portfolio and has decided to increase the asset allocation in Japanese equity by 1 billion yen. The manager is very bullish on the Japanese economy. It will take a week to transfer the money to Japan and build the portfolio of Japanese shares. The manager believes there is a good chance that the Japanese stock market will rise quickly. What should the manager do?

SOLUTION

Immediately buy futures contracts on the Nikkei index for a value of 1 billion yen. In addition to the few days required for the cash transfer, it may take a few more days to get best execution prices on the desired Japanese shares. The position in Japanese shares is progressively built on the Japanese stock market. As Japanese shares are purchased, the futures exposure should be accordingly reduced.

while retaining the British pound currency exposure. Similarly, the manager might be bullish on a few Australian mining companies, while fearing an adverse movement in both the general level of Australian stock prices and the value of the Australian dollar.

Two major questions must be answered when hedging a specified source of risk:

- Which contract should I use?
- What amount should I hedge?

The answer to the first question is fairly straightforward. The motivation is to reduce, at least temporarily, the exposure to some market risk that could negatively affect a portfolio. The source of risk will dictate the use of some specific stock market index, interest rate, or currency contract.[11] The answer to the second question requires a more detailed study of the optimal hedge ratio to be used.

Currency risk management is addressed in Chapter 11; here, we focus on the hedging approach to a single national market (equity or fixed income).

The Simple Approach: Unitary Hedge Ratio A *hedge ratio* is the ratio of the size of the (short) position taken in futures contract to the size of the exposure (the value of the portfolio to be hedged).

$$\text{Hedge ratio} = \frac{\text{Number of contracts} \times \text{Size} \times \text{Spot price}}{\text{Market value of asset position}} = \frac{N \times \text{Size} \times S}{V} \tag{10.6}$$

[11] If the investor is bearish on a specific security in the portfolio, the only reasonable action is to directly sell that security.

For example, take a portfolio invested in Australian stocks worth A\$1 million. The ASX index is 4,000 and the futures contract has a multiple of A\$25 and trades at 4,050. If you sell $N=10$ contracts, the hedge ratio is equal to

$$h = \frac{10 \times 25 \times 4{,}000}{1{,}000{,}000} = 1$$

Note that to be consistent, both the asset and the futures positions are valued at current market value, using spot prices, not futures prices.[12]

The simplest approach to hedging is to use a *unitary hedge ratio* of 1. In the preceding example, the Australian portfolio is worth 1 million, or 250 stock indexes, and we sell 10 futures contracts ($10 \times 25 = 250$).[13]

Conversely, we can use Equation 10.6 to derive the number of contracts to be sold if we know the hedge ratio that we want to implement:

$$N = h \times \frac{V}{\text{Size} \times S} \tag{10.6'}$$

For example, if we decide to hedge only 50 percent of the portfolio ($h = 0.5$), we can compute that we need to sell $N=5$ contracts.

Minimum-Variance Hedge Ratio Because of cross-hedge and basis risks (discussion follows), it is usually impossible to build a perfect hedge. One objective is to search for minimum variability in the value of the hedged portfolio. Investors usually care about the rate of return on their investments and the variance thereof. It is easy to show the rate of return on a portfolio hedged, R_H, is equal to the rate of return on the original portfolio (unhedged) R minus h times the percentage change in the futures price R_F:

$$R_H = R - h \times R_F \tag{10.7}$$

So, if investors decide to hedge, they would like to set the hedge ratio h to minimize the variance of the return on the hedged portfolio. The optimal hedge ratio h^*, which minimizes the variance of R_H, is equal to the covariance of the asset, or portfolio, return to be hedged with the return on the futures, divided by the variance of the return on the futures (see the derivation in Exhibit 10.6):

$$h^* = \frac{\text{cov}(R, R_F)}{\sigma_F^2} \tag{10.8}$$

This is the *minimum-variance hedge ratio.* Example 10.3 shows how to use this ratio.

This optimal hedge ratio is sometimes called the *regression hedge ratio* because it can be estimated as the slope coefficient of the regression of the asset, or portfolio, return on the futures return:

12 See Hull (2007).

13 If an investor is worried about currency risk on a foreign investment, the simple strategy is to sell the foreign currency forward, for an amount equal to that of the portfolio market value.

EXHIBIT 10.6

Derivation of the Minimum-Variance Hedge Ratio

Assuming you select a specific hedge ratio h, the return on the hedged position is given by Equation 10.7:

$$R_H = R - h \times R_F$$

The rates of return on the portfolio R, and on the future R_F, are uncertain, so the return on the hedged portfolio R_H is also uncertain. An investor trying to minimize the volatility of the hedged portfolio will try to minimize the standard deviation of R_H (or, equivalently, its variance). Let's call σ, σ_F, and σ_H the standard deviations of the original portfolio (unhedged), of the futures, and of the hedged portfolio, respectively. Because the hedge ratio is a fixed parameter, we know that the return on the hedged portfolio is simply the sum of two random variables R and $-h \times R_F$. Hence its variance is given by

$$\sigma_H^2 = \sigma^2 + h^2 \times \sigma_F^2 - 2 \times h \times \text{cov}(R, R_F)$$

The objective is to choose an optimal hedge ratio h^* that minimizes the variance of the hedged portfolio σ_H^2 (or equivalently, its standard deviation σ_H). The risks of the original portfolio and of the futures are known, and the hedge ratio is the decision variable. The optimum is obtained by setting to zero the derivative of the variance of the hedged portfolio:

$$\frac{d\sigma_H^2}{dh} = 2 \times h \times \sigma_F^2 - 2 \times \text{cov}(R, R_F) = 0$$

Hence,

$$h^* = \frac{\text{cov}(R, R_F)}{\sigma_F^2}$$

$$R = \alpha + h^* R_F + \epsilon$$

where

R is the return on the asset or portfolio

R_F is the return on the futures

α is a constant term

ϵ is an error term because the relation between R and R_F is not perfect

Hedge Ratio for Bonds Interest rate risk affects all bond portfolios, but we know the mathematical relation between a movement in the general yield level and the value of a bond portfolio. Chapter 7 introduced the concept of duration or interest rate sensitivity. The approximate percentage price change of the portfolio

EXAMPLE 10.3 MINIMUM-VARIANCE HEDGE

Let's consider a portfolio of small Australian stocks with a value of A$1 million. This portfolio of small stocks is much more volatile than the market. It tends to amplify the movement in the Australian market index by 50 percent. In other words, its beta relative to the market is equal to 1.5, the slope of the regression of the portfolio return on the market index return. The current ASX stock index is 4,000, and the futures contract quotes at 4,050 with a multiple of A$25.

1. What is the optimal hedge ratio?
2. How many futures contracts should you sell?

SOLUTION

1. The minimum-variance or optimal hedge ratio is equal to 1.5. Whenever the market drops by X percent, the portfolio tends to drop by $1.5X$ percent. If the value of the portfolio is A$1 million, the manager should sell A$1.5 million worth of stock index futures.
2. Using Equation 10.6′, we find that we should sell

$$N = h^* \times \frac{V}{\text{Size} \times S} = 1.5 \times \frac{1{,}000{,}000}{25 \times 4{,}000} = 15 \text{ contracts}$$

is equal to the duration times the change in market yield (in percent). Mathematically, this can be written as

$$\frac{\Delta P}{P} = -D_p \times \Delta r$$

where

P is the average price of the bond portfolio (i.e., the market value divided by the par value)

ΔP is a small change in P

D_p is the duration(or interest rate sensitivity)of the portfolio

Δ_r is a small change in market yield

Then it can be shown[14] that the optimal hedging policy that reduces the impact of an up-movement Δr in yields is such that the hedge ratio would be

$$h^* = \frac{P \times D_p}{F \times D_F} \tag{10.9}$$

14 The futures price follows price movements in the cheapest-to-deliver bond, so it has the same duration as that bond: $\Delta F/F = -D_F \times \Delta r$. Equation 10.9 is derived by equating the "dollar" capital loss on the portfolio and the "dollar" gain on the futures position for any small movement in the interest rate Δr.

where D_F is the duration of the cheapest-to-deliver bond for the futures contract. The intuition is that one should adjust the hedge ratio to reflect the difference in interest rate sensitivity (duration) between the portfolio and the futures price. If the portfolio has a duration of 5 and the futures has a duration of 10, one should adopt a hedge ratio of roughly 50 percent.

An Imperfect Hedge A hedge is seldom perfect for at least two reasons:

- Basis risk
- Correlation, or cross-hedge, risk

The portfolio's value depends on the spot price, while hedging is done using futures whose price differs from the spot price by the basis. The basis varies over time in a somewhat unpredictable manner. For example, interest rates, which are part of the cost of carry, vary over time. To reduce basis risk, one should select contracts' maturity to match the investment horizon over which risk is to be managed.

The chance of matching a futures contract to a specific portfolio of bonds or stocks is slim. A cross-hedge has to be constructed in order to hedge the volatility of specific securities in a portfolio, so a hedge is often built with a contract that is only partly correlated with the portfolio to be hedged. This induces correlation, or cross-hedge, risk. For example, a portfolio invested only in shares of a specific industry would be hedged by contracts on the general stock index. But the evolution of the value of a specific industry and that of the stock market as a whole are not similar. Various techniques attempt to determine an optimal hedge ratio, but correlation risk remains.

The Pros and Cons of Hedging Futures allow a manager to monitor the market risk exposures of a portfolio. If a manager temporarily fears an adverse movement in some market (equity, interest rate, or currency), he can sell the proper amount of futures and buy them back after fears have materialized or disappeared. This is much less costly, in terms of transaction costs, than first selling the securities and then buying them back. It could also be that the manager likes the specific securities held in the portfolio but fears a drop in the overall market. Selling futures on the market allows the manager to capture the excess performance (alpha) on the portfolio.

However, hedging could turn out to be painful if the market goes up contrary to expectations, because futures have a symmetric profit/loss structure. Assume that a manager has temporarily hedged a well-diversified portfolio of French stocks by selling futures on the CAC index. Contrary to expectations, the French stock market goes up by 10 percent, so that the capital gain on the portfolio is offset by an equivalent loss on the futures position. That is a cash loss because of the marking-to-market procedure. The client who focuses on that visible loss might be very upset with the manager, although it might have been a wise ex ante risk management decision. Psychologically, it would have been less visible to reduce the French risk exposure by simply selling stocks, despite higher transaction costs. Those psychological considerations are often a factor in a manager–client relationship. This could also lead managers to manage their market risks by using contracts with asymmetric profit/loss structures such as options.

Swaps

Futures are short-term contracts with a maturity rarely exceeding a few months. Risk often extends well past such a short time horizon, however. This is especially the case when dealing with interest rate and currency risks. In dealing with longer-term exposures, investors frequently rely on swaps. Swaps are used extensively by banks to manage risk exposure on their assets and liabilities. Some other types of corporations also use swaps extensively. In investment management, swaps are used in the construction of structured products and in dynamic arbitrage strategies, such as the strategies followed by numerous hedge funds.

The Principles of a Swap

Definition A *swap* is a contract whereby the two parties agree to a periodic exchange of cash flows. On each payment date, only a net payment is made (the obligations of the two parties are netted). A swap resembles a back-to-back loan arrangement but is packaged into a single contract, as opposed to two separate loans.[15] On each swap payment date, the two cash flows are netted and a payment is made by the party owing money. In swap jargon, each side of the swap is called a *leg*. For example, an interest rate swap in euros could have a 5.10 percent fixed interest rate as one leg, and six-month Euribor, the euro floating interest rate, as the other leg. A swap is simply a contract stating the formula to be used to compute the net amount paid or received on each payment date. A swap must be studied independently of any initial borrowing or lending operation that motivates it. An important point to remember is that swaps appear off-balance-sheet. They are simply commitments to make future payments. A swap can be regarded as a long-term package of periodic forward contracts.

Market Organization The swap market is an OTC market in which major commercial and investment banks participate. They belong to the *International Swaps and Derivatives Association* (*ISDA*). Typically, an investor wishing to arrange a swap will call one or several banks specialized as swap dealers and providing swap rate quotes. The quotes are the interest rates on the swap.[16] Dealers quote a bid–ask spread because the investor does not indicate the side she wishes to take. For example, a five-year interest rate swap in euros could be quoted as 5.10 to 5.15 percent fixed against Euribor, meaning that the dealer is willing to pay 5.10 percent and receive Euribor, or receive 5.15 percent and pay Euribor.

---

[15] In currency back-to-back loans, each party lends money to the other party for the same initial amount but in different currencies and at respective market interest rates.

[16] Swap dealers use different conventions to quote interest rates (linear, actuarial, etc.), so it is important to clarify the conventions used when a quote is made.

As for any forward contract, there is no organized secondary swap market. This can be a problem because swaps are long-term contracts. An investor wishing to get out of a swap has three alternatives:

- *Agree on a voluntary termination with the original counterparty.* This popular agreement is simple and implies only a lump-sum payment to reflect the changes in market conditions, but it requires the agreement of the other party.
- *Write a mirror swap with the original counterparty.* A swap is reversed by writing an opposite swap contract with the same maturity and amount but at current market conditions. The difference between a mirror swap and a termination is that the settlement is paid over the remaining maturity of the swap, and some credit risk remains on the differential interest rate payment.
- *Write a reverse swap in the market with another counterparty.* This is the easiest deal to arrange but has two drawbacks. First, it is difficult and expensive to find a swap that exactly offsets the previous one in all its terms. Second, engaging in another swap doubles credit risk.

The Different Instruments

Historically, three major types of swaps were offered in the marketplace: currency swaps, interest rate swaps, and currency–interest rate swaps. Recently, many other types of swaps have been successfully offered.

Currency Swaps A *currency swap* is a contract to exchange streams of fixed cash flows denominated in two different currencies. A typical currency swap can be illustrated by using the following example. An investor enters in a five-year swap with a bank to receive yen and pay dollars for 100 million. In this swap, \$100 million and ¥10 billion are the principal amounts (called notional principals) because the spot exchange rate is ¥100 per \$. The fixed interest rates are 2 percent on the yen leg and 6 percent on the dollar leg, and payments are annual; these are the current market conditions in each currency. Each year, the investor will receive ¥200 million (the annual interest of 2% on the Japanese yen principal of ¥10 billion) minus \$6 million (the annual interest of 6% on the U.S. dollar principal of \$100 million) valued at the then-current spot ¥ per \$ exchange rate. When this amount is negative, the investor will pay it. After five years, the principal amounts of ¥10 billion and \$100 million valued at the then-current spot ¥ per \$ exchange rate are netted and the net amount owed is paid.

Currency swaps may involve an exchange of principal at initiation of the swap when one of the parties has an actual need for the principal amount in a particular currency. However, we will consider the case where such a need is absent. Because the swap is designed to have the same principal value in yen and dollars at the time of contracting (¥10 billion equals \$100 million at the spot exchange rate of $\$/¥ = 100$, or 100 yen per dollar), there is no initial payment between the two parties. Future swap payments depend on the evolution of the \$/¥ exchange rate, S_t. On each of the first four swap payment dates t, the investor will receive in millions of yen

$$200 - (S_t \times 6)$$

or in millions of dollars

$$(200/S_t) - 6$$

If this figure is positive, the investor will receive this amount from the bank; if this figure is negative, the investor will have to pay it.

On the fifth payment date, the investor will receive the balance of the last interest and principal, or in million yen

$$10{,}200 - (S_5 \times 106)$$

To motivate the type of swap just illustrated, suppose that a European company had issued an international bond in yen a few years ago, with five years remaining on its maturity. The company is now worried that the yen will strongly appreciate against all currencies. By entering the previously discussed swap to receive yen and pay dollars, the company is basically transforming its yen liability into a dollar liability.

Interest Rate Swaps An *interest rate swap* is a contract to exchange streams of cash flows in the same currency but based on two different interest rates. The most common interest rate swaps are U.S. dollar swaps involving a fixed interest rate and a floating rate. The floating-rate index used is generally the six-month London interbank offer rate (LIBOR). As on a floating-rate note, the floating-rate leg is generally reset on a date that precedes the payment date, with a lead equal to the maturity of the floating interest rate. For example, the six-month LIBOR is preset six months before the next swap payment date. Interest rate swaps in euros are generally indexed on Euribor (see Example 10.4).

The uncertainty over the future swap payments on date *t* stems from the evolution of the floating rate. Interest rate swaps do not involve exchange of principal, because the same amount and currency are involved on both legs of the swap.

EXAMPLE 10.4 SWAP PAYMENT

An investor has entered a three-year interest rate swap for €1 million, receiving fixed at 5.10 percent and paying six-month Euribor. Payments are semiannual, and interest rates are computed linearly (i.e., the semiannual rate is obtained by dividing the annualized rate by 2). At some later reset date, the six-month Euribor is at 4 percent. What is the payment six months later (i.e., on the following payment date)?

SOLUTION

The investor receives a payment of

$$\text{Payment} = \left(\frac{5.1\% - 4\%}{2}\right) \times 1{,}000{,}000 = 5{,}500 \text{ euros}$$

Currency–Interest Rate Swaps A *currency–interest rate swap* is a contract to exchange streams of cash flows in two different currencies, one with a fixed interest rate and the other with a floating interest rate. For example, an investor could decide to swap a five-year yen obligation with a fixed interest rate of 2 percent into a five-year dollar obligation at the six-month LIBOR plus 0.25 percent. Future swap payments are uncertain because of the evolution of both the exchange rates and the floating interest rate.

Other Swaps Swaps are often customized products. Banks quote swap rates for generic, or plain-vanilla, swaps, but customers often require some specific features on their swaps to match some specific characteristics of their existing liabilities or assets. Furthermore, exotic swaps are being marketed. Swaps are often part of a more complex package of securities offered to a customer as a way to reduce its financing costs, speculate, or manage an interest rate or currency position. This package is tailor-made to take advantage of some specific aspect of the market environment, such as supply/demand imbalance and tax or regulation considerations.

Some interest rate swaps involve two floating rates; these are often referred to as *basis swaps.* A typical example is the exchange of a LIBOR-indexed obligation for a Treasury bill rate–indexed obligation. This basis swap is known as a Treasury–Eurodollar spread (TED spread swap). Another example is the exchange of obligations indexed on the one-month and the six-month LIBOR. A *forward swap* begins at some specified future date, but with the binding terms set in advance. An *amortizing swap* has a regular fixed or floating coupon on one leg and a zero coupon on the other leg. Hence, the counterparties exchange a future stream of coupons for a large lump sum. Amortizing swaps can be designed to have this lump sum paid at contracting or to have it paid at maturity. A *total return swap* has a regular fixed or floating coupon on one leg and the total return on some asset on the other leg. An *equity swap* is an exchange of a fixed or floating coupon against the return on some equity index. This is a form of total return swap. An equity swap is sometimes used to invest in a foreign stock market without making the necessary transactions in the cash market.

Credit derivatives have been the fastest-growing segment of the swap market. A *default swap* (or *credit swap*) is an exchange of a fixed or floating coupon against the payment of a loss caused by default on a specific loan or bond. For example, an institutional investor could be holding some corporate bonds of doubtful quality. The investor could then enter a default swap with a payment of a fixed coupon on one leg, and the receipt of an amount equal to the default loss on the corporates, if any. Credit derivatives, such as default swaps, have been very successful, and their design is sometimes quite complex.

Swaps Valuation

We now turn to the important question of the value of a swap contract. At the time of contracting, the two parties agree on the terms of the swap. The value of the swap at the time of contracting is zero. However, as market conditions change over time, so does the value of the swap. Swaps are treated as off-balance-sheet items, but this does not mean they should not be valued periodically to reflect current market value.

This is true for nonfinancial corporations publishing annual or quarterly accounting reports. Financial institutions, and portfolio managers, need to value their derivatives position frequently, ideally daily.

The financial profession uses standard methods to value a swap. We will first assume that there is no credit (default) risk for either party to the swap. Later, we will introduce credit risk.

Valuation in the Absence of Credit Risk Let's take the example of the five-year yen/dollar swap introduced earlier. At the time of issue, interest rates in the two currencies (6% in dollars and 2% in yen) are set at prevailing market conditions, so that there is no actual exchange of money. In our example, \$100 million is worth ¥10 billion at the current exchange rate, and no money need be exchanged to enter into this swap agreement. The market value of this currency swap is zero on the contracting day. However, the market value of this swap will change because of movements in interest rates and in the spot exchange rate. The question is: How should we value a swap in the secondary market? For example, assume that the corporation entered this swap contract to pay dollars and receive yen and wants to sell it a year later. How should we price this swap?

Two approaches can be used:

- Value a currency swap as a package of long-term forward currency contracts.
- Value a swap as a portfolio of two bonds.

A currency swap can be broken down into a series of forward currency contracts for each cash flow. In our example, the swap can be treated, at time of contracting, as a package of five forward contracts with maturity from one to five years, as depicted in Exhibit 10.7. We can price the swap as a sum of forward currency prices. In other words, we can unbundle the package of forward currency contracts.

There are two problems with this approach, however. First, it is not obvious that a fixed bundle of contracts would be priced exactly as the sum of its components, because markets are incomplete and unbundling a package of contracts is difficult. Second, forward contracts are not frequently traded for long-term maturities, so forward currency rates have to be inferred from interest rate yield curves, as discussed in Chapter 7. As a matter of fact, it is more common to derive forward currency prices from swap prices rather than the reverse.

Currency swaps can be treated as a portfolio of two bonds, short in one currency and long in the other. Basically, the swap is treated as a back-to-back loan, and each leg of the swap is valued separately. The value of this hedged portfolio changes if interest rates in either of the two currencies move or if the spot exchange rate moves. Let's denote $P_1(r_\$)$ and $P_2(r_¥)$ as the respective values of the dollar and yen bonds, given the current market interest rates $r_\$$ and $r_¥$ on bonds in the two currencies. Then the yen value of the swap, given the spot exchange rate S expressed as yen per dollar, is

$$\text{Swap value} = P_2(r_¥) - S \times P_1(r_\$) \tag{10.10}$$

EXHIBIT 10.7

Valuing a Currency Swap as a Package of Forward Currency Contracts (in millions)

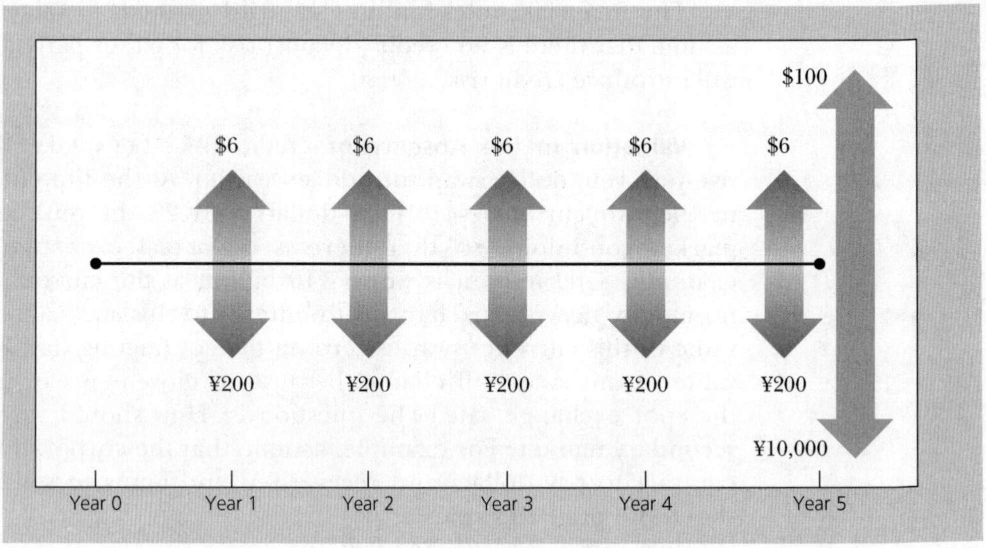

This is the value of a swap to pay dollars and receive yen. The dollar value of the swap is simply deducted from the yen value of the swap by dividing by the spot exchange rate S. The value of the swap for the other party, which agreed to pay yen and receive dollars, is exactly the opposite of that computed in Equation 10.10. Example 10.5 illustrates the valuation of a currency swap as a portfolio of two bonds.

The only practical problem with this approach is determining the relevant market interest rates used on both legs of the swap. For each cash flow on the fixed-rate leg, we should use a zero-coupon term structure. The practice in the finance profession is to derive a zero-coupon structure from the current swap rates quotations and use it to price outstanding swaps. This term structure is usually called *zero swap rates.*

Interest rate swaps can be valued likewise using a portfolio of a fixed-rate bond and a floating-rate bond. The floating-rate leg is assumed to have a market value that remains set at par on the reset date (see Chapter 7). The fixed-rate leg is valued as described earlier, using the current zero swap rates. The same applies to a mixed currency–interest rate swap.

Valuation in the Presence of Credit Risk The swap quotations should differ for a party with credit risk. For example, an AAA bank quoting swap rates to an A customer is likely to increase the bid–ask spread on the swap rates. Typically, the credit *quality spread* for an A party would be from one to five basis points on either side.

EXAMPLE 10.5 *VALUATION OF A CURRENCY SWAP*

One hundred million U.S. dollars are swapped against ten billion yen. The spot exchange rate is ¥/$ = 100; the interest rates on dollars and yen are 6 percent and 2 percent, respectively. The maturity of the contract is five years, and interest coupons are swapped once a year. At time of contracting, the two interest rates were equal to the market yield to maturity on five-year bonds in dollars (6%) and yen (2%). Assume that a year later, the yield curves in dollars and yen are flat and that interest rates have dropped to 4 percent on U.S. dollar bonds and 1 percent on yen bonds. The spot exchange rate has dropped to ¥/$ = 90. A swap payment of ¥340 million has just been made (200 − 90 × 6). What is the new value of the swap for the party that agreed to receive yen and pay dollars?

SOLUTION

We value the two bonds implied in the swap separately. The dollar bond was worth $100 million (its par value) when the swap was contracted with dollar interest rate of 6 percent. A year later, the bond is worth $103.55 million at the current market yield of 5 percent. This is the present value of a stream of yearly coupons of $6 million and a principal of $100 million repaid in four years, discounted at 4 percent:

$$P_1 = \frac{6}{(1.05)} + \frac{6}{(1.05)^2} + \frac{6}{(1.05)^3} + \frac{106}{(1.05)^4} = 103.55$$

Similarly, the yen bond was worth ¥10 billion (its par value) when the swap was contracted, with a yen interest rate of 2 percent. A year later, the bond is worth ¥10,390 million at the current market yield of 1 percent. This is the present value of four yearly coupons of ¥200 million and a principal of ¥10 billion repaid in four years, discounted at 1 percent. The yen value of the swap (to pay dollars and receive yen) is equal to

$$\text{Swap value (in million yen)} = 10{,}390 - 90 \times 103.55$$
$$= ¥1{,}071 \text{ million, or } \$11.9 \text{ million}$$

For the other party, the swap now has a value of −¥1,071 million.

A quality spread of a few basis points may seem small as compensation for the risk of default on a swap.[17] However, the potential losses on swaps, especially interest rate swaps, are much smaller than for a loan. The default risk does not apply to the principal and interest payments, but only to the differential in

[17] Duffie and Huang (1996) studied the quality spread that should be paid by a risky party (e.g., rated A or Baa) over the AAA rate on a bond issuance and on a swap, as a function of its credit quality. They found that if a quality spread of 100 basis points is required on a bond, it should only be around 1 basis point on an interest rate swap of similar maturity.

interest payments in the case of an interest rate swap. The default risk also applies to the differential in principal repayment in the case of a currency swap, so the quality spread should be somewhat higher. Further, note that the default of a risky customer will affect the bank (the other party) only if the interest rate and currency movements are such that the customer is in a position to owe money to the bank. If the market conditions are such that the swap has a negative value for the bank, the default of the customer will not imply an additional loss for the bank.

Swap contracts specify how the swap will be terminated in case of bankruptcy of one of the parties. These termination clauses can vary across swaps and market participants. The most common clause is the "full two-way payments" option proposed in the ISDA master agreement. Under this clause, a party is deemed to default on the swap if it becomes insolvent on its debt. All outstanding swaps are "netted," and the settlement is based on the replacement values of the outstanding swaps. In other words, the net market value of the swap position between the two parties is computed using standard methods and quotes from major swap dealers.

Use of Swaps

As usual in finance, the major motivations for using swaps are return and risk. Companies use swaps to reduce their financing costs (return motivation). They also use swaps to manage their long-term exposure to currency and interest rate risks, especially when they are faced with risks to existing assets and liabilities. For example, if a U.S. corporation borrowed in Swiss francs two years ago and is concerned about an anticipated strong appreciation of the Swiss franc, a U.S. dollar/Swiss franc swap can be used to transform the Swiss franc liability into a U.S. dollar liability.

Cost Benefits of Swaps The usual argument for the use of swaps in new borrowing is cost savings. The main motivation in the early stage of the market was to take advantage of borrowing cost differentials between two markets to raise funds cheaply. It must be stressed that by itself, the swap does not provide a cost benefit, but it does provide a bridge across several financing markets. Given competition, swaps are priced at fair value, but they allow the transfer of some cost advantage obtained by borrowing in one market to another market.

Simple Cost-Financing Advantage The motivation for a classic currency swap can be illustrated in the following hypothetical example. A supranational borrower (say, the World Bank) can tap the U.S. dollar market on favorable terms but would prefer to borrow Swiss francs because of the low interest rate in that market and because it needs to diversify its financing currencies. Supranational borrowers, such as the World Bank, the EU, or the European Investment Bank, are not favorites of Swiss investors, who prefer nonstate borrowers. Alternatively, a large U.S. corporation can borrow on very attractive terms in the foreign Swiss franc market but needs dollars. Each party is better off borrowing in the market in which it holds a comparative advantage and then entering a swap with a bank to obtain the desired structure of cash flows. For example, the supranational borrower issues a bond in the U.S. dollar market and swaps the proceeds for the low-interest-rate Swiss francs. Conversely, the U.S. corporation issues a Swiss franc bond and swaps the francs for dollars. Each party is bound to benefit from this swap by obtaining funds more cheaply than if it had directly accessed its desired currency market.

The idea is to use financing on a specific market in which a borrower has a *comparative advantage* and to transfer that advantage to another market or currency by making a swap at prevailing market conditions. The swap helps only as a bridge across markets. However, these cost savings based on the comparative advantage of some companies in some market segments are a form of market inefficiency. Financial arbitrage, such as a swap, exploits these market inefficiencies. As the volume of swaps increases, these simple inefficiencies are bound to disappear; they are arbitraged away.

More Complex Engineering Many swap dealers believe that the growth of the market depends on the ability to identify and exploit new arbitrage opportunities as they develop in world markets. Many of these temporary or persistent arbitrage opportunities are caused by the regulatory and fiscal environment. For example, some domestic firms have access to subsidized lending (some government agency subsidizes part of the interest cost) at home but wish to borrow foreign currencies to finance their foreign operations. Example 10.6 illustrates some financial engineering that could be done in response to a particular regulatory and fiscal environment.

Swaps are similarly used in complex investment strategies to take advantage of some excess risk-adjusted return (alpha) in one market and transfer it to another market. This comparative advantage transfer is sometimes referred to as *alpha transfer.*

A Word of Caution Swaps are often offered as part of a package that replicates an existing security at a cost advantage. However, investors must be careful to verify that this synthetic replication is indeed perfect, and that the apparent cost benefits are not simply due to higher assumed risks. Let's take the example of a synthetic fixed-rate loan in euros sold to a corporate customer by a bank. The customer wishes to borrow fixed-rate euros for 10 years. This can be done by issuing a bond at a yield of 7 percent. Instead, the bank suggests borrowing short-term, by issuing six-month commercial paper (CP) and entering an interest rate swap in euros to receive floating and pay fixed. The CP is supposed to be rolled over every six months. The corporation can currently borrow through CP at Euribor + 1/2 percent and enter a 10-year swap paying a fixed 6 percent and receiving Euribor. If the corporation rolls over its CP every six months, it re-creates with the swap the economic position of borrowing fixed. The net annual cost to the corporation is 6.5 percent (6% − Euribor + Euribor + 1/2 %) compared with 7 percent on a fixed-rate bond. The cost benefit appears to be 50 basis points. However, the synthetic position is not exactly equal to the fixed-rate bond. If the corporation's credit quality deteriorates over time, its short-term borrowing costs will increase, as the quality spread over Euribor could move from 0.5 percent to 1 percent or more. Actually, if the corporation experiences severe financial problems, it could even face a situation in which it cannot issue more CP. This is called *rollover risk.* If the corporation borrows fixed at 7 percent, it knows that the rate will remain fixed whatever its future credit quality. To summarize, investors should exercise caution when faced with large cost benefits on fairly simple synthetic packages.

EXAMPLE 10.6 SOME COMPLEX ENGINEERING

An interesting example can be found in the yen market, in which Japanese regulatory pressure is strongly felt. In the 1990s, three Japanese regulatory and fiscal situations could have led to an interesting packaging of securities:

1. The Ministry of Finance limited the amount of foreign currency (non-yen) bonds held by Japanese institutions, such as pension funds and insurance companies.
2. A dual-currency bond issued in yen, with interest payments in yen but principal repayment in a foreign currency, qualified as a yen bond for purposes of the yen limit imposed by the Ministry of Finance. This was attractive to Japanese institutions as a legal way to invest in foreign currency assets.
3. Zero-coupon bonds were taxed as non-income-generating assets. At maturity, the difference between the nominal value and the purchase price of the bond was taxed as capital gain, at a lower tax rate than income. Zero-coupon bonds were attractive to taxable Japanese investors.

In response to this regulatory and fiscal environment, a corporation wanting to borrow U.S. dollars could instead have engaged in the following operations:

- Issue a five-year dual-currency bond[18] with a 4 percent interest coupon in yen and principal repayment in dollars (Bond A). The repayment value would have been $100 million, and the issue amount would have been 10 billion yen. The spot exchange rate was 100 yen/dollar.
- Issue a five-year zero-coupon yen bond with the same maturity as the dual-currency bond and a nominal value of 10 billion yen (Bond B). There would be no interest payment, simply a principal repayment of 10 billion yen in five years.
- Enter into an agreement to swap a five-year yen fixed-rate obligation of 10 billion yen, with an annual interest rate of 4 percent (400 million yen), for a fixed-rate dollar obligation. This is a yen/dollar currency swap where the corporation receives yen and pays dollars. The dollar leg has a principal of $100 million and a coupon $c\%$ set at the conditions prevailing in the swap market. So, the dollar leg has a coupon of $c\% \times$ $100 million = C million dollars.

1. What is the currency exposure and the resulting position for the corporation?
2. What is the motivation of the corporation for entering into this complex package?

[18] See the description of dual-currency bonds in Chapter 7.

SOLUTION

1. Let's look at the economic position taken. The combination of the zero-coupon and dual-currency loan is equivalent to a straight yen bond, with a principal of 10 billion yen and annual coupons of 400 million yen, plus a U.S. dollar zero-coupon bond with a nominal value of $100 million. The reasoning is simple if we look at the cash flows by currency, as shown in Exhibit 10.8. The corporation ends up with a pure dollar exposure by swapping the yen obligation of 10 billion yen for a U.S. dollar obligation.
2. The motivation is to reduce the borrowing cost in dollars. The issue of the two bonds would capitalize on a regulatory and a fiscal attraction to Japanese investors, and therefore could be done on attractive (low-cost) terms. But the final product for the corporation would be a U.S. dollar loan, at a cheaper cost than a straight U.S. dollar loan, because the cost benefit is transferred from Japanese yen to U.S. dollars.

EXHIBIT 10.8

Cash Flows

	Payments (in millions)	
	Yen	**Dollar**
Before swap (dual currency and yen bonds)		
Year 1: Interest	400^A	0
Year 2: Interest	400^A	0
Year 3: Interest	400^A	0
Year 4: Interest	400^A	0
Year 5: Interest	400^A	0
Year 5: Principal	$10{,}000^B$	100^A
After swap (dual currency and yen bonds plus swap)		
Year 1: Interest	0	C
Year 2: Interest	0	C
Year 3: Interest	0	C
Year 4: Interest	0	C
Year 5: Interest	0	C
Year 5: Principal	0	100 + 100

^{A}Cash flow from Bond A.

^{B}Cash flow from Bond B.

Risk Management Interest rate swaps can be used to alter the exposure of a portfolio of assets or liabilities to interest rate movements. Swaps are all the more useful when assets or liabilities cannot be traded, as is the case for bank loans.

Risk management using swaps requires several steps:

1. Identify the source of uncertainty that could induce losses.
2. Measure the amount of exposure to this risk.
3. Identify the type of swaps that could best be used to hedge the risk.
4. Decide on the amount of hedging that should be undertaken. It is useful to start from the risk-minimizing hedge and to deviate from this neutral position as a function of expectations and risk aversion.

The risk management process is illustrated in Example 10.7.

For the same reasons that swaps can be used to hedge risks on existing positions, they can also be used to take speculative bets on interest and exchange rates. Corporations have often used swaps as investment vehicles. They regard swaps as highly leveraged long-term contracts that help them capitalize on predictions about exchange rate or interest rate movements. Although swaps are off-balance-sheet contracts, their risks should be clearly accounted for.

Options

Forward, futures, and swap contracts have a symmetric profit-and-loss structure. Options are very different contracts.

Introduction to Options

Definition In general, an *option* gives the buyer the right, but not the obligation, to buy or sell an asset, and the option seller must respond accordingly. Many types of option contracts exist in the financial world. The two major types of contracts traded on organized options exchanges are *calls* and *puts.*

A *call option* gives the buyer of the option contract the right to buy a specified number of units of an *underlying asset* at a specified price, called the *exercise price* or *strike price,* on or before a specified date, called the *expiration date* or *strike date.* A *put option* gives the buyer of the option contract the right to sell a specified number of units of an underlying asset at a specified price on or before a specified date. In all cases, the seller of the option contract, the *writer,* is subject to the buyer's decision to exercise or not, and the buyer exercises the option only if it is profitable to her. The buyer of a call benefits if the price of the asset is above the strike price at expiration. The buyer of a put benefits if the asset price is below the strike price at expiration.

The buyer of an option acquires something of value. A buyer can make a profit, potentially large, if the asset price moves in the right direction. A buyer will let the option expire worthless if the asset price moves in the wrong direction. Such an attractive profit-and-loss structure has a price: This is the option price, or *option premium,* that has to be paid to purchase the option. This premium is received by the seller of the option.

EXAMPLE 10.7 RISK MANAGEMENT WITH SWAPS

Let's consider a small British bank that provided a loan in euros to a top-quality customer that had to finance an acquisition in Germany. The amount of the loan is €50 million, with a fixed annual coupon of 7 percent and three years remaining. The British bank finances this euro fixed-rate loan by rolling over short-term borrowing on the Eurocurrency market. This bank is mostly domestic, and this loan and its associated euro floating-rate borrowing are the only asset and liability in euros appearing on the bank's balance sheet. The current six-month rate on Euribor is 6 percent, and the bank fears a rise in euro interest rates that would affect short- and long-term rates in a similar fashion. This interest rate increase is specific to the Eurozone, and no particular movements in the exchange rates are predicted.

How could this bank use interest rate swaps to hedge the risk that the euro interest rate will rise?

SOLUTION

The following analysis of this simple example could be performed:

1. The source of risk is a movement in the general level of euro interest rates. This can be seen in two ways. In terms of annual cash flows, the rise in interest rates will increase the financing costs (floating) of the bank without a corresponding increase in its interest income (fixed). However, the overall impact on the bank is best measured by looking at the change in market value of its assets and liabilities. A rise in euro interest rates should not affect the value of the floating-rate borrowing; however, the value of the fixed-rate loan would drop as market yields increase. A rise in euro interest rates would hurt the bank; a drop in euro interest rates would benefit the bank.
2. The amount at risk is €50 million, the market value of the exposed asset.
3. A euro interest rate swap is a good hedge against this risk. The bank should enter into a swap to pay fixed and receive floating.
4. The risk-minimizing strategy would be to swap €50 million. If the bank is very sure of its rate prediction, it could enter a swap for a larger amount. This would be equivalent to "speculating" on this prediction.

The complete definition of an option must clearly specify how the option can be exercised. A *European-type option* can be exercised only on the expiration date. An *American-type option* can be exercised at any time until the expiration date. American options are used on most of the organized options exchanges in the world. Both types of options can be freely traded at any time until expiration.

Market Organization The organization of the market for listed, or traded, options is somewhat similar to that of the futures market. An options clearing corporation, or clearinghouse, plays a central role. All option contracts are represented by bookkeeping entries on the computers of the clearinghouse corporation. As soon as a buyer and a seller of a particular contract decide to trade, the clearinghouse steps in and breaks the deal down into two option contracts: one between the buyer and the clearinghouse acting as seller, and the other between the seller and the clearinghouse acting as buyer. This procedure completely standardizes the contracts. It allows an investor to close a position by simply selling out the options held, while a seller may buy options to close a previous position. If a buyer decides to exercise an option, the clearinghouse randomly selects a seller of the option and issues an exercise notice. Selling an option entails a sizable risk. Hence, selling an option (a naked sale) requires a margin deposit.[19]

In most cases, investors offset their positions by making a reverse trade before the expiration date. Option buyers usually find it more profitable to resell an option on the market than to exercise it. There are times, however, when exercising an option is more profitable; this can be the case for a call option on a stock, when a large dividend is about to be paid on the underlying stock. Listed options markets can be found all over the world.

There is also an OTC market with banks writing European-type currency options tailored to the specific needs of commercial customers. This interbank market has developed successfully for interest rate and currency options.

The Different Instruments

Currency Options Markets in currency options have developed to cope with the volatility of exchange rates. Currency options are now traded on markets throughout the world. Three types of currency options contracts are negotiated:

1. *Over-the-counter currency options* are not tradable and can be exercised only at maturity; that is, they are European-type options.[20] Commercial customers often turn to a bank when they need a large amount of options of this type for a specific date. For example, a German car exporter may expect a payment of $20 million, three months from now, to be transferred into euros. Listed options do not offer this specific expiration date, and the amount involved may be too large for the volume of transactions on the options exchange. Moreover, a commercial exporter would not be interested in the possibility of early exercise or sale of the options anyway. Once the bank has written the option, it uses forward contracts or listed currency options to actively hedge the position it has created. Options are also written for longer terms (over two years) than the maturity available on the exchange-listed options.
2. *Spot currency options* are traded on some exchanges. When a currency option is exercised, foreign currency must be physically delivered to a bank account, usually in the country in whose currency the delivery is made. The Philadelphia stock exchange trades option contracts on currencies.

---

[19] The seller of a call can deposit as collateral the asset on which the option is written (*covered option*).

[20] European-type options are generally used in OTC markets because they are simpler. But any type of option can be negotiated in such a customized market.

3. Other listed currency options are *options on currency futures* contracts. For example, the CME trades options on its own currency futures.[21]

To offer more flexibility, options exchange also offers the possibility of writing some customized options in terms of expiration date, amount, and option type.

Currency options are quoted in several ways. Interbank currency options are basically traded in the fashion desired by the investor. Typically, U.S. options are quoted in terms of U.S. dollars per unit of foreign currency. The quotations from various options markets are published in slightly different formats, but they all include the same information. For example, Exhibit 10.9 reports quotes for £/$ options. The contract size is £31,250, and the option prices are expressed in U.S. cents per pound. The first column gives the strike price (the dollar value of one pound) and the next columns give the option premium (in U.S. cents per pound) for different expiration months of calls and puts. The call British pound April 1.620 quoted in Philadelphia is an option contract giving the right to buy 31,250 pounds at a strike price of 1.620 dollars per British pound on or before April. At the time (February 18), the spot exchange rate was 1.633 dollars per British pound, and the premium was 2.63 cents per British pound. If the British pound had gone up, the price of the option would have increased and the holder of the call would have profited. An investor could also have bought a British pound put, which would have given the investor the right to sell 31,250 British pounds at a fixed strike price. For example, the put British pound April 1.620 was worth 1.32 cents per British pound. If the British pound had depreciated (i.e., if its value had gone down in terms of U.S. dollars), the holder of the put would have profited.

EXHIBIT 10.9

Currency Options Quotations: February 18

PHILADELPHIA Sterling OPTIONS £31,250 (cents per pound)

	Calls			Puts		
Strike Price	**Mar**	**Apr**	**May**	**Mar**	**Apr**	**May**
1.620	2.01	2.63	3.11	0.63	1.32	1.77
1.630	1.38	2.10	2.56	0.97	1.75	2.21
1.640	0.94	1.67	2.13	1.44	2.22	2.69

Previous day's volume, calls–puts 422. Previous day's open interest, calls 1,553, puts 19,754.

Source: Financial Times, February 19, 1999

21 The price of an option on spot and futures exchange rates may differ slightly. Technical differences are also important. For example, spot currency options on the Philadelphia stock exchange and futures currency options on the CME do not expire on the same day of the month.

Stock Options Trading in listed options started with options on individual common stocks. Markets have developed throughout the world to the point at which options are now traded on all major stocks. In most countries, the national stock exchange or an associated options exchange trades options on domestic companies listed on the stock exchange.

Stock options are usually protected against capital adjustments, such as splits or stock rights, but not against dividend payments. This is why it can be more profitable to exercise a call option just before a dividend is paid than to keep it and lose the dividend.

Options on stock indexes have also developed in most countries. They can be options on the stock index or on the stock index futures contract. All settlement procedures require cash rather than physical delivery of an index. The cash settlement is based on the calculated value of the index at the time of expiration.

Interest Rate Options Listed options are traded on the interest rate futures contracts (bonds, and short-term deposits) described previously. Options use the same convention as futures. For example, a put on Euribor with a strike of 97 percent and the exercise month June is quoted on February 19 at 0.10 percent. The underlying asset is a three-month Euribor futures contract with a nominal value of €1 million and delivery in June. Following the futures convention, the premium on one option contract is 0.10 percent of €1 million divided by four, or €250. This gives the investor the right to sell one Euribor futures contract in June at a price of 97 percent (i.e., to borrow in June for three months at a 3 percent interest rate). If Euribor futures quote at 96 percent on expiration, the put option contract will be worth 1 percent times €1 million divided by four, or €2,500.

Also, some interest rate options are traded OTC. Example 10.8 shows an interest rate call option (cap) based on LIBOR. Typically, OTC options such as caps and floors (a type of interest rate put) are longer-term options on short-term interest rates.

The basic contract in an interest rate *cap option* is an agreement between the buyer and the seller of the option, stating that if a chosen rate, such as the three-month LIBOR, is above the agreed-on strike price at prespecified dates in the future, the seller will reimburse the buyer for the additional interest cost until the next specified date. A floor option has the reverse characteristics. A five-year cap on the three-month LIBOR can be broken down into a series of 19 European options with quarterly strike dates. The option premium may be paid in the form of a single front-end price (e.g., 2% of the amount specified in the option) or a yearly cost paid up regularly (e.g., 0.5% per year).

Option Valuation

Profit and Loss at Expiration The profit-and-loss structure of an option that is held until expiration is shown in Exhibit 10.10. The strike price K is assumed to equal the spot price at the time of contracting. The profit at expiration depends on the spot price at expiration.

Exhibits 10.10a and 10b show the profit structures for long and short positions in an underlying asset, illustrating the profit structure for buying and

EXAMPLE 10.8 PAYMENTS ON A CAP

Consider a five-year 6 percent cap on the three-month LIBOR for $1 million. The current LIBOR is 5 percent, and the yearly cap premium is an annualized 0.5 percent paid quarterly. You buy such a cap. What would be the quarterly payment on the cap in the following situations?

1. LIBOR stays below 6 percent, the strike price.
2. LIBOR moves up to 8 percent.

SOLUTION

1. If LIBOR stays below 6 percent over the next five years, the cap option will be useless. Each quarter in which LIBOR is below 6 percent, you will have to pay the premium of 0.5 percent annualized, hence, a payment of

$$\$1 \text{ million} \times \left(\frac{0.5\%}{4}\right) = \$1{,}250$$

2. If LIBOR is equal to 8 percent on a quarterly payment date, you will receive the difference between LIBOR and the strike rate of 6 percent, minus the premium payment of 0.5 percent:

$$\$1 \text{ million} \times \left(\frac{8\% - 6\% - 0.5\%}{4}\right) = \$3{,}750$$

A cap can benefit a borrower who has a LIBOR-indexed loan. For a 0.5 percent premium payment, the cap buyer gains protection from a LIBOR-based interest cost increase because a rise in LIBOR above the strike rate yields an offsetting gain on the cap.

selling futures. We see that the profit structures on these two positions exactly mirror each other. This stems from the fact that for any dollar increase in the spot price of the asset, the buyer of futures earns a dollar profit and the seller loses a dollar.

The profit structures for options must take premiums into account. The buyer and the writer of a call option have opposite profit opportunities at expiration. The maximum loss for an option buyer is limited to the premium, although the profit may be quite large. The reverse holds true for the option writer, which is why Exhibit 10.10c and 10d also are mirror images of each other. Another way of saying this is that the risk structure of options is asymmetric when compared with a direct investment in the spot or futures market. That is, though the option buyer risks losing the premium, the seller of that same option bears the risk of an almost unlimited loss.

Valuation Models Option premiums fluctuate so rapidly as a function of price movements in underlying assets that computerized models are necessary to properly value them. To understand how options are valued, recall both the parameters that

EXHIBIT 10.10
Profits and Losses from Various Positions

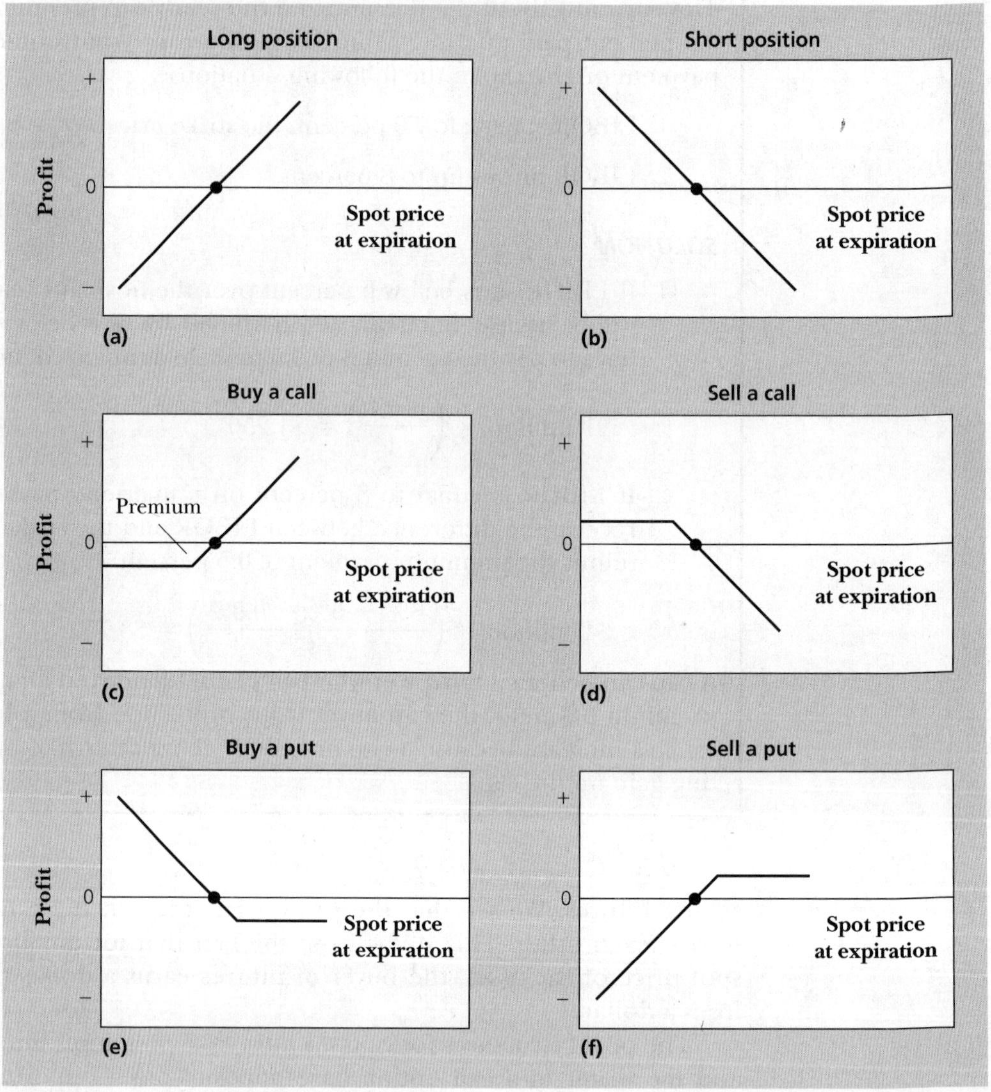

determine option premiums and the famous valuation formula proposed by Black and Scholes (1973).[22]

Most options traded in the world are American options in the sense that they can be exercised any time before expiration, which means that premiums must at least equal the profit an investor could obtain by immediately exercising the option. *Intrinsic value* is the value of an option that is immediately exercised. A rational option buyer would never exercise a call when the underlying asset price

[22] See also Hull (2007) and Kolb (2007).

EXHIBIT 10.11

Call Option Intrinsic Value as a Function of Asset Price

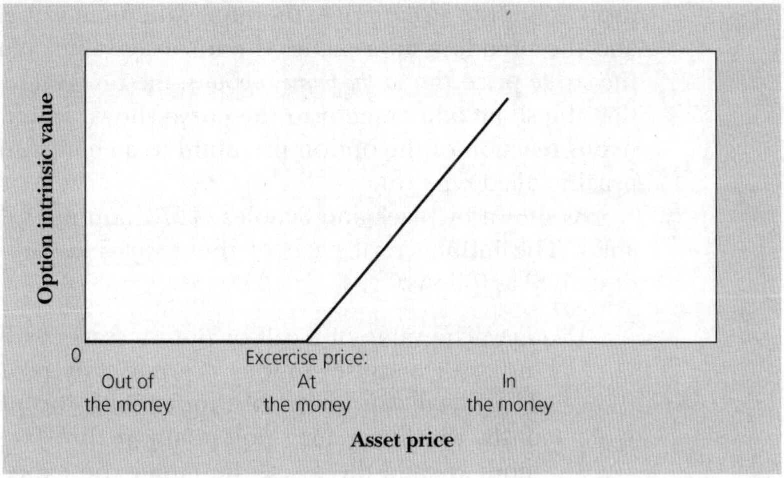

is below the strike price, because he would lose money. This is said to be an *out-of-the-money option,* and its intrinsic value is zero. When an asset price is above the strike price, the call is said to be *in the money,* and its intrinsic value is the difference between the asset price and the strike price. The intrinsic value of a call as a function of asset price is shown in Exhibit 10.11.

An option will generally sell above its intrinsic value; the difference between an option's market value and its intrinsic value is called its *time value.* At any time before expiration, call option premiums vary with the underlying asset prices along a curve similar to that shown in Exhibit 10.12 (dashed line). For very low values of the asset price relative to the strike price, the intrinsic value is zero and the time value of the option is close to zero because the probability that the option will ever

EXHIBIT 10.12

Call Option Value as a Function of Asset Price

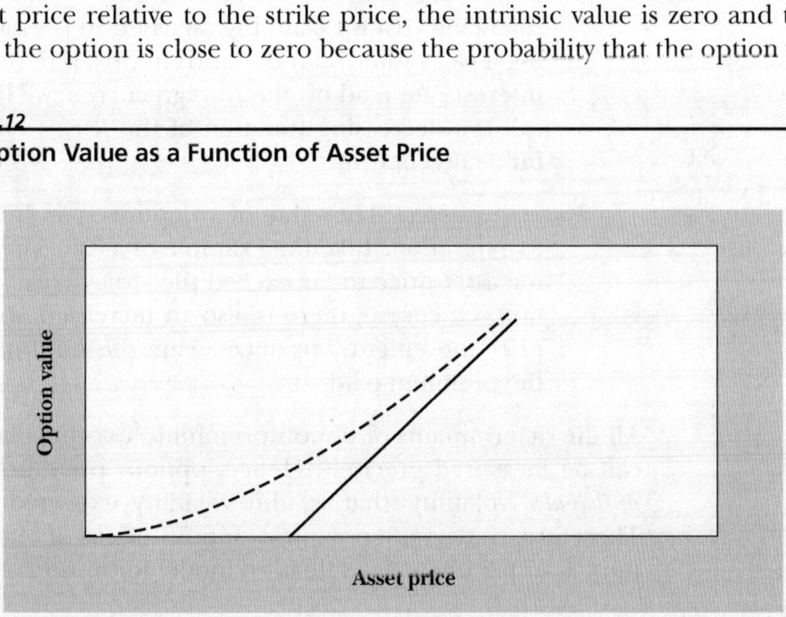

be exercised is almost zero. For very high asset prices relative to the strike price, the option premium is almost equal to the option's intrinsic value. The option is almost sure to be exercised at expiration because it is unlikely that the asset price will ever drop below the strike price; therefore, the time value of the option is close to zero and the premium approaches the intrinsic value. When the asset price is close to the strike price (an *at-the-money option*), the time value of the option is largest. Note that the slope of a tangent to the curve shown in Exhibit 10.12 gives the instantaneous reaction of the option premium to a change in the asset price. This slope is usually called *delta* (δ).

As shown by Black and Scholes (1973), option values depend on just four variables. The influence of each of these variables on call and put options can be described as follows:

Volatility: The value of a call or put increases with the volatility of the underlying asset because options are perfectly protected against downside risk. The buyer can never lose more than the premium paid. Yet, simultaneously, the buyer may potentially realize large gains on the upside. The more volatile the asset, the larger the expected gain on the option and, hence, the larger its premium.

Asset price relative to strike price: The value of an option depends critically on its strike price relative to its current asset price. The lower the asset price relative to the strike price, the lower the premium for a call (the higher for a put).

Interest rate: The value of a call (put) is an increasing (decreasing) function of the *domestic* interest rate. Buying a call enables an investor to lay claim to an asset, although making a much smaller capital investment than required to buy the asset outright. A call reduces the opportunity or financing cost for claiming an asset. In the case of a currency option, buying a call rather than the currency itself deprives the buyer of the foreign interest rate paid on the foreign currency. Hence, the value of a currency call is a decreasing function of the *foreign interest rate.* The reverse is true for a currency put.

Time to expiration: The value of an option is an increasing function of the time to expiration. Take the example of a call. The opportunity for the underlying asset price to far exceed the strike price increases with time to expiration. Of course, there is also an increased opportunity for a large adverse price movement, but once again, the call holder's loss is always limited to the premium paid.

All the determinants of option premiums, except volatility of the underlying asset, can be measured precisely. Hence, options premiums are directly related to the *anticipated* volatility, that is, the volatility expected to prevail until expiration. Therefore, traders often express options prices in terms of implicit volatility. From these four parameters, a valuation model for options can be constructed. Analytical valuation models have been derived for European-type options, which cannot be exercised until expiration. They offer an operational approximation for American-type options, which can be exercised at any time; this is the case for a majority of options traded in the world. The most famous valuation model was developed by Black and Scholes and is currently used on options markets worldwide. It is a fairly complex mathematical formula which is explained in derivatives textbooks such as Hull (2007), Chance (2003), and Kolb (2007).

Use of Options

Options can be put to several uses. Selling (writing) options allows an investor to pocket income if the option expires worthless, but the risks are huge if the price of the underlying asset moves in an unfavorable direction. *Covered call writing* is the sale of a call option written on assets held in the portfolio, but the risk is that the assets will have to be delivered if the option is exercised. Hence, selling options is a strategy left to specialized investors. Some strategies involve dynamic trading based on sophisticated valuation models and are again reserved for specialists. In traditional portfolio management, options are mainly used either to invest in a specific security or market, while limiting the downside risk potential, or for temporarily insuring some types of portfolio risk. In both cases, investment managers only buy options—they do not sell them. Options are also used in constructing some structured notes designed for the specific need of some investors, mostly institutional.

Speculation with Limited Risk The buyer of an option can take a position in the underlying asset with a limited downside risk, namely, the option premium. For example, the call British pound April 1.620 quoted in Exhibit 10.9 gives the right to buy 31,250 pounds at a strike price of 1.620 dollars per British pound, and the option premium is 2.63 cents per British pound. An investor could speculate on an appreciation of the pound against the dollar by buying one contract on 31,250 pounds and paying $\$0.0263 \times 31{,}250 = \$821.875$. If the pound rises to \$1.800 by April, the investor will make a profit equal to the difference between the spot and the strike price, minus the option premium. This will be a profit per contract of

$$31{,}250 \times (1.800 - 1.620 - 0.0263) = 4{,}803.125 \text{ dollars}$$

This is less than the pound appreciation because of the cost of the call premium. But if the pound drops in value by April, the investor will lose only the premium that she paid initially.

Insurance Options provide a unique tool with which to insure portfolios. *Insuring* means that a portfolio is protected against a negative performance while it retains its positive performance potential. By contrast, hedging with futures removes both negative and positive performance potentials. The case of insuring against currency risks is detailed in Chapter 11. Example 10.9 illustrates how to insure an equity portfolio against market risk.

EXAMPLE 10.9 INSURING AGAINST MARKET RISK

A portfolio manager has an allocation of €4 million to French equity. The French portfolio is well diversified and tracks the local CAC stock index. The manager believes that the French market offers excellent returns prospects. However, the manager is worried that French elections taking place next month (April) could lead to a severe market correction. Although the probability of such an outcome is quite small, the manager wishes to insure against it. The current value of the CAC index is 4,000. Futures on the CAC with maturity in June also trade at 4,000. Put options with maturity in June trade as follows:

Strike Price	Premium (€ per unit of index)
3,900	30
4,000	100

CAC options and futures have a multiple of €10 times the index. Thus, the total premium for one put with exercise price €3900 is 30 × €10 = €300, for example. The manager hesitates between selling 100 futures contracts, buying 100 puts with a strike of 3,900, or buying 100 puts with a strike of 4,000.

1. Calculate the outcome of each strategy if the CAC is equal to 3,500, 4,000, or 4,500 at expiration of the contracts in June.
2. Recommend a strategy to the portfolio manager.

SOLUTION

1. The value of the portfolio under the various strategies is given below:

Value of CAC at expiration	Initial Portfolio (No Futures or Options)	Portfolio Hedged with Futures	Portfolio Insured with Puts 3,900	Portfolio Insured with Puts 4,000
3,500	3,500,000	4,000,000	3,870,000	3,900,000
4,000	4,000,000	4,000,000	3,970,000	3,900,000
4,500	4,500,000	4,000,000	4,470,000	4,400,000

2. Hedging with futures provides the best protection in case of a drop in the market, but it deprives the manager of any profit potential. Buying puts provides protection in case of a market drop while keeping most of the upside potential (the put premium is deducted from the portfolio value). Given the manager's expectations, buying puts is a natural strategy. Out-of-the-money puts are cheaper, so they are more attractive in case of an up-movement, but offer less protection in case of a down-movement. To get the best downside protection while retaining upside potential, the portfolio manager should buy 100 puts with a strike price of 4,000.

Structured Notes A *structured note* is a bond issued with some unusual option-like clause.[23] These notes are bonds issued by a name of good credit standing and can therefore be purchased as investment-grade bonds by most institutional investors,

EXAMPLE 10.10 GUARANTEED NOTE

Consider the guaranteed note on the Nikkei described previously:

1. Value the call option implicit in the bond.
2. Assume that you offer a similar bond but with a coupon set at zero. What is the equity participation that you could offer?

SOLUTION

1. The present value of the straight bond is

$$P = \frac{3}{1.08} + \frac{103}{(1.08)^2} = 91.08\%$$

Because the bond is issued at 100 percent, the implicit value of 50 percent of a call option on the Nikkei is therefore equal to

$$100 - 91.08\% = 8.92\%$$

and the implicit value of 100 percent of one call option on the Nikkei index is equal to

$$2 \times (100 - 91.08) = 17.84\%$$

2. There is clearly a negative relation between the amount of the guaranteed coupon and the participation rate that can be offered in the option. For example, a structured note with a zero coupon will leave more money to invest in the call option:

$$P = \frac{0}{1.08} + \frac{100}{(1.08)^2} = 85.73\%$$

The difference between the redemption value and the current market value of the zero-coupon bond (14.27% = 100 − 85.73) can be invested by the issuer in call options. The remaining question is to determine the number of call options that can be purchased with this amount. The number of call options that can be purchased is equal to the participation rate that is set in the structured note. In the example, one call option on the Nikkei index is worth 17.84, and 14.27 is available to invest in options. Hence, this allows a participation rate of

$$14.27/17.84 = 80\%$$

instead of 50 percent, as above.

[23] Some other examples of structured notes offered to international investors are discussed in Chapter 7.

even those that are prevented by regulations from dealing in derivatives. Another attraction for investors is that these structured notes offer some long-term options that are not publicly traded. Structured notes with equity participation are in strong demand in many countries, especially in Europe, where they are sometimes called *guaranteed notes.*

Guaranteed notes with equity participation are bonds having guaranteed redemption of capital and a minimum coupon; in addition, some participation in the price movement of a selected index is offered if this price movement is positive. For example, let's consider a two-year note that guarantees the initial capital (redemption at 100%) plus an annual coupon of 3 percent and offers a 50 percent participation rate in the percentage price appreciation in the Japanese Nikkei index over the two years. At time of issue, the yield curve was flat at 8 percent. The 50 percent participation rate works as follows: If the stock index goes up by x percent, the investor will get 50 percent of x. For example, if the Nikkei stock index goes up by 30 percent from the time of issue to the time of redemption, the option will yield a profit of 15 percent and the bond will be redeemed for 115 percent. The participation rate is, in effect, the percentage of a call option on the index obtained by the investor. In summary, the structured note can be viewed by investors as the sum of

- a straight bond with a coupon of 3 percent
- plus 50 percent of an at-the-money call option on the Nikkei.

All of these bonds can be analyzed as the sum of a straight bond with a low coupon plus an option play (see Example 10.10).

Summary

- Derivatives offer high financial leverage and liquidity. Major derivative contracts are futures and forward contracts, swaps, and options.
- Futures contracts are standardized in terms of size and delivery dates. They may be freely traded on the market. They are marked to market every day so that profits and losses are immediately realized.
- Forward contracts are private contracts between two parties. They are customized in terms of size and delivery date and have to be held until delivery. The margin is set once and never revised.
- Futures contracts have a symmetrical payoff structure.
- Futures prices are usually broken down into the spot, or cash, price of the asset plus a basis. The basis is referred to as a discount, or premium, for currency or stock index contracts.
- The major question in futures valuation is how to determine the theoretical value of the basis. This is usually done using an arbitrage argument taking offsetting positions in the spot and futures or forward markets. The cost of

carrying this arbitrage puts limits on the basis. In all cases, the basis tends to reflect the financing cost of holding a cash position minus the income lost, if any, in holding a futures position. Various technical aspects render the valuation of bond futures more difficult.

- Futures and forward contracts are used to hedge assets or portfolios of assets against price risk. Several types of hedges can be designed. Two major decisions are the contracts to be used and the amount of hedging. Because few futures contracts exist, investors must often engage in cross-hedging by using contracts that are close, but not identical, to the assets to be hedged. The aim is to use contracts whose futures price most closely correlates with that of the type of risk to be hedged.
- Perfect hedges can seldom be created because of basis risk (unexpected fluctuations in the basis) and cross-hedge risk (imperfect correlation between the asset and the contract). Hedging strategies range from a simple approach using a unitary hedge ratio to a minimum-variance optimization approach.
- Swaps are long-term periodic forward contracts.
- Currency swaps involve the exchange of obligations in two currencies. Interest rate swaps involve the exchange of two obligations in the same currency: one with a fixed interest rate, the other with a floating rate. Currency–interest rate swaps involve the exchange of a fixed interest rate in one currency for a floating interest rate in another currency.
- Swaps are used to transfer a comparative advantage enjoyed in one market to another market. They are often part of a complex financing or investment package. Swaps also are used to manage a company's long-term exposure to currency and interest rate risk.
- Swaps are generally valued as a portfolio of two bonds. Credit risk on a swap involves smaller potential losses than on a bond. This explains why the quality spread (the difference between the swap rate for parties with and without credit risk) amounts to only a few basis points.
- Options, like futures, are leveraged instruments but have an attractive asymmetric risk–return characteristic. Calls and puts are the major types of options traded on organized exchanges.
- Exchange traded options are written on all types of financial instruments, including commodities, currencies, individual stocks, stock indexes, fixed-income instruments, and interest rates. Options exist on spot asset prices as well as on futures contracts.
- The valuation of options is somewhat complex. Analytical valuation models have been derived for European-type options, which cannot be exercised until expiration. They offer an operational approximation for American-type options, which can be exercised at any time up to and including the expiration date—the case for a majority of options traded in the world.

- Options can be used to invest in a specific security or market, while limiting the downside risk potential. They are also used to "insure" an existing portfolio. For example, buying a put on an asset (or portfolio) allows the reduction, or elimination, of loss in case of a drop in value of the asset. In-the-money options offer better protection than out-of-the-money options, but at a higher cost.
- Options are also used in constructing some structured notes designed for the specific need of some investors, mostly institutional.

Problems

1. In Chicago, the size of a yen futures contract is 12.5 million yen. The initial margin is \$2,025, and the maintenance margin is \$1,500. You decide to buy 10 contracts, with maturity in June, at the current market futures price of \$0.01056 per ¥. The contract expires on the second-to-last business day before the third Wednesday of the delivery month (expiration date: June 17). Today is April 1, and the spot exchange rate is \$0.01041 per ¥. Indicate the cash flows on your position if the following prices are subsequently observed. (Assume that spot and futures prices stay equal to the previous quotes on the dates that are not indicated in the following table.)

	April 1	April 2	April 3	April 4	June 16	June 17
Spot \$/¥	0.01041	0.01039	0.01000	0.01150	0.01150	0.01100
Futures \$/¥	0.01056	0.01054	0.01013	0.01160	0.01151	0.01100

2. Eurodollar futures contracts are traded on the CME with a size of \$1 million. The initial margin is \$540, and the maintenance margin is \$400. You are the treasurer of a corporation, and we are at April 1. You know that you will have to pay cash for some goods worth \$10 million that will be delivered on June 17. In turn, you will sell those goods with a profit, but you will not receive payment until September 17. Hence, you know that on June 17, you will have to borrow \$10 million for three months. Today is April 1, and the current 3-month LIBOR is 6.25 percent. On the CME, the Eurodollar futures contract with June delivery is quoted at 93.280 percent. The contract expires on the second business day before the third Wednesday of the delivery month (expiration date: June 17).

a. What is the forward interest rate implicit in the Eurodollar futures quotation (93.280%) on April 1? Why is it higher than the current three-month Eurodollar rate (6.25%)?

b. What position would you take in futures contracts to lock in a three-month borrowing rate for June 17?

c. On June 17, the Eurodollar futures contract quotes at 91 percent, while the current Eurodollar rate in London is 9 percent. You unwind your position on that date. Describe the cash flows involved.

3. Consider a currency trader based in Germany. The current spot exchange rate is €1.1 per \$1. The risk-free rate in the United States is 5 percent per year, and the euro risk-free rate is 8 percent per year. The current forward price on a one-year contract is €1.15 per \$1.

a. Calculate the arbitrage-free forward price.

b. Based on the current forward price of €1.15 per \$1, indicate how the trader can earn a risk-free arbitrage profit.

4. Consider a currency trader based in the United States. The current spot rate is \$0.90 per euro. The risk-free rate in the United States is 7 percent, and the euro risk-free rate is 5 percent. The current forward price on a one-year contract is \$0.85 per euro.

a. Calculate the arbitrage-free forward price.

b. Based on the current forward price of \$0.85 per euro, indicate how the trader can earn a risk-free arbitrage profit.

5. A pension fund manager expects a cash inflow of \$250 million in two weeks. He wishes to avoid missing a significant increase in equity prices over the next two weeks. Assume that the beta of the portfolio under management is 1.1. A stock index futures contract is quoted at 1225 and has a multiplier of 250. The current stock index is also 1225.

a. Indicate whether the pension fund manager should undertake a long hedge or a short hedge.

b. How many contracts should be bought or sold?

6. Consider a portfolio manager who wishes to reduce the allocation to equities in his portfolio by \$500 million. The manager is concerned that equity prices may drop quickly. Assume that the beta of the portfolio under management is 0.90. A stock index futures contract is quoted at 1052 and has a multiplier of 250. The current stock index stands at 1050.

a. Indicate how the portfolio manager can reduce the exposure to equities by using stock index futures.

b. How many contracts should be bought or sold?

7. A U.S. company has issued floating-rate notes with a maturity of 10 years, an interest rate of six-month LIBOR plus 25 basis points, and total face value of \$10 million. The company now believes that interest rates will rise and wishes to protect itself against this by entering into an interest rate swap. A dealer provides a quote on a 10-year swap whereby the company will pay a fixed rate of 5 percent and receive six-month LIBOR. Interest is paid semiannually. Assume the current LIBOR rate is 4 percent. Indicate how the company can use a swap to convert the debt to a fixed rate. Calculate the first net payment and indicate which party makes the payment. Assume that all payments are semiannual and made on the basis of 180/360.

8. Consider a bank that is currently lending \$25 million at an interest rate of six-month LIBOR plus 65 basis points. The loan maturity is two years and calls for semiannual payments. The bank expects interest rates to fall and wishes to hedge against this by entering into an interest rate swap. A dealer provides the following quotes on swaps:

a. The bank will pay a fixed rate of 5.05 percent and receive six-month LIBOR.

b. The bank will receive a fixed payment of 5.25 percent and pay a floating rate of LIBOR plus 25 basis points.

Indicate which swap the bank should choose. How might the swap hedge the bank against a decline in interest rates? Assume that all payments are semiannual and made on the basis of 180/360.

9. Suppose a U.S. company enters into a currency swap with a counterparty in which the U.S. company pays a fixed rate of 5 percent in euros and the counterparty pays a fixed rate of 6 percent in dollars. The notional principals are \$50 million and €45 million.

The spot exchange rate is €0.90 per dollar. Payments are made semiannually on the basis of 30 days per month and 360 days per year.

a. Calculate the initial exchange of payments that takes place at the beginning of the swap if the parties have no immediate need for each other's currency.
b. Indicate how to calculate the semiannual payments.
c. Indicate how to calculate the final exchange of payments that takes place at the end of the swap.
d. Describe a scenario in which the U.S. company might wish to enter into this currency swap.

10. Suppose a British company enters into a currency swap in which the counterparty pays a fixed rate of 6.5 percent in dollars and the British company pays a fixed rate of 5.5 percent in pounds. The notional principals are £25 million and $41.25 million. The spot exchange rate is $1.65 per pound. Payments are made annually, and the parties have no immediate need for each other's currency.

a. Calculate the initial exchange of payments that takes place at the beginning of the swap.
b. Indicate how to calculate the annual payments.
c. Describe a scenario in which the British company might wish to enter into this currency swap.

11. Four years ago, a Swiss firm entered into a currency swap of $100 million for 150 million Swiss francs, with a maturity of seven years. The swap fixed rates are 8 percent in dollars and 4 percent in francs, and swap payments are annual. The Swiss firm contracted to pay dollars and receive francs. The market conditions for zero swap rates (i.e., rates to be used to discount the two legs of the swap) are now (exactly four years later) as follows:

Spot exchange rate: 1.5 Swiss francs/U.S. dollar

The current structure of zero swap rates:

Maturity (years)	**U.S. Dollar (% annual)**	**Swiss Franc (% annual)**
1	9	5
2	9.5	5.75
3	10	6
4	10.25	6.25
5	10.75	6.5
6	11	7
7	11.5	7.5

a. Calculate the swap payments at the end of the fourth year (i.e., today).
b. Right after this payment, what is the market value of the swap to the Swiss firm?

12. A French corporation plans to invest in Thailand to develop a local subsidiary to promote its French products. The creation of this subsidiary should help boost its exports from France. The Thai baht is pegged to a basket of currencies dominated by the U.S. dollar, so borrowing in U.S. dollars would reduce the currency risk on this investment. The corporation needs to borrow $20 million for five years. A bank has proposed a five-year dollar loan at 7.75 percent. The French government wishes to support this type of foreign investment helping French exports. A French government agency can subsidize a 1.50 percent improvement in euro interest costs. In other words, the corporation can get a five-year, €22 million loan at 7.5 percent instead of the current market rate of 9 percent. The current spot exchange rate is €1.1 per dollar. A bank offers to write a currency swap for a principal of $20 million, whereby the corporation would pay dollars at 7.75 percent and receive euros at 9 percent. What could the corporation do to obtain a loan in dollars, its desired currency position, while capturing the French interest rate subsidy? What is the cost saving compared with directly borrowing in dollars?

13. Susan Fairfax is president of Reston. She realizes that her $10 million holding of Reston stock presents a problem in terms of diversification and specific risk for her total portfolio of $12 million ($10 million in Reston stock plus a $2 million savings portfolio). A major brokerage firm has reviewed her situation and proposed an equity swap having the following features:

Term:	3 years
Notional principal:	$10 million
Settlement frequency:	Annual, commencing at end of year 1
Fairfax pays to broker:	Total return on Reston stock
Broker pays to Fairfax:	Total return on S&P 500 stock index

Ignore the tax consequences of the swap transaction, and assume that Fairfax plans to renew the contract at the expiration of its three-year term.

a. Justify advising Fairfax to enter into the swap, including in your response
   i. a description of the swap's effect on Fairfax's total portfolio, and
   ii. two reasons why use of such a swap may be superior to an alternative strategy of selling a portion of the Reston stock.

b. Explain one risk to be encountered by Fairfax under each of the three following scenarios, assuming that she enters the swap at the beginning of year 1. Your answer must cite a different risk for each scenario.
   i. At the end of year 1, Reston stock has significantly outperformed the S&P 500 index.
   ii. At the end of year 1, Reston stock has significantly underperformed the S&P 500.
   iii. At the end of year 3, Fairfax wants to negotiate a new three-year swap on the same terms as the original agreement, adjusted for the new market value of her Reston holding.

14. a. Calculate the payoff at expiration for a call option on the euro in which the underlying is at $0.90 at expiration, the options are on 62,500 euros, and the exercise price is
   i. $0.75
   ii. $0.95

b. Calculate the payoff at expiration for a put option on the euro in which the underlying is at $0.90 at expiration, the options are on 62,500 euros, and the exercise price is
   i. $0.75
   ii. $0.95

15. A U.S. investor believes that the dollar will depreciate and buys one call option on the euro at an exercise price of $1.10 per euro. The option premium is $0.01 per euro, or $625 per contract of 62,500 euros (Philadelphia).

a. For what range of exchange rates should the investor exercise the call option at expiration?

b. For what range of exchange rates will the investor realize a net profit, taking the original cost into account?

c. If the investor had purchased a put with the same exercise price and premium, instead of a call, how would you answer the previous two questions?

16. You are currently borrowing $10 million at six-month LIBOR + 50 basis points. The LIBOR is at 4 percent. You expect to borrow this amount for five years but are worried that LIBOR will rise in the future. You can buy a 6 percent cap on six-month LIBOR over the next five years with an annual cost of 0.5 percent (paid semiannually). Describe the evolution of your borrowing costs under various interest rate scenarios.

17. A lender makes a loan of $5 million that carries an interest rate of six-month LIBOR + 125 basis points and matures in two years. The lender is worried about a decline in the LIBOR rate and in order to hedge against this risk decides to purchase a 5 percent floor on six-month LIBOR over the next two years. The annual floor premium is 0.75 percent (paid semiannually). Indicate the annualized lending rates if LIBOR rates are above and below 5 percent.

18. You hold a diversified portfolio of German stocks with a value of €50 million. You are getting worried about the outcome of the next elections and wish to hedge your German stock market risk. However, you like the companies that you hold and believe that the German stock market will do well in the long run. Transaction costs are too high to sell the stocks now and buy them back in a few weeks. Instead, you decide to use DAX futures or options to temporarily protect the value of your portfolio. Current market quotations are as follows:

DAX index value:	Spot, 5,000
	June futures, 5,000
DAX call June 5,000:	62
DAX put June 5,000:	60
DAX put June 4,950:	30
DAX put June 4,900:	10

The standard contract size is €25 times the index for futures and €5 times the index for options.

a. What would you do to hedge your portfolio with futures?
b. What would you do to insure your portfolio with options?
c. Calculate the results of the four protection strategies: selling June futures, buying puts June 5000, buying puts June 4,950, and buying puts June 4,900. Look at the value of your portfolio, assuming that it follows the movements in the market exactly. Assume that the DAX index in June is equal to 4,800, 4,900, 5,000, 5,100, and 5,200, successively.

19. Consider a U.S. portfolio manager holding a portfolio of French stocks. The market value of the portfolio is €20 million, with a beta of 1.2 relative to the CAC index. In November, the spot value of the CAC index is 4,000, and the price of a futures contract on the CAC index for December delivery is 4,000. The dividend yield, euro interest rates, and dollar interest rates are all equal to 4 percent (flat yield curves).

a. The portfolio manager fears a drop in the French stock market (but not the euro). The size of CAC index futures contracts is €10 times the CAC index. There are futures contracts quoted with December delivery. How many contracts should he buy or sell to hedge the French stock market risk?
b. Puts on the CAC index with December expiration and a strike price of 4,000 sell for 50. Assume the standard contract size for the index options is €10 times the CAC index. How many puts should he buy or sell to insure the portfolio? Compare the

results of this insurance with the hedge suggested previously. Assume that the CAC index in December is equal to 3,800, 4,000, and 4,200, successively.

c. Suppose the manager fears a depreciation of the euro relative to the U.S. dollar. Will the previously mentioned strategies protect against this depreciation?

20. You are an investment banker considering the issuance of a guaranteed note with stock index participation for a client. The current yield curve is flat at 8 percent for all maturities. Two-year at-the-money calls trade at 17.84 percent of the index value; three-year at-the-money calls trade at 20 percent of the index value. You are hesitant about the terms to set in the structured note. You know that if you guarantee a higher coupon rate, the level of participation in the stock appreciation will be less.

a. Your supervisor asks you to compute the "fair" participation rate that would be feasible for various guaranteed coupon rates and maturities. Based on the current market conditions (as described), estimate the participation rates that are feasible with a maturity of two or three years and a coupon rate of 0, 1, 2, 3, 5, and 7 percent.

b. Explain the relationship between the amount of the guaranteed coupon and the participation rate that can be offered.

Bibliography

Black, F., and Scholes, M. "The Pricing of Options and Corporate Liabilities," *Journal of Political Economy*, May/June 1973.

Chance, D. *Analysis of Derivatives for the CFA® Program*, Charlottesville, VA: AIMR, 2003.

Cornell, B., and Reiganum, M. "Forward and Futures Prices: Evidence from the Foreign Exchange Market," *Journal of Finance*, December 1981.

Duffie, D., and Huang, M. "Swap Rates and Credit Quality," *Journal of Finance*, 51(3), July 1996.

Fleming, J., and Whaley, R. E. "The Value of the Wildcard Option," *Journal of Finance*, March 1994.

Hull, J. C. *Fundamentals of Futures and Options Markets*, 6th ed., Upper Saddle River, NJ: Prentice Hall, 2007.

Kolb, R. W., and Overdhal, J. A. *Futures, Options and Swaps*, 5th ed., Malden, MA: Blackwell, 2007.

11

Currency Risk Management

LEARNING OUTCOMES

After completing this chapter, you will be able to do the following:

- Demonstrate how to protect a portfolio against currency risks
- Demonstrate how to hedge the current value of a foreign investment
- Discuss the difference between translation and economic risk
- Discuss the factors to consider in hedging the future value of a foreign investment
- Discuss how to hedge multicurrency portfolios
- Discuss how to insure a portfolio against currency risks using currency options
- Discuss dynamic hedging strategies with currency options
- Calculate the future value of a portfolio under several alternative strategies, including no hedging, hedging with futures, and insuring with options with different strike prices
- Discuss methods to reduce currency exposure and to take positions in foreign markets without incurring excessive exchange rate risk and without using currency futures, forwards, or options as hedging vehicles
- Explain the various factors that can influence the strategic currency hedging policy
- Explain the various approaches to currency overlay management

The traditional international investment strategy is first to decide on an international asset allocation. An allocation breaks down a portfolio by both asset class (short-term deposit, bond, equity, sectors) and country or currency of investment (U.S. dollar, British pound, euro). The resulting allocation can be used to form a matrix of currencies and asset classes. Ten percent of a typical portfolio's value may be allocated to Japanese stocks, five percent to international bonds, and so forth. Specific bonds and stocks are selected using the various techniques discussed in previous chapters. Once a portfolio is structured, it must be managed according to changes in expectations and risks.

Derivative instruments, such as options and futures, are used domestically to hedge risks. They protect a manager from being forced to arbitrage or liquidate a large part of her portfolio. For example, interest rate futures or options may be used to hedge a long-term bond portfolio if fears about a rise in interest rates suddenly materialize. The use of financial futures and options in controlling portfolio risk is described in textbooks that deal with domestic investment. The most important area of risk management in international investment is currency risk. This chapter is therefore devoted to currency risk management. Most portfolio managers are often confronted with practical problems such as these:

- Currency risks can strongly affect the performance of an international portfolio. What proportion of the currency exposure should be hedged?
- A U.S. investor is bullish about her portfolio of Australian stocks but is concerned that the Australian dollar may drop sharply in the wake of local elections. On the other hand, the Australian dollar may appreciate strongly as a result of these elections.
- A Japanese investor holds British gilts. He expects the long-term U.K. interest rate to drop, which in turn would cause a depreciation of the pound that will offset the capital gain on the bond in pound terms.

This chapter is intended to assist the reader in better handling situations of this kind. The first three sections of this chapter deal with techniques of currency management using currency futures or forward contracts, currency options, and other methods. The last section deals with currency management in a portfolio context. We review strategic currency management, namely, the "neutral" or "long-term" policy for currency hedging. We also review tactical currency management, often referred to as *currency overlay*. In this final section, we discuss currencies as a separate asset class.

Hedging with Futures or Forward Currency Contracts

Either futures or forward currency contracts may be used to hedge a portfolio. They differ in several ways, as outlined in Chapter 10. Futures are exchange traded contracts while forwards are over-the-counter (OTC) contracts. Currency forwards are sometimes referred to as *currency swaps*. Portfolio managers tend to primarily use forward contracts in currency hedging. But forward and futures contracts allow a manager to take the same economic position. Therefore, in this chapter, the generic term *futures* will denote both futures and forward (or swap) contracts.

The Basic Approach: Hedging the Principal

Hedging with futures is very simple. An investor takes a position with a foreign exchange contract that offsets the currency exposure associated with the principal being hedged. In other words, a citizen of Country A who wants to hedge a portfolio of assets denominated in currency B would sell a futures contract to exchange currency B for currency A. The size of the contract would equal the market value ("principal") of the assets to be hedged. For example, a U.S. investor with £1 million invested in British gilts (treasury bonds) would sell futures for £1 million worth of dollars. The direction of a foreign exchange rate contract is often confusing because it involves the exchange rates of two currencies.

On the Chicago Mercantile Exchange (CME), investors can buy and sell contracts of £62,500 wherein the futures price is expressed in dollars per pound. The same size contract is also found on the London International Financial Futures Exchange (LIFFE). Let us assume that on September 12, a U.S. investor can buy or sell futures with delivery in December for 1.95 dollars per pound; the spot exchange rate is 2.00 dollars per pound. Throughout this chapter, we will use the shortcut notation "/" to mean "per"; hence, \$2.00/£ means 2.00 dollars per pound. In order to hedge her £1 million principal, the investor must sell a total of 16 contracts. Now let us assume that a few weeks later, the futures and spot exchange rates drop to \$1.85 and \$1.90, respectively, whereas the pound value of the British assets rises to 1,010,000. The hedge is undertaken at time 0, and we study the rate of return on the portfolio from time 0 to a future time t. We introduce the following notation:

V_t is the value of the portfolio of foreign assets to hedge, measured in foreign currency at time t (e.g., £1 million)

V_t^* is the value of the portfolio of foreign assets measured in domestic currency (e.g., \$2 million)

S_t is the spot exchange rate: domestic currency value of one unit of foreign currency quoted at time t (e.g., \$2.00/£)

F_t is the futures exchange rate: domestic currency value of one unit of foreign currency quoted at time t (e.g., \$1.95/£)

R is the rate of return of the portfolio measured in foreign currency terms, $(V_t - V_0)/V_0$

R^* is the rate of return of the portfolio measured in domestic currency terms, $(V_t^* - V_0^*)/V_0^*$

s is the percentage movement in the exchange, $(S_t - S_0)/S_0$

In this example, the pound value of the British assets appreciates by 1 percent and the pound exchange rate drops by 5 percent, causing a loss in the dollar value

EXHIBIT 11.1
Relationships between Portfolio Value and Rate of Return

	Period 0	Period t	Rate of Return (%)
Portfolio value (in pounds) V	1,000,000	1,010,000	1.00
Portfolio value (in dollars) V^*	2,000,000	1,919,000	−4.05
Exchange rate (\$/pound) S	2.00	1.90	−5.00
Futures rate (\$/pound) F	1.95	1.85	−5.00

on the portfolio of 4.05 percent (see Exhibit 11.1). In absolute dollar terms, this loss in portfolio value is \$81,000:

$$V_t^* - V_0^* = V_t S_t - V_0 S_0 \tag{11.1}$$

Hence, \$1,919,000 − \$2,000,000 = (£1,010,000 × \$1.90/£) − (£1,000,000 × \$2.00/£) = −\$81,000. On the other hand, the realized gain on the futures contract sale is \$100,000, as follows:

$$\text{Realized gain} = V_0(-F_t + F_0) \tag{11.2}$$

Hence, £1,000,000 × (\$1.95/£ − \$1.85/£) = \$100,000. Therefore, the net profit on the hedged position is \$19,000:

$$Profit = V_t S_t - V_0 S_0 - V_0(F_t - F_0) \tag{11.3}$$

Hence, *Profit* = −\$81,000 + \$100,000 = \$19,000. The rate of return in dollars on the hedged position, R_H, can be found by dividing the profit in Equation 11.3 by the original portfolio value $V_0 S_0$. We find

$$R_H = \frac{V_t S_t - V_0 S_0}{V_0 S_0} - \frac{F_t - F_0}{S_0} = R^* - R_F \tag{11.4}$$

where R_F is the futures price movement as a percentage of the spot rate $(F_t - F_0)/S_0$.

In the example, we find

$$\text{Hedged return} = R_H = \frac{19{,}000}{2{,}000{,}000} = 0.95\%$$

This position is almost perfectly hedged, because the 1 percent return on the British asset is transformed into a 0.95 percent return in U.S. dollars, despite the drop in value of the British pound. The slight difference between the two numbers is explained by the fact that the investor hedged only the principal (£1 million), not the unexpected return on the British investment (equal here to 1 percent). The 5 percent drop in sterling value applied to this 1 percent return exactly equals 1% × 5% = 0.05 percent.

The exact relationship between dollar and pound returns on the foreign portfolio is as follows:

$$R^* = R + s(1 + R) \tag{11.5}$$

Hence, $R^* = 1\% - 5(1.01)\% = -4.05$ percent.

The currency contribution $R^* - R$ is equal to exchange rate variation plus the cross-product sR (equal here to 0.05%). When the value of the portfolio in foreign currency fluctuates widely, the difference can become significant over long periods. This implies that the amount of currency hedging should be adjusted periodically to reflect movements in the value of the position to be hedged. A portfolio manager could decide to hedge the expected future value of the portfolio rather than its current (principal) value. This practice could be risky if expectations do not materialize, and therefore this approach is applied only for fixed-income securities to hedge both the principal value and the yield to be accrued. Still, periodic adjustment of the currency hedge would be required to cover unexpected capital gains or losses on the price of the fixed-income securities.

The hedge result could also be affected by the basis, that is, the difference between the futures and the spot prices. Basis risk is discussed on page 495.

Another illustration of a hedged portfolio is provided in Example 11.1.

EXAMPLE 11.1 HEDGED PORTFOLIO

You are French and own a portfolio of U.S. stocks worth \$1 million. The current spot and one-month forward exchange rates are €1 per \$. Interest rates are equal in both countries. You are worried that the results of U.S. elections could lead to a strong depreciation of the dollar and you decide to sell forward \$1 million to hedge currency risk. A week later, your U.S. stock portfolio has gone up to \$1.02 million, and the spot and forward exchange rates are now €0.95 per \$. Analyze the return on your hedged portfolio.

SOLUTION

The U.S. stock portfolio went up by 2 percent, but the dollar lost 5 percent relative to the euro. If the portfolio had not been hedged, its return in euros would have been

$$\frac{1{,}020{,}000 \times 0.95 - 1{,}000{,}000 \times 1}{1{,}000{,}000 \times 1} = -3.1\%$$

As per Equation 11.3, your profit on the hedge portfolio in euros is

$$\begin{aligned}\text{Profit} &= 1{,}020{,}000 \times 0.95 - 1{,}000{,}000 \times 1 - 1{,}000{,}000 \times (0.95 - 1)\\ &= 19{,}000\end{aligned}$$

The rate of return on the hedged portfolio in euros is equal to 19,000 per 1,000,000 = 1.9 percent, which is very close to the 2 percent portfolio rate of return in dollars. The difference comes from the fact that the dollar capital gain on the U.S. portfolio (2%) was not hedged and suffered the 5 percent currency loss.

We could also directly apply Equation 11.4:

$$R^* - R_F = -3.1\% + 5\% = 1.9\%$$

Minimum-Variance Hedge Ratio

The objective of a currency hedge is to minimize the exposure to exchange rate movement. If the foreign investment were simply a foreign currency deposit—a fixed amount of local currency—it would be sufficient to sell forward an equivalent amount of foreign currency to eliminate currency risk. However, a problem appears when the foreign currency value of a foreign investment reacts *systematically* to an exchange rate movement. For example, a drop in the value of the British pound could lead to an increase in the value of a British company (measured in pounds). This is because this pound depreciation will increase the pound value of cash flows received from abroad, as well as make the company's products more attractive abroad. Another example is provided by bonds issued in a country that has an exchange rate target. A depreciation in its domestic currency will lead the country to raise its interest rates, pushing local bond prices down. In both cases, there is a covariance[1] between the asset return measured in local currency and the exchange rate movements. The covariance between asset returns and movements in the local currency value is negative in the first case and positive in the second case.

One objective is to search for minimum variability in the value of the hedged portfolio. Investors usually care about the rate of return on their investment and the variance thereof. So, if they decide to hedge, investors would like to set the hedge ratio h to minimize the variance of the return on the hedged portfolio. Although the hedge ratio was defined in Chapter 10, it bears repeating that it is the ratio of the size of the short futures position in foreign currency to the size of the currency exposure (value of the portfolio in foreign currency). For example, the hedge ratio is 1 if an investor has a portfolio of British gilts worth 1 million pounds and decides to sell forward 1 million pounds in futures currency contracts. It is easy to show that the rate of return on a hedged portfolio, R_H, is equal to the rate of return on the original portfolio (unhedged), R^*, minus h times the percentage change on the futures price R_F:

$$R_H = R^* - h \times R_F \tag{11.6}$$

The return on a hedged portfolio with a 50 percent hedge ratio is illustrated in Example 11.2.

As shown in Chapter 10, the optimal hedge ratio h^*, which minimizes the variance of R_H, is equal to the covariance of the portfolio return[2] to be hedged with the return on the futures, divided by the variance of the return on the futures:

$$h^* = \frac{\text{cov}(R^*, R_F)}{\sigma_F^2} \tag{11.7}$$

[1] Remember that the covariance between two variables is equal to the correlation times the product of the standard deviations of the two variables.

[2] In Chapter 10, we used R as the generic notation for any asset return. In Chapter 11, we introduce the notations h^* to denote the optimal hedge ratio and R^* and R to differentiate between returns measured in the investor's domestic currency (R^*) and in the foreign currency (R). Equation 11.8 should be applied to R^*, the asset return in domestic currency, which is the currency relevant to the domestic investor.

This optimal hedge ratio is sometimes called the *regression hedge ratio* because it can be estimated as the slope coefficient of the regression of the asset, or portfolio, return on the futures return:

$$R^* = a + h^* R_F + \text{Error term} \tag{11.8}$$

where R^* is the return on the asset or portfolio measured in the investor's domestic currency, R_F is the return on the futures, and a is a constant term.

To get a better understanding of this minimum-variance hedge ratio, it is useful to substitute the value of R^* given in Equation 11.5 into Equation 11.6. From now on, we will further assume that the cross-product term of Equation 11.5 is small and will drop it.[3] We find

$$R_H = R + s - hR_F \tag{11.9}$$

The futures exchange rate differs from the spot exchange rate by a "basis" equal to the interest rate differential (see Chapters 1 and 10). Let's first assume that the basis is zero (interest rates equal in the two currencies) and remains so over time. Hence, the futures exchange rate is equal to the spot exchange rate. Then the rate of return on a futures contract, $R_F = (F_t - F_0)/S_0$, is equal to the spot exchange rate movement, $s = (S_t - S_0)/S_0$. Equation 11.9 can now be written as follows:

$$R_H = R + s(1 - h) \tag{11.10}$$

EXAMPLE 11.2 PORTFOLIO WITH A 50 PERCENT HEDGE RATIO

You are French and own a portfolio of U.S. stocks worth $1 million. The current spot and one-month forward exchange rates are €1 per $. Interest rates are equal in both countries. You are worried that the results of U.S. elections could lead to a strong depreciation of the dollar and decide to hedge 50 percent of the portfolio value against currency risk ($h = 0.5$). A week later, your U.S. stock portfolio has gone up to $1.01 million, and the spot and forward exchange rates are now €0.95 per $. Analyze the return on your hedged portfolio.

SOLUTION

The U.S. stock portfolio went up by 1 percent, but the dollar lost 5 percent relative to the euro. If the portfolio had not been hedged, its return in euros would have been

$$R^* = \frac{1{,}010{,}000 \times 0.95 - 1{,}000{,}000 \times 1}{1{,}000{,}000 \times 1} = -4.05\%$$

According to Equation 11.6, the return on your 50 percent–hedged portfolio is

$$R_H = R^* - h \times R_F = -4.05\% - 0.5 \times (-5\%) = -1.55\%$$

---

[3] This assumes very frequent adjustment of the currency hedge to follow movements in the value of the portfolio.

and the minimum-variance hedge ratio is equal to

$$h^* = \frac{\text{cov}(R^*,R_F)}{\sigma_F^2} = \frac{\text{cov}(R+s,s)}{\sigma_s^2} = 1 + \frac{\text{cov}(R,s)}{\sigma_s^2} \tag{11.11}$$

where σ_s^2 is the variance of the exchange rate movement. Equation 11.11 shows the minimum-variance hedge ratio as the sum of two components, h_1 and h_2, linked to different aspects of currency risk:

- Translation risk ($h_1 = 1$)
- Economic risk ($h_2 = \frac{\text{cov}(R,s)}{\sigma_s^2}$)

Translation Risk *Translation risk* comes from the translation of the value of the asset from the foreign currency to the domestic currency. It would be present even if the foreign currency value of the asset were constant (e.g., a deposit in foreign currency). The hedge ratio of translation risk is 1.

This is usually taken to mean that a currency hedge should achieve on a foreign asset the same rate of return in domestic currency as can be achieved on the foreign market in foreign currency terms. For example, a U.S. investor would try to achieve a dollar rate of return on a British gilts portfolio equal to what he could have achieved in terms of pounds. Creating a perfect currency hedge is equivalent to nullifying a currency movement and translating a foreign rate of return directly into a similar domestic rate of return. Considering only translation risk, the optimal amount to hedge is determined by finding the value of h such that the hedged return in domestic currency terms R_H closely tracks the return in foreign currency terms R.

Equation 11.10 can be written as

$$R_H - R = s(1 - h) \tag{11.12}$$

To minimize the variance of $R_H - R$, we must obviously set a hedge ratio of 1. This is basically the strategy of "hedging the principal" outlined previously.

Economic Risk *Economic risk* comes when the foreign currency value of a foreign investment reacts systematically to an exchange rate movement. This is in addition to translation risk. Let's take again the example of a country that has an exchange rate target. A depreciation in its local currency will lead the country to raise its interest rates, pushing local bond prices down. So, there is a positive covariance between bond returns, measured in local currency, and the exchange rate movement. An investor from abroad will lose twice from the foreign currency depreciation. First, the percentage translation loss will be equal to the percentage depreciation of the foreign currency. Second, the value of the investment measured in foreign currency itself will drop.

The hedge ratio required to minimize this economic risk can be estimated by $\text{cov}(R,s)/\sigma_s^2$. This is the slope that we would get on a regression of the foreign currency return of the asset on the exchange rate movement.

Hedging Total Currency Risk If an investor worries about the total influence of a foreign exchange rate depreciation on her portfolio value, measured in domestic currency, she should hedge both translation and economic currency risk. In this approach, the objective is to minimize the overall influence of an exchange rate movement, whether direct or indirect, on the asset return in domestic currency. The objective is not to try to minimize the tracking error between R_H and R (translation risk).

Most portfolio managers care only about translation risk, so they adopt a unitary hedge ratio if they try to minimize the impact of currency risk. From a portfolio accounting standpoint, currency loss is simply stated as the difference in return when measured in domestic and foreign currencies, $R^* - R$. So, minimizing accounting currency losses is an objective choice. Also, the sensitivity of an asset value to an exchange rate movement has to be estimated from some economic model and/or from historical data. Even though estimates might be imprecise and unstable, hedging only translation risk might not be optimal from an economic viewpoint.

In practice, stock returns and currency movements are quite independent. If a foreign asset's returns are uncorrelated with short-term currency movements, a hedge ratio of unity is a reasonable strategy. Bonds returns and currency movements tend to exhibit a more significant correlation because currencies react to interest rate movements and vice versa. But the short-term correlation between bond returns and currency movements is still low.

Implementation As mentioned above, a regression between asset returns and currency returns is the simplest way to estimate the minimum-variance hedge ratio (Equations 11.8 and 11.11). This can be performed using time series such as 100 data points for past weekly returns. Taking the example of a U.S. investor calculating the optimal hedge ratio for his diversified British equity portfolio, the procedure would be as follows:

- Collect a weekly time series of the dollar price of the British pound (£:$).
- Calculate the weekly percentage price movement (rate of return) for this exchange rate.
- Collect a weekly time series of dollar returns on the British equity portfolio. As this is a diversified British equity portfolio, an easy alternative is to collect returns on a British stock index calculated in dollar terms (the investor's domestic currency).
- Run a simple regression (ordinary least square) between the equity return and the currency return. This can be done on a spreadsheet.
- The slope of this regression is the optimal hedge ratio h^*, as used in Example 11.3

Alternatively, one could get a direct estimate of the economic risk by running a regression between the pound return on the British equity index, namely, the British equity return measured in local currency (the British pound) and the exchange rate

EXAMPLE 11.3 PORTFOLIO WITH MINIMUM-VARIANCE HEDGE RATIO

You are French and own a portfolio of U.S. stocks worth $1 million. The current spot and one-month forward exchange rates are €1 per $. Interest rates are equal in both countries. You are worried that the results of U.S. elections could lead to a strong depreciation of the dollar. You have observed that U.S. stocks tend to react favorably to a depreciation of the dollar. A broker tells you that a regression of U.S. stock returns on the euro per dollar ($:€) percentage exchange rate movements has a slope of −0.20. In other words, U.S. stocks tend to go up by 1 percent when the dollar depreciates by 5 percent.

1. Discuss what your currency hedge ratio should be.
2. A week later, your U.S. stock portfolio has gone up to $1.01 million and the spot and forward exchange rates are now €0.95 per $. Analyze the return on your hedged portfolio.

SOLUTION

1. These are the factors to consider:
   - To hedge only translation risk would require a hedge ratio of 1 (100%).
   - To hedge economic risk would require an additional hedge ratio of −20%.

   The minimum-variance hedge ratio reflecting both translation and economic risk should therefore be 80 percent.

2. Let's now study the return on the optimally hedged portfolio under the proposed scenario. Using Equation 11.10, we find that the return on the hedged portfolio is equal to 0 percent (remember that we neglected the cross-product term). So, we have removed the overall impact of the currency movement. But we do not track the rate of return in foreign currency.

movement. The slope of that regression added to 100 percent would also yield the optimal hedge ratio h^*.

One should be aware that this is only a statistical estimate based on past data. Qualitative considerations based on an economic assessment of future relationships between asset values and currencies could help refine this estimate.

The Influence of the Basis

Note that the minimum-variance hedge, as described, is not necessarily optimal in a risk–return framework:

- Futures and spot exchange rates differ by a basis. Changes in the basis can affect hedging strategies, creating *basis risk*.

- Futures and spot exchange rates differ by a basis. Over time, the percentage movement in the futures and in the spot exchange rate will differ by this basis. In the long run, the return on the hedged portfolio will differ from the portfolio return achieved in foreign currency by the basis, even with a hedge ratio of 1.

These two aspects are now addressed.

Basis Risk Forward (or swap) and futures exchange rates are directly determined by two factors: the spot exchange rate and the interest rate differential between two currencies. The forward discount, or the premium—which is the percentage difference between the forward and the spot exchange rates—equals the interest rate differential for the same maturity as the forward contract. In futures jargon, we say that the basis equals the interest rate differential. If we express the exchange rate as the dollar value of one pound (e.g., $\$/£ = 2.00$) and call $r_\$$ and $r_£$ the interest rates in dollars and pounds, respectively, with the same maturity as the futures contract, the relation known as interest rate parity is

$$\frac{F}{S} = \frac{1 + r_\$}{1 + r_£} \text{ and } \frac{F - S}{S} = \frac{r_\$ - r_£}{1 + r_£} \quad (11.13)$$

Note that the interest rates in equation 11.13 are period rates, not annualized. They equal the annualized rates multiplied by the number of days until maturity and divided by 360 days. Because interest rate parity is the result of arbitrage on very liquid markets, it technically holds at every instant (see Chapters 1 and 2). Changes in the basis have an impact on the quality of the currency hedge. Although currency risk is removed by hedging, some additional risk is taken in the form of *basis risk.* But this basis risk is quite small.

The correlation between futures and spot exchange rates is a function of the futures contract term. Futures prices for contracts near maturity closely follow spot exchange rates because at that point the interest rate differential is a small component of the futures price. To illustrate, consider the futures price of British pound contracts with 1, 3, and 12 months left until delivery. The spot exchange rate is currently \$2.00 per pound, and the interest rates and the calculated values for the futures are as given in Exhibit 11.2. The 1-month futures price should equal \$2.00 plus the 1-month interest rate differential applied to the spot rate. The interest rate

EXHIBIT 11.2

Importance of Interest Rate Differentials to Futures Prices

	Maturity		
	One Month	Three Months	Twelve Months
Pound interest rate (%)	14	13.5	13
Dollar interest rate (%)	10	10	10
Futures price (dollars per pound)	1.993	1.983	1.947
Interest rate component (dollars)	–0.007	–0.017	–0.053
Spot rate: £1 = \$2.00.			

differential for 1 month equals the annualized rate differential of −4 percent multiplied by 30 days and divided by 360 days, or divided by 12:

$$F = S + S\frac{r_{\$} - r_{£}}{1 + r_{£}} = 2.00 - 2.00\frac{\frac{4}{12}\%}{1 + \frac{14}{12}\%}$$

Hence, $F = 1.993$.

We see, then, that even though the interest rate differential is very large, its effect on the one-month futures price is minimal, because the spot exchange rate is the driving force behind short-term forward exchange rate movements. This is less true for long-term contracts. More specifically, a reduction of 1 percentage point (100 basis points) in the interest rate differential causes a futures price movement of approximately 0.25 percentage point (3/12) for the three-month contract and 1 percentage point (12/12) for the one-year contract, as compared with 0.08 percentage point (1/12) for the one-month contract. So, basis risk is very small compared with the currency risk that is being hedged.

Another factor that can affect the quality of the hedge is that movement in the interest rate differential (basis) could be correlated with movement in the spot exchange rate itself.

Expected Hedged Return and the Basis We have so far focused on minimizing risk. A hedge ratio of 1 will minimize transaction risk. But in the long run, the return on the hedged portfolio will differ from the portfolio return achieved in foreign currency by the interest rate differential, even with a hedge ratio of 1. Although we can minimize, or even eliminate, the variance of $R_H - R$, it is impossible to set them equal. This is because we can hedge only with futures contracts with a price F different from S. Over time, the percentage movement in the futures price used in the hedge, R_F, will differ from the percentage movement in the spot exchange rate, s, which affects the portfolio by the interest rate differential.

Implementing Hedging Strategies

A major decision in selecting a currency hedge, whether it be with a forward (or swap) contract or with a futures contract, is the choice of contract terms. Short-term contracts track the behavior of the spot exchange rates better, have greater trading volume, and offer more liquidity than long-term contracts. On the other hand, short-term contracts must be rolled over if a hedge is to be maintained for a period longer than the initial contract. For long-term hedges, a manager can choose from three basic contract terms:

1. Short-term contracts, which must be rolled over at maturity
2. Contracts with a matching maturity, that is, contracts that match the expected period for which the hedge is to be maintained
3. Long-term contracts with a maturity extending beyond the hedging period

EXHIBIT 11.3

Three Hedging Strategies for an Expected Hedge Period of Six Months

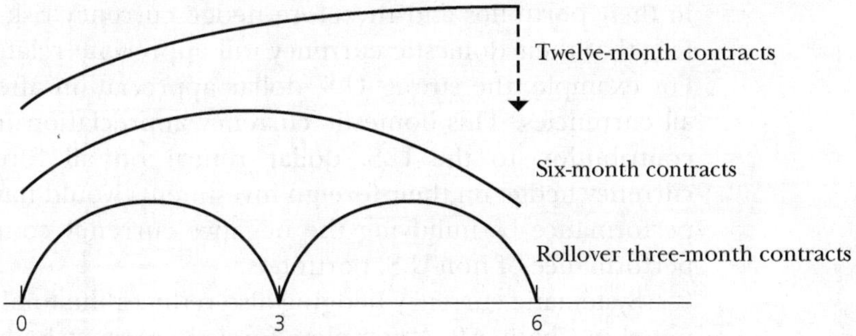

Contracts for any of the three terms may be closed by taking an offsetting position on the delivery date. This avoids actual physical delivery of a currency. Exhibit 11.3 depicts three such hedging strategies for an expected hedge period of six months. The results of the strategy depend on the evolution of interest rates and, hence, of the basis. Any contract maturity different from six months implies basis risk.

Another consideration in choosing a hedging strategy is transaction costs. Rolling over short-term contracts generates more commissions because of the larger number of transactions involved.

It must also be stressed that the market value of the investment to be hedged varies over time. To maintain a desired hedge ratio, the hedge amount should be adjusted frequently to reflect changes in asset market prices. Practically, this cannot be done on a continuous basis because of transaction costs. Forward contracts of small size can be expensive to arrange and will entail a staggering of maturity dates difficult to manage because they are arranged for a fixed duration (e.g., one month or six months). Futures are easier to use for frequent adjustments because they are of small size and traded with a few fixed maturity dates rather than a fixed duration.

Longer hedges can be built using currency swaps, which can be arranged with horizons of up to a dozen years. However, currency swaps are used primarily by corporations in the currency management of their assets and liabilities. Portfolio managers usually take a shorter horizon.

Hedging Multiple Currencies

Cross-hedges are sometimes used for closely linked currencies. For example, a U.S. investor could use euro futures to hedge the currency risk in Swiss stocks, because the Swiss franc and the euro are highly correlated. Futures and forward currency contracts are actively traded only for the major currencies. International portfolios are often invested in assets in Norway, Sweden, Singapore, and other countries where futures contracts in the local currency are sometimes not actively traded.

In these cases, investors must try to find contracts on other currencies that are closely correlated with the investment currencies.

Some investment managers fear the depreciation of only one or two currencies in their portfolios and therefore hedge currency risk selectively. Other managers fear that their domestic currency will appreciate relative to all foreign currencies. For example, the strong U.S. dollar appreciation after 2000 was realized against all currencies. This domestic currency appreciation induced a negative currency contribution to the U.S. dollar return on all foreign portfolios. An overall currency hedge on their foreign investments would have drastically improved their performance by nullifying the negative currency contribution to the total dollar performance of non-U.S. portfolios.

Systematic currency hedging also reduces the total volatility of the portfolio, as noted in Chapter 9. A complete foreign currency hedge can be achieved by hedging the investments in each foreign currency. This is not feasible for many currencies, however, and is very cumbersome administratively. Also, it is not necessary to hedge each currency component in a multicurrency portfolio. In a portfolio with assets in many currencies, the residual risk of each currency is partly diversified away. Optimization techniques can be used to construct a hedge with futures contracts in only a few currencies (e.g., yen, euro, and sterling). Although the residual risk of individual currencies is not fully hedged, the portfolio is well protected against a general appreciation of the home currency.[4] Another alternative is to use contracts on a basket of currencies as offered by some banks.

The stability of the estimated hedge ratios is crucial in establishing effective hedging strategies, especially when cross-hedging is involved. Empirical studies indicate that hedges using futures contracts in the same currency as the asset to be hedged are very effective but that the optimal hedge ratios in cross-hedges that involve different currencies are somewhat unstable over time.[5]

In practice, a diversified international portfolio can be hedged using only the futures contracts available in a few currencies by following this procedure:

- Select the most independent major currencies with futures contracts available. For a U.S. investor, these may be the yen, the euro, and the pound. For a Swiss investor, these may be the yen, the euro, the pound, and the U.S. dollar.
- Calculate the hedge ratios jointly by running a multiple regression of the domestic currency returns of the portfolio (U.S. dollar return for a U.S. investor) on the futures returns in the selected currencies. With the example of three currencies, we have

$$R^* = a + h_1 R_{F1} + h_2 R_{F2} + h_3 R_{F3} + \text{Error term} \tag{11.14}$$

---

[4] For an empirical examination of the multicurrency betas of international portfolios, see Adler and Simon (1986).

[5] See Eaker and Grant (1987), Dale (1981), and Grammatikos and Saunders (1983). The importance of basis risk (movements in interest rate differential) for determining the risk-minimizing hedge ratio has been illustrated by Briys and Solnik (1992). Kroner and Sultan (1993) derive risk-minimizing dynamic hedging strategies if the distribution of returns changes over time and follows some GARCH process.

- Use the estimates of the regression coefficients h_1, h_2, and h_3 as the hedge ratios in each currency. Because the spot currency movement is the major component of futures volatility, the hedge ratios obtained would be fairly close if we used currency movements in the regression instead of futures return.

Of course, this procedure requires historical data on the portfolio and will work well only if the estimated regression coefficients are stable over time.

Insuring and Hedging with Options

Two approaches are used for reducing currency risk exposure with options. The traditional method exploits the asymmetric risk–return characteristic of an option, so that it is used as an *insurance* vehicle. The second approach takes into account the dynamics of the relationship between the option premium and the underlying exchange rate. This second approach is closer to a *hedging* technique.

Insuring with Options

Many investors focus on the characteristics of options at expiration. Currency options are purchased in amounts equal to the principal to be hedged. It is not trivial to determine which options to use (calls or puts), because they involve the rate of exchange between two currencies. Consider a U.S. investor with £1 million of British assets. Let us assume that on the Philadelphia Stock Exchange he buys British pound puts for December with a strike price of 200 U.S. cents per pound. The contract size is £12,500. A British pound put gives him the right, but not the obligation, to sell British pounds at a fixed exercise (or strike) price with payment in dollars. Similarly, a British pound call gives him the right to buy British pounds with U.S. dollars. Note that a call to buy British pounds with U.S. dollars is equivalent to a put to sell U.S. dollars for British pounds. Options markets in some countries sometimes offer reverse contracts, so that investors must be sure they understand the position they are taking. In all cases, however, a good hedge implies buying options (puts or calls), not selling or writing them.

Suppose the spot exchange rate is $2.00 per pound. The strike price for the December put is 200 cents per pound (or $2.00 per pound), and the premium is 6 cents per pound. The investor must buy puts for £1 million, or 80 contracts. In this traditional approach, puts are treated as insurance devices. If the pound drops below $2.00 at expiration, a profit will be made on the put that exactly offsets the currency loss on the portfolio. If the pound drops to $1.90, the gain on the puts at expiration is

$$80 \times 12{,}500 \times (2.00 - 1.90) = \$100{,}000$$

The advantage of buying options rather than futures is that options simply expire if the pound appreciates rather than depreciates. For example, if the British pound moves up to $2.20, the futures contract will generate a loss of $200,000, nullifying the currency gain on the portfolio of assets. This does not happen with options that simply expire. Of course, investors must pay a price for this asymmetric risk structure, namely, the premium, which is the cost of having this insurance.

Note that the cost of the premium prevents a perfect hedge. In the previous example, the net profit on the put purchase equals the gain at expiration minus the premium. If we call V_0 the number of pounds, P_0 the premium per £, and K the strike (or exercise) price, the net dollar profit on the put at the time of exercise t is

$$\text{Net dollar profit} = V_0(K - S_t) - V_0P_0 \text{ when } K > S_t$$
$$= -V_0P_0 \text{ otherwise} \quad (11.15)$$

That is, when $K > S_t$, we have net dollar profit = £ quantity × (Exercise price − Spot price) − £ quantity × Premium per pound, but the investor loses the premium otherwise.

Hence, if the pound drops to \$1.90, the net dollar profit is

$$£1{,}000{,}000 \times (\$2.00/£ - \$1.90/£) - £1{,}000{,}000 \times \$0.06/£ = \$40{,}000$$

This profit does not cover the currency loss on the portfolio (equal to roughly \$100,000), because the option premium cost \$60,000. An alternative solution is to buy out-of-the-money puts with a lower exercise price and a lower premium. But with those, exchange rates would have to move that much more before a profit could be made on the options. In general, what is gained in terms of a lower premium is lost in terms of a lower strike price for the put option.

In fact, this approach does not allow for a good currency hedge except when variations in the spot exchange rate swamp the cost of the premium. Instead, this approach uses options as insurance contracts, and the premium is regarded as a sunk cost. Note, however, that options are usually resold on the market rather than left to expire; when the option is resold, part of the initial insurance premium is recovered. On the other hand, the approach still exploits the greatest advantage of options, namely, that an option can be allowed to expire if the currency moves in a favorable direction. Options protect a portfolio in case of adverse currency movements, as do currency futures, and maintain its performance potential in case of favorable currency movements, whereas futures hedge in both directions. The price of this asymmetric advantage is the insurance cost implicit in the time value of the option. To summarize, using options allows us to insure a portfolio against currency losses, rather than hedge it, and the option premium is the insurance cost. The use of currency options is illustrated in Example 11.4.

Dynamic Hedging with Options

Listed options are traded continually, and positions are usually closed by reselling the option in the market instead of exercising it. The profit is therefore completely dependent on market valuation. The dynamic approach to currency-option hedging recognizes this fact and is based on the relationship between changes in option premiums and changes in exchange rates.

The definition of a full currency-option hedge is simple and similar to the one given previously. A full hedge is a position in which every dollar loss from currency

EXAMPLE 11.4 INSURING WITH OPTIONS

You are a U.S. investor holding a portfolio of European assets worth €1 million. The current spot exchange rate is \$1 = 1 euro but you fear a depreciation of the euro in the short term. The three-month forward exchange rate is \$0.9960 = 1 euro. You are quoted the option premiums for calls euro and puts euro with a three-month maturity. These are options to buy (call) or sell (put) one euro at the dollar exercise price mentioned for each option. The contract size on the CME is €125,000. The quotations are as follows:

Euro Options (All Prices in U.S. Cents per Euro)

Strike	Call Euro	Put Euro
105	0.50	6.50
100	2.10	3.00
95	6.40	0.50

You decide to use options to insure your portfolio.

1. Should you buy (or sell) calls (or puts)? What quantity?
2. You decide to buy at-the-money puts, puts 100 (strike price of 100 U.S. cents) for €1 million. Suppose that you can borrow the necessary amount of dollars to buy these puts at a zero interest rate. Calculate the result at maturity of your strategy, assuming that the euro value of your portfolio remains at €1 million.
3. You have the choice of three different strike prices. What is the relative advantage of each option? What is the advantage relative to hedging, using forward currency contracts?

SOLUTION

1. To insure, you need to buy options. Here, you want to be able to translate euros at a fixed exchange rate, so you should buy euro puts for €1 million, or eight contracts.
2. You buy at-the-money puts on €1 million. The cost (premium) is equal to

   $$€1{,}000{,}000 \times \$0.03/€ = \$30{,}000$$

   If the euro rises in value, the put will expire worthless. If the euro depreciates, the gain on the option (per euro) will be equal to the difference between \$1 and the spot exchange rate at maturity (in dollars per euro). For example, if the spot exchange rate is \$0.90 = 1 euro, the gain on the puts will be

   $$€1{,}000{,}000 \times (\$1/€ - \$0.90/€) = \$100{,}000$$

But the original portfolio is now worth only $900,000 (€1,000,000 × 0.90). The net result is a dollar portfolio value equal to

$900,000 − $30,000 + $100,000 = $970,000

The simulation of the dollar value of the position for a different value of the exchange rate at maturity is given in the first column of the following table. The portfolio is insured for down movements in the euro and benefits from up movements. But the cost of the insurance premium has to be deducted in all cases.

Exchange Rate at Maturity (U.S. Cents per Euro)	Using Puts 100	Using Puts 105	Using Puts 95	Hedging with Forward
110	1,070,000	1,035,000	1,095,000	996,000
105	1,020,000	985,000	1,045,000	996,000
100	970,000	985,000	995,000	996,000
95	970,000	985,000	945,000	996,000
90	970,000	985,000	945,000	996,000

3. The preceding table simulates the results of using the various options as well as the forward. An "expensive" option (in-the-money, put 105) gives better downside protection at the expense of a lesser profit potential in case of an appreciation of the euro. A "cheap" option (out-of-the-money, put 95) provides less downside protection but a larger profit potential. Using forward contracts freezes the value of the portfolio at $996,000. You are well protected on the downside, but you cannot benefit from an appreciation of the euro. You will decide on the strategy, depending on your scenario for the euro exchange rate. If a depreciation of the euro seems very likely, you will hedge; if a depreciation seems very unlikely, you will buy out-of-the-money options, which are the cheapest. The other two strategies lie in between.

movement on a portfolio of foreign assets is covered by a dollar gain in the value of the options position.

We know that an option premium is related to the underlying exchange rate, but in a complex manner. Exhibit 11.4 shows the relationship we usually observe for a put. Beginning with a specific exchange rate, say, £:$ = 2.00, a put premium can go up or down in response to changes in the exchange rate. The slope of the curve at point A denotes the elasticity of the premium in response to any movements in the dollar exchange rate. In Exhibit 11.4, the premium is equal to 6 cents when the exchange rate is 200 U.S. cents per pound, and the slope of the tangent at point A equals −0.5. This slope is usually called delta (δ).

In this example, a good hedge would be achieved by buying two pound puts for every pound of British assets. One pound put is defined here as a put option on

EXHIBIT 11.4

Value of Pound Puts in Relation to the Exchange Rate

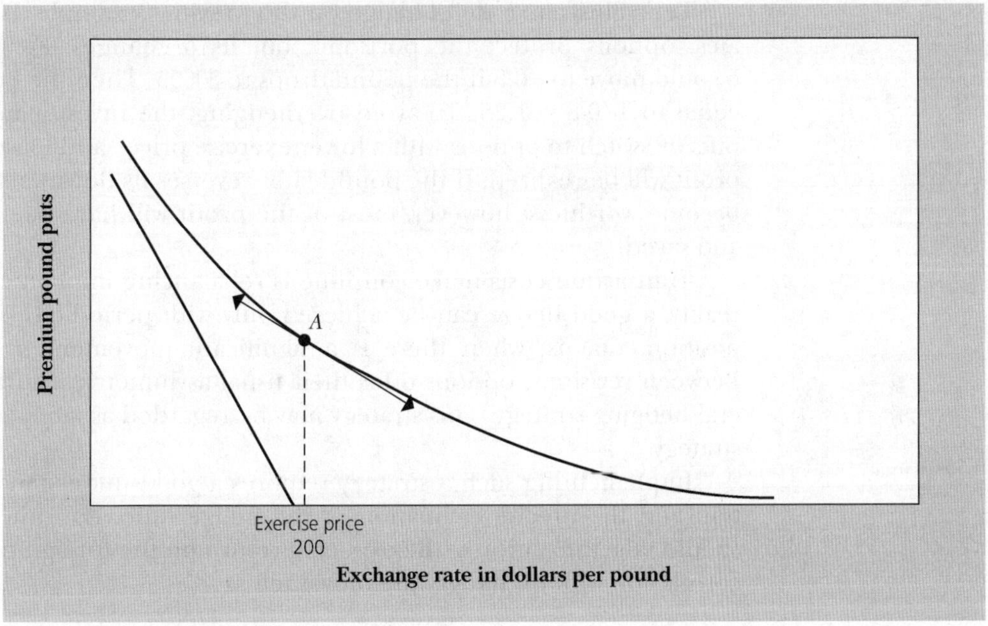

one unit of British currency. One contract includes several pound puts, depending on the contract size. If the pound depreciated by 1 U.S. cent, each put would go up by approximately 0.5 cents, offsetting the currency loss on the portfolio. In general, if n pound put options are purchased, the gain on the options position is

$$\text{Options gain} = n(P_t - P_0) \tag{11.16}$$

where P_t is the put value at time t, and P_0 is the put value at time zero. For small movements in the exchange rate,

$$P_t - P_0 = \delta(S_t - S_0) \tag{11.17}$$

Hence, the gain on the options position is

$$\text{Options gain} = n(P_t - P_0) = n \times \delta \times (S_t - S_0) \tag{11.18}$$

Assuming that the value of the portfolio in foreign currency remains constant at V_0, the gain (loss if negative) on the portfolio in domestic currency is equal to

$$\text{Portfolio gain} = V_0 \times (S_t - S_0) \tag{11.19}$$

A good currency hedge is obtained by holding $n = -V_0/\delta$ options. The hedge ratio is equal to $-1/\delta$. The profit on the options position offsets the currency loss on the portfolio. In the example, the hedge ratio is equal to two as $\delta = -0.5$. One should buy two pound puts for every pound of portfolio value.

We must emphasize that δ and the hedge ratio vary with the exchange rate, so that the number of options held must be adjusted continually. This strategy is called the *delta hedge.*

Let's illustrate a delta hedge on the previous example. If the pound depreciates, options protect the portfolio, but its δ changes. For example, the slope δ could move to -0.8 if the pound drops to \$1.95. Then the hedge ratio should be equal to $1/0.8 = 1.25$. To avoid overhedging, the investor must either sell some puts or switch to options with a lower exercise price (and lower δ); in both cases, a profit will be realized. If the pound later reverses its downward trend, the puts will become worthless; however, most of the profit will have been realized previously and saved.

Transaction costs make continuous rebalancing impractical and expensive. In reality, a good hedge can be achieved only with periodic revisions in the options position, that is, when there is a significant movement in the exchange rate. Between revisions, options offer their usual asymmetric insurance within the general hedging strategy. This strategy may be regarded as a mixed hedging insurance strategy.

Implementing such a strategy requires a good understanding of option valuation and the precise estimation of the hedge ratio. As with futures, the strategy should take into account the expected return on the foreign portfolio, as well as its correlation with exchange rate movements.

Implementation

Hedging strategies with options can be more sophisticated than those with forwards or futures for two reasons: The hedge ratio of options fluctuates but is constant for futures; and an investor can play with several maturities and exercise prices with options only.

A hedging strategy can combine futures and options.[6] Futures markets are very liquid and have low transaction costs. Options offer the advantage of an asymmetric risk structure but have higher costs, in terms of both the fair price for this insurance risk structure and their transaction costs.

If a hedging decision is necessary because an investor faces an increasing volatility in exchange rates and doesn't have a clear view of the direction of change, currency options are a natural strategy. In the scenario described at the beginning of this chapter, Australian elections created uncertainties about the future of the Australian dollar. In that case, options would have allowed the investor to hedge a drop in the Australian dollar while maintaining the opportunity to profit in case it rose.

Where the direction of a currency movement is clearly forecasted, currency futures provide a cheaper hedge. In setting the hedge, however, investors should take into account the expected return on the portfolio and its correlation with currency movements.

---

6 For a detailed description of currency options strategies, see the *Currency Options Strategy Manual* by the Chicago Mercantile Exchange, as well as various brochures prepared by options exchanges.

Other Methods for Managing Currency Exposure

Many methods are used to reduce currency exposure and to take positions in foreign markets without incurring excessive exchange risk. First, an investor can rearrange a portfolio so as to increase its risk level in a foreign market without increasing its currency exposure. For stocks, this means buying equities with higher betas (relative to the market index) and selling those with lower betas. This makes the portfolio more sensitive to local market movements without increasing its sensitivity to currency fluctuations. For bonds, this means adjusting the duration of the foreign portfolio to increase the portfolio's sensitivity to foreign interest rates without increasing its currency exposure.

An international portfolio manager who wants to invest in countries where the currency is expected to weaken has a few choices. She can buy common stock outright and hedge the exchange risk with currency futures or options, or buy options on the stock. For example, a U.S. investor may want to buy call options on the British firm ABC rather than ABC shares. The reason is simple: If ABC stock goes up by the same percentage as the British pound drops, the dollar value of a direct investment in ABC stock will remain unchanged. On the other hand, options on ABC will yield both a pound profit and a dollar profit. With options, currency fluctuations affect mostly the translation of the profit into dollars, not the principal. The price quotations given in Exhibit 11.5 illustrate how this strategy works.

The dollar profit of buying one share of ABC is zero because the currency loss on the principal offsets the capital gain in pounds. If the investor had instead purchased an option, the profit per share would have been $36 (= $52.50 – $16.50) despite the currency loss. Also, note that the initial investment in options is only $16.50 compared with $300 for shares. The difference could have been invested in U.S. cash instruments. Because the initial foreign currency investment in an option is very small, the currency impact is always limited compared with a direct investment in the asset.

A similar approach can be used to invest in an entire foreign market rather than only specific securities. This is done by buying stock index futures or options. Like any futures, stock index futures limit an investor's foreign currency exposure to the margin. Any realized profit can be repatriated immediately in the domestic currency. For example, a Swiss investor who is bullish on the U.S. stock market, but

EXHIBIT 11.5

Price Quotations on ABC Shares

	Prices December 1	Prices January 15	Price Variation (%)
Dollars per pound	1.50	1.25	
Pounds per dollar	0.667	0.800	+20
ABC stock (in pounds)	200	240	+20
ABC stock (in dollars)	300	300	0
ABC February 200 options (in pounds)	11.0	42	
ABC February 200 options (in dollars)	16.5	52.5	

EXAMPLE 11.5 · BUYING STOCK INDEX FUTURES

A European portfolio manager wishes to increase her exposure to Japanese stocks by €10 million, without taking much foreign exchange risk. Futures contracts are available on the TOPIX index. Each contract is for ¥1,000 times the index. The current futures price of the TOPIX index is 1,000, and the spot exchange rate is ¥100 per euro. What strategy could she adopt using those contracts?

SOLUTION

She would buy TOPIX futures contracts to gain an overall exposure in the Japanese stock market corresponding to €10 million, or ¥1 billion at the current exchange rate. The number of contracts N to be bought is determined as follows:

$$N = \frac{\text{¥}1{,}000{,}000{,}000}{\text{Multiplier} \times \text{Index value}} = \frac{\text{¥}1{,}000{,}000{,}000}{\text{¥}1{,}000 \times 1{,}000} = 1{,}000 \text{ contracts}$$

The futures contracts are not exposed to currency risk. However, she also has to deposit a margin in yen that can be hedged against currency risk.

not on the U.S. dollar, can buy Standard & Poor's 500 Index futures. In addition, hedging the margin deposited in dollars against currency risk would provide the Swiss investor with complete currency protection. Stock index options can likewise be used. The use of stock index options is illustrated in Example 11.5. A similar strategy applies to bond investments. For example, a U.S. investor who is bullish on interest rates in the United Kingdom can buy gilt futures on the LIFFE rather than bonds, and thereby simultaneously hedge against exchange risk. Other alternatives include buying bond warrants.

Futures and options on foreign assets reduce currency exposure as long as an investor does not already own the assets in question. In addition, costs involved in taking such positions are less than those for actually buying foreign assets and hedging them with currency futures or options. On the other hand, if the assets are already part of a portfolio, more conventional methods of currency hedging are probably better, especially for assets that will remain in the portfolio for a long time.

Investors also should be aware of the currency impact on an investment strategy involving different types of instruments whose currency exposures are not identical. As an illustration, let's consider the following strategy. A U.S. investor buys Australian natural resource companies stock for A$1 million and sells stock index futures for the same amount to hedge the Australian stock market risk. The beta of this portfolio relative to the Australian market is assumed to be 1. The motivation for this strategy is the belief that natural resource stocks are undervalued relative to the Australian market. The U.S. investor believes that the portfolio will generate a positive alpha ("alpha strategy"). Such a position, which is long in stocks and short in futures, is not exposed to Australian stock market risk; however, it does require an Australian dollar net investment, and is therefore exposed to the risk of the Australian dollar. A depreciation of the Australian dollar would induce a currency loss in the stock position that would not be offset by a currency gain on the stock index futures.[7] This is illustrated in Example 11.6.

Several investment vehicles and strategies may be used either to take advantage of or to hedge against monetary factors. Many of these strategies have been discussed before, so we already know that they usually involve a combination of investments in money, capital, and speculative markets. For example, a British investor expecting a weak U.S. dollar and falling U.S. interest rates could buy long-term U.S. bonds, or zero coupons, to maximize the sensitivity of her portfolio

EXAMPLE 11.6 CURRENCY RISK FOR ALPHA STRATEGIES

On September 1, an American investor buys Australian natural resource companies stock for A$1 million and sells ASX stock index futures (December maturity) for the same amount to hedge the Australian stock market risk. The ASX contract has a multiplier of A$25. The current ASX futures price is 2,000. The investor sells 20 contracts.

The Australian dollar drops from 1.0 U.S. dollar on September 1 to 0.90 U.S. dollar on October 1. In the same period, the ASX index and the ASX futures price drop by 10 percent (in A$), while the portfolio only loses 7 percent (in A$). What is the profit or loss on this alpha strategy in Australian dollars and in U.S. dollars if the investor does not engage in currency hedging?

SOLUTION

Calculations are detailed in the following table (the margin deposit is neglected here). The investor would have realized a gain of A$30,000 corresponding to the 3 percent return difference between the portfolio and the market (alpha). If the US$/A$ exchange rate had remained stable at 1, this would have translated into a US$30,000 profit. Instead, the 10 percent depreciation of the Australian dollar induced a loss of 73,000 U.S. dollars. To reduce the impact of currency movements, the investor should have hedged the stock portfolio against currency risk.

	Futures Market	Stock Market
September 1 (A$:US$ = 1)	Sell 20 December ASX futures at 2,000	Buy natural resource stocks; cost = A$1,000,000, US$1,000,000
October 1 (A$:US$ = 0.9)	*Market declines 10%, but natural resource stocks decline 7%*	Sell natural resource stocks; proceeds = A$930,000,
	Buy 20 December ASX futures at 1,800	US$837,000
	Profit on futures = A$100,000, US$90,000	Loss on stocks = A$70,000, US$163,000
	Net loss on trade = US$73,000	

[7] As a matter of fact, there will even be an additional small currency loss in the initial margin deposited for the futures contracts.

EXHIBIT 11.6

A Strategy Matrix of Alternative Investments in the U.S. Dollar Fixed-Income Markets

Dollar strength

Group I

A. Long-maturity bonds
B. Long-maturity mortgage-related securities
C. CATS
D. Zero-coupon bonds
E. Money market plus bond options/futures/warrants
F. Bond warrants
G. Financial options—bull strategies
H. Financial futures—bull strategies
I. Currency options—$ bull strategies
J. Currency futures—$ bull strategies
Government yield curve arbitrage—bull strategies

Group II

A. Money market
B. Eurodollar FRNs
C. Repurchase agreements
D. "Cash and carry"
E. Hedged nondollar money market
F. Short-maturity bonds
G. Financial options—bear strategies
H. Financial futures—bear strategies
Government yield curve arbitrage—bear strategies
Currency options—$ bull strategies
Currency futures—$ bull strategies

Falling dollar interest rates

Rising dollar interest rates

Group IV

A. Hedged long-maturity bonds
B. GNMA forward plus base-currency money market
C. Reverse repos (overnight) plus base-currency money market
D. Government yield curve arbitrage—bull strategies
CATS
Zero-coupon bonds
Bond warrants
Financial options—bull strategies
Financial futures—bull strategies
Currency options—$ bear strategies
Currency futures—$ bear strategies

Group III

A. Hedged money market
B. Hedged Eurodollar FRNs
C. Reverse repos to maturity plus base-currency money market (for loss-constrained portfolios)
D. Currency options—$ bear strategies
E. Currency futures—$ bear strategies
F. Government yield curve arbitrage—bear strategies
Financial options—bear strategies
Financial futures—bear strategies

Dollar weakness

Securities/strategies are generally listed with the more traditional, or less risky, at the top of each group; the more highly leveraged, or risky, are toward the bottom of the list. In some instances, the same instruments/strategies appear in more than one quadrant. In such cases, they appear only with a code letter in that quadrant where they are especially appropriate. They appear without a code letter in the other quadrants.

Source: J. Hanna and P. Niculescu. "The Currency and Interest Rate Strategy Matrix: An Investment Tool for Multicurrency Investors," Bond Market Research, Salomon Brothers Inc., September 1982. Reprinted with permission.

to U.S. interest rate movements and, at the same time, to hedge against exchange risk with currency futures or options. A matrix of alternative investments in the U.S. dollar fixed-income markets is given in Exhibit 11.6. Each quadrant represents a specific scenario concerning U.S. interest rates and the U.S. dollar. Group I, for example, represents a set of strategies designed to capitalize on a strong U.S. dollar and falling dollar interest rates.

The purpose in outlining strategies is to help an investor to take advantage of his specific forecasts with respect to interest rates and currencies. Of course, the actual performance of these strategies depends on the accuracy of the investor's forecasts. A similar strategy matrix can be designed for nondollar investments, although the absence of speculative markets in some currencies sometimes limits the range of strategies an investor can choose.

Strategic and Tactical Currency Management

Currency management must be addressed at the strategic and tactical level. Investors must decide on the foreign currency exposure they wish to retain in the long run. This is a strategic policy decision, where a "neutral" allocation is decided in the absence of specific priors on currencies. Such a policy results in a neutral or benchmark hedge ratio for the long run. In the short run, the amount of currency hedging can deviate from this benchmark based on tactical considerations. Tactical management of the currency exposure is often delegated to currency overlay managers. Some investors even regard currency as a special asset class with attractive risk–return characteristics.

Strategic Hedge Ratio

Investors must decide on the amount of currency exposure that should be hedged in their strategic allocation. For private investors, the approach to currency management is specified in the investment policy statement. For institutional investors, the strategic currency decision takes the form of a benchmark hedge ratio assigned to managers. Unfortunately, theory does not provide a clear-cut answer for the optimal hedge ratio to be used (see Chapters 4 and 9). In the absence of simple, widely accepted recommendations for a passive benchmark, simple hedging rules with a fixed hedge ratio are commonly adopted.

A traditional approach is simply to choose the hedging policy that minimizes the variance (risk) of the international portfolio. With the additional assumption that the correlation between asset returns and currency returns is small and unstable, this choice leads to a benchmark hedge ratio of 100 percent. All currency risk should be hedged. Basically, currency risk is treated as additional uncertainty with unpredictable return; it should be eliminated to the extent possible. Several large institutional investors use such a benchmark hedge ratio (e.g., CalPERS in 2007). However, several factors could be taken into account to determine the benchmark hedge ratio.

Total Portfolio Risk The traditional approach is to focus solely on the risk of the international segment of the total portfolio. But currencies provide an element of diversification to domestic assets. The contribution of currency risk should be measured at the level of the total portfolio (domestic and international investments), not at the level of international investments taken in isolation. It is often claimed that currency risk does not add a significant amount of uncertainty to the total portfolio when the international allocation is small (typically 10%). So the optimal passive hedge ratio is likely to depend on the proportion of international assets in the total portfolio: The lower the proportion of international assets, the lower the benchmark hedge ratio.

Asset Types Different asset prices react differently to currency movements. Correlation between asset returns and currency returns can be different across asset types. Stock prices from emerging countries are more sensitive to the value of the local currency than stock prices from developed countries. International bond portfolios could justify a different benchmark hedge ratio than international equity portfolios. The lower the correlation between portfolio return and currency movements, the lower the benchmark hedge ratio should be.

Investment Horizon It is often stated that exchange rates revert to fundamentals over the long run, so currency risk tends to diminish over long horizons. Hence, long-term investors should worry less about currency risk and possibly adopt a no-hedging policy. But, as referenced in Chapter 3, empirical work indicates that it might take a very long time for exchange rates to revert to fundamentals. The longer the investor's time horizon, the lower the benchmark hedge ratio should be.

Prior Beliefs on Currencies Some investors believe that their own base currency is structurally weak (strong). This would lead them to adopt a lesser (higher) hedge ratio. In the old days (e.g., 1960s and 1970s), currencies like the French franc or British pound were regarded as depreciating currencies, and few investors from those countries considered any amount of currency hedging.

Costs There are two components in hedging cost. The first one is related to trading, namely, transaction costs in the form of fees, commissions, and bid–ask spreads. Currency hedging entails rather small transaction costs but poses a cumbersome administrative burden. The administrative and monitoring tasks should not be underestimated. The hedging policy is dynamic; contracts in many currencies have to be rolled over periodically and adjusted to changes in the asset portfolio. There is also the need for active multicurrency cash management as margins change and profits/losses are realized at contract expirations. Some money managers believe that removing currency risk is not worth the cost and effort. The second cost component is the interest differential, as described in earlier chapters. To hedge, one has to sell foreign currencies forward at their forward price, which differs from the spot exchange rate used to value assets. For

EXHIBIT 11.7

Distribution of Benchmark Hedge Ratio for Investors from Different Base Currencies

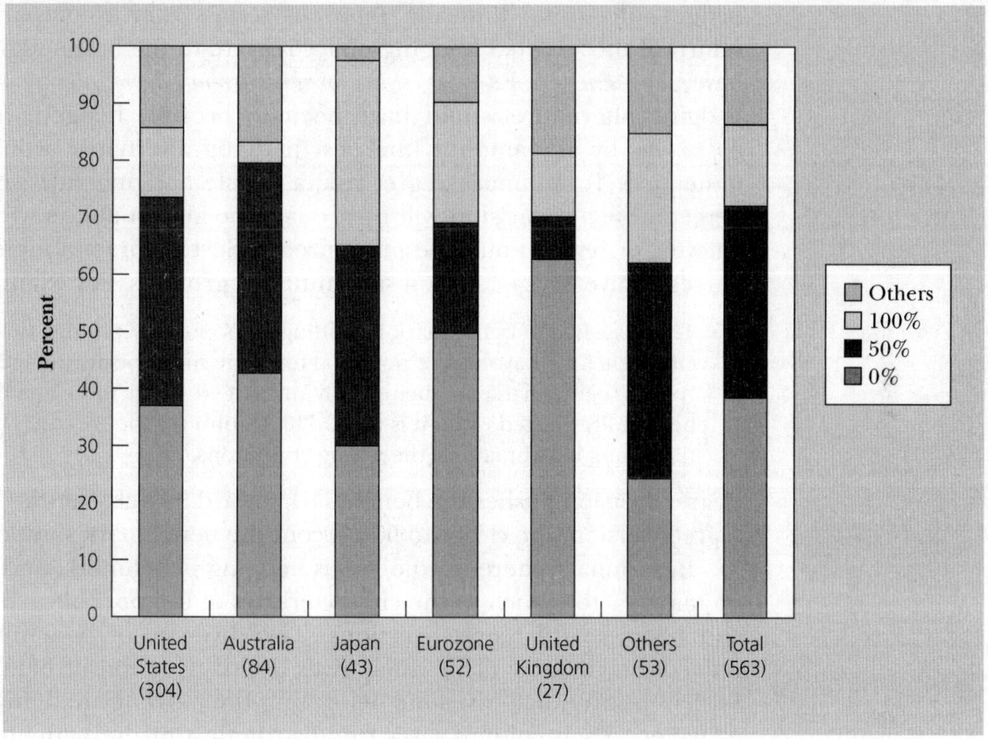

Source: Based on Harris, L., "Is There Still Alpha to Be Gained in Active Currency Management?" Russell/Mellon, 2005.

example, when a Japanese investor hedges her U.S. assets against currency risk, she sells dollars forward against yen and must pay the U.S. dollar interest rate while receiving the yen interest rate. The difference (or basis) is the spread between the two interest rates. In 2007, the interest rate spread between the United States and Japan was on the order of 4 percent. This is not a transaction cost, but it is still a sure cost to be borne by a hedger. Hedging will become attractive only if the actual dollar depreciation is larger than this basis. Up to 2007, Japan has structurally been a low-interest-rate country, making foreign currency hedging less attractive for Japanese investors.[8] In general, the higher the perceived costs of hedging, the lower the benchmark hedge ratio should be.

Is Regret the Proper Measure for Currency Risk? Currencies are an emotional investment. A wrong hedging decision can lead to a vast amount of regret. For example, a U.S. investor who decided not to hedge currency risk would have incurred a currency loss of some 40 percent on Eurozone assets from late 1998 to

[8] This is a different argument from the forecast that the yen might be "temporarily" overvalued (undervalued), leading to a tactical decision to decrease (increase) the hedge ratio used by Japanese investors.

late 2000, with huge regret at not having been fully hedged. Conversely, a fully hedged investor would have missed the 50 percent appreciation of the euro from late 2001 to late 2004; again, there is a huge regret at not having made the "right" hedging decision.[9] Basically, *regret risk* stems from a comparison of the ex post return of the adopted hedging policy relative to the best hedging policy that could have been chosen. Ex post, *if the foreign currency depreciates* by any amount, the best hedging alternative would have been to be fully hedged. *If the foreign currency appreciates* by any amount, the best hedging alternative would have been to be unhedged. To minimize regret risk, a simple hedging rule would be to hedge 50 percent. Such a decision will turn out to be almost always wrong ex post, but the amount of regret would be minimized.[10] Several practitioners have justified a 50 percent naïve hedge ratio on such intuitive grounds. For example:

> The 50% hedge benchmark is gaining in popularity around the world as it offers specific benefits. It avoids the potential for large underperformance that is associated with "polar" benchmark, i.e. being fully unhedged when the Canadian dollar is strong or being fully hedged when it is weak. This minimizes the "regret" that comes with holding the wrong benchmark in the wrong conditions.[11]

Regret aversion pushes the benchmark toward 50 percent; the higher the investor's regret aversion, the closer to 50 percent the benchmark should be.

In summary, there is no obvious hedging benchmark, and the choice depends on many factors, such as the characteristics of the portfolio, the investor's horizon, and his risk and regret aversions. The diversity of benchmark hedge ratios is reflected in Exhibit 11.7, which gives the distribution of benchmark hedge ratios for 563 institutional investors delegating the currency hedging decision to overlay managers. Each column gives the distribution of the benchmark hedge ratio for investors from a given base currency, that is, a region (e.g., the first column is the distribution for U.S. investors) as well as the number of accounts in that base currency. The last column gives the distribution of all accounts. The 0 percent, 50 percent, and 100 percent hedging policies are the most common benchmarks, but their acceptance varies across investors' country of residence.

Currency Overlay

The currency management of the international portfolio is often delegated to a specialized manager called the *currency overlay manager.* This decision is based on the assumption that the primary manager of the international assets does not have the currency expertise of the currency overlay specialist. The composition of the portfolio is periodically transferred to the currency overlay manager, who decides

---

[9] Furthermore, selling short an appreciating foreign currency leads to cash losses on the forward position that have to be covered by the sale of assets—a forced decision that is highly visible, painful, and easily criticized.

[10] Michenaud and Solnik (2006) propose a modelization of optimal currency hedging under risk and regret aversion. See also Gardner and Willoud (1995) and Statman (2005).

[11] Chrispin (2004) p.2.

on the positions taken in currencies and manages currency risk. In the currency overlay approach, currencies are regarded as financial prices that require the expertise of a specialist. Note that the currency overlay manager could be an external manager or simply a specialized team among the organization managing the portfolio. A client who uses several managers for an international portfolio can delegate the management of the aggregate currency position to a single currency overlay manager.

The role of the currency overlay manager is to manage currency risks within the existing portfolio, hedging part or all of the currency exposure of the international portfolio. It is not to take naked speculative positions in currencies. Typically, the client assigns to the currency overlay manager a benchmark hedge ratio that reflects the investor's desired neutral currency exposure. The tactical currency management on the portfolio is delegated to the currency overlay manager. The client also sets some parameters indicating how much an active currency overlay manager can deviate from the assigned benchmark. This is done in the forms of bounds on the actual hedge ratio used by the currency overlay manager or a maximum level of tracking error relative to the benchmark. Other parameters include the set of currencies and instruments that can be used by the manager.

Several types of tactical approaches are used in currency overlay.

Management of the Currency Risk Profile Exchange rate movements are assumed to be unpredictable and no attempt is made to forecast future returns. But currency risk is managed through dynamic hedging or option-based approaches. The strategy attempts to create an asymmetric risk profile protecting from downside losses while allowing capture of some upside potential. This is pure active risk management.

Technical Approach The currency markets are the most liquid markets in the world. But many of the major market participants are very different from those found on equity and bond markets. These market participants do not follow the usual paradigm of return and risk optimization. For example, central banks intervene to manage their cash positions in various currencies and to satisfy some inflation or balance of payments objectives. Corporate treasurers participate when business transactions create cash inflows or outflows in foreign currency. In many cases, the supply and demand for currencies that affect the exchange rate are non-profit-driven and may result in some temporary market inefficiencies in the price quoted for currencies. Some currency overlay managers claim that they can exploit these inefficiencies. They develop models that attempt to identify predictable price patterns in exchange rates and in their volatility. These technical models are used to generate superior returns within controlled currency risk management.

Fundamental Approach Economic analysis could help detect undervalued or overvalued currencies. We discussed various forecasting methods in Chapters 2 and 3. The basic idea is that economic data can help predict future exchange rate movements. A fair value is determined for each currency, and the hedge ratio is adjusted upward (downward) when a foreign currency trades above (below) its fair value. Of course, sophisticated models have been developed that incorporate both the technical and fundamental approach in a risk-controlled framework. Ultimately, the success of these strategies depends on the predictability of exchange rates.

Currency overlay is a complex process in which costs must be minimized. While diversified equity portfolios are invested in a large number of countries and currencies, liquid currency forward and option contracts exist only for major currencies. It is feasible to hedge the currency risk on investments in many emerging markets, but the cost can be significant and the instruments are often illiquid. Hence, active currency managers typically use only a few major currencies and often resort to cross-hedging. For example, hedging in euros could be used to cover investments in Swedish kronor.

It should be stressed that an investment management approach that separates the asset allocation decision from currency exposure decisions is not ideal. Jorion (1994) proposed a mean-variance analysis of currency overlay. He found that currency overlays are suboptimal. It is better to optimize simultaneously the asset allocation and the currency hedging decision rather than to adopt a two-step currency overlay approach. In the two-step, suboptimal approach, asset allocation is optimized first (without taking currencies into consideration) and currency hedging is optimized second, assuming the asset allocation as given (currency overlay). But if the correlation between currency movements and asset returns is small, the difference between the optimal and the two-step approach will be small in terms of risk optimization.

Currencies as an Asset Class

Currency overlay is restricted to the management of the currency exposure of an existing portfolio. The next step is to offer funds that specialize in currency management. The definition of what constitutes an asset class is beyond the scope of this book. But there is no doubt that the currency market is huge and liquid, and that the drivers of exchange rates are somewhat different from those of other asset classes. The correlation between currency movements and equity returns is low. Even the correlation between currency movements and bond returns is relatively low. Hence, managers are now offering hedge funds and products that solely invest in currency instruments. They apply strategies outlined above to generate superior returns (alpha) with low correlation with other asset classes. But the objectives are somewhat different from those of a traditional currency overlay manager:

- Traditional currency overlay managers focus primarily on hedging an existing portfolio against currency risks. They manage the currency exposure of a portfolio to generate an attractive risk profile compared to a passive hedging benchmark.
- Currency funds typically use a LIBOR or other cash benchmark, on an absolute return basis. They will use currencies to generate a positive alpha. These funds are sometimes called *currency for alpha* funds.

Summary

- Currency futures, forwards, and option contracts are used primarily to protect a portfolio against currency risks. Managers adapt their hedging strategies to their expectations of an asset's performance in foreign currency and of exchange rate movements.
- The basic approach to the use of currency futures contracts is to hedge the foreign currency value of the foreign asset. Managers would sell short currencies in the amount of an asset's value. Ideally, investors should hedge the future value of an investment, taking into account the expected price change and income.
- The hedge ratio is the ratio of the size of the short futures position in foreign currency to the value of the portfolio in foreign currency.
- The covariance between the asset return and the exchange rate movement should be considered. A minimum-variance hedge sets a hedge ratio that minimizes both translation risk and economic risk. Translation risk comes from the fact that the principal value of a foreign asset is translated at the exchange rate, so that a movement in the exchange rate affects the domestic currency value of the asset. Economic risk comes from the fact that the foreign currency value of a foreign asset can be influenced by a movement in the exchange rate.
- The interest rate differential is the forward basis, the percentage difference between the futures and the spot exchange rates. Basis risk affects the quality of currency hedging.
- Because a currency hedge must use futures (or forward) exchange rates, not spot exchange rates, the return on the hedged asset will differ over time from the return on the asset measured in foreign currency by the interest rate differential.
- Hedging strategies for multicurrency portfolios usually involve the use of futures in the major currencies. The instability of the estimated hedge ratios reduces the effectiveness of hedging strategies.
- Currency options are used for their asymmetric risk–return characteristics. They provide insurance against adverse currency movements while retaining the profit potential in case of a favorable currency movement. There is a cost associated with this attractive insurance characteristic. More dynamic hedging strategies can also be implemented using currency options. They require option valuation models to estimate the hedge ratio.
- Other methods can be used to manage the currency exposure of international portfolios. Leveraged instruments on foreign assets, such as futures and options, have little currency exposure, because the capital invested in foreign currency is very small compared with the value of the underlying asset. The impact of a currency movement on a combined position of several assets and contracts should be studied carefully.
- Currency management must be addressed at the strategic and tactical level. Investors must decide on the foreign currency exposure they wish to retain in

the long run. This is a strategic policy decision, where a "neutral" allocation is decided in the absence of specific priors on currencies. Many factors can affect the choice of a strategic hedge ratio.

- A currency overlay approach is sometimes used in international investment management. Some clients delegate the currency management of the international portfolio to a specialized currency overlay manager. This strategy is based on the assumption that the primary manager of the international assets does not have the currency expertise of the currency overlay specialist. The composition of the portfolio is periodically transferred to the currency overlay manager, who decides on the positions taken in currencies and manages currency risk.

Problems

Note: In these problems, the notation / is used to mean "per." For example, ¥158/$ means "¥158 per $".

1. A U.S. investor holds a portfolio of Japanese stocks worth ¥160 million. The spot exchange rate is ¥158/$, and the three-month forward exchange rate is ¥160/$. The investor fears that the Japanese yen will depreciate in the next month but wants to keep the Japanese stocks. What position can the investor take based on three-month forward exchange rate contracts? List all the factors that will make the hedge imperfect.
2. Consider a German portfolio manager who holds a portfolio of U.S. stocks currently worth $5 million. In order to hedge against a potential depreciation of the dollar, the portfolio manager proposes to sell December futures contracts on the dollar that currently trade at €1.02/$ and expire in two months. The spot exchange rate is currently €0.974/$. A month later, the value of the U.S. portfolio is $5,150,000, and the spot exchange rate is €1.1/$, while the futures exchange rate is €1.15/$.
   a. Evaluate the effectiveness of the hedge by comparing the fully hedged portfolio return with the unhedged portfolio return.
   b. Calculate the return on the portfolio, assuming a 50 percent hedge ratio.
3. Consider a U.S. portfolio manager who holds a portfolio of French stocks currently worth €10 million. In order to hedge against a potential depreciation of the euro, the portfolio manager proposes to sell December futures contracts on the euro that currently trade at $1/€ and expire in two months. The spot exchange rate is currently $1.1/€. A month later, the value of the French portfolio is €10,050,000 and the spot exchange rate is $1.05/€, while the futures exchange rate is $0.95/€.
   a. Evaluate the effectiveness of the hedge by comparing the fully hedged portfolio return with the unhedged portfolio return.
   b. Calculate the return on the portfolio, assuming a 35 percent hedge ratio.
4. A Dutch investor holds a portfolio of Japanese stocks worth ¥160 million. The current three-month dollar/euro forward exchange rate is $1.2/€, and the current three-month $:¥ forward exchange rate is ¥160/$. Explain how the Dutch investor could hedge the €:¥ exchange risk, using $:¥ and €:$ forward contracts.
5. You are a U.S. investor and currently have a portfolio worth €100 million in German bonds. The current spot exchange rate is €2/$. The current one-year market interest rates are 6 percent in the euro area and 10 percent in the United States. One-year

currency options are quoted with a strike price of $0.50/€; a call on euros is quoted at $0.01 per euro, and a put on euros is quoted at $0.012 per euro. You are worried that inflation in euro area will cause a drop in the euro. You consider using forward contracts or options to hedge the currency risk.

a. What is the one-year forward exchange rate $:€?
b. Calculate the dollar value of your portfolio, assuming that its euro value stays at €100 million; use $:€ spot exchange rates equal in one year to 1.6, 1.8, 2, 2.2, and 2.4. First consider a currency forward hedge, then a currency option insurance.
c. What could make your forward hedge imperfect?

6. You are a Swiss investor who has $10 million in short-term dollar deposits. You are worried that the dollar will drop relative to the Swiss franc in the next month. You care only about the Swiss franc value of your assets. Currency options exist that would guarantee that the $10 million would be worth a minimum amount of Swiss francs in one month (in March), if the dollar dropped, but would benefit from a dollar appreciation. The March forward exchange rate is $0.7389/SFr (or SFr1.3534/$). The quotes for Swiss franc currency options in Chicago are as follows:

March SF Options (all prices in US$ per SFr)

Strike	Call SFr	Put SFr
0.73	0.0243	0.0154

a. What minimum portfolio value in SFr can you *guarantee* for March, using these options? Make the simplifying assumption that all interest rates are equal to zero and that you can buy exactly the desired number of SFr options. You must use some of the $10 million to get the options.
b. What would be the difference if you used forward contracts?

7. You are a U.S. investor who holds a portfolio of French stocks. The market value of the portfolio is €20 million, with a beta of 1.2 relative to the CAC index. In November, the spot value of the CAC index is 4,000. The exchange rate is $1.1/€. The dividend yield, euro interest rates, and dollar interest rates are all equal to 4 percent (flat yield curves).

a. You fear a drop in the French stock market (but not the euro). The size of CAC index contracts is €10 times the CAC index. There are futures contracts quoted with March delivery. How many contracts should you buy or sell to hedge the French stock market risk?
b. You are optimistic about the French stock market [different scenario from part (a)] but fear a depreciation of the euro. How many euros should you sell forward?
c. You have the following quotes in Chicago on euro options, maturity March. Should you buy or sell calls or puts to insure against currency risk? What is the premium?

March Euro Options (all prices in US$ per euro)

Strike	Call Euro	Put Euro
1.10	0.021	0.02

d. Calculate the result of your strategies (unhedged, hedged with March forward, insured with March options), assuming that your French stock portfolio is still worth €20 million in March. Simulate for different values of the spot €:$ in March, namely, €1 = $1, $1.1, $1.2.

8. The spot exchange rate is 10 Mexican pesos (MXP) per U.S. dollar. Today is November 4. The three-month interest rates are 12 percent in pesos and 8 percent in dollars. A Mexican peso call traded in Chicago with a strike price of $0.10 per peso has a premium of $0.005. The peso call gives the right to buy one peso for a strike price of $0.10. A Mexican peso put traded in Chicago with a strike price of $0.10 per peso has a premium of $0.0062. The size of the option contract is MXP 500,000. Both calls and puts can be exercised on February 4 (in three months).

a. What is the three-month forward exchange rate $:MXP?
b. You are Mexican and will receive $1 million U.S. on February 4. Should you buy or sell pesos forward to hedge your future dollar cash flow? How many pesos will you get on February 4 if you hedge?
c. Should you buy or sell peso calls or puts to insure your cash flow? Assuming that you have some cash available to buy the options, how many option contracts should you buy? Calculate the resulting peso cash flows on February 4 for spot exchange rates of 8, 9, 9.5, 10, 10.5, 11, and MXP12/$.

9. A U.S. investor is attracted by the high yield on British bonds but is worried about a British pound depreciation. The currency market data are as follows:

	United States	**United Kingdom**
Bond yield (%)	7	12
Three-month interest rate (%)	6	8
Spot exchange rate, £:$ = 2		

A bond dealer has repeatedly suggested that the investor purchase hedged foreign bonds. This strategy can be described as the purchase of foreign currency bonds (here, British pound bonds) with simultaneous hedging in the short-term forward or futures currency market. The currency hedge is rolled over when the forward or futures contract expires.

a. What is the current three-month forward exchange rate (£:$)?
b. Assuming a £1 million investment in British bonds, how would you determine the exact hedge ratio necessary to minimize the currency influence?
c. When will this strategy be successful (compared with a direct investment in U.S. bonds)?

10. Futures and forward currency contracts are not readily available for all currencies. However, many currencies are closely linked. For example, many European countries, which are not part of the euro, attempt to maintain a close link with the euro.

An American investor has a portfolio of Danish stocks that she wishes to hedge against currency risks. No futures contracts are traded on the Danish kroner, so she decides to use euro futures contracts traded in Chicago, because both countries belong to the European Union. Here are some quotes:

Value of the portfolio	DKK 100 million
Spot exchange rates	DKK6.6/$
	$1.10/€
Futures price (contract of €125,000)	$1.11/€

How many euro contracts should the U.S. investor trade?

11. Consider a U.S. investor who owns a portfolio of Japanese securities worth ¥160 million. In order to hedge currency risk, he considers buying currency puts on yen instead of selling futures contracts. In Philadelphia, a yen put with a strike price of $0.62 per 100 yen and three-month maturity is worth \$0.007 per 100 yen (0.007 cents per yen). The current exchange rate is ¥158/\$.

Assume that three months later the portfolio is still worth ¥160 million. Compare the results of the following two currency-hedging strategies for values of the exchange rate three months later of ¥140/\$, ¥150/\$, ¥158/\$, ¥170/\$, and ¥180/\$. In the first strategy, the investor sells ¥160 million forward; in the second strategy, he buys yen puts for ¥160 million.

12. On October 1, a Swiss investor decides to hedge a U.S. portfolio worth \$10 million against exchange risk, using Swiss franc call options. The spot exchange rate is SFr2.5/\$ or \$0.40/SFr. The Swiss investor can buy November Swiss francs calls with a strike price of \$0.40/SFr at a premium of \$0.01 per Swiss franc. The size of one contract is SFr62,500. The delta of the option is estimated at 0.5.

a. Reflecting this delta, how many Swiss franc calls should the investor buy to *hedge* (not insure) the U.S. portfolio against the SFr/\$ currency risk (*dynamic* or *delta* hedge)?

A few days later, the U.S. dollar has dropped to SFr2.439/\$, or \$0.41/SFr, and the dollar value of the portfolio has remained unchanged at \$10 million. The November 40 Swiss franc call is now worth \$0.016 per Swiss franc and has a delta estimated at 0.7.

b. What is the result of the hedge?
c. How should the hedge be adjusted?

13. You are a French investor holding a portfolio of U.S. stocks worth \$10 million. You wish to engage in a dynamic hedge of the €:\$ exchange risk by buying € calls. On April 1, a June 100 € call is quoted at \$0.02 per euro. This gives you the right to buy one euro for \$1 in June. The delta of this call is equal to 0.5. The spot exchange rate is \$1/€. The size of an option contract is €125,000.

a. How many € calls should you buy to get a good dynamic hedge?

A few days later, your portfolio is still worth \$10 million. The dollar, however, has dropped to \$1.1/€. The call is now worth \$0.11, and its delta is equal to 0.9.

b. What is the result, in euros, of your strategy?
c. Has the hedge resulted in a net gain or loss?
d. What should you do to rebalance your hedge?

14. Why is a purchase of a futures contract or an option on a foreign asset not exposed to much currency risk? Take the following example for a U.S. investor on the British stock market:

	November	December
FTSE 100 index	6,000	6,100
FTSE 100 December futures	6,030	6,100
FTSE Call December 6,050	20	50
\$/£ spot rate	2.00	1.80

The FTSE 100 is an index of the top one hundred British stocks. One FTSE futures contract has a multiplier of £10. The margin deposit is £1,500 per contract. FTSE options have a contract size of £10 times the index. What is the dollar amount of currency loss per index unit if the U.S. investor had bought

a. the index in the form of stocks (e.g., £6,000 worth of an FTSE index fund)?
b. a December futures on FTSE?
c. a December 6,050 FTSE call?

15. The current yield curve is much lower in the United States than in Great Britain. You read in the newspaper that it is unattractive for a U.S. investor to hedge currency risk on British assets. The same journal states that British investors should hedge the currency risk on their U.S. investments. What do you think?

16. Salomon Brothers proposes to investors a contract called a *range forward contract.* Here is an example of such a U.S. dollar/British pound contract:

The contract has a size of £100,000 and a maturity of three months. At maturity, the investor will purchase the pounds at a price that is a function of the spot exchange rate.

- If the spot exchange rate at maturity is less than $1.352/£, the investor will pay $1.352 to get one pound.
- If the spot exchange rate at maturity is between $1.352/£ and $1.470/£, the investor will pay the current spot exchange rate to get one pound.
- If the spot exchange rate at maturity is more than $1.470/£, the investor will pay $1.470 to get one pound.

Assume that you are a British exporter who will receive $10 million in three months that will have to be transferred into British pounds at the time. Currently, the spot and forward exchange rates are $1.4200/£ and $1.4085/£, respectively.

a. Explain why such a range forward contract could be attractive if you fear a depreciation of the dollar during the three months.
b. Explain why Salomon Brothers can sell such a contract at a very low price.

17. You are a British exporter who knows in December that you will receive $15 million in three months (March). The current spot exchange rate is $1.5/£, and the March forward exchange rate is also $1.5/£. Calls on the British pound are quoted by your bank for the exact amount that you desire, as follows:

March Sterling Options (all prices in $ per £)

Strike	Call £
1.50	0.03
1.55	0.015
1.60	0.005

Calculate the £ value of the $15 million received in three months, assuming that the £:$ spot exchange rate in March is equal to 1.3, 1.4, 1.5, 1.6, 1.7, and 1.8 dollar per pound. Perform this calculation under five different scenarios about your hedging decision in December:

- You do nothing.
- You hedge with forward contracts.
- You insure with calls 150.
- You insure with calls 155.
- You insure with calls 160.

Put all of these figures in a table, and discuss the relative advantages of the various strategies.

18. Consider a U.S. portfolio manager who invests £5,000,000 in shares of a U.K. company. In order to hedge the stock market risk, he sells FTSE stock index futures that expire in three months. The current price of the FTSE stock index futures contract is 4,098 with a multiplier of £10. The current exchange rate is $1.58/£. One month later, the investment in the U.K. company is worth £5,022,000. The FTSE stock index futures price is now 4,200 and the exchange rate is \$1.65/£.

a. Calculate the number of futures contracts that the portfolio manager must sell.
b. Calculate the profit or loss in dollar terms and pound terms.

19. Consider a French portfolio manager who invests \$10,000,000 in shares of a U.S. company. In order to hedge the stock market risk, he sells S&P 500 stock index futures that expire in three months. The current price of the S&P 500 stock index futures contract is 902 with a multiplier of \$250. The current exchange rate is €1.2/\$. One month later, the investment in the U.S. company is worth \$10,050,000. The S&P 500 stock index futures price is now 890, and the exchange rate is €0.98/\$.

1. Calculate the number of futures contracts that the portfolio manager must sell.
2. Calculate the profit-or-loss in euro terms and dollar terms.

20. The HFS Trustees have decided to invest in international equity markets and have hired Jacob Hind, a specialist manager, to implement this decision. He has recommended that an unhedged equities position be taken in Japan, providing the following comment and data to support his views:

Appreciation of a foreign currency increases the returns to a U.S. dollar investor. Because appreciation of the yen from 100¥/\$ to 98¥/\$ is expected, the Japanese stock position should not be hedged.

Market Rates and Hind's Expectations	**United States**	**Japan**
Spot rate (direct quote)	n/a	100
Hind's 12-month currency forecast	n/a	98
One-year Eurocurrency rate (% per annum)	6.00	0.80
Hind's 1-year inflation forecast (% per annum)	3.00	0.50

Assume that the investment horizon is one year and that there are no costs associated with currency hedging. State and justify whether Hind's recommendation should be followed. Show any calculations.

Bibliography

Adler, M., and Simon, D. "Exchange Rate Surprises in International Portfolios," *Journal of Portfolio Management*, Winter 1986.

Briys, E., and Solnik, B. "Optimal Currency Hedge Ratios and Interest Rate Risk," *Journal of International Money and Finance*, December 1992.

Chrispin, G. "Managing Currency Risk—The Canadian Perspective," *State Street Global Advisors, Essays and Perspectives*, 2004.

Dale, C. "The Hedging Effectiveness of Currency Futures Markets," *Journal of Futures Markets*, Spring 1981.

Eaker, M., and Grant, D. "Cross-Hedging Foreign Currency Risks," *Journal of International Money and Finance*, March 1987.

Gardner, G. W., and Wuilloud, T. "Currency Risk in International Portfolios: How Satisfying Is Optimal Hedging?" *Journal of Portfolio Management*, 21, 1995.

Grammatikos, T., and Saunders, A. "Stability and the Hedging Performance of Foreign Currency Futures," *Journal of Futures Markets,* Fall 1983.

Hanna, J., and Niculescu, P. "The Currency and Interest Rate Strategy Matrix: An Investment Tool for Multicurrency Investors," Bond Market Research, Salomon Brothers, September 1982.

Jorion, P. "Mean/Variance Analysis of Currency Overlays," *Financial Analysts Journal,* May–June 1994.

Kroner, K. F., and Sultan, J. "Time-Varying Distributions and Dynamic Hedging with Foreign Currency Futures," *Journal of Financial and Quantitative Analysis,* December 1993.

Michenaud, S., and Solnik, B. "Applying Regret Theory to Investment Choices: Currency Hedging Decisions," Working Paper, August 2006.

Statman, M. "Hedging Currencies with Hindsight and Regret," *Journal of Investing,* Summer 2005.

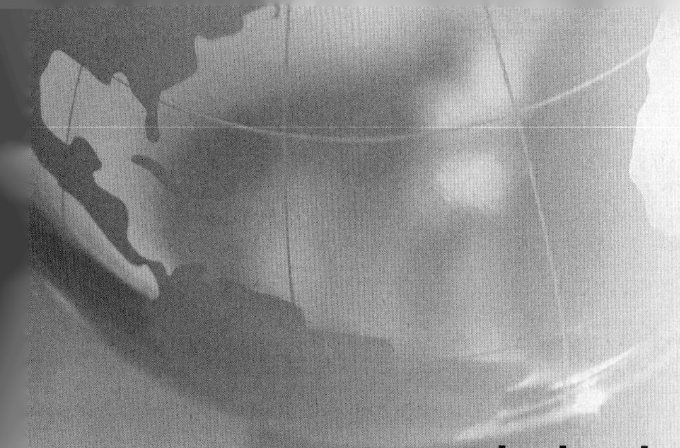

12

Global Performance Evaluation

LEARNING OUTCOMES

After completing this chapter, you will be able to do the following:

- Explain the three steps of global performance evaluation: measurement, attribution, and appraisal
- Calculate, explain, and contrast the following measures for computing a rate of return: money-weighted return and time-weighted return
- Explain why time-weighted returns should be used in performance evaluation and discuss the problems that arise when approximate methods are used
- Calculate and explain the effect of currency movements on the portfolio rate of return calculated in its base currency
- Explain the decomposition of portfolio return into yield, capital gains in local currency, and currency contribution, and calculate those components of portfolio return
- Explain the purpose of global performance attribution and calculate the contribution of market allocation, currency allocation, and security selection
- Interpret the results of performance attribution for a global portfolio
- Explain the impact of currency management on performance
- Explain the difficulties in calculating a multiperiod attribution and discuss various practical solutions
- Calculate and discuss total risk and tracking error for a portfolio
- Calculate and interpret the Sharpe ratio and the information ratio for a portfolio
- Explain how risk budgeting is used in global performance evaluation
- Discuss the various biases that may affect performance appraisal
- Discuss the characteristics of different global and international benchmarks used in performance evaluation

The management of a global portfolio is a complex task with numerous parameters to take into account. The portfolio's performance and risk can be attributed to many management decisions, including the choice of instruments, markets, currencies, and individual securities. This book has shown the wide variety of institutional features, investment techniques, and concepts that a capable international money manager must master. Given this complexity, a detailed and frequent evaluation of the performance and risk of global portfolios is required, for both the investment manager and the client. A money management firm typically has several portfolio managers with responsibility for a large number of accounts under diverse mandates. It is of the utmost importance for the firm to perform an in-house assessment of the performance of each account and manager, of the risks and bets taken, and of the areas in which expertise, or lack of expertise, has been demonstrated. Performance must be attributed to the various investment decisions of the manager. From an external viewpoint, clients wish to compare the performance of competing money managers and judge their investment skills; this requires that performance on managed accounts be analyzed in a comparable fashion and that proper risk adjustment be performed. This chapter deals with the principles, mathematics, and implementation of performance evaluation in a global context. By nature, performance evaluation is quite technical and requires equations. But each equation is illustrated by a simple example to facilitate comprehension of the calculations.

The first section of this chapter details the principles and objectives of *global performance evaluation* (*GPE*). Because performance evaluation can be quite complex in a global environment, a good understanding of the basic return measurement concepts is required, and some words of caution are in order. The second section details performance attribution in multicurrency, multiasset portfolios: The return relative to a benchmark is attributed to the major investment decisions. The final step of a GPE is to analyze investment skills. Performance appraisal, discussed in the third section, requires one to consider the risks taken to determine whether the manager has a true ability to add value. The final section deals with some implementation issues and discusses various performance standards, especially Global Investment Performance Standards (GIPS).

The Basics

Principles and Objectives

GPE can be separated into three components:

- Performance measurement
- Performance attribution
- Performance appraisal

Clients (individual investors, plan sponsors) and investment managers focus on different aspects of this process. GPE can be conducted by the investment manager using a proprietary system or some specialized software. It is also performed by consultants offering a GPE service. The latter service also allows one to compare performance with that of a universe of investment managers.

Performance Measurement The core of GPE is to calculate rates of return on the portfolio and its various segments. Performance is then measured by comparing these returns with those on preassigned benchmarks. Performance is a return relative to that of a benchmark. In a global context, it is important to be able to measure the return on various portfolio segments (e.g., European equity, yen bonds) both in the local currency of the investment and in the base currency of the investor. This is an added complexity compared with the performance measurement of domestic portfolios. *Performance measurement* is the GPE component by which returns are calculated over a measurement period for the overall portfolio and various segments.

Performance measurement should not be confused with accounting valuation. Multicurrency accounting systems keep track, on a daily basis, of all transactions, including forward commitments, and provide a valuation of the account based on current market prices from around the world and computed in one *base currency* (also called the *reference currency*). The base currency is the currency chosen by the investor to value the portfolio; for example, a British pension fund would use the British pound as base currency. Every item, including stocks, bonds, alternative investments, derivatives, and, of course, cash, is included in an accounting valuation.

GPE systems measure the return on a portfolio and various portfolio segments over a short *measurement period*, usually on a monthly basis but sometimes daily. These returns are then compounded over longer *performance evaluation periods* (a quarter, a year, or several years). A huge amount of valuation and transaction information is synthesized into a few return figures. So, the way rates of return are calculated to synthesize the information is of great importance (as we discuss later). The quality of data is an important issue that will affect the method used and the reliability of the results. Using short measurement periods (ideally, daily) allows one to generate more precise performance numbers but also better risk estimates.

At the end of the measurement process, one should be able to answer questions such as these three:

- What is the total return on the portfolio over a specific period, and its performance relative to a benchmark?
- What are the total returns on each segment of the portfolio, in local and base currencies, and the performance relative to their benchmarks?
- What is the volatility of the portfolio and its tracking error?

The major focus of performance measurement is to perform correct calculations of return.

Performance Attribution Managers and clients need to understand how the total performance was reached. *Performance attribution* is the GPE component by which the total portfolio performance is attributed to major investment decisions taken by the manager. For example, a manager is assigned the MSCI World index as benchmark for a global equity portfolio with the British pound as base currency. A country allocation different from that of the index could result in currency gains or losses, as well as market gains or losses relative to the index. Even with the same country weights, the manager could decide to favor some industries or investment styles worldwide; this decision could again result in superior return.

To quantify performance attribution, detailed calculations need to be performed, as illustrated in the next section. In particular, we need to account for exchange rate translation, a source of complexity in performance attribution. One should also try to attribute the total risk of the portfolio to major investment decisions, and again currency risk could be of importance.

At the end of the performance attribution process, one should be able to answer questions such as these:

1. What is the breakdown of the return in terms of capital gains, currency fluctuations, and income?
2. To what extent are returns explained by asset allocation, country weighting, industry weighting, investment style selection, currency selection and hedging, or individual security selection?
3. How is the total risk of the portfolio explained by the major investment decisions outlined in question 2?

Performance Appraisal Clients wish to know if their managers possess true investment skill. *Performance appraisal* is the GPE component by which some judgment is formulated on the investment manager's skills. It requires one to look at performance over longer horizons, taking into account the risks borne. Risk-adjusted measures are used.

The choice of benchmarks used to appraise performance is important, and again the multicurrency environment makes it a more difficult issue (e.g., should benchmarks be currency-hedged?). At the end of the performance appraisal process, one should be able to answer questions such as

- Has the manager provided a good risk-adjusted performance over some long-run horizon?
- How does the manager compare with a peer group (i.e., a universe of managers with similar investment objectives)?
- Is the performance due to luck, higher risks taken, or true investment skill?
- Is there evidence of unusual expertise and added value in a particular market (e.g., Japanese stocks or British bonds) or dimension (industry, style, currency overlay, etc.)?

The goal of GPE is ambitious and the conclusions drawn are of significant importance. Unfortunately, technical and conceptual problems arise, due in part to the quality of the data used as inputs to the analysis. These problems are present to some extent in a domestic performance evaluation, but they are magnified in an international setting, in which a detailed GPE requires the calculation of rates of return on various segments and in different currencies. The method used to calculate a rate of return is of significance.

Calculating a Rate of Return

The rate of return[1] is typically calculated on a short measurement period (say, one month) and then compounded over a performance period (say, one year). The first, and somewhat unexpected, problem encountered in performance evaluation is the method to be used in calculating a basic rate of return on a portfolio or on a portfolio segment for a specific measurement period.

The rate of return over a measurement period is easy to calculate if there are no cash flows in or out of the portfolio. Its return r is simply equal to the change in value over the period $(V_1 - V_0)$ divided by the initial value V_0:

$$r = \frac{V_1 - V_0}{V_0} \quad \text{or} \quad 1 + r = \frac{V_1}{V_0} \tag{12.1}$$

The rate of return is not annualized but applies to the measurement period.

However, let's now assume that a cash flow C_t took place on day t during the period.[2] Then the calculation of the rate of return is less obvious. The problem is that the capital invested has changed over the period, so a simple formula such as Equation 12.1 cannot be used.

There are two very different approaches to calculating a rate of return in the presence of interim cash flow:

- The *money-weighted return*[3] (*MWR*) concept captures the return on the *average invested capital*. It is a measure of the net enrichment of the client, taking cash flows into account.

- The *time-weighted return* (*TWR*) concept captures the return *per dollar invested* (or per unit of base currency).[4] It is a measure of the performance of the manager independently of the cash flows to the portfolio. In other words, the TWR measures the performance that would have been realized had the same capital been under management during the whole period. It allows meaningful comparisons with a passive index or with other managers.

---

[1] It must be stressed that rates of return discussed in this chapter are not annualized. They are the return over the period considered.

[2] We use the convention that a positive cash flow is an addition to the portfolio and that a negative cash flow is a withdrawal from the portfolio (a reduction in invested capital). This convention is changed from previous editions of this book.

[3] It is often called *dollar-weighted return* in the United States.

[4] The traditional label *time-weighted* sometimes leads to confusion. It simply means that only time matters in calculating the rate of return, but not the amount of invested capital.

We now detail the various methods, exact or approximate, to measure the MWR and TWR and illustrate them in simple examples such as Example 12.1.

Money-Weighted Return Financiers are accustomed to using discounting to calculate the rate of return on an investment with multiple cash flows. This MWR is sometimes called an *internal rate of return* (*IRR*). It is the discount rate that sets the present value of future cash flows (including the portfolio final value) equal to the initial investment (the start-of-period value).

The MWR can be calculated for any measurement period. The time index t of a cash flow C_t is expressed as a fraction of the length of the measurement period. It is simply the number of days from the start of the period, divided by the number of days in the period:

$$t = \frac{\text{Number of days since start of period}}{\text{Total number of days in measurement period}}$$

So t starts from zero at the start of the measurement period and moves to 1 at the end of the measurement period. In general, the MWR is the value of r in the following equation:

$$V_0 = \sum_t \frac{-C_t}{(1+r)^t} + \frac{V_1}{(1+r)^1} \tag{12.2}$$

The cash flows C_t enter with a negative sign because of the convention that a positive C_t is a contribution made by the client to the portfolio, while a negative C_t is a cash flow withdrawn by the client.

EXAMPLE 12.1 SIMPLE PORTFOLIO: RATE OF RETURN

Consider a simple portfolio with a single cash flow during the measurement period. For simplicity, the measurement period is supposed to be one year.[5] The details on the portfolio are as follows:

- Value at start of the year is $V_0 = 100$
- Cash withdrawal on day t is $C_t = -50$
- The cash outflow takes place 30 days after the start of the period, or at $t = 30/365 = 0.082$ year
- Value on day t, before the cash flow, is $V_t = 95$
- Final value at year-end is $V_1 = 60$

What would be the rate of return using Equation 12.1?

SOLUTION

If Equation 12.1 were applied directly, we would find a rate of return of $(60-100)/100 = -40$ percent, which is clearly incorrect.

[5] In practice, it is typically one month, as shown in the example on page 549.

Example 12.2 shows the money-weighted return calculation for the simple portfolio introduced in Example 12.1 with its single cash flow during the measurement period.

Again, the MWR is *not* annualized; it is the average return over the measured period, taking into account the amount of capital invested. Its calculation does not require one to value the portfolio at the time of cash flows. Computers can easily calculate an internal rate of return; it can also be done on a spreadsheet. With today's computing power, this is a trivial task. However, the calculation can yield multiple answers when there are negative and positive cash flows, and it is sensitive to measurement errors and the exact dating of cash flows. For ease of calculation, some approximations to MWR were developed.

Approximation to the MWR: Dietz Method A linear approximation to the MWR can be obtained by calculating a simple ratio as proposed by Dietz. This is an "accounting" measure of the return on the average invested capital and is obtained by dividing the profit on the portfolio by the average capital invested during the period:

$$MWR_1 = \frac{\text{Profit}}{\text{Average invested capital}} \tag{12.3}$$

Everyone agrees on the profit over the period: It is the change in value of the portfolio minus the net cash flow (sum of all cash flows). The only question remaining is how to compute the average invested capital. This is obtained by weighting each cash flow by the amount of time it is held in the portfolio. In general, each cash flow taking place at time t has a weight in the average capital equal to $1 - t$. Hence, the formula[6] is

EXAMPLE 12.2 SIMPLE PORTFOLIO: MONEY-WEIGHTED RETURN

What is the MWR of the simple portfolio in Example 12.1?

SOLUTION

In the example, the internal rate of return is the value of r in the following equation:

$$100 = \frac{50}{(1+r)^{30/365}} + \frac{60}{1+r}$$

Thus, the MWR is equal to

$$r = \text{MWR} = 18.37\%$$

---

6 It can be easily verified that this is just the linear approximation to the internal rate of return. Simply multiply both sides of Equation 12.2 by $1 + r$ and replace $(1 + r)^{1-t}$ by its first-order linear expansion $1 + r(1 - t)$. Then Equation 12.2 becomes

$$V_0(1+r) = -\sum_t C_t(1 + r(1-t)) + V_1 \text{ or } r = \frac{V_1 - V_0 - \sum_t C_t}{V_0 + \sum_t (1-t)C_t}$$

which is identical to Equation 12.4. The first-order approximation works well for small values of r.

$$\text{MWR}_1 = \frac{\text{Profit}}{\text{Average invested capital}} = \frac{V_1 - V_0 - \sum_t C_t}{V_0 + \sum_t (1-t) C_t} \tag{12.4}$$

Generally, the Dietz method gives a reasonable approximation to the MWR for short measurement periods (up to one month).

A further crude approximation could be performed. Rather than keeping track of the timing of the cash flows, one assumes arbitrarily that the net cash flow takes place at the middle of the period. Then, the average invested capital is simply equal to the starting capital plus 50 percent of the net cash flow. The resulting rate of return is

$$\text{MWR}_2 = \frac{\text{Profit}}{\text{Average invested capital}} = \frac{V_1 - V_0 - \sum_t C_t}{V_0 + \frac{1}{2}\sum_t C_t}$$

This formula, sometimes called the original Dietz method, can provide a poor approximation of the MWR (see Example 12.3). Given today's data processing capabilities, it is a trivial task to keep track of the timing of cash flows and calculate their weighted average. Use of the original Dietz method is hard to justify any longer.

Time-Weighted Return By contrast with the MWR methods, the time-weighted rate of return (TWR) is the performance per dollar invested (or per unit of base currency) and is calculated independently of the cash flows to or from the portfolio.

In other words, the TWR measures the performance that would have been realized had the same capital been under management over the whole period. This method is necessary for comparing performance among managers or with a passive benchmark. The TWR is obtained by calculating the rate of return between each cash flow date and chain-linking those rates over the total measurement period. As mentioned, the rate of return over a period without cash flows suffers no controversy, and the TWR simply compounds the rates of return per unit of base currency. Calculating a TWR with interim cash flows requires the valuation of a portfolio each time a cash flow takes place. Basically, a daily valuation is required. Let's call V_t the value of the portfolio just before the cash flow takes place. In the presence of a single cash flow, C_t, during the measurement period, we need to calculate the rate of return from the start of the measurement period until the cash flow takes place, and then from the date of the cash flow till the end of the period.

The rate of return for the first subperiod, from zero to t, is given by r_t.

$$1 + r_t = \frac{V_t}{V_0}$$

where the value of the portfolio just before the cash flow takes place is V_t.

The rate of return for the second subperiod, from t to 1, is given by r_{t+1}:

$$1 + r_{t+1} = \frac{V_1}{(V_t + C_t)}$$

EXAMPLE 12.3 SIMPLE PORTFOLIO: APPROXIMATIONS TO THE MWR

Calculate an approximation to the MWR of the simple portfolio, using the Dietz method.

SOLUTION

In Example 12.1, a cash flow of 50 was removed after 30 days, so that it was not available for investment during 335 days of the one-year measurement period. Hence, this approximation to the MWR yields a rate of

$$\text{MWR}_1 = \frac{\text{Profit}}{\text{Average invested capital}} = \frac{60 - 100 + 50}{100 - \dfrac{365 - 30}{365} \times 50} = \frac{10}{54.11} = 18.48\%$$

The difference from the correct MWR is 0.11 percent over a year. The original Dietz method yields an approximate MWR of

$$\text{MWR}_2 = \frac{\text{Profit}}{\text{Average invested capital}} = \frac{60 - 100 + 50}{100 - \dfrac{1}{2} \times 50} = \frac{10}{75} = 13.33\%$$

Although MWR_1 is close to MWR (18.48% instead of 18.37%), MWR_2 is very different (13.33%).

where the value of the portfolio just after the cash flow is $V_t + C_t$.

The total TWR[7] over the measurement period, r, is obtained by chain-linking:

$$(1 + r) = (1 + r_t)(1 + r_{t+1}) = \frac{V_t}{V_0} \times \frac{V_1}{(V_t + C_t)} \tag{12.5}$$

If there are more cash flows during the measurement period, we need to calculate a rate of return between each cash flow date and chain-link them as done here.

The MWR is useful for measuring the return of invested capital: It gives an assessment of the *client's* net enrichment over the measurement period. However, everyone agrees that the TWR is the preferred method for measuring and comparing the performance of money managers. To evaluate the *manager's ability*, the comparison should be independent of the cash movements imposed by clients. Benchmarks or peer groups are not affected by the same cash flows. Example 12.4 demonstrates why the TWR must be used for performance evaluation.

Returns over Long Horizons: A Word of Caution Once rates of return are calculated over a measurement period, they are geometrically chain-linked[8] over

[7] Remember that the rates of return are not annualized.

[8] A *geometric* average uses compounding of rates of return. This is different from an *arithmetic* average, which uses a simple summation of rates of return.

EXAMPLE 12.4 SIMPLE PORTFOLIO: TIME-WEIGHTED RETURN

Calculate the TWR of the simple portfolio. Contrast the result with the MWR found in Example 12.2.

SOLUTION

In the example, the portfolio was worth 95 at the time cash was withdrawn, so the TWR is equal to 26.67 percent, as shown here:

Rates of return

$$1 + r_t = \frac{95}{100} \qquad r_t = -5\%$$

$$1 + r_{t+1} = \frac{60}{45} \qquad r_{t+1} = 33.33\%$$

$$1 + r = 0.95 \times 1.3333 = 1.2667 \qquad r = \text{TWR} = 26.67\%$$

Clearly, the various methods of calculating a rate of return yield very different results: from 13.33 percent to 26.67 percent. In the example, the client withdrew some funds just before a bull market, so the invested capital was smaller in the bull market than in the bear market. This is why the MWR is less than the TWR in the example.

longer performance periods (a quarter, one or several years). For example, the quarterly return can be calculated from three monthly returns, using the formula

$$r_q = (1 + r_1) \times (1 + r_2) \times (1 + r_3) - 1 \tag{12.6}$$

where r_q is the portfolio quarterly return and r_1, r_2, and r_3 are the monthly returns in months 1, 2, and 3.

An exact TWR cannot be calculated for a portfolio or its various segments unless the portfolio is valued at the date of any addition or withdrawal of funds. With a high level of cash flow activity, this may be costly. A compromise that has been tried is to calculate MWRs over measurement periods of one month, and to chain-link them over a longer performance period. One must be aware, however, that a discrepancy in a monthly return (between the calculated MWR and the true TWR) will subsist permanently in the chain-linked performance.[9] There is no technical reason to expect the discrepancy to be offset in the next month. In a world in which clients increasingly focus on alphas relative to passive benchmarks, the magnitude of the potential discrepancy between an MWR and a true TWR over a month has significant importance. To avoid serious distortions, one should revalue the portfolio on each large cash flow (as recommended by GIPS).

[9] Further, if an approximation to the MWR is used, such as the original Dietz method, there is an additional source of error.

The shorter the measurement period used for an MWR, the smaller the discrepancy. And reliable daily valuation should be the goal of any asset management firm.

To conduct a detailed GPE, one should calculate the return for the various segments of the portfolio. This allows one to judge the contribution of various investment decisions to total performance. In the international context, the problems associated with using monthly MWR figures are compounded by the multicurrency and multimarket nature of performance measurement. In a detailed international analysis of the performance of each national segment, shifting funds between markets creates the same cash flow problem. Because these internal cash flows are frequent, the portfolio should be valued frequently. Time differences and lags in reporting of international transactions can introduce various statistical problems with daily valuation. But using monthly MWR for the various segments leads to the same problem discussed previously. An illustration is given in Example 12.5.

The importance of exact computations cannot be overstressed. Astute stock selection is supposed to be a significant contribution made by a manager. This is computed as a residual, subtracting the currency and market effects from the overall performance of the portfolio's segments. Unfortunately, this residual is also the repository for a variety of errors arising from poor data, incorrect calculations and approximations, and transaction costs.

Frequent calculation of return is also needed to estimate operational risk measures, especially on a global portfolio. A few years of monthly data (the usual

EXAMPLE 12.5 VALUING STOCK SELECTION ABILITY ON A JAPANESE EQUITY PORTFOLIO

Consider a £10 million fund that is restricted to a 10 percent investment in Japan. One hundred million yen (£1 million) is invested in the Japanese stock market and managed by a local money manager. The British fund's trustee wants to evaluate the manager's security selection skill in this market. Assuming a fixed exchange rate (i.e., ¥100 per £ rate), we will consider the following scenario. The Japanese manager invests ¥100 million in the Japanese stock index, via an index fund, thereby exactly tracking the index. After two weeks, the index rises from 100 to 130, and the fund's trustee asks the manager to transfer ¥30 million to a falling market (such as the U.K. market) in order to keep within the 10 percent limitation on Japanese investment and rebalance the asset allocation to its desired target. Over the next two weeks, the Japanese index loses 30 percent of its value (falling to 91), so that by the end of the month, the Japanese portfolio is down to ¥70 million. The MWR approximation, using the Dietz method, and the TWR of the portfolio are indicated in Exhibit 12.1. If a consultant performed a GPE using the Dietz method, what would be his conclusion regarding the security selection ability of the manager in Japan? Would his conclusion be correct?

EXHIBIT 12.1

TWR and Dietz Approximation to MWR for a Hypothetical Japanese Portfolio

	Day				
	0	15	30	TWR %	MWR %
Index	100	130	91	–	–
Portfolio before transfer	100	130			
Portfolio after transfer		100	70	−9	0

SOLUTION

The TWR on the Japanese portfolio is −9 percent; that is the performance of the Japanese index, which was perfectly tracked and fell from 100 to 91. The MWR computed by the consultant will be 0 percent (a net profit equal to zero, divided by some average capital), wrongly implying that the manager outperformed the Japanese market and has great skills in Japanese stock selection. In fact, the manager precisely tracked the Japanese market and no more.

practice is five years) are required to obtain statistically significant estimates of an overall fund's volatility, and this assumes stationary currency and market returns over that period, as well as a constant risk objective on the part of the manager. These assumptions are risky (especially for currencies) in light of the marked instability that many financial markets have displayed over time.

Performance Attribution in Global Performance Evaluation

The exact measurement of returns is an important task in a domestic as well as global performance evaluation. Performance attribution is more difficult in a GPE because a portfolio can be invested in many different national markets and because prices are quoted in different currencies on these markets.

To conduct a detailed global performance attribution, a portfolio is broken down into various segments according to type of asset and currency. Each homogeneous segment (say, Japanese stocks) is valued separately in its local currency as well as in the base currency of the portfolio. Thus, Japanese stocks are valued in yen as well as in the investor's base currency.

In Example 12.6, we introduce a sample international portfolio designed to assist the reader in understanding the concepts and performing attribution and calculations in a practical and intuitive manner.

EXAMPLE 12.6 INTERNATIONAL PORTFOLIO: TOTAL RETURN

A U.S. investor has invested $100,000 in an international equity portfolio (which we will call the international portfolio) made up of Asian and European stocks. On December 31, the portfolio is invested in 400 Sony shares listed in Tokyo and 100 BMW shares listed in Frankfurt. She wants to beat some international index used as benchmark. This benchmark has an equal weight in the Japanese stock index and in the European stock index. She uses the U.S. dollar as the base currency. All necessary data are given in Exhibit 12.2. There were no cash flows in the portfolio, nor were any dividends paid. No dividends were paid on the market indexes either. What is the total return on the international portfolio in dollars, and how does it compare to the benchmark return?

EXHIBIT 12.2

International Portfolio: Composition and Market Data

Portfolio	Number of Shares	Price (in local currency)		Portfolio Value on Dec. 31		Portfolio Value on Mar. 31	
		Dec. 31	Mar. 31	Local Currency	Base Currency (dollar)	Local Currency	Base Currency (dollar)
Japanese Stocks							
Sony	400	10,000	11,000	4,000,000	40,000	4,400,000	41,905
European Stocks							
BMW	100	600	600	60,000	60,000	60,000	61,224
Total					*100,000*		*103,129*

Market Data	Dec. 31	Mar. 31
International index benchmark ($)	100	98.47
Japanese index (¥)	100	105
European index (€)	100	95
Yen per dollar ($: ¥)	100	105
Euro per dollar ($: €)	1	0.98

SOLUTION

On March 31, her portfolio has gained 3.13 percent ((103,129 − 100,000)/100,000), while the benchmark (international index) has lost 1.53 percent in dollars ((98.47 − 100)/100). The performance of the portfolio relative to the benchmark is therefore a positive 4.66 percent. Of course, she will want to know why her portfolio had such a good performance over the quarter.

The Mathematics of Multicurrency Returns

The basic unit of measurement is the rate of return on each segment before any cash movement between segments. To avoid a notational crisis, all time indexes are indicated with superscripts, and specific portfolio segments are indicated with subscripts. We now present the rate of return calculations for a specific segment, both in its local currency and in the investor's base currency.

Return in Local Currency If we call V_j the value of one segment j, in local currency, the rate of return in local currency for period t is given by

$$r_j = \frac{V_j^t - V_j^{t-1} + D_j^t}{V_j^{t-1}} = \frac{V_j^t - V_j^{t-1}}{V_j^{t-1}} + \frac{D_j^t}{V_j^{t-1}} = p_j + d_j \tag{12.7}$$

where

D_j is the amount of dividends or coupons *paid* during the period

p_j is the capital gain(price appreciation) in percent

d_j is the yield in percent

Further precision is needed for fixed-income segments. In most countries, as well as on the Eurobond market, accrued interest A is computed and quoted separately from the quoted price of a bond P. An investor must pay both the price and accrued interest to the seller. Therefore, the total *value* of the bond is $V = P + A$. The rate of return on the bond segment is given by

$$r_j = \frac{V_j^t - V_j^{t-1} + D_j^t}{V_j^{t-1}} = \frac{P_j^t - P_j^{t-1}}{P_j^{t-1} + A_j^{t-1}} + \frac{A_j^t - A_j^{t-1} + D_j^t}{P_j^{t-1} + A_j^{t-1}} = p_j + d_j \tag{12.8}$$

Return in Base Currency The base currency rate of return is easily derived by translating all prices[10] into the base currency 0 at exchange rate S_j:

$$r_{j0} = \frac{V_j^t S_j^t + D_j^t S_j^t - V_j^{t-1} S_j^{t-1}}{V_j^{t-1} S_j^{t-1}}$$

where r_{j0} is the segment return in base currency 0, while r_j is the segment return in its local currency and s_j is the number of units of currency 0 per unit of currency j. After some algebraic reshuffling, this may be written as

$$r_{j0} = p_j + d_j + s_j(1 + p_j + d_j), \text{ or}$$

$$r_{j0} = p_j + d_j + c_j \tag{12.9}$$

Total return in base currency = Capital gain component + Yield component + Currency component

where s_j denotes the percentage exchange rate movement, and c_j denotes the influence of the exchange rate movement on the estimated return in the base currency. Note that the currency component c_j is equal to zero if the exchange rate movement s_j is zero. If s_j is not zero, c_j differs slightly from s_j because of the cross-product terms.

---

[10] For simplicity, assume that the dividend is paid at the exchange rate prevailing at the end of the period.

The compounding of currency and market movements on a foreign security is illustrated in Exhibit 12.3. The value of a foreign investment is represented as a rectangle, where the horizontal axis represents the exchange rate and the vertical axis represents the value of the investment in local currency. As an illustration, consider a U.S. investor holding £10,000 of British assets with an exchange rate of $/£ = 2. The dollar value of the assets is represented by area A, or $20,000. Later, the British assets have gone up by 10 percent to £11,000, and the pound has appreciated by 5 percent to $/£ = 2.10. The total dollar value is now £23,100, or a gain of 15.5 percent. The dollar gain, if the currency had not moved, is represented by area B (10 percent of initial value). Because of the currency movement, this gain is transformed to a total gain of 15.5 percent, equal to the sum of areas B, C, and D. Area C plus D is the currency component of the total return. Note that it can be seen as a pure exchange rate movement (area D) and a cross-currency market term (area C). It is equal to the exchange rate movement applied to the final pound value of the investment, not its initial value.

Total-Return Decomposition

The first objective of GPE is to decompose the portfolio's total return, measured in base currency, into the three main sources of return:

- Capital gain (in local currency)
- Yield
- Currency

EXHIBIT 12.3

Market and Currency Gains

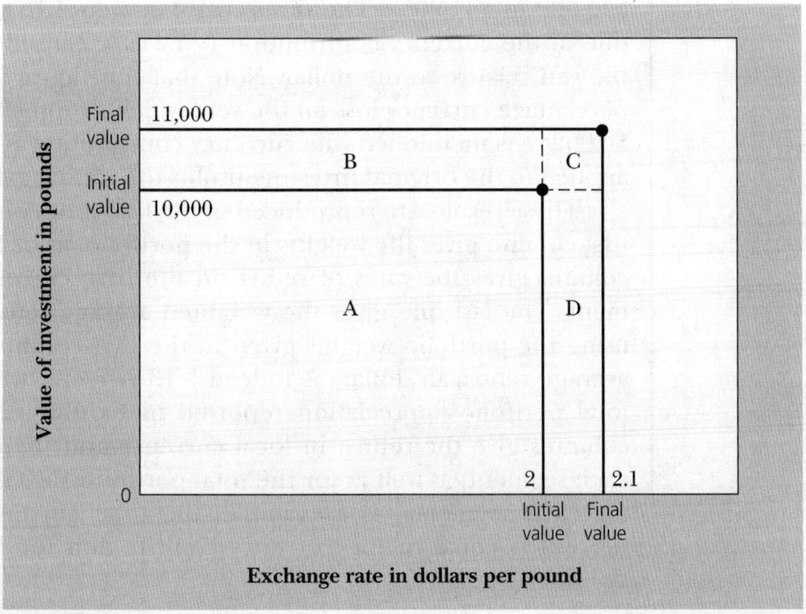

The total return is simply the weighted average of the returns on all segments. Over period *t*, the total portfolio's return *r* is computed in the base currency as follows:

$$r = \sum_j w_j r_{j0} = \sum_j w_j(p_j + d_j + c_j)$$

where w_j represents the percentage of segment *j* in the total portfolio at the start of the period, and the sign $\sum_j$ means that we sum over all segments *j*. The various sources of return may be regrouped into three components:

$$r = \underset{\text{Capital gain component}}{\sum_j w_j p_j} + \underset{\text{Yield component}}{\sum_j w_j d_j} + \underset{\text{Currency component}}{\sum_j w_j c_j} \quad (12.10)$$

Example 12.7 is an important example to demonstrate total return decomposition.

EXAMPLE 12.7 INTERNATIONAL PORTFOLIO : TOTAL RETURN DECOMPOSITION

Let's now return to the sample international portfolio and its international benchmark. Decompose the total return into capital gain, yield, and currency components. Perform a similar calculation for the benchmark.

SOLUTION

There is no yield, so we will focus on the other components of return. The Japanese shares went up by 10 percent in the first quarter (from ¥10,000 per share to ¥11,000). The rate of return in yen on the Japanese equity segment is 10 percent (from ¥4 million to ¥4.4 million). When translated into dollars, the rate of return of the Japanese equity segment becomes 4.76 percent (from \$40,000 to \$41,905). The difference between 4.76 percent and 10 percent is due to the currency contribution (−5.24%), caused by a drop in the value of the yen relative to the dollar. Note that this figure is not exactly equal to the percentage currency loss on the yen, which dropped from ¥100 = \$1 to ¥100 = \$0.9524. As mentioned, the currency contribution is equal to the currency loss applied to the original investment plus the capital gain.

These results are reproduced in the first four columns of Exhibit 12.4. The first column gives the weights in the portfolio, as of December 31. The second column gives the rates of return in the base currency (dollar) for each segment. The last line gives the weighted average return for the total portfolio, using the portfolio weights given in the first column. Note that the weighted average return in dollars is indeed 3.13 percent, which is consistent with the total portfolio appreciation reported in Exhibit 12.2. The third and fourth columns give the return in local currency and the currency contribution for each segment, as well as for the total portfolio (by taking the weighted average for each segment). For example, the total currency contribution of −0.87 percent is equal to the currency contribution for Japanese equity (−5.24%)

EXHIBIT 12.4

International Portfolio: Total Return Decomposition

	(1) Portfolio Weights	(2) Rate of Return in $	(3) Rate of Return in Local Currency	(4) = (2) − (3) Currency Contribution	(5) Market Index	(6) = (3) − (5) Security Selection
Japanese Stocks	40%	4.76%	10.00%	−5.24%	5.00%	5.00%
European Stocks	60%	2.04%	0.00%	2.04%	−5.00%	5.00%
Total Portfolio	**100%**	**3.13%**	**4.00%**	**−0.87%**	**−1.00%**	**5.00%**

multiplied by the weight of Japanese equity in the total portfolio (40%), plus the currency contribution of European equity (2.04%) multiplied by the weight of European equity in the total portfolio (60%).

In the end, the total portfolio return of 3.13 percent can be decomposed as a nice capital gain in local currency of 4.00 percent, minus a currency loss of −0.87 percent. Note that columns 3 and 4 add up to column 2. Columns 5–6 are discussed in Example 12.8.

The Japanese index gained 5 percent from 100 to 105 yen, but the yen depreciated from \$:¥ = 100 to \$:¥ = 105. The dollar return on the Japanese index is calculated by simply dividing the index by the \$:¥ exchange rate. The Japanese index in dollar terms was unity on December 31 (100/100) and remains unity on March 31 (105/105). Hence, the dollar return on the Japanese market equals 0 percent (constant index in dollars). Similarly, the European index return is −5 percent in euros, but the euro strengthened from \$:€ = 1 to \$:€ = 0.98. So the European index return is −3.06 percent in dollars, and the currency contribution is +1.94% = −3.06% − (−5%). To get the return decomposition for the international benchmark, we simply take the weighted average of the return decomposition for the Japanese and European market indexes as shown in Exhibit 12.5. We verify that the benchmark return in dollars is a loss of 1.53 percent. The benchmark's total return all comes from

EXHIBIT 12.5

International Benchmark: Total-Return Decomposition

	(1) Benchmark Weights	(2) Rate of Return in $	(3) Rate of Return in Local Currency	(4) Currency Contribution
Japanese Index	50%	0.00%	5.00%	−5.00%
European Index	50%	−3.06%	−5.00%	1.94%
Benchmark	**100%**	**−1.53%**	**0.00%**	**−1.53%**

an average currency contribution of −1.53 percent. The local currency returns of the Japanese and European market indexes offset each other.

Note that in Exhibit 12.5 we calculated the currency contributions on the Japanese index as −5 percent and on the European index as +1.94 percent. The currency contributions for the Japanese and European segments of the international portfolio shown in Exhibit 12.4 are slightly different (−5.24% and 2.04%). This is because the currency loss applies both to the original principal and also to the capital gain. Because the Japanese portfolio had a better capital appreciation (10%) than the Japanese index (5%), it has more currency exposure to the yen and therefore lost more. Similarly, the European portfolio had a slightly better currency gain.

Performance Attribution

A manager's relative performance may be measured by making several comparisons. The basic idea is to provide a comparison with some passive benchmarks for all major investment decisions. Active management decisions will induce deviations from the benchmarks' returns. Some of the many management decisions that are commonly analyzed are discussed next.

Security Selection A manager's security selection ability is determined by isolating the local market return of the various segments. Let's call I_j the return, in local currency, of the market index corresponding to segment j (e.g., the Tokyo Stock Exchange index). Remember that market indexes are usually price-only indexes (do not reflect dividends). Assuming a portfolio has market-index-average risk, the return derived from security selection is simply $p_j - I_j$. The rate of return on segment j (Japanese stocks) may be broken down into the following components:

$$r_{j0} = I_j + (p_j - I_j) + d_j + c_j$$

The total portfolio return may be written as

$$r = \underbrace{\sum w_j I_j}_{\text{Market return component}} + \underbrace{\sum w_j (p_j - I_j)}_{\text{Security selection contribution}} + \underbrace{\sum w_j d_j}_{\text{Yield component}} + \underbrace{\sum w_j c_j}_{\text{Currency component}} \qquad (12.11)$$

The first term on the right-hand side of Equation 12.11 measures the performance that would have been achieved had the manager invested in a local market index instead of individual securities. This contribution is calculated net of currency movements, which are picked up by the last term in the formula. The second term measures the contribution made by the manager's individual security selection. It is simply the weighted average of the security selection on each segment.

EXAMPLE 12.8 INTERNATIONAL PORTFOLIO: SECURITY SELECTION

Calculate the overall contribution of security selection to the performance of the sample international portfolio.

SOLUTION

These calculations are given in the last columns of Exhibit 12.4. Column 5 is the market index return component and column 6 is the contribution of security selection. The return on the Japanese index is 5 percent in yen, while the Japanese segment of the portfolio returns 10 percent in yen. Hence, the contribution of security selection on the Japanese market is 5 percent. The return on the European index is −5 percent in euros, while the European segment of the portfolio returns a flat 0 percent in euros. Hence, the contribution of security selection on the European market is 5 percent. So columns 5 and 6 simply add up to column 3.

To derive information at the international portfolio level, we take the weighted average of the figures reported for the various segments, using the portfolio weights reported in column 1. Hence, the overall contribution of security selection at the portfolio level, reported in column 6 of Exhibit 12.4, is equal to

$$\text{Security selection contribution} = 0.40 \times (5\%) + 0.60 \times (5\%) = 5\%$$

We can see that the sample international portfolio had a return in local currency equal to 4 percent (column 3). If the investor has passively allocated 0.40 of her portfolio to the Japanese stock index and 0.60 to the European stock index, she would have taken a capital loss of −1 percent (column 5):

$$\text{Market index return} = 0.40 \times (5\%) + 0.60 \times (-5\%) = -1\%$$

However, superior security selection (+5%) led to an actual portfolio gain, in local currency, of +4 percent.

The market indexes used as benchmark are sometimes total-return indexes, meaning that they include dividends paid on the stocks making up the index. To calculate the contribution of security selection, one has to be consistent in the treatment of dividends. Hence, one must compare the total return (capital gain plus yield) on the segment to that of the market index. The return derived from security selection on segment j would simply be $p_j + d_j - I_j$. The calculations here assume that the indexes are price-only indexes, but the extension to total-return indexes is straightforward.

Asset Allocation Another step in performance attribution is to study the performance of the total portfolio relative to that of a global benchmark. This comparison is usually made with respect to the return I^* on an international index, such as the MSCI, the EAFE index, or the World index. The objective is to assess the portfolio manager's ability as measured by the difference in return, $r - I^*$.

To do this, additional notation is required. Let's call I_{j0} the return on market index j, translated into base currency 0. We have

$$I_{j0} = I_j + C_j$$

where C_j is the currency component of the index return in base currency, that is, $C_j = s_j\,(1 + I_j)$. Let's call w_j^* the weight of market j in the international benchmark chosen as a standard. In base currency, the return on this international index equals

$$I^* = \sum w_j^* I_{j0}$$

Equation 12.11 may be rewritten and transformed into Equation 12.12 by simultaneously adding $\Sigma w_j^* I_{j0}$ and subtracting $\Sigma w_j^* I_{j0} = \Sigma w_j^* (I_j + C_j)$:

$$r = \sum w_j^* I_{j0} + \sum (w_j - w_j^*) I_j + \sum (w_j c_j - w_j^* C_j) + \sum w_j d_j + \sum w_j (p_j - I_j) \quad (12.12)$$

International benchmark return I^* + Market allocation contribution + Currency allocation contribution[11] + Yield component + Security selection contribution

This breakdown allows us to estimate the contribution to total performance of any deviation from the standard asset allocation, $w_j - w_j^*$.

The word *contribution* in this context indicates performance relative to a selected benchmark; the word *component* refers to a breakdown of the portfolio's total return. Equation 12.12 states that a manager's relative performance, $r - I^*$, can be attributed to the following three factors (after allowing for the yield on the portfolio):

1. *A market allocation different from that of the index:* This factor is a source of positive performance for the manager who overweights ($w_j > w_j^*$) the best-performing markets and underweights the poorest-performing markets.

2. *A currency allocation different from that of the index:* This factor is a source of positive performance for the manager who overweights ($w_j > w_j^*$) the best-performing currencies and underweights the poorest-performing currencies. So, it is possible for a manager to have chosen his markets very effectively (resulting in a positive market allocation contribution) but be penalized by adverse currency movements (resulting in a negative currency allocation contribution). The market allocation and currency allocation contributions are sometimes combined into a single allocation contribution. The impact of currency management is further discussed below.

3. *Superior security selection:* This three-factor breakdown of relative performance is the simplest of many possibilities. GPE services use a variety of similar approaches and employ graphics in presenting their results. Example 12.9 illustrates such an analysis.

---

[11] Remember that c_j and C_j are close to s_j, the exchange rate movement, so that the currency allocation contribution is close to $\Sigma\,(w_j - w_j^*)\,s_j$.

EXAMPLE 12.9 INTERNATIONAL PORTFOLIO: GLOBAL PERFORMANCE ATTRIBUTION

You are to perform a global performance attribution for the sample international portfolio. In particular, you must find the major reason for the good performance of the portfolio relative to its benchmark. Discuss the impact of currencies on performance. To assist you, results of calculations already performed for the portfolio and the benchmark are summarized in Exhibit 12.6.

EXHIBIT 12.6

Summary of Previous Results

	(1)	(2)	(3)	(4)
	Weights	Rate of Return in $	Rate of Return in Local Currency	Currency Contribution
International Portfolio				
Japanese stocks	40%	4.76%	10.00%	−5.24%
European stocks	60%	2.04%	0.00%	2.04%
Total portfolio	**100%**	**3.13%**	**4.00%**	**−0.87%**
Benchmark				
Japanese Index	50%	0.00%	5.00%	−5.00%
European Index	50%	−3.06%	−5.00%	1.94%
Benchmark	**100%**	**−1.53%**	**0.00%**	**−1.53%**

SOLUTION

The portfolio returned 3.13 percent compared to −1.53 percent for the benchmark, a performance of 4.66 percent relative to the benchmark. This performance can be attributed to various investment decisions:

- *Market allocation*: The benchmark has equal weights (0.50) in Japan and Europe, while the investor allocated weights of 0.40 to Japan and 0.60 to Europe. Let's now study the impact of the market allocation decision to underweight Japan compared to the benchmark (0.40 instead of 0.50). This resulted in a negative deviation from the benchmark as the Japanese index gained 5 percent. The resulting underperformance due to the underweighting of 0.10 applied to a gain of 5 percent is

  $$-0.10 \times 5\% = -0.5\%$$

  The overweighting in Europe was also an unfortunate decision, because the European market went down in euro terms. The resulting underperformance due to the overweighting of 0.10 applied to a loss of −5 percent is

  $$0.10 \times (-5\%) = -0.5\%$$

The net market allocation contribution is equal to

$$\text{Market allocation contribution} = -0.10 \times (5\%) + 10\% \times (-5\%) = -1\%$$

- *Currency allocation contribution*: The currency loss on the portfolio has been calculated before as −0.87 percent. This is evidence that currency risk is not hedged. However, the benchmark had a worse currency loss of −1.53 percent. The difference comes primarily from the currency/country weights. Compared to the benchmark, the manager underweighted the yen (0.40 compared to 0.50) and overweighted the euro (0.60 compared to 0.50). This turned out to be a good currency decision as the euro went up against the dollar while the yen went down against the dollar. The contribution of the currency allocation compared to the benchmark is equal to

$$\text{Currency allocation contribution} = -0.87\% - (-1.53\%) = 0.66\%$$

Hence, the asset allocation deviation relative to the benchmark led to a negative performance on the markets and a positive performance on the currencies. We have no information on the motivations for the investor's decisions, but it could be that she decided to overweight Europe and underweight Japan because of currency considerations.

- *Security selection contribution*: Calculations for security selection contribution appear in Example 12.8. The result is a positive contribution of security selection equal to 5 percent.

To summarize, the portfolio return could be attributed as follows:

Benchmark return	−1.53%
Market allocation contribution	−1.00%
Currency allocation contribution	0.66%
Yield component	0.00%
Security selection contribution	5.00%
Portfolio return	3.13%

These figures allow us to conduct a global performance evaluation. The portfolio had a great return (+3.13%) compared to the benchmark (−1.53%). However, the added value does not come from the asset allocation decision. The decision to overweight Europe relative to Japan led to a loss on the markets (−1%) and a gain on the currencies (0.66%). The major contributor to the performance is the individual stock selection on each market (+5%). The excellent selection of securities explains the superior performance of International Portfolio.

Market Timing Asset allocation varies over time, so that over a given performance period, *market timing* makes a contribution due to the time variation in weights, w_j. Moreover, the contribution made by market timing can be further broken down and measured for each segment (e.g., Japanese equity).

Industry and Sectors We presented a GPE in which performance is attributed to country allocation. Equity managers often focus on the global industry allocation across countries. Hence, another line of analysis is to attribute performance to the industry weighting chosen by the manager. Attribution along global industry lines is gaining in importance.

Factors and Styles Performance within a segment can further be attributed to the choice of investment style (see Sharpe, 1992). For example, a manager could favor value stocks over growth stocks in his European portfolio. Differences in portfolio return can be explained by the relative allocation between value and growth stocks. Hence, performance would be attributed not along country lines but along style lines. This investment style approach is less common outside the United States. Various factors are sometimes favored by investment managers using factor models. Once a manager takes investment positions on various factors within a national market segment, a GPE system can analyze how much of the performance relative to the national market index, or globally, can be attributed to each factor bet.

Risk Decomposition Just as the total rate of return is decomposed into its main contributors, the total risk of a portfolio can be decomposed along the same lines. The counterpart of *performance attribution* in the return dimension is called *risk allocation* (or *risk budgeting*) in the risk dimension. This is discussed in the performance appraisal section of the chapter, after risk measures are introduced.

More on Currency Management

We now turn to the issue of active currency management and currency hedging. A few managers claim that they are "passive" on currencies, meaning that they do not take views on currency and simply accept the currency exposures that result from their international investment choices. This definition of the term *passive currency management* can be misleading because investment choices will result in a positive currency exposure that can lead to significant losses if foreign currencies depreciate, with a negative contribution to the total return on the portfolio. Another definition of *passive currency management* is that the manager does not take any currency risk exposure and therefore fully hedges any currency exposure.

A major issue is the benchmark that is assigned to the portfolio manager. If the benchmark is fully hedged against currency risk, then taking any currency exposure in the portfolio is an active decision. On the other hand, if the assigned benchmark is not hedged against currency risk, then the passive (neutral) decision on currencies is achieved by matching the currency weights in the benchmark. Deviating from the benchmark currency composition is an active currency decision. Hence, "passive" currency management has to be defined relative to the benchmark being assigned. A special situation can arise when currency management is delegated to a *currency overlay manager* (see Chapter 11). Then currency management is not a concern for the manager of assets: The resulting currency exposure is managed by the currency overlay manager. The asset manager does not have to worry about the contribution of currencies to the return on the portfolio because his performance is evaluated net of currency return.

In general, there are two major ways to analyze active currency exposure relative to a benchmark.

Deviations from Benchmark Currency Weights An asset allocation that carries currency weights that differ from the currency weights in the benchmark will result in active currency exposure. This situation was extensively discussed above. In the international portfolio example, the portfolio had country weights (40% in Japan and 60% in Europe) that were different from those in the benchmark (equally invested in both countries). This weighting created a currency exposure relative to the benchmark. It could be that the manager had no views on the currencies and simply chose this tactical asset allocation because the European market looked more attractive than the Japanese market. But one should be aware that currency movements by themselves can induce losses or gains relative to the benchmark. An alternative is to use currency hedging to offset the deviations of currency weights relative to the benchmark. On the other hand, the asset allocation of the international portfolio could have been the result of active currency management, whereby the manager desired to increase the currency exposure to the euro and reduce the currency exposure to the yen.

Using Derivatives Numerous strategies based on derivatives can be used to manage currency exposure, as outlined in Chapter 11. The most common one is to engage in currency hedging with forward/futures currency contracts. It is important to be able to calculate the impact of currency hedging on the return of a portfolio.

Part of the total portfolio could be hedged against currency risk. This is usually done by *selling forward* foreign currencies against the base currency. A *forward currency purchase* is equivalent to being long in foreign cash (receiving the foreign short-term interest rate R_j) and short in the domestic, or base currency, cash (paying the domestic short-term interest rate R_0). A *forward currency sale* is just the reverse position. Using the linear approximation,[12] the forward purchase of currency j has a pure currency component equal to the percentage exchange rate movement s_j (change in the domestic currency value of one unit of foreign currency) plus the interest rate differential (foreign minus domestic):

$$c_j^f = s_j + R_j - R_0$$

Remember that over short periods, the interest rate differential is small relative to the exchange rate movement, so c_j^f is quite close to the exchange rate movement s_j.

[12] See Chapters 1 and 2; see also Ankrim and Hensel (1994) and Singer and Karnosky (1995).

Assume that the portfolio is hedged by forward currency sale for a proportion w_j^f in currency j. This means that the forward position in currency j represents $-w_j^f$ percent of the total value of the portfolio. There is a negative sign because we are selling forward currency contracts, not buying them. If currency hedging positions are taken on several currencies, the net contribution of currency hedging to the total return on the portfolio will be

$$-\sum_j w_j^f c_j^f \tag{12.13}$$

Hence, the contribution of currency j is fully hedged when $w_j^f = w_j$. Note, however, that the hedge will be good only if the amount of hedging is periodically adjusted to reflect changes in the asset value to be hedged. In case of an asset price appreciation, the value of the assets to be hedged increases, and so should the amount of hedging. This is illustrated in Example 12.10. In performance attribution, the return on the currency hedge, as measured above, is included in the analysis of the currency contribution.

To summarize, the overall currency component of the portfolio return can be viewed as the sum of

- the currency component of the passive benchmark,
- the currency allocation contribution (deviations from benchmark currency weights), and
- the return on the currency hedges.

EXAMPLE 12.10 INTERNATIONAL PORTFOLIO: IMPACT OF CURRENCY HEDGING IN PERFORMANCE ATTRIBUTION

Let's assume that the manager of the sample international portfolio decided to fully hedge the euro currency risk by selling forward €60,000 to buy dollars on December 31. The interest rates in euros and dollars are equal, so the forward exchange rate is equal to the spot exchange rate. What would be the contribution of the currency hedge to the return on the European equity segment and on the total portfolio?

SOLUTION

On December 31, 60,000 euros are worth \$60,000 and represent 60 percent of the portfolio. This is the same weight as the European equity segment. The forward currency position is to be short in 60,000 euros. On March 31, the exchange rate is equal to €0.98 per dollar, or \$1.0204 per euro. The euro has gone up by 2.04 percent. Hence, the short forward position in 60,000 euros is now worth \$61,224.50. Because this is a short position whose value has gone up, there is a loss of \$1,224.50. Relative to the initial European equity investment, this is a percentage loss of 1,224.50/60.000 = 2.04 percent. Note that the currency hedge exactly offsets the currency contribution on the European equity segment. The short sale of euros achieved a perfect hedge and nullified the currency impact on European equity. In this case, the result is unfortunate because the euro appreciated.

The contribution of the hedge to the overall portfolio return is calculated by dividing the dollar loss on the hedge by the initial value of the portfolio, giving a rate of return of −1,224.50/60.000 = −1.22 percent. This result could be obtained by direct application of Equation 12.13, where we have $w_j^f = 0.60$ and $c_j^f = 2.04$ percent for the European segment (and zeros for the Japanese segment):

$$-\sum_j w_j^f c_j^f = -0.60 \times 2.04\% = -1.24\%$$

This negative currency return on the hedging position will reduce (i.e., worsen) the currency contribution in the attribution analysis performed in previous examples.

Note that the hedge is perfect because the euro value of the hedge position remained the same over time. The hedge would have been imperfect for the yen position because its value went up by 10 percent from December to March. A progressive adjustment to the hedge amount would have been required to improve the hedging efficacy.

Multiperiod Attribution Analysis

In performance attribution, the return on a portfolio is compared to that on a benchmark, and the difference is decomposed into a number of attributes (security selection, market allocation, currency contribution, etc.). While many decompositions of performance have been designed along various attributes (or effects), it is common industry practice to provide a *linear additive* decomposition for a basic (short) time period such as one month or one quarter. These single-period attributes are then accumulated over several periods to allow for performance valuation over one or several years. The question arises as to how this accumulation of single-period results is conducted. Unfortunately, this is a difficult task.

While clients and managers like the simplicity of the linear additivity of the various attributes, additivity does not fare well with compounding (linking) returns over many periods. Because of the mathematical complexity of the issue, we will resort to simple examples.

Single Attribute Let's first consider a portfolio solely invested in one market. The original value of the portfolio is 100. The return on that portfolio is denoted R. The benchmark is simply the market index with a return denoted $\overline{R}$. The difference between the portfolio and benchmark return is simply attributed to security selection with a contribution S. We consider two successive periods (say, two months), and we have

$$R_1 - \overline{R}_1 = S_1$$

and

$$R_2 - \overline{R}_2 = S_2$$

Let's consider the following example:

- The portfolio returns 25 percent in period 1 and 20 percent in period 2.
- The market index (benchmark) went up by 20 percent in period 1 and 10 percent in period 2.
- Hence, the contribution of security selection (attribute return) was 5 percent in period 1 and 10 percent in period 2.

The benchmark market movement over the two months is not the sum of the two monthly returns, or $\overline{R}_1 + \overline{R}_2 = 30$ percent. Returns need to be compounded (linked). If the benchmark value was 100 in period 0, it went up to 120 in period 1 and to $132 = 120 \times (1.10)$ in period 2. In period 2, the 10 percent rise is applied not only to the original value of the benchmark but also to its capital gain in period 1. One earns "interest on interest," so the two-period benchmark return is given by

$$1 + \overline{R} = (1 + \overline{R}_1) \times (1 + \overline{R}_2)$$

or

$$\overline{R} = (1 + \overline{R}_1) \times (1 + \overline{R}_2) - 1 = 1.20 \times 1.10 - 1 = 32\%$$

The benchmark return over two months is 32 percent. Similarly, the two-period return on the portfolio is not the simple sum of the portfolio return in each period, or $R_1 + R_2 = 45$ percent. It is the compounded (linked) return:

$$1 + R = (1 + R_1) \times (1 + R_2)$$

or

$$R = (1 + R_1) \times (1 + R_2) - 1 = 1.25 \times 1.20 - 1 = 50\%$$

The portfolio return is 50 percent, not 45 percent. It went up from 100 in period 0 to 125 in period 1 and 150 in period 2.

Let's now look at the two-period contribution of security selection S. A simple idea would be to take the sum of the two monthly attributes, or $S_1 + S_2 = 15$ percent. Another idea would be to compound (link) the two monthly attributes:

$$(1 + S_1) \times (1 + S_2) - 1 = (1.05) \times (1.10) - 1 = 15.5\%$$

However, we can easily get the correct figure by calculating directly the two-period attribute as the difference between the two-period portfolio return and benchmark return. By definition, the two-month contribution of security selection must be the difference between the two-month portfolio return (50%) and the two-month benchmark return (32%). We get

$$S = R - \overline{R} = 50\% - 32\% = 18\%$$

Clearly, the correct multiperiod attribute (18%) is not equal to either the simple sum (15%) or the compounded return (15.5%):

$$S = R - \overline{R} \neq (R_1 - \overline{R}_1) + (R_2 - \overline{R}_2)$$
$$S = R - \overline{R} \neq (1 + R_1 - \overline{R}_1) \times (1 + R_2 - \overline{R}_2) - 1$$

The reason a simple addition or compounding of the single-period attributes will not yield the multiperiod value of the attribute is fairly intuitive. In period 1, the security selection contribution of 5 percent (25% − 20%) applies to the original (period 0) portfolio value of 100. But in period 2, the security selection contribution of 10 percent (20% − 10%) applies to the period 1 value of the portfolio of 125. An intuitive way to accumulate the attribute is as follows:

- The past attribute (here, 10%) would compound with the benchmark return in period 2 if there is no active investment choice being made in period 2.
- To the extent that there is an active investment choice in period 2, the contribution of the choice will be earned on the portfolio value at the end of the previous period (here, period 1).

In mathematical terms, we have

$$S = R - \overline{R} = (R_1 - \overline{R}_1) \times (1 + \overline{R}_2) + (R_2 - \overline{R}_2) \times (1 + R_1) = S_1 \times (1 + \overline{R}_2) + S_2 \times (1 + R_1) \quad (12.14)$$

Equation 12.14 is the key to two-period attribution and will be used throughout the remainder of this section. (Its multiperiod extension is given as Equation 12.15.) In words, the two-period attribute can be decomposed into the first-period attribute compounded at the second-period benchmark rate of return plus the second-period attribute compounded at the first-period portfolio rate of return. We summarize the situation in a table where we multiply the quantities that are screened and then sum the two results to get the two-period attribute of 18 percent.

	Period 1	Period 2	Total Period
International Portfolio (1 + Return)	1.25	1.20	1.5
Benchmark (1+ Return)	1.20	1.10	1.32
Attribute (Return)	0.05 or 5%	0.10 or 10%	0.18 or 18%

Here,

$$S = (5\% \times 1.10) + (10\% \times 1.25) = 18\%$$

When there is a *single* attribute, there is a direct way to calculate the multiperiod contribution of the attribute. We simply calculate the multiperiod return on both the portfolio and the benchmark and then take the difference. But what can we do if there are several attributes? Taking the difference in multiperiod returns between the portfolio and the benchmark will yield the total effect of the many attributes but will not disentangle the effect for each attribute. To do so, we need to get the detailed attribution for each period as the composition of the portfolio, and hence its exposure to each attribute, changes over time.

Multiple Attributes Let's first consider decomposition with two commonly used attributes, security selection and market allocation. For simplicity, there are only two attributes, but the analysis can be directly extended to numerous attributes. Similarly, one of the attributes could be currency contribution or allocation. The multiperiod analysis is not specific to the attributes chosen in the example.

For exposition, we will assume the data shown in the following table (details are provided in Example 12.11 to follow).

	Period 1	**Period 2**	**Total Period**
International Portfolio (1 + Return)	1.22	1.1625	1.41825
Benchmark (1 + Return)	1.1	1.125	1.2375
Attribute (Return)	0.12 or 12%	0.0375 or 3.75%	0.18075 or 18.075%
Security selection	10%	4%	16.130% = 10 × 1.125 + 4 × 1.22
Market allocation	2%	−0.25%	1.945% = 2 × 1.125 + (−0.25) × 1.22

For each short period, we can calculate the performance of the portfolio relative to the benchmark and decompose it additively into two attributes: security selection (S) and market allocation (A). In the example, the performance in period 1 can be decomposed as

$$R_1 - \overline{R}_1 = S_1 + A_1$$

or

$$22\% - 10\% = 10\% + 2\% = 12\%$$

The portfolio beats the benchmark by 12 percent, with 10 percent attributed to security selection and 2 percent attributed to market allocation.

For period 2, we get

$$R_2 - \overline{R}_2 = 16.25\% - 12.50\% = S_2 + A_2 = 4.00\% - 0.25\% = 3.75\%$$

The portfolio beats the benchmark by 3.75 percent, with 4 percent attributed to security selection and −0.25 percent attributed to market allocation.

For the total period, we get $R = 41.825$ percent and $\overline{R} = 23.75$ percent. This can be verified by compounding the portfolio and benchmark rates of return in periods 1 and 2. For example, $41.825\% = 1.22 \times 1.1625 - 1$. Hence, the performance relative to the benchmark is 18.075 percent.

The difficult question is: How is this performance attributed to security selection and market allocation? As we shall see, the solution involves multiplying the screened returns in the first column by similarly color-coded returns in the second. Before showing that approach, we will mention another approach that is unfortunately often taken.

This alternative, but *incorrect,* approach is to simply compound the attributes over the short periods. The compounded effects would be

$$\text{Security selection compounded} = S_{comp} = (1.10) \times (1.04) - 1 = 14.40\%$$

$$\text{Market allocation compounded} = A_{comp} = (1.02) \times (0.9975) - 1 = 1.75\%$$

EXAMPLE 12.11 MULTIPERIOD ANALYSIS

A portfolio of $100 million is invested in European and Japanese stocks at the start of period 1. The country weights in the portfolio are 60 percent in Europe and 40 percent in Japan. At the end of period 1, the portfolio value went up to $122 million. To evaluate performance, the investor uses a composite benchmark made up of 50 percent of the European equity index and 50 percent of the Japanese equity index. All calculations are performed in base currency, the U.S. dollar, and indexes are total-return indexes (dividends are reinvested). Over the first period, the European index went up by 20 percent and the Japanese index remained flat, so the benchmark gained 10 percent. Detailed return data are given in Exhibit 12.7. At the end of period 1, the country allocation was changed to 55 percent in Europe and 45 percent in Japan. At the end of period 2, the portfolio was up to $141,825,000, while the composite benchmark gained 23.75 percent over the two periods.

1. Attribute the performance to security selection and market allocation for *each* of the two short periods: period 1 and then period 2.
2. Attribute the performance to security selection and market allocation for the total period (i.e., linked over the two short periods).

EXHIBIT 12.7

Data on Portfolio and Benchmark

PORTFOLIO			BENCHMARK	
Country Component	**Country Weights**	**Rate of Return in Base Currency**	**Country Weights**	**Rate of Return in Base Currency**
Period 1				
Europe	0.60	30.0%	50.0%	20.0%
Japan	0.40	10.0%	50.0%	0.0%
Total Portfolio	100%	**22.0%**		**10.0%**
Period 2				
Europe	0.55	5.0%	50.0%	10.0%
Japan	0.45	30.0%	50.0%	15.0%
Total Portfolio	100%	**16.25%**		**12.5%**
Compounded over overall period				
Europe		36.5%		32.0%
Japan		43.0%		15.0%
Total		**40.30%**		**23.75%**

SOLUTION

1. Detailed calculations are given in Exhibit 12.8. In period 1, the portfolio beat the benchmark by 12 percent: 10 percent can be attributed to security selection and 2 percent to market allocation:

$$\text{Security selection} = 0.60 \times (30\% - 20\%) + 0.40 \times (10\% - 0\%)$$
$$= 6\% + 4\% = 10\%$$
$$\text{Market allocation} = 0.10 \times (20\% - 10\%) - 0.10 \times (0\% - 10\%)$$
$$= 1\% + 1\% = 2\%$$

In period 2, the portfolio beat the benchmark by 3.75 percent. Of this 3.75% performance, 4 percent can be attributed to security selection and −0.25 percent to market allocation:

$$\text{Security selection} = 0.55 \times (5\% - 10\%) + 0.45 \times (30\% - 15\%)$$
$$= -2.75\% + 6.75\% = 4\%$$
$$\text{Market allocation} = 0.05 \times (10\% - 12.5\%) - 0.05 \times (15\% - 12.5\%)$$
$$= -0.125\% - 0.125\% = -0.25\%$$

2. It is straightforward to calculate the total returns on the portfolio and on the benchmark. We get $R = 41.825$ percent and $\overline{R} = 23.75$ percent. Hence, the portfolio overperformed its benchmark by 18.075 percent.

A quick and dirty approach to calculate the attribution to security selection and market allocation over the two periods would be to link (compound) the single-period attributes. The results are given in Exhibit 12.8 in the line titled "Total Portfolio Unadjusted." The linking of the two single-period attributions to security selection yields a rate of 14.4 percent:

$$(1 + 10\%) \times (1 + 4\%) - 1 = 14.4\%$$

Similarly, the linking of the two single-period attributions to market allocation yields a rate of 1.745 percent:

$$(1 + 2\%) \times (1 - 0.25\%) - 1 = 1.745\%$$

The sum of these two terms is clearly not equal to the performance of the portfolio over the total period (18.075%). As explained in the text, this method is faulty. Instead, Equation 12.14 should be used for each attribute. Results are given in the last line of Exhibit 12.8. The multiperiod contributions of security selection and market allocation are 16.130 percent and 1.945 percent, respectively. These two attributes do add up to 18.075 percent, the multiperiod performance of the portfolio.

EXHIBIT 12.8

Multiperiod Performance Attribution

Country	Portfolio Country Weights	Rate of Return on Portfolio Segment	Rate of Return on Market Benchmark	Performance	Attribution to Security Selection	Attribution to Market Allocation
Period 1						
Europe	0.60	30.0%	20.0%		6.00%	1.00%
Japan	0.40	10.0%	0.0%		4.00%	1.00%
Total Portfolio	100%	**22.0%**	**10.0%**	**12.00%**	**10.00%**	**2.00%**
Period 2						
Europe	0.55	5.0%	10.0%		−2.75%	−0.125%
Japan	0.45	30.0%	15.0%		6.75%	−0.125%
Total Portfolio	100%	**16.25%**	**12.5%**	**3.75%**	**4.00%**	**−0.25%**
Linked over Total Period						
Total Portfolio Unadjusted				18.075%	14.400%	1.745%
Total Portfolio Adjusted				**18.075%**	**16.130%**	**1.945%**

Clearly, the sum of the two attributes (14.40% + 1.75% = 16.15%) does not equal the performance of the portfolio over the total period (18.075%). The difference is 1.925 percent. As mentioned above, the difference comes from the fact that the portfolio value changes over time, so that each period attribute return should be applied to a different base value.

A quick and dirty adjustment is to assign this difference to each attribute proportionally to the attribute contribution. For example, security selection represents 14.40/16.145 = 89 percent of the sum of the two effects. Hence, we would allocate 89 percent of the unexplained performance difference to security selection and 11 percent to market allocation.

The second approach, then, is to use the highly recommended method of Equation 12.14. For each attribute:

- The past attribute would compound with the benchmark return in period 2, if no active investment choice is being made in period 2.
- To the extent that there is an active investment choice in period 2, the contribution of the choice will be earned on the portfolio value at the end of the previous period (here, period 1).

Let's take the example of security selection. We have

$$S = (10\% \times 1.125) + (4\% \times 1.22) = 16.130\%$$

For market allocation, we replace S with A in Equation 12.14 and find

$$S = (2\% \times 1.125) + (-0.25\% \times 1.22) = 1.945\%$$

We now verify that the sum of the two attributes is equal to the performance on the overall period:

$$S + A = 16.130\% + 1.945\% = 18.075\% = R - \overline{R}$$

So far, we have considered only two short periods, but the method can be generalized to compounding over a larger number of periods, say, from period 0 to period t. We use the subscript t for returns on the short period t and the superscript c for cumulative returns from 0 to period t (included).The cumulative attribute up to period t, S_t^c, is equal to the sum of

- The cumulative attribute up to period $t-1$, S_{t-1}^c, compounded at the benchmark return for period t, $\overline{R}_t$
- The attribute for the short period t, S_t, compounded at the cumulative portfolio return up to period $t-1$, R_{t-1}^c.

$$S_t^c = R_t^c - \overline{R}_t^c = S_{t-1}^c \times (1 + \overline{R}_t) + S_t \times (1 + R_{t-1}^c) \tag{12.15}$$

Different Methodologies It should be noted that the method presented here is not the only one used by performance evaluation services. In all methods, some choices have to be made on how to allocate cross products. Cross products inevitably appear when there are many attributes, even in a single-period analysis. Take the example of a manager who chose to overweight a country where he is simply tracking the country index and his overweight turns to an underweight at the end of the period of good performance for the index (as in period 1 of Example 12.5). The good performance of the portfolio relative to its composite benchmark is in part due to the cross-product of asset allocation and security selection. Here, we chose (as is commonly done) to allocate that cross product to security selection. But cross products also creep in when single-period returns are linked in a multiperiod analysis. Different methods make different choices on the allocation of these cross products to the various attributes. Hence, different methods can lead to slightly different attribution results. Discussion of various methods is provided in Bonafede, Foresti, and Matheos (2002) and Carino (2002).

An Example of Output

Graphic displays of performance attribution are proposed by most external GPE services. These services collect information on a large number of portfolios with comparable investment mandates. Exhibit 12.9 presents the comparison of the performance of a specific portfolio with that of a universe of managers with a similar mandate (non–North American equity). The performance attribution is presented here for one year. The left side of Exhibit 12.9 gives the total return on the fund,

EXHIBIT 12.9

Analysis of Performance: Non–North American Equity Return in U.S. Dollars: One year (in percent)

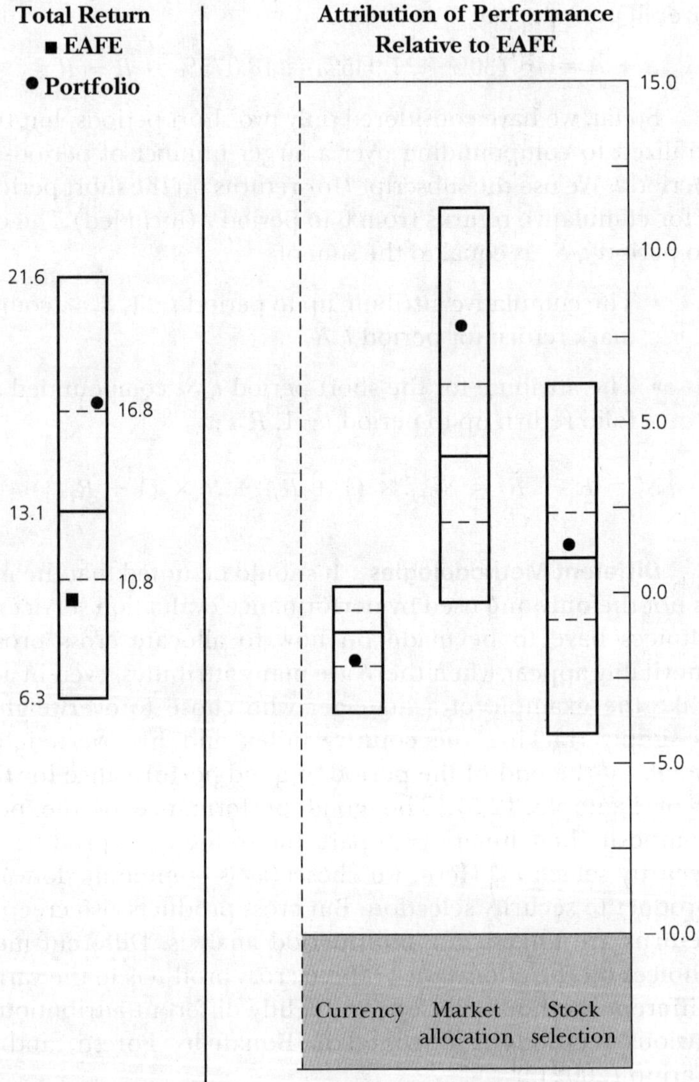

17.3	−2.0	7.7	1.6	Your portfolio (●)
19	69	15	36	Percentile rank
13.1	−1.2	4.0	1.0	Universe median

Source: Used by permission of InterSec Research.

the MSCI EAFE index, and a universe of 117 portfolios. The return of the studied portfolio is represented by a dot; that of the EAFE index is represented by a square. The distribution of the same statistics for the universe of managed funds surrounds the dot. For example, the return on the portfolio is 17.3 percent over the year, whereas the EAFE index went up by only 10.0 percent. The median of the universe had a return of about 13.1 percent (*full line*). The first quartile of the distribution (top 25 percent of the universe) is around 16.8 percent *(dashed line)*, whereas the third quartile (bottom 25 percent of the universe) is around 10.8 percent (*other dashed line*). The best manager had a return of 21.6 percent; the worst one had a return of 6.3 percent. The portfolio ranked quite high in the universe; on a percentile scale of 0 to 100, its rank is 19. The performance relative to the EAFE index is attributed in the right side of Exhibit 12.9. The relative performance of the portfolio is 7.3 percent (a return of 17.3 percent minus the return on the EAFE index of 10.0 percent). This can be decomposed into a market allocation contribution of 7.7 percent, a currency allocation contribution of 22.0 percent, and a stock selection contribution of 1.6 percent. The manager ranked high in the universe on asset allocation and stock selection but poorly on currency allocation.

Performance Appraisal in Global Performance Evaluation

The final stage of GPE is to appraise the investment skills of a manager. Because short-term results can be due to chance, rather than skills, a long horizon must be used. Performance may result from the level of risk taken by the manager, rather than from true investment skill. So, performance should be appraised after adjusting for risk.

Risk

The final calculation step in GPE is to analyze the risks borne by the portfolio. The most common approach to global investment involves two steps.

- *First*, the investor decides on an asset allocation across various asset classes (domestic equity, European equity, international bonds, emerging markets, etc.) based on expected returns and risks for the various asset classes. At this level, risk measures are calculated on *absolute* returns (i.e., not returns in relation to a benchmark).
- *Second*, an actively managed portfolio is constructed for each asset class, and a benchmark is assigned. Within each asset class, the risk of the portfolio is measured *relative* to this benchmark.

In practice, two types of risk measures are widely used.

Total or Absolute Risk: Standard Deviation The risk of the total portfolio is measured by the standard deviation of total returns over time. It is sometimes called *absolute risk*, because it does not value risk relative to a benchmark. If the standard deviation is calculated over T periods, the standard deviation σ_{tot} is given by

$$\sigma_{tot} = \sqrt{\frac{1}{T-1}\sum_{t=1}^{T}(r_t - \bar{r})^2} \tag{12.16}$$

The standard deviation is usually annualized[13] and expressed in percent per year. In other words, if the standard deviation is computed with monthly returns, the result is multiplied by $\sqrt{12}$.

If a global benchmark is assigned to the total portfolio, the standard deviation of the total portfolio and of the global benchmark can be compared. A regression of total portfolio returns on the benchmark returns allows one to calculate the beta of the portfolio relative to the benchmark.

The total risk of a portfolio is not the only relevant measure of risk. Investors who are interested primarily in diversification typically spread their assets among several funds. Pension funds, for example, invest abroad partly to diversify their domestic holdings. Calculating the correlation of an international portfolio to a domestic benchmark reveals whether the benefits of diversification have been achieved. A low correlation means that there are great international diversification benefits.[14]

Other risk measures, such as VaR (value at risk), are closely linked to the standard deviation.

Relative Risk: Tracking Error Investors measure how closely their portfolio, or segment of a portfolio, tracks a benchmark. Active managers take positions to beat a benchmark, but they also assume risks because they deviate from the benchmark. The *tracking error* is the standard deviation of returns in excess of the benchmark's returns. For any period *t*, the excess return in relation to a benchmark is given by

$$er_t = r_t - I_t$$

And the tracking error is

$$\sigma_{er} = \sqrt{\frac{1}{T-1}\sum_{t=1}^{T}(er_t - \overline{er})^2} \tag{12.17}$$

The tracking error is usually annualized and expressed in percent per year. Tracking error is sometimes called *active risk*. In the hope of positive performance, an active manager will deviate from the passive benchmark, thereby taking active risk. The tracking error quantifies this active risk. Example 12.12 illustrates tracking error for the International Portfolio.

---

[13] The standard deviation computed on monthly (or daily) returns is annualized by multiplying by the square root of the number of months (or days) in a year.

[14] Some services compute betas rather than correlation coefficients to derive the same type of information. (A beta coefficient is equal to the correlation coefficient times the ratio of the standard deviation of the portfolio over that of the market index.)

EXAMPLE 12.12 INTERNATIONAL PORTFOLIO TOTAL RISK AND TRACKING ERROR

In the International Portfolio, the investor is interested to know the tracking error of the Japanese (European) segment of her portfolio relative to the Japanese (European) stock index. These calculations are performed in the local currency, yen or euros. She also wants to know the tracking error of the total portfolio relative to the benchmark, in dollars. Finally, she wants to know how the total risk of her portfolio compares with that of the benchmark. Annualized risk estimates for the simple portfolio are reported in Exhibit 12.10. Standard deviations are calculated using daily returns, and then annualized. Comment on these figures.

SOLUTION

The tracking errors are very large, which is not surprising, because this portfolio is very poorly diversified. The total risk is much higher than that of the benchmark (24% compared with 20%). The information ratio reported in Exhibit 12.10 is discussed in the next section on risk-adjusted performance.

EXHIBIT 12.10

Tracking Error and Total Risk of International Portfolio

Portfolio Segment	Total Risk (% per year)	Tracking Error to Relevant Benchmark (% per year)	Information Ratio (annualized)
Japanese stocks		6%	3.33
European stocks		8%	2.50
Total portfolio	24%	7%	2.66
Benchmark	20%	0	0

Risk estimates are often unstable over time because they are derived from a mixture of many types of assets and sources of uncertainty. Currency markets are particularly prone to periods of calm followed by periods of extreme volatility. Portfolios that are low risk during one period can experience a larger standard deviation, or beta, during the next period. That is why an analysis of both past and present risk exposures is necessary. Again, frequent return data are required to obtain statistically significant risk estimates. Further insights can be gained by a detailed risk decomposition, as discussed in the next section.

Risk-Adjusted Performance

In a domestic setting, performance measurement services often attempt to rank managers on their risk-adjusted performance. It seems attractive to derive a single number, taking into account both performance and risk.

Sharpe Ratio The usual approach to risk-adjusted performance measurement is to calculate a *reward* (mean excess return over the risk-free rate) *to variability* (standard deviation of returns) ratio. This measure, introduced by Sharpe, is known as the *Sharpe ratio*,[15] which is both simple and intuitive. Let's note $\bar{r}$, the ex post mean return on the portfolio; R_0, the risk-free interest rate; and σ_{tot}, the total risk of the portfolio, where all variables have been annualized. Then, the Sharpe ratio is equal to

$$\text{Sharpe ratio} = \frac{\bar{r} - R_0}{\sigma_{tot}} \tag{12.18}$$

This reward-to-variability measure is intuitive, because it measures the return in excess of the risk-free rate (risk premium) per unit of risk taken.

However, the Sharpe ratio should be used only for the investor's global portfolio. A portfolio whose objective is to be invested in foreign assets to diversify risk of the domestic assets cannot be evaluated separately from the total portfolio. The standard deviation of the foreign portfolio will get partly diversified away in the global portfolio. The pertinent measure of risk of a portfolio of foreign assets should be its *contribution* to the risk of the global portfolio of the client (see Jorion and Kirsten, 1991). Other methods are the ratio of mean excess return to the market risk (β) (the Treynor ratio) and the Jensen measure.[16] Unfortunately, the application of these methods poses some problems, as outlined by Roll (1978), in a domestic context. The problems are even worse in an international context, in which investors disagree on what constitutes the "passive" world market portfolio, and these methods are seldom used.

The Sharpe ratio focuses on the total risk of the portfolio (uncertainty of absolute returns). But a manager who is assigned a benchmark will measure the risk of deviations from the benchmark's return.

Information Ratio When an investor measures performance relative to benchmarks, the *information ratio* is used.[17] The information ratio, IR, is defined as the ratio of the excess return from the benchmark, divided by the tracking error relative to the benchmark:

$$\text{IR} = \frac{er}{\sigma_{er}} \tag{12.19}$$

where *er* is the excess return over the benchmark for some observed period (often called *alpha*), and the tracking error σ_{er} is defined in Equation 12.17. A manager attempting to "beat" a benchmark takes some active bets and therefore incurs tracking error. The information ratio measures whether the excess return generated (often called *alpha*) is large relative to the tracking error incurred. Grinold and Kahn

---

[15] Sharpe (1994) extends the definition to include a Sharpe ratio relative to any benchmark.

[16] See Reilly and Brown (2003).

[17] A good discussion of the information ratio can be found in Grinold and Kahn (1995) and Goodwin (1998).

(1995) assert that an IR of 0.50 is "good" and that an IR of 1.0 is "exceptional." In practice, very few managers achieve an IR of 0.5 over a long period of time, so an IR of 0.2 or 0.3 realized over a few years is regarded as excellent by the profession.

Example 12.13 appraises the information ratios for the segments of the international portfolio and shows the Sharpe ratio calculation for the total portfolio.

If risk is a complex, multidimensional notion, no single reward-to-risk ratio can be used, and we are left with a more qualitative discussion of the risk–return trade-off. GPE services display risk–return performance comparisons for the universe of managers they evaluate. An example for World equity portfolios is reproduced in Exhibit 12.11. Each point in the exhibit is one managed portfolio from a universe of 45 portfolios with a global equity mandate. The annualized rate of return over four years is given on the Y axis. The annualized standard deviation is given on the X axis. The large dot represents the MSCI World index, which is a natural benchmark. The median return (about 12%) and risk (about 9.75%) of the universe are represented by a straight line. The best portfolios should lie in the upper left quadrant of this graph (more return and less risk).

EXAMPLE 12.13 INTERNATIONAL PORTFOLIO: INFORMATION RATIOS AND SHARPE RATIO

Analyze the information ratio for the international portfolio and calculate its Sharpe ratio.

SOLUTION

Performance is measured over a very short period of time (one quarter), so it is hard to conclude whether the good performance is the result of luck or of some true stock selection expertise. The Japanese stocks outperformed the Japanese benchmark by 5 percent over the quarter, an annualized 20 percent rate.[18] This leads to a 3.33 information ratio (20/6). The various information ratios are reported in Exhibit 12.10; they are all good. We can also compute the Sharpe ratio for the total portfolio. The risk-free dollar interest rate is 10 percent. Hence, for this portfolio of non–U.S. stocks,

$$\text{Sharpe ratio} = \frac{3.13 \times 4 - 10}{24} = 0.105$$

Again, because this international portfolio of non-U.S. stocks is only part of the global portfolio of our investor, it is somewhat unfair to compare the ex post risk premium realized to the total risk of the international portfolio. The total risk (24%) looks very high, but it would get partly diversified away in the global portfolio of the investor that also includes U.S. stocks. So, the risk contribution of the international portfolio is smaller than 24 percent, while the realized excess return is unquestionable.

[18] For illustration purposes, we use a simple arithmetic average to calculate the annualized mean return. In practice, returns should be compounded (geometric average).

EXHIBIT 12.11

Risk–Return Performance Comparisons: World Equity Portfolios (U.S. dollars)
Four years

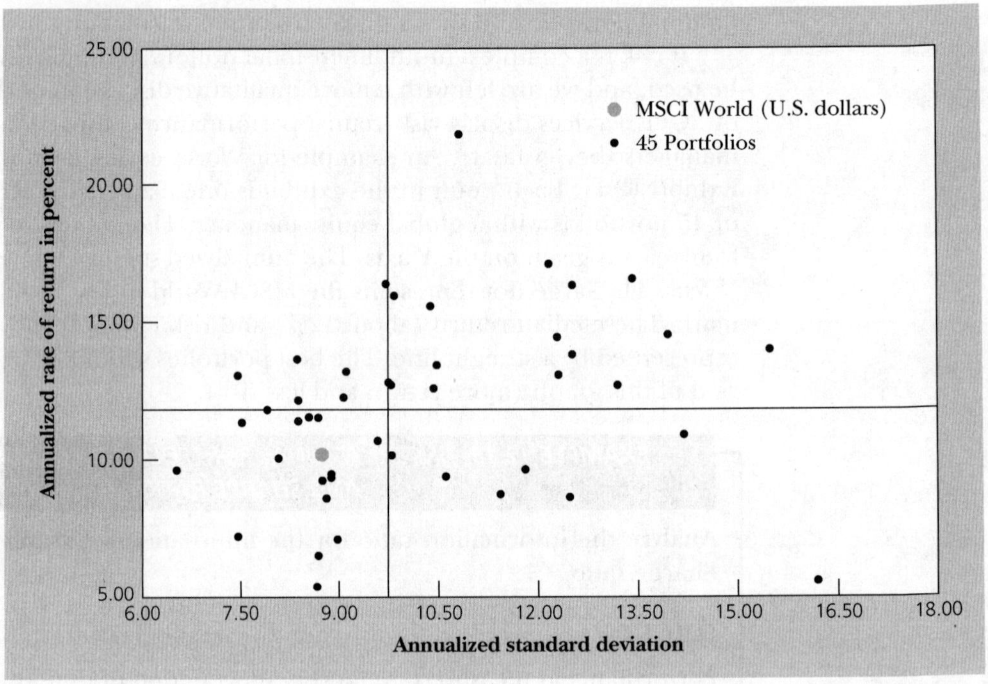

Risk Allocation and Budgeting

Just as the total portfolio performance can be attributed to the various investment decisions (*performance attribution*), the total risk can be decomposed into the various risk exposures taken by the manager (*risk allocation*). This leads to a better understanding of the total risk borne.

In GPE, a client will judge in which areas its investment managers have skills; that is, they can add value relative to a passive benchmark. Based on the performance appraisal, the client will then decide to allocate more active risk to those managers. This process is called *risk budgeting.* In other words, the client will allow some managers to have a large tracking error, because they expect to add value in their segment, but will allow some other managers to have only a small tracking error. For example, a pension plan could assign a 4 percent tracking error to a European equity manager and to a currency overlay manager, but a minimal tracking error to an Asian equity manager.

So, the total risk (standard deviation) of a portfolio is the result of decisions at two levels:

- The *absolute risk allocation* to each asset class: This is a traditional asset allocation approach, wherein the risk on each asset class is measured using passive benchmarks. The risk of active managers who deviate from their benchmarks is not introduced at this level.
- The *active risk allocation* of managers in each asset class: This is the risk budgeted to generate alphas relative to each benchmark.

Such a risk decomposition can be quite complex in a global portfolio, because risks are correlated and, hence, not additive. The currency risk dimension is always an important element in GPE.

Because the investment policy statement usually contains risk objectives and constraints, it is important that a GPE be able to provide a consistent risk analysis at the various levels of the investment process, from the strategic allocation to the appraisal of each manager.

Some Potential Biases in Return and Risk

GPE is used by a client, in part, to evaluate and select managers on the basis of their historical track records. However, it is difficult to separate expertise from luck. Past performance is not necessarily a good indicator of future performance, and switching from one manager to the next is a costly process. It is important not to overestimate the statistical significance of performance comparisons to prevent inefficient churning of the portfolio and management changes based on insignificant information.

Performance appraisal requires that both return and risk measures be unbiased. Performance standards such as GIPS (see the next section on implementation) attempt to ensure the reliability of the data presented, but it is hard to differentiate between past performance due to luck or to true investment skills that will lead to superior performance in the future. Furthermore, several problems can introduce severe biases in performance appraisal. This is typically the case for some asset classes, such as alternative investments or hedge funds. Past return-and-risk figures can be biased estimates of the future for a variety of reasons:

- Infrequently traded assets
- Option-like investment strategies
- Survivorship bias: return
- Survivorship bias: risk

Following are discussions of some of these problems, with an illustration of hedge funds performance appraisal.

Infrequently Traded Assets Some assets trade infrequently. This is the case for many alternative assets that are not exchange traded, such as real estate or private equity. This is also the case for illiquid exchange traded securities or over-the-counter instruments often used by hedge funds. Because prices used are not up-to-date market prices, they tend to be smoothed over time.[19] For example, the appraisal process used in real estate introduces a smoothing of returns, because properties are appraised only infrequently. The internal rate of return methodology used in private equity also introduces a smoothing of returns. The infrequent nature of price updates in the alternative asset world induces a significant downward bias to the measured risk of the assets. In addition, correlations of alternative investment returns with conventional equity and fixed income returns, and among the alternatives, are often close to zero or even negative, because of the smoothing effect and the absence of market-observable returns. The bias can be large,[20] so that the true risk can be larger than the reported estimates.

Option-like Investment Strategies Risk measures used in performance appraisal assume that portfolio returns are normally distributed. Many investment strategies followed by hedge funds have some option-like features that violate the normality assumption. For example, hedge funds following so-called arbitrage strategies will generally make a "small" profit when asset prices converge to their arbitrage value, but they run the risk of a huge loss if their arbitrage model fails. Standard deviation or traditional VaR measures understate the true risk of losses.

Survivorship Bias: Return As discussed in Chapter 8, unsuccessful investment funds and managers tend to disappear over time. Only successful ones search for new clients and present their track records. This fact creates a *survivorship bias*. This problem is acute with hedge funds because they often do not have to comply with performance presentation standards. It is not uncommon to see hedge fund managers present the track records of only their successful funds, omitting those that have been closed. If a fund begins to perform poorly, perhaps even starting to go out of business, it may stop reporting its performance entirely, thus inflating the reported average performance of hedge funds. Hedge fund indexes and databases may include only funds that have survived. Funds with bad performance disappear and are removed from the database that is used by investors to select among existing funds. Most academic studies suggest that survivorship bias overstates return by 200 to 400 basis points per year. Malkiel and Saha (2005) estimated the average annual bias in performance to be 442 basis points.

To illustrate the concept of survivorship bias, let's take a hypothetical example of a world in which no managers have any investment skill; that is, the markets are fully efficient and any outperformance is purely due to luck. At the end of any period, there will still be hedge fund managers and funds who will report, by luck, a good

---

[19] See, for example, Terhaar, Staub, and Singer (2003).

[20] See, for example, Asness, Krail, and Liew (2001).

performance ex post. They will survive, and the others will disappear. All existing funds will tend to report excellent track records, and the average[21] past performance of the group of all existing funds will be positive. But the question is whether those surviving managers will deliver a superior performance in the future.

Survivorship Bias: Risk A similar survivorship bias applies to risk measures. Investors shy away from high risk, as well as from negative performance. Hedge funds that exhibited large downside shocks in the past tend to disappear. So, the average reported risk of existing funds will tend to be lower than had all funds been included in the calculation. But there is no guarantee that the same strategy will also be low risk in the future. Examples abound of hedge funds that were regarded as low risk but lost all of their capital.

Implementation of Performance Evaluation

In-house performance measurement is useful in determining the strengths and weaknesses of an investment organization. This is even more important in a global than in a domestic setting because of the larger number of factors influencing return and risk. The development of a GPE system requires some sophisticated information technology, given the enormous mass of data that must be summarized into a few performance figures. The diversity of instruments, quotation, time zones, trading techniques, and information sources, renders the analysis susceptible to errors. However, a good investment organization should be able to master this issue.

Once an investment organization is able to generate reliable and detailed return-and-risk numbers, two issues have to be addressed:

- What are the benchmarks used to evaluate performance?
- What are the standards used for performance presentation?

More on Global Benchmarks

Manager Universes and Customized Benchmarks The traditional approach to evaluate the performance of an asset manager has been to compare the return on the managed fund with that of peers (other managers). This process is referred to as *peer group* or *manager universe* comparison. Managers are compared even if the investment policies followed in the portfolio are widely different. A criticism often voiced is that this approach "mixes apples and oranges." This peer group approach is understandable if the client delegates to the manager the task of setting the

[21] There is also a self-selection bias in the publicly available databases and indexes of alternative investment funds. Managers choose to be included in these databases only if they have had a good past performance, and their good-performance history for the previous years is instantly incorporated in the database (backfilling bias). See Fung and Hsieh (2002).

investment policy of the fund and its strategic, or long-term, allocation. A comparison of returns of managers with balanced mandates is meaningful.

However, most institutional investors have now taken the responsibility of setting the investment policy of their overall fund. They translate this investment policy into benchmarks and assign a customized benchmark to each of their managers. The performance of an asset manager should be judged relative to the customized benchmark that has been assigned to him or her, not relative to the universe of all managers. Some individual investors also set benchmarks in their investment policy statement.

Comparison with benchmarks has become the rule for the U.S. pension fund industry. Other types of clients, however, such as foundations and endowment funds, still resort to comparisons with manager universes. In the early 1990s, peer group comparison was the dominant method used to evaluate the performance of U.K. pension scheme managers. But a majority of British pension schemes moved to comparison with customized benchmarks during the 1990s. For example, the Unilever Superannuation Fund made the move to scheme-specific benchmarks in 1996, as described in the following Concepts in Action feature.

Choosing benchmarks in a global setting is not an easy task, especially if the benchmark spans several countries/currency (e.g., European equity or non-dollar bonds). Important issues in constructing customized international benchmarks are

- individual country/market weights;
- countries, industries, and styles; and
- currency hedging.

CONCEPTS IN ACTION *LESSONS FROM THE UNILEVER/MERRILL CASE*

. . . a peer group benchmark arrangement conflates the two big tasks facing the stewards of our pension assets: setting long-term policy on the one hand, and implementing it on the other.

The original objectives of the Unilever scheme called for Merrill and its other managers to "maximise long-term returns subject to an acceptable level of risk normally associated with a balanced approach to fund management". This really was a 'managers know best' approach. By contrast, the new benchmark had a target rate of return of the benchmark plus 1%, as measured over three years, and a downside risk tolerance of −3%, as measured over any trailing four calendar quarter period. Effectively, the more precise wording of the new objectives, and the specification of a benchmark portfolio, reflected the greater responsibility taken by the client for setting the scheme's investment policy. Indeed, the Pension Act of 1995 seems to demand that trustees, not managers, take on this responsibility.

Source: Extract from Mark Tapley, "Lessons from the Unilever/Merrill case," *IPE*, May 2002, p. 36.

Individual Country/Market Weights Standard international equity indexes are weighted by market capitalization. Some clients prefer equity indexes whose national allocation is based on different sets of weights—for example, relative national gross domestic product (GDP). This gives each country a weight proportional to its economic importance in world production, rather than the size of its financial market. The problem with international indexes based on GDP weights is that they are difficult and costly to track in a managed portfolio. GDP figures are adjusted only every few months, whereas stock market prices move continuously; hence, the portfolio must be continuously rebalanced to adjust to GDP weights. This can be costly in terms of transaction costs. Replicating a GDP-weighted benchmark is not practically feasible because rebalancing would be needed whenever country weights differ from market-capitalization weights.

National bond markets have market capitalizations that depend on the budget deficit of the country. Governments that run large budget deficits must issue more bonds to finance the deficits. It is unclear why the country/currency allocation should favor lax fiscal/budget policies. Again, the choice of national weights is an important investment policy decision.

Countries, Industries, and Style The traditional approach to international equity investing has been a top-down country allocation. So, it was natural to assign to managers country or regional benchmarks. However, many believe that industry factors have grown to be more important than country factors. Hence, it could be natural to assign benchmarks that favor global or regional industry allocation rather than country allocation. Similarly, many believe that investment styles are important in explaining differences in global portfolio returns. So, it could be natural to assign benchmarks along investment styles. For example, an asset manager that specializes in value stocks could be assigned an international value benchmark, allowing the manager to invest internationally in value stocks.

Global industry and style approaches are different ways to slice global portfolios. Hence, global benchmarks could be customized along country/regional lines but also along global industry lines or global style lines.

Currency Hedging Publicly available market indexes are generally not hedged against currency movements. But a client could decide to assign to an asset manager a customized benchmark that is fully hedged against currency risk. This is because the client does not wish to take on any currency risk, or because the client decides to delegate currency management to a separate currency-overlay manager. Some clients even decide to apply to the benchmark an arbitrary hedge ratio, between zero and 100 percent; it is not uncommon to see pension plans assigning international benchmarks that are 50 percent hedged against currency risk.

It should be noted that a fully hedged benchmark does not mean that the asset manager can neglect the currency dimension. This is because the value of corporations is influenced, in a different way, by currency movements (see Chapter 4).

Global Investment Performance Standards and Other Performance Presentation Standards

Some countries have adopted performance presentation standards that apply to global portfolios. In the United States, various regulations apply to different types of portfolios. Mutual funds have to follow rules mandated by the Securities and Exchange Commission (SEC). Corporate pension funds apply the Employee Retirement Income Security Act (ERISA). Public pension funds follow regulations set by federal or local governments. These performance presentation regulations are not very restrictive and provide little guidance for internationally diversified portfolios.

CFA Institute (formerly known as AIMR) implemented Performance Presentation Standards (AIMR-PPS) for North American asset managers in the late 1980s and subsequently developed the *Global Investment Performance Standards* (*GIPS*), which are voluntary guidelines for the ethical presentation of investment performance. In 2005, a new version of GIPS was published to be used worldwide. As of 2006, GIPS replaced the AIMR-PPS and are being adopted by many countries. The CFA Institute believes that the establishment and acceptance in all countries of performance presentation standards based on GIPS are vital steps in facilitating the availability of comparable investment performance history on a global basis. Global standardization of performance reporting guidelines allow investors to compare investment firms on a global level and allow these investment firms to compete for business on an equal footing with investment firms in other countries. GIPS are a set of detailed, ethical principles intended to promote full disclosure and fair representation by investment managers in reporting their investment results to existing and prospective clients. A secondary objective is to ensure uniformity in reporting so that results are directly comparable among investment managers. To this end, some performance presentation aspects are mandatory, whereas others are only recommended. GIPS carefully detail the calculation and presentation of historical records of performance by base currency.

Clearly, prospective and existing clients of investment management firms benefit from a global standard, by having a greater degree of confidence in the performance numbers presented by investment management firms. Performance standards, uniform in all countries, are required so that clients can readily compare investment performance among firms. GIPS have become the standards for presenting performance to institutional clients worldwide. This can be explained by the recognized quality of GIPS, the fast-growing number of CFA charterholders in all countries, and the pressures of global competition in asset management. An investment manager that presents historical performance figures that are not GIPS compliant is at a clear competitive disadvantage.

The concept of composites is central to GIPS. All portfolios managed by an investment firm must enter the composites. A *composite* is an aggregation of a number of portfolios into a single group that is representative of a particular investment objective or strategy. The composite return is the asset-weighted average of the performance results of all the portfolios in the composite. The idea is that an investment firm cannot present to existing or prospective clients a track record that is based only on a few selected accounts. Composites therefore ensure that prospective clients have a fair and complete representation of a manager's past performance record. Each composite must comprise portfolios or asset classes representing a similar strategy or investment objective. For each composite, the firm must select a benchmark that reflects the investment strategy of the composite, and the benchmark return must be presented for the same period for which the composite return is presented. Time-weighted rates of return, adjusted for cash flows, are required.[22] Investment firms must meet all the requirements set forth in GIPS to claim compliance. GIPS also detail the verification procedures that a third-party verifier must follow to establish that an investment firm claiming compliance with GIPS has adhered to the standards.

As mentioned, CFA Institute strongly encourages all countries to adopt GIPS as their performance presentation standards. Where existing laws, regulations, or industry standards already impose performance presentation standards, investment firms are strongly encouraged to meet both sets of requirements and to disclose any possible conflicts. For example, British actuaries have set rules for U.K. pension funds. The National Association of Pension Funds (NAPF) has established British standards requiring that performance be calculated by an outside service. This British industry practice of relying on outside services to calculate and present historical performance makes the aggregation into a composite more difficult if different outside services are used for different portfolios. A diversity of outside services is the rule for large investment firms, with many clients requesting that performance be calculated by their preferred actuarial service. However, a U.K. version of GIPS has now been adopted by the NAPF. Industry practices in continental Europe lag behind Anglo-American standards. Only recently has the focus been on performance among Europeans, partly because of institutional investors' extensive reliance on in-house portfolio management. But national performance presentation standards are likely to be formulated in the near future, given the development of pension funds and the internationalization of competition among investment managers.

Japan used to rely extensively on book-value accounting of performance. In other words, unrealized profits or losses were not included in the calculation of the total rate of return. Deregulation and competition are progressively pushing Japan toward the Anglo-American approach to performance measurement. In all countries, GIPS are increasingly used on a voluntary basis.

[22] The authoritative statement of the GIPS, and associated guidelines, can be found on the CFA Institute Web site at www.cfainstitute.org.

Summary

- Global performance evaluation is conducted in three steps: measurement, attribution, and appraisal.
- The rate of return on a portfolio or on one of its segments can be measured using various methods to account for cash flows. Money-weighted rates measure the return on the average invested capital, whereas time-weighted rates measure the return per unit of invested currency. The time-weighted rate should be used for performance evaluation.
- Global performance evaluation is important to understanding how performance has been achieved. A good performance evaluation relies on the quality and availability of data, and the problems are magnified in the international context. Frequent cash flows among the various portfolio segments are a major problem, and calculation of the performance of each segment (e.g., Japanese equity) requires the valuation of segments on each cash flow date.
- In a global setting, the investment rate of return should be decomposed into the return made in local currency (capital gain/loss plus yield) and the currency return component (from the local currency to the base currency of the account).
- In active management, superior performance can result from any of the major investment decisions: asset allocation, currency allocation, market timing, and security selection on each market. The total performance should therefore be broken down and attributed to the various management decisions (performance attribution).
- The realized performance should be appraised in light of the risk assumed. Risk is measured in absolute terms (*total or absolute risk*) but also relative to some benchmarks *(tracking error).* Each measure gives useful, but different, information. Because risk reduction is an important motivation for international investing, the contribution to the risk of the overall fund of an investor could be considered when studying the absolute risk of an international portfolio. Risk-adjusted return can be measured on absolute risk *(Sharpe ratio)* or relative risk *(information ratio).* Just as the total portfolio returns can be attributed to the various investment decisions *(performance attribution),* the total risk can be decomposed into the various risk exposures taken by the manager *(risk allocation).*
- Performance is measured relative to some benchmarks. In a global setting, the choice of benchmarks is an important decision that reflects investment policy; many alternatives are available.
- Global standardization of performance reporting guidelines allows investors to compare investment firms on a global level and allows investment managers to compete globally. Performance presentation standards are a set of detailed, ethical principles intended to promote full disclosure and fair representation by investment managers in reporting their investment results to existing and prospective clients. GIPS are a set of standards developed by CFA Institute that are widely adopted worldwide by managers of institutional assets.

Problems

1. A client invested €100 at the start of the month. Assume that the manager tracks an assigned benchmark index. After 20 days, the portfolio gained 10 percent (value = €110), as did the index, and the client added an extra €50 (total portfolio value = €160). From day 20 to day 30, the portfolio, and the index, lost 9.09 percent—the final portfolio value is €160 × (1 − 0.0909) = €145.46. What are the rates of returns using the various methods outlined in the text? Which rate should you use to evaluate the performance of the manager relative to its benchmark?

2. You are managing a portfolio worth $200 at the start of the period. After one month, the value of the portfolio is up to $220, and the client, who needs cash, withdraws $40. Two months later, the portfolio is still worth $180. Give various measures of the return on the portfolio over the three-month period.

3. You own a portfolio of British assets worth £100,000 on January 1. The portfolio is worth £90,000 on January 10, and you withdraw £20,000. On January 20, the value of your portfolio has gone up to £90,000, and you add £50,000. On January 31, your portfolio is worth £145,000. Compute the rate of return in January, using the methods proposed in this text.

4. A U.S. pension fund wants to invest $1 million in foreign equity. Its board of trustees must decide whether to invest in a commingled index fund tracking the EAFE index or to give the money to an active manager. The board learns that this active manager turns the portfolios over about twice a year. Given the small size of the account, the transaction costs are likely to be an average of 1.5 percent of each transaction's value. The active manager charges 0.75 percent in annual management fees, and the indexer charges 0.25 percent. By how much should the active manager outperform the index to cover the extra costs in the form of fees and transaction costs on the annual turnover?

5. You are a French investor holding some U.S. bonds. Over the month, the value of your bond portfolio goes from $1 million to $1.05 million. The exchange rates move from €1 per dollar to €1.02 per dollar.

a. What is your rate of return in dollars?

b. What is your rate of return in euros?

c. Is the difference exactly equal to the percentage movement in the exchange rate? If not, why?

6. You own a portfolio of Swedish and American stocks. Their respective benchmarks are the OMX and S&P 500 indexes, and the Swedish and American portfolios are closely matched to their benchmarks in risk. There have been no movements during the year (cash flows, sales or purchase, dividends paid). Valuation and performance analysis is done in Swedish kronor (SKr). Here are the valuations at the start and the end of the year:

	January 1	**December 31**
Swedish stocks	SKr600,000	SKr660,000
U.S. stocks	SKr600,000	SKr702,000
Total	SKr1,200,000	SKr1,362,000
Exchange rate	SKr6 per $	SKr5.4 per $
OMX index	100	120
S&P index	100	125

a. What is the total return on the portfolio?
b. Decompose this return into capital gain, yield, and currency contribution.
c. What is the contribution of security selection?

7. An American investor has invested $100,000 in a global equity portfolio made up of U.S., Asian, and European stocks. On December 31, the portfolio is invested in 500 IBM shares listed in New York, 200 Sony shares listed in Tokyo, and 50 BMW shares listed in Frankfurt. He wants to beat the World index used as benchmark. This index has a 50 percent weight in the U.S. stock index, a 25 percent weight in the Japanese stock index, and a 25 percent weight in the European stock index. The country components of the portfolio have average risk relative to their respective country indexes. He uses the U.S. dollar as base currency. On March 31, his portfolio has gained 4.065 percent, while the World index gained only 0.735 percent in dollars. He wishes to understand why his portfolio had such a good performance over the quarter. All necessary data are given in the following tables. There were no cash flows in the portfolio, nor any dividends paid.
   a. Decompose the total return on the portfolio into capital gains (in local currency) and currency contribution.
   b. What is the contribution of security selection?
   c. Attribute the performance relative to the benchmark (World index) to the various investment decisions.

Global Equity Portfolio: Composition and Market Data

		Price (in local currency)		Portfolio Value on Dec. 31		Portfolio Value on Mar. 31	
Portfolio	**Number of Shares**	**Dec. 31**	**Mar. 31**	**Local Currency**	**Dollar**	**Local Currency**	**Dollar**
U.S. stocks							
IBM	500	100	105	50,000	50,000	52,500	52,500
Japanese stocks							
Sony	200	10,000	11,000	2,000,000	20,000	2,200,000	20,952
European stocks							
BMW	50	600	600	30,000	30,000	30,000	30,612
Total					*100,000*		*104,065*

Market Data	**Dec. 31**	**Mar. 31**
World index ($)	100	100.735
U.S. index ($)	100	103
Japanese index (¥)	100	105
European index (€)	100	95
Yen per dollar	100	105
Euro per dollar	1	0.98

8. A U.S. pension plan hired two international firms to manage the non-U.S. equity portion of its total portfolio. Each firm was free to own stocks in any country market included in the MSCI EAFE index and free to use any form of dollar and/or nondollar cash or bonds as an equity substitute or reserve. After three years had elapsed, the records of the managers and the EAFE index were as shown in the following table:

Summary: Contributions to Return

	Currency	Country Selection	Stock Selection	Cash/Bond Allocation	Total Return Recorded
Manager A	−9.0%	19.7%	3.1%	0.6%	14.4%
Manager B	−7.4	14.2	6.0	2.8	15.6
Composite of A&B	−8.2	16.9	4.5	1.7	15.0
EAFE index	−12.9	19.9	—	—	7.0

The "Country Selection" column gives the local-currency return that would have been achieved if the portfolio were invested in country indexes rather than specific stocks. You are a member of the plan sponsor's pension committee, which will soon meet with the plan's consultant to review manager performance. In preparation for this meeting, you go through the following analysis:

a. Briefly describe the strengths and weaknesses of each manager, relative to the EAFE index data.

b. Briefly explain the meaning of the data in the Currency column.

9. Your discussion with a client has turned to the measurement of investment performance, particularly with respect to international portfolios.

Performance and Attribution Data: Annualized Returns for Five Years Ended 12/31/2008

International Manager/Index	Total Return	Country/Security Selection	Currency Return
Manager A	−6.0%	2.0%	−8.0%
Manager B	−2.0	−1.0	−1.0
EAFE index	−5.0	0.2	−5.2

a. Assume that the data in this table for Manager A and Manager B accurately reflect their investment skills and that both managers actively manage currency exposure. Briefly describe one strength and one weakness for each manager.

b. Recommend and justify a strategy that would enable the fund to take advantage of the strength of each of the two managers while minimizing their weaknesses.

10. A U.S. portfolio manager has a global equity portfolio with investments in the United States, United Kingdom, and France. The local currency values of the equity investments on December 31, 2006, and December 31, 2007, are shown in the following table. The performance of the portfolio manager is measured against the World index, which has 60 percent weight in the U.S. stock index, a 20 percent weight in the U.K. stock index, and a 20 percent weight in the French stock index. Assume that no dividends were paid and there were no cash flows in the portfolio during the year. The base currency is the U.S. dollar. The country components of the portfolio have average risk relative to their respective country indexes. Use the information provided in the following tables to answer the questions asked.

Country	Dec. 31, 2006 Local Currency Value	Dec. 31, 2007 Local Currency Value
United States	$50,000,000	$55,000,000
United Kingdom	£20,000,000	£20,500,000
France	€25,000,000	€32,000,000

Market Data	Dec. 31, 2006	Dec. 31, 2007
World index ($)	780	834.622
U.S. index ($)	760	829
U.K. index (£)	1,090	1,148
France index (€)	950	1,009
Pounds per dollar	0.65	0.62
Euros per dollar	1.1	1.2

a. Calculate the local currency return and dollar return on the portfolio for the period December 31, 2006, to December 31, 2007.

b. Decompose the total return on the portfolio into the following components:
- Capital gains in local currency
- Currency contribution

c. Decompose the total return on the portfolio into the following components:
- Market component
- Security selection contribution
- Currency component

d. Carry out a global performance evaluation for the portfolio relative to the World index. Make sure the global performance attribution identifies the following components:
- Benchmark return
- Market allocation
- Currency allocation
- Security selection

11. A U.S. pension fund has a domestic portfolio with an expected return of 10 percent and a standard deviation of 12 percent. It also invests in a foreign equity fund that has an expected dollar return of 11 percent and a dollar standard deviation of 20 percent. The correlation of the foreign and U.S. portfolio is 0.2. The current dollar interest rate is 8 percent. Would you say that the foreign equity portfolio is attractive from a risk–return viewpoint?

12. Consider a U.S. pension fund with the following performance:

	Percentage Total Portfolio (%)	Total Dollar Return (%)	Standard Deviation of Return (%)	Correlation with U.S. Stock Index
U.S. equity	90	10	15	0.99
Foreign equity	10	11	20	−0.10

Is the risk–return performance of the foreign portfolio attractive?

13. You are provided with annual rates of return for a portfolio and relevant benchmark index for the years 2008 to 2012. Calculate the tracking error for the portfolio.

Year	Portfolio Return	Benchmark Return
2008	12%	14%
2009	14%	10%
2010	20%	12%
2011	14%	16%
2012	16%	13%

14. You are provided with annual return, standard deviation of returns, and tracking error to the relevant benchmark for three portfolios. Calculate the Sharpe ratio and information ratio for the three portfolios and rank them according to each measure.

Portfolio	Return	Standard Deviation	Tracking Error
1	13.50%	19.00%	6.50%
2	16.25%	24.00%	8.00%
3	17.00%	23.00%	7.00%
Benchmark	13.00%	20.00%	
Risk-free	5.00%		

15. A hedge fund group specializes in strategies related to a market whose index increased by 20 percent during a year in which the group's three funds began at equal size but with different strategies. Here is the performance of the three funds over the year, before and after management fees set at 20 percent of gross profits:

Fund	Gross Return	Net Return
A	40%	32%
B	30%	24%
C	−10%	−10%

One can observe that the average performance of the three funds is exactly equal to the performance of the market index. By year end, most clients had left fund C and so it was closed. At the beginning of the next year, the hedge fund group launched an aggressive publicity campaign among portfolio managers, stressing the remarkable performance of fund A. For clients responding to the publicity campaign and asking about its other funds, the hedge fund group discussed fund B, and claimed that their average performance across funds was 35 percent. What do you think of this publicity campaign?

16. Investment markets are highly competitive and professional investors now dominate the marketplace. What should the average performance of all investors be, compared with market indexes? If international investment managers, as a group, beat some national market index, what does it tell us about the performance of local investment managers? Would you reach the opposite conclusion if international managers underperform, as a group, relative to some local market index?

17. A client has given you $100 million to invest abroad in an equity GDP-indexed fund. There are only two foreign countries, A and B, and their GDPs are currently equal to $100 billion each. Their respective stock market capitalizations are $150 and $100 billion. The performance of the fund is compared monthly with the GDP-weighted index. Assume that exchange rates remain fixed and that there are no new listings on the stock markets, so that national market capitalizations go up and down in line with movements in the national stock indexes. Here are the stock market indexes and the published GDPs for the next six months:

Month	GDP-A	GDP-B	Index A	Index B
0	100	100	100	100
1	100	100	95	110
2	100	100	100	100
3	102	101	100	120
4	102	101	105	125
5	102	101	110	135

a. Calculate the values at the end of each month of the two international indexes: GDP-weighted index and market capitalization–weighted index. In both cases, use the international weights (GDP and market cap) that are valid at the start of the month.
b. Assume that you build a portfolio using two national index funds. What operation should you do each month to track the GDP-weighted index?

18. a. Explain how total portfolio risk can be decomposed into various risk exposures, and indicate why risk decomposition can be a complex exercise.
b. Explain what is meant by the term *risk budgeting.*

19. List and explain three factors that introduce potential biases in performance and risk measurement of portfolios.

20. Mr. Smith is a foreign investor who has an account with a small Luxembourg bank. He does not pay taxes on his account. He gave a complete management mandate to the bank and wants to judge the performance of the manager. He is using the U.S. dollar as his base currency.
a. He is looking at the two most recent valuation monthly reports, which are given in Exhibit A, and wonders how to compute the performance. He reads in the financial press that the MSCI World index has risen by 2 percent this month (in U.S. dollars). Basically, he would like to answer the following questions:
   i. What is the total return on his portfolio?
   ii. What are the sources of this return; that is, how much is due to capital appreciation, yield, and currency movements?
   iii. How good is the manager in selecting securities on the various markets?

You must give him precise, quantified information that will help him to answer these questions. (First, compute the return for each segment of the portfolio and its components, that is, price, yield, and currency; then combine these returns to answer the last two queries.)

b. Mr. Smith is aware that cash flows, as well as movements among the various segments of his portfolio, may obscure his analysis. He tries to compute the performance during the next month where the manager has been more active.

He wants to make sure he understands how a valuation report is constructed before doing his analysis. He gets the following information to prepare his own version of the valuation report:

Cash flow: Mr. Smith added $10,000 to his account.
Transactions: The manager sold the 500 Exxon. The total proceeds of the sale, net of commissions, were $20,000. He bought 400 Pernod-Ricard on the Paris Bourse for a total cost of $30,860.
Income received: A semiannual coupon was paid on the EIB bond for a total receipt of $575. AMAX dividends were $357.

Market Prices on February 28

AMAX	24	Dollar/yen	0.0047
Hitachi	880	Dollar/euro	1.05
TDK	6,000	U.S. stock index	103
Club Méditerranée	85	Japan stock index	97
Pernod-Ricard	72	France stock index	110
Government 6% 92	92	Yen bond index	101
(accrued interest, 1.55%)		World index	104
EIB 8.5% 93	98		
(accrued interest, 0.62%)			

EXHIBIT A

Account Valuation Reports (explanation)

The valuation report is set up following a standard method:

- Column 1 describes the security and its quotation currency.
- Column 2 gives either the number of securities for common stocks or the nominal invested for fixed income.
- Column 3 gives the market price in local currency. For bonds, this is given in percentage of the nominal (par) value.
- Column 4 gives the accrued interest as the percentage of the nominal (par) value. Usually, a yen bond with a coupon of, say, 8% will bear an interest of 8/365% per day. This is cumulated in the accrued interest column until the coupon is paid (semiannual, here).
- Column 5 gives the capital amount in base currency (here, U.S. dollars). It is the market price (column 3), multiplied by the column 2 value, multiplied by the exchange rate.
- Column 6 gives the amount of accrued interest in base currency. It is the accrued interest in percentage (column 4), multiplied by the column 2 value, multiplied by the exchange rate.
- Columns 7 and 8 give subtotals in capital and percentage.

Account Valuation for Mr. Smith, December 31

(1) Description of Security	(2) Number of Securities or Nominal	(3) Market Price (local currency)	(4) Accrued Interest (%)	(5) Capital Amount ($)	(6) Accrued Interest ($)	(7) Subtotal ($)	(8) Subtotal (%)
Equity							
United States (in $)							
AMAX	1,000	24.50		24,500			
Exxon	500	37.25		18,625		43,125	29.8
Japan (in yen)							
Hitachi	10,000	800		34,320			
TDK	1,000	6,500		27,885		62,205	43.0
France (in euros)							
Club Med	200	77		18,326		18,326	12.7
Bonds							
Yen							
Govt. 6% 92	2,000,000	91.0%	0.52%	7,807	45		
EIB 8.5% 93	3,000,000	98.5%	3.47%	12,677	447	20,976	14.5
Cash							
U.S. dollars	0			0	0	0	0
Total				**144,140**	**492**	**144,632**	**100**

Exchange rates:
Yen = 0.00429 dollars
Euro = 1.19 dollars

Market indexes (price only):
U.S. stocks = 100
Japanese stocks = 100
French stocks = 100
Yen bonds = 100
World index = 100

EXHIBIT A (CONTINUED)

Account Valuation for Mr. Smith, January 30

(1) Description of Security	(2) Number of Securities of Nominal	(3) Market Price (local currency)	(4) Accrued Interest (%)	(5) Capital Amount ($)	(6) Accrued Interest ($)	(7) Subtotal ($)	(8) Subtotal (%)
Equity							
United States (in $)							
AMAX	1,000	23.50		23,500			
Exxon	500	38.00		19,000		42,500	28.8
Japan (in yen)							
Hitachi	10,000	820		36,900			
TDK	1,000	6,100		27,450		64,350	43.5
France (in euros)							
Club Med	200	87		19,140		19,140	12.9
Bonds							
Yen							
Govt. 6% 92	2,000,000	90.0%	1.04%	8,100	94		
EIB 8.5% 93	3,000,000	96.9%	4.16%	13,081	562	21,837	14.8
Cash							
U.S. dollars	0			0	0	0	0
Total				**147,171**	**656**	**147,827**	**100**

Exchange rates:
Yen = 0.0045 dollars
Euro = 1.10 dollars

Market indexes (price only):
U.S. stocks = 102.5
Japanese stocks = 98
French stocks = 108
Yen bonds = 99
World index = 102

Mr. Smith has no indication of the exact day of the transactions, and it would be too complicated to break down the month into subperiods, anyway. He therefore decides to make the assumption that every transaction or cash flow occurred just before the end of the month and at the month-end exchange rate. To help him, you should

i. establish a new valuation report (see Exhibit A),
ii. discuss the methodology for adjusting for cash movements, and
iii. analyze the manager's performance.

21. A European investor holds a portfolio worth $1 million invested in American stocks. The dollar just went down against the euro (the base currency), and the investor wonders what the result would have been if she had hedged the dollar risk. In the past month, the U.S. stock portfolio went up by 1 percent, and the dollar went down from one euro per dollar to 0.95 euro per dollar. The one-month interest rates (annualized) are 5 percent in dollars and 4 percent in euros.

What would have been the one-month rate of return on the portfolio in base currency (euros) if the investor had decided on the following strategies?

a. No currency hedging
b. 50 percent currency hedge
c. 100 percent currency hedge

22. A portfolio of $100 million is invested in European and Japanese stocks at the start of period 1. The country weights in the portfolio are 60 percent in Europe and 40 percent in Japan. At the end of period 1, the portfolio value went up to $110 million. To evaluate performance, the investor uses a composite benchmark made up of 50 percent of the European equity index and 50 percent of the Japanese equity index. All calculations are performed in base currency, the U.S. dollar, and indexes are total-return indexes (dividends are reinvested). Over period 1, the European index went up by 20 percent and the Japanese index gained 10 percent, so the international benchmark gained 15 percent. Detailed return data are given below. At the end of period 1, the country allocation was changed to 40 percent in Europe and 60 percent in Japan. At the end of period 2, the portfolio was up to $120.120 million, while the composite benchmark gained 29.375 percent over the two periods.
a. Attribute the performance to security selection and market allocation for *each* of the two short periods: period 1 and then period 2.
b. Attribute the performance to security selection and market allocation for the total period (i.e., linked over the two short periods).

PORTFOLIO			**BENCHMARK**	
Country Component	**Country Weights**	**Rate of Return in Base Currency**	**Country Weights**	**Rate of Return in Base Currency**
Period 1				
Europe	0.60	10.0%	50.0%	20.0%
Japan	0.40	10.0%	50.0%	10.0%
Total Portfolio	100%	**10.0%**		**15.0%**
Period 2				
Europe	40.0%	5.0%	50.0%	10.0%
Japan	60.0%	12.0%	50.0%	15.0%
Total Portfolio		**9.2000%**		**12.5%**
Compounded over entire period				
Europe		15.5%		32.0%
Japan		23.2%		26.5%
Total		**20.120%**		**29.375%**

Bibliography

Ankrim, E. M., and Hensel, C. R. "Multicurrency Performance Attribution," *Financial Analysts Journal*, March/April 1994.

Asness, C., Krail, R., and Liew, J. "Do Hedge Funds Hedge?" *Journal of Portfolio Management*, Fall 2001.

Bonafede, J. K., Foresti, S. J., and Matheos P. "A Multi-period Linking Algorithm That Has Stood the Test of Time," *Journal of Performance Measurement*, Fall 2002.

Carino, D. "Refinements in Multi-period Attribution," *Journal of Performance Measurement*, Fall 2002.

CFA Institute, *Global Investment Performance Standards (GIPS) Handbook*, 2nd ed., Charlottesville, VA, 2006.

Fung W., and Hsieh, D. A. "Hedge-Fund Benchmarks: Information Content and Biases," *Financial Analysts Journal*, January/February 2002.

Goodwin, T. H. "The Information Ratio," *Financial Analysts Journal*, July/August 1998.

Grinold, R. C., and Kahn, R. N. *Active Portfolio Management*, Chicago: Irwin, 1995.

Jorion, P., and Kirsten, G. "The Right Way to Measure International Performance," *Investing*, Spring 1991.

Malkiel, B., and Saha, A. "Hedge Funds: Risk and Return," *Financial Analysts Journal*, 61(6), November/December 2005.

Reilly, F., and Brown, K. *Investment Analysis and Portfolio Management*, 7th ed., Orlando: South-Western, 2003.

Roll, R. "Ambiguity When Performance Is Measured by the Securities Market Line," *Journal of Finance*, September 1978.

Sharpe, W. F. "Asset Allocation: Management Style and Performance Measurement," *Journal of Portfolio Management*, Winter 1992.

Sharpe, W. F. "The Sharpe Ratio," *Journal of Portfolio Management*, Fall 1994.

Singer, B. D., and Karnosky, D. S. "The General Framework for Global Investment Management and Performance Attribution," *Journal of Portfolio Management*, Winter 1995.

Terhaar, K., Staub, R., and Singer, B. "Asset Allocation: The Alternatives Approach," *Journal of Portfolio Management*, Spring 2003.

13

Structuring the Global Investment Process

LEARNING OUTCOMES

After completing this chapter, you will be able to do the following:

- Discuss the functions of and relationships among the major participants in the global investment industry
- Discuss the components of a formal investment policy statement (IPS)
- Evaluate the appropriateness of an investment policy statement for a global investor
- Discuss the role of capital market expectations in strategic and tactical asset allocation
- Interpret capital market data and capital market expectations in the context of strategic asset allocation for a global investor
- Compare and contrast the major choices—active/passive, top-down/bottom-up, style, global/specialized, currency, quantitative/subjective—available to a global investor in structuring the global investment decision-making process
- Evaluate the appropriateness, in terms of implementing the investment policy statement and strategic or tactical asset allocation, of fund/manager choices available to a global investor
- Discuss the important issues—particularly scope, weights, and currency allocation—in choosing a global benchmark for strategic asset allocation
- Compare and contrast alternative approaches to hedging currency risk in strategic asset allocation
- Discuss the determinants of effective global tactical asset allocation
- Compare and contrast strategic and tactical asset allocation in the global context
- Describe and evaluate the components of the global asset allocation process
- Design an appropriate strategic asset allocation for a global investor

- Interpret capital market data and capital market expectations in the context of tactical asset allocation for a global investor
- Design an appropriate tactical asset allocation for a global investor
- Evaluate the implications of a portfolio performance analysis for a global investor
- Summarize the primary issues that must be addressed by an investor contemplating global investment

An investment organization that is planning to offer global investment products to its clients first needs the information on institutions and techniques provided earlier in this book. Then the manager needs to properly structure the entire global investment decision process, from research to management and control. Among the many global investment organizations in the world today, there are a great variety of approaches that reflect different investment philosophies and strategies.

This chapter is organized as follows. The first section is a brief tour of the global investing industry. The second section reviews the various approaches to choosing a global investment philosophy to propose to a client. The rest of the chapter discusses the various steps of the global portfolio management process. As discussed in the third section, the client's objectives, constraints, and requirements are specified in an investment policy statement that forms the basis for the strategic asset allocation. Finally, capital market expectations are formulated for use in determining the asset allocation. This crucial step in a world with many equity, debt, and currency markets is discussed in the fourth section. Some important issues in terms of global asset allocation are then discussed. Strategic asset allocation and tactical asset allocation are usually viewed as two different steps of the asset allocation process. The chapter concludes with an example of how to structure and quantify the global investment process.

A Tour of the Global Investment Industry

Readers unfamiliar with the global investment scene often ask for a brief presentation of the major players. There are several types of participants in the global investment arena: investors (private or institutional), investment managers, brokers, consultants and advisers, and custodians. Some players belong to several categories.

Investors

Private Investors Investors belong to two broad categories: private and institutional. The term *private investor* usually refers to an individual or a small group of individuals, such as those represented by a family trust. Private investors have many ways to invest globally. They can buy foreign shares listed on their domestic markets. They can also buy, through a broker, foreign shares not listed domestically. They can buy mutual funds that diversify across multiple international markets or funds that invest only in specific markets. Finally, they can have their money managed by investment professionals; high-net-worth individuals are a clientele actively sought by many investment management firms. Whether a private or institutional investor, the client should prepare, with the manager, a policy statement outlining the investment goals and the risks that can be taken. This procedure is all the more important in global investing, in which the investment universe is enormous, as are the potential returns, costs, and risks.

Institutional Investors The term *institutional investor* is generally used to describe an organization that invests on behalf of others, such as a mutual fund, pension fund, or charitable organization or an insurance company. A variety of institutional investors exist. *Mutual funds* pool money from investors and invest it in financial assets to achieve a stated investment objective. Mutual funds are offered to the public at a listed price reflecting the market value of the fund's assets. Mutual funds are called *unit trusts* in the United Kingdom or *Sociétés d'Investissement à Capital Variable* (*SICAV*) in France, Belgium, and Luxembourg.

Retirement provisions are diverse throughout the world and even within each country. Basically, two very different philosophies can be found. Many countries have a *pay-as-you-go* system: Active workers pay for the pensions of retired workers. Workers, and their employers, do not contribute to the future pensions of the employees; they do not "capitalize" their contributions. Rather, these contributions are immediately paid to the current retirees. Except for some minimal technical reserves, there is no money to be invested, because it is immediately disbursed.

In a *capitalized contribution* system, employers contribute to a *pension fund*, which capitalizes all contributions and pays them back at the time of retirement. In this case, pension funds are considered long-term institutional investors. In general, a basic social security (pay-as-you-go) system tends to coexist with supplementary pension funds (sometimes called *second pillar*).

The investment approach of pension funds is greatly affected by the way future benefits are planned. There are basically two types and a combination thereof. A *defined benefit* (DB) pension plan promises to pay beneficiaries a defined income after retirement. This benefit depends on factors such as the workers' salary and years of service. The contributions are based on an actuarial rate of return assumption; capitalized at this actuarial rate, the contributions should be equal to the promised benefits. If the investment performance of the pension assets is insufficient, over time, to meet this assumption, the employer may have to increase its contribution to cover the shortfall. Therefore, the corporation carries the risk of the pension plan. This type of plan leads to investment policies that focus on meeting the return objective over the long term while reducing the risk of a major shortfall in the near term.

Defined contribution (DC) pension plans are increasingly favored worldwide. In a defined contribution plan, the amount of contributions is set, usually as a percentage of wages, but future benefits are not fixed. If the rate of return on invested assets is high, large benefits will be paid at time of retirement. If the rate of return is low, smaller benefits will be paid.

For either type of plan, a board selects a long-term asset allocation. Investment management is either delegated to external managers, done in-house, or a combination of both. The selection of investment managers is a lengthy process, often assisted by consultants. External managers are given a mandate, detailed in an investment brief. For example, one manager could be selected to manage a portfolio invested in emerging stock markets. The mandate will state the investment objective (e.g., "Outperform the S&P/IFC composite index") and provide guidelines on the type of investments that are acceptable and the amount of risk that can be taken.

In a traditional pension fund, all contributions are pooled and the total money is managed collectively. A recent trend is to give more investment decision power to each employee. The plan sponsor offers a range of asset allocations and investment products from which each employee can select. Hence, external investment managers have to pass two selection hurdles: the plan sponsor and the individual investors. Pension reforms in many countries follow the U.S. model and give employees some flexibility in asset allocation.

Endowments and foundations accumulate the contributions made to charitable and educational institutions. Endowments are long-term investment portfolios formed from donated funds and restricted to maintaining their principal over time. Foundations are entities that provide grants to accomplish the purposes of the original donor or donors. They have a variety of horizons (some are designed to terminate after a specific number of years) and spending rates (some have legally determined minimum spending rates), but most foundations have in common the need to meet their spending entirely from investment returns. Endowments and foundations tend to have great investment freedom because they operate under fewer regulatory constraints than other institutional investors. As a result, their return objective tends to focus on total return over the long run. Their investment policies are often the most aggressive among institutional investors, with many having extensive global and alternative investments.

Insurance companies form another major category of institutional investors. Life insurance companies collect premiums for insuring lives, and these premiums are invested until claims are paid. Insurance companies are heavily regulated in each country and state in which they operate. They tend to adopt conservative investment policies, focusing on fixed-income assets, in order to assure their claim-paying ability. Global asset allocation is often limited by regulatory constraints. Property and casualty insurance companies operate under a different regulatory framework that is somewhat more permissive in all countries. The investment policy of any insurance company depends on its surplus. Loosely speaking, the surplus is the difference between the total value of the invested assets and the expected claim payments. Although the assets matching the expected claim payments are typically invested in domestic bonds, the surplus can be invested in riskier assets, including global investments.

Investment Managers

Investment managers form a diverse group. It is hard to offer a single classification of asset managers. They range from the asset management department of banks to independent boutiques specializing in offering specific investment products. Some managers offer a diversified menu of products (much like a supermarket) and basically charge a fee based on the assets under management, while others offer only a specialized product promising high investment performance and may charge fees linked to their performance. Some asset managers cater to retail as well as institutional clients, while others, sometimes less known by the public, serve the needs of only one type of client, such as a pension fund. Others, such as hedge funds, are a highly specialized type of asset manager. Many asset managers now offer global investment capabilities, either directly or through joint ventures with foreign partners. U.S. asset managers that offer global investment management to U.S. pension funds can easily offer a similar product to British, Dutch, or Swiss pension funds, so competition among managers has truly become global.

Brokers

Stockbrokers, or *brokers*, have traditionally played an important role in asset management, both in terms of implementing security trades and in research of companies and markets. They have a large staff of financial analysts who cover companies domestically and sometimes worldwide. This financial analysis is called *sell side* because brokers use this research to sell trading ideas to investors (*buy side* analysts work for investment managers and institutional investors). In many countries, the standards of professional conduct are lax compared with those in the United States or the United Kingdom. However, all CFA charterholders and CFA candidates must follow the CFA Institute Code of Ethics and Standards of Professional Conduct, wherever they work and invest. Many brokers also act as investment banks, but the independence of sell-side analysts must be maintained.

Major global brokers have offices in all major financial centers and cover most markets in the world. Other brokers specialize in some niches (e.g., European small-cap stocks). Bond brokers provide extensive research on interest rates, exchange rates, and company and country risk. The research efforts at these brokerage houses have moved in two directions. As a result of their excellent research capabilities, brokers moved successfully into investment banking. Financial analysts extended their approach to cover mergers and acquisitions as well as corporate finance. Others applied their research expertise and knowledge of the financial markets to asset management. Asset management is a low-margin business compared with investment banking, but profits are much more stable. Brokers in Japan have always offered asset management, and this service is now a major priority for the big U.S. brokerage houses, which are marketing their asset management skills in Europe and Asia.

Consultants and Advisers

Consultants and advisers provide several types of advice and play a major role in the asset management industry. Although they are better known for their work with the pension fund market, they are also employed by other investors, such as insurance companies, endowments, foundations, and high-net-worth individuals. Independent consulting firms have traditionally advised U.S. pension funds, while actuaries played a similar role in the United Kingdom. For many years, consultants played no role in most other countries, but this situation changed dramatically in the late 1990s.

Consultants can help with all the actuarial calculations of pension plan obligations, such as liabilities to plan members and technical reserves. These calculations depend on many factors, such as the age structure of plan members, retirement patterns, the plan's benefits formula, and so on. Although these actuarial calculations are often performed in-house in the United States and other countries, the United Kingdom traditionally requires the intervention of external actuaries. Consultants also focus on services such as recommending asset allocation, selecting investment managers, and monitoring performance, and they may give tax and legal advice.

Major consultants measure the performance of a large number of managers with different mandates. Hence, they maintain a database that allows them to compare the performance of a universe of managers. But probably the most sensitive role of consultants, which has spread throughout Europe and the United States, is their assistance in the process of selecting, hiring, and firing external managers. Some commentators state that pension fund sponsors are relieved to share their fiduciary responsibilities with consultants who have a worldwide reputation and are used by numerous other pension funds. When looking for an external manager, a pension fund typically prepares a *request for proposal* (*RFP*) or *request for information* (*RFI*), which specifies the type of manager sought. The consultant organizes the selection process by sending out the RFP or RFI in the form of a questionnaire to be completed by prospective managers. Based on the responses and the consultant's own research on the managers, a short list is established, and managers on this list make a presentation to the pension fund, detailing their case. The board of the pension fund decides, with the consultant's advice, which manager(s) will be selected. It should be noted that the arrangement between pension plan sponsors and consultants varies considerably. Some plan sponsors delegate much of the decision-making process regarding manager hiring and firing to the consultant, while others prefer to make the decision themselves and use the consultant in an advisory role. Many consulting firms advise only domestic institutional clients. But some consulting firms have developed a client base in many countries, either by growing globally or by participating in a global network of consultants.

A new trend for pension consultants is to go one step further and offer multimanager funds or funds of funds (FoFs). The consultant does not manage money directly but creates a fund of selected managers. This approach has caused some controversy over a potential conflict of interest in the advisory capacity.

Individual investors are also in need of professional advice for the management of personal or family assets. As discussed earlier, the taxable environment of private investors poses a challenge, and tax systems vary markedly across countries, even within the same region. For example, the tax environment is different for each country in the European Union. Hence, advisers tend to be domestic rather than global players, but they may be part of a global network.

Custodians

Securities owned by investors are deposited with a custodian, which often uses a global network of subcustodians. Given the complexities of global investing due to national differences in taxation, trading, and settlement procedures, an efficient and reliable custodian is a necessity. Accurate information from around the world should be gathered rapidly. Automated trade notification is necessary. Computer-to-computer links with the subcustodians, clearing services, and the manager should be set up. Income collection should be swift and correctly reported. Tax recovery should be automated and carefully checked with each government. Securities-lending facilities should be available in most markets. Finally, a cash management system in many currencies should be implemented. Cost and reliability are two important features of custodial services.

Information technology is an important component of custodial services. With the high development costs of such software, many banks have sold their custodial activities, and further consolidation is expected in the future because economies of scale can be significant in this business.

Global Investment Philosophies

Global investment has grown rapidly among institutional investors of all nationalities. Investment managers worldwide can no longer treat foreign investments as an exotic, minor consideration, and they must now have a clear view of how to approach global investing. An investment management organization must make certain major choices in structuring its global decision process, based on several factors:

- Its view of the world regarding security price behavior
- Its strengths, in terms of research and management
- Cost aspects
- Its location and prospective domestic/global marketing strategy

Similarly, investors will select managers based on the same factors, as well as their ability to control currency risks. These important choices are discussed in the following sections in terms of investment philosophy and strategy from the viewpoint of a fund manager. But individual or institutional investors face exactly the same choices when deciding on their approach to global investing and their selection of fund managers. The global approach to equity is more complex than the approach to bonds, so some of the points discussed next are primarily relevant for equity portfolio management.

The Passive Approach

A fund managed according to a passive approach simply attempts to reproduce a market index of securities. This type of fund is often called an *index fund*. The sole purpose of an index fund is to exactly track the return on a selected market index, to capitalize on its long-term performance while keeping all costs at a minimum. The passive approach is an extension of modern portfolio theory, which claims that the market portfolio should be efficient. In the United States, the domestic index fund approach is supported by extensive empirical evidence of the efficiency of the stock market. A similar domestic index fund approach has developed in the United Kingdom and, more recently, in other European countries and Japan. Large pension funds have moved extensively to indexing their domestic assets.

The trend toward global indexing is strongly felt among institutional investors. It is now common to see funds that passively replicate some international index (e.g., some Europe or ex U.S. benchmark) or a World index. While institutional investors can invest in dedicated passive portfolios, retail investors can choose from some passive mutual funds, including exchange traded funds (ETFs) that track some international index.

The basic argument supporting the passive indexing approach is that the alternative, an active strategy, requires above-average ability in forecasting markets, currencies, and security valuation. Forecasting is never easy; moreover, it entails higher commissions and costs. With a passive strategy, the fund can achieve the full benefits of global risk diversification without incurring these high costs.

Various indexing methods can be used:

- *Full replication:* All securities in the index are bought, with proper weighting. This method is impossible globally, given the huge number of securities involved.

- *Stratified sampling:* This approach tracks the index by holding a representative sample of securities. The securities are grouped according to various criteria (country, firm's size, industry, yield), and the index fund sample attempts to replicate the characteristics of the index across the various criteria.

- *Optimization sampling:* This is a sampling method using factor models to minimize the tracking error of the index. It is a sophisticated statistical method based on a large number of factors, or firm attributes, and using optimization techniques based on historical relationships.

- *Synthetic replication:* A stock index can be replicated by using a futures contract on the index plus a cash position. The fair pricing of the futures ensures that the index is closely tracked and that transaction costs are low. For some investors, legal aspects regarding the use of derivatives constrain the implementation of this approach on a global scale. Another problem is that futures contracts tend to be written on indexes based on a subset of the broad market, while natural market benchmarks are broadly based indexes. Stock index swaps are also used.

Although indexing does reduce costs, perfect tracking of a global index is not feasible. For example, whenever a dividend is paid in one currency—say, the Australian dollar—it should be reinvested simultaneously in all global securities with proper weights, which is an impossible task. Indexing requires superior computer, administrative, and trading technology, but it does result in large economies of scale. Because the quality of the indexer shows up quickly, and objectively, in the form of a low tracking error, only the best indexers are likely to capture a large market share of this management style. A remaining issue, discussed later, is the choice of the global benchmark to be passively tracked.

The Active Approach

In an active strategy, investors place bets on the various factors that affect securities' behaviors. A benchmark is often imposed in the mandate set by the client, and it will clearly guide the structure of the portfolio. Active deviations from the benchmark can lead to superior performance. Of course, the strategy itself depends on the investor's view of the world. Active decisions of a portfolio manager show up at various levels:

- *Regional/country allocation:* This is the choice of national markets and currencies. The manager can select long-term weights that differ from those of market indexes, such as the EAFE index. This long-term allocation is often called *strategic asset allocation.* Periodic, temporary revisions in the weights can be justified by changes in market expectations or risk estimates. This is often called *tactical asset allocation.* Allocation decisions also are discussed later in the chapter.
- *Sector/industry selection:* The globalization of the economy pushes some managers to allocate funds across worldwide industries rather than countries. This is more commonly done when managing a portfolio within integrated regions such as Continental Europe.
- *Style selection:* Some managers believe that companies with similar attributes tend to have similar stock price behavior. Common style decisions are value versus growth stocks or small versus large firms.
- *Security selection:* To achieve a given asset allocation, managers can engage in active selection of securities within each asset class and conduct pair arbitrage between two similar securities.
- *Market timing:* Managers can resort to market timing to temporarily increase or reduce the exposure in one or more markets or currencies. This is a short-term trading tactic (as opposed to long-run strategies for allocating assets) that often involves the use of derivatives.
- *Currency hedging:* Managers can actively manage their currency position.

A few additional dimensions can be found in the active management of global debt securities (see Chapter 7):

- *Sector selection/credit selection:* Managers can deviate from a bond benchmark by overweighting some market sectors or investing in higher credit risk, such as low-credit-rating bonds and emerging debt. This strategy leads to an increase in yield but also in credit risk.

- *Duration/yield curve management:* In each currency market, the manager can adjust the duration of the portfolio according to forecasts about changes in the level of interest rates and shapes of the yield curve.
- *Yield enhancement techniques:* Numerous techniques are proposed to add value to the performance of the basic strategy; these include lending securities, using swaps and other derivatives, investing in complex bonds, and doing pairs arbitrage.

A manager can be active in some dimensions and not in others. For example, active asset allocation management can be achieved using national index funds for each market. Conversely, a manager could follow a fixed asset allocation, using active security selection within each market.

The risk diversification argument is usually at the heart of the rationale of both active and passive global money managers. In the quickly changing global environment, active money managers must be able to evaluate and control the risk of their portfolios as rapidly as possible. Taking active bets on markets, currencies, or securities could result in portfolios that turn out to be quite risky and do not provide the global risk diversification benefits so widely claimed.

Following is a review of major choices to be made in active global asset management. It focuses primarily on equity because the management of portfolios of debt securities is more technical and is addressed in Chapter 7.

Balanced or Specialized

Investment managers for private clients have traditionally been balanced money managers. For example, a European bank advising a private client will suggest both the global asset allocation and the selection of each security for the portfolio; the bank will advise on all aspects of private wealth management. The asset allocation covers all asset classes: equity, debt securities, alternative investments, and cash, as well the currency hedging policy.

Even for pension assets, the approach of having a single balanced manager or, at most, a few can be used. In this case, the investment policy statement can be quite loose, with objective statements such as "Maximize long-term returns subject to an acceptable level of risk normally associated with a balanced approach to fund management."[1]

By contrast, the specialization approach involves hiring managers who specialize in particular investment areas, such as Japanese stocks, European growth stocks, or emerging market debt. The trend toward specialized global management is based on the hypothesis that no manager is an expert on all markets, although some managers can be superior on one or a few markets.

---

[1] Extract from Mark Tapley, "Lessons from the Unilever/Merrill Case," *IPE*, May 2002, p. 36.

For a client, the central question in the specialized approach is how to decide on asset allocation. Because asset allocation is potentially the most profitable and important investment management decision, it seems a bit odd to deprive asset managers of this important opportunity to add value. This specialization constraint is especially problematic in equity management when listed companies compete globally and stock markets are increasingly correlated. To study European equity, one must compare European firms with their U.S. and Asian competitors. If an equity manager is expert on European equity, she should (must) also be expert on global equity.

Industry or Country Approach

Asset managers should structure their investment processes along the major factors affecting security prices:

- If a manager believes that the nationality of a company is a major factor affecting the return and risk on the company's stock, then the global portfolio should be structured primarily according to country or region. The allocation to countries/regions is a major investment decision; then stocks are selected within countries. Although there is a tendency to presume that the country of origin or the head office of a multinational firm is irrelevant, a close look at human resource and hiring/firing constraints will reveal that such an idealized world is not yet here.
- If a manager believes that the industry or sector in which a company operates is a major factor affecting its return and risk, then the global portfolio should be structured primarily according to industry or sector. The allocation to industries/sectors is a major investment decision, and then stocks are selected within global industries.
- If a manager believes that the major factors affecting the return and risk on the company's stock are specific to that company (quality of management, cost structure relative to competition, prospects for its products, etc.), the manager should rely primarily on company analysis.

Top-Down or Bottom-Up

Both domestically and globally, portfolio managers use either a top-down or a bottom-up approach or combination to the investment process.

- *Top-down approach:* The manager using a top-down approach first allocates his assets across asset classes and then selects individual securities to satisfy that allocation. The most important decision in this approach is the choice of markets and currencies. In other words, the global money manager must choose from among several markets (stocks, bonds, or cash) as well as a variety of currencies. Once these choices have been made, the manager selects the best securities available in each market. In global equity portfolios, a manager following the country approach decides on the percentage allocated to the various countries and then selects the best stocks in each market; a manager following the industry approach decides on the percentage allocated to the various global industries and then selects the best stocks in each industry.

- *Bottom-up approach:* The manager using a *bottom-up investing* approach studies the fundamentals of many individual stocks, from which she selects the best securities (regardless of their national origin or currency denomination) to build a portfolio. For example, a manager may be bullish on car manufacturers and buy shares in all of them (GM, Toyota, Volkswagen, Peugeot, and others), or the manager may buy shares in only the best oil company in the world, regardless of its national origin. The product of this approach is a portfolio with a market and currency allocation that is more or less the random result of the securities selected. Implicit in this approach is the manager's greater concern with risk exposure in various sectors than with either market or currency risk exposure. But currency risk or market exposure can be hedged.
- *Top-down/bottom-up approach:* Some investment organizations attempt to combine a top-down with a bottom-up approach, but this is not easy to achieve. The rationale for combining the two often cites risk control. For example, a top-down manager may choose to limit exposure to a particular country when the bottom-up manager would decide otherwise. The entire investment decision process has to be consistent, and sophisticated risk management tools are needed. A manager typically bases his security selection on worldwide company analysis. Factor models are used to control the exposure to countries and industries. Pair trades between companies in the same industry (but different countries) or in the same country (but different industries) allow the manager to satisfy risk objectives in terms of geographic and sector/industry allocation, while taking advantage of superior company analysis (see Example 13.1).

Style Management

In previous chapters, we talked about style managers who construct portfolios based on some attributes of companies. This approach has been extended to global investing. Common style decisions are value versus growth stocks or small versus large firms. In the 1980s and early 1990s, a simple strategy that favored small and value stocks yielded above-average returns in the United States. The simplest global extension was to choose stocks based on the firm's size and its price-to-book ratio. However, style analysis does not extend globally in a simple manner (see Michaud, 1999). For example, a firm of a given size may look small in the United States and rather big in France. Similarly, a given style indicator, such as the price-to-book ratio, which works well in identifying a value factor in one country, may not work in another country, in part due to accounting differences. To define a value stock,

EXAMPLE 13.1 PAIR TRADES

You own a well-diversified global portfolio mimicking the World index. You wish to retain the same regional and industry exposure as the World index. You believe that Total, a French oil company, is undervalued (much lower P/E) relative to ExxonMobil. You also believe that BMW is overpriced relative to General Motors. You own $100,000 of ExxonMobil shares and $120,000 of BMW shares. What could you do?

SOLUTION

- Sell the shares of ExxonMobil in the portfolio and buy $100,000 of Total shares.
- Sell $100,000 of the BMW shares and buy $100,000 of General Motors shares.

The net result will leave unchanged the asset allocation to European and American stocks. It will also leave unchanged the global industry allocation.

managers resort to different indicators in different countries. Careful analysis is required to derive style factors that would apply to companies in all countries. Furthermore, a given style factor is not necessarily synchronized across countries. For example, value stocks could underperform growth stocks in France, while the reverse could simultaneously be true in Germany. Finally, no style can systematically outperform others forever. This was amply demonstrated by the poor relative performance of small stocks and value stocks in the late 1990s. This does not mean that active style management cannot achieve superior performance. Style rotation strategies can add value if the manager can forecast when a given style will become favored by market participants (or lose favor).

Currency

Some managers treat currencies only as residual variables; their currency breakdowns are determined by the countries, industries, and securities they select for their portfolios. They generally consider currency risk a necessary evil and argue that currency movements are impossible to predict and wash out in the long run anyway, because it is the real economic variables that ultimately determine a portfolio's performance.

Other managers fully hedge their foreign portfolios or decide on a permanent hedge ratio based on a historical estimate. Full hedging is based on the belief that foreign currency risk premiums are small or unpredictable and, hence, that investors are not compensated for carrying foreign exchange risk. Others adopt a passive, uniform currency-hedging strategy with a fixed hedge ratio different from 100 percent (e.g., 50%). Various currency hedging policies are reviewed in Chapter 11.

Still other managers take a proactive tactical approach to currency forecasting. They try to minimize the contribution currency makes to total risk, and cash in on opportunities created by currency movements.

At the extreme end of the spectrum is a breed of global money managers, called *currency overlay managers*, who actively manage the currency exposure of a portfolio and often resort to currency options and forward or futures contracts for selective hedging and speculation. Currency overlay managers do not manage the portfolio itself. The client transfers the composition of the portfolio managed by another party on a daily basis. This other party makes no currency-hedging decisions but only manages the assets. The currency overlay managers take currency positions on the portfolio using currency derivatives. Some even offer pure currency products attempting to generate high returns from currency plays.

Naturally, the approach an investment manager takes toward currencies leads to very different portfolio strategies. The question of currency hedging is raised again later in this chapter.

Quantitative or Subjective

Whether a manager employs a quantitative or a subjective decision-making process, a great deal of information is required before portfolios are constructed. Quantification of the investment process is very helpful in global investment management because of the large number of parameters and decision variables involved. Quantification can be applied to various models or aids used in the global investment process, including the following:

- Econometric or technical forecasting models of markets and currencies
- Global asset allocation optimizers
- Dividend-discount models, factor models, duration models, or option valuation models (for quantitative assessment of individual securities)
- Risk management models
- Performance and risk analysis

Managers who favor the subjective approach argue that the global environment is too complex to permit formal quantification. They think that models based on past data are not helpful because constant changes in the global environment distort such models. Quantitative managers also believe that the global environment is complex, but they eventually come to the opposite conclusion regarding the helpfulness of models. Models are used to extract from past data some useful lessons for the future. An advantage of a purely quantitative approach is that it is highly disciplined and therefore avoids some emotional reactions that can lead to poor decisions and impaired performance.

Many managers rely on subjective judgment but make use of some quantitative models in their portfolio management process. Others tend to follow models but inject some judgment as they think appropriate.

The Investment Policy Statement

An *investment policy statement (IPS)* is the cornerstone of the portfolio management process. The IPS is prepared by the advisor and the client and serves as the governing document for the portfolio manager and for all investment decision making. The IPS is extensively discussed in Maginn et al. (2007), and we summarize only its main features and stress aspects that should be taken into account when investing globally. A case study, used as example throughout this chapter, details the preparation of such a document. The case circumstances are described in Example 13.2.

EXAMPLE 13.2 JOHN BOUDERI CASE CIRCUMSTANCES

Leigh Brennan is a financial advisor working with John Bouderi.[2] Bouderi retired at age 60 in March, selling the business and receiving net proceeds after tax of $1.5 million. Because Bouderi is Australian, the dollar symbol in this case refers to Australian dollars. He is looking forward to a long retirement because his parents lived a relatively healthy life to an old age. He expects to do the same.

BACKGROUND

Bouderi's wife died ten years ago. He has two children, both now in their late twenties and self-sufficient. Although Bouderi has no grandchildren now, he hopes for them someday and would like to provide a financial legacy for them. He desires a comfortable retirement and is determined that this objective not be jeopardized by poor investment decisions. Bouderi has developed an understanding of investments, gained primarily from years of personal study and observing markets, and has begun to develop and implement his own investment strategy.

Given his long time horizon, Bouderi initially decided to invest $600,000 in direct purchase of Australian equities. Although he understood the benefits of global investing, he limited his initial investments to Australian issues such as AMP, ANZ, and Westpac. This decision was due partially to his familiarity with the companies, but also because he felt that the Australian market had shown strong performance. A subsequent 5% drop in the Australian stock market made Bouderi question his decision to invest solely in Australian shares.

The $900,000 remaining was added to an existing money market account, bringing the total money market balance to $1 million. The account currently yields 5 percent and will be used to cover his living expenses while awaiting further investment.

The first several meetings between Bouderi and Brennan were devoted to evaluating Bouderi's current financial circumstances in detail. He provided the following information on his financial situation.

[2] Case developed with Jan Squires, CFA, and Victoria Rati, CFA.

Assets

Residence in Sydney, Australia; market value:	$1,000,000
Domestic equity portfolio:	570,000
Money market account:	1,000,000
Total:	$2,570,000
Estimated after-tax annual income desired:	$90,000

Immediate Plans

1. Take a family vacation in Europe: estimated cost $50,000
2. Sell existing home and purchase smaller retirement home for approximately 520,000.
3. Place net cash proceeds from home transactions in investment portfolio
4. Establish a trust for any future grandchildren with initial contribution of $100,000

Expected investable assets after completion of immediate plans: $1,900,000 (= $2,570,000 – $50,000 – $520,000 – $100,000)

Liabilities

Current home is fully paid off; no mortgage or any other loans are outstanding.

RISK AND RETURN OBJECTIVES

Brennan next conducted several interviews to determine Bouderi's investment goals and to identify any constraints that might limit his achieving those goals.

Desired Return

Bouderi desires to lead a comfortable retirement, with an income that keeps pace with inflation. He prefers steady returns consistent with a modest level of risk and desires a return from equity investments of 10 percent annually before tax. For his overall portfolio, he decides that 7 to 8 percent annually before tax would be acceptable.

Required Return

Brennan believes that Bouderi's required equity return is in excess of 9 percent, given total investment assets, liquidity needs, time horizon, and inflation protection needs. Bouderi finally agrees with Brennan's figure, but he is concerned about the level of risk a higher return target will bring to the portfolio.

Risk Tolerance

Bouderi's personal investing style suggests he is prudent, diligent, and methodical. This is consistent with the approach he took in running his business. Despite his recent experience in the equity market, he still believes that it is necessary to take calculated risks to realize appropriate rewards.

In their final discussion about risk tolerance, Bouderi indicates his willingness to accept a possible 10 percent decline in the value of his portfolio in any one year in order to achieve his objectives. Brennan also introduces the concepts of ability and willingness to take risk. She discusses the idea that ability to take risk is determined by such factors as wealth position, annual spending requirements, and inflation expectations. Bouderi realizes that the two concepts of ability and willingness may be substantially different but is unsure how to combine them to understand his own risk position.

IPSs vary in terms of content, especially between private and institutional clients. IPSs for private clients often reflect a balanced mandate to manage the whole wealth. But an IPS could be more specialized and target specific asset classes. For example, an investor could give a mandate to manage international assets and prepare an IPS accordingly. A well-constructed policy statement typically includes a summary of the various elements:

1. *Client description and purpose:* The IPS starts with a brief description of the client and the purpose of the establishment of the investment policy statement. It could detail the duties and investment responsibilities of the various parties involved.

2. *Return and risk objectives:* Establishing objectives for return and risk is an important step for individual as well as institutional clients. The manager must be sure that investment goals, especially the return objective, are attainable within the client's risk tolerance. Some institutional investors set quantified objectives. For example, a British pension plan could set as an objective for a manager to outperform the World equity index, ex U.K, by 3 percent per year, with a maximum annual tracking error of 4 percent. Return is measured as total return from income and capital appreciation, which is specified as real or nominal, and as pretax or after-tax. Investors have stated return desires that may or may not be realistic. Nevertheless, the adviser and the client also must determine the investor's required return, the return that must be achieved on average. The required return is necessary, as contrasted with the stated return, which may be more in the nature of a hope. The return objective must be set to achieve the investor's required return balanced with the investor's risk tolerance. *Risk tolerance* is the capacity to accept risk; risk aversion is the inability and unwillingness to take risk. Risk tolerance is a function both of the investor's ability and his willingness to take risk. An investor may have more willingness to take risk than he has ability to accept the consequences of large losses. Ability is a function of such characteristics as income needs and asset base, as well as liquidity requirements and time horizon. With basic statistics and the simplest

assumption of returns being independent and normally distributed, the sample mean and standard deviation can be used to explore the probability of losses for the investor. If these are found to be tolerable, the investor's risk tolerance may need calibration.

3. *Constraints:* All economic and operational constraints on the investment portfolio should be identified in the IPS. Portfolio constraints generally fall into one of five categories:

    - Liquidity requirements stem from liquidity events when the investor must make specific cash payments higher than normal long-term net cash flows. An example of a liquidity event is the planned purchase of a house in one year. Even though stocks are liquid, their future price is uncertain. The liquidity requirement constrains asset allocation because the portfolio should include risk-free government securities targeted to supply the cash required. As a practical matter, the presence of both liquidity risk (the need to sell less marketable assets) and price risk (the risk of fluctuations in market prices) means that the investor must anticipate liquidity requirements by holding some proportion of assets that are *both* liquid and relatively low-risk.
    - Time horizon is the period associated with the investor's objectives. Long-term horizons are generally considered to be those over ten years, but many investor horizons are multistage horizons, mixtures of short- and long-term objective horizons. A long-term retirement objective and a short-term college financing objective would produce a multistage time horizon. Because different investments are appropriate for different horizons, the investor's time horizon constrains asset allocation.
    - Tax concerns constrain asset allocation decisions because taxable investors must look for after-tax returns in their taxable portfolios, as well as plan for tax payments on retirement distributions in their tax-deferred portfolios.
    - Legal and regulatory factors constrain asset allocation because they may rule out certain investments. In some countries, pension funds are limited to certain asset classes. Legal and regulatory factors are constraints external to the investor and imposed by others.
    - Unique circumstances constrain asset allocation. They include constraining factors other than liquidity requirements, time horizon, tax concerns, and legal and regulatory factors. These other constraints are internal to the investor and limit his choice of investments or asset classes. Investor preferences, investment knowledge, staff, and capabilities are examples of unique circumstances. Typical constraints are illustrated in Example 13.3.

4. *Asset allocation considerations:* The IPS can state some asset allocation objectives and constraints that have to be followed by the manager. These can be varied, and a few examples are listed. In particular, the IPS could set out the following points:

EXAMPLE 13.3 JOHN BOUDERI INVESTMENT CONSTRAINTS

With agreement on investment objectives, Brennan and Bouderi must consider the constraints on portfolio choice and the attainment of objectives.

TIME HORIZON

Based on Bouderi's family history of longevity and his current good health, Brennan determines that he can be expected to experience another twenty years of active retirement.

LIQUIDITY

Apart from funding the trip to Europe and establishment of the trust, Bouderi has no unusual liquidity requirements.

TAX ISSUES

All income earned by Bouderi, regardless of source, is assumed to be taxed at a 15 percent annual rate.

LEGAL AND REGULATORY ISSUES

Neither Bouderi nor Brennan has identified any material legal or regulatory issues facing Bouderi, including the establishment of the trust.

UNIQUE CIRCUMSTANCES

- The anticipated exchange of homes within the next year will increase the size of Bouderi's portfolio substantially.
- The $100,000 to be set up as a trust for his future grandchildren would establish an investment account to manage the funds on behalf of the future beneficiaries. A share of the funds would be available to each grandchild at age 21. Should there be no grandchildren, the funds would be available to Bouderi's children for their retirement. He may add to this trust in later years. These assets will be held separately, and once the trust is established, they are no longer part of Bouderi's portfolio.

- Give a global balanced mandate to the manager giving its "best effort" to satisfy the risk/return investment goals of the client.
- Set a specific benchmark for the manager, as done by institutional clients who use several specialized managers.
- List the asset classes that can be considered, thereby excluding various types of investments (e.g., derivatives, emerging markets, shares of "unethical" firms, etc.).

- Set constraints on the allocation to be followed at all times. For example, the IPS could state that no more than 40 percent of the portfolio should be allocated to international investments and that the foreign currency exposure should not exceed 20 percent of the portfolio.
- Outline the investment philosophy to be followed by the manager.

Some IPSs include the strategic asset allocation to be used in the portfolio, but we maintain a distinction between the IPS and the determination of the strategic asset allocation. This process is addressed in the section on global asset allocation.

5. *Schedule for review and monitoring:* Feedback and control of the portfolio are essential in reaching investment goals. The IPS can include a schedule for review of the investment performance and of the IPS itself. *Performance evaluation* is a critical step in the review of the portfolio and is discussed in Chapter 12. The client should be provided with rates of return for the portfolio on a periodic basis (*performance measurement*), but that is not sufficient. *Performance attribution* allows us to understand the sources of performance. So many factors can affect the performance of a global portfolio that global performance attribution is crucial in understanding why and how the portfolio performed as it did. Finally, *performance appraisal,* typically conducted over a long period of time, should enable the client to judge whether the manager is doing a good job.

   The IPS also could include monitoring and rebalancing guidelines. Because of price movements, the composition of the portfolio will progressively deviate from the strategic asset allocation. Rebalancing the portfolio entails transaction costs, and some guidelines have to be established regarding rebalancing. More generally, changes in capital market expectations, or in the client's investment objectives and constraints, would dictate revisions in the portfolio. The illustration of a typical IPS continues in Example 13.4.

Capital Market Expectations

Capital market expectations are expectations about the future distributions of returns to asset classes, including expected returns, volatility of returns, and correlation of returns. Formulating capital market expectations is potentially the most rewarding part of global asset management, but it is also the most difficult. The formulation process is usually decomposed into three steps:

- Defining asset classes
- Formulating long-term expectations used in strategic asset allocation
- Formulating shorter-term expectations used in tactical asset allocation

EXAMPLE 13.4 JOHN BOUDERI INVESTMENT POLICY STATEMENT

Brennan prepared an initial investment policy statement for John Bouderi's review. After several discussions and further fact-finding by Brennan, the following IPS was approved by Bouderi.

SUMMARY

This investment policy statement outlines the goals and objectives of John Bouderi (the client) and the long-term investment strategy that is proper for the achievement of his financial goals. These goals include providing a retirement income and meeting several near-term spending plans.

To fund his retirement, Bouderi sold his share of the family business. The investment returns from this portfolio are his sole means of support.

In order to achieve a comfortable retirement, this statement will outline the return-and-risk objectives, acceptable asset classes for inclusion in the portfolio, portfolio strategies, and any constraints on achieving these goals.

OBJECTIVES

Return Requirement

A return requirement of 9.6 percent is established.

A total return of 4.7 percent after inflation, taxes and investment expenses is required to meet the anticipated annual spending needs of $90,000 in current dollars. Taking into account expected annual inflation of 3 percent and a tax rate of 15 percent gives a required nominal total return of 9.1 percent on an annualized basis, before expenses. The return requirement of 9.6 percent reflects an initial estimate of annual transaction costs and investment management expenses of 50 basis points.

Such a return is expected to meet after-tax income needs in real terms over an extended time horizon. A return of approximately 1 percent in excess of this amount is desirable to provide modest long-term growth, but is not required.

Risk Tolerance

The risk tolerance of the client is best described as average to slightly below average. To meet the return requirement, it is understood that risk must be taken. Although a fluctuation in portfolio value is expected, the portfolio should be constructed to minimize the likelihood that the portfolio declines by more than 10 percent in any one year. The achievement of a stable portfolio with predictable returns is a highly desired outcome.

CONSTRAINTS

Time Horizon

Bouderi has a two-stage time horizon:

- The next year, defined by several substantial liquidity events, outlined below.
- The remainder of his retirement period, expected to be at least twenty years.

Liquidity

The following liquidity events are expected to occur in the next year:

- $50,000 outflow for a European trip
- $100,000 outflow for a trust for future grandchildren
- $480,000 net inflow from sale and purchase of homes

No liquidity events past the next year are known to exist, apart from meeting annual spending requirements.

Tax Issues

The client faces a maximum tax rate of 15 percent on all income, regardless of the source. He has no outstanding tax liabilities or unresolved issues with the taxing authorities.

Legal and Regulatory Issues

The client faces no material legal or regulatory constraints; his desire to establish a trust for his grandchildren is not expected to present any unusual problems or concerns.

Unique Circumstances

- The timing of establishing the trust for Bouderi's grandchildren, though material, is largely indeterminate.
- The anticipated exchange of homes, though material, is largely indeterminate.

ACCEPTABLE INVESTMENTS

In order to meet the return objective, the following asset classes have been identified as acceptable within the framework of a diversified portfolio:

- Australian equities
- Debt instruments of the Australian government
- Debt instruments of Australian corporations
- Equity investments in the United States
- Equity investments in Europe
- Money market instruments

Both active and passive strategies may be employed. It is understood that active strategies may employ higher risk in order to exceed a benchmark return and that results may not meet expectations.

It is understood that investments outside Australia add currency risk to the portfolio. Hedging strategies designed to mitigate this risk are acceptable.

FREQUENCY OF REVIEW

This investment policy statement and the resulting strategic asset allocation should be reviewed periodically to ensure that they remain appropriate to the client's needs and circumstances. They should be reviewed again if a material event occurs. Material events would include, but not be limited to, the following:

- The exchange of homes, resulting in net proceeds substantially different than the anticipated $480,000 inflow
- Bouderi's health deteriorating markedly

Quantified performance evaluation will be provided detailing the contribution of currency risk and asset allocation.

The client further understands the importance of his understanding the investment strategies adopted and the role his ability and willingness to tolerate risk will play in meeting his objectives.

Defining Asset Classes

An asset class is a set of "homogeneous" securities, those whose prices are affected by a common factor. The segmentation of asset classes is usually based on various criteria:

- Asset type (e.g., debt, equity, real estate)
- Geography (e.g., domestic vs. international, or regional breakdown)
- Sector (e.g., technology stocks, energy stocks, intermediate bonds, high yield bonds)
- Style (e.g., growth vs. value stocks)

The segmentation and its number of categories depend on the size of the portfolio and the characteristics of the investor. An institutional investor with a long horizon can include private equity and other illiquid alternative investments, but this would not be the case for an elderly individual investor with little wealth. Individual investors tend to consider few asset classes, and a typical breakdown could include domestic equity, international equity, domestic bonds, international bonds, domestic real estate, and cash. A large institutional investor usually considers a more detailed breakdown, which could include U.S. equity, European equity, Asian equity, emerging-market equity, investment-grade domestic bonds, high-yield domestic bonds, international bonds, inflation-linked bonds, emerging-market debt, and so on.

Long-Term Capital Market Expectations: Historical Returns

Long-term capital market expectations, perhaps over the next five or ten years, are now used to determine the strategic asset allocation of a portfolio. Several approaches are used. As suggested by Maginn et al. (2007),[3] two basic approaches are used to formulate long-term expectations: historical returns and forward-looking returns.

Historical records for mean returns, volatility, and correlation can simply be projected to repeat in the future; however, there are many limitations in using past returns to directly formulate expectations on future returns.

Economic conditions in the past, especially the distant past, may not be relevant for the future. A market that has done exceptionally well (or poorly) in the past because of some specific events (e.g., liberalization of the economy) may not do so in the future because that specific event will not repeat. The exceptional equity risk premium in the twentieth century (6 percent for U.S. stocks) was caused by two factors:

- Earnings per share grew steadily.
- Valuation multiples, such as the price/earnings ratio, grew dramatically over time.

Stock prices went up in part because of real growth, but more importantly, because valuation multiples rose impressively until 2000. To expect a similar equity risk premium in the future, an analyst must make the assumption that valuation multiples will continue upward to unprecedented levels.[4]

Another problem is the quality of past data. For example, many countries had fixed-income markets that were controlled by their local governments until the 1980s. This was typically the case for Continental Europe. Bond yields and cash rates were not market rates but rates that governments regulated so that they could borrow cheaply. Various capital and currency controls, as well as regulations of institutional investors, forced local investors to purchase fixed-income securities with low returns. This is an explanation for the negative historical real yields in many countries. Fixed-income markets are now open worldwide.

Problems also arise when looking at historical volatility and correlation. Correlation across equity and bond markets in the past is likely to change over time because of market integration worldwide. The problem in using unadjusted historical estimates of volatility and correlation is even more acute for alternative investments. Some assets trade infrequently. This is the case for many alternative assets that are not exchange traded, such as real estate or private equity. This is also the case for illiquid exchange traded securities or over-the-counter instruments often used by hedge funds. Because prices used are not up-to-date market prices, they tend to be smoothed over time.[5] For example, the appraisal process used in real estate introduces a smoothing of returns because properties are appraised only infrequently. The internal rate of return methodology used in private equity also introduces a smoothing of returns. The infrequent nature of price updates in the alternative asset world induces a significant downward bias to the measured risk of the assets. In addition, correlations between alternative investment returns and

[3] See Chapter 4, "Capital Market Expectations," in Maginn et al. (2007).

[4] An interesting discussion is provided by Arnott and Bernstein (2002).

[5] See Chapter 8 and Terhaar, Staub, and Singer (2003).

conventional equity and fixed-income returns, and among the alternative asset returns themselves, are often close to zero because of the smoothing effect and the absence of market-observable returns. The bias can be large, so that the true risk is larger than the reported estimates. Traditional indexes of hedge fund returns also suffer from a serious survivorship bias (only good-performing hedge funds are included in the database) that biases historical return measures for this asset class.[6]

Long-Term Capital Market Expectations: Forward-Looking Returns

Although the past can be useful to forecast the future, simply extrapolating past risk–return measures is not sufficient. A useful approach is to derive long-term estimates that would be consistent with market equilibrium. In an integrated world financial market, expected returns should reflect the risks borne by investors. Although events could create attractive investment opportunities in the short run, long-term capital market expectations that are consistent with market equilibrium are useful to guide investment strategy. An interesting approach has been developed by Singer and Terhaar (1997) and Terhaar, Staub, and Singer (2003). This approach uses the international capital asset pricing model (ICAPM)[7] as an anchor but takes into account market imperfections, such as segmentation and illiquidity. The approach can be summarized in three steps:

- Calculate an updated covariance matrix[8] (volatility and correlation of asset classes).
- Use the ICAPM to infer expected returns for each asset class.
- Adjust expected returns for possible market segmentation and illiquidity.

The historical covariance matrix serves as the starting point, but it is adjusted to reflect some of the biases mentioned previously for infrequently traded assets and is updated to be forward-looking. A multifactor updating approach ensures consistency of the updated matrix.

The expected return on an asset class is equal to the risk-free rate plus a risk premium. The ICAPM states that the risk premium on any asset class should be proportional to its beta with the world market portfolio:

$$RP_i = \beta_{iM} RP_M \tag{13.1}$$

where

RP_i is the risk premium for asset class i

β_{iM} is the beta of asset class i

RP_M is the risk premium on the world market portfolio

---

[6] See Asness, Krail, and Liew (2001).

[7] See Chapter 4.

[8] Remember that the covariance between two assets is equal to the product of the standard deviation (volatility) of the two assets times their correlation. So, the covariance matrix contains all risk information on asset classes.

We assume that the risk premium on any currency is equal to zero. This assumption could be relaxed if we assume that a specific currency is undervalued and will revert to its fundamental purchasing power parity (PPP) value in the long run (see Chapter 2).

Plotting the risk premiums versus the betas would result in all the points lying on a straight line. Equation 13.1 can be rewritten by replacing β_{iM} by its value:

$$\beta_{iM} = \rho_{iM}\frac{\sigma_i}{\sigma_M}$$

$$RP_i = \rho_{iM}\frac{\sigma_i}{\sigma_M}RP_M = \rho_{iM}\sigma_i\frac{RP_M}{\sigma_M} \tag{13.2}$$

or

$$\frac{RP_i}{\sigma_i} = \rho_{iM}\frac{RP_M}{\sigma_M} \tag{13.3}$$

where σ_i and σ_M are the standard deviations of returns of asset class i and of the market portfolio, and ρ_{iM} is the correlation of returns between asset class i and the market portfolio.

Equation 13.3 simply states that the expected reward-to-risk ratio (RP_i/σ_i), the Sharpe ratio of an asset class, is equal to the Sharpe ratio of the market portfolio times the correlation of the asset class with the market portfolio. The lower the correlation, the lower the Sharpe ratio of an asset class. In a fully integrated world, the risk premium on an asset reflects the risk-diversification property of the asset. An asset with a correlation of 0.5 with the market portfolio should have a Sharpe ratio equal to half that of the market. This is because half of the volatility of asset i can be diversified away and therefore should not be rewarded by a risk premium.

However, world financial markets are not fully integrated, and equilibrium pricing of some asset classes (e.g., emerging equity markets or private equity) should reflect their partial segmentation from the world market. To illustrate, let's consider an asset class, called emerging market in Example 13.5, that is fully segmented. The ICAPM does not hold for this asset class. Local investors cannot invest abroad, and they dominate the local market. They will require a high risk premium on this asset class because its total risk cannot be diversified away in a global portfolio. The risk premium is set in isolation by local investors, reflecting the total risk σ_i of the segmented asset class without regard to its diversification ability. If the market were integrated in the world market, global investors would set a lower risk premium (higher price), reflecting the fact that part of the risk of this asset class can be diversified away in a global portfolio (correlation less than 1). In a way, global investors can take advantage of segmented markets. In practice, some markets are partly segmented, so the equilibrium risk premium on these assets should be somewhat higher than what is dictated by a fully integrated ICAPM, but less than under full segmentation. This is illustrated in Example 13.5.

Similarly, to hold illiquid assets, investors require compensation in the form of an illiquidity premium to be added to the risk premium dictated by the ICAPM, which assumes liquid markets. While the expected return on an illiquid asset can therefore look high, such an asset has the unpleasant characteristic that any sale of

EXAMPLE 13.5 RISK PREMIUM

Suppose all investors in the world have similar risk aversion and require a Sharpe ratio of 0.2 on their diversified portfolios. The world market portfolio has a volatility of 20 percent. An emerging-market asset has a volatility of 30 percent and a correlation of 0.5 with the world market portfolio. The beta of the emerging-market asset class is

$$0.5 \times 30\%/20\% = 0.75$$

1. What is the equilibrium risk premium for the market portfolio?
2. Assuming full integration, what is the equilibrium risk premium for the emerging market?
3. Assuming full segmentation, what is the equilibrium risk premium for the emerging market?

SOLUTION

1. The equilibrium Sharpe ratio required for a well-diversified portfolio is 0.2. Hence, the risk premium on the world market portfolio is 4 percent:

$$0.2 = \frac{RP_M}{\sigma_M} = \frac{RP_M}{20\%}$$

$$RP_M = 4\%$$

2. If we assume full integration, the ICAPM tells us what the Sharpe ratio should be for the emerging market:

$$\frac{RP_i}{\sigma_i} = \rho_{iM}\frac{RP_M}{\sigma_M} = 0.5 \times \frac{4\%}{20\%} = 0.10$$

Hence, $RP_i = 0.10 \times \sigma_i = 3$ percent. This is also equal to beta times the risk premium on the world market:

$$0.75 \times 4\% = 3\%$$

3. If we assume full segmentation, the ICAPM does not hold, and the emerging market is priced locally, reflecting its total volatility. Local investors search for a Sharpe ratio of 0.20 for a diversified portfolio, so

$$\frac{RP_i}{\sigma_i} = 0.20$$

Hence, $RP_i = 0.2 \times \sigma_i = 6$ percent.

a sizable order cannot be achieved quickly except at a significant price discount. Estimating the premium that is required by market participants to compensate for the illiquidity of an asset class is a difficult task.[9]

[9] Terhaar, Staub, and Singer (2003) calculate illiquidity premiums for a full array of asset classes.

These equilibrium expected returns are used to "guide" the formulation of long-term capital market expectations. Additional forward-looking factors could be considered to adjust those expectations, but managers should ensure that the long-term risk and return assumptions are consistent.

Short-Term Capital Market Expectations

The definition of *short term* varies according to the investor, but *long term* typically refers to ten years or more and *short term* to less than a year or a few years. Changes in market environment and valuations could suggest that some assets are under- or overvalued. This can happen when investors have become very optimistic on some asset class and asset prices have risen well above their perceived intrinsic values. The opposite can occur when pessimism prevails. Many forecasting and valuation techniques are used, from subjective to quantitative. Some have been reviewed in previous chapters. For example, Chapters 2 and 3 suggested approaches to forecasting currency movements, and Chapter 6 dealt with equity valuation. Short-term capital market expectations will suggest (temporary) tactical deviations from the strategic asset allocation, as discussed in the following section.

Example 13.6 details the capital market expectations in the John Bouderi case.

EXAMPLE 13.6 JOHN BOUDERI CURRENCY VIEW AND CAPITAL MARKET EXPECTATIONS

Brennan's firm supplies her with some capital market expectations, summarized below. These were derived from long-term history and a forward-looking model.

Capital Market Expectations

Asset Class	Expected Return	Standard Deviation
Domestic equity	11%	15%
European equity	14	21
U.S. equity	12	19
Government bonds	6	7
Corporate bonds	7	9
Money market	5	2

A final part of her firm's analysis confirmed Brennan's opinion that the Australian dollar was undervalued and that the undervaluation will get corrected in the long run at a rate of 2 to 3 percent per year. She confirmed her conclusion by reviewing a report prepared by her firm and based on some IMF data. The report studied the purchasing power value of the Australian dollar over the past twenty years. Twenty years ago, the Australian dollar was stable and regarded as fairly priced relative to the U.S. dollar. In the table that follows, period 1 refers to twenty years ago and period 2 to the present. The period 1 exchange rate between the U.S. dollar (US$) and the Australian dollar (A$)

was A$:US$ = 1.1279, or 1.1279 U.S. dollars per Australian dollar. The period 2 exchange rate had moved to A$:US$ = 0.5106.

Time Period	**1**	**2**
End-of-period exchange rate A$:US$	1.1279	0.5106
CPI Australia	44.4	114.8
CPI U.S.	64.6	116.2
PPP value of A$:US$	1.1279	0.7847

Assuming that the Australian dollar was fairly priced relative to the U.S. dollar in period 1, its period 2 value as dictated by PPP can be calculated by adjusting by the inflation differential between the United States and Australia:

$$\text{PPP value in period 2} = 1.1279 \times \frac{116.2}{64.6} \times \frac{44.4}{114.8} = 0.7847$$

The theoretical PPP value of the Australian dollar is US$0.7847, while the actual spot exchange rate at the end of period 2 was US$0.5106, or a 35 percent undervaluation.

Brennan knows that the possibility of a strong Australian dollar raises the question of hedging the currency risk of the non-Australian investments. She wants to hear John's reaction to the capital market expectations and exchange rate data she has presented.

JOHN BOUDERI'S REACTION

Bouderi finds the projected returns from outside Australia compelling, but he is concerned about the increased volatility of European and U.S. markets. Brennan explains the benefits of adding asset classes with a low correlation to the Australian market. To support her position, she provides a table of historical correlation information, along with the expected correlations developed by the research department of her firm.

Bouderi concurs with Brennan's rationale for global investing from a diversification standpoint, but he understands that this will add a new risk to his portfolio due to currency fluctuations. He has read of investors who have lost substantial sums speculating on currency movements and wonders whether currency hedging is worth the expense or risk. He expresses doubts about hedging: "I am familiar with currency fluctuations because Bestbuilt [his company] buys many of its supplies from Asian firms. Some years it would hurt us, some years it would help, but in the long run it seemed to balance out. Isn't the same true with global investing?"

Brennan replies that fine-tuned risk management is an important component of global asset management. If currency fluctuations induce pure risk without return compensation, it makes sense to hedge to avoid excessive volatility in portfolio returns. Currency-hedging transaction costs are low.

Furthermore, an appreciation of the Australian dollar is likely, and that will induce a currency loss on foreign investments. Although it is true that currency fluctuations tend to balance out in the long run, it may take many, many years before that happens, and Bouderi is starting from a point at which the Australian dollar seems extremely low. Something like a 50 percent hedging strategy would be a reasonable middle-of-the-road position, given current market expectations and the fact that there is currently no forward premium to pay. An advantage is that the 50 percent strategy would also minimize regret.

Global Asset Allocation: From Strategic to Tactical

The most important global investment decision is asset allocation. The first step for a global investor is to decide on a *strategic asset allocation* (*SAA*), or the structure of the portfolio for the long term. This decision is based on long-term capital market expectations. The process of periodically adjusting asset allocation to reflect changes in the market environment is referred to as *tactical asset allocation* (*TAA*).

Strategic Asset Allocation

The SAA is derived by conducting an asset allocation optimization using long-term capital market expectations. For portfolio management with *individual clients,* the objectives and constraints indicated in the investment policy statement play a big role in the optimization. In *institutional* investment management, the SAA often takes the form of an investable benchmark that is assigned as an objective by the sponsor to the manager(s). Because the performance of the portfolio is measured against it, this benchmark provides a strong guide to the manager's investment strategy. The question that remains is the choice of the proper global benchmark. There are three important issues:

- The scope of the benchmark
- The set of weights chosen
- The investor's attitude toward currency risk

Scope of the Global Benchmark A truly global investor should include all asset classes, domestic and foreign, in the global benchmark. This global benchmark could then be broken down into various sub-benchmarks that can be assigned to different investment managers. In practice, many investors treat domestic and foreign investments as different asset classes. For example, a Dutch investor could decide to invest 50 percent of its assets out of the Netherlands, with half invested in foreign stocks and half in foreign bonds. Then the Dutch investor could assign some world equity index to the foreign equity manager and some world bond index to the foreign bond manager. These global indexes should then be calculated by excluding the Netherlands from the indexes. Note that the global asset allocation will be strongly biased toward Dutch assets because 50 percent of the assets are invested domestically, so the natural benchmark for the total assets of the fund will not be a market capitalization–weighted world index. Further note that within equity, the distinction is often made between investments in developed and emerging markets, which are usually treated as different asset classes.

Weights in the Global Benchmark A whole range of approaches is used to determine the benchmark weights. The simplest, most common approach is to use a *published global market index.* The weights are proportional to the relative market capitalizations (caps). A market cap–weighted index is a natural implication of the theory. It can be easily replicated in a passive strategy because the weights change in line with price movements in the portfolio. This type of global index is widely published and is commonly used by institutional investors worldwide. Hence, the performance can easily be compared across funds and managers.

Some investors are using *GDP country weights* instead of market-cap country weights. The idea is interesting because it gives each country a weight proportional to its economic strength. But implementing this approach is not easy, and it is fairly costly in a passive portfolio that must be rebalanced each time a new GDP figure is published or revised in any country. The same problem occurs if a given stock market goes up or down while the GDP weights stay constant.

The inclusion of bonds and alternative investments in a variety of currencies makes the concept of a world market portfolio very difficult to measure and implement. Investors seldom consider the world market portfolio of all assets a practical global investment strategy. Most investors exhibit a strong home bias in their investment strategy. This attitude is often justified, because foreign investments are regarded as more risky and costly due to lack of information/familiarity, currency risk, transaction costs, and differential tax treatments. A large investor will therefore treat each asset class separately, for example, assigning separate benchmarks for domestic equity, international equity, domestic bonds, and so on. This policy leaves open the question of the strategic global asset allocation across all asset classes. Different investor groups should follow different core strategies that reflect their situations and comparative advantages in terms of costs, taxes, and risks; therefore, private and institutional investors may select a *customized* global strategic asset allocation. This allocation is then translated into a customized benchmark combining indexes for each asset class. Studies by Blake, Lehmann, and Timmermann (1999) and Brinson, Singer, and Beebower (1991) show that the asset allocation decision is a major determinant of returns on U.K. and U.S. pension plans. So, the weights chosen are of great importance for performance. Optimization techniques are often used, based on long-term capital market expectations and on characteristics and constraints of the investor (see the next section).

Institutional investors face constraints in the form of various regulations that they must follow. But deviating from the peer group also poses a "business" risk. For example, a pension sponsor that decides to have a much greater international allocation than its peers is under severe pressure in times when international investments underperform domestic investments. So, the current asset allocation of peers is also a form of benchmark. The asset allocation of British and Dutch pension funds, for example, is much more global than that of U.S., German, and Swiss pension funds. Pension funds in some small countries have a majority of their investments abroad. The equity allocation also differs markedly, with British funds typically investing some 60 percent of their assets in stocks while French funds typically invest 10 percent. All of these numbers are for an "average" pension fund; they vary greatly across funds and change over time. Nevertheless, the obvious picture is that institutional investors do not follow a uniform investment strategy across the world.

Currency Allocation in the Benchmark Should foreign investments be systematically hedged against currency risks? This question has led to an extensive controversy (already addressed in Chapters 4 and 9). The international CAPM (ICAPM) provides useful insights on risk management. The basic conclusion from theoretical research is that the optimal portfolio is the world market portfolio *partly hedged* against currency risk (see Chapter 4). *Partly hedged* means that all foreign assets are optimally hedged when the market is in equilibrium. We can objectively observe the world market portfolio; we can use world market caps as weights for the benchmark. Although investment managers may disagree as to the exact benchmark to use, all of these portfolios approximate the investable world portfolio and are observable. The problem is identifying the optimal hedge ratios, because theory tells us that optimal hedge ratios are a function of the asset to be hedged, and their values depend on unobservable parameters such as relative preferences of different nationals, risk aversions, and the net foreign investment position of each country. The existence of currency risk premiums is central to the determination of optimal hedge ratios. Exchange rates, like interest rates and stock prices, are financial prices, and risk premiums are justified. Unfortunately, these currency risk premiums cannot be measured directly and are likely to be unstable over time. So, *pragmatic shortcuts* are necessary:

- A first pragmatic possibility is *full hedging*. The motivation for a full-hedging policy is based on the assumption that we cannot tell whether currency risk premiums are positive or negative; hence, the sole objective is to minimize the risk. Therefore, we hedge 100 percent and use a fully hedged or unitary-hedge benchmark as the strategic benchmark.[10] Full hedging is simply focusing on minimizing the volatility of the foreign part of the portfolio. This simple approach has been severely attacked from several angles:
  - First, theory tells us that currency risk premiums should exist if some countries are net foreign investors (e.g., Japan) or exhibit more risk aversion than others (see Chapter 4).

---

[10] Many practitioners use Pérold and Schulman (1988) as a justification for a unitary hedge ratio (100% hedge). Actually, Pérold and Schulman do consider the case of a zero-currency-risk premium, but they advocate taking into account the correlation between currency and market risk to determine the "full" hedge ratio.

- Second, even if we were doing only a passive, risk-minimization hedge and cared only about risk, not about expected return, we would take into account the correlation between the currency risk and the asset risk. In the presence of correlation between currency and market risk, we should use "regression" hedges, which will generally not equal 1 because of the correlation between asset returns and currency movements.

- Third, the relevant measure of risk should not be the volatility of the foreign assets taken in isolation, but their contribution to the total risk of the global portfolio (domestic and foreign). Indeed, currencies provide an element of monetary risk diversification for the domestic portfolio. As long as the proportion of foreign assets in the total portfolio is small (e.g., less than 10%), the contribution of currency risk is minimal, and it is not worth the trouble and costs to engage in systematic currency hedging (see Nesbitt, 1991, and Jorion, 1989).

- A second pragmatic alternative often proposed is *no hedging*. This approach refutes the assumption that full currency hedging reduces the volatility of return on foreign assets. The question raised is the investor's time horizon. A pension fund has a long-term objective and should not be concerned with short-term risk, such as monthly or quarterly volatility. Given the structure of its liabilities, a pension fund should instead focus on the risk that a sufficient return will not be realized over a long horizon, for example, five or ten years. Froot (1993) shows, theoretically and empirically, that the risk-minimizing currency hedge is a function of the investment horizon. With a horizon of ten years, foreign stocks display a greater return volatility when hedged than unhedged. The reason for this finding is the mean reversion in exchange rates. Over the short run, currency returns are explained mostly by changes in the real exchange rate. In the very long run, the purchasing powers of two currencies tend toward parity, and exchange rate trends are explained mostly by the inflation differential between the two currencies. Another motivation for this approach is that systematic currency hedging can be a costly process. The job of a fund trustee or an investment manager is at stake in the short run, so whether that person will feel comfortable with measuring performance and risk solely on such a long horizon is another question. Also, significant deviations from PPP persist in the long run.

- A third pragmatic shortcut is to use *universal hedge ratios* (or arbitrary hedge ratios). Black (1990) used theory, and some restrictive assumptions, to come up with a 0.75 hedge ratio. Gastineau (1995) suggested a 0.5 hedge ratio. As mentioned in Chapter 4, Black had to make many extreme assumptions to derive his universal hedge ratio.[11] For example, all countries should have exactly the same amount of investment abroad (no net foreign investment)

[11] For a criticism of this model, see Adler and Solnik (1990) and Adler and Prasad (1992).

and no inflation. Also, he postulated that all investors should have an identical risk aversion, and so on. Even if the principle that each investor should use exactly the same hedge ratio for every single asset were to be accepted, the exact value of the universal hedge ratio is still arbitrary because it is based on a forecast of the future return and volatility of the world market portfolio. If investors are to make so many "arbitrary" assumptions in order to derive a universal hedge ratio of, say, 0.75, why not simply assume the result at the start? In a sense, Gastineau's "Why bother?" approach is cleaner. He assumes that 0.5 is the best. Why 0.5? Because it is halfway between 0 and 1, neither of which is appropriate. A wrong hedging decision can lead to a vast amount of regret over not having taken the best decision. For example, a U.S. investor who decided not to hedge currency risk would have incurred a currency loss of some 40 percent on Eurozone assets from late 1998 to late 2000, with huge regret at not having been fully hedged. Conversely, a fully hedged U.S. investor would have missed the 50 percent appreciation of the euro from late 2001 to 2005, again, with huge regret at not having made the "right" hedging decision. Basically, regret risk stems from a comparison of the ex post return of the adopted hedging policy relative to the best hedging policy that could have been chosen. To minimize regret risk, a simple hedging rule would be to hedge 50 percent. Such a decision will turn out to be almost always wrong ex post, but the amount of regret will be minimized. Several practitioners have justified a 50 percent naive hedge ratio on such intuitive grounds.

To summarize, the extent of strategic currency hedging remains an open theoretical and empirical question. Because hedge ratios differ across assets and currencies, depending on unobservable foreign asset positions, utility functions, individual risk aversion, and inflation, no simple practical solution or theoretically unquestionable benchmark exists, or ever will, for currency allocation. In the absence of a natural benchmark dictated by theory or systematic empirical observation, investors have taken various routes. Some use different currency-hedging strategies for different asset classes. For example, the foreign stock benchmark can be unhedged while the foreign bond benchmark is fully hedged because currency risk is relatively more important for bonds than for stocks. Currency-hedged global indexes are now available for both stocks and bonds from the major index providers, so performance of fully hedged portfolios can easily be assessed.

Tactical Asset Allocation

Active managers adjust their asset allocations periodically, typically monthly but sometimes more often, to reflect changes in the market environment. This strategy is called *dynamic* or *tactical asset allocation* (*TAA*). TAA is the process of deciding which *asset classes* are attractively or unattractively priced, and making short-term departures from the long-term policy by buying more of the attractive markets and reducing the holding of unattractive markets. Through this process, the aim is to add value by achieving a higher return than would be achieved by simply holding the portfolio defined by the long-term policy. Adjustments made are *conditional* on new information, so deviations from the SAA are based on short-term developments and reflect forecasts on market trends in the next few months. This is typically the case when it is perceived that investors have become too optimistic (pessimistic) on some asset class, pushing asset prices very high (low) relative to fundamentals. How to exploit these forecasts depends on the investment philosophy chosen by the investment manager (see the earlier discussion of various philosophies).

Some managers use a systematic quantitative approach to TAA, in which adjustments strictly follow some *disciplined* risk–return optimization process. A set of variables is used to evaluate the relative attractiveness of markets, namely, their risk premium. Typical variables used are the level of the dividend yield, the level of the interest rate, the spread between long-term yields and cash rates, and so on.[12] The holdings of an equity market with a low dividend yield (relative to its historical average) would be adjusted downward on the premise that the market is overpriced and will soon revert to normality. Rebalancing is done automatically in a disciplined fashion to prevent emotions or fads from influencing the TAA.

Other managers base their revision on various models of currencies, interest rates, and equity markets to determine the fundamental value (or fair value) of various asset classes (i.e., their fair price). TAA decisions are made if market prices come to deviate significantly from their fundamental value. While many of the inputs are quantitative, the TAA decisions are not automatic; they take into account the current market environment. Efforts are made to understand why those discrepancies have arisen. Some of these discrepancies could be explained by theories grounded in behavioral finance. Finding that an asset class is overvalued will not be useful in TAA unless the market corrects the discrepancy fairly quickly. Other managers simply use a subjective assessment of changes in the current market environment.

The proposed asset allocation for the John Bouderi case is discussed in Example 13.7.

Global Asset Allocation: Structuring and Quantifying the Process

The global asset allocation process described, with its separation between strategic and tactical asset allocations, is common among *institutional* investors such as pension funds. *Private* investors make less use of benchmarks and tend to state their investment objectives in a less formal manner. They sometimes seem to care more about absolute returns than about deviations from a prespecified benchmark, but this does not mean that the investment process should not be structured. We will discuss an adaptable global investment process.

[12] There is some evidence that the direction of worldwide stock and bond prices can be predicted to some extent by using a set of information variables. This fact does not necessarily imply that these markets are inefficient; predictability could also be explained by a time variation in risk premiums justified by a change in the socioeconomic environment. In statistical jargon, the strategic asset allocation could be based on long-term, unconditional risk premiums; the tactical asset allocation could be based on conditional risk premiums.

EXAMPLE 13.7 BOUDERI ASSET ALLOCATION AND HEDGING

Brennan had analyzed possible asset allocations using her firm's optimization model. She selected the asset allocation shown below. She chose a mix close to the efficient frontier and meeting all of Bouderi's objectives, following the liquidity events.

Asset Class	Proposed Asset Allocation	Proposed Dollar Asset Allocation	Expected Return	Standard Deviation
Domestic equity	30%	$570,000	11%	15%
European equity	15	285,000	14	21
U.S. equity	15	285,000	12	19
Government bonds	12	228,000	6	7
Corporate bonds	25	475,000	7	9
Money market	3	57,000	5	2
Total	100%	$1,900,000*	9.82%	8%

*Includes proceeds of $480,000 from the home transactions and $150,000 expenses for the trip to Europe and the trust.

Given her capital market expectations, Brennan believes that foreign currency hedging was in order. She reviews her thinking and explains her reasoning to Bouderi:

"Interest rates in Australia, Europe, and the United States are comparable, so the forward discount/premium is equal to zero. Currency hedging will exactly offset any loss caused by depreciation of foreign currencies against the Australian dollar, without having to pay a forward premium. Of course, any potential foreign currency gain would also be eliminated. Full hedging would be a natural strategy, given expectations, but it can take a very long time before currencies revert to their PPP value. Furthermore, having some foreign currency exposure in the portfolio could provide some risk-diversification elements in case of a sudden surge of inflation in Australia. Also, John, you seem reluctant to do any hedging. A 50 percent hedge ratio seems a reasonable middle-of-the-road strategy and could be easily implemented with foreign currency forward contracts."

Bouderi agrees, and Brennan explains the details. To minimize transaction costs, the hedge will consist of buying a one-year-maturity forward contract for Australian dollars equal to half the amount initially invested in U.S. dollars and euros (selling forward U.S. dollars and euros). The hedge amount will be rebalanced yearly. Brennan realizes that this static hedging policy means that the hedge ratio will diverge from 50 percent as the value of foreign equity moves up or down. All expected returns provided in Brennan's mix reflect this hedging strategy.

Apart from the obvious technical and practical problems inherent in investing abroad, the key issue in global investing is how to structure the *asset allocation* process. Essential to this decision process are a variety of uncertain forecasts concerning exchange rates, interest rates, and stock market patterns. The task is further complicated by the fact that many of these variables are, to varying degrees, interdependent in the global context. For example, all the major stock markets are linked, but some are more closely linked than others, depending on the integration of the underlying economies. Global industry factors cut across borders. Similarly, a change in the interest rate of one currency will affect the exchange rates and interest rates of other currencies, but not to the same degree. Domestic asset allocation is simplified by the fact that an investor chooses from a limited variety of assets, namely, cash, bonds, common stocks, and possibly alternative assets. In the global context, however, these choices are multiplied by the number of countries and currencies available, which can, in and of themselves, present certain practical problems. For example, an investor may be bullish on the Japanese stock market but not on the yen. The complexity of the global scene, which involves so many interactions, makes quantification all the more useful and calls for computer technology. Any added value should be transferred immediately and efficiently to all accounts, even if they have diverse objectives and constraints as stated in their IPSs.

This section describes a quantified system or process for portfolio management based on a top-down approach that is currently used by several global money management firms, primarily in private banking. Because it is internally consistent, it avoids the pitfalls sometimes found in the bottom-up approach. The purpose of this system is to ensure the most efficient use of existing expertise within an organization and a rapid implementation of new investment ideas in all accounts. The system must therefore be structured along the lines of the major common factors affecting a security's price behavior. A different model of the world capital market would lead to a different system. We will discuss here a *balanced* approach centered along a *country investment philosophy*, but an investment philosophy focusing on worldwide industry factors, or both country and industry factors, could also be considered.

Our portfolio management system has four major stages: research and market analysis, asset allocation optimization, portfolio construction, and performance and risk control. The attraction of the system lies not in its components but in the way it integrates the four stages, with the aid of computers, to benefit money managers and their clients. The idea is not to generate more reliable forecasts but to use currently available forecasts better. That goal requires capitalizing most efficiently on the existing expertise within an organization. A diagram of this system is shown in Exhibit 13.1.

Research and Market Analysis

To cope with the complexity and rapid changes of the global environment, a manager must have the technological tools to analyze and interpret large streams of data. Ideally, everyone involved in the investment decision process—analysts, investment committee members, and managers—should operate with a common electronic system (the *platform*) that allows a free flow of data and research findings between decision makers.

EXHIBIT 13.1

An Integrated Investment Process

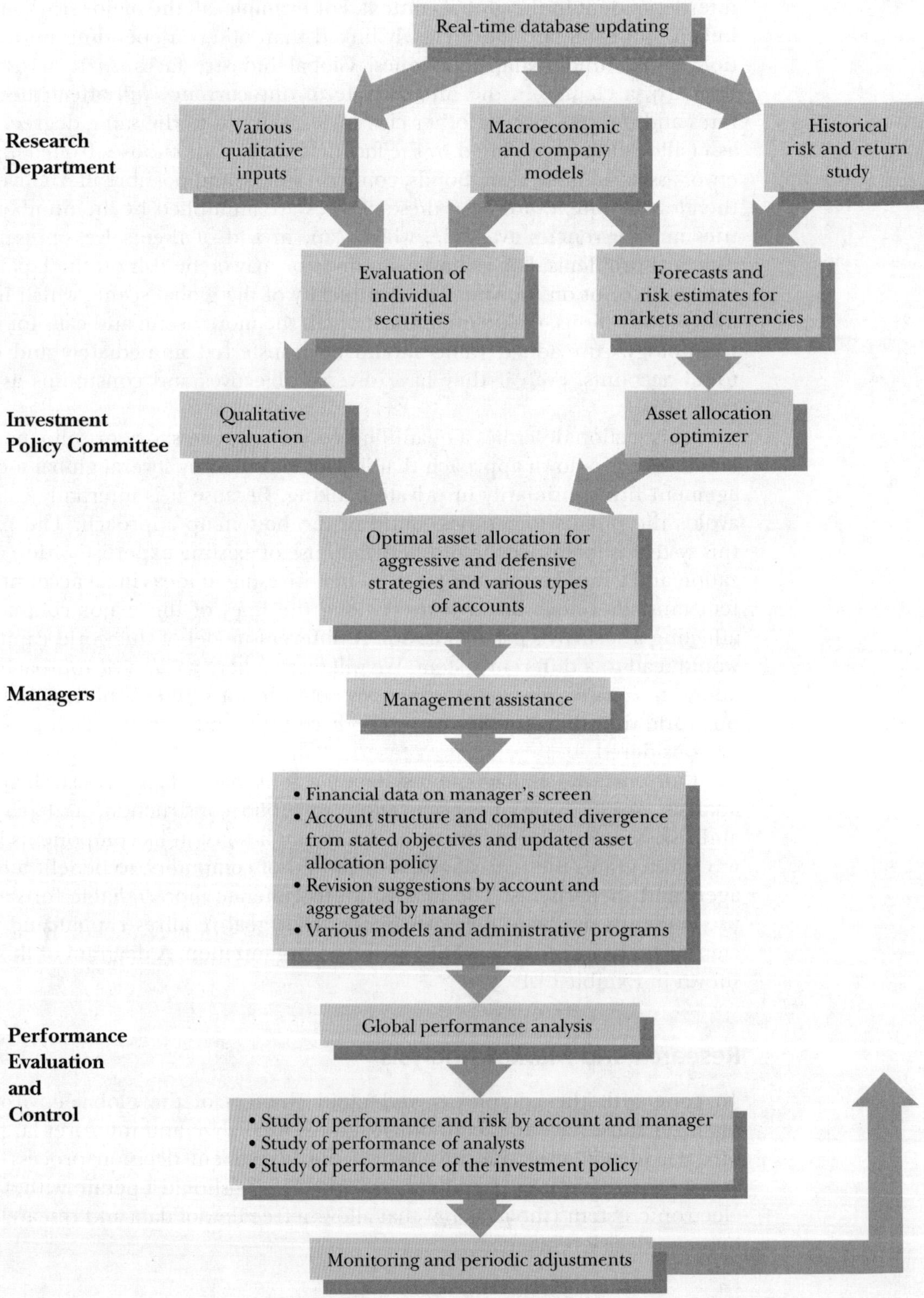

To monitor markets, a large global database with online connections to major outside databank services is necessary. The database available on the platform should contain price histories on markets and individual securities, as well as economic statistical data. Ideally, the data should cover several previous years and should be updated daily. All reports and recommendations produced by research analysts should be available instantly on the platform. Another major use of the platform is the development and revision of forecasts on currencies, interest rates, commodity prices, and national stock indexes. The manager should then translate these forecasts into estimates of total returns in particular base currencies. Similarly, risk parameters for markets and securities should be available on the platform and frequently updated.

Asset Allocation Optimization

The objective of any investment strategy is to achieve a superior performance for a given level of risk. This can be done through subjective discussion among the members of an investment strategy committee or by using formal optimization models. Given the investment philosophy selected, an investment strategy should aim to achieve an efficient asset allocation by regions/country (or currency) and type of investment (stocks, bonds, money markets). Toward this end, a mean-variance quadratic program is often used to merge the forecasts and risk estimates generated by an investment organization. Providing it is optimal, the resulting asset allocation will outperform a passive strategy only to the extent that the organization's forecasts reflect superior expertise in one or more markets, such as stocks, bonds, or currency. Also, the allocation must conform to the objectives and constraints set out in the IPSs of the various accounts managed by an organization. Some accounts permit only equity investment, others impose restrictions on selling short, and still others do not permit investment in specific asset classes. Plainly, constraints such as these will affect the potential return on an account, as will the choice of risk level or any other limitation.

Unless currency risk is systematically hedged, optimal asset allocations will differ according to the client's base currency. In theory, managers should care about real returns, not nominal returns. They should consider the returns calculated in the currency of the investor and adjusted by the appropriate inflation rate. Because the volatility of inflation rates is very small compared with that of most asset returns or currency movements, the use of real or nominal returns would not make much difference in the results of the optimization procedure.[13]

The optimization can be conducted on absolute returns. It also can be conducted relative to a prespecified benchmark, with return and risk being measured in deviation from the benchmark. This is the case when an SAA is first determined (the benchmark) and tactical revisions are considered based on the current market

[13] Some institutional investors take the structure of their liabilities into account to determine the appropriate investment strategy. The risk of the assets is measured relative to that of the liabilities rather than in absolute terms. But the modeling of the liabilities is a difficult task. This process is called asset/liability management (ALM).

environment. The SAA is optimized based on long-term capital market expectations when the IPS is drafted. The SAA can be periodically revised (e.g., once a year) following the same process. Tactical deviations from this SAA can be implemented more frequently based on an optimization using short-term capital market expectations and taking transaction costs into account.

Portfolio Construction

Active security selection in each market is a natural complement to active market selection. A research department should maintain on the platform an *active list* of individual securities in each market. This regularly updated list should provide a manager with an analyst's recommendation, possibly in the form of an expected return in local currency, as well as major risk characteristics of the security, including sensitivities to various factors and, for bonds, actuarial yields and a measure for duration. The manager can then use this active securities list to construct the portfolio according to the asset allocation strategy of a specific client. Multifactor risk models are necessary to control the active risks taken in security selection.

Managers of a large number of medium-sized accounts find that rebalancing those accounts to reflect even modest alterations in the client's investment policy or the firm's strategy is extremely time-consuming and unduly repetitive. Reacting to a major policy or strategy change takes even longer. To cope with this problem, a manager should first value each portfolio in the asset allocation format. Next, each manager should modify the new investment strategy so that it reflects client IPS guidelines for his major classes of accounts. The extent of this modification will depend on the type of client, the base currency, and the size of the account. Total transaction costs and taxes (e.g., on realized capital gains) must be taken into account. Any deviations of the current asset allocation appear on the manager's screen. Drawing on the active securities list, a computer program will make sell-and-buy recommendations for stocks and bonds that would enable the account to satisfy the new asset allocation guideline. The manager can either validate the proposed transactions on the screen or make his own decisions. The market orders and attendant paperwork required for implementing the validated transactions can be generated automatically by the computer. The use of pooled investment funds simplifies the process.

More quantitatively oriented managers would probably make extensive use of the models described elsewhere in this book. They could adjust the sensitivity of the portfolio to specific market factors in each cell of the asset allocation; for example, a manager who is bullish on interest rates in Britain could select sterling bonds with a long duration to increase the sensitivity to a drop in sterling bond yields. Futures and options can be used to react to sudden threats of a large market movement in some currency or asset classes. At this level, fine-tuning of the risk management of the portfolio should come into play.

Performance and Risk Control

The final step in the investment process is to monitor the performance and risk of individual portfolios. A common problem is that all money managers are outspoken about global risk diversification, but many do not use a structured allocation process to achieve it. This problem is all the more serious for managers with active strategies, who tend to concentrate on a few currencies and markets and are therefore vulnerable to the high risk associated with those currencies and markets.

Performance control should be driven by an organization's daily accounting system. As mentioned in Chapter 12, the objective is to be able to answer the following questions about a portfolio and, in doing so, to assess the effectiveness of its manager:

- What is the total return on the fund over a specific period?
- What is the breakdown of the return in terms of capital gains, currency fluctuations, and income?
- To what extent is the performance explained by asset allocation, market timing, currency selection, or individual security selection?
- How does the overall return compare with that of certain benchmarks?
- Is there evidence of particular expertise in various asset classes and markets?
- Has the risk-diversification objective been achieved?
- How aggressive is the manager's strategy? How does this compare with the goals of the client?

The characteristics and use of an account review of a global performance evaluation system are discussed in Chapter 12. It should be stressed that the performance of a research department should also be studied to pinpoint the areas of expertise. This can be done by constructing mock portfolios based on analyst recommendations for each country and comparing the subsequent returns with those on the corresponding national indexes. An illustration of performance evaluation for the John Bouderi case is provided in Example 13.8.

In this chapter, we have examined the global investment industry and an integrated investment process for asset management. The performance report and presentation come at the end of the process, and they provide feedback as the process is continuously repeated. Because everything in asset management is global, all the chapters in this book support the process.

EXAMPLE 13.8 PERFORMANCE EVALUATION OF THE BOUDERI PORTFOLIO

A year has passed, so Brennan meets with John Bouderi for a scheduled review of the investment policy statement and a review of his portfolio's performance for the year. After a general discussion, Brennan moves on to discuss portfolio performance for the year. She has prepared an informal presentation and several performance reports. Based on her experience with Bouderi's reaction to quarterly performance reports, she knows that John finds it difficult to understand the sources of international equity performance, although he has become much more willing to accept hedging after all the reading he has done about it. At their meeting the previous year to set up the strategic asset allocation, Brennan and Bouderi had agreed on an unhedged benchmark for the international equity portion of the portfolio. The passive benchmark had a 60 percent weight in the U.S. index and a 40 percent weight in the European index. Brennan had encouraged Bouderi to follow performance against this benchmark.

GLOBAL PERFORMANCE EVALUATION

Bouderi's portfolio has appreciated by 11 percent before taxes and inflation. Brennan gives him several reports, including the performance report shown below. Bouderi wants to compare the performance of the unhedged portfolio with the unhedged benchmark and then reflect on the impact of currency hedging. The Australian dollar has appreciated over the year against most currencies by approximately 5 percent. After reviewing the document, Bouderi feels happy with the performance of his international portfolio.

PERFORMANCE REPORT FOR INTERNATIONAL PORTFOLIO

Your international equity portfolio rose from \$570,000 to \$630,285 (a gain of \$60,285 or 10.58%). An additional gain of \$14,492 came from the forward currency contracts in which we sold forward US\$79,800 and €79,800 for \$285,000 forward. So, the total value of the international portfolio is \$644,777, or a total return of 13.12 percent in Australian dollars. Net of currency hedging, the return was 10.58 percent, which is only 0.09 percent below the return on your unhedged benchmark (10.67 percent). All data and calculations are reported in the tables herein.

The performance of your *unhedged* international equity portfolio relative to the benchmark is explained by two factors:

- Your U.S. equity investments had exactly the same return as the U.S. index component of the benchmark, namely, 12 percent in Australian dollars. But your European equity investments overperformed the European equity index by $0.47\% = 9.15\% - 8.68\%$. Because European equity accounted for 50 percent of your international investments, the contribution of security selection to total return is a positive $0.24\% = 50\% \times 0.47\%$.

- Your asset allocation was more heavily weighted toward European equity (50% weight) than the benchmark (40% weight). Because European equity underperformed U.S. equity, this made your international portfolio underperform the benchmark. The contribution to performance of the asset allocation decision is –0.33 percent.

Hence:[14]

Portfolio return = Benchmark return + Asset allocation + Security selection

10.58% = 10.67% − 0.33% + 0.24%

The currency hedge that you applied contributed an additional 2.54 percent to your performance. You sold forward US$79,800 (countervalue $142,500), that is, half of your U.S. dollar exposure. You did this at a forward rate[15] of A$:US$ = 0.56, or US$:A$ = 1.7857 (equal to 1/0.56). The exchange rate has now moved to A$:US$ = 0.59, or US$:A$ = 1.6949 (equal to 1/0.59). So, you can buy back the US$79,800 for $135,254, with a gain of $7,246 = 142,500 − 135,254. A similar gain is made on the forward euro sale, and the total gain is $14,492. Hence, hedging has given an additional return of 2.54% = 14,492/570,000.

The total return on the international equity portfolio is 13.12 percent, well above your benchmark return of 10.67 percent.

Index	July Previous	July Current In Local Currency	July Current In A$	Return in A$
United States	100	118	112	12.00%
Europe	100	114.50	108.68	8.68%
Benchmark	100	116.25	110.67	10.67%
A$:US$	0.56	0.59		
A$:€	0.56	0.59		

Note: Weights in the benchmark are 60 percent United States and 40 percent Europe.

	July Previous In Local Currency	July Previous In A$	July Current In Local Currency	July Current In A$	Return in Local Currency	Return in A$	Contribution to Portfolio Return
U.S. stocks	159,600	285,000	188,328	319,200	18%	12%	6.00%
Europe stocks	159,600	285,000	183,540	311,085	15%	9.15%	4.58%
Currency futures		0		14,492			2.54%
Total		570,000		644,777			13.12%

Note: All local currency values are converted at the exchange rates given above. Starting weights in the portfolio are 50 percent U.S. stocks and 50 percent European stocks.

[14] Let's denote R, R_{US}, and R_{EU} as the returns on the portfolio and on the U.S. and European segments; I, I_{US}, and I_{EU} as the returns on the benchmark and on the U.S. and European indexes; and SS_{EU} as the security selection return on European equity. We have

$$R - I = 0.5R_{US} + 0.5R_{EU} - (0.6I_{US} + 0.4I_{EU}) = 0.5I_{US} + 0.5(I_{EU} + SS_{EU}) - (0.6I_{US} + 0.4I_{EU})$$
$$= (0.5 - 0.6)I_{US} + (0.5 - 0.4)I_{EU} + 0.5SS_{EU} = -0.33\% + 0.24\%$$

[15] The forward rate is equal to the spot rate because interest rates are equal in the three countries.

Summary

- There are several types of participants in the global investment arena: investors (private or institutional), investment managers, brokers, consultants and advisers, and custodians. Some players belong to several categories.
- Major choices in terms of investment philosophy and strategy must be made by an investment firm structuring its global investment process. These choices are based on a view of the global behavior of security prices. A major question is how active a global strategy should be. In an active strategy, a manager can decide on (1) global asset allocation by type of asset and currency, (2) security selection, and (3) market timing. An active manager can also selectively hedge certain types of risks, such as currency risk. Another question is whether the major emphasis should be on market analysis (top-down approach) or on security analysis (bottom-up approach). Yet another important question is whether the focus should be on regional/ country factors or on global factors that cut across countries, such as industry factors. These and other choices dictate how the investment process should be structured.
- The client's objectives, constraints, and requirements are specified in an investment policy statement (IPS), which then forms the basis for the strategic asset allocation.
- Capital market expectations are expectations about the future distributions of returns to asset classes, including expected returns, volatility of returns, and correlation of returns. Formulating capital market expectations is potentially the most rewarding part of global asset management, but it is also the most difficult. The formulation process is usually decomposed into three steps:
  - Defining asset classes
  - Formulating long-term expectations used in strategic asset allocation
  - Formulating shorter-term expectations used in tactical asset allocation
- The most important global investment decision is the selection of an asset allocation. The first step for a global investor is to decide on a strategic asset allocation, or the structure of the portfolio for the long term. This choice is based on long-term capital market expectations. The process of periodically adjusting asset allocation to reflect changes in the market environment is referred to as tactical asset allocation.
- The strategic asset allocation is formalized through one or several benchmarks set as guidelines to investment managers. Important questions must be resolved:
  - The scope of the global benchmark
  - The weights in the global benchmark
  - The attitude toward currency risk and hence the currency allocation in the global benchmark

- Structuring and quantifying the investment process is a difficult task because of the large number of parameters involved. A disciplined and efficient approach calls for a partly quantified, integrated system. The objective is to make optimal use of all expertise and to control risk.
- For a global investor, multiperiod portfolio performance evaluation is essential. Careful performance evaluation disentangles attributes and also allows a comparison of hedged and unhedged positions.

Problems

1. Distinguish between sell-side and buy-side analysts.
2. Describe the difference between a pay-as-you-go retirement system and a capitalized contribution system.
3. Compare the margins in asset management and investment banking.
4. List four indexing methods, and specify why tracking of a global index is so difficult.
5. Describe four approaches to currency management for portfolios.
6. A retiree, James Timor, has an asset base of €1,900,000. Taking into account annual inflation of 3 percent, taxes of 15 percent, management fees of 50 basis points, his objectives, his constraints, and his annual spending needs of €90,000, his financial advisor recommended an asset allocation with an expected return of 9.82 percent and a standard deviation of 8 percent. The advisor based this on the following calculations:

Principal		€1,900,000
Return rate	0.0982	186,580
Management expenses	0.005	−9,500
Inflation	0.03	−57,000
Tax rate	0.15	−27,987
Annual spending		92,093

During the next year, Timor's return is negative 6.18 percent. He has a scheduled meeting with his advisor. If his portfolio's returns are normally distributed and independent, what is the probability of a loss of 6.18 percent or more in one year? What is the probability of three years in a row of returns of less than 9.82 percent?

7. Timor is unnerved a little by losing over €100,000 last year in his portfolio that had begun the year at €1,900,000. He is now more risk averse and wants to decrease his allocation to stocks and increase his allocation to government securities. What is the effect of this sequence of events on Timor's ability to spend €90,000 annually? If his risk tolerance had not changed, what advice would have helped him meet his objectives? What difficulty does his change in risk tolerance create?
8. An individual planning to retire at the end of three years has a defined benefit of $30,000 per year not protected against inflation. In her planning, she uses a thirty-year

life expectancy in retirement. She receives an offer of a lump sum payment of $215,000 with an explanation that (1) money in hand is much more valuable than money in the future; (2) she can earn 11 percent or more annually on the stock market if she had the money now; and (3) she could use the money now to pay off a few debts. The risk-free rate is three percent. Analyze the merits and assumption of the offer.

9. An individual planning to retire at the end of three years has savings of approximately $212,000. In his planning, he uses a thirty-year life expectancy in retirement. He calculates his spending needs at $30,000 per year. He thinks he can earn 11 percent or more annually on the stock market. The risk-free rate is three percent. How much should this individual have saved to meet his pseudo-liabilities of $30,000 per year? Can he meet his spending needs by investing his $212,000 in the stock market?

10. For an individual planning to retire in ten years, with a thirty-year life expectancy in retirement, and with living expenses that will grow with inflation, what is the risk-free investment?

11. An investor holds an aggressive growth mutual fund and was forced to sell it at an inopportune time when the fund had lost a considerable amount of money. She is upset at being forced out of the fund and claims that this endangers her ability to meet critical return and risk objectives. Is the investor correct in her appraisal of the consequences of being forced out of the fund?

12. A forty-year old employee has never before belonged to a defined-contribution retirement plan. Upon seeing the investment alternatives available in the plan, she determines that she needs to tilt her portfolio toward aggressive growth funds to make up for lost time. Discuss the merits of this catch-up strategy.

13. If an asset class has a 0.25 correlation with the market portfolio, and the market portfolio has a Sharpe ratio of 0.2, what would you expect as the Sharpe ratio of the asset class?

14. Suppose the equilibrium Sharpe ratio required for a well-diversified portfolio is 0.25, the world market portfolio has a volatility of 19 percent, and the emerging markets have a volatility of 32 percent and a correlation of 0.45 with the world market portfolio. What would be the risk premium on the world market portfolio? What should be the emerging Sharpe ratio, risk premium, and beta?

15. Criticize the full hedging approach, the approach that sets a unitary hedge ratio.

16. Discuss the merits of a 50 percent hedging ratio.

17. Bouderi's portfolio was hedged with a 50 percent hedge ratio. Examining just his U.S. equity exposure of A$285,000, suppose he had been fully hedged at the A$:US$ = 0.56 forward rate. Over his portfolio performance measurement period, the exchange rate moved to A$:US$ = 0.59. What would the currency hedge have contributed in additional performance to the un-hedged U.S. equity portfolio return?

18. Bouderi's portfolio was hedged with a 50 percent hedge ratio. Examining just his U.S. equity exposure of A$285,000, suppose he sold U.S. dollars forward at A$:US$ = 0.56 forward rate. Over his portfolio performance measurement period, the exchange rate moved to A$:US$ = 0.50. What would the currency hedge have contributed in negative performance to the un-hedged U.S. equity portfolio return?

Bibliography

Adler, M., and Prasad, B. "On Universal Currency Hedges," *Journal of Financial and Quantitative Analysis*, February 1992.

Adler, M., and Solnik, B. Letter to the Editor, "The Individuality of 'Universal' Hedging," *Financial Analysts Journal*, May/June 1990.

Arnott, R. D., and Bernstein, P. L. "What Risk Premium Is Normal?" *Financial Analyst Journal*, March/April 2002.

Black, F. "Equilibrium Exchange Rate Hedging," *Journal of Finance*, July 1990.

Blake, D., Lehmann, B., and Timmermann, A. "Asset Allocation Dynamics and Pension Fund Performance," *Journal of Business* 9, 1999.

Brinson, G., Brian, P., Singer, D., and Beebower, Gilbert L. "Determinants of Portfolio Performance II: An Update," *Financial Analysts Journal* 47(3), 1991.

Froot, K. A. "Currency Hedging over Long Horizons," NBER Working Paper No. 4355, May 1993.

Gastineau, G. L. "The Currency Hedging Decision: A Search for Synthesis in Asset Allocation," *Financial Analysts Journal*, May/June 1995.

Jorion, P. "Asset Allocation with Hedged and Unhedged Foreign Stocks and Bonds," *Journal of Portfolio Management*, Summer 1989.

Krail, R. J., Asness, C. S., Liew, J. M. "Do Hedge Funds Hedge?" *The Journal of Portfolio Management*, Fall 2001.

Maginn, J., Tuttle, D., McLeavey, D., and Pinto, J. *Managing Investment Portfolios*, 3rd ed. New Jersey: Wiley, 2007.

Nesbitt, S. L. "Currency Hedging Rules for Plan Sponsors," *Financial Analysts Journal*, March/April 1991.

Pérold, A., and Schulman, E. "The Free Lunch in Currency Hedging: Implications for Investment Policies and Performance Standards," *Financial Analysts Journal*, May/June 1988.

Singer, B., and Terhaar, K. *Economic Foundations of Capital Market Returns*, Charlottesville, VA: Research Foundation of the Institute of Chartered Financial Analysts, 1997.

Terhaar, K., Staub, R., and Singer, B. "Appropriate Policy Allocation for Alternative Investments," *Journal of Portfolio Management*, Spring 2003.

Glossary

accrued interest Interest earned but not yet due and payable. This is equal to the next coupon to be paid on a bond multiplied by the time elapsed since the last payment date and divided by the total coupon period. Exact conventions differ across bond markets.

actuarial yield The total yield on a bond, obtained by setting the bond's current market value equal to the discounted cash flows promised by the bond. Also called *yield to maturity.*

agency trade A trade in which a broker acts as an agent only, not taking a position on the opposite side of the trade.

AIMR See *CFA Institute.*

American Depositary Receipt (ADR) A certificate of ownership issued by a U.S. bank to promote local trading in a foreign stock. The U.S. bank holds the foreign shares and issues ADRs against them.

American-type option An option that can be exercised at any time before expiration.

amortizing swap An interest rate swap with a decreasing notional principal amount.

arbitrage The simultaneous purchase of an undervalued asset or portfolio and sale of an overvalued but equivalent asset or portfolio, in order to obtain a riskless profit on the price differential. Taking advantage of a market inefficiency in a risk-free manner.

arbitrage approach A common approach used to value derivative securities, based on an arbitrage strategy involving the underlying securities.

ask price The price at which a market maker is willing to sell a security; also called *offer price.*

asset allocation Dividing of investment funds among several asset classes to achieve diversification.

at-the-money option An option for which the strike (or exercise) price is close to (at) the current market price of the underlying asset.

back-to-back Transactions in which a loan is made in one currency against a loan in another currency.

balance of payments A record of all financial flows crossing the borders of a country during a given time period (a quarter or a year).

balance of trade See *Trade balance.*

base currency A reference currency chosen by an investor to value a portfolio.

basis The difference between the futures (or forward) price of an asset and its spot (or cash) price. The basis can be expressed as a value or as a percentage of the spot price.

basis point One hundredth of 1 percent (0.01%).

basis risk The risk that arises from fluctuation in the basis.

basis swap An interest rate swap involving two floating rates.

bear floating-rate note (bear FRN) A note that benefits investors if interest rates rise.

bearer security A negotiable security. All cash flows paid on the security are remitted to its bearer. No register of ownership is kept by the issuing company.

benchmark A standard measurement used to evaluate the performance of a portfolio. The benchmark may be some passive index or the aggregate performance on a universe of comparable portfolios (see *Composite*).

benchmark bond A bond representative of current market conditions and used for performance comparison.

beta (β) A statistical measure of market risk on a portfolio; traditionally used to estimate the elasticity of a stock portfolio's return relative to the market index.

bid–ask spread The difference between the quoted ask and bid prices.

bid price The price at which a market maker is willing to buy a security.

bilateral arbitrage With reference to currencies, an arbitrage involving two currencies only.

Black-Scholes or Black-Scholes-Merton formula A standard option pricing formula derived by F. Black and M. Scholes and also by R. Merton.

bond A long-term debt security with contractual obligations regarding interest payments and redemption.

book value The accounting value of a firm.

bottom-up investing With respect to investment approaches, a focus on selecting individual securities with whatever allocation of money to asset classes, countries, or industry securities results.

bourse A French term often used to refer to a stock market.

Brady bonds Bonds issued by emerging countries under a debt-reduction plan named after Mr. Brady, former U.S. Secretary of the Treasury.

break-even exchange rate The future exchange rate such that the return in two bond markets would be even for a given maturity. Also called *implied forward exchange rate.*

Bretton Woods The site of a 1944 conference that led to the establishment of a semifixed exchange rate system.

broker An agent who executes orders to buy or sell securities on behalf of a client in exchange for a commission.

bull floating-rate note (bull FRN) A floating-rate note whose coupon increases if interest rates drop; an inverse floater.

call auction See *Fixing.*

call option A contract giving the right to buy an asset at a specific price on or before a specified date.

cap A contract on an interest rate, whereby at periodic payment dates, the writer of the cap pays the difference between the market interest rate and a specified cap rate if, and only if, this difference is positive. This is equivalent to a stream of call options on the interest rate.

cap option A contract on an interest rate, whereby the seller of the cap option periodically pays to the buyer the difference between the market interest rate and the specified cap rate if, and only if, this difference is positive. This is equivalent to a stream of call options on the interest rate.

capital account A component of the balance of payments that reflects unrequited (or unilateral) transfers corresponding to capital flows entailing no compensation (in the form of goods, services, or assets). Examples include investment capital given (without future repayment) in favor of poor countries, debt forgiveness, and expropriation losses.

capital asset pricing model (CAPM) An equilibrium theory that relates the expected return of an asset to its market risk (see *Beta*).

cash-and-carry arbitrage An arbitrage strategy with a simultaneous spot purchase and forward sale of an asset. The reverse transaction (borrowing the asset, selling it spot, and buying it forward) is known as a reverse cash and carry, or as a carry-and-cash arbitrage. These arbitrages lead to a relation between spot and forward, or futures, prices of the same asset.

cash settlement A procedure for settling futures contracts in which the cash difference between the futures price and the spot price is paid instead of physical delivery.

CFA Institute The global, not-for-profit association of investment professionals that awards the CFA designation; formerly the Association for Investment Management and Research (AIMR).

chartism A subjective forecasting analysis based on the study of charts; also called *technical analysis.*

clean price The price of a bond obtained as the total price of the bond minus accrued interest. Most bonds are traded on the basis of their clean price.

clearinghouse An organization that settles and guarantees trades in some financial markets.

closed-end fund An investment company with a fixed number of shares. New shares cannot be issued and the old shares cannot be redeemed. Shares are traded in the marketplace, and their value may differ from the underlying net asset value of the fund.

collateralized debt obligation (CDO) A set of structured notes backed by a pool of assets such as a portfolio of bonds or loans.

composite A universe of portfolios with similar investment objectives.

conditional correlation Correlation of two variables conditional on some information set.

conditional variance Variance of a variable conditional on some available information set.

consumer price index (CPI) A price index defined on a basket of goods consumed.

contract for difference (CFD) A contract between an investor and a broker in which the investor receives (or pays) the difference between the price of the underlying share when the contract is closed and the price when the contract was opened.

convertible bond A type of corporate debt that can be exchanged for shares of stock.

convexity A measure of the change in duration with respect to changes in interest rates.

co-opetition A term from game theory referring to cooperation along the value chain.

cost of carry The cost associated with holding some asset, including financing, storage, and insurance costs. Any yield received on the asset is treated as a negative carrying cost.

covered option An option position that is offset by an equal and opposite position in the underlying security.

credit spread A yield premium required by investors who purchase risky corporate bonds; also called *quality spread.*

cross rate The exchange rate between two currencies, derived from their exchange rates with a third currency.

currency exposure The sensitivity of the asset return, measured in the investor's domestic currency, to a movement in the exchange rate.

currency-option bond A bond in which the coupons and/or the principal may be paid in more than one currency, at the option of the bondholder.

currency overlay In currency risk management, the delegation of the management of currency risk in an international portfolio to a currency specialist.

currency swap A contract to exchange streams of fixed cash flows denominated in two different currencies.

current account A component of the balance of payments covering all current transactions that take place in the normal business of the residents of a country, such as exports and imports, services, income, and current transfers.

data mining Refers to spurious associations that arise by chance when performing repeated studies of a database.

dealer An agent that buys and sells securities as a principal (for its own account) rather than as a broker for clients. A dealer may function, at different times, as a broker or as a dealer. Sometimes called a *market maker.*

default risk The risk that an issuer will be unable to make interest and principal payments on time.

default swap An exchange of a fixed or floating coupon against the payment of a loss caused by default on a specific loan or bond; also called *credit swap.*

delta (δ) Ratio of change in the option price to a small change in the price of the underlying asset. Also equal to the derivative of the option price with respect to the asset price.

delta hedge A dynamic hedging strategy using options with continuous adjustment of the number of options used, as a function of the delta of the option.

derivatives Securities bearing a contractual relation to some underlying asset or rate. Options, futures, forward, and swap contracts, as well as many forms of bonds, are derivative securities.

devaluation Deliberate downward adjustment of a currency against its fixed parity.

direct exchange rate The amount of local or domestic currency required to purchase one unit of foreign currency.

direct quote An exchange rate quotation that gives the value of the foreign currency in terms of units of the domestic currency.

distressed investing An investment strategy that relies on purchase of securities in companies that are in poor financial condition.

dual-currency bond A bond with coupons fixed in one currency and principal repayment fixed in another currency.

duration A measure of an option-free bond's average maturity. Specifically, the weighted average maturity of all future cash flows paid by a security, in which the weights are the present value of these cash flows as a fraction of the bond's price. More importantly, a measure of a bond's price sensitivity to interest rate movements (see *Modified duration*).

EAFE index A stock index for Europe, Australia, and the Far East published by Morgan Stanley Capital International.

early stage With reference to venture capital financing, the stage associated with moving into operation and before commercial manufacturing and sales have occurred. Includes the start-up and first stages.

earnings multiplier See *Price–earnings ratio.*

econometric model A statistical model that analyzes complex correlations between variables.

economic risk As used in currency risk management, the risk that arises when the foreign currency value of a foreign investment reacts systematically to an exchange rate movement.

efficient frontier The set of all efficient portfolios for various levels of risk.

efficient market A market in which any relevant information is immediately impounded in asset prices.

efficient portfolio A portfolio that provides the best expected return for a given level of risk.

electronic communication networks Order-driven trading systems in which the book of limit orders plays a central role.

electronic crossing networks Order-driven trading systems in which market orders are anonymously matched at prespecified times at prices determined in the primary market for the system.

employee stock options Employee compensation in the form of company stock.

endogenous growth theory A theory of economic growth that does not assume that the marginal productivity of capital declines as capital is added.

euribor Interbank offer rate for short-term deposits in euros. Euribor is determined by an association of European banks.

euro The common currency of many European countries.

eurobond See *International bond.*

eurocurrency market Interbank market for short-term borrowing and lending in a currency outside of its home country. For example, borrowing and lending of U.S. dollars outside the United States. Thus, it is an offshore market escaping national regulations. This is the largest money market for several major currencies.

European Monetary System A formal arrangement linking some, but not all, of the currencies of the EU.

European Union (EU) A formal association of European countries founded by the Treaty of Rome in 1957. Formerly known as the EEC.

European-type option An option that can be exercised only at expiration.

exchange traded funds (ETFs) A type of mutual fund traded like other shares on a stock market, having special characteristics particularly related to redemption, and generally designed to closely track the performance of a specified stock market index.

ex-dividend A synonym for "without dividend." The buyer of a security ex-dividend does not receive the next dividend.

exercise price A specified price at which the buyer of an option can purchase an asset on or before a particular date; also called *strike price.*

expected return The rate of return that an investor expects to get on an investment.

expiry The expiration date of a derivative security.

face value The amount paid on a bond at redemption and traditionally printed on the bond certificate. This face value excludes the final coupon payment. Sometimes referred to as *par value.*

fair value The theoretical value of a security based on current market conditions. The fair value is the value such that no arbitrage opportunities exist.

financial account A component of the balance of payments covering investments by residents abroad and investments by nonresidents in the home country. Examples include direct investment made by companies, portfolio investments in equity and bonds, and other investments and liabilities.

fixed exchange rate regime A system in which the exchange rate between two currencies remains fixed at a preset level, known as official parity.

fixing A method for determining the market price of a security by finding the price that balances buyers and sellers. A fixing takes place periodically each day at defined times. Sometimes called a *call auction.*

flexible or floating exchange rate system A system in which exchange rates are determined by supply and demand.

floating-rate note (FRN) A bond issued with variable quarterly or semiannual interest rate payments, generally linked to LIBOR; also called a *floater.*

floor option A contract on an interest rate, whereby the writer of the floor option periodically pays to the buyer the difference between a specified floor rate and the market interest rate if, and only if, this difference is positive. This is equivalent to a stream of put options on the interest rate.

foreign bond A bond issued by a foreign company on the local market and in the local currency (e.g., Yankee bonds in the United States, Bulldog bonds in the United Kingdom, or Samurai bonds in Japan).

foreign currency risk premium The expected movement in the (direct) exchange rate minus the interest rate differential (domestic risk-free rate minus foreign risk-free rate).

foreign exchange The purchase (sale) of a currency against the sale (purchase) of another.

foreign exchange controls Various forms of government-imposed controls on the purchase (sale) of foreign currencies by residents or on the purchase (sale) of local currency by nonresidents.

foreign exchange expectation A relation that states that the forward exchange rate, quoted at time 0 for delivery at time 1, is equal to the expected value of the spot exchange rate at time 1. When stated relative to the current spot exchange rate, the relation states that the forward discount (premium) is equal to the expected exchange rate movement.

foreign exchange parity A foreign exchange rate of two currencies that is officially fixed by international agreement.

forex See *foreign exchange.*

formative stage With respect to venture capital financing, the seed and early stages.

forward contract A customized contract to buy (sell) an asset at a specified date and a specified price (forward price). No payment takes place until maturity.

forward discount or premium Refers to the percentage difference between the forward exchange rate and the spot exchange rate (premium if positive, discount if negative).

forward exchange rate A rate contracted today but with delivery and settlement in the future, usually 30 or 90 days away.

forward rate agreement (FRA) An agreement between two parties that will apply to a future notional loan or deposit.

franchise value In P/E ratio analysis, the present value of growth opportunities divided by next year's expected earnings.

full price (or dirty price) The total price of a bond, including accrued interest.

fund of funds (FOF) An investment fund that invests in a selection of hedge funds.

fundamental value The intrinsic value of an asset at a point in time.

futures contract A standardized contract to buy (sell) an asset at a specified date and a specified price (futures price). The contract is traded on an organized exchange, and the potential gain/loss is realized each day (marking to market).

generally accepted accounting principles (GAAP) A set of accounting standards followed in the United States.

generic See *plain-vanilla.*

gilt (or gilt-edged) A U.K. government bond.

Global Investment Perfomance Standards (GIPS) A global industry standard for the ethical presentation of investment performance results promulgated by CFA Institute.

gold standard An international monetary system in which the parity of a currency is fixed in terms of its gold content.

gray market A forward market for newly issued bonds before the final terms on the bond are set.

gross domestic product (GDP) Total value of a country's output produced by residents within the country's physical borders.

gross national product (GNP) Total value of a country's output produced by residents both within the country's physical borders and abroad.

group of seven (G-7) The seven countries (Canada, France, Germany, Italy, Japan, the United Kingdom, and the United States) that meet periodically to enhance cooperative action on international economic matters. [The Group of Eight (G-8) includes Russia.]

growth stock A corporation whose market price per share is relatively high compared to its earnings per share, indicating high EPS growth potential if the stock is correctly priced.

hedge funds Investment funds that may use any type of strategy in the search for absolute returns.

hedge ratio The percentage of the position in an asset that is hedged with derivatives.

hedging The process of reducing the uncertainty of the future value of a portfolio by taking positions in various derivatives (e.g., forward and futures contracts).

Herfindahl index A measure of industry concentration equal to the sum of the squared market shares of the firms in the industry.

implementation shortfall With respect to execution costs, the difference between the value of the executed portfolio or share position and the value of the same portfolio at the time the trading decision was made.

implied forward exchange rate See *Break-even exchange rate.*

implied volatility The volatility of an asset that is implicit in the current market price of an option (using a standard Black-Scholes-Merton formula).

in-the-money option An option that has a positive value if exercised immediately. For example, a call when the strike price is below the current price of the underlying asset, or a put when the strike price is above the current price of the underlying asset.

index funds Investment funds that exactly track the returns on selected market indexes.

index-linked bond A bond whose interest rate payments and/or redemption value are contractually linked to some specified index (e.g., a commodity price).

indirect exchange rate The amount of foreign currency required to purchase one unit of domestic currency.

indirect quote An exchange rate quotation that gives the value of the domestic currency in terms or units of the foreign currency.

information ratio The ratio of excess return over the benchmark to tracking error relative to the benchmark.

initial margin The amount that an investor must deposit to open a position in futures and some other derivatives; also used to refer to the initial equity required when a stock is purchased using borrowed money.

initial public offering (IPO) The first sale of a company's stock to the public; also, a public resale of a company that was acquired in a leveraged buyout and then taken private.

insuring The process of setting a minimum level for the future value of a portfolio by taking positions in various derivatives (e.g., options).

interest rate parity (IRP) An arbitrage process that ensures that the forward discount or premium equals the interest rate differential between two currencies.

interest rate swap A contract to exchange streams of fixed-interest-rate for floating-interest-rate cash flows denominated in the same currency.

internal rate of return (IRR) The discount rate that equates the present value of a future stream of cash flows to the initial investment.

international bond A bond underwritten by a multinational syndicate of banks and placed mainly in countries other than the country of the issuer.

International CAPM (ICAPM) An equilibrium theory that relates the expected return of an asset to its world market and foreign exchange risks.

International Capital Market Association (ICMA) An association formed in 1969 to establish uniform trading procedures in the international bond markets; formerly known as the International Securities Market Association (ISMA) or the Association of International Bond Dealers (AIBD).

International Fisher relation The assertion that the interest rate differential between two countries should equal the expected inflation rate differential over the term of the interest rates.

International Monetary Fund (IMF) An organization set up in 1944 to promote exchange rate stability and to assist member countries facing economic difficulties.

International Capital Market Association (ICMA) An association formed in 1969 to establish uniform trading procedures in the international bond markets. Formerly named AIBD and ISMA.

International Swaps and Derivatives Association (ISDA) An association of swap dealers formed in 1985 to promote uniform practices in the writing, trading, and settlement procedures of swaps and other derivatives.

intrinsic value The value that would be obtained on an option if it were to be exercised immediately.

investment company A firm that issues (sells) shares, and uses the proceeds to invest in various financial instruments or other assets.

investment policy statement (IPS) A document prepared by an investment advisor and a client to guide investment decisions.

later stage With respect to venture capital financing, the stage after commercial manufacturing and sales have begun. Later-stage financing includes second-stage, third-stage, and mezzanine financing.

Leverage The relation between the value of the asset position and the amount of equity invested.

leveraged buyout Purchase of a company financed primarily through borrowing, often with the intent of taking the company private and eventually reselling it.

LIBMEAN The average of LIBID and LIBOR.

limit order An order to buy or sell a security at a specific price or better (lower for a buy order and higher for a sell order).

limit pricing Pricing below average cost to deter entry into an industry.

local currency (foreign currency) exposure The sensitivity of the asset return, measured in the asset's local currency, to a movement in the exchange rate.

London Interbank Bid (LIBID) The rate quoted to a top-quality lender on the London interbank market.

London InterBank Offer Rate (LIBOR) The rate at which international banks lend on the Eurocurrency market. This is the rate quoted to a top-quality borrower. The most common maturities are one month, three months, and six months. There is a LIBOR for the U.S. dollar and a few other major currencies. LIBOR is determined by the British Banking Association in London. See also *Euribor*.

long hedge A hedge involving the purchase of forward or futures contracts in anticipation of a spot purchase. Also known as anticipatory hedge.

maintenance margin The minimum margin that an investor must keep on deposit in a margin account at all times.

margin deposit The amount of cash or securities that must be deposited as guarantee on a futures position. The margin is a returnable deposit.

margin trading An arrangement in which an investor borrows money or shares from a broker to finance a transaction.

market impact With reference to execution costs, the difference between the actual execution price and the market price that would have prevailed had the manager not sought to trade the security.

market maker An institution or individual quoting firm bid and ask prices for a security and standing ready to buy or sell the security at those quoted prices; also called a *dealer.*

market order An order to buy (sell) immediately at the best obtainable price.

market portfolio An investment portfolio made up of all assets traded in proportion to their market capitalization.

marking to market Procedure whereby potential profits and losses on a futures position are realized daily. The daily futures price variation is debited (credited) in cash to the loser (winner) at the end of the day.

mezzanine financing With respect to venture capital financing, capital provided to prepare for the step of going public. Also known as *bridge financing.*

minimum-variance hedge ratio The hedge ratio that is expected to minimize the variance of the rate of return on the hedged portfolio; also called *regression hedge ratio.*

modified duration Measure of a bond's price sensitivity to interest rate movements. Equal to the duration of a bond divided by one plus its yield to maturity.

money-weighted return (MWR) A rate of return measure corresponding to the internal rate of return; captures a return on average invested capital.

mutual fund An open-end investment company; also called *unit trust* in the United Kingdom and some other countries.

neoclassical growth theory A theory of economic growth that assumes that the marginal productivity of capital declines as more capital is added.

net asset value (NAV) The market value of the assets owned by a fund.

offer price The price at which a market maker is willing to sell a security; also called *ask price.*

official reserves The amount of reserves owned by the central bank of a government in the form of gold, Special Drawing Rights, and foreign cash or marketable securities.

open-end fund An investment company that continuously offers to sell new shares, or redeem them, at prices based on the market value of the assets owned by the fund (net asset value).

open interest The total number of futures or option contracts that have not been closed out by offset or fulfilled delivery.

option premium The price of an option.

order-driven market A market without active market makers in which buy-and-sell orders directly confront each other; an auction market.

out-of-the-money option An option that has no value if exercised immediately. For example, a call when the strike price is above the current price of the underlying asset, or a put when the strike price is below the current price of the underlying asset.

over-the-counter (OTC) A market for securities made up of dealers. It is not an organized exchange, and trading usually takes place by telephone or other electronic means.

par value The principal amount repaid at maturity of a bond; also called *face value.*

par yield curve The yield curve drawn for government coupon bonds of different maturities that trade at, or around, par.

parity relations Guidelines for global investment that describe the theoretical relationship between inflation rates, interest rates, and foreign exchange rates.

pegged exchange rate regime A system in which a country's exchange rate in relation to a major currency is set at a target value (the peg) but allowed to fluctuate within a small band around the target.

performance appraisal The assessment of an investment record for evidence of investment skill.

performance attribution The attribution of investment performance to specific investment decisions (such as asset allocation and country weighting).

performance measurement The global performance evaluation component by which returns are calculated over a measurement period for a portfolio and various segments.

pip The smallest incremental move an exchange rate can make, i.e., the last decimal place in a quote.

plain-vanilla Refers to a security, especially a bond or a swap, issued with standard features. Sometimes called *generic.*

point One percent (1%).

predatory pricing Pricing below average cost to drive competitors out of the industry.

present value The current worth of a future cash flow. Obtained by discounting the future cash flow at the market-required rate of return.

price-driven market A market in which dealers (market makers) adjust their quotes continuously to reflect supply and demand; also known as a dealer market.

price–earnings ratio (P/E ratio) The ratio of the stock market price to the earnings per share. Sometimes called *earnings multiplier.*

principal trade A trade through a broker who guarantees full execution at specified discount/premium to the prevailing price.

purchasing power parity (PPP) A theory stating that the exchange rate between two currencies will exactly reflect the purchasing power of the two currencies.

put option A contract giving the right to sell an asset at a specified price, on or before a specified date.

quality spread See *credit spread.*

random walk theory A theory stating that all current information is reflected in current security prices and that future price movements are random because they are caused by unexpected news.

rating evaluation Performed by a credit rating agency, such as Moody's or Standard & Poor's, to assign a rating to an issue's investment quality.

real exchange rate The exchange rate adjusted by the inflation differential between the two countries.

real foreign currency risk The risk that real prices of consumption goods might not be identical in different countries. Also known as *real exchange rate risk* or *purchasing power risk.*

real interest rate The interest rate adjusted by the inflation rate of the country.

regression hedge ratio See *minimum-variance hedge ratio.*

regret risk The risk that an investor will be disappointed by the actual return of an investment policy in comparison to the best policy that could have been chosen.

risk allocation The decomposition of the risk of a portfolio into the various risk exposures taken by a manager.

risk aversion Describes the fact that investors want to minimize risk for the same level of expected return. To take more risk, they require compensation by a risk premium.

risk budgeting In a portfolio management context, the setting of risk limits for individual managers.

risk premium The difference between the expected return on an asset and the risk-free interest rate.

risk tolerance An investor's capacity to accept risk, which depends on both willingness and ability to take investment risk.

seed stage With reference to venture capital financing, the stage associated with product development and market research.

settlement price The official closing price of a futures contract set by the clearinghouse at the end of the day and used for marking to market.

Sharpe ratio The ratio of mean excess return (return minus the risk-free rate) to standard deviation of returns (or excess returns).

short hedge A hedge involving the sale of forward or futures contracts to cover the risk of a long position in the spot market.

short sale The sale of a security not owned by the seller at the time of trade.

sinking fund Bond provision that requires the bond to be paid off progressively rather than in full at maturity.

sovereign risk The risk that a government may default on its debt.

special drawing right (SDR) An artificial official reserve asset held on the books of the IMF.

special purpose entities (SPEs) Off-balance-sheet arrangements that allow corporations to isolate, and sometime disguise, some financial risk.

spot exchange rate A quote for an immediate currency transaction.

spot price Current market price of an asset; also called *cash price.*

spread Difference between the ask and the bid quotations. Also refers to a mark-up paid by a given borrower over the market interest rate paid by a top-quality borrower.

standard deviation of return A common measure of risk, often calculated using a time series of returns observed over the past. Equal to the square root of the variance.

straight bond Refers to a plain-vanilla bond with fixed coupon payments and without any optional clauses.

strategic asset allocation The allocation to the major investment asset classes that is determined to be appropriate, given the investor's long-run investment objectives and constraints.

strike price See *Exercise price.*

structured note A bond or note issued with some unusual, often option-like, clause.

style investing An investment philosophy that prefers corporations with particular attributes.

swap A contract whereby two parties agree to a periodic exchange of cash flows. In certain types of swaps, only the net difference between the amounts owed is exchanged on each payment date.

swaption An option to enter into a swap contract at a later date.

tactical asset allocation Short-term adjustments to the long-term asset allocation to reflect views on the current relative attractiveness of asset classes.

technical analysis A forecasting method for asset prices based solely on information about past prices (see *chartism*).

term structure See *yield curve.*

time-weighted return A rate of return measure that captures the rate of return per unit of currency initially invested.

time value The difference between an option's market value and its intrinsic value.

tombstone (or **tumbstone**) Advertisement that states the borrower's name, gives the conditions of an issue, and lists the various banks taking part in the issue.

top-down approach With respect to investment approaches, the allocation of money first to categories such as asset classes, countries, or industry followed by the selection of individual securities within each category.

tracking error The standard deviation of returns in excess of benchmark returns; also called *active risk.*

trade balance The balance of a country's exports and imports; part of the current account.

tranche Refers to a portion of an issue that is designed for a specific category of investors. French for "slice."

translation risk Risk arising from the translation of the value of an asset or flow from a foreign currency to the domestic currency.

triangular arbitrage With respect to currencies, an arbitrage involving three currencies only.

uncovered interest rate parity The assertion that expected currency depreciation should offset the interest differential between two countries over the term of the interest rate.

underlying asset Refers to a security on which a derivative contract is written.

underwriter An agent or sponsor that guarantees final placement of bonds at a set price to the borrower.

unitary hedge ratio A hedge ratio equal to 1.

value at risk (VaR) A money measure of the minimum loss that is expected over a given period of time with a given probability.

value chain The set of transformations to move from raw material to product or service delivery.

value stock A corporation whose market price per share is relatively low compared to its earnings per share, indicating low EPS growth potential if the stock is correctly priced.

variation margin Profits or losses on open positions in futures and option contracts that are paid or collected daily.

volatility A measure of the uncertainty about the future price of an asset. Typically measured by the standard deviation of returns on the asset.

wholesale price index (WPI) A price index defined on a basket of goods produced.

withholding tax A tax levied by the country of source on income paid.

World Bank A supranational organization of several institutions designed to assist developing countries. The International Bank for Reconstruction and Development (IBRD) and the International Finance Corporation (IFC) are the more important members of the World Bank group.

writer of an option A term used for the person or institution selling an option and therefore granting the right to exercise it to the buyer of the option.

yield curve A curve showing the relationship between yield (interest rate) and maturity for a set of similar securities. For example, the yield curve can be drawn for U.S. Treasuries or for LIBOR. Typically, different yield curves are drawn for zero-coupon bonds (zero-coupon yield curve) and for coupon bonds quoted at par (par yield curve).

yield to maturity (YTM) The total yield on a bond obtained by equating the bond's current market value to the discounted cash flows promised by the bond; also called *actuarial yield.*

zero-coupon bond A bond paying no coupons until final redemption. Such bonds trade at a discount to their face value so that the price differential (face value minus market price) ultimately provides a return to the investor commensurate with current interest rates.

图书在版编目（CIP）数据

国际投资：第 6 版：英文/索尔尼克，麦克利维著．—北京：中国人民大学出版社，2011.5
经济学经典教材·金融系列
ISBN 978-7-300-13623-3

Ⅰ.①国… Ⅱ.①索…②麦… Ⅲ.①国际投资-双语教学-高等学校-教材-英文 Ⅳ.①F831.6

中国版本图书馆 CIP 数据核字（2011）第 069358 号

高等学校经济类双语教学推荐教材
经济学经典教材·金融系列
国际投资（第六版）
布鲁诺·索尔尼克
丹尼斯·麦克利维 著
Guoji Touzi

出版发行	中国人民大学出版社		
社　　址	北京中关村大街 31 号	**邮政编码**	100080
电　　话	010－62511242（总编室）		010－62511770（质管部）
	010－82501766（邮购部）		010－62514148（门市部）
	010－62515195（发行公司）		010－62515275（盗版举报）
网　　址	http://www.crup.com.cn		
经　　销	新华书店		
印　　刷	涿州市星河印刷有限公司		
规　　格	215 mm×275 mm　16 开本	**版　　次**	2011 年 6 月第 1 版
印　　张	41.5 插页 1	**印　　次**	2021 年 1 月第 3 次印刷
字　　数	863 000	**定　　价**	89.00 元

教学支持说明

中国人民大学出版社经济分社与人大经济论坛（www. pinggu. org）于 2007 年结成战略合作伙伴后，一直以来都以种种方式服务、回馈广大读者。

为了更好地服务于教学一线的任课教师与广大学子，现中国人民大学出版社经济分社与人大经济论坛做出决定，凡使用中国人民大学出版社经济分社教材的读者，填写以下信息调查表后，发送电子邮件、邮寄或者传真给我们，经过认证后，我们将会向教师读者赠送人大经济论坛论坛币 200 个，向学生读者赠送人大经济论坛论坛币 50 个。

教师信息表	学生信息表
姓名： 大学： 院系： 教授课程： 联系电话： Email： 论坛 id： 使用教材： 论坛识别码（请抄下面的识别码）：	姓名： 所读大学： 所读院系： 所读专业： 入学年： QQ 等联系方式： Email： 论坛 id： 使用教材： 论坛识别码（请抄下面的识别码）：

我们的联系方式：
Email：gaoxiaofei11111@sina. com
邮寄地址：北京市中关村大街甲 59 号文化大厦 1506 室中国人民大学出版社经济分社，100872
传真号：010-62514775

附：人大经济论坛（www. pinggu. org）简介

人大经济论坛依托中国人民大学经济学院，于 2003 年成立，致力于推动经济学科的进步，传播优秀教育资源。目前已经发展成为国内最大的经济、管理、金融、统计类在线教育和咨询网站，也是国内最活跃和最具影响力的经济类网站：

• 拥有国内经济类教育网站最多的关注人数，注册用户以百万计，日均数十万经济相关人士访问本站；

• 是国内最丰富的经管类教育资源共享数据库和发布平台；

• 提供学术交流与讨论的平台、经管类在线辞典、数据定制和数据处理分析服务、免费的经济金融数据库、完善的经管统计类培训和教学相关软件。

论坛识别码：pinggu _ com _ 1545967 _ 4210768

PEARSON

北京培生信息中心
北京市东城区北三环东路 36 号
北京环球贸易中心 D 座 1208 室
邮政编码：100013
电话：(8610)57355171/57355169/57355176
传真：(8610)58257961

Beijing Pearson Education
Information Centre
Suit 1208, Tower D, Beijing Global Trade Centre,
36 North Third Ring Road East,
Dongcheng District, Beijing, China 100013
TEL: (8610)57355171/57355169/57355176
FAX: (8610)58257961

尊敬的老师：

您好！

为了确保您及时有效地申请教辅资源，请您务必完整填写如下教辅申请表，加盖学院的公章后传真给我们，我们将会在 2～3 个工作日内为您开通属于您个人的唯一账号以供您下载与教材配套的教师资源。

请填写所需教辅的开课信息：

采用教材			□中文版 □英文版 □双语版
作　者		出版社	
版　次		ISBN	
课程时间	始于　年　月　日	学生人数	
	止于　年　月　日	学生年级	□专科 □本科 1/2 年级 □研究生 □本科 3/4 年级

请填写您的个人信息：

学　校			
院系/专业			
姓　名		职　称	□助教 □讲师 □副教授 □教授
通信地址/邮编			
手　机		电　话	
传　真			
official email(必填) (eg: XXX@ruc. edu. cn)		email (eg: XXX@163. com)	
是否愿意接受我们定期的新书讯息通知：　□是　□否			

系/院主任：__________(签字)

(系/院办公室章)

______年______月______日

Please send this form to: Service. CN@pearson. com

Website: www. pearsonhighered. com/educator

中国人民大学出版社经济类英文原版教材

(一)国际贸易系列

序号	中文书名	英文书名	作者	Author	定价(元)	出版年份	ISBN
1	国际经济关系(第六版)	International Economic Relations,6e	琼·E·斯佩罗	Joan E. Spero	43	2009	978-7-300-10635-9
2	国际贸易(第六版)	International Trade,6e	丹尼·R·阿普尔亚德等	Dennis R. Appleyard	45	2009	978-7-300-10342-6
3	国际经济学(第二版)	International Economics,2e	W·查尔斯·索耶等	W. Charles Sawyer	36	2009	978-7-300-10074-6
4	国际商务谈判(第五版)	International Business Negotiation,5e	罗伊·J·列维奇等	Roy J. Lewicki	39	2008	978-7-300-09795-4
5	国际商法	International Business Law	约翰·H·威尔斯等	John H. Willes	46	2008	978-7-300-09687-2
6	国际商务(第五版)	International Business,5e	里基·W·格里芬等	Ricky W. Griffin	45	2008	978-7-300-09686-5
7	国际营销(第三版)	International Marketing,3e	汉斯·米尔鲍尔等	Hans Muhlbacher	56	2008	978-7-300-09408-3
8	世界经济(第四版)	World Economics,4e	詹姆斯·格伯	James Gerber	25	2008	978-7-300-09688-9

(二)金融系列

序号	中文书名	英文书名	作者	Author	定价(元)	出版年份	ISBN
1	国际投资(第六版)全文影印版	Global Investments, 6e	布鲁诺·索尔尼克等	Bruno Solnik	69	2011	978-7-300-13623-3
2	金融学(第二版)全文影印版	Financial Economics, 2e	兹维·博迪等	Zvi Bodie	59	2011	978-7-300-13174-0
3	债券市场:分析与策略(第七版)	Bond Markets, Analysis and Strategies, 7e	弗兰克·J·法博齐	Frank J. Fabozzi	69	2010	978-7-300-12647-0
4	国际货币与金融(第七版)	International Money and Finance, 7e	迈克尔·梅尔文	Michael Melvin	36	2010	978-7-300-12483-4
5	资本市场:机构与工具(第四版)	Capital Markets, Institutions and Instruments, 4e	弗兰克·J·法博齐等	Frank J. Fabozzi	55	2010	978-7-300-12202-1
6	国际投资(第六版)	Global Investments, 6e	布鲁诺·索尔尼克等	Bruno Solnik	49	2010	978-7-300-11792-8
7	风险与保险原理(第九版)	Fundamentals of Risk and Insurance, 9e	埃米特·J·沃恩等	Emmett J. Vaughan	48	2008	978-7-300-08817-4
8	银行管理(第六版)	Bank Management and Financial Services, 6e	彼得·S·罗斯等	Peter S. Rose	46	2007	978-7-300-08510-4
9	跨国公司财务管理(第八版)	Multinational Financial Management, 8e	艾伦·C·夏皮罗	Alan C. Shapiro	43	2007	978-7-300-08156-4
10	金融工程	Financial Engineering Principles	佩里·H·博蒙特	Perry H. Beaumont	26	2007	978-7-300-08110-6
11	投资学	Basic Investments	赫伯特·B·梅奥	Herbert B. Mayo	40	2007	978-7-300-08155-7
12	公司理财(第五版)	Fundamentals of Corporate Finance, 5e	理查德·A·布雷利等	Richard A. Brealey	41	2007	978-7-300-07991-2
13	金融学(第四版)	The Financial System and the Economy, 4e	莫琳·伯顿等	Maureen Burton	39	2007	978-7-300-08019-2
14	金融市场与机构(第五版)	Financial Markets Institutions, 5e	弗雷德里克·S·米什金等	Frederic S. Mishkin	52	2007	978-7-300-07992-9

(三)财税系列

序号	中文书名	英文书名	作者	Author	定价(元)	出版年份	ISBN
1	财政学(第九版)	Public Finance,9e	大卫·N·海曼	David N. Hyman	29	2009	978-7-300-10752-3
2	税收筹划原理	Principles of Taxation	萨莉·M·琼斯等	Sally M. Jones	45	2009	978-7-300-10307-5

(四)经济系列

序号	中文书名	英文书名	作者	Author	定价(元)	出版年份	ISBN
1	卫生经济学(第六版)	The Economics of Health and Health Care,6e	舍曼·富兰德等	Sherman Folland	68	2011	978-7-300-13175-7
2	计量经济学基础(第五版)	Basic Econometrics,5e	达摩达尔·N·古扎拉蒂等	Damodar N. Gujarati	49	2010	978-7-300-12464-3
3	微观经济学	Microeconomics: A Modern Approach	安德鲁·斯科特	Andrew Schotter	49	2010	978-7-300-12004-1
4	宏观经济学:理论与政策(第九版)	Macroeconomics: Theories and Policies,9e	理查德·T·弗罗恩	Richard T. Froyen	49	2010	978-7-300-12053-9

序号	中文书名	英文书名	作者	Author	定价（元）	出版年份	ISBN
5	货币金融学(商学院版)	The Economics of Money, Banking, and Financial Markets	弗雷德里克·S·米什金	Frederic S. Mishkin	69	2010	978-7-300-12082-9
6	宏观经济学(第三版)	Macroeconomics,3e	斯蒂芬·D·威廉森	Stephen D. Williamson	45	2009	978-7-300-11089-9
7	计量经济分析(第六版)	Econometric Analysis,6e	威廉·H·格林	William H. Greene	49	2009	978-7-300-11206-0
8	金融学(第二版)	Financial Economics,2e	兹维·博迪等	Zvi Bodie	48	2009	978-7-300-11139-1
9	宏观经济学(第二版)	Macroeconomics,2e	斯蒂芬·D·威廉森	Stephen D. Williamson	68	2009	978-7-300-08767-2
10	中级微观经济学——理论与应用(第十版)	Theory and Application of Intermediate Microeconomics, 10e	尼克尔森等	Walter Nicholson	66	2009	978-7-300-08830-3
11	国际经济学(第十版)	International Economics,10e	罗伯特·J·凯伯	Robert J. Carbaugh	49.80	2009	978-7-300-08831-0
12	统计学——在管理和经济学中的应用(第六版)	Statistics for Management and Economics,6e	杰拉德·凯勒等	Gerald Keller	75	2007	978-7-300-08539-5